TERRORISM
& COMMUNICATION

TERRORISM
& COMMUNICATION

A Critical Introduction

JONATHAN MATUSITZ

University of Central Florida

Los Angeles | London | New Delhi
Singapore | Washington DC

Los Angeles | London | New Delhi
Singapore | Washington DC

FOR INFORMATION:

SAGE Publications, Inc.
2455 Teller Road
Thousand Oaks, California 91320
E-mail: order@sagepub.com

SAGE Publications Ltd.
1 Oliver's Yard
55 City Road
London EC1Y 1SP
United Kingdom

SAGE Publications India Pvt. Ltd.
B 1/I 1 Mohan Cooperative Industrial Area
Mathura Road, New Delhi 110 044
India

SAGE Publications Asia-Pacific Pte. Ltd.
3 Church Street
#10-04 Samsung Hub
Singapore 049483

Acquisitions Editor: Matthew Byrnie
Editorial Assistant: Stephanie Palermini
Production Editor: Laura Stewart
Copy Editor: Matthew Sullivan
Typesetter: C&M Digitals (P) Ltd.
Proofreader: Eleni Georgiou
Indexer: Enid Zafran
Cover Designer: Candice Harman
Marketing Manager: Liz Thornton
Permissions Editor: Karen Ehrmann

Printed in the United States of America

Library of Congress Cataloging-in-Publication Data

Matusitz, Jonathan Andre, 1976-

Terrorism and communication : a critical introduction / Jonathan Matusitz.

p. cm.
Includes bibliographical references and index.

ISBN 978-1-4522-4028-2 (pbk.)

1. Terrorism and mass media. 2. Terrorism.
3. Communication—Political aspects. I. Title.

P96.T47.M38 2013
363.325—dc23   2012026843

This book is printed on acid-free paper.

12 13 14 15 16 10 9 8 7 6 5 4 3 2 1

Contents

3 Terrorism as a Communication Process: The Media

4 Terrorism as a Communication Process: The Audience

6 Terrorism as Social Construction of Reality 137

7 Stereotyping Terrorists 163

8 Interpreting Terrorism through Rhetoric   185

11 Organizational Structure and Leadership in Terrorism   281

12 Diffusion of Innovations (DoI) and Terrorism

Preface

OVERVIEW OF THE TEXTBOOK

Terrorism and Communication provides a conceptual look at terrorism from a deeply communicative perspective. This is the first textbook to examine terrorism in relation to all major aspects of communication.

An important premise of this textbook is that terrorism is essentially a message. Communication is indispensable for a terrorist cause, not just to garner attention, but also to ensure its longevity and very survival. The victims' identities are not necessarily important to the terrorists, as long as the victims are members of a large group and the attack sends the intended message to the much larger population (i.e., an entire nation and possibly the entire world). Each chapter isolates a particular dimension of terrorism and communication, exposes the contexts and processes involving the main participants in terrorism (i.e., terrorists, targets, media, and audience), and examines the ways in which terrorism has, and will always have, the same objective: to send a message to cause change. Throughout all chapters, about twenty areas of communication are covered: two-way communication (i.e., David Berlo's Model of Communication), mass communications, media theory, visual communication, semiotics, intercultural communication, social constructionism, political communication, rhetoric, persuasion, linguistics (e.g., euphemisms, etc.), group dynamics, organizational communication, globalization, international communication, new media, interpersonal communication, nonverbal communication, conflict management, and crisis communication. Definitions of key terms, examples, data, facts from experts, theories, case studies, topic coverage, speech excerpts, and models and tables are provided to enhance and enrich understanding of how terrorism functions within communication contexts.

Another important premise of this book is that a symbiotic relationship exists between terrorism and the media. Without established methods of communication, terrorists depend on the media to communicate their objectives and interpret their signals. The media are considered tools for terrorists, providing the familiar "oxygen for publicity." After all, the media become very instrumental in forming interpretations of events. As terrorism scholar Walter Laqueur (1976) explains it, "[T]he media are the terrorist's best friend. The terrorist act by itself is nothing; publicity is all" (p. 104). On the other hand, media outlets can boost their ratings by covering terrorist incidents.

A third important premise is that globalization, which allows international communication channels to be exploited to the fullest, has given terrorism unprecedented ubiquity. The Internet, in particular, enables terrorism to travel with just a few mouse clicks away. And thanks to borders becoming increasingly porous, GTT (global transnational terrorism) offers non-state actors weapons and organization structures never used before. One organizational tactic is the use of autonomous sleeper cells, which require practically no leadership or vertical structure.

PREVIEW OF ALL CHAPTERS

Chapter 1 introduces the complex definition of terrorism. At best, there is a "most universally accepted" definition of it, which is the following: *terrorism* is the use of violence to create fear (i.e., terror; psychic fear) for (1) political, (2) religious, or (3) ideological reasons. This chapter also compares old and new terrorism: while old terrorism strikes only selected targets, new terrorism is indiscriminate; it causes as many casualties as possible. In Chapter 2, terrorism is described as a dynamic, two-way communication process between a sender (the terrorist) and a receiver (the audience). The chapter argues that the real objective of terrorism is persuasion. To understand how the communication process works and creates terrorism for the audience, three forms of communication of terrorism are analyzed: social noise, the signature method, and the conduit metaphor. Chapter 3 highlights the symbiotic relationship between terrorism and the media. Terrorists need the media or else their cause would be less known. Conversely, a terrorist act that just happened or that is going to happen may be a major scoop for the media; the audience ratings will likely increase. In fact, government officials have a tendency to associate the media with terrorists' success or failure. Because the media select events that are newsworthy, terrorists select targets and locations that will be given high priority by news organizations. Examples of this are the Munich massacre and the Oklahoma City bombing.

In Chapter 4, terrorists are described as participating in a dialogue with various audiences beyond their immediate target. Terrorism is a spectacle, like a form of drama or theater. The audience is the public character of terrorism: it is both the second party (immediate target of the message) and the third party (target beyond the immediate target of the message) of terrorism. Chapter 5 explores how terrorism is framed by the media and examines the ways in which conventional frames about terrorism can influence public opinion. Framing gives priority to facts, images, or developments over others. Media interpretations of terrorism have become one-sided: terrorism has increasingly come to refer to acts associated with agents and supporters of foreign-based terrorist movements such as Al Qaeda, rather than with the violence of homegrown activists and radicals. Also part of the framing strategy is censorship. For example, in the Afghan War, there have been instances of military-imposed censorship on reporters.

Chapter 6 discusses terrorism as a social construct. The construction of terrorism is what people agree on through consensus. Language is essential to the social construction of reality. A striking response to 9/11 was the upsurge of symbolism across the U.S. (e.g., patriotic slogans), which led to an American collective identity: patriotism, memorialization, and celebration. This chapter also explores the pivotal role that culture plays in shaping how terrorism is perceived.

Chapter 7 looks at the use of stereotypes in response to terrorism. There are diverse ways for stereotyping the enemy: guilt by association, linguistic profiling, and so on. A direct consequence is stigmatization (an invisible sign of condemnation) of the "Other"; Arabs and Muslims have been stigmatized as a result of guilt by association. This chapter also explores related issues including discursive imperialism (a type of discourse that berates the enemy's culture), racism, and stereotyping in Hollywood movies.

In Chapter 8, terrorism is interpreted through rhetoric. This chapter examines rhetorical appeals used in both the Global War on Terror (GWOT) and the Iraq War, and explores rhetorical strategies used in response to terrorism such as Othering, enemification, evilification, Orientalism, Occidentalism, or the "us vs. them" dichotomy. The chapter offers in-depth analysis of the rhetorical strategies of the Bush and Obama administrations' counterterrorism efforts, as well as rhetorical strategies used by terrorists themselves.

Chapter 9 describes the use of euphemisms for terrorism and how they play an active role in the lives of many Americans. Euphemisms, in place of natural language, can be used to obscure issues through deliberate deception or to provide tactful language. For example, the act of bombing has been romanticized with nicer language. Ultimate consequences of euphemisms are obscurantism (intentionally keeping the facts from becoming known, which has a direct effect on our thinking process) and glossocracy (government or ruling through distorted language).

In Chapter 10, terrorism is described from the perspective of group dynamics. Many people become terrorists through indoctrination techniques, which are very efficient in small groups and Communities of Practice (CoPs). The role of Social Identity Theory (SIT) fits well to organizations like Al Qaeda, where new members are taught to hate the out-group (i.e., America and the West) and to avenge humiliations against the ummah (the global Muslim community). In addition, terrorist groups tend to rely heavily on symbols to solidify their in-group cohesion. For example, for Hamas, key symbols have contributed to Palestinian identity. These symbols include Zionist presence, the rise of Islamic awakening, and the signing of the Oslo Accords.

In Chapter 11, terrorist organizations are described through an organizational communication perspective. For instance, in the pyramidal (or hierarchical) structure, leaders are at the top and passive supporters at the bottom. In the horizontal structure, where there is no pyramid of command, the organization is divided according to particular tasks and loosely organized cells. With respect to leadership, two leadership types are described: authoritarian leadership and charismatic leadership. The important role of terrorist cells is something to behold. The clandestine cell structure has vague leadership and organizational configurations. It protects the cell and gives a group certain secretiveness. Likewise, a sleeper cell lies dormant until it wakes up or decides to conduct missions.

In Chapter 12, Diffusion of Innovations (DoI) theory explains how innovations (i.e., ideas or movements) are diffused through certain channels over time across society and diverse cultures. Opinion leaders and change agents are diffusers of ideas: they sway people's attitudes or behavior in a desired fashion and, in the process, infuse innovative extremist ideologies into entire populations. Put simply, most of the jihad problem today can be traced back to Iran, beginning in 1979. The urge to change the world was diffused across all Muslim and Arab nations. A more extreme version of DoI is mimetism, the theory explaining the capacity of imitation (to mimic), which one mind diffuses to another mind. A meme can be disseminated through vertical transmission or horizontal transmission.

Chapter 13 looks at the impact of globalization and the Global Village of cyberspace on terrorism. Global transnational terrorism (GTT), along with its violent non-state actors (VNSAs), is analyzed. Globalization, thanks to international trade and transportation, has given new opportunities for terrorist groups to obtain and use better and deadlier weapons. Modern-day technologies diffuse power and level the playing field for terrorists. Terrorism also plays a huge role in cyberspace. Terrorism exploits the Global Village. Terrorists also communicate via predetermined codes that are generally transmitted through old personal messenger systems. Such a method is steganography (an ancient practice of concealing messages within texts, pictures, and objects). Lastly, terrorists can turn into cyberterrorists. *Cyberterrorism* is the use of information technology (e.g., the Internet or computer systems) as a method to mount attacks.

Chapter 14 examines interpersonal communication in terrorism, beginning with an exploration of hostage negotiation. One psychological and communicative method for solving a hostage crisis is relational development, the idea that relationships evolve into stages as a result of interpersonal dialogue. Because relational development was used during the Moluccans' hijacking in the Netherlands in 1975, the remaining hostages were safely released. Negotiation is discourse. The second part of the chapter is about the role of interpersonal communication in interrogation of suspected terrorists. In any case where interrogation has the objective of extracting reliable information, a rapport-based method is first recommended, using an approach of personal appearance (including appropriate age), good conduct, and tactful communication.

In Chapter 15, both international communication and international dialogue are important when facing terrorists one-on-one. Negotiating with terrorists is difficult as parties may have different objectives and cultural backgrounds. Various tactics and strategies in negotiation are listed and described. The concept of third-party intervention can be useful in that an individual (or team of people) can help the conflicting parties manage or resolve it. Another important method is diplomacy. A specific type of diplomacy is multi-track diplomacy, the combination of five track diplomacies: Track I, Track II, Track III, Track IV, and Track V. For instance, Track II diplomacy is celebrity diplomacy, in which a rock star like Bono will step in to improve inter-civilizational diplomacy.

Chapter 16 explores how crisis communication responds to terrorism, and how it may be used to improve terrorism preparedness. Crisis response through the web and movable phones is also discussed in this chapter. The chapter also examines intelligence about terrorism, and the ways in which intelligence may be thwarted by both misinformation (inaccurate information that is disseminated unintentionally) and disinformation (deliberately inaccurate information, including the spread of fabricated intelligence).

CHAPTER 1

What Is Terrorism?

After reading this chapter, you will be able to

- discuss the most universally accepted definition of terrorism, and competing definitions of terrorism proposed by various scholars and institutions;
- explain the history of terrorism and the different types of terrorism today, comparing old terrorism with new terrorism;
- discuss the fifteen causes that explain why people resort to terrorism; and
- describe the various facets of the terrorist's identity.

TERRORISM: ORIGIN OF THE WORD

To begin, it seems appropriate to define the term *terrorism*. Within terrorism lies the word *terror*. **Terror** comes from the Latin *terrere*, which means "frighten" or "tremble." When coupled with the French suffix *isme* (referencing "to practice"), it becomes akin to "practicing the trembling" or "causing the frightening." Trembling and frightening here are synonyms for fear, panic, and anxiety—what we would naturally call terror. The word terror is over 2,100 years old. In ancient Rome, the **terror cimbricus** was a state of panic and emergency in response to the coming of the Cimbri tribe killers in 105 BCE. This description of terrorism as being rooted in terror is an example of etymology. **Etymology** is the study of the origin and evolution of words. From this standpoint, language is organic, changeable, fluctuating, depending on the needs of thinkers and speakers over time and place.[1]

The word terrorism, in and of itself, was coined during the French Revolution's Reign of Terror (1793–1794). In the **Reign of Terror** (*Le Gouvernement de la Terreur*), a group of rebels, the Jacobins, used the term when self-reflexively portraying their own actions in—and explanations of—the French Revolution. The Reign of Terror was a campaign of large-scale violence by the French state; between 16,000 and 40,000 people were killed in a little over a year. It is not surprising, then, that the French National Convention proclaimed in

1

September 1793 that "terror is the order of the day." Maximilien Robespierre, a frontrunner in the French Revolution, declared in 1794 that "terror is nothing other than justice, prompt, severe, inflexible." The very first official definition of terrorism in French was provided several years later. In 1798, the French released the supplement for the dictionary of the **Académie Française**, an elite French learned body on matters dealing with the French language. In this supplement, the term was explained as the "système, régime de la terreur" (i.e., "government of terror"). The English version of the word terrorism is attributed to a British man's depiction of the bloodshed he had witnessed from afar in France, where the revolution was happening. Sir Edmund Burke commented on the French Revolution and warned about "thousands of those hell hounds called terrorists."[2]

TERRORISM: DEFINITION

While the Reign of Terror was a product of the French government, in modern times, terrorism denotes the killing of humans by nongovernment political actors for various reasons—usually as a political statement. This interpretation came from Russian radicals in the 1870s. Sergey Nechayev, the founder of People's Retribution in 1869, viewed himself as a terrorist. In the 1880s, German anarchist writer Johann Most helped promote the modern gist of the word by giving out "advice for terrorists."[3] Worldwide, many governments are incredibly averse to defining terrorism because they are worried about how an official definition of terrorism would expose the legitimacy of self-proclaimed combats of national liberation. In certain countries, the word has become virtually synonymous with political opponents. For instance, the Chinese call pacific Tibetan Buddhists vicious terrorists. In Zimbabwe, President Robert Mugabe regards the democratic opposition in a similar fashion.[4] Terrorism is a pejorative term. When people employ the term, they characterize their enemies' actions as something evil and lacking human compassion. Terrorism is considered worse than war, torture, or murder. A **pejorative term** is a term that is fraught with negative and derogatory meanings.[5]

Studies have found more than 200 definitions of terrorism. In fact, Simon (1994)[6] reports that at least 212 different definitions of terrorism exist across the world; 90 of them are recurrently used by governments and other institutions. Schmid and Jongman (1988),[7] two researchers at the University of Leiden (Netherlands), adopted a social science approach to figure out how to best define terrorism. They gathered over a hundred academic and official definitions of terrorism and examined them to identify the main components. They discovered that the concept of violence emerged in 83.5% of definitions; political goals emerged in 65%; causing fear and terror in 51%; arbitrariness and indiscriminate targeting in 21%; and the victimization of civilians, noncombatants, neutrals, or outsiders in 17.5%. What Schmid and Jongman actually did was a content analysis of those definitions. A **content analysis** is a careful, thorough, systematic analysis and interpretation of the content of texts (or images) to identify patterns, themes, and meanings.[8] Merari (1993) found that, in the U.S., Britain, and Germany, there are three common elements that exist in the legal definitions of terrorism of those countries: (1) the use of violence, (2) political objectives, and (3) the aim of propagating fear in a target population.[9]

Definitions from Various Scholars and Institutions

Throughout the years, various scholars have attempted to define terrorism. Yet, the term is so loaded with conceptual problems that a totally accepted definition of it still does not exist. The irony is that the recurrent theme of terrorism has become the daily part of the political drama of modern times. One just needs to turn on the TV to hear about it constantly. Below is a list of definitions of terrorism by some of the most distinguished scholars and institutions on the matter:

- Walter Laqueur: "Terrorism is the use or the threat of the use of violence, a method of combat, or a strategy to achieve certain targets... [I]t aims to induce a state of fear in the victim, that is ruthless and does not conform with humanitarian rules... [P]ublicity is an essential factor in the terrorist strategy."[10]

- Bruce Hoffman: "Terrorism is ineluctably political in aims and motives, violent—or, equally important, threatens violence, designed to have far-reaching psychological repercussions beyond the immediate victim or target, conducted by an organization with an identifiable chain of command or conspiratorial cell structure (whose members wear no uniform or identifying insignia), and perpetrated by a subnational group or non-state entity."[11]

- Alex Schmid and Albert Jongman: "Terrorism is an anxiety-inspiring method of repeated violent action, employed by (semi-)clandestine individual, group, or state actors, for idiosyncratic, criminal, or political reasons, whereby—in contrast to assassination—the direct targets of violence are not the main targets. The immediate human victims of violence are generally chosen randomly (targets of opportunity) or selectively (representative or symbolic targets) from a target population, and serve as message generators."[12]

- David Rapoport: terrorism is "the use of violence to provoke consciousness, to evoke certain feelings of sympathy and revulsion."[13]

- Yonah Alexander: terrorism is "the use of violence against random civilian targets in order to intimidate or to create generalized pervasive fear for the purpose of achieving political goals."[14]

- Stephen Sloan: the definition of terrorism has evolved over time, but its political, religious, and ideological goals have practically never changed.[15]

- League of Nations Convention Definition of Terrorism (1937): terrorist acts are "all criminal acts directed against a State and intended or calculated to create a state of terror in the minds of particular persons or a group of persons or the general public."[16]

- U.S. Department of Defense Definition of Terrorism: terrorism refers to "the calculated use of unlawful violence or threat of unlawful violence to inculcate fear; intended to coerce or to intimidate governments or societies in the pursuit of goals that are generally political, religious, or ideological."[17]

- U.S. Department of State: terrorism is "premeditated, politically motivated violence perpetrated against noncombatant targets by subnational groups or clandestine state agents."[18]

- Arab Convention for the Suppression of Terrorism: terrorism is "any act or threat of violence, whatever its motives or purposes, that occurs in the advancement of an individual or collective criminal agenda and seeking to sow panic among people, causing fear by harming them, or placing their lives, liberty or security in danger, or seeking to cause damage to the environment or to public or private installations or property or to occupying or seizing them, or seeking to jeopardize a national resources."[19]

As one can see, there are problems about attaining an all-inclusive definition. As Yasser Arafat, late Chairman of the PLO (the Palestine Liberation Organization), notably said in a 1974 speech before the United Nations, "[O]ne man's terrorist is another man's freedom fighter." This statement exemplifies the ease with which politicians' biases can influence their definitions of terrorism. In line with these contentions, a public opinion poll was conducted in Palestine on December 21, 2001. The poll found that 98.1% of the Palestinians surveyed agreed or strongly agreed that "the killing of 29 Palestinians in Hebron by Baruch Goldstein at al Ibrahimi mosque in 1994" should be called terrorism, whereas 82.3% of the same respondents disagreed or strongly disagreed that "the killing of 21 Israeli youths by a Palestinian who exploded himself at the Tel Aviv Dolphinarium" should be called terrorism.[20] Trying to define terrorism is like being in an Alice-in-Wonderland universe; it is a concept that no one can clearly define and even involves actors that no one can specifically identify. While some definitions are precise, others lack important aspects of terrorism (e.g., global connections, ideological roots, etc.).

Most Universally Accepted Definition

There is no universally agreed-on definition of terrorism. At best, we have a "most universally accepted" definition of terrorism, which is the following: **terrorism** is the use of violence to create fear (i.e., terror, psychic fear) for (1) political, (2) religious, or (3) ideological reasons (**ideologies** are systems of belief derived from worldviews that frame human social and political conditions). The terror is intentionally aimed at noncombatant targets (i.e., civilians or iconic symbols), and the objective is to achieve the greatest attainable publicity for a group, cause, or individual. The meaning of terrorism is socially constructed.[21] Terrorism is different from murder, assault, arson, demolition of property, or the threat of the same; the reason is that the impact of terrorist violence and damage reaches more than the immediate target victims (e.g., government or military). It is also directed at targets consisting of a larger spectrum of society (e.g., civilians or even society as a whole). Terrorism is distinct from regular crime because of its powerful objectives. The change is desired so desperately that the inability to achieve change is perceived as a worse consequence than the deaths of civilians. Terrorist acts are both mala prohibita acts and mala in se acts. **Mala prohibita acts** are "crimes that are made illegal by legislation"; **mala in se acts** are crimes "that are immoral or wrong in themselves."[22]

Terrorism is, first and foremost, a method, and it is used in times of peace and conflict. A **terrorist organization** is an illicit clandestine organization that generally consists of planners, trainers, and actual bombers/killers. A terrorist organization can have various structures, such as an identifiable hierarchy of command, a horizontal structure where leaders are non-identifiable or have no major role, or a cell structure where the terrorists can be "lone wolves." Terrorism is also asymmetric warfare. **Asymmetric warfare** refers to the use of random/unpredictable violence by a weak group (i.e., one with a smaller force) against a stronger power (i.e., military, government, or even society in general) to gain advantage. Asymmetrical warfare is fought between grossly unequal sides. The less powerful force does not attack the more powerful force under the conventional rules of war because it cannot win by following these tactics. The centrality of asymmetric warfare is the use of unexpected and unconventional tactics in combat. This is similar to the notion of **war without front lines**, a war waged in the shadows against an indescribable enemy, without a clear understanding of where it would lead or how it would end.[23]

U.S. DEPARTMENT OF STATE'S LIST OF CURRENT TERRORIST ORGANIZATIONS

This section lists both Foreign Terrorist Organizations (FTOs) and Domestic Terrorist Organizations (DTOs)—that is, U.S. terrorist groups—that are currently active or believed to be active. Terrorist groups that are no longer operational were not included. The sources come from the U.S. Department of State:[24]

Foreign Terrorist Organizations (FTOs)	Domestic Terrorist Organizations (DTOs)
Abu Nidal Organization (ANO)	Alpha 66
Abu Sayyaf Group (ASG)	Animal Liberation Front (ALF)
Al-Aqsa Martyrs Brigade (AAMS)	Army of God (AOG)
Al-Shabaab	Aryan Nations (AN)
Ansar al-Islam (AAI)	Black Liberation Army (BLA)
Army of Islam (AOI)	Coalition to Save the Preserves
Asbat al-Ansar	The Covenant, the Sword, and the Arm of the Lord (CSA)
Aum Shinrikyo (AUM)	Earth First!
Basque Fatherland and Liberty (ETA)	Earth Liberation Front (ELF)
Communist Party of the Philippines/	
New People's Army (CPP/NPA)	Greenpeace
Continuity Irish Republican Army (CIRA)	Hardesty Avengers

(Continued)

(Continued)

Foreign Terrorist Organizations (FTOs)	Domestic Terrorist Organizations (DTOs)
Gama'a al-Islamiyya (Islamic Group)	Jamaat ul-Fuqra
HAMAS (Islamic Resistance Movement)	Jewish Defense League (JDL)
Harakat ul-Jihad-i-Islami/Bangladesh (HUJI-B)	Phineas Priesthood (Phineas Priests)
Harakat ul-Mujahidin (HUM)	Sea Shepherd Conservation Society (SSCS)
Hezbollah (Party of God)	
Indian Mujahideen (IM)	
Islamic Jihad Union (IJU)	
Islamic Movement of Uzbekistan (IMU)	
Jaish-e-Mohammed (JEM) (Army of Mohammed)	
Jemaah Islamiya organization (JI)	
Jundallah	
Kahane Chai (Kach)	
Kata'ib Hizballah (KH)	
Kongra-Gel (KGK, formerly Kurdistan Workers' Party, PKK, KADEK)	
Lashkar-e Tayyiba (LT) (Army of the Righteous)	
Lashkar i Jhangvi (LJ)	
Liberation Tigers of Tamil Eelam (LTTE)	
Libyan Islamic Fighting Group (LIFG)	
Moroccan Islamic Combatant Group (GICM)	
Mujahedin-e Khalq Organization (MEK)	
National Liberation Army (ELN)	
Palestine Liberation Front (PLF)	
Palestinian Islamic Jihad (PIJ)	
Popular Front for the Liberation of Palestine (PFLP)	
PFLP-General Command (PFLP-GC)	

Foreign Terrorist Organizations (FTOs)	Domestic Terrorist Organizations (DTOs)
al-Qaida in Iraq (AQI)	
al-Qa'ida (AQ)	
al-Qa'ida in the Arabian Peninsula (AQAP)	
al-Qaida in the Islamic Maghreb (formerly GSPC)	
Real IRA (RIRA)	
Revolutionary Armed Forces of Colombia (FARC)	
Revolutionary Organization 17 November (17N)	
Revolutionary People's Liberation Party/ Front (DHKP/C)	
Revolutionary Struggle (RS)	
Shining Path (Sendero Luminoso, SL)	
Tehrik-e Taliban Pakistan (TTP)	
United Self-Defense Forces of Colombia (AUC)	

BRIEF HISTORY OF TERRORISM

Terrorism is an old tactic. Accounts of terrorism existed before the word itself was invented. This was confirmed by specific artifacts located fifty miles south of Mosul in Iraq. Assurnasirpal, the conqueror and king of Assyria (884–860 BCE), enforced his rule on conquered territories by erecting stone monuments. Written on them, in cuneiform, is the following:

> I built a pillar over against his city gate and I flayed all the chiefs who had revolted, and I covered the pillar with their skin. Some I walled up within the pillar, some I impaled upon the pillar on stakes... Many captives from among them I burned with fire, and many I took as living captives. From some I cut off their noses, their ears and their fingers, of many I put out the eyes. I made one pillar of the living and another of heads.

Assurnasirpal's exercise of terror is particularly obvious.[25] Several ancient writers in antiquity advocated **tyrannicide** (the killing of tyrants) as a way to have an ideal society and to please the gods. **Regicide** (the killing of kings) happened quite frequently during the Roman age. The best-known political tragedy in ancient Rome was perhaps the assassination of Julius Caesar in 44 BCE. Other Roman emperors also had a violent death: Caligula and Galba. In 9 CE, Germanic tribes conducted guerrilla attacks against passing Roman brigades. In that year, Hermann the Cheruscan ("Arminius"), a Germanic "freedom fighter," deserted the Roman army and organized "the great revolt of Germania" (Gundarsson). In an extraordinary spectacle of Barbarian resistance to the Roman occupiers, Arminius's forces attacked Roman legionnaires as they passed through the deeply wooded region of Teutoburger Wald. Three Roman legions were entirely eliminated in the Battle of Teutoburger Wald; the Romans were immediately booted out of Germania and back past the Rhine. Approximately 15,000 Roman soldiers were killed and hundreds more slain after being taken prisoner. For the Romans, such Barbarian resistance would have been considered terrorism.[26]

Another early terrorist group was the **Sicarii** (66–73 CE), a Zealot-affiliated religious sect fighting against Roman occupiers in Palestine and Jerusalem (the City of David), Jewish traitors, and Jewish moderates who had sold their souls to Hellenistic influences. The Sicarii opposed the law that Jews pay taxes to Rome and refused to acknowledge the power of the Roman Emperor (Vitellius). They were persuaded that political change could come only through violent acts. Hence, they adopted terrorism as their tactic.[27] For example, after investigating a target's routine every day, hiding nearby a temple's entrance, they knew the perfect time to cut the target's throat. In fact, **sica** (the first four letters of the group's name) means "short sword." The Sicarii's most fundamental justification was that all means were legitimate to achieve political and religious liberation. They wanted to show the world who they were, but eventually the terrorists lost and committed mass suicide in Masada in 73 CE, which coincides with the destruction of the Second Temple in Jerusalem by Titus (the Emperor's son).[28]

During the Middle Ages, in 11th century Persia, the **Assassins** were a religious sect striking terror against the empire of Saladin and resisted the armies of the Ottoman Empire. As Chaliand and Blin (2007)[29] noted in their influential book, *The History of Terrorism, from Antiquity to Al Qaeda*, the Assassins' assassination of Nizam al-Mulk, the Persian grand vizier of the dominant Turkish Seljuq sultans, was one of the chief terrorist attacks in human history. The word *assassin* allegedly comes from the drug hashish, which some scholars believe al-Sabbah's followers ate before committing acts of terrorism in the name of Allah. They called themselves **hashashins**—meaning "hashish eaters." The Assassins killed numerous people, including fellow Sunni Muslims and Christians. Suicide missions were customary, and some Crusader leaders were so frightened by the Assassins that they paid tribute to them; in exchange, the Assassins would not attack them. The Assassins were exceptionally good at doing disguise, stealth, and surprise killings. Therefore, the word **assassination** was invented to describe this tactic. A major part of the Assassins' belief was the paramount righteousness of their cause and procedure. To slay or be slain was seen as a positive gesture because it was done in the name of Allah and secured a place in paradise after death. As the Qur'an explains it, "Allah has purchased of the believers their persons and their goods; for theirs in return is the garden of Paradise: they fight in His cause, and slay and are slain: a promise binding on Him in truth" (Qur'an 9:111). This belief in ultimate justification and reward is adopted by many contemporary Islamist terrorists. The Assassins made a profound impact on the modern era.[30]

From the 13th to the 19th century, the **Thugs of India** were among the many worshippers of the Hindu Goddess Kali, the destroyer. The Thugs of India were also called Thuggees or the Thuggee cult (from which the English word *thug* is derived). Thugs strangled sacrificial victims (typically travelers) with a phansi (a noose) in the name of Kali and then robbed, ritually mutilated, and buried them. Offerings were to be made to Kali. The number of Thuggee victims was, on average, 20,000 a year.[31]

The more "avant-garde" version of terrorism occurred during the French Revolution in the 1790s (as discussed in the first paragraphs of this chapter). Eighty years later, during the Franco-Prussian War (1870–1871), Germany faced drastic resistance from the locals in foreign territories it had occupied. The French guerrilla attacks and the asymmetric warfare during the Franco-Prussian War had a deep impact on the German General Staff. Protecting their homeland against the German soldiers, French and Russian peasants were considered terrorists or **franc-tireurs** ("free shooters").[32]

Terrorism became an issue on the international agenda in 1934, when the League of Nations took the first major step toward making terrorism highly illegal and punishable. In doing so, it drafted a convention for the prevention and punishment of terrorist acts.[33] A few years later, the **Stern Gang**, a militant Zionist group founded by Avraham Stern, was making headlines. The group's objective was to expel the British authorities from Palestine, allow unlimited immigration of Jews, and create a Jewish state. A similar Jewish terrorist group, **Irgun**, operated in the British mandate of Palestine between 1931 and 1948. A notorious Irgun act was the bombing of the King David Hotel (the headquarters of the British Forces in Palestine) in Jerusalem in 1946, killing ninety-one people.[34] To have a clear idea of what modern terrorism looks like, one needs to pay particular attention to the next two sections: the first section gives some descriptive statistics on terrorist attacks or casualties from the 1970s until today; the second section compares, in detail, "old terrorism" with "new terrorism."

STATISTICS ON PRESENT-DAY TERRORISM

Terrorism began to make headlines again in the 1970s and reached a pinnacle in the mid-1980s. From 1975 to 1984, the average number of reported terrorist attacks increased from ten per week to nearly ten every day.[35] In 1985, Jenkins observed that 10% of the world's countries accounted for 60% of the world's terrorist attacks.[36] Li and Schaub (2004)[37] examined international terrorist incidents within 112 countries from 1975 to 1997. They discovered that the Middle East had the highest proportion of international terrorist incidents. Europe ranked second. Africa, Asia, and the Americas experienced considerably fewer international terrorist attacks—approximately 69%, 65%, and 33%, respectively, in comparison with the Middle East. More than 80% of arrested terrorists in Europe and the U.S. are members of the Muslim Diaspora, mostly second- and third-generation immigrants.[38] **Diaspora** refers to the dispersal of an ethnic or religious group worldwide and away from a founded or ancestral homeland. Once applied to Jews only, the concept of Diaspora today applies to any ethnic or religious group.[39]

On 9/11, America experienced the worst terrorist attack on its soil, committed by Al Qaeda ("The Base"). On that fateful day, Al Qaeda killed more people than the Irish Republican Army had killed in thirty-five years. According to a 2006 Gallup poll, involving over 50,000 interviews in various nations, 7% of the 1.3 billion Muslims in the world—90 million people—see the 9/11 attacks as "completely justified." The current Global War on Terror (GWOT), initiated by President George W. Bush, is the most all-encompassing counterterrorist campaign in history and the most important fight since the fall of the Berlin Wall.[40] Since then, the number of terrorist attacks worldwide has increased significantly. As a case in point, from 2001 to 2005 alone, they rose from 1,732 to 4,995. A year later, they rose to 6,659.[41]

RAND Corporation

RAND Corporation, a California-based nonprofit global policy institution, has been a major frontrunner in terrorism and counterterrorism studies since the 1970s. RAND, which stands for **R**esearch **AN**d **D**evelopment, is widely considered the yardstick of measure for comprehensive data on international and domestic terrorism. According to RAND Database of Worldwide Terrorism Incidents, the number of deaths as a result of terrorist attacks in Europe and North America from 2000 to 2010 was 4,873. Of those 4,873 people killed, 4,703 were casualties of attacks committed by Muslim terrorists. That is over 96%. On closer analysis, in the U.S., 3,000 people were killed by Muslim terrorists; in Russia and Eastern Europe, the number of deaths was 1,452; and in Western Europe, the number was 251. Only 170 terrorism casualties in the U.S., Russia, Eastern Europe, and Western Europe were not caused by Muslim terrorist attacks. Even if we remove the infamous September 11, 2001 attacks from this RAND statistic, the percentage of casualties due to Islamist terror is still 90%.

By comparison, RAND reports that, during the same period (2000–2010), the Madrid attacks alone (executed by an Al Qaeda–inspired terrorist cell on March 11, 2004) caused three times as many fatal human losses as the deaths of all combined attacks by the IRA, ETA, Corsican separatists, right-wing extremists, and all other non-Muslim terrorists in Europe.[42] ETA is an armed Basque terrorist organization active in France and Spain that has killed between 850 and 900 people since 1968.[43] Corsican terrorists have also been active in France and Corsica (an island that is French territory). Since the 1960s, separatists from the Front for the National Liberation of Corsica have attacked French mainlanders in their enduring fight for independence.[44] Yet, in both the ETA and Corsican cases, the terrorist attacks have produced starkly fewer casualties (comparatively speaking).

Muslim Support for Terrorism in the U.S.

In 2009, Muslim Americans composed only 0.8% of the total U.S. population (this was the equivalent of roughly 2.4 million Muslims living in the U.S.).[45] Nevertheless, according to a report by the Pew Research Center (2007),[46] over twice as many Muslim Americans under the age of thirty as older Muslims think that suicide bombings are often or sometimes justifiable in the defense of Islam (15% vs. 6%). I could have included many statistics on terrorist attacks or support of terrorism in other places besides the U.S. and Europe (e.g., the Middle East, South Asia, Africa, or South America), but for lack of space and time, I deemed important to stick to the main issues of this chapter.

OLD TERRORISM VS. NEW TERRORISM

Walter Laqueur (1999),[47] a prominent terrorism expert, suggests that "there has been a radical transformation, if not a revolution, in the character of terrorism" (p. 4). Laqueur compares old terrorism with new terrorism. **Old terrorism** is terrorism that strikes only selected targets. **New terrorism** is terrorism that is indiscriminate; it causes as many casualties as possible. Another major feature of new terrorism is the increasing readiness to use extreme indiscriminate violence. Laqueur argues that "the new terrorism is different in character, aiming not at clearly defined political demands but at the destruction of society and the elimination of large sections of the population" (p. 81).[48] Terrorism has changed because of a paradigm shift. A **paradigm** is a pattern, worldview, or model that is logically established to represent a concept. A paradigm is a way of interpreting the world that has been accepted by a group of people and that can be useful for politicians and thinkers to design policy agendas. When a paradigm changes, the whole group experiences a **paradigm shift**.

Many scholars argue that the paradigm shift from old to new terrorism occurred at some point in the 1990s, with the 1993 bombing of the World Trade Center in New York and the 1995 sarin gas attack in the Tokyo subway system by **Aum Shinrikyo** (a deadly Japanese cult).[49] Supporters of the concept of new terrorism identify the strict compliance with religion, predominantly radical Islam, as one of its main characteristics. While old terrorism was mainly secular in its focus and drive, new terrorism works hand-in-glove with religious fanaticism. New terrorism rejects all other ways of life and advocates a categorical and inflexible worldview consistent with the belief of the religion. New terrorism is also increasing.[50] Gurr and Cole (2000)[51] examined the sixty-four international terrorist organizations that existed in 1980; they found that only two of them were religious organizations (only 3% in total). By 1995, the number of religious terrorist organizations rose sharply to twenty-five out of fifty-eight (43% in total). It was an increase of 40% in just fifteen years.

Classical, Modern, and Postmodern Terrorism

For Ganor (2002),[52] the comparison between old and new terrorism can be articulated through the differences between classical, modern, and postmodern terrorism. **Classical terrorism** means that group warfare is direct; it is aimed at specific targets with few casualties (e.g., assassinations) or wreaks havoc on "non-significant" facilities. The damage is fairly low because the terrorist acts are perpetrated to achieve a specific political objective. In **modern terrorism**, a more indirect approach is used; attacks are more indiscriminate and destruction is much higher, inflicting hundreds of casualties. Although conventional weapons are used in modern terrorism, they are used to create mass fatalities. **Postmodern terrorism** has the objective of altering the reality of the conflict (with its enemy) by the very act of terrorism—such as using CBRN (chemical, biological, radiological, and nuclear weapons; pronounced C-BURN) weapons or attacks against symbols of the enemy—to materially demolish as much of their adversary as possible. The objective here is to eliminate the source of conflict itself.[53]

Four Waves of Terrorism

The comparison between old and new terrorism can also be explained through the evolution of terrorism in four waves, the Fourth Wave being new terrorism. The **First Wave** was in the late 19th and early 20th centuries. The **Second Wave** was the colonial wave, confined within national geographical boundaries from 1921 until today. The **Third Wave** was the contemporary wave; it introduced international terrorism, crossing national boundaries, which began in the 1960s.[54] The September 11, 2001 terrorist attacks gave rise to the Fourth Wave of terrorism (both for the U.S. and nations worldwide). The **Fourth Wave** is symbolized by religious justification for killing, international scope, unparalleled gory tactics and weapons, and dependence on technologies of modernity. The latter consists of communications, ease of global travel (i.e., moving across borders), and accessibility to finances and **WMDs** (weapons of mass destruction). In the Fourth Wave, terrorism has reached a global phase. The use of any weapon is justifiable. The "Other" is now a legitimate target. No distinction among targets should be taken into account. Terrorism, then, becomes **bellum omnium contra omnes** (the war of all against all). The Fourth Wave suggests a **Culture of Terror**, which refers to a collapse (both physically and figuratively) of America and the West through massive killings, the constant availability and uses of WMDs or CBRN weapons, and religious legitimation for terrorist attacks against civilians in any country that is considered Satan, infidel, or apostate (i.e., religious rebel). For example, the intent of Aum Shinrikyo to kill people in Tokyo subways in 1995 (through sarin poison gas attacks) was to punish everyone: infidels and faithful alike. This heralds the reality of sacred apocalyptic terrorism.[55]

Clash of Civilizations

Proposed by Samuel Huntington (1996),[56] the **Clash of Civilizations** posits that cultural and religious differences between civilizations worldwide have become the primary source of terrorism today. This can be easily observed in the concept of new terrorism. Terrorists want to produce a Clash of Civilizations or cause radical changes in the U.S. presence in the Middle East. The Clash of Civilizations is akin to the **War of Ideas**, where ideals and ideologies clash between the West and the Muslim world (which continues to oppose Western political forms such as democracy). Both the Clash of Civilizations and the War of Ideas give rise to a controversial concept: the **new world order**, a wide-ranging global agenda intended to change the world, establish new ideologies, and eventually replace sovereign nation-states.

Generally, religious terrorists compose their own community or population. They are not worried about upsetting their supporters with their terrorist attacks. They view themselves as people accountable only to God. New terrorists may not even deny responsibility for their acts of destruction. They oppose any type of negotiation.[57] As Morgan (2004)[58] explains it, "[T]oday's terrorists don't want a seat at the table; they want to destroy the table and everyone sitting at it" (p. 30).

Box 1.1   Jihad

Jihad is an Arabic word meaning "struggle." According to the Qur'an (where jihad appears forty-one times), Muslims have the duty of fighting enemies and invading non-Muslim territories to spread Islam. The belief is that the violent elimination of apostate regimes, the slaughter of the **People of the Book** (monotheistic non-Muslims, mostly Jews and Christians), and the removal of **kafir** (those who disbelieve in Allah) are justified in the cause of jihad. This has driven non-state actors (e.g., Al Qaeda) to commit terrorism.[59] The **greater jihad** is the struggle a person has within him- or herself to fulfill what is right. On account of human pride, selfishness, and sinfulness, believers must continually wrestle with themselves and accomplish what is right and good. The **lesser jihad** refers to the external, physical effort to defend Islam (including terrorism) when the Muslim community is under attack.[60]

The key characteristics of modern jihad ideology include (1) hakimiyya (true sovereignty of Allah over nation-states or civil laws), (2) Islamic society and upholding hisba (praising good, forbidding evil) by following the **sharia** (i.e., "Islamic law"; the required implementation of virtuous vs. materialistic, status-driven behavior based on group interpretation), (3) the necessity for jihad, (4) occupation of Muslim lands (used as justification for jihad as individual duty), (5) **martyrdom** (i.e., "dying or suffering as a hero"; martyrdom is associated with jihad and praised through videos, poetry, songs, and web postings), and (6) takfir (i.e., "disbelief in Allah"; non-Muslim governments are viewed as infidels and unwilling to be subdued by Islamic law. Therefore, it is an object of jihad).[61]

Jihadists have near enemies and far enemies. **Near enemies** are Muslim governments and forms of Islamic law that do not embrace the jihadist view. If non-Islamic powers or countries outside the jurisdiction of Islam (i.e., the West, the U.S., and Israel) do not embrace the jihadist view, they are referred to as the **far enemy**.[62]

Typically, radical Islam is singled out as the principal source of this Clash of Civilizations, with Al Qaeda being the foremost and most obvious example. Of particular relevance are members of the **mujahedin** (or **mujahideen**). The mujahedin are "Muslims doing the jihad" (see Box 1.1), or Muslims engaged in terrorist acts against the Western infidels to fulfill the new Islamic world order. The **new Islamic world order** refers to an expressed will to power and a tremendous ambition to rebuild a **Caliphate** (a great Arab-Muslim state).[63] Gunaratna (2007)[64] found that Al Qaeda recruits new affiliates from seventy-four different nations and among no less than forty different nationalities. Al Qaeda is an Islamist movement. A difference needs to be made between *Islamic* and *Islamist*. While **Islamic** means "Muslim-related," **Islamist** is an extreme version of Islamic and has connotations of militancy and terrorism. Therefore, there is a distinction between Islam and Islamism.[65]

In *The Terrorist Next Door*, Erick Stakelbeck (2011)[66] interviewed Al Qaeda prisoners about their motives to attack America and the West. Their response was that Islamist ideology drives them to engage in terrorism—not the Israeli–Palestinian conflict or poverty. Another aspect of the Clash of Civilizations is the model of **Jihad vs. McWorld**, proposed by scientist Benjamin Barber (1995).[67] This model describes the struggle between jihad and "McWorld" (globalization and the political process controlled by corporations). For instance, Barbie dolls are perceived as anti-Islamic; importing them in Iran is punishable by law. In Saudi Arabia, the mutaween (the country's religious police) have announced that Barbie dolls, with their revealing clothing, endanger morality. The Muslim version of Mickey Mouse is not the same as its U.S. counterpart. The Muslim Mickey wears a Jellabiya (a long robe) and carries a misbaha (a necklace; prayer beads). In 2002, in Pakistan, crowds organized by Islamist groups destroyed and looted Kentucky Fried Chicken and McDonald's restaurants, while burning American flags.[68]

New Organizational Structures

Another major characteristic of new terrorism is its ultra-flexible networked and less hierarchical organizational structure, enabled by state-of-the-art technologies. Terrorist groups within these networks become very autonomous but are still connected through advanced communication and common objectives. In this manner, terrorist organizations can adjust more easily to various situations. Although members may communicate with their leaders, groups can operate independently.[69] From a social network perspective, new terrorist organizations adopt a mixture of the **hub and spoke design** (where nodes in the network communicate with the center) and the **wheel design** (where nodes communicate with each other without having to go through the center).[70] Arquilla, Ronfeldt, and Zanini (1999)[71] remark that terrorist leadership follows a "set of principles [that] can set boundaries and provide guidelines for decisions and actions so that members do not have to resort to a hierarchy—'they know what they have to do'" (p. 51).

Often, new terrorists only come together to commit their terrorist acts and then disassemble. They do not receive training or logistical support from state supporters. Rather, they depend on support networks and instructions on the web. By using information and communication technologies, new terrorists can communicate secretly and reduce distances more easily. Their massive range of communication toolkit includes mobile phones, satellite phones, and the web to prepare for their upcoming terrorist attacks, communicate with other terrorist factions, and spread their message across the globe.[72] The financing of new terrorism does not stem from funds received from state backers; it comes from illegal channels such as drug trafficking, credit card fraud networks, and money laundering. Conversely, their financing is sometimes based on legal business investments, donations from the wealthy, and charities.[73]

WHY DOES TERRORISM EXIST? FIFTEEN CAUSES

Why do people resort to terrorism? The reasons are complex and plentiful. The factors that motivate people to join and remain in terrorist groups can be religious, economic, social, psychological, retaliatory, and so forth. Below is a list of fifteen causes, based on an extensive examination of journal articles and books on terrorism written by various experts on the matter.

Religion: religious fanaticism is an extreme sense of ideological zeal complemented by a focused and unrelenting set of activities that express the high dedication of one or more people to their own belief system(s). Radical religious Islamism has been identified as a root cause of terrorism. The Islamist attacks against civilians from Glasgow to Jakarta confirm that many Islamists are ideologically determined to engage in terrorism.[74] In the early 1950s, Hizb ut-Tahrir (The Liberation Party) advocated the collapsing of Arab regimes and the formation of an Islamic state. In 1952, Jordan and all other Arab states banned the party. Ironically, European countries such as Great Britain have permitted Islamic parties to establish ideological roots. Ex-Islamist Ed Husain, the author of *The Islamist*, argues that this British course of action was a blunder, as proved by the 2005 London bombings committed by Islamist terrorists.[75] Mohammed Atta, a leader of the September 11, 2001 attacks, carried with him writings from the Holy Qur'an that urged him and others to stay firm in their desire to carry out the attacks and pursue the rewards of martyrdom.[76] Based on Islamic writings, one of the rewards of martyrdom is a place in heaven (for men), with 80,000 servants and 72 virgins.[77] As one Hamas fighter said, "Before I start shooting, I start to concentrate on reading verses of the Qur'an because the Qur'an gives me the courage to fight the Israelis."[78] Some Christians have also committed acts of religious extremism. For example, in the U.S., radical Christian killers have been involved in abortion-clinic bombings and militia actions. Likewise, in Northern Ireland, Catholics and Protestants have perpetrated terrorist acts.

Oppression: terrorism can be the result of groups' portrayal of governments (and their actors) as oppressive. Terrorism, then, feeds on the desire to reduce the power of opponents. In autocratic societies, military-occupied areas, or even in the international arena where political expression is limited, groups opposing the current state of affairs may engage in terrorism as a principal method of expression and not as a last resort. Especially in the case of nationalist-separatist movements (e.g., ETA, Hamas), terrorists often invoke the unfairness of their treatment by governments that deprive them of identity, dignity, security, and freedom as the main reason for joining terrorist groups.[79] Chechen Black Widows are reported to retaliate against Russians for their own experience of rape by the Russian military or for the deaths of their husbands and male family members and friends. Consequently, the Black Widows turn to terrorism as a way to reclaim their personal or family honor.[80] In the late 1800s, Andrei Zhelyabov, a leader of People's Will (a terrorist organization) and the architect of many political assassinations (e.g., the bombs that killed Czar Alexander II), resorted to terrorist activities as a promise to revenge the many crimes by the monarchist regime that he experienced directly. His favorite aunt was raped by her land master (and it was ignored by the police); because he took part in a harmless protest against arbitrary grading practices, he was expelled from his university without right to reapply; and finally, he sat in jail for four months for sending a kindly note to an imprisoned friend. These feelings of oppression shaped and reinforced Zhelyabov's determination to use terrorism against the ruling elite.[81]

Historical grievances: terrorists target governments and groups they view as responsible for historical injustices. Chechen terrorists have defended their terrorist attacks by alluding to Russia's long-lasting rejections of Chechen desire for independence, and the old and cruel history of Russian invasion of Chechnya dating back to the 17th century.[82] The Basque separatist movement ETA, Sikh extremists (in India), the IRA, the ANC (in South Africa), and pro-Palestinian terrorist groups have all looked for vengeance for historical grievances.[83] Reports on Palestinian suicide bombers systematically refer to historical grievances, such as resentment, humiliation, sorrow, and the aspiration for vengeance and retaliation. Resentment and revenge are a major principle in the writings of the Shi'ite thinkers of jihad. Jihadists exploit collective narratives of humiliation and revenge to rationalize the need to kill themselves, civilians, and even fellow Muslims, as is the case in Iraq.[84] For Crenshaw (1981),[85] avenging comrades or the community is "the single common emotion that drives the individual to become a terrorist" (p. 394).

Violations of international law: in the terrorist's mind, a wrong can be the violation of some basic right treasured by the terrorist. The right may have been infringed on by a historical incident, such as a war or multiple violations of international law (e.g., genocide and unlawful dispossession of local inhabitants). The **international rule of law** is the standard by which all nations are subject to and bound by supranational legal covenants. Enduring conduct such as extended military occupation or foreign domination in violation of U.N. resolutions may be a major cause. According to Imre, Mooney, and Clarke (2008),[86] Palestinians demanded but were not granted justice through the U.N. and other legal channels. Other examples of violations of international law include the failure of Britain to protect the rights of Palestinians after the Balfour Declaration (1917), the failure of the Paris Peace Conference to grant Arab autonomy under the Treaty of Sèvres (1920), and the annexation of Palestinian territory by Jews in the 1940s and the resulting eviction of thousands of Palestinians from their land.

Relative deprivation: multiple scholars have found a strong link between poverty and terrorism.[87] In view of the 70% adult unemployment rate in Gaza, the GDP of less than $1,000 throughout the Palestinian Territories, the very limited economic opportunities due to the unsettled Israeli–Palestinian conflict, and the cultural prominence of the male wage-earner role, it is easy to allude to the possibility that relative deprivation has helped trigger Palestinian terrorism.[88] Sageman (2004)[89] describes how the Core Arabs (from Saudi Arabia, Egypt, Yemen, and Kuwait) sent abroad to study by their rich families were rejected, underemployed, and possibly discriminated against. Hence, they found themselves in a state of relative deprivation in comparison with the natives of their host countries. The Maghreb Arabs living or born in France may experience such relative deprivation too. In both cases, the Arabs' perception of relative deprivation may have been assuaged by their espousal of radical Islam; this is a way for them to rebuild their dignity, to be "born again," and to disseminate their values. In Peru, the popularity of the Shining Path (Sendero Luminoso) in the 1960s, where government economic restructurings initially gave hope but then failed, is another historical case of relative deprivation.[90]

Hatred toward the global economic hegemony: countries that express hatred toward the global economic hegemony will produce more terrorist groups. The background that gave birth to Al Qaeda, namely Afghanistan and Pakistan, symbolizes this notion.[91] Many terrorists abhor the World Trade Organization (WTO). According to the Bureau of Economic Analysis, the September 11, 2001 attacks shattered $16 billion of private and government property, including structures, computer equipment, and software. The loss is of the same degree as that caused by Hurricane Andrew in 1992 and the California earthquake of 1994.[92]

Financial gain: terrorism can be used for sheer financial gain. Generally, corporate hostage taking in Central and South America, and hostage taking by the Abu Sayyaf group in the Philippines, happens more out of a desire to earn a ransom than achieving political goals. In 1987, the Iran-Contra scandal concluded with an arms-for-hostage deal, even when the Reagan administration initially refused to negotiate with terrorists.[93] After Palestinian bombers commit suicide, their families earn subsequent social status and are usually secured a financial reward.[94]

Racism: racism can be a powerful method for dehumanizing adversaries and accomplishing moral disengagement. Gottschalk and Gottschalk (2004)[95] found that both Palestinian and Israeli terrorists draw on stereotypes and racism to dehumanize the other group. Similarly, the FBI-watched **Aryan Brotherhood** (a group of devious bikers formed in U.S. prisons) identifies with Nazi ideals (as noticed with their Nazi symbols) and has vowed to remove the Jewish and Black races out of the earth.

Guilt by association: for terrorists, you are the company that you keep. For example, the 2004 Madrid train bombings were executed by an Al Qaeda–inspired terrorist cell. One of the motives was Spain's involvement in the Iraq War, where the country had troops. Likewise, since decolonization in continents like Africa and South America, the West has been the target of terrorist attacks because it has been accused of making local minorities of Westernized people become comprador ruling elites. **Comprador ruling elites** are Third World ruling elites perceived to be in power (despite being shady, incompetent, and sanguinary) because the West put them or has kept them in power. In exchange, those elites fulfill the economic needs of the West. Because they have become Westernized in the process, the comprador ruling elites are culturally close to those in power in the West. Accordingly, the latter is blamed for the substandard quality of Third World governance because of a partnership between corrupt Third World elites and their backers in the West.[96]

Supporting sympathizers: because terrorism is the weapon of the oppressed, an important goal is to push the stronger power (e.g., U.S.) into unleashing against the terrorists' perceived support base. Such acts of retaliation, cruelty, and counterterrorism often turn the stronger power into a support for sympathizers, like a recruiting driver for the terrorist cause. For example, a chief Al Qaeda objective would have been to trigger U.S. retaliation so that the U.S. was seen as violently repressive.[97]

Mortality salience: mortality salience refers to anxiety over one's own death. Research by Tom Pyszczynski and his colleagues (2006)[98] examined the effect of mortality salience on Iranian and U.S. students and their respective espousal of martyrdom (terrorism) or extreme military intervention (counterterrorism). When Iranian students answered questions about their own demise, they rated the student who advocated martyrdom as higher than the student who opposed it. However, among politically conservative U.S. students, mortality salience increased advocacy for extreme military interventions by U.S. forces.

Narcissism: people with certain narcissistic dispositions are more prone to committing terrorist acts.[99] Suellwold (1981)[100] observed a high percentage of angry paranoids among members of the Baader-Meinhof Group, a German terrorist group active from the 1970s to the 1990s. A common characteristic among many of these terrorists is a propensity to externalize—to look for outside sources to blame for personal inadequacies. Without being bluntly paranoid, terrorists over-rely on the ego defense of projection. Other prominent characteristics were a defensive grandiosity and a larger-than-life self-absorption with little concern for others' feelings. Crenshaw (1990)[101] observed various self-satisfying or self-aggrandizing motives for resorting to terrorist behavior and an increase in personal status for terrorists whose actions are praised by their communities, or at least by their fellow group members. Lastly, by analyzing the social backgrounds of forty neo-Nazi males, together with two case studies, Hamm (2004)[102] concluded that his subjects aspired to fame within their subculture and that "this insatiable need to be famous was, in fact, so strong that it outweighed every other motivational factor" (p. 337).

Sensation-seeking: another variable suggested as a reason for being drawn to the path of terrorism is sensation-seeking. Here, sensation-seeking denotes the inherent risk and excitement that a terrorist career may provide. Researchers contend that it is highly plausible that sensation-seekers are more likely to join an organization that uses violent tactics.[103] Sensation-seeking entails personal reward, including the thrill of the combative lifestyle and a feeling of empowerment through violence. The appeal and excitement of terrorism, perhaps the fascination for some individuals, lie in part in the physical danger it involves. Some terrorists have been reported to be stress-seekers seeking to increase the emotional intensity or the level of activation of the organism. Stress-seekers meticulously plan their behavior, respond more to internal than external necessities, and frequently repeat stressful activities. Moreover, repetition of the stressful situation becomes not only addictive and fanatical but also escalatory; the stress-seeker is forced to perform more to achieve the same high.[104]

Failure of conventional channels of expression: in democratic civilizations, the use or threat of using terrorist violence is seen by some scholars, like Chomsky (2006),[105] as the definitive failure of conventional channels of political expression and legitimate systems of authority. A related concept is the **Death of Statecraft**, whereby diplomats fail to negotiate with their counterparts or nation-states do not attempt at engaging in communicative action. As a result, people deploy more lethal actions. Terrorism, then, becomes a by-product of violations of diplomacy and other forms of political expression.[106]

Communication and publicity: this is a major premise of this book, and several chapters are devoted to communication and publicity. In essence, by killing adversaries or innocent civilians, terrorists seek to publicize their cause, communicate demands, air grievances to bulldoze authorities, sway the public policy agenda, or gain concessions. If publicity is constrained or unsatisfactory to the group's tactical goals, the group's terrorist violence will probably escalate. After the British press and population reacted to the London terrorist bombings of July 7, 2005 (and the failed attacks two weeks later) with defiance and a stiff upper lip, **Ayman al-Zawahiri**, Al Qaeda's new #1 (also called "the Egyptian doctor"), felt compelled to issue additional threats through the Qatar-based Al Jazeera TV station.[107]

CASE STUDY: ANDERS BEHRING BREIVIK'S MANIFESTO

On July 22, 2011, **Anders Behring Breivik**, then only 32 years old, was the perpetrator of two successive terrorist attacks on the government, the civilian population, and a summer camp in Norway. In total, 77 people were killed and 151 were injured. This was the most devastating attack on Norwegian soil since World War II. In his 1,500-page manifesto, titled *2083: A European Declaration of Independence,*[108] in which he slightly modified his name to Andrew Berwick, he describes his reasons for taking actions against Europe's real enemies. One of the reasons, writes Breivik, is "the rise of cultural Marxism/multiculturalism in Western Europe." This is made clear in the following excerpt:

> Multiculturalists/cultural Marxists usually operate under the disguise of humanism. A majority are anti-nationalists and want to deconstruct European identity, traditions, culture and even nation states. As we all know, the root of Europe's problems is the lack of cultural self-confidence (nationalism). Most people are still terrified of nationalistic political doctrines thinking that if we ever embrace these principles again, new "Hitler's" will suddenly pop up and initiate global Armageddon... Needless to say; the growing numbers of nationalists in Western Europe are systematically being ridiculed, silenced and persecuted by the current cultural Marxist/multiculturalist political establishments. This has been a continuous ongoing process which started in 1945. This irrational fear of nationalistic doctrines is preventing us from stopping our own national/cultural suicide as the Islamic colonization is increasing annually. This book presents the only solutions to our current problems. You cannot defeat Islamisation or halt/reverse the Islamic colonization of Western Europe without first removing the political doctrines manifested through multiculturalism/cultural Marxism.

The "rise of cultural Marxism/multiculturalism" has somewhat of a correlation with the "hatred toward the global economic hegemony" mentioned as one of the fifteen causes in the previous section. On looking at the list of victims who fell at the hands of Breivik, one would quickly notice that few of them were actually Muslims or Arabs. Rather, many victims were young Norwegians with left-wing tendencies. A deduction could be that Breivik's reason to kill them had to do with guilt by association. From this vantage point, it is not just Muslim immigrants who pose a threat to European values, but also those who support Islamic immigration. Based on the excerpt above, it also seems like Breivik was attempting to break the sacred cow of the political left: multiculturalism, or what he refers to as "cultural Marxism." The latter, he claims, would eventually lead to "national/cultural suicide." By extension, racism was another cause or motivator for the Norwegian terrorist to enact his "final solution." In any case, as he expressed it clearly, he was convinced that his manifesto "presents the only solutions to our current problems."

THE TERRORIST IDENTITY

By and large, **identity** refers to the distinct personality of a person. It is a set of character-istics, called **identity cues**, which a person has. These identity cues (e.g., skin color, style of dress, communicative style, sexual orientation, family background, etc.) make him or her definitively recognizable or known. There are three categories of human identity: natural (or innate) identity (born with an identity, at least some aspects of it, such as gender or race), ascribed identity (an identity attributed by others), and self-ascribed identity (an identity that one has created for oneself).[109] So, who is the terrorist? What is his or her identity? Long-established research on terrorism has indicated that the terrorist identity tends to be ascribed or self-ascribed.[110]

Ascribed Terrorist Identity

During the Cold War against the Soviet Union, Ronald Reagan and others in the White House frequently referred to the Afghan fighters as freedom fighters and mujahedin. However, twenty years later, after nineteen skyjackers—instructed by the late Osama bin Laden, the six-foot-five Afghan man hiding in a cave (and later in a compound in Pakistan)—reduced key U.S. symbols into shambles, their act was labeled terrorism by the George W. Bush administration.[111] President Bush employed the terms *terrorists* and *axis of evil*. What followed immediately after 9/11 was a rhetorical process of legitimizing the terrorism label. Politicians and media pundits made public statements intended to validate the label. Press conferences, State of the Union addresses, and Al Qaeda videos served to legitimate labels in remarkable and effective ways.[112] In regard to the conflict with Osama bin Laden, Pilon (2001)[113] quotes Attorney General John Ashcroft, at a National Press Club luncheon, as say-ing that Americans were "at war against international terrorism." The axis of evil became the presidential refrain.

U.S. presidential ascriptions of terrorists' identities and methods have focused immensely on the unacceptable levels of death and destruction caused by terrorism. They stress the unacceptable aspect of terrorist incidents through the use of descriptors such as terrorism, terrorist act, massacre, atrocity, tragedy, calamity, indiscriminate slaughter, ruthless murder, butchery, cruel oppression, monstrous brutality, intimidation, subjugation, suppression, suf-fering, persecution, tyranny, horror, scourge, treachery, barbarism, acts of savagery, evil, and sadism.[114] Likewise, as Reverend Jerry Falwell said on *60 Minutes* in 2002, "I think Muhammad was a terrorist. I read enough of the history of his life written by both Muslims and non-Muslims, that he was a violent man, a man of war." It is very simple: if Robin Hood steals and keeps all the goodies, then it is a crime. If Robin Hood steals from the rich and gives the good-ies to the poor, then he would be a terrorist to one side and a hero to the other side.

Self-Ascribed Terrorist Identity

We use political labels: we refer to the bad ones as terrorists. They do not. The terror-ists, as their opponents call them, rarely identify themselves as such. Generally, they use other terms or terms pertaining to their situation, such as enemy combatants, freedom fighters, guerrillas, liberators, militants, paramilitary groups, patriots, revolutionaries, rebels, separatists, unlawful combatants, vigilantes, or any word with a similar meaning in other languages and cultures. While some Western pundits call militant groups and individuals in the Arab world terrorists, the latter call themselves mujahedin (jihadi terrorists), **Fedayeen** (suicide squads who are not bombers), and so forth. In fact, such Arabic words have entered the English lexicon for the past few decades.[115]

Based on unstructured interviews with Irish and European terrorists, Taylor and Quayle (1994)[116] reported that many respondents became terrorists as a result of their own creation of a new identity. Strentz (1981)[117] classifies three types of self-ascribed terrorist identity. The Leader is the chief ideologue and commander of the terrorist group and views him- or herself as the Anointed One chosen for bringing political, social, or ideological change. The Idealist is usually portrayed as a young, naïve, or oppressed person attracted to a terrorist organization. Just like the Leader, he or she hopes to create political, social, or ideological change. However, the Idealist does not give orders but follows them. The Opportunist displays antisocial traits, suffers from identity confusion, or does not see him- or herself as fitting any major personality mold in current society. By joining a terrorist organization, the Opportunist aspires to gain a sense of purpose and self-worth—"a place in the sun."[118] Typically, he or she already has a track record of criminal conduct that predates his or her membership with the terrorist organization.

A thorough study of terrorists' self-ascribed identities examined Germany's **Baader-Meinhof Group**, also called the **Red Army Faction**, one of Europe's most vicious post–World War II terrorist organizations. Researchers methodically reviewed major documents for each terrorist: perinatal, pediatric, preschool, lower school, grade school, high school, and university records. Researchers also interviewed the terrorists' relatives, neighbors, and classmates. Remarkably, no psychological differences emerged between the Baader-Meinhof Group terrorists and demographically matched controls. This is evidence that terrorists' behavior is sometimes rooted in the identity type they create for themselves later in life.[119] Let us look at this in further detail. Böllinger (1981)[120] conducted interviews with eight members of the German terrorist group. Böllinger found that some of the respondents' over-controlling parents, preventing them from becoming autonomous, led to identity crises. These youths became Idealists willing to engage in violent struggle and sacrificing their lives in attacks. Causing drastic societal change by liberating themselves and joining a terrorist organization was a major motive for such youths.

By the same token, those respondents with identity confusion saw themselves as Opportunists. After being distressed by a sense of isolation, they took part in terrorist acts as an adaptive response to the discomfort of anomie.[121] **Anomie** is a sense of social confusion and separation, a reaction against or withdrawal from the mainstream controls of society. The name Baader-Meinhof is a combination of the two founders' last names: Andreas Baader and Ulrike Meinhof. Baader was a historian's son, and Meinhof was an art historian's daughter. Meinhof was a graduate student in philosophy. Originally, the two founding members had no ill intentions and were actually peacemakers, taking reasonable political actions. Because their peaceful efforts were fruitless, Baader and Meinhof started to wear their Leader's hat: they recruited new members, radicalized their organization, and committed extremely violent acts.[122]

This anecdote is evocative of the works of psychiatrist Frantz Fanon (1965),[123] who posited that extreme self-determination to create change frees not only the body but also self-identity. Menachem Begin (1977),[124] Prime Minister of Israel from 1977 to 1983, confirmed this mode of thinking with his maxim, "We fight, therefore we are." In their tenacious search for identity, people turning to terrorism may act alone (e.g., Charles Bishop, the 15-year-old who crashed his airplane into a bank in 2002, leaving a suicide note in which he acknowledged he had identified with Al Qaeda) or may be enthusiastic about joining groups—a move offering an immediate grafting of identity.[125]

Terrorists' Educational and Family Backgrounds

Contrary to popular opinion, many terrorists come from mainstream educational and family backgrounds. The Aum Shinrikyo sect was composed of many specialists, including scientists and engineers. Scores of Baader-Meinhof terrorists were noticeably middle class. More recently, thorough studies of Islamist terrorists have categorized them as middle class, with a large percentage of engineers and physicians. Osama bin Laden came from a family with exceptional wealth in Saudi Arabia. Many terrorists have been exposed to the academic and cultural milieus of the West. As a case in point, terrorist Mohammed Atta came from a middle-class Egyptian background. Although he became a well-respected academic in Germany (and throughout the Western academic world), he was found to be a suspected mastermind of the September 11, 2001 attacks. He was flying the plane that crashed into the North Tower.[126]

Sageman (2004)[127] observed that 73% of the jihadists he studied were married and most of them had children. They came from upper- or middle-class families. Only a fairly small proportion (27%) came from working-class or poor families. This challenges assumptions that terrorism is a result of personal poverty or deprivation (although some cases are, of course). Bakker (2006)[128] noticed comparatively high levels of marriage among jihadists. An important conclusion here is that family commitments have certainly not prevented people from espousing jihad. Sageman also found that many jihadist marriages are to wives who share deep-seated ideological beliefs defending jihadism (or that the wives' families adopt those beliefs). Hence, marriage is essentially a supporting environment for jihadist views, and not a restraining influence.

Krueger and Maleckova's (2003)[129] study of 129 Hezbollah terrorists who died in action in the Middle East from 1982 to 1994 revealed that they had received better education and had earned more than non-terrorist Lebanese of the same age group and regional background. Pape's (2005)[130] study of suicide terrorists found that many of them came from privileged backgrounds. By the same token, research on non-jihadist terrorist groups generates similar results. For example, Hewitt (2003)[131] observed that members of the **Weather Underground**, a U.S. radical left organization that committed terrorist acts against the U.S. government, came mostly from middle- and upper-class families.

The Gender of the Terrorist

Since the beginning of modern terrorism, women have sometimes been the leaders and intellectual drivers, as it was the case in the U.S.-based Weather Underground, in Italy's Red Brigades, and Germany's Baader-Meinhof Group. As one can expect, the majority of female terrorists have been followers.[132] According to Harmon (2000),[133] today "more than 30% of international terrorists are women, and females are central to membership rosters and operational roles in nearly all insurgencies" (p. 212). Other figures range from 20% to 30% for many domestic and international terrorist groups. In general, left-wing organizations have exceedingly more female members than right-wing ones.[134] There are a few possible explanations for gender differences between ordinary crime and terrorism: terrorist actions (e.g., making bombs explode) may require less physical ability than many ordinary crimes (e.g., robbery); women may be tactically valuable because they can approach targets more closely without experiencing the same degree of scrutiny as men.

These differences imply that, in regard to gender, terrorism resembles white-collar crime more than other types of crime.[135] Between 1985 and 2006, 225 female suicide bombers from various terrorist organizations were identified and dozens of women were arrested after the suicide missions failed.[136] Pape (2005)[137] gathered data on 462 suicide bombers between 1980 and 2003 (including both genders). Fifty percent of the cases involved Muslim terrorists in Lebanon and Palestine who were linked to Al Qaeda, and most of the rest were Kurds, Chechens, and Tamil Tigers. Pape found that the proportion of women differed significantly across these groups, ranging from no women among the Al Qaeda terrorists to over 50% of women for the Chechens and Kurds.

The Age of the Terrorist

Mahan and Griset (2007)[138] observed that suicide terrorists are typically male aged 17 to 23. In his study of suicide terrorists, Pape (2005)[139] found that the average age ranged from 21.1 years for Lebanese Hezbollah and Palestinian terrorists to 29.8 years for Chechens. Part of this age difference lies in the median age differences in the populations from which suicide terrorists came: the median ages of the Lebanese and Palestinian groups were roughly ten years younger than that of the Chechens. In brief, in comparison with the results for regular crime, the correlation between age and terrorism seems to be stronger than the correlation between gender and terrorism. Pape also confirmed that, put side-by-side with men, women terrorists are on average older. For instance, the 48 women suicide terrorists in his survey were much older than the 213 men. Over 60% of the males were between 19 and 23, and only about 25% were 24 or older. On the other hand, only 40% of the females were between 19 and 23 and almost 50% were 24 or older. Part of this age difference lies in the fact that female suicide terrorists are sometimes widows of men killed by the government or the military. This situation is so common among female Chechen suicide bombers that they are often referred to as **Black Widows**. Finally, the average age of the left-wing terrorist is usually lower than other kinds of terrorists. In fact, many of them do not even have a high-school diploma.[140]

SUMMARY

Terrorism is an ancient practice that has existed for over 2,000 years. There is no universally agreed-on definition of terrorism. At best, there is a "most universally accepted" definition of it, which is the following: terrorism is the use of violence to create fear (i.e., terror; psychic fear) for (1) political, (2) religious, or (3) ideological reasons. Of particular relevance is the comparison between old and new terrorism. While old terrorism strikes only selected targets, new terrorism is indiscriminate; it causes as many casualties as possible. New terrorism is synonymous with Sam Huntington's (1996) "Clash of Civilizations," the idea that cultural and religious differences between civilizations across the world have become the primary source of terrorism today. This chapter also lists and describes fifteen causes that explain why people resort to terrorism. The last section of this chapter deals with the terrorist identity. Many terrorists have an ascribed identity (i.e., it is imposed on them) or self-ascribed identity (i.e., they choose it). In addition, many of them come from middle- and upper-class backgrounds, are young, and increasingly include females.

KEY TERMS

anomie   21

assassination   8

asymmetric warfare   5

bellum omnium contra omnes   12

caliphate   13

Clash of Civilizations   12

classical terrorism   11

content analysis   2

Culture of Terror   12

Death of Statecraft   18

diaspora   9

etymology   1

far enemy   13

Four Waves of terrorism   12

greater jihad   13

hub and spoke design   14

identity   20

identity cues   20

ideologies   4

international rule of law   16

Islamist   13

jihad   13

Jihad vs. McWorld   14

lesser jihad   13

mala in se acts   4

mala prohibita acts   4

martyrdom   13

modern terrorism   11

mujahedin   13

near enemy   13

new Islamic world order   13

new terrorism   11

new world order   12

old terrorism   11

paradigm   11

paradigm shift   11

pejorative term   2

People of the Book   13

postmodern terrorism   11

regicide   7

Reign of Terror   1

sharia   13

terror   1

terror cimbricus   1

terrorism   4

terrorist organization   4

tyrannicide   7

War of Ideas   12

wheel design   14

WMDs   12

ENDNOTES

1. Burgess, Mark (2003). *A Brief History of Terrorism*. Washington, D.C.: Center for Defense Information (CDI); Tuman, Joseph S. (2009). *Communicating Terror: The Rhetorical Dimensions of Terrorism* (2nd ed.). Thousand Oaks, CA: Sage.

2. Burke, Edmund (1790). *Reflections on the Revolution in France* (Ed. C. C. O'Brien, 1969, London: Penguin Books); Shane, Scott (2010, April 3). Words as Weapons: Dropping the "Terrorism" Bomb. *The New York Times*, p. WK1; Tuman, Joseph S. (2003). *Communicating Terror: The Rhetorical Dimensions of Terrorism*. Thousand Oaks, CA: Sage.

3. Crenshaw, Martha (1995). *Terrorism in Context*. University Park: Pennsylvania State University Press.

4. International Bar Association (2003). *International Terrorism: Legal Challenges and Responses*. Ardsley, NY: Transnational Publishers; Moeller, Susan D. (2002). A Hierarchy of Innocence: The Media's Use of Children in the Telling of International News. *The International Journal of Press/Politics, 7*(1), 36–56.

5. White, Jonathan R. (2011). *Terrorism & Homeland Security* (7th ed.). Belmont, CA: Wadsworth.

6. Simon, Jeffrey D. (1994). *The Terrorist Trap*. Bloomington: Indiana University Press.

7. Schmid, Alex, & Jongman, Albert (1988). *Political Terrorism: A New Guide to Actors, Authors, Concepts, Data Bases, Theories, and Literature*. Amsterdam: North Holland, Transaction Books.

8. Berg, Bruce L. (2009). *Qualitative Research Methods for the Social Sciences* (7th ed.). Boston: Allyn & Bacon.

9. Merari, Ariel (1993). Terrorism as a Strategy of Insurgency. *Terrorism and Political Violence, 5*(4), 213–251.

10. Laqueur, Walter (1987). *The Age of Terrorism* (2nd ed.). Boston: Little & Brown, p. 143.

11. Hoffman, Bruce (2006). *Inside Terrorism* (2nd ed.). New York: Columbia University Press, p. 43.

12. Schmid, Alex, & Jongman, Albert (1988). *Political Terrorism: A New Guide to Actors, Authors, Concepts, Data Bases, Theories, and Literature*. Amsterdam: North Holland, Transaction Books, p. 28.

13. Rapoport, David C. (1977, November 26). The Government Is Up in the Air over Combating Terrorism. *National Journal, 9*, 1853–1856.

14. Alexander, Yonah (1976). *International Terrorism: National, Regional and Global Perspectives*. New York: Praeger, p. xiv.

15. Sloan, Stephen (2006). *Terrorism: The Present Threat in Context*. Oxford: Berg Publishers.

16. League Convention (1937). Convention for the Prevention and Punishment of Terrorism. Article 1(2)

17. Joint Chiefs of Staff DOD (2008). *Department of Defense Dictionary of Military and Associated Terms*. Washington, D.C.: DOD.

18. U.S. Department of State (1996). *Patterns of Global Terrorism: 1995*. Washington, D.C.: U.S. Department of State.

19. Arab Convention for the Suppression of Terrorism (1998). *Arab Convention on Terrorism*. Cairo: Council of Arab Ministers of the Interior and the Council of Arab Ministers of Justice.

20. Khalil Shikaki (2001, December 21). Palestinian Survey Research, http://www.pcpsr.org.survey/polls/2001/p3a.html.

21. Barnett, Brooke, & Reynolds, Amy (2009). *Terrorism and the Press: An Uneasy Relationship*. New York: Peter Lang; Hoffman, Bruce (2006). *Inside terrorism* (2nd ed.). Columbia University Press; Jenkins, Brian (1983). Research in Terrorism: Areas of Consensus, Areas of Ignorance. In Burr Eichelman, David A. Soskis, & William H. Reid (Eds.), *Terrorism: Interdisciplinary Perspectives* (pp. 153–177). Washington, D.C.: American Psychiatric Association; Schmid, Alex P., & de Graaf, Janny (1982). *Violence as Communication: Insurgent Terrorism and the Western News Media*. Beverly Hills: Sage.

22. Rush, George E. (2002). *The Dictionary of Criminal Justice* (5th ed.). Guildford, CT: McGraw-Hill, pp. 204–205.

23. Hoge, James F., Jr., & Rose, Gideon (2001). *How Did This Happen? Terrorism and the New War*. New York: Public Affairs; Mansdorf, Irwin J., & Kedar, Mordechai (2008). The Psychological Asymmetry of Islamist Warfare. *Middle East Quarterly, 15*(2), 37–44; White, Jonathan R. (2011). *Terrorism & Homeland Security* (7th ed.). Belmont, CA: Wadsworth.

24. U.S. Department of State (2011, September 15). *Foreign Terrorist Organizations*. Washington, D.C.: U.S. Department of State. Retrieved December 18, 2011 from http://www.state.gov/s/ct/rls/other/des/123085.htm

25. Roux, George (1966). *Ancient Iraq*. Baltimore, MD: Penguin Books.

26. Gibbon, Edward (1974). *The History of the Decline and Fall of the Roman Empire*. New York: AMS Press; Imre, Robert, Mooney, T. Brian, & Clarke, Benjamin (2008). *Responding to Terrorism*. Farnham, England: Ashgate; Laqueur, Walter (1999). *The New Terrorism: Fanaticism and the Arms of Mass Destruction*. London: Oxford University Press; Wells, Peter S. (2003). *The Battle That Stopped Rome*. New York: W.W. Norton & Company.

27. Matusitz, Jonathan (2008). Similarities between Terrorist Networks in Antiquity and Present-Day Cyberterrorist Networks. *Trends in Organized Crime, 11*(2), 183–199; Matusitz, Jonathan (2011). Social Network Theory: A Comparative Analysis of the Jewish Revolt in Antiquity and the Cyberterrorism Incident over Kosovo. *Information Security Journal: A Global Perspective, 20*(1), 34–44.

28. Ben-Yehuda, Nachman (1998). Where Masada's Defenders Fell. *Biblical Archaeology Review 24*(6), 32–39; Laqueur, Walter (1999). *Terrorism and History*. Oxford: Oxford University Press; Roth, Cecil (1959). The Zealots in the War of 66–73. *Journal of Semitic Studies, 4*, 332–355.

29. Chaliand, Gérard, & Blin, Arnaud (2007). *The History of Terrorism, from Antiquity to Al Qaeda*. Berkeley: University of California Press.

30. Anderson, Sean K., & Sloan, Stephen (2003). *Terrorism: Assassins to Zealots*. Lanham: Scarecrow Press; Lewis, Bernard (1987). *The Assassins: A Radical Sect in Islam*. New York: Oxford University Press; Martin, Gus (2010). *Understanding Terrorism: Challenges, Perspectives, and Issues*. Thousand Oaks, CA: Sage.

31. Martin, Gus (2010). *Understanding Terrorism: Challenges, Perspectives, and Issues*. Thousand Oaks, CA: Sage.

32. Nabulsi, Karma (1999). *Traditions of War*. Oxford: Oxford University Press; Ticehurst, Rupert (1997). The Martens Clause and the Laws of Armed Conflict. *International Review of the Red Cross, 317*, 125–134.

33. Sinclair, Andrew (2003). *An Anatomy of Terror: A History of Terrorism*. London: Macmillan.

34. Hoffman, Bruce (1999). *Inside Terrorism*. New York: Columbia University Press.

35. Risks International. (1985). *Major Incidents of Terrorism: 1970–1984*. Alexandria, VA: Risks International.

36. Jenkins, Brian M. (1985). Terrorism Prone Countries and Conditions. In Ariel Merari (Ed.), *On Terrorism and Combating Terrorism* (pp. 25–40). Frederick, MD: University Publications of America.

37. Li, Quan, & Schaub, Drew (2004). Economic Globalization and Transnational Terrorist Incidents: A Pooled Time Series Analysis. *Journal of Conflict Resolution, 48*(2), 230–258.

38. Bakker, Edwin (2007). *Jihadi Terrorists in Europe*. The Hague: Netherlands Institute of International Relations; Sageman, Marc (2008). *Leaderless Jihad: Terror Networks in the Twenty-First Century*. Philadelphia: University of Pennsylvania Press.

39. Braziel, Jane Evans (2008). *Diaspora: An introduction*. Malden, MA: Blackwell.

40. Jackson, Richard (2005). *Writing the War on Terrorism: Language, Politics and Counter-Terrorism*. Manchester, England: Manchester University Press.

41. Martin, Gus (2010). *Understanding Terrorism: Challenges, Perspectives, and Issues*. Thousand Oaks, CA: Sage.

42. RAND (2011). *RAND Database of Worldwide Terrorism Incidents*. Santa Monica: RAND Corporation. Retrieved April 6, 2011 from http://www.rand.org/nsrd/projects/terrorism-incidents.html

43. Pontvieux, Delphine (2010). *ETA—Estimated Time of Arrest*. Chicago: Miss Nyet Publishing.

44. Martin, Gus (2010). *Understanding Terrorism: Challenges, Perspectives, and Issues*. Thousand Oaks, CA: Sage.

45. Pew Research Center (2009). *Mapping the Global Muslim Population*. Washington, D.C.: Pew Research Center. Available at http://pewforum.org/newassets/images/reports/Muslimpopulation/Muslimpopulation.pdf

46. Pew Research Center (2007). *Muslim Americans: Middle Class and Mostly Mainstream*. Washington, D.C.: Pew Research Center. Available at http://pewresearch.org/assets/pdf/muslim-americans.pdf

47. Laqueur, Walter (1999). *The New Terrorism: Fanaticism and the Arms of Mass Destruction*. London: Oxford University Press, p. 4.

48. Laqueur, Walter (1999). *The New Terrorism: Fanaticism and the Arms of Mass Destruction*. London: Oxford University Press, p. 81.

49. Carter, Ashton B., Deutch, John, & Zelikow, Philip (1999). Catastrophic Terrorism. *Foreign Affairs, 77*(6), 80–94; Hoffman, Bruce (1998). *Inside Terrorism*. London: St. Andrew's University Press; Laqueur, Walter (2003). *No End to War: Terrorism in the Twenty-First Century*. New York: Continuum.

50. Juergensmeyer, Mark (2000). *Terror in the Mind of God: The Global Rise of Religious Violence*. Berkeley: University of California Press.

51. Gurr, Nadine, & Cole, Benjamin (2000). *The New Face of Terrorism: Threats from Weapons of Mass Destruction*. London: I.B. Tauris.

52. Ganor, Boaz (2002). Defining Terrorism: Is One Man's Terrorist Another Man's Freedom Fighter? *Police Practice and Research, 3*(4), 287–304.

53. Sinai, Joshua (2004). Forecasting Terrorists' Proclivity to Embark on CBRN Warfare. *International Studies Review, 7*, 133–154.

54. Rapoport, David (1988). Introduction. In David Rapoport (Ed.), *Inside the Terrorist Organizations* (pp. 2–10). New York: Columbia University Press.

55. Crelinsten, Ronald D. (1988). Images of Terrorism in the Media: 1966–1985. *Terrorism, 12*, 167–198; Jenkins, Brian M. (2000). Terrorism. In Edgar F. Borgotta (Ed.), *Encyclopedia of Sociology* (pp. 3137–3141). New York: Macmillan; Lifton, Robert J. (2000). *Destroying the World to Save It: Aum Shinrikyo, Apocalyptic Violence, and the New Global Terrorism*. New York: Picador; Rapoport, David (1988). Introduction. In David Rapoport (Ed.), *Inside the Terrorist Organizations* (pp. 2–10). New York: Columbia University Press; Weigert, Andrew J. (2003). Terrorism, Identity, and Public Order: A Perspective from Goffman. *Identity: An International Journal of Theory and Research, 3*(2), 93–113; Wittebols, James H. (1991). Politics and Coverage of Terrorism: From Media Images to Public Consciousness. *Communication Theory, 1*, 253–266.

56. Huntington, Samuel P. (1996). *The Clash of Civilizations and the Remaking of World Order*. New York: Simon & Schuster.

57. Hoffman, Bruce (1995). "Holy Terror": The Implications of Terrorism Motivated by a Religious Imperative. *Studies in Conflict and Terrorism, 18*(4), 271–284; Whine, Michael (2002). *The New Terrorism*. Herzliya, Israel: International Policy Institute for Counter Terrorism.

58. Morgan, Matthew J. (2004). The Origin of the New Terrorism. *Parameters, XXXIV*(1), 30–31.

59. Imre, Robert, Mooney, T. Brian, & Clarke, Benjamin (2008). *Responding to Terrorism*. Farnham, England: Ashgate.

60. Martin, Gus (2010). *Understanding Terrorism: Challenges, Perspectives, and Issues*. Thousand Oaks, CA: Sage.

61. Ansari, Hamied (1984). The Islamic Militants in Egyptian Politics. *International Journal of Middle East Studies, 16*, 136–140; Zeidan, David (2001). The Islamic Fundamentalist View of Life as a Perennial Battle. *Middle East Review of International Affairs, 5*(4), 10–21.

62. Gerges, Fawaz (2005). *The Far Enemy: Why Jihad Went Global*. New York: Cambridge University Press.

63. Alexander, Jeffrey C. (2004). From the Depths of Despair: Performance, Counterperformance, and "September 11." *Sociological Theory, 22*(1), 88–105; Sageman, Marc (2004). *Understanding Terror Networks*. Philadelphia: University of Pennsylvania Press.

64. Gunaratna, Rohan (2007). Ideology in Terrorism and Counter Terrorism: Lessons from Combating al Qaeda and al Jemaah Islamiyah in Southeast Asia. In Anne Aldis & Graeme Herd (Eds.), *The Ideological War on Terror: Worldwide Strategies for Counterterrorism* (pp. 21–34). New York: Routledge.

65. Badran, Margot (2001). Understanding Islam, Islamism, and Islamic Feminism. *Journal of Women's History, 13*(1), 47–52.

66. Stakelbeck, Erick (2011). *The Terrorist Next Door: How the Government Is Deceiving You about the Islamist Threat*. New York: Regnery Publishing.

67. Barber, Benjamin R. (1995). *Jihad vs. McWorld*. New York: Crown.

68. Jandt, Fred (2010). *An Introduction to Intercultural Communication: Identities in a Global Community* (6th ed.). Thousand Oaks, CA: Sage; Le Feber, Walter (2002). The Post September 11 Debate over Empire,

Globalization, and Fragmentation. *Political Science Quarterly, 117*(1), 9–10; Zirinski, Roni (2005). *Ad Hoc Arabism: Advertising, Culture, and Technology in Saudi Arabia.* New York: Peter Lang.

69. Gunaratna, Rohan (2002). *Inside Al Qaeda. Global Network of Terror.* London: Hurst; Spencer, Alexander (2006). Questioning the Concept of "New Terrorism." *Peace Conflict & Development, 8,* 1–33.

70. Simon, Steven, & Benjamin, Daniel (2000). America and the New Terrorism. *Survival, 42*(1), p. 70.

71. Arquilla, John, Ronfeldt, David, & Zanini, Michele (1999). Networks, Netwar and Information-Age Terrorism. In I. O. Lesser, B. Hoffman, J. Arquilla, D. F. Ronfeldt, M. Zanini, & B. M. Jenkins (Eds.), *Countering the New Terrorism* (pp. 39–88). Santa Monica: RAND.

72. O'Brien, Kevin A. (2003). Information Age, Terrorism and Warfare. *Small Wars and Insurgencies, 14*(1), 183–206; Tsfati, Yariv, & Weimann, Gabriel (2002). WWW.Terrorism.com: Terror on the Internet. *Studies in Conflict and Terrorism, 25*(5), 317–332.

73. Raphaeli, Nimrod (2003). Financing of Terrorism: Sources, Methods, and Channels. *Terrorism and Political Violence, 15*(4), 59–82.

74. Imre, Robert, Mooney, T. Brian, & Clarke, Benjamin (2008). *Responding to Terrorism.* Farnham, England: Ashgate; Prus, Robert (2005). Terrorism, Tyranny, and Religious Extremism as Collective Activity: Beyond the Deviant, Psychological, and Power Mystiques. *The American Sociologist, 36*(1), 47–74.

75. Husain, Ed (2007). *The Islamist: Why I Joined Radical Islam in Britain, What I Saw Inside and Why I Left.* New York: Penguin.

76. Islam, Muhammad Q., & Shahin, Wassim N. (2001). Applying Economic Methodology to the War on Terrorism. *Forum for Social Economics, 31*(1), 7–26.

77. Hadith #2687: "The smallest reward for the people of Heaven is an abode where there are 80,000 servants and 72 houri [virgins], over which stands a dome decorated with pearls, aquamarine and ruby, as wide as the distance from al-Jabiyyah to San'a."

78. Jaffar (2000, October 23). Interview with Jamil Hamad: First Person: I Shot an Israeli. *Time.*

79. Crenshaw, Martha (1986). 1986. The Psychology of Political Terrorism. In Margaret G. Hermann (Ed.), *Political Psychology* (pp. 379–413). San Francisco: Jossey-Bass; Post, Jerrold M., Sprinzak, Ehud, & Denny, Laurita M. (2003). The Terrorists in Their Own Words: Interviews with 35 Incarcerated Middle Eastern Terrorists. *Terrorism and Political Violence, 15,* 171–184; Taylor, Maxwell, & Quayle, Ethel (1994). *Terrorist Lives.* London: Brassey's.

80. McCauley, Clark, & Moskalenko, Sophia (2008). Mechanisms of Political Radicalization: Pathways toward Terrorism. *Terrorism and Political Violence, 30*(3), 415–433.

81. Tessendorf, K. C. (1986). *Kill the Tzar! Youth and Terrorism in Old Russia.* New York: Atheneum.

82. Tishkov, Valery (2004). *Chechnya: Life in a War-Torn Society.* Berkeley: University of California Press.

83. Imre, Robert, Mooney, T. Brian, & Clarke, Benjamin (2008). *Responding to Terrorism.* Farnham, England: Ashgate.

84. Hafez, Mohammed M. (2007). Martyrdom Mythology in Iraq: How Jihadists Frame Suicide Terrorism in Videos and Biographies. *Terrorism and Political Violence, 19*(1), 95–115; Moghaddam, Fathali (2007). Mayhem, Myths, and Martyrdom: The Shi'a Conception of Jihad. *Terrorism and Political Violence, 19*(1), 125–143.

85. Crenshaw, Martha (1981). The Causes of Terrorism. *Comparative Politics, 13*(4), 379–399.

86. Imre, Robert, Mooney, T. Brian, & Clarke, Benjamin (2008). *Responding to Terrorism.* Farnham, England: Ashgate.

87. Harmon, Christopher C. (2000). *Terrorism Today.* London: Frank Cass; Hasisi, Badi, &, Pedahzur, Ami (2000). State, Policy, and Political Violence: Arabs in the Jewish State. *Civil Wars, 3,* 64–84; Schmid, Alex (1983). *Political Terrorism: A Research Guide to the Concepts, Theories, Databases and Literature.* Amsterdam: North Holland.

88. Bennet, J. (2004, July 15). In Chaos, Palestinians Struggle for Way Out. *The New York Times, 1,* 10–11.

89. Sageman, Marc (2004). *Understanding Terror Networks.* Philadelphia: University of Pennsylvania Press.

90. Palmer, David Scott (1995). Revolutionary terrorism of Peru's Shining Path. In Martha Crenshaw (Ed.), *Terrorism in Context* (pp. 249–308). University Park: Pennsylvania State University Press.

91. Louw, P. Eric (2003). The "War against Terrorism": A Public Relations Challenge for the Pentagon. *Gazette: The International Journal for Communication Studies, 65*(3), 211–230.

92. International Monetary Fund. (2001, December 18). *World Economic Outlook: The Global Economy after September 11*. Press release.

93. Islam, Muhammad Q., & Shahin, Wassim N. (2001). Applying Economic Methodology to the War on Terrorism. *Forum for Social Economics, 31*(1), 7–26.

94. Bouhana, Noémie, & Wikström, Per-Olof H. (2008). *Theorizing Terrorism: Terrorism as Moral Action*. London: University of College London Research Reports.

95. Gottschalk, Michael, & Gottschalk, Susan (2004). Authoritarianism and Pathological Hatred: The Social Psychological Profile of the Middle Eastern Terrorist. *American Sociologist, 32*, 38–59.

96. Louw, P. Eric (2003). The "War against Terrorism": A Public Relations Challenge for the Pentagon. *Gazette: The International Journal for Communication Studies, 65*(3), 211–230; Lulat, Y. G.-M. (2005). *A History of African Higher Education from Antiquity to the Present: A Critical Synthesis*. Santa Barbara: Praeger.

97. Bassiouni, M. Cherif (1979). Prolegomenon to Terror Violence. *Creighton Law Review, 12*(3), 745–780; Kelly, Michael J., & Mitchell, Thomas H. (1981). Transnational Terrorism and the Western Elite Press. *Political Communication and Persuasion, 1*(3), 269–296; Thornton, Thomas Perry (1964). Terror as a Weapon of Political Agitation. In Harry Eckstein (Ed.), *Internal War: Problems and Approaches* (pp. 71–99). New York: The Free Press.

98. Pyszczynski, Tom, Abdollahi, Abdolhossein, Solomon, Sheldon, Greenberg, Jeff, Cohen, Florette, & Weise, David (2006). Mortality Salience, Martyrdom, and Military Might: The Great Satan Versus the Axis of Evil. *Personality and Social Psychology Bulletin, 32*(4), 525–537.

99. Post, Jerrold M. (1987). Rewarding Fire with Fire: Effects of Retaliation on Terrorist Group Dynamics. *Terrorism, 10*, 23–36.

100. Suellwold, Liselotte (1981). In Herbert Jäger, Gerhard Schmidtchen, & Liselotte Suellwold (Eds.), *Analysen Zum Terrorismus 2: Lebenslauf-Analysen*. Darmstadt, Germany: Deutscher Verlag.

101. Crenshaw, Martha (1990). Questions to Be Answered, Research to Be Done, Knowledge to Be Applied. In Walter Reich (Ed.), *Origins of Terrorism: Psychologies, Ideologies, Theologies, States of Mind* (pp. 247–260). New York: Cambridge University Press.

102. Hamm, Mark S. (2004). Apocalyptic Violence: The Seduction of Terrorist Subcultures. *Theoretical Criminology, 8*(3), 323–339.

103. Victoroff, Jeff (2005). The Mind of the Terrorist: A Review and Critique of Psychological Approaches. *Journal of Conflict Resolution, 49*, 3–42; Zuckerman, Marvin (2002). Genetics of Sensation Seeking. In Jonathan Benjamin, Richard P. Ebstein, & Robert Belmaker (Eds.), *Molecular Genetics and the Human Personality* (pp. 193–210). Washington, D.C.: American Psychiatric Publishing.

104. Crenshaw, Martha (1990). Questions to Be Answered, Research to Be Done, Knowledge to Be Applied. In Walter Reich (Ed.), *Origins of Terrorism: Psychologies, Ideologies, Theologies, States of Mind* (pp. 247–260). New York: Cambridge University Press; Klausner, Samuel Z. (1968). The Intermingling of Pain and Pleasure: The Stress-Seeking Personality in Its Social Context. In Samuel Z. Klausner (Ed.), *Why Man Takes Chances: Studies in Stress Seeking* (pp. 137–168). New York: Doubleday.

105. Chomsky, Noam (2006). *Failed States: The Abuse of Power and the Assault on Democracy*. New York: Metropolitan Books.

106. Imre, Robert, Mooney, T. Brian, & Clarke, Benjamin (2008). *Responding to Terrorism*. Farnham, England: Ashgate.

107. Oliver, Mark (2005, August 4). Al-Qaeda Warns of More London Destruction. *The Guardian*, p. A1.

108. Breivik, Anders Behring (2011). *2083: A European Declaration of Independence*. Retrieved December 18, 2011 from http://www.kevinislaughter.com/wp-content/uploads/2083 + - + A + European + Declaration + o f + Independence.pdf

109. Afshar, Halah, Aitken, Rob, & Franks, Myfanwy (2005). Feminisms, Islamophobia and Identities. *Political Studies, 53*(2), 262–283; Lichtensetin, Heinz (1961). Identity and Sexuality. A Study of Their Interrelationship in Man. *Journal of the American Psychoanalytic Association, 9*, 179–260; *New Oxford American Dictionary* (2010). Oxford: Oxford University Press.

110. Bakker, Edwin (2006). *Jihadi Terrorists in Europe, Their Characteristics and the Circumstances in Which They Joined the Jihad: An Exploratory Study*. The Hague: Clingendael Institute; Lifton, Robert J. (2000).

Destroying the World to Save It: Aum Shinrikyo, Apocalyptic Violence, and the New Global Terrorism. New York: Picador; Sageman, Marc (2004). *Understanding Terror Networks*. Philadelphia: University of Pennsylvania Press; Sageman, Marc (2008). *Leaderless Jihad*. Philadelphia: University of Pennsylvania Press.

111. Best, Steven, & Nocella II, Anthony J. (2004). Defining Terrorism. *Animal Liberation Philosophy and Policy Journal, 2*(1), 1–18.

112. Heath, Robert L., & O'Hair, Dan (2008). Terrorism: From the Eyes of the Beholder. In Dan O'Hair, Robert Heath, Kevin Ayotte, & Gerald R. Ledlow (Eds.), *Terrorism: Communication and Rhetorical Perspectives* (pp. 17–41). Cresskill, NJ: Hampton Press.

113. Pilon, R. (2001, December 10). *Right, Center, and Left Support Free and Open Debate in Wartime: Dissent Does Not Give Aid, Comfort to Enemy*. Remarks delivered at the National Press Club meeting, Washington, D.C., by the vice president for legal affairs and director, Center for Constitutional Studies, Cato Institute, Washington, D.C.

114. Winkler, Carol (2008). Recalling U.S. Terrorism History in Contemporary Presidential Discourse. In Dan O'Hair, Robert Heath, Kevin Ayotte, & Gerald R. Ledlow (Eds.), *Terrorism: Communication and Rhetorical Perspectives* (pp. 193–217). Cresskill, NJ: Hampton Press.

115. Abrahamian, Ervand (2008). *A Modern History of Iran*. Cambridge: Cambridge University Press; Rea, Tony, & Wright, John (1993). *The Arab-Israeli Conflict*. Oxford: Oxford University Press.

116. Taylor, Maxwell, & Quayle, Ethel (1994). *Terrorist Lives*. London: Brassey's.

117. Strentz, Thomas (1981). The Terrorist Organizational Profile: A Psychological Role Model. In Yonah Alexander & John Gleason (Eds.), *Behavioral and Quantitative Perspectives on Terrorism* (pp. 86–104). New York: Pergamon.

118. Taylor, Maxwell, & Quayle, Ethel (1994). *Terrorist Lives*. London: Brassey's.

119. McCauley, Clark (2002). Psychological Issues in Understanding Terrorism and the Response to Terrorism. In Chris E. Stout (Ed.), *The Psychology of Terrorism: Theoretical Understandings and Perspectives, Vol. III. Psychological Dimensions to War and Peace* (pp. 3–29). Westport, CT: Praeger.

120. Böllinger, Lorenz (1981). Die entwicklung zu terroristischem handeln als psychosozialer prozess: Begegnungen mit beteiligten. In H. Jäger, G. Schmidtchen, and L. Süllwold (Ed.), *Analyzen zum terrorismus 2: Lebenslaufanalysen*. Darmstadt, Germany: DeutscherVerlag.

121. Victoroff, Jeff (2005). The Mind of the Terrorist: A Review and Critique of Psychological Approaches. *Journal of Conflict Resolution, 49*(1), 3–42.

122. McCauley, Clark & Segal, Mary D. (1989). Terrorist Individuals and Terrorist Groups: The Normal Psychology of Extreme Behavior. In Jo Groebel & Jeffrey F. Goldstein (Eds.), *Terrorism* (pp. 39–64). Seville, Spain: Publicaciones de la Universidad de Sevilla.

123. Fanon, Frantz (1965). *The Wretched of the Earth*. London: MacGibbon and Kee.

124. Begin, Menachem (1977). *The Revolt: Story of the Irgun*. Jerusalem: Steimatzky's Agency.

125. Rosenberg, Debra, Waddell, Lynn, & Smalley, Suzanne (2002, January 21.). A Troubled Teenager's Tragic Flight Plan. *Newsweek*.

126. Lifton, Robert J. (2000). *Destroying the World to Save It: Aum Shinrikyo, Apocalyptic Violence, and the New Global Terrorism*. New York: Picador; Sageman, Marc (2008). *Leaderless Jihad*. Philadelphia: University of Pennsylvania Press; Stout, Chris E. (2002). *The Psychology of Terrorism: Theoretical Understandings and Perspectives, Vol. III. Psychological Dimensions to War and Peace*. Westport, CT: Praeger.

127. Sageman, Marc (2004). *Understanding Terror Networks*. Philadelphia: University of Pennsylvania Press.

128. Bakker, Edwin (2006). *Jihadi Terrorists in Europe, Their Characteristics and the Circumstances in Which They Joined the Jihad: An Exploratory Study*. The Hague: Clingendael Institute.

129. Krueger, Alan B., & Maleckova, Jitka (2003). Education, Poverty and Terrorism: Is There a Causal Connection? *Journal of Economic Perspectives, 17*(4), 119–144.

130. Pape, Robert A. (2005). *Dying to Win*. New York: Random House.

131. Hewitt, Christopher (2003). *Understanding Terrorism in America: From the Klan to al Qaeda*. London: Routledge.

132. Nacos, Brigitte L. (2005). The Portrayal of Female Terrorists in the Media: Similar Framing Patterns in the News Coverage of Women in Politics and in Terrorism. *Studies in Conflict & Terrorism, 28*, 435–451.

133. Harmon, Christopher C. (2000). *Terrorism Today*. London: Frank Cash.

134. Nacos, Brigitte L. (2005). The Portrayal of Female Terrorists in the Media: Similar Framing Patterns in the News Coverage of Women in Politics and in Terrorism. *Studies in Conflict & Terrorism, 28*, 435–451.

135. Forst, Brian (2008). *Terrorism, Crime and Public Policy*. Cambridge: Cambridge University Press.

136. Von Knop, Katharina (2007). The Female Jihad: Al Qaeda's Women. *Studies in Conflict & Terrorism, 30*, 397–414.

137. Pape, Robert A. (2005). *Dying to Win*. New York: Random House.

138. Mahan, Sue G., & Griset, Pamala L. (2007). *Terrorism in Perspective* (2nd ed.). Thousand Oaks, CA: Sage.

139. Pape, Robert A. (2005). *Dying to Win*. New York: Random House.

140. Laqueur, Walter (1987). *The Age of Terrorism* (2nd ed.). Boston: Little & Brown.

CHAPTER 2

Terrorism as a Communication Process: Tactics

After reading this chapter, you will be able to

- explain terrorism as a dynamic, two-way communication process between a sender (the terrorist) and a receiver (the audience);
- discuss persuasion as the objective of terrorism; and
- identify and describe three forms of terrorism as a communication process: social noise, the signature method, and the conduit metaphor.

COMMUNICATION: DEFINITION

Communication is the act of conveying a message from a sender to a receiver. The study of communication in Western culture has a history of approximately 2,500 years and is reported to have originated in Greece with Aristotle's *Rhetoric and Poetics*. For Aristotle, the process of communication involved the speaker, the speech act, the audience, and a purpose. He contended that all communication is persuasion and entails people as senders and receivers of messages. The study of communication lived on through Roman rhetorical theory, continental traditions, and about 200 years in the U.S.[1] As Harold Lasswell (1948)[2] famously said, communication is the act or process of "who says what in which channel to whom with what effect" (p. 38). In his view of communication, Lasswell identified several essential elements: a sender (who), a message (says what), a medium (in which channel), a receiver (to whom), and a purpose (with what effect). Lasswell's model suggests that communication is purposeful and is meant to have an impact on the audience.

Berlo's Model of Communication

David Berlo's (1960)[3] **Model of Communication**, largely inspired by Shannon and Weaver's (1949)[4] "mathematical model" of a one-way, direct transmission of messages, stresses that communication is a dynamic process because both the sender and receiver are interconnected and influence each other. Unlike Shannon and Weaver's model of communication, Berlo's model, as seen in his ten components of communication (see below), stresses other important aspects such as feedback and context:

(1) Source: the person who has an idea, an intention to communicate. Examples are Osama bin Laden (through his taped speeches), Al Jazeera, the White House, or a maimed victim being interviewed.

(2) Encoding: the process of turning the idea into a symbol. When using symbols to communicate, human beings assume that the other person shares and understands their symbol system. These symbolic meanings are sent both verbally and nonverbally. Nonverbal symbols can communicate powerful meanings. An example is the image of Osama bin Laden on his white horse, as shown by Joseph Tuman (2010)[5] in his book titled *Communicating Terrorism*. Muslims believe that Prophet Muhammad's horse was white (the one he mounted on his journey from Mecca to Jerusalem). Osama bin Laden on a white horse was a potent symbol of a desire for conquest.[6] Conversely, in May 2006, the U.S. Department of Defense (DOD) took a jab at Al-Zarqawi by depicting him, in an outtake, as a fool unable to handle a weapon. Al-Zarqawi was a militant Islamist killed in Iraq by U.S. forces later that year. The DOD's satire was to convey the idea that even an international terrorist like Al-Zarqawi can be mocked and then eliminated.

(3) Message: the encoded thought. While encoding is the process, the message is the resulting entity. Each message can have more than one meaning, and many different degrees. For example, the message "We will retaliate" can mean "We will bombard the whole region," "We will launch airstrikes," "We will send troops," "We will join forces with our allies," "We will enforce an embargo," or "We will capture the enemies and put them on trial."

(4) Channel (or medium): the means by which the encoded message is sent. The channel may be face-to-face communication, the television, the radio, print media, or electronic media (i.e., Internet).

(5) Noise: anything that distorts the message encoded by the source. There are many types of noise: (a) external noise (sights, sounds, stimuli that deflect our attention away from the message; listening to music while writing a paper is external noise); (b) internal noise (thoughts and feelings interfering with the message. For example, thinking of the terrorist attack that struck your hometown yesterday will distract you from attending to the message); (c) semantic noise (alternative meanings of the source's message can get us sidetracked. For example, a speaker's use of unwarranted curse words can make us wonder why the speaker used curse words that distracted from the message); and (d) cultural noise (occurs when the receiver's culture is so different from the sender's that the message is understood in a different or unanticipated way).[7]

(6) Receiver: the person attending to the message.

(7) Decoding: the opposite of encoding. The receiver is ascribing meanings to the symbols received.

(8) Receiver's answer (or reaction): the receiver's response after he or she has received and decoded the message. The receiver's reaction can range from taking no action to doing something or taking actions that the source had or had not anticipated.

(9) Feedback: the part of the receiver's response that the source knows and to which the source attends and assigns meaning. With feedback, communication becomes a two-way process.

(10) Context: an important component of communication. Context means culture, setting, or background; it is the environment in which communication takes place.

This model is also called the **hypodermic model**, in which the sender of the message selects an appropriate communication channel (e.g., face-to-face, phone, radio, e-mail, etc.) and sends a message to the receiver.[8] Corman, Thethewey, and Goodall (2007)[9] created a similar model called the **Message Influence Model**. The model conceptualizes messages as a conduit for conveying information from a source to a receiver. The purpose of the message is to have an effect on the receiver so that he or she understands the information in the same way as the source. If not, the sender needs to persuade the receiver to change his or her attitudes.

TERRORISM AS A COMMUNICATION PROCESS

Terrorism is essentially a communication process. It is disseminated through public communication and publicized through mass communication. Terrorism is a communicative act because it is aimed at a very large audience beyond the direct targets. The objective of terrorism is to create fear and signs of fear. Overall, terrorist attacks produce fewer casualties than what was intended, but the attacks imprint signs, messages, and images on our minds. They create interferences—those internal noises discussed in Berlo's Model of Communication. The audiences of terrorism, in turn, communicate with one another—both individually and collectively, and both directly and indirectly. This whole process is part of a bigger loop that will also feed back to the terrorists. In most situations, the interactions between all the audiences already existed before the communication loop established by the terrorist message.[10]

The terrorist has a message to send. The violence—a medium in and of itself—is conveyed to the immediate receiver, typically with devastating effects. This is interpersonal communication, in the same way that one sends a punch in the face or letter in the mail. As a form of interpersonal communication, terrorist violence requires killing or maiming of the victim to be effective. Nevertheless, the goal of most terrorism is not killing but change, usually a change in the audience's behavior or beliefs. As such, terrorism seeks to modify the behavior or beliefs of the public.[11]

Communicating Terrorism: A Model

Joseph Tuman (2003)[12] conceived a **model of terrorism as a communication process**: the terrorist conveys a message to a target audience (i.e., the general public, the government, an organization, etc.) by committing an act of violence. The message, in and of itself, is not the violence. Instead, it is encoded within such an activity. Terrorism as a communication process has a rhetorical facet that is separate from the simple force (or intimidation) linked to violence for its own sake. Terrorist acts may well serve to trigger discourse among target audiences. The process of encoding depends on the context: the symbolic tone of the violence and the capacity for using different media to send such a message. The target audience decodes this message by also depending on the context: the methods and tools the audience has for interpreting the situation—what Tuman refers to as "constructing its own sense of reality" (p. 19). As shown in Figure 2.1, a terrorist act does not work with a one-way communication process. Rather, the terrorist message is two-way (interactive) because the first message creates some kind of response, which will then be fed back to the terrorist either directly (i.e., through government action, evidence of public discourse, etc.) or indirectly (i.e., through the explanation of the response by the media).

Figure 2.1 Tuman's Model of Terrorism as a Communication Process

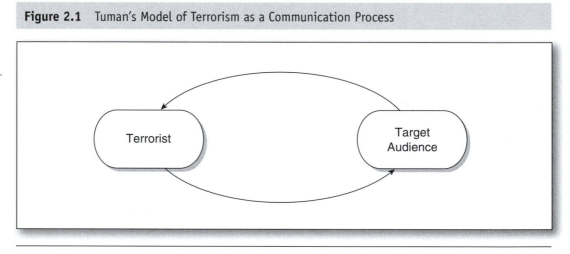

Source: Communicating Terror: The Rhetorical Dimensions of Terrorism, by Joseph S. Tuman, 2003, Thousand Oaks, CA: Sage. Copyright 2003 by Sage Publications. Reprinted with permission.

Act of Terrorism

Terrorists may try to cause fear, panic, and chaos, or attract attention to an issue or condition that the media, political institutions, or academic conferences have given scant or no treatment. The terrorists may also try to cause the government or institution (which was just attacked or coerced by an act of violence) to surrender to the demands (made by the terrorists). Given these circumstances, the real objective of terrorism as a communication process is persuasion. In this case, the goal of terrorism would be to persuade the audience that chaos and fear will ensue, to persuade them to seriously consider an issue they have ignored, or to persuade them to take actions they would not otherwise take.[13] To have a basic understanding of how the communication process works and creates terrorism for the audience, we must analyze three forms of communication of terrorism: social noise, the signature method, and the conduit metaphor. First, it might prove interesting to look at the Collective Communication Model of Terrorism.

Collective Communication Model of Terrorism

Terrorism is an act, a process, a plan intended to cause a response. Since communication is an interactive process between the sender and the receiver, it follows that the terrorist is the sender of the message and the target audience is the receiver of the message. This process is fundamentally communicative. Communication functions as the conduit for carrying terrorism motives. Until we recognize and understand the supremacy of communication within terrorism, we will continue to be oblivious to this communicative impact on our lives.[14] What is the symbolic expression of terrorism? Terrorism has long been acknowledged to be a violent vehicle for communication. Hence, the terrorist act itself is purposely created to attract attention and, through the publicity that it produces, to communicate a message. As Schmid and de Graaf (1982)[15] observed about thirty years ago, "Without communication there can be no terrorism" (p. 9).

Fischer and colleagues (2010)[16] refer to this description of "terrorism as a communication process" as the **Collective Communication Model of Terrorism (CCMT)**. CCMT posits that the psychological and behavioral impacts of terrorist threats can be seen as a collective communication process that occurs between terrorists and their potential targets. Based on this model, terrorists are considered the senders of a particular collective message (e.g., "stop oppressing our culture"); a terrorist act as the collective message itself (through its performance, manner, and targets); and the potential targets as its collective receivers (who construe the aims of the terrorist attack as a function of their [the victims'] distinctive attributes, such as race, religion, or social identities). The perception of terrorism as a dynamic and two-way process between collective senders, messages, and receivers follows the same logic as David Berlo's Model of Communication: terrorism comes from a source and can be successful conveyed as a message (i.e., reaching its collective aim), and the message can be interpreted as rational or irrational (i.e., cultural noise, depending on the context).

COMMUNICATION OF TERRORISM: SOCIAL NOISE

According to Schmid and de Graff (1982), "[T]errorism can best be understood as a violent communication strategy. There is a sender, the terrorist, a message generator, the victim, and a receiver, the enemy and/or the public" (p. 15). In the past, however, terrorism was limited in its capacity to spread its messages in a way that differs considerably from modern methods. Before the invention of television and its images, terrorism could not be portrayed by the media that existed at the time. Depictions of terrorist acts could only be accessible by a few individuals. This is analogous to Plato's *Republic*, where his ideal society was limited to the number of residents who could be reached through a single human voice. In the Middle Ages, the area around an English parish was defined by the reach of the church bell, and the first North American immigrants (i.e., in their farms) settled within shouting distance of each other.[17] In all cases, as it was for most terrorist acts, the reason was simple: communication was limited because the capacity to transmit messages was limited.

Terrorists had to find a strategy to get their messages across to large audiences. The best method was to be attention-grabbing, what Simonson (2001)[18] refers to as *social noise*. **Social noise** is a practice of being conspicuously noticeable by means of noisy or controversial actions. When social noise leads to public disorder, it carries over long distances and, by instilling uncomfortable stirs or sensations in the audience, eventually influences social life. Social noise draws attention to a critical aspect of public communication: its ability to fascinate or frighten the public on the basis of both form and content. Today, social noise would be akin to **shock advertising** (or *shockvertising*), a form of advertising that is controversial, distressing, and graphic.[19]

Like shock advertising, social noise intentionally, rather than accidentally, communicates a message to the audience by warning, upsetting, and affronting the audience. Social noise validates the statement made by Chalfont (1980)[20] that "terrorism would be impotent without publicity" (p. 79). Communication is indispensable for a terrorist cause, not just to garner attention, but also to ensure its longevity and very survival. Without effective communication, a terrorist organization would be incapable to maintain a constant flow of new recruits, motivate existing members, and enlarge its base of active supporters and passive sympathizers (on which terrorism also thrives).[21] There are two examples of terrorism as social noise that should be discussed: Propaganda by the Deed and martyrdom.

Propaganda by the Deed

At the end of the 19th century and at the beginning of the 20th, the anarchist movement adopted the Propaganda by the Deed, a phrase that encapsulated both terrorist violence and its professed political purpose. **Propaganda by the Deed** means that terrorism becomes a tool of communication to galvanize the masses and trigger a revolution. For German anarchist Gustav Landauer (2005),[22] the objective was to arouse others to transform society. Historically, anarchism without violence was rarely fruitful. To get their messages across, anarchists needed to find a way to be "noisy." One particular tactic allowed them to do that: dynamite. Terrorism spread quickly in the second half of the 19th century as a result of Nobel's invention of dynamite in 1866. Dynamite became the supreme democratic weapon, "the great equalizer" allowing revolutionaries to fulfill their dream of overcoming the mighty power of the state. In fact, the propagandists called it the **philosophy of the bomb** (the idea that bombing enemies was the only viable social noise and means of social change).[23]

Their deeds included the bombing of politicians' and world leaders' houses (or headquarters), and the assassinations of central political figures, including President William

McKinley in 1901. Leon Czolgosz, the young man who killed McKinley, was driven by the benefits of making anarchist sentiment known to the public. As social noise, Propaganda by the Deed was justified as the necessary counterpart to state repression and the repressive nature of the bourgeois state.[24] Based on the Collective Communication Model of Terrorism (CCMT), the communicative purpose of terrorism suggests that it is a social endeavor, where both terrorists and the audience need to be involved to make the message meaningful. It is a two-way relationship; this is where feedback and context come into play. Terrorists are involved in various and complex social interactions with their targets, the state, and the audience in general.

Propaganda by the Deed is similar to what Iviansky (1977)[25] called **individual terror**, a form of revolutionary terror involving the murder of isolated individuals with the purpose of promoting a political movement or causing political changes. The distinction between traditional political assassination and individual terror is simple: in the first one, the killer's purpose is the assassination of the target (e.g., a high-profile figure such as a king or dictator) whose removal would allow political changes. Hence, choosing the right person to kill is of utmost importance. In the second one, individual terror, the choice of the target is secondary to the primary goal: creating social noise, and bringing undivided attention to a political movement and promoting that movement. This main distinction explains differences in tactics. While traditional political assassination tends to be clandestine (i.e., a clean job), individual terror is only efficient insofar as it receives wide publicity for the act.

Propaganda by the Deed is also similar to **demonstrative terrorism**, a type of terrorism enacted mainly for publicity reasons, particularly the three following reasons: (1) to recruit new members; (2) to gain attention to protests, accusations, and pains from soft-liners on the other side; and (3) to receive attention from third parties who might put pressure on the other side.[26] Organizations that count on demonstrative terrorism include the Orange Volunteers (Northern Ireland), the National Liberation Army (Colombia), and the Red Brigades (Italy).[27] Demonstrative terrorism is social noise because it communicates the message that a group can no longer be ignored.

The First Chechen War shared a lot in common with the First Palestinian Intifada: mass protests against what they considered invaders, deep yearning for nationalism and independence, and an open relationship with the Western media. Before the First Intifada (1987–1993), terror was already used as an attention-grabbing strategy. In the First Chechen War (1994–1996), terrorism was used to attract new recruits and bring worldwide attention to their fight for independence. These acts, comparable to Palestinian terror attacks, demonstrated that the Chechens' social cry could no longer be disregarded.[28] These elements created social noise for the Chechen state and provided an opportunity for supporting a move for independence. It was their window of opportunity.

Martyrdom

Martyrdom is another window of opportunity to gain worldwide attention. Martyrdom means dying or suffering as a hero, so a martyr could be a terrorist for the West but a hero for terrorist groups (and their sympathizers). There have been exclusive interviews with Palestinian and Afghani martyrs' wives, who sing the praises of their husbands' decisions to die as martyrs (e.g., in suicide attacks). Creating social noise is an art in and of itself, and it is usually planned thoroughly. After months of training, the "hero" is assigned a target, blows himself up, kills multiple people in the process, and gains widespread attention to his cause. By extension, to avoid overloading their audiences with too much information or same-as-usual political and theological rhetoric, Islamic leaders simplify their message by using emotional stories that create the image of the heroic martyr. Social noise can also be achieved through online video clips, biographies of martyrs, audio recordings, online magazines, and still images posted online. These narratives of heroes rely on fundamental themes of humiliation, spiritual commitment, and redemption to make their enemies look bad and inspire their Muslim audiences to make heroic sacrifices too (Box 2.1).[29] The depiction of martyrs in video clips and biographies is very propagandistic and, likely, does not represent the entirety of their motivations. Groups seek to achieve a high level of social noise by manipulating narratives, not to insinuate that such mythologies portray the true motivations of the martyrs.[30]

Box 2.1:   Martyrdom Videos

A **martyrdom video** is a video recording, usually from Islamist activists, advocating the participation in a suicide attack and the death as a hero during the intended actions. The video includes a speech by the terrorist preparing to be a martyr for their cause. While the videos are usually of substandard quality, some of them include text, music, and soppy/emotional clips. In these videos, the future martyr sits or stands in front of a black Islamic flag. In this regard, social noise can be a form of **visual rhetoric**, the art of visual persuasion, visual communication, and visual images. It is a strategy whereby visual images communicate a message to influence an audience.[31] For propaganda purposes, martyrdom videos are widely circulated by the groups behind them, particularly after the suicide attack has occurred. The videos are also created to preserve the audience's memory of the martyrs and to justify and praise their actions. The videos may also "lock" the future martyrs by making them committed soldiers who will carry their actions to the fullest. In doing so, the future martyrs make a public statement of commitment from which they cannot backtrack.[32]

Upon examining jihadist/terrorist martyrdom videos, it appears that still images, websites, sermons devised to inspire youths to accept violent forms of jihadist ideology, and filmatic montages such as those of the **Baghdad Sniper** (an alleged Islamist sniper, featured in propaganda videos, who has killed over 600 U.S. soldiers) all exemplify the strong importance given to emotive narratives. **Emotive narratives** are stories loaded with emotional appeals and often combined with pictures. In this particular instance, in a campaign to escalate indignation and anger within the wider Muslim community, emotive narratives portray Muslims as being mistreated or humiliated. These emotional appeals tend to be juxtaposed against pictures of Muslims shown fighting U.S. troops in Iraq and Afghanistan, or resisting power in other conflict areas such as Chechnya and Kashmir. The objective is always the same: to provoke emotional responses and convert them into political action.[33]

The dominant narratives in martyrdom videos, audio recordings, biographies, and the like center on three themes often presented in a sequence (as if it were a three-act play). The first act describes the harsh humiliation and suffering inflicted on Muslims (e.g., in Iraq and in other places), implying a conspiracy by the Western "crusaders" to harm Muslims and stereotype them for punishment. The second act shows the ineffectualness of current Muslim regimes and their complicity with the West, implying that they put the Muslim world in danger by being the servants of their Western "masters." The final act guarantees Muslim victory thanks to devout and heroic recruits who have worked hard to avenge the grief and humiliation of their fellow Muslims through faith in Allah, sacrifice in combat, and morality in their cause. The presentation of the three narratives is sometimes done separately, but frequently they are staged together to expose a problem, a source of the problem, and a solution to the problem.[34] By elevating the martyrs to the status of immortal or remarkably moral beings who sacrifice their lives for Allah and the Muslim world, jihadists create social noise by (1) deflecting attention away from their killings and (2) turning a blind eye on the victims they harm.

COMMUNICATION OF TERRORISM: THE SIGNATURE METHOD

Terrorism is fundamentally a communication process. Its objective is to communicate threats and instill feelings of anxiety, even among members of the public far removed from its immediate vicinity. To achieve this, terrorist groups use various tactics. Terrorism, indeed, is a tactic, not an enemy, and it is often random and unpredictable. Yet, the tactics can remain the same for some groups. A **signature method** is a method that becomes the identifier or the familiar tactic of a terrorist group. The signature method becomes strongly associated with the operational activities of the group. By using the same method, over time the terrorist group leaves an inscription that often speaks for the ideology and communicative intent of the group.[35] This is analogous to a situation in which a boy sends love letters to a girl on a weekly basis. The source, sender, message, receiver, and context tend to remain the same.

Signature Methods in History

As explained in Chapter 1, one of the early terrorist groups in antiquity was the Sicarii. The Sicarii needed publicity, and they used a signature method to make themselves known to the public. The Sicarii would go to places where they could gash the Romans' throats (and those who supported them) in public. They used very visible and visual acts of violence against Roman legionnaires or Jewish citizens that the Sicarii viewed as guilty of apostasy or disloyalty. Their killings regularly occurred in broad daylight and in the presence of witnesses, in thronged marketplaces or on holidays. The word *Sicarii* comes from *sica*, a short sword to kill targets.[36] By using the same method of public killings, the Sicarii (members of the Jewish faith) sent a two-fold message: to refuse paying taxes to Rome and to refuse acknowledging the authority of the Roman Emperor (Vitellius). Today, Muslim insurgents in the Philippines use an identical signature method: their sica is the **bolo**, the emblematic bush knife so unique to the Philippines and which has killed many opponents (and civilians) in broad daylight.[37] Likewise, during the peak of the French Revolution in September 1793, the Reign of Terror was formally declared and implemented, causing the execution of thousands of people through the **guillotine**, a device for decapitation. Executions were carried out in the presence of large audiences and were accompanied by extraordinary publicity, thus propagating the intended fear.[38]

The IRA's Signature Methods

During the Irish War of Independence (1919–1921), Michael Collins, Director of Intelligence for the Irish Republican Army (IRA), used the term **selective terrorism** and opposed the employment of indiscriminate terror attacks. In the early 1920s, this IRA's signature method consisted of selectively targeting the British military, the police force it sponsored, and those who supported the United Kingdom. The tactics and targets tended to remain the same. The message was always the same too: turning Ireland into a British-free independent nation.[39] Later, a signature method was the use of homemade devices in complex attacks, such as the barrack busters developed by the IRA.[40] **Barrack buster** is the nickname given to a homemade mortar developed since the 1970s. Barrack busters epitomized the desperate resistance of the IRA (usually poor and outnumbered) against the rich and powerful Britons in Northern Ireland. A third signature method used by the IRA (and Italy's Red Brigades) was known as **kneecapping**—firing a shot in the back of a victim's knee joint, thus shooting off the kneecap. By damaging a target's knee for life, making it impossible for the person to walk adequately again, the tactic of kneecapping carried with it the message of making the person suffer, so the public becomes aware that terrorists, too, have power and that the battle is not over.[41] Kneecapping had the deliberate effect of terrifying all journalists, fearful that any of them might be the next, random target.

A signature method is a way of notifying the audience about the look and feel of a terrorist organization. If the signature method is terrifying, and if the audience is well familiar with it, it becomes a force multiplier that affects the audience and that reaches short-term, mid-term, or long-term objectives. In combat terms, a **force multiplier** aims at increasing the impact power of a method without increasing the number of people involved in an attack. An important purpose is to maximize the gravity and length of the psychological impact and to produce far-reaching ramifications beyond the immediate victims or targets. The signature method, then, affects not only victims but the wider population as well.[42]

Suicide Bombings

Suicide bombing is the act of blowing oneself up and other people in the process. To the eyes of terrorists, suicide bombings are considered efficient tactics because they cost fewer lives than any traditional military tactic and blowing up unprotected civilians is much easier than targeting soldiers. This signature method has grown popular over the past three decades. The number of suicide bombings has increased from an average of 3 to 4 per year during the 1980s to 180 per year between 2000 and 2005, and from 81 in 2001 to 460 in 2005. Suicide bombing, of course, has been popularized with the September 11, 2001 terrorist attacks (i.e., "detonating" aircrafts by smashing them into buildings), killing roughly 3,000 people, and the suicide bombings in London (on double-deck buses) on July 7, 2005, killing 52 people.[43] Suicide bombers, or **shahids**, have become role models for many young Muslim militants.[44] In fact, during the Second Intifada, the second Palestinian uprising in the Palestinian–Israeli conflict, which began in September 2000, it has been reported that there were so many volunteers to be shahids that recruiters and dispatchers had an unparalleled pool of candidates, with one interviewee asserting that they were flooded with applicants.[45]

A chief purpose of suicide bombing is the successful achievement of something gigantic before dying. The aphorism, "One man willing to throw away his life is enough to terrorize a thousand," was conceived by Wu Ch'I, a Chinese military philosopher. This quote resembles the statement, "Kill one man, terrorize a thousand." As in the 2004 Madrid train bombings, suicide bombers like to emulate Al Qaeda's signature method of synchronized explosions against symbolic or economic targets, an approach greatly promoted by Osama bin Laden in several recorded speeches. Pape (2005),[46] an expert on suicide bombings, stated that 95% of suicide attacks in recent times have sent the same specific message to the global community: the forces that occupy a state from a disputed territory *must withdraw now*. Suicide bombings, then, serve to demoralize various parties—particularly the targeted civilians and the leadership of the terrorists' enemies.

Kidnappings and Hijackings

Another signature method includes kidnappings and hijackings. For example, the Colombian Revolutionary Armed Forces (FARC), an anti-government faction since 1964, abducts prominent figures and, in exchange for their release, demands the release of the incarcerated FARC members.[47] This tactic is referred to as **redemptive terrorism**, a form of terrorism that attempts to coerce a higher force into ceding specific human (e.g., prisoners) or material (e.g., money) resources. Redemptive terrorism typically consists of kidnapping civilian hostages as a bargaining piece in exchange for a specific concession. Many hijackings in the Middle East, such as those by Hezbollah and the Popular Front for the Liberation of Palestine, illustrate the basic format of this category of terrorism.[48]

On June 14, 1985, Hezbollah terrorists hijacked **TWA Flight 847** on its way to Rome from Athens and forced the aircraft to land at Beirut International Airport. The thirty-nine U.S. passengers on board were sent to various secret locations in West Beirut. Hezbollah ordered the U.S. to talk the Israelis into releasing 766 Lebanese prisoners who had been transferred to Israel during its departure from parts of southern Lebanon eight days before. After a succession of deliberations involving many intermediaries, the 766 Lebanese prisoners were released, followed by the liberation of the U.S. captives on July 1, 1985.[49] Similarly, to put an end to the Iran hostage crisis, President Ronald Reagan freed almost $8 billion in Iranian assets in exchange for the fifty-two U.S. hostages.[50]

Hafez (2007)[51] states that the tactics of kidnappings and hijackings send messages that serve to achieve key objectives: (1) showing the world that negotiating with terrorists is possible; (2) appealing to potential recruits inside and outside of terrorist organizations' territories; (3) justifying to the public the kidnapping of victims or hijacking of airplanes; (4) legitimizing the organizations that engage in violence; and (5) defying the authorities of the West and outside of the Muslim world.

Beheadings

The Islamic signature method of beheading infidels dates back to Muhammad's Battle of Medina, his third battle, which took place in 627. For Muhammad, any person insulting or opposing him (or his people) deserved such excruciating death. This is in accordance with Allah's command to "smite the necks" of the "unbelievers" (Qur'an 47:4). On winning the Battle of Medina, Muhammad passed an execution sentence against the Qurayza Jews, and 600–900 Qurayza males were beheaded (except for those who chose to become Muslims).[52]

A **beheading video** is a U.S. colloquial term that became popular during President W. Bush's Global War on Terror (GWOT). Beheading videos are videos released by Islamist terrorist groups showing interviews by hostages taken by those groups. The introduction or prologue to these videos shows the captive alive and pleading for his life—sometimes accompanied by his kidnappers (who stand behind), sometimes not. At the end of the video, one of the captors is shown to pull his knife out and behead (slowly) the hostage. The objective of the terrorist group is to make demands that are broad and clear, such as total withdrawal of the captive's nation's military forces from a specific Middle Eastern country. Habitually, the beheading video is released a few days later. Then, the video is uploaded to the Internet by the terrorists and distributed by traditional news media or by web-based services such as blogs.

The most famous beheading video is about Jewish-American journalist Daniel Pearl.[53] On January 23, 2002, *Wall Street Journal* reporter Daniel Pearl was abducted. A month after Pearl's kidnapping, on February 21, 2002, the U.S. State Department confirmed that Pearl was beheaded. CBS showed a three-and-a-half minute video of Pearl in which he was speaking. At one point on the video, Pearl said, "My father is Jewish, my mother is Jewish, I am Jewish." Then, his throat was chopped off and his severed head was held aloft. In the Pearl video, three edited sections were montaged, music video–style, with footage from Palestine, Chechnya, Kashmir, and Bosnia, and with a voiceover of a radical diatribe against the "enemies of Islam."

CBS was scorned by most U.S. media, by the White House, and by Pearl's family, which said that CBS had helped the terrorists to spread "their message of hate and murder." By making the Pearl beheading video available worldwide, the terrorists had, indeed, accomplished their goal. Here, the terrorists were aided by a major U.S. news network. In May 2004, Nick Berg, another Jewish-American man, a contractor, was kidnapped and beheaded in Iraq. "Nick Berg" was the second most popular search on Google, following "American Idol." A month later, when American engineer Paul Johnson, Jr., was decapitated, his name was the most popular search on Google. As CBSnews.com news director Michael Sims observed, any news stories with graphic violence trigger an astronomical record in photo and video viewing online.[54]

Underpublicized Signature Methods

The aforesaid signature methods are well-known types that are widely discussed in the literature. A few important signature methods, however, have been underpublicized in the media. For example, during the Rwandan Civil War in the early 1990s, in addition to the 800,000 people who were killed, hundreds of thousands of females (both underage and adult) were victims of mass rape—this was the signature method of the Hutu majority against the Tutsi minority. Mass rape during ethnic conflict causes mass trauma and is considered a method of destruction of an ethnic group.[55] According to the 1948 *Convention on the Prevention and Punishment of the Crime of Genocide*,[56] inflicting severe bodily or mental harm to people of an ethnic, national, or religious group, or "deliberately inflicting on the group conditions of life calculated to bring about its physical destruction in whole or in part" constitutes genocide.

Another signature method that has been underrepresented is the one used by the **Earth Liberation Front** (**ELF**), a European eco-terrorist organization that, according to its website, engages in "economic sabotage and guerrilla warfare to stop the exploitation and destruction of the environment." ELF's sister organization is the **Animal Liberation Front** (**ALF**), another European-based terrorist group that commits unlawful actions in quest of animal liberation. The signature tactics of ELF consist of attacks on property (not humans), including arson, sabotage, and vandalism. The objective is to cause substantial economic damage. Most of ELF targets are research laboratories, multinational corporations (MNCs), and logging businesses.[57] In like manner, a signature tactic of ALF is the destruction of laboratories (i.e., for the sake of animals) to hold back the restocking process or make animal research impossible.[58]

COMMUNICATION OF TERRORISM: THE CONDUIT METAPHOR

Historically, terrorism spread quickly thanks to a set of developments consisting of the invention of the rotary press, the advent of the telegraph, and the spectacular increase in public literacy. Terrorist acts committed in one location could now be rapidly communicated to another. A single, militant incident could now be observed by a nationwide constituency.[59] As French anarchist Leon Lehautier once remarked, "If my protest does not attract a scandal which forcibly attracts attention to my grievances, it is as if I am not complaining at all." Dynamite ensured that terrorists, with relative ease, could now "attract a scandal."[60] The progress of the media guaranteed that the terrorists' grievances would now be caught by an ever larger audience.[61] In the 19th century, Russian revolutionaries became the first anti-government militants to exploit the printing press to the fullest extent to publicize their cause. Leaflets and other printed documents were issued by The People's Will (Narodnaya Volya) and other related groups. **Narodnaya Volya** was a Russian terrorist organization notorious for the assassination of Czar Alexander II of Russia. Narodnaya Volya propagated its political agenda through all layers of the Russian populace. The organization's newspapers, *Narodnaya Volya* and *The Worker's Gazette*, popularized the concept of political war against the autocracy.[62]

In communicative terms, this exploitation of the media to make a terrorist cause known or visible is referred to as the conduit metaphor. The **conduit metaphor** is the notion that, when communicating, humans use the media for encoding purposes—that is, (1) putting ideas into words, signs, or symbols; (2) moving them along a conduit (e.g., channel or medium); and (3) getting them across to the receiving end.[63] According to the perspective of the conduit metaphor, terrorism is a communicative strategy that thrives on the **oxygen of publicity**.[64] The oxygen of publicity was a phrase used in the 1980s by Margaret Thatcher, then prime minister (PM) of Britain, to refer to the daily IRA bombings and killings reported on the newspapers' front pages and the 6 p.m. TV news, giving terrorists free publicity in the process.[65] The terrorist organization was using daily newspapers as a successful conduit. In like fashion, the Red Brigades were nicknamed **weekend terrorists**. Their terrorist acts were frequently committed on Saturday because they knew that, in Italy, newspaper circulation on Sunday was the highest. Terrorism, then, was timely, committed to guarantee substantial media coverage.[66]

Popular Front for the Liberation of Palestine

News coverage greatly influences political action by putting pressure on leaders to act in media-determined crisis situations. Absence of a media conduit works in the opposite direction too. We can look at the case of kidnapping of over 600 people by the **Popular Front for the Liberation of Palestine (PFLP)** in 1970. Founded in 1967, the PFLP is a Palestinian Marxist movement considered a terrorist organization by over thirty countries (including the U.S., the European Union, Australia, and Canada). In 1970, four airliners en route to New York were hijacked, three of which landed in Jordan. At that time, there was poor satellite television coverage because of limited resources and high costs. Therefore, public awareness of the situation through the mass media was limited. There was no guarantee that conventional news media (broadcast or print) would make press releases on the story. Even if they were to release the story, editors would frame the story as presented to mainstream news audiences. Given these circumstances, President Nixon did not feel pressured to find a quick fix for the situation; the hostages were held for more than three weeks.

Today, news media organizations are more numerous and act as a conduit for terrorists.[67] It was no accident that Palestinian terrorism began disseminating in Europe in the early 1970s, exactly when the media became more able to broadcast live. Until aircrafts hit the Twin Towers, the "Black September" attack of the 1972 Munich Olympics was the world's most widely witnessed terrorist event (as a "live" event). In the 1970s, when modern international terrorism was born, dramatic media-attention-grabbing terrorist attacks with destructive power were prominent in the Middle East and Western Europe. It was not until 1979 when Iranian students took over the U.S. Embassy in Tehran that international terrorism became a deeply emblazoned topic in U.S. foreign policy, in the U.S. news media, and in public consciousness.[68]

Osama bin Laden Videotapes

From October 2001 until his death on May 1, 2011, Osama bin Laden videotapes, disseminated profusely through both television and the Internet, had a massive appeal in the major part of the Muslim world. In 2007, an Al Qaeda spokesman described the strategic influence of Osama bin Laden videotapes in the Arab world:

Sheikh Osama knows that the media war is not less important than the military war against America. That's why Al Qaeda has many media wars. The Sheikh has made Al Qaeda's media strategy something that all TV stations look for. There are certain criteria for the stations to be able to air our videos, foremost of which is that it has not taken a previous stand against the mujahedeen. That maybe explains why we prefer Al Jazeera to the rest.[69]

The conduit for Osama bin Laden's messages was **Al Jazeera television**, a small and fast-growing Arabic news channel based in Qatar which, on October 7, 2001, started releasing the first of many exclusive videotapes of Osama bin Laden. Many complained that Al Jazeera was becoming a platform for bin Laden and his Al Qaeda acolytes.[70] Yet, international news networks wanted to air his speeches too. CNN eventually made a temporary arrangement with Al Jazeera, working out deals to benefit from the same exclusives that the small Qatari new station was enjoying. Over time, many videotapes were released and most were aired. The Osama bin Laden videotapes consisted of fairly sophisticated messages. Directed not only at his Muslim audience in the Middle East—a fact evoked by his speeches in Arabic and his selection of Al Jazeera as the conduit for broadcast—his videotapes were also aimed at a wider global audience, including the U.S., its allies, and the neutral nations that President W. Bush had warned in his speeches.[71]

On November 3, 2001, bin Laden released another videotape where he was attacking the West, the U.N., and Israel, and describing all of the developing events as essentially a religious war against Islam started by the "Crusader" West. On December 27, 2001, bin Laden released another video tape stating the following: "Terrorism against America deserves to be praised because it was a response to injustice, aimed at forcing America to stop its support for Israel, which kills our people." In the recording, bin Laden denounced attacks by the U.S. against Islamic groups. He said his message was a review of events following 9/11, and in this speech he neither claimed nor denied responsibility for the September 11, 2001 attacks.[72] On September 7, 2007, his first new appearance in close to three years, a completely new videotape of Osama bin Laden was released. The target of his message was now an even wider audience. In the tape, he condemned large corporations, Congressional Democrats, the GWOT, and the PM of Great Britain. He strongly urged individuals to convert to Islam. He also cited the name of Sarkozy, the new President of France, and the concept of global warming.[73]

Joseph Tuman (2003)[74] looked closely at several early Osama bin Laden videotapes. Tuman asserted that the image fashioned by his appearance hinted at an attitude of open indifference and defiance to the U.S. Here, a certain mildness and placidity in bin Laden's demeanor came across. Recalling David Berlo's Model of Communication, bin Laden's encoding process demonstrated that powerful nonverbal symbols can communicate equally powerful meanings. In the videos, he did not look angry or visually fanatical—both traits that the audience would expect given his reputation, history, and content of his messages in other videos. Yet, here, he projected a sense of gentleness that conveyed either inner strength or a bogus sense of confidence. His voice was soft and confident. There was a discrepancy between the harsh discourse and menacing tone of his words and the tranquil appearance of his delivery. This was no coincidence. Airing these videos was a conduit for affirming his leadership in facing the U.S. and Israel, while also continuing to terrorize Americans by jogging their memory about the September 11, 2001 terrorist attacks.

All three forms of communication of terrorism—social noise, the signature method, and the conduit metaphor—are examples of **social communication** in that they offer approaches as to how the communication of terrorism can be noticed, transmitted, and understood, and as to what impact those forms have on society. This very section on the conduit metaphor serves as the basis, in the next two chapters, for understanding the role of the media in analyzing terrorism as a communication process. The next two chapters will deal, respectively, with the media and the audience.

SUMMARY

Terrorism is a dynamic, two-way communication process between a sender (the terrorist) and a receiver (the audience). It tends to follow David Berlo's (1960) Model of Communication, in which the sender of the message selects an appropriate communication channel (e.g., face-to-face, phone, radio, e-mail, etc.) and sends a message to the receiver. This is what Joseph Tuman (2003) theorized in his model of "terrorism as a communication process." Given these circumstances, the real objective of terrorism is persuasion. To have a basic understanding of how the communication process works and creates terrorism for the audience, three forms of communication of terrorism were analyzed: (1) social noise, (2) the signature method, and (3) the conduit metaphor. Examples of social noise are Propaganda by the Deed (a tool of persuasion to galvanize the masses and trigger a terrorist revolution) and martyrdom (dying or suffering as a hero and telling the world about it through online video clips, audio recordings, etc.). The signature method refers to a "signature" of a terrorist group that becomes strongly associated with the operational activities of that group. Contemporary examples are suicide bombings, kidnappings, hijackings, and beheadings. The conduit metaphor, which thrives on the "oxygen of publicity," refers to human use of the media for encoding purposes (e.g., the multiple videos released by Osama bin Laden to communicate his missions to the world).

KEY TERMS

Al Jazeera television   47

barrack buster   42

beheading video   44

Berlo's Model of Communication   34

Collective Communication Model (of Terrorism)   37

communication   33

conduit metaphor   45

demonstrative terrorism   39

emotive narratives   40

force multiplier   42

guillotine   42

hypodermic model   35

individual terror   39

ENDNOTES

1. Jandt, Fred (2010). *An Introduction to Intercultural Communication: Identities in a Global Community* (6th ed.). Thousand Oaks, CA: Sage.

2. Lasswell, Harold D. (1948). The Structure and Function of Communication in Society. In Lymon Bryson (Ed.), *The Communication of Ideas* (pp. 37–51). New York: Institute for Religious and Social Studies.

3. Berlo, David K. (1960). *The Process of Communication: An Introduction to Theory and Practice*. New York: Holt, Rinehart and Winston.

4. Shannon, Claude E., & Weaver, Norbert (1949). *The Mathematical Theory of Communication*. Urbana: University of Illinois Press.

5. Tuman, Joseph S. (2010). *Communicating Terror: The Rhetorical Dimensions of Terrorism*. Thousand Oaks, CA: Sage.

6. Eljahmi, Mohamed (2006). Libya and the U.S.: Qadhafi Unrepentant. *Middle East Quarterly, 13*(1), 11–20.

7. Jandt, Fred (2010). *An Introduction to Intercultural Communication: Identities in a Global Community* (6th ed.). Thousand Oaks, CA: Sage.

8. Bineham, Jeffery L. (1988). A Historical Account of the Hypodermic Model in Mass Communication. *Communication Monographs, 55*(3), 230–246.

9. Corman, Steven R., Thethewey, Angela, & Goodall, Bud (2007). *A 21st Century Model for Communication in the Global War of Ideas: From Simplistic Influence to Pragmatic Complexity*. Tempe, AZ: Consortium for Strategic Communication.

10. Miller, Claude, Matusitz, Jonathan, O'Hair, Dan, & Eckstein, Jacqueline (2008). The Role of Communication and the Media in Terrorism. In Dan O'Hair, Robert Heath, Kevin Ayotte, & Gerald R. Ledlow (Eds.), *Terrorism: Communication and Rhetorical Perspectives* (pp. 43–66). Cresskill, NJ: Hampton Press.

11. Williams, John J. (1998). The Failure of Terrorism as Mass Communication. *Turkish Journal of Police Studies, 1*(4), 37–52.

12. Tuman, Joseph S. (2003). *Communicating Terror: The Rhetorical Dimensions of Terrorism*. Thousand Oaks, CA: Sage.

13. Tuman, Joseph S. (2003). *Communicating Terror: The Rhetorical Dimensions of Terrorism*. Thousand Oaks, CA: Sage.

14. O'Hair, Dan, & Heath, Robert (2005). Conceptualizing Communication and Terrorism. In Dan O'Hair, Robert Heath, & Gerald Ledlow (Eds.), *Community Preparedness, Deterrence, and Response to Terrorism: Communication and Terrorism* (pp. 1–12). Westport, CT: Praeger.

15. Schmid, Alex P., & de Graaf, Janny (1982). *Violence as Communication: Insurgent Terrorism and the Western News Media*. Beverly Hills, CA: Sage.

16. Fischer, Peter, Fischer, Julia K., Weisweiler, Silke, & Frey, Dieter (2010). Terrorism as Collective Communication: The Collective Communication Model of Terrorism (CCMT). *Social and Personality Psychology Compass, 4*(9), 692–703.

17. Schafer, R. Murray (1994). *The Soundscape: Our Sonic Environment and the Tuning of the World.* Rochester, VT: Destiny Books.

18. Simonson, Peter (2001). Social Noise and Segmented Rhythms: News, Entertainment, and Celebrity in the Crusade for Animal Rights. *The Communication Review, 4*(3), 399–420.

19. Saunders, D. (1998). *Shock in Advertising.* London: B.T. Batsford.

20. Chalfont, Lord (1980). Political Violence and the Role of the Media: Some Perspectives—the Climate of Opinion. *Political Communication and Persuasion: An International Journal, 1*(1), 79–81.

21. Hoffman, Bruce (2007). Countering Terrorist Use of the Web as a Weapon. *CTC Sentinel, 1*(1), 4–6.

22. Landauer, Gustav (2005). *Anarchism in Germany.* Montreal: Black Rose Books.

23. Carlson, Joseph R. (1995). The Future Terrorists in America. *American Journal of Police, 14*(3), 71–91.

24. Cahm, Caroline (2002). *Kropotkin: And the Rise of Revolutionary Anarchism, 1872–1886.* Cambridge: Cambridge University Press.

25. Iviansky, Ze'ev (1977). Individual Terror: Concept and Typology. *Journal of Contemporary History, 12*, 143–163.

26. Pape, Robert A. (2003). The Strategic Logic of Suicide Terrorism. *American Political Science Review, 97*(3), 343–361.

27. Clutterbuck, Richard (1975). *Living with Terrorism.* London: Faber & Faber; Edler Baumann, Carol (1973). *Diplomatic Kidnappings: A Revolutionary Tactic of Urban Terrorism.* The Hague: Nijhoff; St. John, Peter (1991). *Air Piracy, Airport Security, and International Terrorism.* New York: Quorum Books.

28. Younis, Mona (2000). *Liberation and Democratization: The South African and Palestinian National Movements.* Minneapolis: University of Minnesota Press.

29. Hafez, Mohammed M. (2007). Martyrdom Mythology in Iraq: How Jihadists Frame Suicide Terrorism in Videos and Biographies. *Terrorism and Political Violence, 19*(1), 95–115.

30. Hafez, Mohammed M. (2006). Suicide Terrorism in Iraq: A Preliminary Assessment of the Quantitative Data and Documentary Evidence. *Studies in Conflict and Terrorism, 29*, 1–27; Hafez, Mohammed M. (2007). Martyrdom Mythology in Iraq: How Jihadists Frame Suicide Terrorism in Videos and Biographies. *Terrorism and Political Violence, 19*(1), 95–115.

31. Olson, Lester C., Finnegan, Cara A., & Hope, Diane S. (2008). *Visual Rhetoric: A Reader in Communication and American Culture.* Thousand Oaks, CA: Sage.

32. Durodi, Bill (2007). Fear and Terror in a Post-Political Age. *Government & Opposition, 42*(3), 427–450.

33. Wright-Neville, David, & Smith, Debra (2009). Political Rage: Terrorism and the Politics of Emotion. *Global Change, Peace & Security, 21*(1), 85–98.

34. Hafez, Mohammed M. (2007). Martyrdom Mythology in Iraq: How Jihadists Frame Suicide Terrorism in Videos and Biographies. *Terrorism and Political Violence, 19*(1), 95–115.

35. Martin, Gus (2010). *Understanding Terrorism: Challenges, Perspectives, and Issues.* Thousand Oaks, CA: Sage.

36. Ben-Yehuda, Nachman (1998). Where Masada's Defenders Fell. *Biblical Archaeology Review 24*(6), 32–39; Laqueur, Walter (1999). *Terrorism and History.* Oxford: Oxford University Press; Roth, Cecil (1959). The Zealots in the War of 66–73. *Journal of Semitic Studies, 4*, 332–355.

37. Parman, Jose (2007). *Arnis Self-Defense: Stick, Blade, and Empty-Hand Combat Techniques of the Philippines.* Berkeley, CA: Blue Snake Books.

38. Weimann, Gabriel (2008). The Psychology of Mass-Mediated Terrorism. *American Behavioral Scientist, 52*(1), 69–86.

39. White, Jonathan R. (2011). *Terrorism & Homeland Security* (7th ed.). Belmont, CA: Wadsworth.

40. Graeme, Steven (2010). Terrorist Tactics and Counter-Terrorism. In Andrew Silke (Ed.), *The Psychology of Counter-Terrorism* (pp. 152–163). New York: Routledge.

41. Martin, Gus (2010). *Understanding Terrorism: Challenges, Perspectives, and Issues.* Thousand Oaks, CA: Sage.

42. Cvrtila, Vlatko, & Perešin, Anita (2008). The New Anti-Terrorist Strategy as an Answer to Mega Terrorism. In Iztok Prezelj (Ed.), *The Fight against Terrorism and Crisis Management in the Western Balkans* (pp. 35–46). Fairfax, VA: IOS Press; Hoffman, Bruce (2003). *The Logic of Suicide Terrorism*. Santa Monica: RAND; White, Jonathan R. (2011). *Terrorism and Homeland Security* (7th ed.). Belmont, CA: Wadsworth.

43. Atran, Scott (2006). The Moral Logic and Growth of Suicide Terrorism. *The Washington Quarterly, 29*(2), 127–147.

44. Sageman, Marc (2008). A Strategy for Fighting International Islamist Terrorists. *Annals of the American Academy of Political and Social Science, 618*, 223–231.

45. Schweitzer, Y. (2007). Palestinian Istishhadia: A Developing Instrument. *Studies in Conflict & Terrorism, 30*(8), 683–685.

46. Pape, Robert A. (2005). *Dying to Win*. New York: Random House.

47. Forero, Juan (2003, May 6). Rebels Execute 10 Hostages in Colombia. *The New York Times*, p. A14.

48. Gambill, Gary C. (1998). The Balance of Terror: War by Other Means in the Contemporary Middle East. *Journal of Palestine Studies, 109*, 55–57.

49. Wright, Robin (1989). *In the Name of God: The Khomeini Decade*. New York: Simon and Schuster.

50. Abrahms, Max (2005). Al Qaeda's Miscommunication War: The Terrorism Paradox. *Terrorism and Political Violence, 17*, 529–549.

51. Hafez, Mohammed M. (2007). Martyrdom Mythology in Iraq: How Jihadists Frame Suicide Terrorism in Videos and Biographies. *Terrorism and Political Violence, 19*(1), 95–115.

52. Neuman, Jake (2009). *Islam: Evil in the Name of God*. New York: Felibri.com.

53. Heuston, Sean (2005). Weapons of Mass Instruction: Terrorism, Propaganda Film, Politics, and Us: New Media, New Meanings. *Studies in Popular Culture, 27*(3), 59–74.

54. Moeller, Susan D. (2009). *Packaging Terrorism: Co-Opting the News for Politics and Profit*. New York: Wiley-Blackwell.

55. Sharlach, Lisa (2000). Rape as Genocide: Bangladesh, the Former Yugoslavia, and Rwanda. *New Political Science, 22*(1), 89–102.

56. *Convention on the Prevention and Punishment of the Crime of Genocide* (1948, December 9). Paris: United Nations General Assembly.

57. Leader, Stefan H., & Probst, Peter (2003). The Earth Liberation Front and Environmental Terrorism. *Terrorism and Political Violence, 15*(4), 37–58.

58. Likar, Lawrence E. (2011). *Eco-Warriors, Nihilistic Terrorists, and the Environment*. Westport, CT: Praeger.

59. Avrich, Paul (1984). *The Haymarket Tragedy*. Princeton, NJ: Princeton University Press; Laqueur, Walter (1987). *The Age of Terrorism*. Boston: Little, Brown; Schmid, Alex P., & de Graaf, Janny (1982). *Violence as Communication: Insurgent Terrorism and the Western News Media*. Beverly Hills, CA: Sage.

60. Leites, Nathan, & Wolf, Charles (1970). *Rebellion and Authority: An Analytic Essay on Insurgent Conflicts*. Santa Monica, CA: RAND.

61. McCormick, Gordon H. (2003). Terrorist Decision Making. *Annual Review of Political Science, 6*, 473–507.

62. Martin, Gus (2010). *Understanding Terrorism: Challenges, Perspectives, and Issues*. Thousand Oaks, CA: Sage; Maynard, John (1962). *Russia in Flux: Before the October Revolution*. New York: Collier Books.

63. Reddy, Michael J. (1979). The Conduit Metaphor: A Case of Frame Conflict in Our Language about Language. In Andrew Ortony (Ed.), *Metaphor and Thought* (pp. 284–297). Cambridge: Cambridge University Press.

64. McNair, Brian (1999). *An Introduction to Political Communication*. London: Routledge; Wardlaw, Grant (1989). *Political Terrorism: Theory, Tactics and Counter-Measures*. Cambridge: Cambridge University Press; Wilkinson, Paul (1997). The Media and Terrorism: A Re-Assessment. *Terrorism and Political Violence, 9*(2), 51–64.

65. Preston, Peter (2001, July 23). We Gave Them the Oxygen. *The Guardian*, p. A1.

66. Sheehan, Thomas (1981). Italy: Terror on the Right. *The New York Review of Books, 27*(21), 10–21.

67. Klopfenstein, Bruce (2006). Terrorism and the Exploitation of New Media. Kavoori, Anandam P., & Todd Fraley (Eds.), *Media, Terrorism, and Theory* (pp. 107–120). New York: Rowman & Littlefield; Nacos, Brigitte L. (1994).

Terrorism and the Media: From the Iran Hostage Crisis to the Oklahoma City Bombing. New York: Columbia University Press; Sparks, Lisa (2005). Social Identity and Perceptions of Terrorist Groups: How Others See Them and How They See Themselves. In H. Dan O'Hair, Robert L. Heath, & Gerald R. Ledlow (Eds.), *Community Preparedness and Response to Terrorism: Communication and the Media* (pp. 13–28). Westport, CT: Praeger.

68. Evans, Ernest (1979). *Calling a Truce to Terror: The American Response to International Terrorism*. Westport, CT: Greenwood Press.

69. Scheuer, Michael (2004). *Imperial Hubris: Why the West Is Losing the War on Terror*. Washington, D.C.: Brassey's, pp. 209–212.

70. Ajami, Fouad (2001, November 18). What the Muslim World Is Watching. *The New York Times*, p. A1; Nawaway, Mohammed, & Iskandar, Adel (2002). *Al-Jazeera: How the Free Arab News Network Scooped the World and Changed the Middle East*. Cambridge, MA: Westview Press, p. 173.

71. Tuman, Joseph S. (2003). *Communicating Terror: The Rhetorical Dimensions of Terrorism*. Thousand Oaks, CA: Sage.

72. bin Laden, Osama (2001, December 27). Terrorism against America Deserves to Be Praised. Transcript of excerpts released by Al Jazeera of a thirty-three-minute video recorded by Osama Bin Laden (from Outlook india.com).

73. Gardner, Frank (2007, September 8). BBC: Trimmed Bin Laden in Media-Savvy War. BBC News.

74. Tuman, Joseph S. (2003). Communicating Terror: The Rhetorical Dimensions of Terrorism. Thousand Oaks, CA: Sage.

Terrorism as a Communication Process: The Media

After reading this chapter, you will be able to

- explain the symbiotic relationship between terrorism and the media, discussing the notion that increased media coverage will lead to further increases in terrorism; and
- describe media terrorism: the sensationalization of terror images to influence the audience.

MEDIA: DEFINITION

Media are transmission channels that are used to store and deliver information. Media are often synonymous with mass communications or news media. They may also refer to a single medium used to communicate any piece of information for any purpose. **Mass communications** include the institutions and methods by which news organizations use technical mechanisms (e.g., press, radio, films) to distribute content to sizable, heterogeneous, and widely diffused audiences.[1] **News media** are news sources like television, radio, and print journalism. They can also be modern sources on the Internet, including news reporting services, the blogosphere, web pages, and propaganda broadcasts. A **news event** is a newsworthy topic that captures broad public attention.[2]

Media take many forms and have grown significantly thanks to the expansion of the Internet. **Print media** consists of newspapers, journals, magazines, and books. **Electronic media** consists of radio, television, facsimile (fax), cell phones, and text messaging. Talk radio can play a very important role in politics and conflict, such as the culture wars in America or the campaign for genocide in Rwanda in 1994. Faxes were a centerpiece for the promotion of student protests in China in 1989—particularly in communicating with backers and advocates outside the nation. Text messaging and digital cameras played an equally important role in Burma during the monks' protests in 2007. The Internet, with its e-mail, interactive chat rooms, blogs, virtual communities, and websites, allows the flow of an amazing range of perspectives and causes at a rate never seen before. Video-sharing websites such as YouTube have greatly contributed to the spreading of "freedom" messages, such as those of student protesters in totalitarian regimes (e.g., China) or those of insurgents in Iraq. The mixture of different technologies—digital cameras, cell phones, and video—has smoothed the progress for the dissemination of messages for both individuals and groups. Put simply, information and images are disseminated widely and quickly.[3]

The media regularly draw on images, videos, expressions, figures (i.e., personalities), places, and events from the past, as well as other media, to establish and to create what currently passes as news. They do so in various ways. Because the audience desperately wants to know the truth, images are more important than words; words, then, are not enough. If we were content with just words, we would not watch, every year, short clips of films now inseparable from the history of landmark events—Zapruder's film of JFK's assassination and the videotape of the planes crashing into the World Trade Center. Images can be used as legal evidence. Stronger than words, they provide moral and emotional testimony. In most cultures, when we hear or read words in our language, we understand; when we see pictures, we know.[4]

Perse and colleagues (2002)[5] also believe that images are more powerful than words. According to these scholars, the media have five purposes: surveillance (media's information-gathering role); correlation (media's explanatory role; that is, its endeavors to clarify and educate); socialization (the process whereby multiple audiences and viewers are connected to the cultural atmosphere of the larger social order); entertainment (the media's role in offering stress relief, recreation, and distraction); and comforting (the process whereby the media serve to bolster and restore public confidence by broadcasting reports from authoritative sources, officials, and leaders).

TERRORISM AND THE MEDIA: A SYMBIOTIC RELATIONSHIP

Terrorism attracts cameras; cameras attract terrorism. It is a **symbiotic relationship**. Bruce Hoffman (2003),[6] a distinguished terrorism expert, made the flat statement that "with the help of the media—willingly or not—terrorism easily reaches global audience. Between media and terrorism, there exists a very interactive (symbiotic) relationship" (p. 128). Other scholars, such as McNair (1999), Wardlaw (1989), and Wilkinson (1997), have also identified a symbiotic relationship between the media and terrorism. This symbiosis is a product of the convoluted interrelationship between the methods used by terrorism and the main priorities of the media.[7] Terrorism needs the media, otherwise the cause of most terrorist groups would be less known. Conversely, an act of terrorism that just happened or that is going to happen may be a major scoop for the media; the audience ratings will likely increase. As political scientist Abraham Miller (1982)[8] wrote,

> Terrorism and the media are entwined in an almost inexorable, symbiotic relationship. Terrorism is capable of writing any drama—no matter how horrible—to compel the media's attention.... Terrorism, like an ill-mannered enfant terrible, is the media's stepchild, a stepchild which the media, unfortunately, can neither completely ignore nor deny. (p. 1)

The boom of modern terrorism, since around 1970, has been associated with mass communications. Researchers indicate that communication satellites are able to give terrorists immediate access to an international audience.[9] The September 11, 2001 terrorist attacks reverberated across the world from satellite to satellite. News disseminated instantaneously from the New York newsrooms to London, Paris, and Moscow, and from Al Jazeera's studios to Islamabad, Tehran, Baghdad, and Mecca. The Al Qaeda-driven incident generated massive coverage in the Western news media with countless stories emphasizing the anguish, suffering, and shock of the victims, their relatives, and witnesses. Years later, the echoes and aftershocks of September 11 are still impacting international affairs, domestic policy, and public opinion.[10] Karber (1971)[11] was one of the first scholars to suggest the communication factor in conceptualizing terrorism. He contended that "as a symbolic act, terrorism can be analyzed much like other mediums of communication" (p. 9). By extension, Brian Jenkins (1983)[12] insists that "terrorism is a product of freedom, particularly freedom of the press" (p. 160).

Carlos Marighella (2008),[13] a key founder of modern revolutionary warfare and author of the *Minimanual of the Urban Guerrilla*, understood the synergistic association between terrorism and the media. He recommended that urban guerrilla warfare adopt three strategies: urbanization of the combat, militarization by means of extreme violence, and manipulation of the media. The last strategy is what he called **armed propaganda**: terrorism and the media feed on each other; it is a strategic communication goal. Terrorists need the media for intensifying their messages, and media need terrorists as an embodiment of the bigger issue of conflict.[14] As Wilkinson (2001)[15] explains, when a person says "terrorism" in a democratic society, he or she also says "media." He continues, "For terrorism by its very nature is a psychological weapon which depends upon communicating a threat to a wider society. This, in essence, is why terrorism and the media enjoy a symbiotic relationship" (p. 177).

Hezbollah's terrorist actions against Israelis were always taped, leading analysts to suggest that there are always at least four actors in a terrorist unit: the perpetrator, a cameraman, a soundman, and a producer.[16] The terrorists' calculated communication goals are intended to legitimize, propagate, and intimidate their audience. Their clever use of the media and the Internet to counterbalance the asymmetrical disadvantages has allowed them to keep producing new generations of terrorists. Terrorist organizations also realized that manipulation of media could be achieved if they contacted news reporters. In doing so, they would acts less like terrorists and more like officials, policymakers, or public relations experts. By granting interviews to reporters, terrorists could offer the promise of a competitive scoop while also ensuring coverage and perhaps more sympathetic treatment in a story.[17] According to Wieviorka (2004),[18] the terrorism–media relationship can be categorized into four different levels:

- Complete indifference: terrorists execute their attacks without taking media coverage into account. The terrorists' objective is to frighten their victims and there is no expectation that the media will be involved.

- Relative indifference: terrorists execute their attacks with an awareness that the mass media could aid in their cause, but are still indifferent to media coverage.

- A media-oriented strategy: terrorists are mindful of and exploit the media to advance their message. After strategic manipulations, the media become incorporated in the terrorist group's actions.

- Complete breakaway: the press (i.e., journalists and reporters) is considered the enemy, and the terrorists will react to the media just like they would react to any enemy. The media are no longer an entity that should be strategically manipulated (as democracy's Achilles' heel). It is instead considered part of a system that must be demolished.

The role of the media is essential for the effect of terrorist attacks on the general audience. As many have stressed for a long time, media reporters serve as facilitators. If there were no oxygen of publicity, no airwaves of Al Jazeera, or no front-page headlines of *The New York Times*, terrorists in general would be unable to achieve many of their goals.[19] Government officials have a tendency to associate the media with terrorists' success or failure, as demonstrated by the case of the Unabomber (see Box 3.1), in which the official publication of his Manifesto in major media outlets was necessary for both the terrorist and people attempting to identify him.

Box 3.1   The Unabomber

Dr. Theodore John "Ted" Kaczynski, a former math professor at Berkeley, was known as the **Unabomber**. The Unabomber was an anarchist against technological progress. He committed a mail bombing spree for over seventeen years, killing three people and harming twenty-three others. In 1995, Kaczynski mailed several letters to some of his former victims and leading media outlets. In the letters, he outlined his objectives and demanded that his fifty-plus page, 35,000-word essay titled "Industrial Society and Its Future" (aka, the **Unabomber Manifesto**) be printed word-for-word in a major newspaper or journal. He stated that if his wish was met, he would terminate his bombing spree. The essay was a manifesto that advocated a global revolution against the effects of modernity and its industrial-technological system.

The U.S. Department of Justice, together with FBI Director Louis Freeh and Attorney General Janet Reno, recommended publication hoping to increase public safety and find a reader who could identify the author of the manifesto. The document was finally published by *The New York Times* and *The Washington Post* on September 19, 1995. The Unabomber was identified by his own relatives.[20] This anecdote, now well-known, confirms the symbiotic relationship between terrorism and the media. One needs the other, and vice versa. At the same time, this anecdote also denotes Wieviorka's third level of terrorism–media relationships: the media-oriented strategy.

The media have become an instrument of modern terrorism, providing a showcase through which individuals carrying out terrorist attacks can flabbergast and terrorize an audience, convert and train possible recruits, and assist and organize a rising network of followers.[21] A showcase is a "glass-fronted cupboard, witted with shelves, in which goods are set out on view for sale or objects for exhibition."[22] If terrorists can exploit the media as a showcase, then, like any good merchant, they will be cautious as to how to expose their causes and actions in the best possible way. Their presentation would be designed to provide information in formats that evoke an anticipated reaction from their viewing audience.

MEDIA AS AMPLIFICATION EFFECT

When terrorist attacks are shown in the media to an audience much larger than what the audience would be at the place where the attacks occur, the terrorists are said to benefit from an **amplification effect**.[23] Zulaika and Douglass (1996)[24] have argued that terrorism "is first and foremost discourse. There is a sense in which the terrorist event must be reported by the media in order for it to have transpired at all" (p. 14). In the words of Schmid and de Graaf (1982),[25] "the most serious effect of media reporting on insurgent terrorism is the likely increase of terroristic activities" (p. 142). A case in point is the lack of media presence in Africa, where terrorists carried out attacks in countries like Angola and Mozambique. For more than a decade, these attacks received little attention from the rest of the world. However, when a comparable number of Palestinians committed terrorist actions in the metropolitan areas of Europe and the Middle East, their attacks and their causes became familiar television audiences around the world. The reason is that, in the metropolitan areas of Europe and the Middle East, the terrorists could be spotted rapidly by reporters and their cameras.[26]

Weimann and Winn's (1994)[27] study investigated 6,714 instances of international terrorism from the late 1960s to the early 1990s. They found a sharp increase in terrorist incidents that applied media-oriented issues (in the selection of victims, place, timing, type of action, contact with media, etc.). Daniel Schorr (1995),[28] of the National Public Radio, wrote, "The phenomenon of blackmailing the news media has grown with the growing importance of the media as a way for terrorists to achieve ego satisfaction" (p. 19). Terrorism's perpetual and unconditional presence in today's media "overdimensionalizes" its ability to reach audiences, amplifying the impacts of its threats and coercion,[29] as exemplified in Box 3.2.

Box 3.2   The Oklahoma City Bombing

The amplification effect is often aided by TV news bulletins. TV news bulletins are focused mainly on what is known as **visual culture**: the importance attached to the visual, as opposed to the oral or written. The attention that a news event receives increases in proportion to the volume of audiovisual components available for it. Many news stations are very much against covering and presenting a story using only narrative or audio material. The availability or absence of audiovisual material is a

(Continued)

(Continued)

decisive factor when selecting which stories will be incorporated in the newscast and which ones will be excluded. This primary trait of mass media has consequences on the preparation and organization of a possible terrorist attack. As a result, terrorists attempt to strike targets based on their location or if their importance will attract the instant attention of the media. This, in turn, guarantees a sufficient amount of images that will ensure one's presence on the news.[30]

Such amplification effect was a motive for the **Oklahoma City bombing** in April 1995, whereby Timothy McVeigh blew up a governmental building. Following his arrest, he stated that he had selected the Alfred P. Murrah Federal Building for his attack because "it was full of open spaces making it easy to take pictures and focus TV cameras." He was so determined to gain publicity that he was sad when he learned that a certain number of children were among his victims. He added that "the death of innocent children could cloud the political message of the bomb."[31] The Oklahoma City bombing is an example of **media-oriented terrorism**, whereby terrorism is deliberately carried out to attract attention from the media and, accordingly, the general public. Targets and locations are chosen because they will be given high priority by news organizations.[32] Because the media select events that are newsworthy, television gives priority to violence indirectly. Different studies point to the fact that the visual report of violence and brutality by the media creates bigger feelings of fear among viewers who are not directly exposed or who have not experienced violence and brutality.[33]

Terrorist incidents using the media for publicity purposes can be called PR disasters (PR for "public relations"). The first form of PR disaster is the **disaster for PR**, which consists mostly of expressive communication, symbolic hatred, a desire for martyrdom, and a crazy, almighty aspiration to dominate the world. The second form is the **disaster created for PR**, which is a strategic and managed intervention, well calculated for an increasingly dominant extremist agenda.[34] Whichever type of PR Timothy McVeigh wanted to adopt is up to the reader to decide. The Oklahoma City bombing certainly embodies Kratcoski's (2001)[35] statement that "if one of the elements of terrorism is the wish to obtain publicity for a cause and create propaganda, the media has obviously overreacted in responding to this desire" (p. 468). One will notice in the Oklahoma City bombing that televised coverage of the impacts of a terrorist attack (particularly if it is "live") creates a paradoxical situation in which the spectators imagine more dreadful scenes than the very witnesses present at the site.[36] Barnhurst (1991)[37] has distinguished two models of the media–terrorism relationship. The **culpable-media model** identifies a causal relationship between media and terrorism, which calls for media regulation. In this model, the media play a dangerous game: "As media cover terrorism, they incite more terrorism, which produces more media coverage" (p. 125). On the other hand, the **vulnerable-media model** considers the media as only victims of terrorism, not causes of it: "Any control on coverage, even a natural one, will be ineffective because terrorists can shift to other forms of communication by striking vulnerable points in the infrastructure of liberal societies" (p. 126). Although involved, the media produce no escape from terrorism.

Media as a Fickle Friend

According to Yungher (2008),[38] terrorists often try to manipulate the media to (1) receive free publicity for their cause, preferably coverage that will portray them in a positive light; (2) cultivate good relationships with the media hoping that the later will share information about the identity of hostages, or information that they might have about law enforcement (e.g., their plans to counterattack, etc.); (3) delegitimize the government by exposing its incompetence; and (4) diffuse information that causes panic and hurts the economy. In line with these contentions, Scott (2001)[39] analyzed data on terrorism from 1978 to 1990 and found a progressive causal relationship between media coverage and terrorism (i.e., increased media coverage resulting in subsequent increases in terrorism). The media, it seems, can be a **fickle friend**, a term alluding to the notion that the media always search for novelty and, from the terrorists' perspective, novelty can be created by the terrorists themselves. Consequently, they attempt to commit terrorist acts in rhythmic succession, or innovate in a way that enables them to recapture the media's favor.[40] Since terrorism is a communicative tactic, it can also be limited by the way media report on terrorist incidents. If media coverage of terrorism were less widespread and more contemplative, public fear might be reduced and attacking innocent targets might lose some of its function as a tool to promulgate political demands.[41]

Terrorists recognize the potential of the media as a weapon. For Ayman al-Zawahiri, now the main Al Qaeda leader, the media is a fickle friend and a big apparatus in Al Qaeda's arsenal. Zawahiri is aware that any attack, especially if it is spectacular, can sensationalize the struggle. All he has to do is consult his own media relations group. When Zawahiri ran Egyptian Islamic Jihad, an affiliate of Al Qaeda, he would always turn to a sub-committee specializing in public relations. After joining Al Qaeda, Zawahiri has continued to rely on his PR friends. Furthermore, he applies his own writings to justify terrorism. He has authored books and pamphlets, playing up support for Muslim victims around the world. Lastly, along with other jihadists, he takes advantage of the Internet.[42]

Photo-sharing and video-sharing websites can sometimes be considered fickle friends as well. Technorati.com, which collects blogs from all over the world, claimed that the first mobile phone pictures of the 2005 London bombings were posted a few minutes after the attacks. Flickr.com, a site that allows users to post photographs for free, had over 300 bombing photos posted within eight hours of the tragedy. Independent Television (ITV), the BBC, MSNBC, *The Guardian*, the *Times of London*, and other outlets requested pictures, through online "solicitation" postings, from witnesses. Those news outlets also hunted for picture-sharing blogs.[43]

Osama bin Laden: A Household Name

Media coverage of Islamist threats changed drastically after Al Qaeda's attacks on September 11, 2001, especially when the U.S. media attempted to answer the question that President George W. Bush had asked in a speech at a joint session of Congress: "Why do they hate us?" At the same time, the perpetrators of 9/11 achieved, possibly, their highest media-dependent goal—specifically, to broadcast their causes, grievances, and demands.[44] While certainly hated by Americans, Osama bin Laden became a household name in the U.S. In the first ten issues after September 11, 2001, *Newsweek* featured the Al Qaeda leader three times on its cover; *Time* twice. During this same period, *Time* showed President George W. Bush's image twice; *Newsweek* not at all. This top coverage of Osama bin Laden was not limited to these two major U.S. news magazines. In the aftermath of the September 11 terrorist attacks, and until the start of the war in Afghanistan on October 7, the U.S. TV networks discussed bin Laden more regularly, prominent newspapers and National Public Radio only slightly less frequently than George W. Bush. This was particularly striking because, during this period, the U.S. president made fifty-four public statements (in various forms), whereas bin Laden did not appear publically at all. Rather, he issued a few faxed and videotaped statements (made by himself and close confrères) that were delivered to the Qatar-based network Al Jazeera.[45]

EXAMPLES OF TERRORISTS' EXPLOITATION OF THE MEDIA

On one occasion, an Algerian terrorist said that he would rather kill a single person in the presence of a news camera than a hundred in the desert where nobody could see them. His statement should be given notice: modern terrorism is a media spectacle.[46] This section lists various examples of terrorists' exploitation of the media, starting with the infamous Munich massacre (Box 3.3) and ending with the even more infamous September 11, 2001 terrorist attacks (Box 3.4).

Box 3.3   The Munich Massacre

The 1972 attack by **Black September**, a Palestinian terrorist group, during the Munich Olympic Games (aka, the **Munich massacre**) was committed before a global audience of close to 800 million viewers. It killed eleven Israeli athletes (after Black September had initially kidnapped numerous Israeli athletes). The Munich massacre was a window of opportunity for Palestinians to introduce the world to the plight of their people living in Israeli-occupied lands. The terrorist attack is a textbook example of perfect success in terms of guaranteeing media attention. It became a catalyst that made terrorism a cost-effective tool of communication, and a method of communication that became a legitimate form of intimidation.[47] As one of the leading Palestinian terrorists, who coordinated the attack, declared, "We recognized that sport is the modern religion of the Western world. We knew that the people in England and America would switch their television sets from any program about the plight of the Palestinians if there was a sporting event on another channel. So we decided to use their Olympics, the most sacred ceremony of this religion, to make the world pay attention to us."[48]

Based on Tuman's (2003)[49] model of terrorism as a communication process described in Chapter 2, the Munich massacre can be explained by following this aforementioned model: (1) sender of message (Black September and possibly the Palestinian Authority), (2) receiver of message (almost 800 million viewers as well as Israeli and Western governments, including the German government since Munich is in Germany), (3) message itself (terrorist act killing eleven Israeli athletes to avenge the plight of the Palestinians), and (4) feedback (reaction of the receiver, including both intended and unintended recipients of the message).

By kidnapping people (i.e., athletes), the Black September terrorists opened channels of communication. The target of their message was a wide and removed audience (i.e., nearly 800 million viewers), such as governments (and their supporters) that the terrorists were protesting against. The hostages and the kidnapping symbolized the message itself, involving specific demands. The reaction of the government(s) (and the entire world) to the terrorists' demands represented the feedback required by the terrorists to establish successful (i.e., two-way) communication. The Munich massacre embodies the notion that the global reporting of terrorism news is the terrorists' first fifteen minutes of fame. In academic terms, this is referred to as **status conferral**, the amount of attention given to particular people. The media confer prestige and empower individuals and groups by legitimizing their authority or status. Acknowledgment by the press, radio, magazines, or newsreels confirms that one is there now, that one is sufficiently important to stand out from the large anonymous crowd, and that one's actions are significant enough to get public notice.[50]

Since around 1970, terrorists have been attentive to their image and cleverly run PR and propaganda campaigns to "package" their causes and actions. Below are selected examples of status conferral in the history of terrorism and the media:

- In mid-1975, the Baader-Meinhof terrorist group negotiated the release of its associates in exchange for a hostage who was being held. Part of the agreement included the television broadcast of communiqués made by Baader-Meinhof.[51]

- In December 1975, Carlos the Jackal (a Venezuelan terrorist who espoused principles linked to communists, Arab nationalists, and Islamists) helped plan the attack on the headquarters of the Organisation of Petroleum Exporting Countries (OPEC) in Vienna. More precisely, he led a unit that assailed OPEC leaders at their meeting and took more than sixty hostages, killing a few of them in the process. Carlos demanded that the Austrian government read statements about the Palestinian cause on the Austrian radio and TV networks every two hours. To avoid the risk of having a hostage executed every fifteen minutes, the Austrian government complied and the statements were broadcast as requested.[52]

- In 1976, Croatian terrorists had a statement published in exchange for liberating hostages from a hijacked airplane.[53]

- In November 1979, Iranian activists stormed the U.S. embassy in Tehran. This shifted the world's attention to the supremacy of Islamic fundamentalism, especially by extending the incident over 444 days. The news program, *Nightline*, was created as a result of the hostage crisis in Tehran, Iran, whereby hostage takers often scheduled demonstrations and made demands during the airing of the program.[54] At the height of the hostage situation, in November and December 1979, three TV networks—ABC News, CBS News, and NBC News—respectively dedicated 54%, 50%, and 48% of their evening news broadcasts to the hostage taking.[55]

- On June 14, 1985, Hezbollah terrorists hijacked TWA Flight 847 heading for Rome from Athens and forced it to land in Beirut. During the journey, the terrorists freed women, children, and non-Americans, until thirty-nine American adult males remained on board. As the hijacking progressed, the media dedicated a remarkable amount of exposure to the incident. The TV networks ABC, CBS, and NBC broadcast close to 500 news reports (i.e., 28.8 per day), and allocated two thirds of their evening news programs to the incident. The hijacking lasted for sixteen days. During this period, CBS allocated 68% of its nightly news broadcasts to the incident while the figures at ABC and NBC were 62% and 63%, respectively. The terrorists skillfully maneuvered the world's media. They accorded carefully choreographed interviews, held press conferences, and selected the information that news outlets should broadcast. Later, it was found that the hijackers had proposed to arrange tours of the airplane for the networks for a $1,000 payment and an interview with the hostages for $12,500. The hostages were freed on June 30, 1985.[56]

- In October 2000, based on TV reports, Al Qaeda arranged for the recording of the suicide bombings of USS Cole in Aden, Yemen. Simulated videos of the Navy destroyer bombings, supposedly made by Al Qaeda for propaganda purposes, have been broadcast on both Al Jazeera and CNN.[57]

Box 3.4   The September 11, 2001 Terrorist Attacks

As stated in a lengthy, in-depth manual of the Afghan jihad used for the instruction of future terrorists in Al Qaeda's training camps, publicity was a paramount consideration in planning the September 11, 2001 terrorist attacks. The manual also advised jihadists to target other sentimental landmarks of the West, such as the Statue of Liberty in New York, Big Ben in London, and the Eiffel Tower in Paris, because destroying them would "generate intense publicity."[58] In their targeting of sentimental landmarks in New York City and Washington, D.C., the 9/11 hijackers generated widespread publicity by all means. As soon as the first airliner hit the North Tower of the World Trade Center (WTC), dreadful images were immediately and continuously emitted through satellites to editors and news anchors who had difficulties making sense of it live before a hypnotized global audience. Beyond the shadow of a doubt, the hijackers timed the WTC attacks to gain maximum media exposure—they anticipated that the cameras would be pointing at the smoking North Tower (i.e., the first tower hit) as the second plane was ready to crash into the South Tower.[59]

In the May 2002 HBO film, *In Memoriam*, the September 11, 2001 terrorist attacks were described as "the most documented event in history." The film was principally a collage of images put together by professional news crews, documentary directors, and nonprofessional videographers and photographers who, in some cases, put their lives at risk to document the event. The September 11, 2001 terrorist attacks dominated virtually all television programs for the next three days without commercial interruptions as the major TV networks concentrated on the tragedy and its aftermath.[60] The attacks served as a "global advertising vehicle,"[61] namely, to advertise Al Qaeda's mission and grievances. As terrorism expert Martha Crenshaw (1981)[62] notes, "[T]he most basic reason for terrorism is to gain recognition or attention" (p. 396).

In all of those cases, the media represented a rewarding opportunity for terrorists. In most of those cases, the media were also forced to collaborate with the terrorists. Hence, the title of this section was about "terrorists' exploitation of the media." Nevertheless, the media coverage of such terrorist events represents a major cultural shift in the viewers' sensitivity toward mass media images, particularly for understanding issues of national security. This, in turn, alters perceptions of risk at home and threats abroad. By being exposed to media depictions of terrorism, the audience can either approach the matter with complacency or hysteria, depending on the viewer's experience and personality. The next section discusses the problems associated with media coverage of terrorism.

PROBLEMS WITH MEDIA COVERAGE OF TERRORISM

Soon after the start of World War I in August 1914, when it became obvious that the soldiers would not come back home for Christmas, France's General Staff agreed in unison: no unaccompanied journalists and photographers on the battlefield. The General Staff viewed the media simply as a channel of intelligence for the enemy. Acrimonious complaints were rehashed about how journalists had caused the French to lose the Franco-Prussian War of 1870 by printing information about the French general's military tactics and the circumstances surrounding the French troops. In more recent times, White House officials attributed the American loss of world standing and credibility during Vietnam to television.[63] This section looks at separate scholarly works, particularly those of Jeffrey Ian Ross (2007)[64] and Cindy Combs (2011),[65] to provide the same chain of reasoning with respect to problems of media coverage. Overall, a dozen combined reasons explain why media coverage of terrorist incidents can be problematic:

Lack of experts focusing on terrorism: only a small number of news organizations employ journalists specializing solely in covering terrorism. From time to time, reporters— like Josh Myers of the *Los Angeles Times*—specialize in covering news on terrorism. Alternatively, news outlets may occasionally rely on experts like Peter Bergen, who frequently appears on CNN.[66]

Editorial discretion: although newsworthy stories exist, it does not mean that they will be selected by an editor or producer. Likewise, even if a story is written or filmed, it does not mean that it will be published or aired. Besides the relationship between journalists and sources, an unwritten agreement exists between reporters and all their editors or producers. This relationship naturally impacts the outcome of news stories on terrorism. Most editors or producers call the shots as to whether, how, and when a story will be reported.[67]

Misinformation given to journalists by national security agencies: many stories published or aired in the media come from official government sources. According to Jenkins (2003),[68] media dependence on law enforcement sources makes a lot of sense because, in spite of all their flaws, agencies such as the FBI tend to be the best-informed organizations in the U.S. They can get access to ample evidence from spies, infiltrators, and surveillance materials. Nevertheless, these agencies can also take advantage of the media for self-serving purposes, especially through so-called *strategic leaks*. This was particularly true after the September 11, 2001 attacks, when federal agencies struggled to be on top of things, hoping to show the American public that they were not dormant but fully energetic on that matter.[69]

Media obstructing antiterrorist endeavors: at times, the media have unintentionally hindered counterterrorist efforts to successfully resolve hostage-type situations. Members of the press have passed into lines of fire and secured zones, and captive and rescue forces have been pictured on live TV as they moved in for an attack. In these incidents, terrorists need only to watch television or listen to a radio newscast to gain the upper hand. Numerous examples like this exist, such as the 1977 Hanafi Muslim invasion of the B'nai B'rith building in Washington.[70]

Dramatic presentation of news: in a ferocious competition for public attention, the press clearly needs to produce a dramatic presentation of the terrorist incident as well as a timely one. During the hijacking of TWA Flight 847 in June 1985, ABC aired lengthy interviews with the captives and the hostage takers. In one of the interviews, a pistol was pointed to the pilot's head in a staged photo-op for the journalists. The press argued that the extreme scrutiny they gave to each aspect of the incident truly protected the hostages. From this perspective, it assumes that the main purpose of the act is to publicize a cause. However, if drama is necessary to prove the gravity of the cause, then the hostages' lives could be endangered by a media demand for drama. If getting hostages killed becomes the cost of drama, then the press may be blamed for increasing the stakes in the hostage "game."[71]

Sensationalization: there is fierce competition among media outlets to be the first to broadcast or publish any story. This influences the method by which news are obtained and described. A news organization can accomplish this in one of two ways: (1) by being the first on the scene or (2) by being the first to report some previously unreported information. It is easier and more sensational for the Western press to refer to terrorists as crazy or evil people.[72] What Americans see on TV drastically influences their political perspectives and behavior. The instant systematic revenge for 9/11 led to the U.S. government's ideal model of a PR-ized war.[73]

Obtaining a scoop: it means being the first to broadcast or publish a story. State-of-the art communications enable and increase the pressure to diffuse news stories in "real time." This gives little time for editing or thoroughly assessing the bearing of such news releases on the situation.[74]

Lack of a "denial of a platform": to impose a denial of a platform means to prevent terrorists from exploiting the free press as a vehicle for their propaganda. This platform is useful not only to increase understanding (and perhaps compassion toward the terrorist's cause) but also to increase substantial support. The 1985 hijacking of TWA Flight 847 in Beirut clearly shed light on the dangers of this platform. The hostage takers allegedly offered reporters tours of the plane for $1,000 and an interview with the captives for $12,500. Governments and news organizations should deny terrorists as much platform as possible.[75]

Absence of consistent focus: the West uses the media as a war instrument; Al Qaeda does it too. To explain this, let us look at Al Qaeda's 1996 "Declaration of War against the United States"—which the Western press barely covered or responded to—and Osama bin Laden's "World Islamic Front for Jihad against Jews and Crusaders," a declaration made in 1998 (two years later) and that received much more media coverage around the world. The difference was bin Laden's efforts to appear in the news media in the two years that led up to this second declaration. However, the television media coverage of this second declaration was microscopic as compared to the coverage of the September 11, 2001 terrorist attacks.[76]

Harming civilians or hostages: a type of media that is absolutely free can cost lives. In the hijacking of TWA Flight 847, radio broadcasts warned the hijackers aboard the Lufthansa aircraft that the captain was sending information to authorities on the ground. The hijackers immediately killed the captain of the plane. The media were free but the cost was the pilot's life.[77]

Harming victims' families: media coverage of terrorist attacks can be very controversial, even with respect to issues of rights to privacy and decisions about the portrayal of delicate or touchy material. For instance, some of these problems emerged in 1994 with uproars over coverage of a terrorist attack on a bus in the center of Tel Aviv: the media had displayed photos of the dead and divulged victims' names even before the families were notified.[78]

Making enemies even angrier: media coverage of Palestinians wounded or killed during conflicts with Israelis fueled the anger of Osama bin Laden's sympathizers as well as Arabs and Muslims in general—many of whom considered bin Laden's extremism fascinating as a response to the exasperation and oppression of their daily lives. For Al Qaeda, watching media coverage of U.S. retaliations in the Muslim world would be seen as advantageous because retaliations could be described as another case of U.S. "bullying" and "aggression." Thus, the rise of future terrorism (aimed at the U.S. and its allies) would have actually been possible thanks to the success of the Afghan War.[79]

As one can see, this exhaustive list of problems points to the fact that media coverage of terrorism can be harmful. Terry Anderson (1993)[80] expressed the following sentiment: "My experience as both journalist and hostage has given me a personal look at terrorists' manipulation of the media and the impact of the media's coverage of such events. The reply seems obvious: Don't give terrorists what they want." As he continued, "Don't give them publicity. Don't report on their demands, or even... on their actions. If they cannot expect publicity, they will go away" (p. 134). And here again: "The media are part of the deadly game of terrorism. Indeed the game can be scarcely played without them. In my experience, publicity has been at once a primary goal and a weapon of those who use terror" (p. 128). Complete censorship, however, is not the solution either. The efficiency of a democratic society is contingent on the freedom of people to make informed decisions. While censorship may contribute to a reduction of terrorism, it could also lead to the reduction of freedom enjoyed by citizens of democratic societies.[81] Nevertheless, there is another problem with media coverage of terrorist incidents: media terrorism.

MEDIA TERRORISM

The debate on the terrorism–media symbiotic relationship prods the following question: does media coverage take the side of terrorists, giving them legitimacy and credibility, as well as inadvertently stimulating more incidents through a contagion effect?[82] A word that was first seen in 14th century English, contagion stems from the Latin word *contagio*, from *contingere*, meaning "to have contact with."[83] Having frequent connotations of disease or mortifying influences, contagion also refers to the rapid communication and dissemination of ideas, doctrines, or emotional conditions.[84] The **contagion effect of media reporting** of terrorism impacts the potential behavior of like-minded extremists. When terrorists manage to get wide exposure or a higher degree of compassion from the media and their audience, future terrorists may be inspired to emulate the methods of the first successful incident. True cases of successful contagion effect include political and commercial kidnappings for payment and concessions in Latin America in the 1960s and 1970s, hijackings in support of Middle Eastern causes (usually Palestinian) from the late 1960s to the 1980s, and the hostage taking of Westerners in Lebanon in the 1980s.[85] There is actually a stronger term for the contagion effect of media coverage of terrorism. The term is *media terrorism*.

Media terrorism refers to media's use of fear, whether the incidents are real or imaginary, to frighten and pressure the masses—in general, to erode or reduce people's ability to think independently. By the same token, media terrorism refers to television's fixation on images of violence. It is violence as popular entertainment.[86] Media terrorism is the concept that media coverage has an overarching goal of broadcasting terrorist violence. Our media-driven culture has fashioned and misshaped our values, creating considerable harm in the process. The media constantly poke, urge, drive, push, and intimidate consumers with fear. Media terrorism exists as long as there is an interpreter to ascribe terrorism a meaning. The media's charge to act with self-discipline is unmistakably of utmost importance.[87] For instance, in Ghana, Dr. Wilberforce Sefakor Dzisah, a communications consultant, has expressed concerns over the skyrocketing rise of irresponsible media practice by a segment of the Ghanaian media. For Dr. Dzisah, this situation poses a serious menace to peace and democracy. Particularly, Ghanaian radio stations are engaging in media terrorism; they call for radical uprisings—including highway pilfering, mass rape, and killing—from the people against others.[88]

According to Josef Ja ab (2005),[89] a Czech politician, at the Council of Europe, "[T]he media are attracted by extreme terrorist acts not only because it is their duty to report on any major event but also because, at the same time, the dramaturgy of terrorism attracts large scale attention." This statement brings to mind another name for media terrorism: second-hand terrorism. Just as there is second-hand smoking (the danger of direct exposure to tobacco smoking), **second-hand terrorism** refers to a practice whereby media outlets excessively stress the possibility for anyone of being a direct victim of terrorism. It discusses the ubiquitous and eternal threat that remains in children's environments—e.g., the media, popular discourse, and government rhetoric—long after terrorist attacks have been perpetrated. In fact, such media terrorism can produce or aggravate a broad range of adverse mental health issues.[90]

A chief objective of media terrorism is to **supersize terrorism**, that is, to overstate the threat of terrorism, and to endorse or authenticate the socially created description of terrorism that it is presently bigger, deadlier, and much more threatening. This tendency to exaggerate the danger of terrorism may symbolize nothing more than signals of a social or moral panic intentionally created to obtain more funding for government agencies and/or to rationalize more limits on civil liberties and human rights by repressive government bodies.[91] By supersizing terrorism, media coverage becomes **infotainment**: it is charged with making news stories entertaining for the public instead of attempting to report the most important information.[92] It also becomes **spectaculturization**, whereby the spectacle of violence is used to confirm the fears of the audience and their feelings of unrest during times of emergency and political uncertainty.[93]

TERRORISM AND THE MEDIA: A SEMIOTIC PERSPECTIVE

Terrorism is symbolic language. It is a semiotic act that functions as a signal, a message, a symbol, and a media image. The images of the aircrafts crashing into the World Trade Center are affixed to our systems. The objective of terrorism is to transmit a meaningful signal, one of which the purpose is to terrify and coerce others. For this reason, terrorism is first and foremost a communication process between terrorists and target audiences.[94] **Semiotics** refers to the study of signs and symbols, especially their processes and systems.[95] As Sebeok (1976)[96] asserts, semiotics is "the exchange of any messages... and the system of signs that underlie them" (p. 60).

Saussurean Semiotics

The study of semiotics was introduced by Ferdinand de Saussure (1959),[97] a Swiss linguist. Semiotics comes from the Greek word *semiotikon*, which means "sign." *Semiotikon*, then, came to embody the study of signs and their interpretation.[98] A **sign** is something that stands for something else. It is made to represent something else. Messages have signs in them, which are sent through sign systems. These sign systems are referred to as **codes**. Meaning can only exist inasmuch as the message receiver understands the code. Semiotics focuses on the interpretation of sign functions and their comprehension of meaning by the receiver.[99] Ferdinand de Saussure was a forerunner in the modern study of language. He supported the theory that signs have two elements: a signifier and a signified. The **signifier** is the visible, or material, part, whereas the **signified** is the absent part. Let us take the example of a flag: the signifier is the flag itself, what people can see and touch; the signified is what the flag represents or symbolizes.[100] The signifier denotes and the signified connotes.

As such, the word *terrorist* is a sign that comprises the two following elements: a signifier (i.e., the word itself) and a signified (i.e., the enemy, the evil ones, the threats to world democracy, etc.). The signifier *terrorist* is seen as a common denominator for describing "a person who launches attacks on premeditated and/or unintended targets" by many governments, such as the government of the U.S., Russia, and Sri Lanka. However, the signified, the perpetrators (and the violent actions they take) are relatively different: Al Qaeda, the Chechens, and the Tamil Tigers. Some terrorist actions symbolize Islamic fundamentalism; others are simple manifestations of revenge against the oppressor. Because the label of signified depends on both the viewer and the context, the concept of terrorism seems to be arbitrary. The signified can also change over time. The only attribute that is stable is the signifier: terrorism.[101] It is the signified aspect of the word that acquires broader political, legal, and cultural overtones. This semiotic understanding of terrorism is important because it can help scholars and practitioners distinguish between the visible part of terrorism (i.e., signifier) and what it symbolizes (i.e., signified).

Peircean Semiotics

Charles Sanders Peirce's (1958 [1931])[102] semiotic framework is made up of a three-part model of signification: (1) the **representamen** (i.e., the actual sign itself; what something is), (2) the **object** (i.e., the "referent"; what the sign refers to or symbolizes), and (3) the **interpretant** (i.e., the viewer's interpretation or the resulting effect in the mind of the interpreter). This framework is what is referred to as Peirce's representamen–object–interpretant model. For Peirce, meaning is a triadic interdependence of these three categories. Terrorism thrives on the media effects of arousing fear. To be viewed as terrorism, terrorist acts need representation. Accordingly, explaining this requires a semiotic examination of this very representation. The semiotics of Charles Sanders Peirce offers such a method.[103]

The *representamen* is the image played time and time again, in the media, of a burning multistory building (i.e., the South Tower of the World Trade Center) after the second hijacked aircraft was shown flying into it. For most members of the audience, it was their very first exposure of an airliner crashing into the World Trade Center. They became cognizant of this only by watching the image on TV. The type of representamen in this instance is a sign that is an absolute and undisputable image: a plane hitting a high-rise building.

The *object* is that the image in question symbolizes an extremely violent terrorist attack; it is a violation of human conscience that is beyond comprehension. In this *object* phase, the audience is putting the two together: a hijacked passenger airliner + crashing into a building = an extremely violent terrorist attack.

The *interpretant* is the resulting effect in the mind of the interpreter; it is the perception that this terrorist event was an intentional and premeditated act of terror—that the terrorists committed it for political and religious purposes and to terrorize a population. In the interpretant phase, the audience uses their mind. Viewers create narratives. The interpretant adds the qualification that the 9/11 massacre was selective and calculatedly chosen.[104] Indeed, in the interpreters' minds, the World Trade Center was deliberately destroyed because it symbolized power—an economic, political, and cultural power. The WTC towers were symbols of New York City's hubris, empire building, supremacy, capitalism, individualism, globalization, contemporary architectural innovation, and secularism. These symbols of power were particularly vulnerable; they represented the weakness of governmental power.[105] As Kappeler and Potter (2005)[106] contend, interpretants are conceptual patterns that help viewers interpret reality and structure their thoughts and beliefs about reality. Momentous targets were selected for their symbolic value, not because an act such as slaughter will automatically cause a financial or tangible effect on the objectives of the perpetrators. It is the interpretant that matters, that is, the viewers' emotional responses. In semiotic terms, the symbolic character of terrorism is amplified by the power of the visual media (i.e., the aftermath of the September 11, 2001 attacks).

The representamen–object–interpretant model was given a "media theory" flavor by Cohen, Adoni, and Bantz (1990)[107] when they conceptualized the omnipresence of the media in our society. For these scholars, we do not live in just one realm of reality; we live in three of them: (1) the real objective world (what is happening "out there"); (2) the symbolic world (how the world is presented and pictured in the media); and (3) the subjective world (the world as the audience views it in their minds; their belief is based on a mixture of direct experiences with the real world and the portrayal of real "things" or "events" in the media).

The Signal-Index Paradigm

Peirce's three-part model also inspired semiotic scholar Robert Jervis (1970)[108] to advance it into a "signal-index" paradigm. Jervis made a distinction between signals and indices. A **signal** is a statement conveyed from a sender to a receiver. It is akin to a promissory note. Conversely, an **index** of the sender's goals is assumed to intrinsically show what the sender intends to accomplish. While signals can be manipulated for various gains, indices are by nature either uncontrollable or not consciously controlled, which provides great discernment as to what the sender really wants.

Abrahms (2005)[109] applied Jervis's signal-index model to Al Qaeda's terrorism. The strongest signal of Al Qaeda is the destruction of the World Trade Center and the grave damage inflicted on the Pentagon. Put another way, its strongest signal is the practice of terrorism. In contrast, Al Qaeda's strongest index is the message that the terrorist organization is fighting the West and all that the U.S. stands for. Terrorism is also an index of Al Qaeda's depravity: by slaughtering 3,000 civilians, Al Qaeda went excessively beyond the simple violation of conventional principles of international conduct. Lastly, terrorism is an index that Al Qaeda covertly embraces maximalist aims; as declared by Osama bin Laden in his 1996 and 1998 fatwas, America and Israel ought to be wiped out, and Islam should be the only religion on earth. Abrahms compared Al Qaeda's actions with President Theodore Roosevelt's actions in the early 1900s. Roosevelt cried out for a crusade to remove terrorists everywhere based on the belief that they would not yield or stop unless their organizations would be broken down. From a semiotic standpoint, Roosevelt only considered the terrorist signal, not the terrorist index. He did not try to determine what the terrorists' ultimate objective or "maximalist goal" was (e.g., undermining democracy in the West, abolishing Christianity and Judaism, etc.).

MEDIA PORTRAYALS OF FEMALE TERRORISTS

In Chapter 1, the role of female terrorists was described with respect to their status and involvement in suicide terrorism. Of particular importance is media's portrayal of female terrorists, which has received negligible attention in the terrorism literature. Media images of female terrorists serve as effective propaganda tools. Women terrorists tend to get more media attention than men because the thought of women, those who deliver life, actually terminating life is distressing. The idea of females acting as instruments of violence runs totally against expectations of femininity. Hence, images of female terrorists garner widespread publicity and diffuse a terrorist organization's message to a larger audience.[110] Evidence shows that media clichés about gender affect the strategic plans and decisions of terrorist organizations and the behavior of female terrorists. Therefore, the intelligence circles, law enforcement, and others involved in counterterrorism operations would benefit greatly from understanding and emphasizing the gap between the stereotypical women terrorists and the importance of gender roles in terrorist organizations. Just as the press finds the looks of women in politics particularly newsworthy, the media also devote much coverage to the physical appearance, the smiles, or the neatly chosen attire of female terrorists that seem to run counter to the image of a tough-looking terrorist.[111]

For instance, in 1995, a year after Idoia Lopez Riano of ETA, the Basque separatist organization, was arrested and accused of killing twenty-three innocent people, Anne McElvoy (1995)[112] reported in the *Times of London* that the female terrorist, under the pseudonym "The Tigress," looked like a Mediterranean movie star and was "one of the few women who manages to look good even in a police shot" (p. A1). The Tigress was also portrayed as "wearing hefty eye make-up, fuchsia lipstick and dangling earrings that tinkle as she tosses her hair of black curls" (p. A1). Likewise, a newspaper article about Wafra Idris, the first female Palestinian suicide bomber, opened with the statement, "She was an attractive, auburn haired graduate who had a loving family and likes to wear sleeveless dresses and make-up" (p. B1).[113] In another press article, Idris was portrayed as a female with "long, dark hair tied back with a black-and-white keffiyeh."[114] A story about the upsurge of "Palestinian women strapping explosives to their bodies and becoming martyrs" on the website of the Christian Broadcasting Network was entitled "Lipstick Martyrs: A New Breed of Palestinian Terrorists."[115]

SUMMARY

There is a symbiotic relationship between terrorism and the media. Terrorism needs the media; otherwise the cause of most terrorist groups would be less known. Conversely, an act of terrorism that just happened or that is going to happen may be a major scoop for the media; the audience ratings will likely increase. In fact, government officials have a tendency to associate the media with terrorists' success or failure. Because the media select events that are newsworthy, terrorists select targets and locations that will be given high priority by news organizations. Examples of this are the Munich massacre and the Oklahoma City bombing. And, of course, the 9/11 terrorists timed the WTC attacks to gain maximum media exposure. In addition, there is a progressive causal relationship between media coverage and terrorism: increased media coverage will lead to subsequent increases in terrorism. Nevertheless, it should be noted that there are a dozen reasons indicating that media coverage of terrorist incidents can be problematic, such as sensationalization and the possibility of harming civilians or hostages. Due to television's fixation on images of violence, media coverage can go as far as taking the side of terrorists (i.e., media terrorism)—wittingly or unwittingly. Finally, terrorism is a semiotic act because terrorism speaks a symbolic language.

KEY TERMS

amplification effect   57

armed propaganda   55

code   67

contagion effect of media reporting   66

culpable-media model   58

disaster created for PR   58

disaster for PR   58

electronic media   53

fickle friend   59

index (semiotics)   69

ENDNOTES

1. Janowitz, Morris (1968). The Study of Mass Communication. In David L. Sills (Ed.), *International Encyclopedia of the Social Sciences* (pp. 40–51). New York: Macmillan.

2. White, Jonathan R. (2011). *Terrorism and Homeland Security* (7th ed.). Belmont, CA: Wadsworth.

3. Crelinsten, Ronald (2007). Terrorism, Counter-Terrorism and the Media. *Counter-Terrorism International Conference, 17,* 19–22.

4. Moeller, Susan D. (2009). *Packaging Terrorism: Co-Opting the News for Politics and Profit.* New York: Wiley-Blackwell.

5. Perse, Elizabeth, Signorielli, Nancy, Courtright, John, Samter, Wendy, Caplan, Scott, Lambe, Jennifer, & Cai, Xiaomei (2002). Public Perceptions of Media Functions at the Beginning of the War on Terrorism. In Bradley S. Greenberg (Ed.), *Communication and Terrorism: Public and Media Responses to 9/11* (pp. 39–52). Cresskill, NJ: Hampton Press.

6. Hoffman, Bruce (2003). *Inside Terrorism.* New York: Columbia University Press.

7. McNair, Brian (1999). *An Introduction to Political Communication.* London: Routledge; Wardlaw, Grant (1989). *Political Terrorism: Theory, Tactics and Counter-Measures.* Cambridge: Cambridge University Press; Wilkinson, Paul (1997). The Media and Terrorism: A Re-Assessment. *Terrorism and Political Violence, 9*(2), 51–64.

8. Miller, Abraham H. (1982). *Terrorism, the Media and the Law.* New York: Transnational Publishers.

9. Alexander, Yonah (1977). Communications Aspects of International Terrorism. *International Problems, 16,* 55–60; Sandler, Todd, & Lapan, Harvey E. (1988). The Calculus of Dissent: An Analysis of Terrorists' Choice of Targets. *Synthese, 76,* 244–261; Schmid, Alex P., & de Graaf, Janny (1982). *Violence as Communication: Insurgent Terrorism and the Western News Media.* Beverly Hills, CA: Sage.

10. Esposito, John L. (2002). *Unholy War: Terror in the Name of Islam.* Oxford: Oxford University Press; Gunaratna, Rohan (2002). *Inside al Qaeda: Global Network of Terror.* New York: Columbia University Press.

11. Karber, Phillip A. (1971). *Terrorism as Social Protest.* Paper Presented at the Southern Political Science Association.

12. Jenkins, Brian (1983). Research in Terrorism: Areas of Consensus, Areas of Ignorance. In Burr Eichelman, David A. Soskis, & William H. Reid (Eds.), *Terrorism: Interdisciplinary Perspectives* (pp. 153–177). Washington, D.C.: American Psychiatric Association.

13. Marighella, Carlos (2008). *Minimanual of the Urban Guerrilla.* St Petersburg, FL: Red and Black Publishers.

14. Weimann, Gabriel, & Winn, Conrad (1994). *The Theater of Terror: Mass Media and International Journalism*. New York: Longman.

15. Wilkinson, Paul (2001). *Terrorism versus Democracy*. London: Frank Cass.

16. Weimann, Gabriel (2008). The Psychology of Mass-Mediated Terrorism. *American Behavioral Scientist, 52*(1), 69–86.

17. Bockstette, Carsten (2008). *Jihadist Terrorist Use of Strategic Communication Management Techniques*. Garmisch-Partenkirchen, Germany: The George C. Marshall European Center for Security Studies.

18. Wieviorka, Michel (2004). *The Making of Terrorism*. Chicago: The University of Chicago Press.

19. Norris, Pippa, Kern, Montague, & Just, Marion (2003). Framing Terrorism. In Pippa Norris, Montague Kern, & Marion Just (Eds.), *Framing Terrorism: The News Media, the Government, and the Public* (pp. 3–21). New York: Routledge.

20. Arnold, Ron (2010). *EcoTerror: The Violent Agenda to Save Nature: The World of the Unabomber*. Bellevue, WA: Merril Press; Chase, Alston (2004). *A Mind for Murder: The Education of the Unabomber and the Origins of Modern Terrorism*. New York: W. W. Norton & Company.

21. Combs, Cindy C. (2011). *Terrorism in the Twenty-First Century*. New York: Longman.

22. *Webster's Dictionary of the English Language* (1991). New York: Lexicon Publications.

23. Combs, Cindy C. (2011). *Terrorism in the Twenty-First Century*. New York: Longman.

24. Zulaika, Joseba, & Douglass, William A. (1996). *Terror and Taboo*. New York: Routledge.

25. Schmid, Alex P., & de Graaf, Janny (1982). *Violence as Communication: Insurgent Terrorism and the Western News Media*. Beverly Hills, CA: Sage.

26. Combs, Cindy C. (2011). *Terrorism in the Twenty-First Century*. New York: Longman.

27. Weimann, Gabriel, & Winn, Conrad (1994). *The Theater of Terror: Mass Media and International Terrorism*. New York: Longman.

28. Schorr, Daniel (1995, May 5). When Alienated, Violent Men Demand to Be Publicized. *Christian Science Monitor*.

29. Soriano, Manuel T. Torres (2008). Terrorism and the Mass Media after Al Qaeda: A Change of Course? *Athena Intelligence Journal, 3*(1), 1–20.

30. Soriano, Manuel T. Torres (2008). Terrorism and the Mass Media after Al Qaeda: A Change of Course? *Athena Intelligence Journal, 3*(1), 1–20.

31. Nacos, Brigitte (2002). *Mass-Mediated Terrorism: The Central Role of the Media in Terrorism and Counterterrorism*. Maryland: Rowman & Littlefield Publishers.

32. Martin, Gus (2010). *Understanding Terrorism: Challenges, Perspectives, and Issues*. Thousand Oaks, CA: Sage.

33. Slone, Michelle (2000). Responses to Media Coverage of Terrorism. *Journal of Conflict Resolution, 44*(4), 508–522.

34. Richards, Barry (2004). Terrorism and Public Relations. *Public Relations Review, 30*, 169–176.

35. Kratcoski, Peter C. (2001). Research Note: Terrorist Victimization: Prevention, Control, and Recovery. *Studies in Conflict and Terrorism, 24*, 467–473.

36. Ganor, Boaz (2005). *The Counter-Terrorism Puzzle: A Guide for Decision Makers*. New Brunswick, NJ: Transaction Publishers.

37. Barnhurst, Kevin (1991). The Literature of Terrorism: Implications for Visual Communications. In A. Odasuo Alali & Kevin K. Eke (Eds.), *Media Coverage of Terrorism* (pp. 112–137). Newbury Park: Sage.

38. Yungher, Nathan I. (2008). *Terrorism: The Bottom Line*. Upper Saddle River, NJ: Pearson Education.

39. Scott, John L. (2001). Media Congestion Limits Media Terrorism. *Defence and Peace Economics, 12*(3), 215–227.

40. Soriano, Manuel T. Torres (2008). Terrorism and the Mass Media after Al Qaeda: A Change of Course? *Athena Intelligence Journal, 3*(1), 1–20.

41. Sirseloudi, Matenia P. (2005). How to Predict the Unpredictable: On the Early Detection of Terrorist Campaigns. *Defense & Security Analysis, 21*(4), 369–386.

42. White, Jonathan R. (2011). *Terrorism & Homeland Security* (7th ed.). Belmont, CA: Wadsworth.

43. Moeller, Susan D. (2009). *Packaging Terrorism: Co-Opting the News for Politics and Profit*. New York: Wiley-Blackwell.

44. Weimann, Gabriel (2008). The Psychology of Mass-Mediated Terrorism. *American Behavioral Scientist, 52*(1), 69–86.

45. Nacos, Brigitte (2003). The Terrorist Calculus behind 9-11: A Model for Future Terrorism? *Studies in Conflict and Terrorism, 26*, 1–16.

46. White, Jonathan R. (2011). *Terrorism & Homeland Security* (7th ed.). Belmont, CA: Wadsworth.

47. Schmid, Alex P., & de Graaf, Janny (1982). *Violence as Communication: Insurgent Terrorism and the Western News Media*. Beverly Hills, CA: Sage.

48. Dobson, Christopher, & Paine, Ronald (1977). *The Carlos Complex: A Pattern of Violence*. London: Hodder and Stoughton.

49. Tuman, Joseph S. (2003). *Communicating Terror: The Rhetorical Dimensions of Terrorism*. Thousand Oaks, CA: Sage.

50. Lazarsfeld, Paul F., & Merton, Robert K. (1948). Mass Communication, Popular Taste and Organized Social Action. In Lyman Bryson (Ed.), *The Communication of Ideas* (pp. 95–118). New York: Harper & Bros.

51. Ross, Jeffrey Ian (2007). Deconstructing the Terrorism-News Media Relationship. *Crime Media Culture, 3*(2), 215–225.

52. Follain, John (1988). *Jackal: The Complete Story of the Legendary Terrorist Carlos the Jackal*. New York: Arcade Publishing.

53. Islam, Muhammad Q., & Shahin, Wassim N. (2001). Applying Economic Methodology to the War on Terrorism. *Forum for Social Economics, 31*(1), 7–26.

54. Daugherty, William J. (2001). *In the Shadow of the Ayatollah: A CIA Hostage in Iran*. Annapolis, MD: US Naval Institute Press.

55. Nacos, Brigitte L. (2010). *Terrorism and Counterterrorism* (3rd ed.). New York: Penguin.

56. Barkan, Steven E., & Snowden, Lynne E. (2000). *Collective Violence*. Boston: Allyn & Bacon; Hoffman, Bruce (1998). *Inside Terrorism*. New York: Columbia University Press; Weimann, Gabriel, & Winn, Conrad (1994). *The Theater of Terror: Mass Media and International Terrorism*. New York: Longman.

57. Islam, Muhammad Q., & Shahin, Wassim N. (2001). Applying Economic Methodology to the War on Terrorism. *Forum for Social Economics, 31*(1), 7–26.

58. Nacos, Brigitte (2003). The Terrorist Calculus behind 9-11: A Model for Future Terrorism? *Studies in Conflict and Terrorism, 26*, 1–16.

59. Virilio, Paul (2002). *Ground Zero*. London: Verso.

60. Kellner, Douglas (2003). September 11, Spectacles of Terror, and Media Manipulation: A Critique of Jihadist and Bush Media Politics. *Logos, 2*(1), 86–102.

61. Bassiouni, M. Cherif (1979). Prolegomenon to Terror Violence. *Creighton Law Review, 12*(3), 745–780, p. 757; Thornton, Thomas Perry (1964). Terror as a Weapon of Political Agitation. In Harry Eckstein (Ed.), *Internal War: Problems and Approaches* (pp. 71–99). New York: The Free Press, p. 82.

62. Crenshaw, Martha (1981). The Causes of Terrorism. *Comparative Politics, 13*(4), 379–399.

63. Moeller, Susan D. (2009). *Packaging Terrorism: Co-Opting the News for Politics and Profit*. New York: Wiley-Blackwell.

64. Ross, Jeffrey Ian (2007). Deconstructing the Terrorism-News Media Relationship. *Crime Media Culture, 3*(2), 215–225.

65. Combs, Cindy C. (2011). *Terrorism in the Twenty-First Century*. New York: Longman.

66. Ross, Jeffrey Ian (2007). Deconstructing the Terrorism–News Media Relationship. *Crime Media Culture, 3*(2), 215–225.

67. Boyd-Barrett, O. (2003). Doubt-Foreclosed: US Mainstream Media and the Attack of September 11, 2001. In Naren Chitty, Ramona Rush, & Mehdi Semanti (Eds.), *Studies in Terrorism: Media Scholarship and the Enigma of Terror* (pp. 147–164). Penang, Malaysia: Southbound Penang; Fishman, Mark (1980). *Manufacturing the News*. Austin: University of Texas Press.

68. Jenkins, Brian (2003). *Images of Terror: What We Can and Can't Know about Terrorism*. Hawthorne, NY: Aldine de Gruyter.

69. Ross, Jeffrey Ian (2007). Deconstructing the Terrorism-News Media Relationship. *Crime Media Culture, 3*(2), 215–225.

70. Ross, Jeffrey Ian (2007). Deconstructing the Terrorism-News Media Relationship. *Crime Media Culture, 3*(2), 215–225; White, Jonathan (2003). *Terrorism: An Introduction*. Belmont, CA: Wadsworth.

71. Combs, Cindy C. (2011). *Terrorism in the Twenty-First Century*. New York: Longman.

72. Chermack, Steven M., Frankie Y. Bailey, Michelle Brown (2003). *Media Representations of September 11*. Westport, CT: Praeger; Hoffman, Bruce (1998). *Inside Terrorism*. New York: Columbia University Press; O'Neil, Michael J. (1986). *Terrorist Spectaculars: Should TV Coverage Be Curbed?* New York: Priority Press; Tuckman, Gaye (1978). *Making News: A Study in the Construction of Reality*. New York: Free Press.

73. Louw, P. Eric (2003). The "War against Terrorism": A Public Relations Challenge for the Pentagon. *Gazette: The International Journal for Communication Studies, 65*(3), 211–230.

74. Combs, Cindy C. (2011). *Terrorism in the Twenty-First Century*. New York: Longman.

75. Ross, Jeffrey Ian (2007). Deconstructing the Terrorism-News Media Relationship. *Crime Media Culture, 3*(2), 215–225.

76. Soriano, Manuel T. Torres (2008). Terrorism and the Mass Media after Al Qaeda: A Change of Course? *Athena Intelligence Journal, 3*(1), 1–20.

77. Combs, Cindy C. (2011). *Terrorism in the Twenty-First Century*. New York: Longman.

78. Shoshani, Anat, & Slone, Michelle (2008). The Drama of Media Coverage of Terrorism: Emotional and Attitudinal Impact on the Audience. *Studies in Conflict & Terrorism, 31*, 627–640.

79. Hoge, James F., Jr., & Rose, Gideon (2001). *How Did this Happen? Terrorism and the New War*. New York: Public Affairs; Louw, P. Eric (2003). The "War against Terrorism": A Public Relations Challenge for the Pentagon. *Gazette: The International Journal for Communication Studies, 65*(3), 211–230.

80. Anderson, Terry (1993). Terrorism and Censorship: The Media in Chains. *Journal of International Affairs, 47*(1), 127–136.

81. Islam, Muhammad Q., & Shahin, Wassim N. (2001). Applying Economic Methodology to the War on Terrorism. *Forum for Social Economics, 31*(1), 7–26.

82. Midlarsky, Manus I., Crenshaw, Martha, & Yoshida, Fumihiko (1980). Why Violence Spreads: The Contagion of International Terrorism. *International Studies Quarterly, 24*(2), 262–298.

83. Kinzelbach, Annemarie (2006). Infection, Contagion, and Public Health in Late Medieval and Early Modern German Imperial Towns. *Journal of the History of Medicine and Allied Sciences, 61*(3), 369–389.

84. Hergenhaun, B.R. (2009). *An Introduction to the History of Psychology*. Belmont, CA: Wadsworth.

85. Martin, Gus (2010). *Understanding Terrorism: Challenges, Perspectives, and Issues*. Thousand Oaks, CA: Sage; Weimann, Gabriel, & Winn, Conrad (1994). *The Theater of Terror: Mass Media and International Terrorism*. New York: Longman.

86. Bok, Sissela (1998). *Mayhem: Violence as Public Entertainment*. Reading, MA: Perseus Books.

87. Krauthammer, Charles (1984). Terrorism and the Media. *Harper's Magazine*, October Issue; Nacos, Brigitte (2002). *Mass-Mediated Terrorism: The Central Role of the Media in Terrorism and Counterterrorism*. Maryland: Rowman & Littlefield Publishers.

88. Mingle, Edmund (2010, November 2). Media Practising Terrorism: Sefakor Dzisah. *The Ghanaian Times*.

89. Jařab, Josef (2005, May 20). *Media and Terrorism*. Strasbourg, France: Council of Europe.

90. Comer, Jonathan S., & Kendall, Philip C. (2007). Terrorism: The Psychological Impact on Youth. *Clinical Psychology: Science and Practice, 14*, 179–212.

91. Boyns, David, & Ballard, James David (2004). Developing a Sociological Theory for the Empirical Understanding of Terrorism. *The American Sociologist, 35*(2), 5–25.

92. Thussu, Daya Kishan (2008). *News as Entertainment: The Rise of Global Infotainment*. Thousand Oaks, CA: Sage.

93. Bruck, P. A. (1992). Crisis as Specular: Tabloid News and the Politics of Outrage. In Marc Raboy & Bernard Dagenais (Eds.), *Media, Crisis, and Democracy: Mass Communication and the Disruption of Social Order*. Newbury Park, CA: Sage.

94. Tuman, Joseph S. (2003). *Communicating Terror: The Rhetorical Dimensions of Terrorism*. Thousand Oaks, CA: Sage.

95. Berger, Arthur (1989). *Signs in Contemporary Culture*. Salem, WI: Sheffield; Eco, Umberto (1986). *Semiotics and the Philosophy of Language*. Bloomington: Indiana University Press; Nöth, Winfried (1995). *Handbook of Semiotics*. Bloomington: Indiana University Press.

96. Sebeok, Thomas A. (1976). *Contributions to the Doctrine of Signs*. Bloomington: Indiana University Press.

97. Saussure, Ferdinand de (1959). *Course in General Linguistics*. New York: McGraw-Hill.

98. Langer, Susanne K., (1953). *Introduction to Symbolic Logic*. New York: Dover.

99. Peirce, Charles Sanders (1958 [1931]). The Collected Papers of Charles Sanders Peirce. In C. Hartshorne & P. Weiss (Eds.), *Peirce: Volumes 1–6*. Cambridge, MA: Harvard University Press.

100. Matusitz, Jonathan (2007). Vexillology, or How Flags Speak. *International Journal of Applied Semiotics, 5*(1), 199–211.

101. Bonham, G. Matthew, Heradstveit, Daniel, Nakano, Michiko, & Sergeev, Victor M. (2007). *How We Talk about the "War on Terrorism": Comparative Research on Japan, Russia, and the United States*. Oslo: Norwegian Institute of International Affairs.

102. Peirce, Charles Sanders (1958 [1931]). The Collected Papers of Charles Sanders Peirce. In C. Hartshorne & P. Weiss (Eds.), *Peirce: Volumes 1–6*. Cambridge, MA: Harvard University Press.

103. Skoll, Geoffrey R. (2007). Meanings of Terrorism. *International Journal for the Semiotics of Law, 20*, 107–127.

104. Mesnard y Mendez, Pierre (2002). Access to an Identification of "Terrorism": Words and Actions. *Rethinking Marxism, 14*(2), 109–121.

105. Miller, Claude, Matusitz, Jonathan, O'Hair, Dan, & Eckstein, Jacqueline (2008). The Role of Communication and the Media in Terrorism. In Dan O'Hair, Robert Heath, Kevin Ayotte, & Gerald R. Ledlow (Eds.), *Terrorism: Communication and Rhetorical Perspectives* (pp. 43–66). Cresskill, NJ: Hampton Press.

106. Kappeler, Victor E., & Potter, Gary W. (2005). *The Mythology of Crime and Criminal Justice* (4th ed.). Long Grove, IL: Waveland Press.

107. Cohen, Akiba, Adoni, Hanna, & Bantz, Charles (1990). *Social Conflict and Television News*. London: Sage.

108. Jervis, Robert (1970). *The Logic of Images in International Relations*. Princeton, NJ: Princeton University Press.

109. Abrahms, Max (2005). Al Qaeda's Miscommunication War: The Terrorism Paradox. *Terrorism and Political Violence, 17*, 529–549.

110. Talbot, Rhiannon (2000). Myths in the Representation of Women Terrorists. *Eire-Ireland, 35*(3), 165–186, p. 180; Von Knop, Katharina (2007). The Female Jihad: Al Qaeda's Women. *Studies in Conflict & Terrorism, 30*, 397–414.

111. Nacos, Brigitte L. (2005). The Portrayal of Female Terrorists in the Media: Similar Framing Patterns in the News Coverage of Women in Politics and in Terrorism. *Studies in Conflict & Terrorism, 28*, 435–451.

112. McElvoy, Anne (1995, September 9). The Trapping of a Tigress. *Times of London*.

113. Walter, Christopher (2002, January 31). Twisted by anger, she turned to terror. *Times of London*.

114. National Public Radio (2002, February 7). *All Things Considered*. Washington, D.C.: National Public Radio.

115. CBN.com, retrieved November 4, 2003.

Terrorism as a Communication Process: The Audience

After reading this chapter, you will be able to

- discuss the audience as both the second party (immediate target of the message) and the third party (target beyond the immediate target of the message) of terrorism;
- identify the six stages of the Yale Model of Persuasion: exposure, attention, comprehension, acceptance, retention, and translation; and
- evaluate and explain the idea that terrorism is a spectacle.

THE AUDIENCE: DEFINITION

The most fundamental principle of any communication endeavor is to understand the audience. By definition, an **audience** is a group of people who participate in an event, either passively (e.g., by merely watching a show or simply attending to a message transmitted by a sender) or actively (e.g., by overtly participating in the event or providing feedback to the message sender). Whether it is passive or active, the audience is the **interpretive community**, reacting or responding to a message.[1] In the previous chapter, the point was made that terrorism is a language. Terrorists "speak" through the actions they take. The set of interactions between terrorist and society represent a dialogue. This dialogue lays the foundations for what the terrorist attempts to do or say. Terrorists take part in a dialogue with various audiences beyond their immediate target, both internal and external to the group. The message may vary for each audience, even within the context of just one act.[2]

Engaging in a dialogue with a human audience indicates that terrorists try to promote change. For example, they may seek to change policies, to coerce a specific action or set of actions, to put off or prevent enactment of policy, to garner support or sympathy, to induce someone into behaving in certain ways, or to paralyze the audience into inaction. Terrorists addressing a human audience have a positivist attitude in that they anticipate that their message be heard, understood, and acted on. To achieve any of this, terrorists need public interaction with the audience.[3] The audience, then, is the **public character of terrorism**. Terrorism is a spectacular public action directed to the psychological and emotional state of the audience observing the disaster. The purpose is to produce, in the audience, a feeling of anxiety, a sense of horror. The audience is both the **second party** (immediate target of the message) and the **third party** (target beyond the immediate target of the message) of terrorism. As we will see in this chapter, terrorist actions can also be deliberately committed against third parties who have nothing to do with the terrorists and their goals. The terrorists' intentions are to force governmental bodies or other structures to meet the terrorists' demands.[4]

From a communicative standpoint, the discussion of audience involves the concept of **proxemics** (the study of space and distance). The audience is always situated within a context of spatial interaction with the message sender. Proxemics was introduced by Edward T. Hall (1966).[5] Hall specified four distance zones. (1) Intimate distance stretches from physical touching to eighteen inches. This zone is occupied by those with whom people are intimate. At this distance, the presence of an intruder is not accepted. For example, teachers who step over students' intimate distance will be perceived as intruders. (2) Personal distance covers eighteen inches to four feet. This is the distance of contact between good friends. This would be a more appropriate distance for teacher and student to discuss private matters such as grades, conduct, personal problems, and so forth. (3) Social distance exists from four to twelve feet. This would be the right distance for interaction between casual friends and acquaintances. And (4) public distance goes from twelve feet to an infinite distance. This is where the media come into play. Audiences from all over the world can witness a terrorist act from a remote distance.

TERRORISM AND THE AUDIENCE: FROM INTIMATE TO PUBLIC DISTANCE

The terrorist act, in and of itself, is expected by its perpetrator not only to accomplish a political, religious, or ideological goal; it is also expected to affect a target audience and modify that audience's behavior in a way that will serve the needs of the terrorist. When terrorism hits, the audience can be the immediate target (i.e., intimate distance). A great number of people will likely be in close proximity and witness the attack directly (i.e., personal and social distance), observing dead or injured people, seeing severe damage or ruins, enduring long hours of separation from kinfolk in an atmosphere of panic, losing a friend, or being forced to relocate to another region. The fourth distance zone, public distance, is the zone in which the remote audience is situated. Television has become a long-distance witness, broadcasting images that come from a world far beyond the viewers' biological vision.[6]

Beyond the Immediate Targets of Terrorism

According to John Williams (1998),[7] two levels of audience exist: (1) the initial, immediate, or direct audience, and (2) the ultimate, delayed, or indirect audience. The former is the target of physical violence, usually innocent civilians. The latter is the intended audience of the terrorists. Statistically, the intended audience will never be physically struck by terrorism. In our three-dimensional world, the audience is never a victim *per se*. Yet, the supremacy of terrorism is that the audience constantly fears of becoming the victim. This fear of victimization gives terrorism a powerful impact or multiplication effect.[8] For example, in the 1970s, the Red Brigades in Italy randomly shot journalists in the kneecap (a very hurting damage) with the calculated effect of terrorizing all journalists. The latter were afraid of being the next, arbitrary target. The Red Brigades also abducted and inhumanely killed former Prime Minister Aldo Moro, a well-respected and beloved politician at that time. The terrorists' purpose was not to take Moro out of power (i.e., the initial, immediate, or direct victim) but to show the Italian audience (i.e., the ultimate, delayed, or indirect audience) that the Italian authorities were ineffective and powerless in preventing terrorism and protecting the nation.[9]

As Nacos (2002)[10] observes, more than just hurting immediate victims, the terrifying "street theater" of terrorism searches for a massive audience through the media. The audience is thought out in advance, before the tragedy actually occurs. The magnitude and distribution of the audience are testimony to the power of terrorism as a method and to the terrorists' ambition to have many people watching (not just many people dead).[11] For the terrorists, the dead are part of the audience, but they do not constitute the core audience. Their death would make them unable to act according to the terrorists' wishes. The terrorists' core audience is that segment in the audience which the terrorists believe they are speaking to. On looking at Osama bin Laden's 1998 fatwa, we know that the audience was America (and the West). In justifying attacks on U.S. facilities, he invoked Allah's will to free holy Muslim territories from occupation by apostates and evil ones. While one would be quick to assume that his audience was Allah, bin Laden was actually sending a message to the U.S. government and the American people, telling the former to get out of Saudi Arabia and telling the latter to force the government to comply. What was even more important was bin Laden's endeavors to reach out to the Muslim community and to persuade them the apostates and evil ones could be ousted. In just one act and statement, Osama bin Laden reached out to three audiences.[12]

Both terrorist acts and the media need a public distance zone in which to function—both need an audience. In a sense, terrorism resembles a reality TV show. Both terrorism and reality TV have made boundaries between the audience at home and the contestants on location blurred so that everybody feels like they are participating. In the case of terrorism, the immediate participant is at all times a victim—a fatal loss or a hostage—who turns into a mediated participant (analogous to the reality television contestant) with whom the viewers can identify. The blurred boundary that exists between observer and participant is important if terrorist acts are to achieve their calculated effect within and on the public zone: either people are victims or they are potential victims—victims in waiting.[13]

Figure 4.1 is Joseph Tuman's (2003)[14] **model of terrorism and its target audiences**. The model shows there are multiple audiences for the terrorist messages. Other target audiences (TAs) besides the immediate TA (i.e., TA1) are involved (i.e., TA2, TA3, TA4, etc.), adding to the size and intricacy of the communication process. In turn, these audiences may communicate with one another or provide feedback independently or together to the terrorists in the manner described in Figure 2.1 (see Chapter 2).

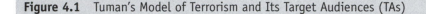

Figure 4.1   Tuman's Model of Terrorism and Its Target Audiences (TAs)

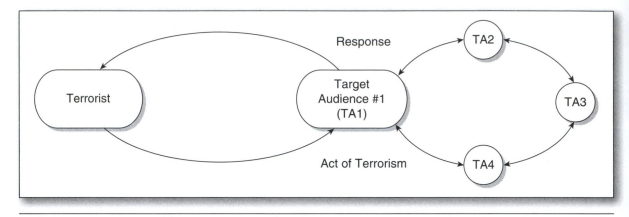

Source: Communicating Terror: The Rhetorical Dimensions of Terrorism, by Joseph S. Turnan, 2003, Thousand Oaks, CA: Sage. Copyright 2003 by Sage Publications. Reprinted with permission.

Based on this model, terrorism is inflicted against one target with the objective of influencing other target audiences. Since the purpose of terrorism is to influence multiple audiences, it follows that acts of terrorism are means of persuasion. **Persuasion** is a form of influence whereby the sender attempts to make the receiver adopt or change an idea, attitude, or action through rational or symbolic methods.[15] It is important to read the Yale Model of Persuasion on the following pages.

An Audience Already Established

In the framework of terrorism, the connections between multiple audiences are already set up before the actual communication loop, created by the terrorist message, surfaces in the media (see Figures 2.1 and 4.1). When multiple audiences interact with each other, they naturally participate in the encoding and decoding of messages. Any audience may communicate directly or indirectly. For instance, detailed images of terrorist destruction of lives will boost the identification of the target audiences (TA2, TA3, or TA4) with the immediate target audience (TA1)—the victims. A central approach for terrorists is to establish audience identification not with the immediate victims but with the terrorist message itself.[16] In this analysis of terrorism, **audience identification** refers to strategic communication adopted by terrorists, in their justification for violence, to attract and engage particular audiences. One way to achieve this is by giving the audience information within a familiar context of meaning.[17]

Generally, terrorists attempt to position themselves as saviors, leaders, or martyrs for some honorable causes. These causes can be liberating victims from an oppressor or promising a newer and more just social and political order. These messages provide an understanding of how terrorists see their actions as leading to a greater good while also convincing the audience that the terrorists' goals are, in fact, necessary. The largest segment of the terrorist audience, the core audience, is the most important message recipient. Therefore, making this audience identify with the terrorist message remains the biggest motivating force for the terrorist.[18]

YALE MODEL OF PERSUASION

Developed by Hovland, Janis, and Kelley (1953),[19] the **Yale Model of Persuasion** explains that a variety of message, source, and audience factors can influence the degree to which audiences can be persuaded; these factors bring about opinion, attitude, affect, and action change. Many terrorist campaigns follow—knowingly or unknowingly—the Yale model. There are two general dimensions of the model: the process of persuasion (six stages) and the variables of persuasion (four types). As the model suggests, an analysis of the process of any persuasion attempt will follow six stages: exposure, attention, comprehension, acceptance, retention, and translation. These stages must be adopted to effectively persuade an audience. The four types of **independent variable** (a thing that causes another thing to change) are source, message, target (i.e., recipient, audience), and channel (i.e., medium of communication).[20] Terrorism should be examined as an effort at persuasive communication. It is a persuasive instrument of (usually) a non-state group that wants significant political change.[21] Below are the six stages of the Yale Model of Persuasion (with the four independent variables included throughout the description):

- Exposure requires that the message get to the audience. For the message to be effective, the terrorist-sender must send the persuasive message through the appropriate channel and to the appropriate audience—one that can produce (directly or indirectly) the desired response. The nature of modern mass media practically ensures that target audiences will receive wide exposure to the terrorists' message. For twenty-four hours a day, almost anywhere in the world, there will be a quasi-instant transmission of news of terrorist acts to several billion viewers.[22]

- Attention can be difficult to achieve at times. The world is an information-overloaded place; news messages compete with others. The message should be crafted to go well with the channel through which it is sent. By their traumatizing nature, terrorist acts make the most of the salience effect, guaranteeing that audiences take notice of the message.[23]

- Comprehension: a terrorist campaign must make sure that the intended recipients understand the persuasive communication. The extent to which the recipient will comprehend the terrorist message is based on factors such as motivation (i.e., "Should I really care about this terrorist attack?"), issue involvement, and culture.[24] Dillard (1994)[25] suggests that message features such as message source, message content, and differences in the audience can have an influence on both the comprehension and emotional impact of the message itself.

- Acceptance: the audience must not only understand the message but also accept it. Osama bin Laden's 1996 and 1998 fatwas (i.e., declarations of war) against America and the West were accepted by many Muslims worldwide. However, other terrorist acts, such as those committed by South Africa's PAGAD (People Against Gangsterism And Drugs), have not been accepted by the audience.

- Retention: a terrorist message must have durable effect, which means that the audience should remember the message for a sufficiently long time so that their behavior changes. A clear example of this is the Madrid train bombing of March 11, 2004. The bombing occurred three days before a national election and completely overshadowed all other issues in the election for the three following days. The devastating acts, which the Spaniards perceived as a punishment for their nation's support of the U.S. invasion of Iraq, unquestionably influenced the outcome of the election.[26]

- Translation entails cognitive change causing behavioral change or the translation of perception into action. For example, in Islamist terrorism, would-be martyrs are promised to be rewarded with a safe place in Paradise and seventy-two virgins if they kill infidels and make the rest of Muslims proud of him (i.e., the martyr). Accordingly, some youth are willing to engage in behavioral change to fulfill Allah's wishes. Influence attempts have a higher probability of success if they are carried out in an environment that enables the translation of changed attitude into changed behavior.[27]

These six stages of persuasion have been effective in many terrorist cases. The outcome seems to be the same: to change the behavior of the audience in a way desired by the terrorist group. The impact of a message significantly depends on how the audience receives it and acts on it.

USES AND GRATIFICATIONS THEORY

Terrorists are well aware of audience needs. They know that Western audiences tend to watch television a lot. Television is just one type of mass media. It can be classified into news media, entertainment media, and into broadcast media. Television is the principal channel of information for the audience to understand terrorism and the Global War on Terror. According to Nielsen ratings, Americans on average watch over four hours of television every day (which is the equivalent of twenty-eight hours per week or two months of uninterrupted TV-watching in a year). In a sixty-five-year lifespan, the average American will have spent nine years watching television.[28] So, it is clear that television is Western audience's preferred type of mass media. During the first two days after 9/11, 81% of Americans were watching television for their main source of information about the tragedy.[29] The theory of **Uses and Gratifications (U&G)**, a traditional framework for understanding the media, posits that the audience matters more than the actual message itself. The key question for U&G is not "what media does to people"; rather, it is "what people do with media."

U&G assumes that audiences are not passive but actively interpret and integrate media into their own lives. The theory also assumes that audiences are in control of choosing media that meet their needs. People, then, will select media that fulfill specific gratifications.

Because of this, various media compete against each other for viewers' gratification.[30] U&G is an example of media logic. **Media logic** looks at the process through which media display or communicate information. Elements of media logic include the distinctive characteristics of each medium and the arrangements used by these media for the news organization, the style in which information is presented, the emphasis on particular attributes of behavior, and the language rules of media communication. People will choose their favorite medium based on these characteristics.[31]

The 1995 Oklahoma City bombing is a good case that explains the effectiveness of U&G in demonstrating how people select a medium to be acquainted with news events. What is incredible is the relatively small status of an immediate target audience (i.e., the 168 victims of the OKC bombing) as compared to the other target audiences. Soon after the 1995 Oklahoma City bombing, the 168 individuals who perished in the attack left behind more than 200 children, 80 grandchildren, and 9 great-grandchildren. One third of Oklahoma City youth polled said that they knew at least one victim killed in the attack.[32] Youth living far away from a terrorist scene are also exposed to a substantial amount of attack-related media coverage. In the wake of the Oklahoma City bombing, 55% of youth living 100 miles away said that they watched a lot of television coverage, and 27% of those youth revealed that they used a lot of print coverage.[33] Likewise, according to a U.S. national survey by Schuster et al. (2001),[34] on September 11, 2001, children watched on average three hours of television news coverage, with 23% of children watching over five hours. In this national survey, only 8% of youth said they were not watching television on September 11, 2001.

AUDIENCE FOR JIHADIST TERRORISTS

In their article titled "Communication and Media Strategy in the Jihadi War of Ideas," communication experts Corman and Schiefelbein (2006)[35] examined how jihadist terrorists view their multiple audiences. The audiences of jihadists are separated into categories. Two basic categories are those of the good guys and the bad guys. The good guys are the backers and supporters of the Islamic expansion, both through violent and peaceful means, throughout the world. The backers and supporters are "good Muslims" who support, emotionally or materially, the jihadists' efforts, and other Muslims who could potentially be involved in what the jihadists do. The latter have quasi-parental attitudes toward the good guys, considering their relationship as one of love, attachment, and advice, and highlighting the good in them and rectifying their mistakes.

The bad guys are any people who are not the good guys. Two varieties of bad guys exist. The apostates are former Muslims who have abandoned their faith. They are the most immediate targets of jihadist contempt (and operations), especially if they head governments or rule entire nations. They represent the main targets of their short-term goals. Occasionally called the *near enemy*, the apostates are the yardstick of measure against which the jihadists describe their social identity. The unbelievers are the non-Muslims, particularly those in America and the West, who are occasionally called the *far enemy*. These non-Muslims constitute an obstacle in the short term because they interfere in the affairs of the Arabian Peninsula. They also appear in the long-term dreams of a global Caliphate.

Other groups that appear in jihadist writings are outsiders. For example, the troublemakers include members of the deposed government, the tribal clans, the hired fighters, and the regular criminals. They are perceived as enemies of the movement, but less dangerous enemies than the bad guys, and maybe good enough to be saved. The Jews are the penultimate targets of the jihadists' struggle. Yet, the level of disdain expressed toward Jews in Corman and Schiefelbein's sample of documents looks very similar to the level accumulated on the apostates. Indeed, the jihadists' plan seems to overthrow the apostates, which will enable the Caliphate to be formed. In turn, the Caliphate will be strong enough to topple the Jews and will then pursue its course toward the West.

9/11 AND ITS EIGHT TYPES OF AUDIENCES

When a tragedy like the September 11, 2001 terrorist attacks occurs, the recipient is the audience. The 9/11 hijackers secretly attacked civilians to produce an extremely frightful state of mind in an audience different than the immediate victims (i.e., 3,000 casualties and symbolic buildings of the capitalist Western world). The phenomenon of terrorism is a spectacular interaction of a social character with multiple, socially significant audiences. Such a mammoth attack involves a multi-actor situation in which eight types of audience can be found. On 9/11, the first audience was the immediate recipient of that fatal demolition—those who were physically present in the World Trade Center (and the very proximate districts of Manhattan), the people working inside the Pentagon, and those unlucky passengers on all airliners that day.[36]

The second audience was the American public who observed and was horrified by the images of the message delivered to them constantly over television, on radio, and in print (i.e., newspapers and magazines). The American public consisted of onlookers, the large audience to the terrorist event. These onlookers watched the dynamics of the incident, public reactions to the tragedy, and political and media evaluations of the attack.[37] The U.S. political system has been significantly mediatized. As a popular medium, television fundamentally affects how Americans perceive the world around them. As Sadkovich (1998)[38] said about the influence of television in the U.S.,

> Television seems able to portray only a limited range of emotions because it lacks linear development and nuance. It homogenizes and reduces complex situations, events and emotions to simple standard items that are almost mythic.... Television precludes careful exegesis in favor of simple explanations of group conflict and reality in general. It invokes and evokes, it does not inform or explain. If television is a dream, it also decides what is real.... As the tube creates and idealizes some groups and ideas by focusing on them, it makes others disappear by ignoring them. Because it is the key source of news for most Americans it has seriously distorted our view of reality. (p. 60)

The third audience consisted of important representatives of our federal and state governments, who were felt obligated to respond to the September 11, 2001 attacks by sending messages of calmness and composure for the public. The third audience included various officials, from New York City Mayor Rudi Giuliani to President George W. Bush and the Joint Chiefs of Staff.[39] The fourth audience was the media establishment. The media's response integrated coverage and treatment of the terrorist message, as well as an internal discourse about what 9/11 stories need to be reported and how they should be framed. The media are the analysts. Analysts interpret the terrorist incident. They are crucial participants because they shape perspectives, interpret tragedies, and publicize labels for the enemy. Journalists are constantly in interaction with various other audiences in the terrorist context.[40]

The fifth audience included America's allies (i.e., Great Britain) or states that might be neutral vis-à-vis terrorism (i.e., Switzerland). The sixth audience was Al Qaeda's own members. For this group, the September 11, 2001 terrorist attacks boosted their own morale by proving that U.S. strength could be defeated (at least temporarily). America's hegemonic apparatus was shown to be weak at its very core.[41] For Al Qaeda's backers, destroying the World Trade Center might have been a cathartic feeling of the kind that Frantz Fanon (1965)[42] discusses: restoring self-respect as the outcome of successfully fighting back against those one perceives as apostates, infidels, and tormentors. Terrorists tend to live secluded from the outside world (i.e., in training camps for a while) and in a perpetual state of alert. They are driven by intense desires to retaliate against some perceived disgrace. Attacks reinforce a group's cohesion and establish solid bonds between its members. Inactivity, on the other hand, causes dissent and desertion. A victorious attack has an ecstatic effect on an often frustrating existence that was subversive or concealed. At the same time, a successful attack contributes to the de-legitimization of the adversary and, as a result, boosts the confidence of the terrorist group. A certain regular rate of attacks is necessary to secure a terrorist group's survival—if they don't use it, they lose it.[43]

The seventh audience consisted of rival terrorist organizations. The terrorists' strategic calculation in a multi-audience scenario also takes intergroup competition into account. Rival terrorist groups have similar goals, compete for resources and support, and seek to garner attention, recognition, prestige, and new potential members. An enormous terrorist attack like 9/11 is certainly a promising tactic for being a leader in the field.[44] The eighth audience was the Muslim world in general. Al Qaeda probably viewed 9/11 as an intermediary to propagandize its missions and grievances on the global Islamic agenda. Since the U.S. and its allies were provoked into retaliation (including the invasion of two Muslim countries—Afghanistan and Iraq), Al Qaeda must have hoped that such Western actions have radicalized many Muslims. This, in turn, serves as a recruiting mechanism for Al Qaeda (and other Islamist organizations). Furthermore, Al Qaeda may have expected that U.S. retaliations create hostility to those Middle Eastern nations considered too closely allied to America.[45]

In regard to the eighth audience, supporters of terrorists can also be patrons—persons who harbor terrorists or offer a supportive environment or system. Supporters will often justify the use of violence as a necessary consequence of a just war. The events of September 11, 2001 unfolded before 1.5 billion Muslims. A certain number of Arab and

Islamic television viewers acclaimed the attacks with great applause. As it was reported authoritatively, some Arabs were shown dancing with joy in the streets. Among Arab rulers, e-mails of satisfaction and victory were exchanged quietly. Among members of the eighth audience, a genuine sense of reunion was felt in the wake of 9/11.

Before committing suicide by flying aircrafts into buildings, terrorists had positioned themselves as martyrs who had fought for a noble cause and had secured a place in Allah's paradise. The infidels, on the other hand, had received warranting punishment, and Allah would also deal with them in an appropriate way.[46] Osama bin Laden made it clear that his core audience is the Muslim world. He wanted his community to return to a state of radical Islamic purity and sanctity (like in Saudi Arabia), a united community that is unhampered by corrupt and corrupted regimes and free of invasion by the infidels. The Saudi regime would be a specific bin Laden's message recipient. The Al Qaeda leader was warning of continued retribution in support of the faithful as long as the occupation and corruption of the infidels were happening.[47]

Looking at the big picture (i.e., all eight audiences), the September 11, 2001 tragedy demonstrates that the magnitude of the attacks were not based on the frequency of Al Qaeda's strikes but on the extent to which these strikes managed to capture the attention of the group's multiple target audiences. When it comes to persuasion and influence building, bigger is usually better. The power of the visual is magnanimous.

MEASURES OF AUDIENCE EFFECTIVENESS

A quintessential aspiration for terrorists is to create a strong link between their methods and the desired outcomes to impact the audience. According to Gus Martin (2010),[48] in *Understanding Terrorism: Challenges, Perspectives, and Issues*, to amplify their impact on the audience, terrorists tend to follow five criteria for audience effectiveness.

Media and political attention: the concentrating of world attention on the terrorists' cause is itself a yardstick of measure for success. In this era of instant media gratification, one essential fact for the terrorist is that success is frequently gauged based on the amount of publicity and attention received. Newsprint and broadcasting exposure are the highest positive rewards in the terrorists' mentality: the only measurable means they have to track their success and evaluate their progress. The June 1985 hijacking of TWA Flight 847, with its journey across several countries and the terrorists' manipulation of world media, is a textbook example of a successful media-centered hijacking incident. Likewise, as one Baader-Meinhof Group member said, "We always immediately looked how the newspapers, especially in Berlin, reacted to our actions, and how they explained them, and thereupon we defined our strategy."[49] Terrorism can also make the audience more aware of another religion (besides Christianity). According to a CBS News survey at the end of February 2002, 55% of Americans responded that they had now more knowledge about Islam than they did before 9/11.[50]

Impacting audiences: to impact viewers, terrorists use Propaganda by the Deed, hoping to provoke audiences to action or trigger a society-level reaction. Victim audiences, remote audiences, and championed groups can all be influenced by a terrorist attack. When such an event occurs, terrorists and their supporters analyze reactions from these audiences. From the terrorists' viewpoint, the efficacy of an attack necessitates successful manipulation of multiple audiences' responses. If a victim audience is effectively manipulated, members of the audience, as Alex Schmid (1982),[51] a renowned expert on terrorism, put it, "change their travel habits or their vacation destinations out of fear of becoming victims. The rationale for this fear is small... but the fear of victimization is real, especially among heavy media consumers" (p. 101). In that case, a process of identification occurs not only with immediate casualties and potential future victims but also with all the people in the audience who share certain "victim characteristics."

Imposing concessions from an enemy interest: the terrorists' adversary embodies an important audience too. Enemy interests will occasionally yield to the demands of a politically violent organization. Concessions differ in degree or scale. They can be short-term and direct concessions or long-term and radical concessions whereby a whole audience (i.e., society) essentially gives in to a movement's cause. At the level of short-term concessions, concessions could be ransoms paid by corporations for the liberation of employees being held hostage. At the long-term level, policies might be modified or autonomy accorded to a national group.

Disruption of normal routines: a useful measure of audience effectiveness is observed in the extent to which normal routines of society are affected or halted by a terrorist attack. Targets can be the commercial transportation industry; they can be selectively attacked so that their operations will be interrupted. In that event, the day-to-day habits of citizens and societal routines will change. In this fashion, numerous people in the larger society react as victims of a fairly weak movement. Murphy, Gordon, and Mullen (2004)[52] found that the September 11, 2001 terrorist attacks greatly disrupted adult value structures in the U.S. They noted that **survival, safety, and security values** increased in importance and **self-esteem and self-actualization values** decreased in importance. The former values refer to comfortable living, being in a world at peace, and enjoying equality, freedom, national security, and deliverance (or redemption). The latter values refer to having feelings of accomplishment, inner harmony, self-respect, and wisdom. In a similar vein, after 9/11, U.S. economic recovery faltered as the stock market went on its worst dip since the Great Depression (a $1.4 trillion drop in a week). The hotel industry incurred $2 billion in losses two months within the attacks, and the U.S. airline industry lost billions of dollars as the amount of passengers dropped by 50%. Then, in subsequent months, it leveled off at 20% below what the levels were before the attacks occurred. The U.S. airline industry suffered $2.2 billion in losses during the first quarter of 2002 as a direct consequence of U.S. travel changes after the September 11, 2001 attacks.[53]

Causing the state to overreact: a measure of audience effectiveness is the nation's enforcement of radical security countermeasures as a reaction to a terrorist attack. In the terrorist environment, the notion of setting up the enemy is widespread. Terrorists expect that the state become intensely repressive, that people suffer, and that the masses soar in rebellion after facing the true character of the enemy. This theory does not always prove true. Terrorists have also been reported to incite repression to expose the iron fist of the government and push more sympathizers to join the terrorists' resistance. The direct corollary is a **downward terror spiral** in which rebels and repressive states escalate their violence.[54] This is the same objective as **destabilizing the enemy**—creating a sense of unrest and heightening a sense of fear that the state or the powers that be are incapable to provide security and stability to its people.[55]

A strange case of an unsuccessful attempt to maximize audience effectiveness (across all five measures) is found in the endeavors of South Africa's **People Against Gangsterism and Drugs** (PAGAD). Established in 1996, PAGAD launched a crusade of violence to object to the values of an "immoral" South African society. PAGAD adopted an anti-government and anti-Western philosophy, supposedly in the best interests of South Africa's Muslims. However, its attacks were mostly directed at "moral" targets. PAGAD chose these targets— mainly in Cape Town—to endorse moralistic Islamic values and expunge non-Islamic elements from society. Among the many targets were fast-food outlets, gay bars, tourist spots, and other icons of Western decadence and immorality. Unfortunately for PAGAD, most South Africans were insignificantly affected. In fact, there was no societal response to PAGAD's attacks (except for revulsion).[56]

EMOTIONAL AND ATTITUDINAL IMPACTS OF TERRORISM ON THE AUDIENCE

Terrorism seeks to use psychological power to attract the attention of the audience and to stimulate, in ideal conditions, behavioral change in that audience. What needs to be discussed now are the emotional and attitudinal impacts of terrorism on the audience. As such, the impacts tend to be fear and trauma, as well as the creation of tertiary identities.

Fear and Trauma

For Kaplan (1981),[57] terrorism is meant to create an enormously fearful state of mind. This fearful state, though, is not directed only to the terrorist victims. Rather, it is directed to an audience who has, in most cases, no relationship to the victims. Oots (1990)[58] insisted that terrorism is caused to "create extreme fear and/or anxiety-inducing effects in a target audience larger than the immediate victims" (p. 146). Opinion polls revealed that the September 11, 2001 terrorist attacks intensified Americans' fears of more terrorist acts to happen and of the possibility that they (or their family members) might become victims themselves. This emotional and attitudinal impact on the targeted population did not decrease when Osama bin Laden and his associates surfaced in the media. On commenting on the effects of 9/11 on the American adversary, bin Laden declared with obvious satisfaction, "There is America, full of fear from north to south, from west to east. Thank God for that."[59]

In 2005, a poll asked U.S. adults to identify "the single most significant event that has happened in your lifetime, in terms of its importance to the U.S. and the world." A low 2% of those polled mentioned the collapse of communism; 3% said it was the Vietnam War; 6% said it was the Iraq War. Only one event was the common denominator among respondents: fully 46% of those respondents cited the September 11, 2001 terrorist attacks as the single most significant event in their lifetime.[60] Immediately after 9/11, polls found that 21 % of Americans all over the nation had a hard time sleeping because of nightmares about the attack and concerns about subsequent attacks.[61] A 10 % rise in the use of mental health services was also reported within thirty days of the attack. Statistics suggest that, nationwide, there was a 4.9 % increase in antidepressant prescriptions during the six months following the attacks, in comparison to the six months before the attacks.[62]

The Madrid terrorist attacks occurred on March 11, 2004. Two weeks later, a large sample was conducted all over Spain: 50 % of the respondents reported depressive symptoms, 47 % acute stress symptoms, and 14 % both. According to some estimates, the number of Spaniards who marched in remembrance across their nation (11.5 million), following the train bombings, was roughly equivalent to 28 % of the country's population (5 % gathered in Madrid alone). In the U.S., that very percentage of people (28 % of the country's population) marching across the nation would have been well over 80 million. These estimates imply a greater emotional and attitudinal impact of the terrorist attack on the mainstream Spaniard.[63]

Many of the impacts of terrorism-generated trauma on children are comparable to the effects of manmade and natural disaster trauma (think of the trauma caused by Hurricane Katrina in 2005). Children differ in their responses to traumatic events. While some children suffer from anxieties and bad memories that wear down with time and emotional support, other children may be more gravely traumatized and suffer long-term problems. Children's reactions include severe stress disorder, posttraumatic stress disorder (PTSD), anxiety, nervous breakdown, regressive behaviors, separation problems, sleep disorders, and attitudinal problems.[64]

In a sample of 17- to 25-year-olds across the U.S., the 9/11 attacks presented effects on identity change.[65] Many U.S. citizens showed a heightened need for human interaction and religious affiliation as a way to cope with such stress and devastation.[66] Case reports are still surfacing about people who have been tempted to commit suicide, more so than before 9/11, as a result of identity confusion.[67] In a study conducted by Rogers and Seidel (2002),[68] emotional reactions to 9/11 were found to be somewhat similar to those of the public after Princess Diana's death in 1997. Such phenomenon is called **mourning sickness**, a collective emotional grieving by individuals at the death of media personalities or victims of violence. According to Rogers (2000),[69] 9/11 caused a widespread outburst of grief, which was partly due to parasocial interaction. **Parasocial interaction** is the extent to which the audience considers having a personal relationship with a celebrity. Millions of Brits attended the memorial service for Princess Diana or viewed her funeral on television.

Tertiary Identities

Tertiary identities are exclusive to those who have indirectly witnessed a terrorist attack. For Lisa Sparks (2005),[70] indirectly affected viewers display terrorism survivorship behaviors just like immediate terrorism survivors would. The direct impact of terrorism also helps illuminate certain terrorism-related social processes. A tertiary identity suggests a **personalization of an attack**, the effect that a terrorist attack has on the audience that is not directly struck by the attack. People, by nature, search for a personal connection to events, a propensity of which the terrorists are well aware. Through the "personalizing" of terrorist attacks, the impact on the target population is extended beyond the directly affected victims to include those who were not even at the scene when the attack happened.[71]

Identities are coded and regulated symbolically. The U.S. audience responded in a way that was in harmony with Al Qaeda's objectives. As the tragedy unfolded, the audience witnessed massive destruction and experienced fears of personal disgrace—almost like losing a family member or dear friend. The inconceivable devastation of colossal buildings and the shocking experience of maiming and violent death were unmistakable and psychologically debilitating. Because many Western viewers identified with people who were directly attacked, they "suffered" the injuries as if these attacks had taken place on their own symbols, bodies, and minds.[72]

As one can see, the concept of tertiary identity was palpable after 9/11. Various online bulletin boards were devoted to discussing the tragedy and sharing feelings of anguish and anger. Most online news outlets had a discussion board consecrated to 9/11. These online news outlets included *The New York Times*, *CNN*, and *USA Today*.[73] Terrorism is essentially indiscriminate. The victims' identities may not be important to the perpetrators, as long as the victims are part of a large group and the attack sends the intended message to the target population. The level at which victims identify with a victim role is extensive. Identification with victims may supersede other focal identifications that may supply positive functions for one's health. Identifying as terrorist victims or survivors, even though one was not physically present when it happened, may bear unhealthy consequences.[74]

On a side note, according to terrorism scholar David C. Rapoport (1977),[75] there is an issue in terrorism studies that has been largely overlooked: while terrorism can induce identification with victims by large segments of the audience, contributing to sensations of helplessness, terror, or anger, there are also people who experience identification with the terrorists themselves. As Corrado (1979)[76] put it, "[T]errorism also satisfies personal identification needs and other emotional needs such as revenge and a sense of potency or power" (p. 198).

IMPACTS OF MEDIA EXPOSURE OF TERRORISM ON THE AUDIENCE

Media coverage of terrorist events is likely to affect the behavior of the audience. As it was explained in the previous section, research has shown that a correlation exists between the amount of exposure to TV coverage of terrorist attacks and viewers' emotional and attitudinal reactions. As a consequence, people with higher levels of media exposure report a higher incidence of symptoms such as PSTD and depression than those who have lower media exposure.[77] A less frequently used term is **fixity**, trauma that media exposure to terrorism causes. Watching the target, location, time, duration, intensity, degree, and meaning of the terrorist attack causes the audience to have the media images anchored in their mind.[78]

Managing Citizens' Fears

In Chapter 3, it was stated that current media practices point to the fact that media and terrorism share a symbiotic relationship. On the one hand, a terrorist attack is a sensationalized story that should be reported and that can boost audience ratings. On the other hand, terrorists exploit the media to engage in a dialogue with a large audience, beyond the immediate victims of an attack, so as to induce fear in society. As the media, in part, regulate the cognitive experience of terrorism by an audience bigger than the immediate victims, and amplify the impact through nonstop reporting of the topic (even to the detriment of other topics), the media play a crucial role in managing citizens' fears (either positively or negatively).[79] According to Roth and Muzzatti (2004),[80] media coverage can serve to magnify the gravity of terrorist incidents, making them look more atrocious and frequent than they really are. Public anxiety is heightened by means of journalistic and linguistic devices. "Special cover story" or "in-depth exposure" style coverage uses spectacular pictures, videos, and sound bites with moralistic discourses. The fear of terrorism tends to be manufactured by a popular culture with an avid appetite for more audiences (e.g., "clients"). The diet is entertainment, with a large quantity of fear.

Much of this rhetoric of fear is powered by agents of social control, who act both as news sources for television reports and as saviors, guardians, and eliminators of the sources of fear. Hence, entertainment, fear, and social control are combining the interests of popular culture with an ever-growing social control industry. The military–media landscape is a big element of programming in an entertainment age controlled by popular culture and communication forms. They share state-of-the-art information technology stimulating visual media and evocative content.[81] Der Derian (2002)[82] noted that "the first and most likely the last battles of the counterterror war are going to be waged on global networks that reach much more widely and deeply into our everyday lives" (p. 11). The **arousal hypothesis** posits that unusual or exceptional media content can intensify a viewer's desire to act aggressively. In fact, terrorism portrayed in the media can raise the likelihood for aggressive behavior from the audience. The **disinhibition hypothesis** rests on the premise that news stories detailing terrorism decrease the inhibition of the viewer to engage in extreme violence, which in turn increases the viewer's readiness to engage in aggressive behavior.[83]

Remarks on Israelis' Reactions

In a study on Israeli undergraduates' reactions to media coverage of terrorism, Weimann (1983)[84] found that the respondents had stronger negative attitudes about terrorists after seeing newspaper extracts of terrorist events. The Israelis' reactions to horrifying images of terrorism from the Israeli–Palestinian conflict have had a profound psychological toll, both short term and long term. Short-term reactions include grief, devastation, fear, phobic avoidance of public places, anger, and pain. Evidence for these short-term reactions can be found in Israeli hotline referrals; there were as high as 30,000 in the year 2001, at the height of terrorism in the Second Intifada. In the same year, long-term effects included a whole variety of post-traumatic symptoms. This was evidenced by an impressive overload of referrals to public and private mental health institutions throughout Israel. It is clear that media viewers risk becoming secondary victims from media exposure.[85] Moral panic has been played up by the media in a manner consistent with entertainment formats. What contributes, in part, to this moral panic is the **fear narrative**, which refers to the widespread communication, symbolic awareness, and expectation that danger is constantly present or imminent. The fear narrative, then, has become a dominant feature of the symbolic environment as the audience defines and experiences it on a daily basis.[86]

Affecting Memory

Terrorists want the audience to observe, to pay attention, and to remember. The media provide the conduit for this. Emotion-loaded media images have been reported to affect memory. Thus, if a viewer strongly experiences certain emotions like anger or sorrow after watching images of an act of extreme violence, these images—those that elicited strong anger and sorrow—would be more easily remembered afterward (as compared to other images). If a viewer strongly feels emotions such as shock or anxiety after watching visuals, he or she is more likely to remember these images than images depicting sorrow or anger. For example, the images people remembered and the emotions they experienced on 9/11 were used to assess the degree of shock and anxiety the audience had vis-à-vis terrorism. Overall, the memory of 9/11 visuals had a deep effect on viewers' shock and anxiety.[87] Similarly, a study by Christianson and Loftus (1987)[88] found that participants who were shown traumatic media content were able to remember the main substance of the media message. The researchers also found that some information seems to be better recalled from very traumatic and emotional events than from non-traumatic regular events. Comparable studies (e.g., Newhagen, 1998)[89] report that visuals that provoke intense emotions such as fear and anger tend to be better recalled.

Perception Is Not Reality

What definitely changed with modern terrorist attacks such as 9/11 were American perceptions of the danger of international terrorism that actually did not match reality. Systematic evidence supplied by the U.S. State Department indicates that the actual dangers from international terrorism have tended to fall around the world. However, post-9/11, American anxieties about the danger of terrorism are much higher. As shown by countless studies, public fear of terrorism surpasses, by far, the actual number of victims of terrorism, which today are lower than victims of homicide, automobile accidents, overdoses, and any number of diseases. At the end of the 1990s, the number of Americans massacred by terrorists was actually lower than those killed by bee stings, choking on sandwiches, or lightning. Nevertheless, terrorism has remained a leading reason on surveys for why Americans are afraid.[90]

According to a study by Rummel (1996),[91] only 518,000 civilians were killed in the 20th century by actual terrorists. By contrast, in the same study, approximately 169 million people were killed by the actions of governments, including 130 million of them killed by their own government—42 million under Stalin alone and 2 million under Pol Pot. Mathematically, the number of civilian killings by terrorists amounts to less than 0.5%. The number of civilian killings as a result of non-state-sponsored terrorist activities is considerably lower: the estimates are that there are 260 state-sponsored terrorism casualties for every non state-sponsored terrorist death. In 1985, 28 million Americans went abroad and 162 were either killed or injured because of terrorism. This translates into a .00058% probability of being a terrorist target. On accounts of terrorism in 1985, 1.8 million Americans modified their travel plans abroad the following year.[92]

Based on these descriptive statistics, one can easily deduce that audience perception does not reflect reality. George Gerbner and colleagues (2002)[93] wrote about the Mean World Syndrome created by the media, particularly television. The **Mean World Syndrome** is a phenomenon whereby the interpretations of the world (through media coverage with violent content) are modified by means of cultivation: audience members are more prone to believing that the world is more dangerous than it truly is. People want to protect themselves more than they should. A direct corollary is the demonization of the enemy, which refers to portraying members of the group to which terrorists belong—for example, Muslims or the bad ones are jihadists—appear to be evil, worthless, or immoral, through the Mean World Syndrome.

Gradual Lessening of Interest

Though terrorists may be aware that they manipulate the media, in choosing calculated targets (for visibility purposes), and achieve sensational violence to guarantee coverage, the opposite is sometimes true. In an era of media saturation, and media already dedicated to coverage of so many stories about violence, death, and tragedy, ensuring coverage of a terrorism story requires visually captivating, spectacular, and destructive violence on a larger and larger scale. Unfortunately, this also means that, with every act of terror, the level for what is dramatic and devastating must be raised. Put simply, if terrorists abduct three missionaries in the Philippines and order the government to release rebel leaders, reporters might release a print news story and local coverage. Conversely, if terrorists blow up an embassy or a supermarket, killing hundreds and injuring more, that story will attract much more attention from the media.[94] It looks like the media constantly have to raise the bar to keep the audience's interest. This gradual lessening of interest is akin to **compassion fatigue**, a gradual avoidance of sensitivity toward dramatic events. It is desensitization. Compassion fatigue may occur as a consequence of media saturation of images of terrorism victims. People, then, grow more resistant and pay less attention to these images.[95] By extension, when one experiences too many terrorist threat warnings, one is said to experience **threat fatigue**.[96]

Then, there is the **media congestion effect**, a phenomenon whereby media coverage of one group singles out coverage of other groups. Factors on both the supply side and the demand side can work against terrorists. On the supply side, terrorists' resources are more limited and governments are much more funded than terrorists. On the demand side, the media do not have an endless source of public interest in any topic. They can find other topics that will raise public interest, *ad infinitum*. Humans' capacity to process information is restricted; many issues vie for the public eye.[97] Even if terrorists continue to contribute to Kelly and Mitchell's (1981)[98] "upward spiral of violence," they may realize that they each draw less media attention as more terrorists compete for the audience's interest. We call this the *media congestion effect*. As Delli Carpini and Williams (1987)[99] state, "On a given evening, other pressing events may push out coverage of terrorist events that would be covered on a less 'busy' evening" (p. 60).

TERRORISM AS SPECTACLE: IT'S ALL FOR THE AUDIENCE

Right after 9/11, opinion polls revealed that virtually all Americans attended to the news of the terrorist attacks (99% or 100% according to surveys) by watching television, listening to the radio, and surfing the web. Worldwide, the interest, fright, and following of the news were equally universal. This was a perfect triumph in regard to the "media exploitation" goal on which the nineteen hijackers throve.[100] The constant replays of the second aircraft hitting the South Tower and its ensuing collapse exemplify the very model of spectacle. In *The Society of the Spectacle*, Guy Debord (1995)[101] explains that the spectacle is the historical moment during which the commodity completes "its colonization of social life. It is not just that the relationship to commodities is now plain to see—commodities are now all [sic] that there is to see; the world we see is the world of the commodity" (p. 29). Constructed into narratives and discourses, spectacles are the core of ideology: "The spectacle is the acme of ideology" (p. 150). For Debord, the **spectacle** refers to a major human event portrayed as a form of drama or theater. From this perspective, terrorism is a spectacle. A terrorist act resembles a play, like political theater, that describes the plight of the perpetrators. The primary function of terrorism is "media spectacle," a language the West knows very well. Terrorism uses the splendid and impressive power of the visual and the image. Through the visual and the image, the media are ally and traitor at the same time, agents of their own creation. Terrorism is strategic violence, typically against symbolic targets with the intent to send a semiotic warning, a persuasive message, a suggestive blow, and a supreme symbol of fear. Such spectacle immerses us and gets us aroused into a frenzy.[102] Terrorism is spectacular through **shock and awe tactics**, tactics that form a traumatic spectacle and that can be justified as a humane method of restraint. Rather than killing a large number of people, it is enough to send them a message by subjecting them to shock and awe tactics.[103]

Commanding the Audience's Gaze

A spectacle is a form of theater. In this context, **theater** refers less to the playing out of spectacular action and more to its etymology in the Greek word for "theater," *theatron*, or a "looking place." As this definition suggests, theater has a looking or visual character.[104] A theater has a visual dimension; it is the idea that terrorist acts are spectacles because they command the viewer's gaze. They are performances that are produced to be seen. To explain this further, let us compare terrorists with assassins and serial killers. For the latter two, killing people is the primary objective. If assassins and serial killers kill a sufficient amount of people and do it "messily enough," they create violent spectacles. However, this is usually not the goal of the assassin or the serial killer. The serial killer will only create drama if he or she wants to attract the attention of the police or the public once the killings have been committed. Generally, serial killers commit their killings secretly. For terrorists, in contrast, the purpose is to create violent displays that both outright command an entire audience's gaze and become deeply anchored into that audience's collective memory.[105]

A distinction needs to be made between physical spectacle and transgressive spectacle. **Physical spectacle** is a situation in which a terrorist act creates a spectacle by overpowering the audience's senses. Deafening howls and blinding flashes attract attention through the monstrous physical impact they have on the viewers' senses. In the case of **transgressive spectacle**, the terrorist act creates a spectacle by commanding the audience's gaze for the simple reason that the terrorist act is such an outrageous infringement on widely established rules, namely the traditional rules of war. By so spectacularly defying the rules of war, terrorists in so doing reject their adversaries as being "of their kind."[106] Commanding the audience's gaze seems to be more like a transgressive spectacle. As noted by Jenkins (1975),[107] "taking and holding hostages increases the drama. The hostages themselves often mean nothing to the terrorists. Terrorism is aimed at the people watching, not at the actual victims. Terrorism is a theater" (p. 4).

The Medium Is the Message

"The medium is the message," Marshall McLuhan's (1964)[108] famous statement in *Understanding Media: The Extensions of Man*, rests on the premise that it is not the ideas that are broadcast that influence society; rather, it is the type of medium itself that will influence it. Information technology has made the immediate airing of the spectacle possible. Information technology allows a globalization of the spectacle in a wide variety of ways, so much so that it can be called **information overload**. Paul Virilio (2000)[109] calls this an information bomb, an unusual name when considering the link between terrorism and the spectacle. The engulfing amount of information that results from one single terrorist attack overloads the audience's senses and generates confusion about the incident. Terrorists like news media coverage because it provides them with maximum publicity for their messages. Media coverage of terrorism amplifies the threat and resultant fear of terrorism to the audience. The yearning for maximum publicity, in turn, creates a tradition in terrorism to meticulously choose targets and participate in types of symbolic action that translate well visually in media exposure. Television is the main medium for all this. The medium is the message again. Bassiouni (1981)[110] refers to such situations as **translating well**, which means that terrorist violence is a dramatic form of spectacle—something that is so engaging that the audience stops and takes notice.

By exploiting this tactic of spectacle, terrorism uses the media (along with the theatrical images and montage) to arrest the audience's attention, hoping in this manner to catalyze unexpected events that will broadcast further terror to the general population. In *Suspensions of Perception*, Crary (1999)[111] extends Debord's and McLuhan's works by stressing that the significance of the spectacle is not so much *what* we see; rather, it is more *that* we see. Today's media are now capable to achieve this capture of the audience's attention and simplify the imperatives of the field of power. This happens thanks to the relationship between the spectacle that the media create, its content (i.e., stories, images, ideas, genres, rhetoric, etc.), and the methods by which this content is processed.[112]

Dawson's Field Hijackings

On September 6, 1970, the Dawson's Field hijackings took place in Jordan. Five jet aircrafts destined to go to New York City were seized by members of the Popular Front for the Liberation of Palestine (PFLP). The PFLP separated the flight crews and Jewish passengers, keeping fifty-six people hostage. On September 12, before their announced deadline, the PFLP bombed the empty planes with explosives, as they were expecting a counterstrike. Most of the reporters at the scene missed the explosions. However, a British television crew from ITN (Independent Television News) caught the explosions on camera. They had been fed streams of information by local Jordanians who had themselves been notified by members of the PFLP. On September 7, 1970, the hijackers organized a media conference for sixty reporters who had entered the zone of what was then called *Revolution Airport*. Clusters of the remaining hostages were gathered on the sand in front of the cameras. Members of the PFLP, among whom was Bassam Abu Sharif, made pro-Palestinian declarations in front of the media. The resulting spectacle, which was watched by numerous viewers worldwide, only served to increase the threshold or standard for what would be perceived as sensationalized, violent terrorism.[113] This is what Shannon Bowen (2008)[114] refers to as **terrorist spectaculars**, whereby large terrorist attacks are carried out to attract rising attention through the intensification of horror.

Culture of Terror

The phrase Culture of Terror was used by Michael Taussig (1987)[115] to depict the spectacle of killing, torture, and evil bewitchment in southwest Colombia from 1969 to 1985. Taussig associates it with Joseph Conrad's descriptions in the novel *Heart of Darkness*. As it is the case with Timothy McVeigh and his Oklahoma City bombing, in a spectacle, no strict line exists between fact and fiction, or between event and representation. The people exposed to media images become collateral damage, or "enemies of God" who should witness live what can happen to them next. The immediate target victims are holy sacrifices whose innocence is meaningless to the eyes of the terrorists. From their standpoint, their innocence makes them suitable sacrificial victims to be shown in front of billions of people. From the standpoint of counterterrorists, broadcasting the killing of the innocent is proof of the absolute, appalling evil and injustice of terrorism.[116] The terrorist spectacle communicates the language of the unspeakable. Terrorists perform and stage the inconceivable. As producers of words and images, and symbolic forms of violence, terrorist acts establish a spectacle of terror that is much more important than the acts themselves. Strategic forms of violence such as detonating bombs in churches are not as essential to their inventory. Their strongest weapon is that very Culture of Terror: the spectacle. It is the media images of destruction that create the mightiest spectacle of all, such as the collapse of the World Trade Center, in which the destruction of one of the most beloved symbols of capitalism was staged, quite consciously, as a symbol in its own right.[117]

TERRORISM AS SPECTACLE: ANALYZING 9/11

The September 11, 2001 terrorist attacks were a textbook example of Propaganda by the Deed. The phrase postulates that, when facing an overwhelmingly powerful enemy, the weaker group needs to accomplish a dramatically daring act to gain attention to their cause.[118] With the advent of television, the potential for successfully performing such a spectacle has been significantly enhanced. The 9/11 terrorist spectacle unwrapped mostly in New York City, one of the most media-saturated places worldwide, and such act turned out to be a deadly spectacle live on television. The images of the airliners crashing into the World Trade Center (WTC) and the collapse of the South and North Towers were played over and over again. The spectacle conveyed the clear message that America was not a fortress; it was vulnerable to terrorist attacks like any other country. The other message was that terrorists could inflict great havoc, and that any human being could be hit by a violent attack at any time.[119]

A Disaster Movie

Heartless, abhorrent, gory, and spectacular at the same time, the terrorist act perpetrated by the nineteen hijackers turned 9/11 into a semiotic rage of television flows, informational and image-based anxiety, and a technological disaster of media spectacle. On 9/11, terrorism was intentionally generating captivating and addictive images like those we see in action flicks. As scholars have pointed out (e.g., Kellner, 2003),[120] the September 11 terror spectacle was akin to explosion scenes in disaster films. In fact, this led Robert Altman, a long-time Hollywood director, to criticize the U.S. movie establishment for allowing directors to make movies that could be copied by terrorists for attacking the U.S. On 9/11, what the world witnessed on television, in the beginning, looked unreal. The audience was not sure whether what was shown on their screens was real or not. Audiences around the world were finally convinced that America was under attack when they saw low-quality video footage. Now, audiences knew it; they were not watching a disaster movie. Rather, as a gargantuan theater scene, the spectacle was real. While it contained images of a disaster movie, it also radicalized the association of the image with reality. Terrorism captures attention through its dramatic and alarming character, resembling more like Hollywood films than prime-time news. Consequently, it inherently fashions, in the audience, a curiosity and a desire to know. The main effect is that human drama of terrorism melts into the psyche of the audience. Terrorism is aimed at an astounded public, foreclosed by the media that perform just as the terrorists want.[121] Soon after the aircrafts smashed into the World Trade Center, videotapes were sold in the Chinese market showing the tragedy, interwoven with scenes from Hollywood disaster movies.[122]

A Horror Movie

Visual images are directly associated with the audience's emotions and attitudes. Otherwise stated, pictorial images may trigger a certain emotion. For example, images of spiders and snakes have demonstrated that they can bring out fear.[123] Thus, in the dramatic footage provided on 9/11, it is very likely that some images were closely linked to emotions such as horror. By looking at scenes of bloody corpses and people jumping off the WTC towers, the audience watching 9/11 was also said to be watching a horror movie.[124] Watching a certain image has led some viewers into the emotion painted in that visual.[125] The 9/11 terrorist attacks generated fear across America because the emotional impact of smashing two skyscrapers into pieces at the very center of the U.S. economy was intense. 9/11 was purposely designed to inspire terror not as a simple by-product, but as the fundamental product of the terrorist act.[126]

A Speech Performance

Now it is clear: 9/11 was the most dramatic and violent human-induced spectacle in modern history. In November 2001, two months after the terrorist attacks, Osama bin Laden discussed his feat. Thinking directly of the nineteen hijackers he had sent, whom he referred to as *vanguards of Islam*, bin Laden gaped with amazement: "Those young men said in deeds, in New York and Washington, speeches that overshadowed other speeches made everywhere else in the world. The speeches are understood by both Arabs and non-Arabs, even Chinese."[127] By enacting a deep-seated symbolic gesture—that is, making the WTC collapse and hitting the Pentagon—the terrorists enacted a speech performance, something akin to the following: we have shown the entire world that we can shatter our enemy's icons of strength and success. Such a speech performance also "speaks" to Al Qaeda's supporters by giving them hope and relief and by garnering support for the group's cause.[128] Around the world, 9/11 boosted morale within radical Islamic groups, anti-American movements, and all those groups that feel powerless in the midst of the U.S.-led global hegemony and America's support of Israel. A case in point was footage of Palestinians celebrating 9/11 by cheering, dancing, and firing shots in the air.[129]

TERRORISM AS SPECTACLE: DRAMATURGICAL ANALYSIS

Yale sociology professor Jeffrey Alexander (2004)[130] published "From the Depths of Despair: Performance, Counter-performance, and 'September 11'" in *Sociological Theory*. Alexander was an inspiration for writing this section on the terrorist spectacle as a form of Dramaturgical Analysis. The theory of **Dramaturgical Analysis** was initially developed by sociologist Erving Goffman (1959).[131] Later, it was reexamined by Kenneth Burke (1972)[132] in his *Dramatism and Development*. According to Dramaturgical Analysis, individuals engage in public performance—activities in the front of observers (i.e., an audience). The objective is to influence the observers' perception of the actors. Performance happens on a front-stage area. The **front-stage** is the physical or social space in which performances are enacted (unlike the **back-stage**, where people are more genuine and less "performing"). Put another way, by acting out in public, people have three key goals: to be seen, to be remembered for being seen, and to be remembered in a specific way.[133]

9/11 as Performance as Political Action

A phrase similar to Dramaturgical Analysis is Performance as Political Action. **Performance as Political Action** rests on the premise that humans participate in a performance-centered method of communicating with the purpose of changing the audience's behavior. More specifically, this theoretical framework is based on understanding the manner in which performers involve audiences and entire communities in an effort to change social behaviors. In the end, Performance as Political Action is successful in mobilizing the audience and gaining awareness.[134] For Jeffrey Alexander, terrorism is a particular kind of political performance. It needs and relies on blood—literally and symbolically—making use of its target's fundamental fluids "to throw a striking and awful painting upon the canvas of social life" (p. 90). Terrorism not only kills; in and through killing, it also intends to gesture in a dramatic style. A terrorist act is like a morality play within the theater of political protest. The allusion to political action is powerful: Oberschall (2004) refers to this as a type of symbolic action in a "complex performative field" and a "dramaturgical framework," or a "bloody drama played out before an audience" (p. 27).[135]

Because terrorist violence is Performance as Political Action, the terrorist performs the part of a moralist: a moral order that must reach some equilibrium.[136] Performative actions have both an apparent and latent symbolic nature. Their obvious messages form against background arrangements of ingrained meaning. Put another way, social performances are like theatrical performances; they embody particular meanings only because they suggest more general, axiomatic meaning frameworks within which their performances are staged. Performances choose, restructure, and create present themes that are less explicit in the immediate context of social life—though these do not exist in a literal sense. Performance is enacted because actors have specific, contingent objectives.[137]

9/11 as Script

A performance is based on a script. A script tells of a terrorist act amid the sacred, profane, and mundane. An excellently scripted story defines fascinating protagonists and terrifying antagonists and places them in a sequence of emotionally laden encounters. Such tense and dynamic action constitutes a plot. Through plotted scenes, spectacular dramas produce emotional and moral effects. Their audiences may go through excitement and delight if the plot is a romance or a comedy, or compassion and suffering if it is a melodrama or tragedy. If the scripted story is good and if the performance of the plot is compelling, the audience will experience catharsis, from which new moral judgments will form and new series of social action will be carried out in turn.[138]

Modern terrorism can be viewed through the lens of production requirements of theatrical engagements. Terrorists focus on script preparation: a worthy story, a memorable progression of events, as well as selection of actors, sets, props, role-playing, and painstaking stage management. Just like successful stage plays or ballet performances, the effective exploitation of media in terrorism demands full attention to detail.[139] A script, in a literal sense, is written for a play that contains a plot, stage/setting, characters, and so forth. In a sociological sense, a script—that is, a sacred cultural script—is a cultural meaning structure that offers individuals tools to interpret and wrap their minds around events.[140] Consistent with Kenneth Burke's notion of dramatism, a full script explains the act (what happened), scene (when or where it happened), agent (who did it), agency (how it was done), and purpose (why it was done) of humans' actions.[141]

As one can see, primarily, a script of social drama is thought up by prospective authors and actors. Nevertheless, in this case, the social drama that the script is written to inspire is directed at audiences consisting of the publics of complex civilizations. In such a social drama, the actors may be governmental authorities or rebels, activists or lazy bums, political leaders or rank-and-file members of social movements, or the imagined audiences of involved citizens. The inspirations and roles of such actors are influenced largely by directors. In this context, directors are the coordinators, thinkers, and leaders of collective action. Because Osama bin Laden was wealthy and was part of a mighty social network, he already had the resources to recruit actors for a growing terrorist organization (something that was never seen before). In addition, he had enough clouts to find the best actors, screen them, and test them before allowing them to work with his production crews.[142]

9/11 as Mise en Scène

Osama bin Laden had a good sense for the story line: it was a script featuring traditional Islamic martyrs (i.e., righteous Al Qaeda heroes) taking their own lives for their sacred honor against wicked Americans with blood on their hands and willing to sell their own mothers. The cunning Al Qaeda director set up secret training camps that enabled backstage rehearsals for public performances to take place. In these training camps, aspiring actors were taught how to play the parts assigned to them devotedly and persuasively in the Al Qaeda script. When the new method acting was mastered with explicit authenticity, the actor-terrorists were placed into performance teams, which carefully planned for the extravagant production of terrorism in Western lands. Osama bin Laden was capable of managing the means of symbolic production. He wanted a global stage and means for killing on a scale much larger, and more dramaturgically convincing, than nobody ever before had been able to get.[143] What bin Laden was creating was a *mise en scène*.

Indeed, such a social drama can be interpreted by the theatrical concept of **mise en scène**, in a literal sense "putting into the scene" (i.e., directing and choreographing). This dramatic performance necessitated mastering the art of symbolic production, which suggests, again, a stage, a setting, and essential theatrical props. In a social drama, mastering such means alludes to the need to build stages for performance in the public imagination and, ultimately, to build access to modern media such as television, print media, radio, and the Internet. Osama bin Laden really presented himself to be highly effective in staging an eminent phase of the long-established performance round of East versus West. In his mind, a new, unparalleled performance could be staged as well. His groundbreaking script was to turn a terrorist act in the U.S. into carnage and to put this performance on the world platform. Osama bin Laden not only placed himself as the **metteur en scène** (i.e., director) of an immensely well-organized and globally televised jihad; he also possessed the awful craftiness and all the indispensable resources to actually place himself in the heart of the *mise en scène*.[144]

Truly, Osama bin Laden became a classic actor involving audiences in a spectacular performance against America and the West. The notion of *mise en scène* is analogous to the notion of staging the scene or focality. In fact, a terrorist spectacle tends to fit all the main criteria for **focality**: a focal place, individual, or event must be well visible, have some unforgettable features, and be associated with a successful story line. Media coverage of terrorism supports all of these criteria. It is also the case that rising actors have advantages of focality. Before September 11, 2001, Al Qaeda was much more marginal than it is today. On that fateful day, the group became focal by managing to carry out the biggest large-scale terrorist attack in the U.S.[145]

9/11 as Choreography

From the perspective of Dramaturgical Analysis, the September 11, 2001 terrorist attack was a perfectly choreographed performance to be played in front of American and global audiences. As a choreographer, Osama bin Laden was able to effectively block (choreograph) Al Qaeda's own movements and gestures and plot crafty response lines (i.e., the anticipated response from the Bush administration). The choreographed movements were practiced before the final performance. As such, Al Qaeda members learned all their script lines and tricks at terrorist training camps and flight schools. Although the spectacle metaphor remains conceptual or theoretical in nature, one has to acknowledge that it is useful for explaining how it can be managed to be recorded for television spectaculars with live breaking news. 9/11 was not only theater but also a televisual spectacular for audiences that rely on television for their understanding of the world. This choreography crosses all boundaries of theatrical events. In the past, most terrorist acts were the occasion for publicity such as news reporting. However, the September 11, 2001 terrorist attack took mass-mediated terrorism to a higher level thanks to the director/choreographer's choices in terms of method, target, timing, and scope. As an act of political performance, 9/11 was artfully executed for maximal symbolic impact.[146]

SUMMARY

Terrorists take part in a dialogue with various audiences beyond their immediate target. For this reason, the audience is the public character of terrorism. As such, the audience is both the second party (immediate target of the message) and the third party (target beyond the immediate target of the message) of terrorism. Terrorism is essentially indiscriminate. The victims' identities may not be important to the perpetrators, as long as the victims are part of a large group and the attack sends the intended message to the target population. The audience is carefully considered in advance, before the tragedy actually occurs. Of importance in this chapter is the Yale Model of Persuasion, according to which the process of any persuasion attempt will follow six stages: exposure, attention, comprehension, acceptance, retention, and translation. Terrorism should be examined as an effort at persuasive communication. These stages must be adopted to effectively persuade an audience. Another important theory is the theory of Uses and Gratifications (U&G), demonstrating for instance how audiences selected television as their main medium to be acquainted with the 1995 Oklahoma City bombing. To measure audience effectiveness, one has to look at Gus Martin's (2010) five criteria: media and political attention, impacting audiences, imposing concessions from an enemy interest, disruption of normal routines, and causing the state to overreact. Nevertheless, impacts of media exposure of terrorism on the audience can cause problems such as fear, trauma, and even gradual lessening of interest. Finally, this chapter demonstrated that terrorism is a spectacle, like a form of drama or theater. As such, it can be akin to a disaster movie, a horror movie, or a speech performance. With respect to the September 11, 2001 attacks, it was a form of Dramaturgical Analysis: indeed, 9/11 was Performance as Political Action, a script, a *mise en scène*, and choreography.

KEY TERMS

arousal hypothesis   91

audience   77

audience identification   80

back-stage   98

compassion fatigue   93

destabilizing the enemy   88

disinhibition hypothesis   91

downward terror spiral   87

Dramaturgical Analysis   98

fear narrative   91

fixity   90

focality   100

front-stage   98

independent variable   81

information overload   95

interpretive community   77

Mean World Syndrome   93

media congestion effect   93

media logic   83

metteur en scène   100

mise en scène   100

mourning sickness   89

parasocial interaction   89

Performance as Political Action   98

personalization of an attack   89

persuasion   80

physical spectacle   94

proxemics   78

public character of terrorism   78

second party   78

self-esteem and self-actualization values   87

shock and awe tactics   94

spectacle   94

survival, safety, and security values   87

terrorist spectaculars   96

tertiary identites   88

theater   94

third party   101

threat fatigue   93

transgressive spectacle   95

translating well   95

Turman's model of terrorism and its target audiences   79

Uses and Gratifications Theory   82

Yale Model of Persuasion   81

ENDNOTES

1. Comer, Jonathan S., & Kendall, Philip C. (2007). Terrorism: The Psychological Impact on Youth. *Clinical Psychology: Science and Practice, 14,* 179–212.

2. Gressang, Daniel S. (2001). Audience and Message: Assessing Terrorist WMD Potential. *Terrorism and Political Violence, 13*(3), 83–106.

3. Gressang, Daniel S. (2001). Audience and Message: Assessing Terrorist WMD Potential. *Terrorism and Political Violence, 13*(3), 83–106.

4. Vasilenko, V. I. (2005). The Concept and Typology of Terrorism. *Statutes and Decisions, 40*(5), 46–56.

5. Hall, Edward T. (1966). *The Hidden Dimension*. New York: Doubleday.

6. Comer, Jonathan S., & Kendall, Philip C. (2007).Terrorism: The Psychological Impact on Youth. *Clinical Psychology: Science and Practice, 14*, 179–212.

7. Williams, John J. (1998). The Failure of Terrorism as Mass Communication. *Turkish Journal of Police Studies, 1*(4), 37–52.

8. Freedman, Lawrence Z. (1983). Why Does Terrorism Terrorize? *Terrorism, 6*(3), 389–401.

9. Williams, John J. (1998). The Failure of Terrorism as Mass Communication. *Turkish Journal of Police Studies, 1*(4), 37–52.

10. Nacos, Brigitte (2002). *Mass-Mediated Terrorism: The Central Role of the Media in Terrorism and Counterterrorism*. Lanham, MD: Rowman & Littlefield Publishers.

11. Jenkins, Brian (1987). The Future Course of International Terrorism. In Anat Kurz (Ed.), *Contemporary Trends in World Terrorism* (pp. 150–159). New York: Praeger.

12. Gressang, Daniel S. (2001). Audience and Message: Assessing Terrorist WMD Potential. *Terrorism and Political Violence, 13*(3), 83–106.

13. Baudrillard, Jean (2002). L'Esprit du Terrorisme. *South Atlantic Quarterly, 101*(2), 403–415.

14. Tuman, Joseph S. (2003). *Communicating Terror: The Rhetorical Dimensions of Terrorism*. Thousand Oaks, CA: Sage.

15. Cialdini, Robert B. (2001). *Influence: Science and Practice* (4th ed.). Boston: Allyn & Bacon.

16. Altheide, David L. (2006). *Terrorism and the Politics of Fear*. Lanham, MD: AltaMira Press.

17. Cordes, Bonnie (1987). When Terrorists Do the Talking: Reflections on Terrorist Literature. *The Journal of Strategic Studies, 10*(4), 150–151.

18. Gressang, Daniel S. (2001). Audience and Message: Assessing Terrorist WMD Potential. *Terrorism and Political Violence, 13*(3), 83–106.

19. Hovland, Carl I., Janis, Irving L., & Kelley, Harold H. (1953). *Communication and Persuasion: Psychological Studies in Opinion Change*. New Haven, CT: Yale University Press.

20. Smith, Bruce L., Lasswell, Harold, & Casey, Ralph D. (1946). *Propaganda, Communication, and Public Opinion*. Princeton, NJ: Princeton University Press.

21. Gerwehr, Scott, & Hubbard, Kirk (2007). What Is Terrorism? Key Elements and History. In Bruce Bongar, Lisa M. Brown, Larry E. Beutler, James N. Breckenridge, & Philip G. Zimbardo (Eds.), *Psychology of Terrorism* (pp. 87–100). New York: Oxford University Press.

22. Gerwehr, Scott, & Hubbard, Kirk (2007). What Is Terrorism? Key Elements and History. In Bruce Bongar, Lisa M. Brown, Larry E. Beutler, James N. Breckenridge, & Philip G. Zimbardo (Eds.), *Psychology of Terrorism* (pp. 87–100). New York: Oxford University Press.

23. Nisbett, Richard E., & Ross, Lee D. (1980). *Human Inference: Strategies and Shortcomings of Social Judgment*. Englewood Cliffs, NJ: Prentice-Hall.

24. Eagly, Alice H., & Warren, Rebecca (1976), Intelligence, Comprehension, and Opinion Change. *Journal of Personality, 44*, 226–242; Petty, Richard E., Harkins, Steven G., & Williams, Kipling D. (1980). The Effects of Group Diffusion of Cognitive Effort on Attitudes: An Information-Processing View. *Journal of Personality and Social Psychology, 38*, 81–92.

25. Dillard, James (1994). Rethinking the Study of Fear Appeals: An Emotional Perspective. *Communication Theory, 4*, 295–323.

26. Gerwehr, Scott, & Hubbard, Kirk (2007). What Is Terrorism? Key Elements and History. In Bruce Bongar, Lisa M. Brown, Larry E. Beutler, James N. Breckenridge, & Philip G. Zimbardo (Eds.), *Psychology of Terrorism* (pp. 87–100). New York: Oxford University Press.

27. Gerwehr, Scott, & Hubbard, Kirk (2007). What Is Terrorism? Key Elements and History. In Bruce Bongar, Lisa M. Brown, Larry E. Beutler, James N. Breckenridge, & Philip G. Zimbardo (Eds.), *Psychology of Terrorism* (pp. 87–100). New York: Oxford University Press.

28. TV-Free America (2007). *Television Statistics*. Washington, D.C.: TV-Free America. Retrieved on April 11, 2011 from http://www.csun.edu/science/health/docs/tv&health.html

29. PEW (2001). The Commons of the Tragedy: How the Internet Was Used by Millions after The Terror Attacks to Grieve, Console, Share News, and Debate the Country's Response. Available at: http://www.pewinternet.org/reports/toc.asp?Report=46.

30. Katz, Elihu (1959). Mass Communication Research and the Study of Culture. *Studies in Public Communication, 2*, 1–6; Katz, Elihu (1987). Communication Research since Lazarsfeld. *Public Opinion Quarterly, 51*, 525–545.

31. Altheide, David L., & Snow, Robert P. (1979). *Media Logic*. Beverly Hills, CA: Sage; Snow, Robert P. (1983). *Creating Media Culture*. Beverly Hills, CA: Sage.

32. Pfefferbaum, Betty, Call, John, & Sconzo, Guy (1999). Mental Health Services for Children in the First Two Years after the 1995 Oklahoma City Terrorist Bombing. *Psychiatric Services, 50*, 956–958; Pfefferbaum, Betty, Nixon, Sara, Krug, Ronald, Tivis, Rick, Moore, Vern, Brown, Janice, Pynoos, Robert, Foy, David, & Gurwitch, Robin (1999). Clinical Needs Assessment of Middle and High School Students Following the 1995 Oklahoma City Bombing. *American Journal of Psychiatry, 156*, 1069–1074.

33. Pfefferbaum, Betty, Seale, Thomas W., Brandt, Edward N., Pfefferbaum, Rose L., Doughty, Debby E., Rainwater, Scott M. (2003). Media Exposure in Children One Hundred Miles from a Terrorist Bombing. *Annals of Clinical Psychiatry, 15*, 1–8.

34. Schuster, Mark A., Stein, Bradley D., Jaycox, Lisa H., Collins, Rebecca L., Marshall, Grant N., Elliott, Mark, Zhou, Annie L., Kanouse, David E., & Berry, Sandra H. (2001). A National Survey of Stress Reactions after the September 11, 2001 Terrorist Attacks. *New England Journal of Medicine, 345*, 1507–1512.

35. Corman, Steven R., & Schiefelbein, Jill S. (2006). *Communication and Media Strategy in the Jihadi War of Ideas*. Tempe, AZ: Consortium for Strategic Communication.

36. Tuman, Joseph S. (2003). *Communicating Terror: The Rhetorical Dimensions of Terrorism*. Thousand Oaks, CA: Sage.

37. Martin, Gus (2010). *Understanding Terrorism: Challenges, Perspectives, and Issues*. Thousand Oaks, CA: Sage.

38. Sadkovich, James J. (1998). *The U.S. Media and Yugoslavia, 1991–1995*. Westport, CT: Praeger.

39. Tuman, Joseph S. (2003). *Communicating Terror: The Rhetorical Dimensions of Terrorism*. Thousand Oaks, CA: Sage.

40. Martin, Gus (2010). *Understanding Terrorism: Challenges, Perspectives, and Issues*. Thousand Oaks, CA: Sage; Tuman, Joseph S. (2003). *Communicating Terror: The Rhetorical Dimensions of Terrorism*. Thousand Oaks, CA: Sage.

41. Louw, P. Eric (2003). The "War against Terrorism": A Public Relations Challenge for the Pentagon. *Gazette: The International Journal for Communication Studies, 65*(3), 211–230, p. 215.

42. Fanon, Frantz (1965). *The Wretched of the Earth*. London: MacGibbon and Kee.

43. Pynchon, Marissa, & Borum, Randy (1999). Assessing Threats of Targeted Group Violence: Contributions from Social Psychology. *Behavioral Science & the Law, 17*, 339–355; Waldmann, Peter (2001). Revenge without Rules: On the Renaissance of an Archaic Motif of Violence. *Studies in Conflict and Terrorism, 24*, 435–450.

44. Sirseloudi, Matenia P. (2005). How to Predict the Unpredictable: On the Early Detection of Terrorist Campaigns. *Defense & Security Analysis, 21*(4), 369–386.

45. Louw, P. Eric (2003). The "War against Terrorism": A Public Relations Challenge for the Pentagon. *Gazette: The International Journal for Communication Studies, 65*(3), 211–230.

46. Alexander, Jeffrey, C. (2004). From the Depths of Despair: Performance, Counterperformance, and "September 11." *Sociological Theory, 22*(1), 88–105.

47. Gressang, Daniel S. (2001). Audience and Message: Assessing Terrorist WMD Potential. *Terrorism and Political Violence, 13*(3), 83–106.

48. Martin, Gus (2010). *Understanding Terrorism: Challenges, Perspectives, and Issues*. Thousand Oaks, CA: Sage.

49. Weimann, Gabriel, & Winn, Conrad (1994). *The Threat of Terror: Mass Media and International Terrorism*. New York: Longman.

50. Cosgrove-Mather, Bootie (2002, February 28). Poll: Americans Feel Safer. *CBS News*.

51. Schmid, Alex P. (1992). Terrorism and the Media: Freedom of Information vs. Freedom from Intimidation. In Lawrence Howard (Ed.), *Terrorism: Roots, Impact, Responses* (pp. 95–115). New York: Praeger.

52. Murphy, Edward F., Jr., Gordon, John D., & Mullen, Aleta (2004). A Preliminary Study Exploring the Value Changes Taking Place in the United States Since the September 11, 2001 Terrorist Attack on the World Trade Center in New York. *Journal of Business Ethics, 50*(1), 81–96.

53. Goodrich, J. N. (2002). September 11, 2001 Attack on America: A Record of the Immediate Impacts and Reactions in the USA Travel and Tourism Industry. *Tourism Management, 23*, 573–580.

54. Martin, Brian (2006). Instead of Repression. *Social Alternatives, 25*(1), 62–66.

55. Combs, Cindy C. (2011). *Terrorism in the Twenty-First Century*. New York: Longman.

56. Shaw, Martin (2002). *Crime and Policing in Post-Apartheid South Africa: Transforming under Fire*. Bloomington: Indiana University Press.

57. Kaplan, Abraham (1981). The Psychodynamics of Terrorism. In Yonah Alexander & John Gleason (Eds.), *Behavioral and Quantitative Perspectives on Terrorism* (pp. 35–50). New York: Pergamon.

58. Oots, Kent (1990). Bargaining with Terrorists: Organizational Considerations. *Terrorism, 13*, 145–158.

59. Osama bin Laden's statement available at http://www.guardian.co.uk./waronterror/story/0,1361,565069,00.html

60. Public Agenda, Special Report on Terrorism (2005). Retrieved on April 14, 2011 from www.publicagenda.org/specials/terrorism/terror_pubopinion10.htm

61. Murphy, Edward F., Jr., Woodhull, Mark D., Post, Bert, Murphy-Post, Carolyn, Teeple, William, & Anderson, Kent (2006). 9/11 Impact on Teenage Values. *Journal of Business Ethics, 69*, 399–421.

62. Boscarino, Joseph A., Galea, Sandro, Ahern, Jennifer, Resnick, Heidi, & Vlahov, David (2002). Utilization of Mental Health Services Following the September 11th Terrorist Attacks in Manhattan, New York City. *International Journal of Emergency Health, 4*(3), 143–156.

63. Muñoz, Manuel, Crespo, María, Pérez-Santos, Eloísa, & Vázquez, Juan (2004). We Were All Wounded on March 11 in Madrid: Immediate Psychological Effects and Interventions. *European Psychologist, 9*, 278–280; Steger, Michael F., Frazier, Patricia A., & Zacchanini, Jose Luis (2008). Terrorism in Two Cultures: Stress and Growth Following September 11 and the Madrid Train Bombings. *Journal of Loss and Trauma, 13*, 511–527.

64. Fremont, Wanda P., Pataki, Caroly, & Beresin, Eugene V. (2005). The Impact of Terrorism on Children and Adolescents: Terror in the Skies, Terror on Television. *Child & Adolescent Psychiatric Clinics of North America, 14*, 429–451; Yehuda, Rachel, McFarlane, Alexander C., & Shalev, Arieh Y. (1998). Predicting the Development of Posttraumatic Stress Disorder from the Acute Response to a Traumatic Event. *Biological Psychiatry, 44*(12), 1305–1313.

65. Dunkel, Curtis S. (2002). Terror Management Theory and Identity: The Effect of the 9/11 Terrorist Attacks on Anxiety and Identity Change. *Identity, 2*(4), 281–301.

66. Alper, Gerald (2002). Up Close and Personal: September 11, through the Lens of a Psychotherapist. *Journal of Loss and Trauma, 7*, 251–261; Dixon, Mark R., Dymond, Simon, Rehfeldt, Ruth Anne, Roche, Bryan, & Zlomke, Kimberly R. (2003). Terrorism and Relational Frame Theory. *Behavior and Social Issues, 12*(2), 129–147.

67. Duggal, Harpreet S., Berezkin, Gennady, & John, Vineeth (2002). PTSD and TV Viewing of the World Trade Center. *Journal of the American Academy of Child and Adolescent Psychiatry, 41*, 494–495; Kettl, Paul, & Bixler, Edward (2002). Changes in Psychotropic Drug Use after September 11. *Psychiatric Services, 53*, 1475–1476.

68. Rogers, Everett M., & Seidel, Nancy (2002). Diffusion of News of the Terrorist Attacks of September 11, 2001. *Prometheus, 20*(3), 209–219.

69. Rogers, Everett M. (2000). Reflections on News Event Diffusion Research. *Journalism & Mass Communication Quarterly, 77*(3), 561–576.

70. Sparks, Lisa (2005). Social Identity and Perceptions of Terrorist Groups: How Others See Them and How They See Themselves. In H. Dan O'Hair, Robert L. Heath, & Gerald R. Ledlow (Eds.), *Community Preparedness and Response to Terrorism: Communication and the Media* (pp. 13–28). Westport, CT: Praeger.

71. Ganor, Boaz (2005). Terrorism as a Strategy of Psychological Warfare. *Journal of Aggression, Maltreatment & Trauma, 9*(1), 33–43.

72. Alexander, Jeffrey, C. (2004). From the Depths of Despair: Performance, Counterperformance, and "September 11." *Sociological Theory, 22*(1), 88–105.

73. Abdulla, Rasha A. (2007). Islam, Jihad, and Terrorism in Post-9/11 Arabic Discussion Boards. *Journal of Computer-Mediated Communication, 12*, 1063–1081.

74. Dunlop, Jean (1990). Peer Groups Support Seniors Fighting Alcohol and Drugs. *Aging, 361*, 28–32; Ganor, Boaz (2005). Terrorism as a Strategy of Psychological Warfare. *Journal of Aggression, Maltreatment & Trauma, 9*(1), 33–43.

75. Rapoport, David C. (1977, November 26). The Government Is Up in the Air over Combating Terrorism. *National Journal, 9*, 1853–1856.

76. Corrado, Raymond R. (1979). Ethnic and Student Terrorism in Western Europe. In Michael Stohl (Ed.), *The Politics of Terrorism* (pp. 191–257). New York: Marcel Dekker.

77. Ahern, Jennifer, Galea, Sandro, Resnick, Heidi, Kilpatrick, Dean, Bucuvalas, Michael, Gold, Joel, & Vlahov, David (2002). Television Images and Psychological Symptoms after the September 11 Terrorist Attacks. *Psychiatry, 65*, 289–300.

78. Danieli, Yael (1998). *International Handbook of Multigenerational Legacies of Trauma*. New York: Kluwer Academic/Plenum Publishing.

79. Kunreuther, H. (2002). Risk Assessment and Risk Management in an Uncertain World. *Risk Assessment, 22*(4), 655–664.

80. Rothe, Dawn, & Muzzatti, Stephen L. (2004). Enemies Everywhere: Terrorism, Moral Panic, and US Civil Society. *Critical Criminology, 12*, 327–350.

81. Altheide, David L. (2006). The Mass Media, Crime and Terrorism. *Journal of International Criminal Justice, 4*, 982–997.

82. Der Derian, James (2002). The War of Networks. *Theory and Event, 5*(4), 10–21.

83. Combs, Cindy C. (2011). *Terrorism in the Twenty-First Century*. New York: Longman.

84. Weimann, Gabriel (1983). The Theater of Terror: Effects of Press Coverage. *Journal of Communication, 3*, 8–45.

85. Lawyer, Steven R., Resnick, Heidi S., Galea, Sandro, Ahern, Jennifer, Kilpatrick, Dean, & Vlahov, David (2006). Predictors of Peritraumatic Reactions and PTSD Following the September 11th Terrorist Attacks. *Psychiatry: Interpersonal and Biological Processes, 69*, 130–141; Shoshani, Anat, & Slone, Michelle (2008). The Drama of Media Coverage of Terrorism: Emotional and Attitudinal Impact on the Audience. *Studies in Conflict & Terrorism, 31*, 627–640; Sontag, Susan (2005). *Regarding the Pain of Others*. Ben-Shemen, Israel: Modan Publishers.

86. Altheide, David L. (2002). *Creating Fear: News and the Construction of Crisis*. Hawthorne, NY: Aldine de Gruyter.

87. Fahmy, Shahira, Cho, Sooyoung, Wanta, Wayne, & Song, Yonghoi (2006). Visual Agenda-Setting after 9/11: Individuals' Emotions, Image Recall, and Concern with Terrorism. *Visual Communication Quarterly, 13*(1), 4–15; Newhagen, John E., & Reeves, Byron (1992). The Evening's Bad News: Effects of Compelling Negative Television News Images on Memory. *Journal of Communication, 42*(2), 25–41.

88. Christianson, Sven-Ake, & Loftus, Elizabeth F. (1987). Memory for Traumatic Events. *Applied Cognitive Psychology, 1*, 225–239.

89. Newhagen, John E. (1998). TV News Images That Induce Anger, Fear and Disgust: Effects on Approach-Avoidance and Memory. *Journal of Broadcasting & Electronic Media, 42*, 265–277.

90. U.S. State Department (2001). *Patterns of Terrorism*. Washington, D.C.: U.S. Department of State; Zulaika, Joseba, & Douglass, William (1997). *Terror and Taboo: The Follies, Fables and Faces of Terrorism*. London: Routledge.

91. Rummel, Rudolph J. (1996). *Death by Government*. New Brunswick, NJ: Transaction Publishers.

92. *Economist, The* (1986). East, West, Home's Best, 300(7455), p. 28. *Economist, The* (1986). Europe Suffers from American Stayaways, 299(7447), 63–64; Edgell, St., David L. (1990). *International Tourism Policy*. New York: Van Nostrand Reinhold; Richter, Linda K., & Waugh, Jr., William L. (1986). Terrorism and Tourism as Logical Companions. *Tourism Management, 7*, 230–238.

93. Gerbner, George, Gross, Larry, Morgan, Michael, Signorielli, Nancy, & Shanahan, James (2002). Growing Up with Television: The Cultivation Perspective. In Jennings Bryant & Dolf Zillmann (Eds.), *Media Effects: Advances in Theory and Research* (pp. 43–67). Mahwah, NJ: Lawrence Erlbaum.

94. Tuman, Joseph S. (2003). *Communicating Terror: The Rhetorical Dimensions of Terrorism*. Thousand Oaks, CA: Sage.

95. Figley, Charles R. (1995). *Compassion Fatigue: Coping with Secondary Traumatic Stress Disorder in Those Who Treat the Traumatized*. New York: Brunner/Mazel.

96. Ungerer, Carl (2004). Issues in Australian Foreign Policy. *Australian Journal of Politics and History, 50*(4), 573–587.

97. Scott, John L. (2001). Media Congestion Limits Media Terrorism. *Defence and Peace Economics, 12*(3), 215–227.

98. Kelly, Michael J., & Mitchell, Thomas H. (1981). Transnational Terrorism and the Western Elite Press. *Political Communication and Persuasion: An International Journal, 1*(3), 269–296.

99. Delli Carpini, Michael, & Williams, Bruce (1987). Television and Terrorism: Patterns of Presentation and Occurrence, 1969 to 1980. *Western Political Quarterly, 40*(4), 45–64.

100. Weimann, Gabriel (2008). The Psychology of Mass-Mediated Terrorism. *American Behavioral Scientist, 52*(1), 69–86.

101. Debord, Guy (1995). *The Society of the Spectacle*. Cambridge, MA: Zone Books.

102. Miller, Claude, Matusitz, Jonathan, O'Hair, Dan, & Eckstein, Jacqueline (2008). The Role of Communication and the Media in Terrorism. In Dan O'Hair, Robert Heath, Kevin Ayotte, & Gerald R. Ledlow (Eds.), *Terrorism: Communication and Rhetorical Perspectives* (pp. 43–66). Cresskill, NJ: Hampton Press.

103. Mitchell, W. J. Thomas (2005). The Unspeakable and the Unimaginable: Word and Image in a Time of Terror. *ELH, 72*(2), 291–308.

104. McGillivray, Glen (2008). Globing the Globe: September 11 and Theatrical Metaphor. *Theory & Event, 11*(4), 10–21.

105. Smith, Matthew Noah (2008). Terrorism, Shared Rules and Trust. *The Journal of Political Philosophy, 16*(2), 201–219.

106. Smith, Matthew Noah (2008). Terrorism, Shared Rules and Trust. *The Journal of Political Philosophy, 16*(2), 201–219.

107. Jenkins, Brian (1975). *International Terrorism*. Los Angeles: Crescent.

108. McLuhan, Marshall (1964). *Understanding Media: The Extensions of Man*. New York: Routledge.

109. Virilio, Paul (2000). *The Information Bomb*. New York: Verso.

110. Bassiouni, M. Cherif (1981). Terrorism and the Media. *Journal of Criminal Law and Criminology, 72*, 1–55.

111. Crary, Jonathan (1999). *Suspensions of Perception*. Cambridge, MA: MIT Press.

112. Schirato, Tony, & Webb, Jennifer (2004). The Media as Spectacle: September 11 as Soap Opera. *Journal for Cultural Research, 8*(4), 411–423.

113. Boyle, Robert P. (1972). International Action to Combat Aircraft Hijacking. *Lawyer of the Americas, 4*(3), 460–473; Raab, David (2004, August 22). Remembrance of Terror Past. *The New York Times*, p. A1; Tuman, Joseph S. (2003). *Communicating Terror: The Rhetorical Dimensions of Terrorism*. Thousand Oaks, CA: Sage.

114. Bowen, Shannon A. (2008). Frames of Terrorism Provided by the News Media and Potential Communication Responses. In Dan O'Hair, Robert Heath, Kevin Ayotte, & Gerald R. Ledlow (Eds.), *Terrorism: Communication and Rhetorical Perspectives* (pp. 337–358). Cresskill, NJ: Hampton Press.

115. Taussig, Michael (1987). *Shamanism, Colonialism, and the Wild Man: A Study in Terror and Healing*. Chicago: University of Chicago Press.

116. Mitchell, W. J. Thomas (2005). The Unspeakable and the Unimaginable: Word and Image in a Time of Terror. *ELH, 72*(2), 291–308.

117. Miller, Claude, Matusitz, Jonathan, O'Hair, Dan, & Eckstein, Jacqueline (2008). The Role of Communication and the Media in Terrorism. In Dan O'Hair, Robert Heath, Kevin Ayotte, & Gerald R. Ledlow (Eds.), *Terrorism: Communication and Rhetorical Perspectives* (pp. 43–66). Cresskill, NJ: Hampton Press.

118. Laqueur, Walter (1977). *Terrorism*. London: Weidenfeld and Nicolson.

119. Kellner, Douglas (2003). September 11, Spectacles of Terror, and Media Manipulation: A Critique of Jihadist and Bush Media Politics. *Logos, 2*(1), 86–102.

120. Kellner, Douglas (2003). September 11, Spectacles of Terror, and Media Manipulation: A Critique of Jihadist and Bush Media Politics. *Logos, 2*(1), 86–102.

121. Lisle, Debbie (2004). Gazing at Ground Zero: Tourism, Voyeurism and Spectacle. *Journal for Cultural Research, 8*(1), 3–21.

122. Buruma, Ian, & Margalit, Avishai (2004). *Occidentalism: The West in the Eyes of Its Enemies*. New York: Penguin.

123. Bower, G. H. (1983). Affect and Cognition. *Philosophical Transactions of the Royal Society of London, 302*, 387–402; Jamieson, Kathleen Hall (1992). *Packaging the Presidency: A History and Criticism of Presidential Campaign Advertising*. New York: Oxford University Press.

124. Strozier, Charles B. (2002). The World Trade Center Disaster and the Apocalyptic. *Psychoanalytic Dialogues: The International Journal of Relational Perspectives, 12*(3), 361–380.

125. Fahmy, Shahira, Cho, Sooyoung, Wanta, Wayne, & Song, Yonghoi (2006). Visual Agenda-Setting after 9/11: Individuals' Emotions, Image Recall, and Concern with Terrorism. *Visual Communication Quarterly, 13*(1), 4–15.

126. Bassiouni, M. Cherif (1979). Prolegomenon to Terror Violence. *Creighton Law Review, 12*(3), 745–780, p. 752.

127. The quotes are taken from the translations of a videotape, presumably made in mid-November 2001 in Afghanistan. Available from http://www.washingtonpost.com/wp-srv/nation/specials.

128. Thornton, Thomas Perry (1964). Terror as a Weapon of Political Agitation. In Harry Eckstein (Ed.), *Internal War: Problems and Approaches* (pp. 71–99). New York: The Free Press.

129. Louw, P. Eric (2003). The "War against Terrorism": A Public Relations Challenge for the Pentagon. *Gazette: The International Journal for Communication Studies, 65*(3), 211–230.

130. Alexander, Jeffrey C. (2004). From the Depths of Despair: Performance, Counterperformance, and "September 11." *Sociological Theory, 22*(1), 88–105.

131. Goffman, Erving (1959). *The Presentation of Self in Everyday Life*. New York: Doubleday.

132. Burke, Kenneth (1972). *Dramatism and Development*. Barre, MA: Clark University Press.

133. Grayson, Kent (1998). Customer Responses to Emotional Labour in Discrete and Relational Service Exchange. *International Journal of Service Industry Management, 9*(2), 126–141.

134. Wood, Julia T. (2004). *Communication Theories in Action: An Introduction*. Belmont, CA: Wadsworth.

135. Oberschall, Anthony (2004). Explaining Terrorism: The Contribution of Collective Action Theory. *Sociological Theory, 22*(1), 26–37.

136. Hughes, H. Stuart (1958). *Consciousness and Society: The Reorientation of Social Thought, 1890–1930*. New York: Vintage Books.

137. Alexander, Jeffrey, C. (2004). From the Depths of Despair: Performance, Counterperformance, and "September 11." *Sociological Theory, 22*(1), 88–105.

138. Alexander, Jeffrey, C. (2004). From the Depths of Despair: Performance, Counterperformance, and "September 11." *Sociological Theory, 22*(1), 88–105.

139. Weimann, Gabriel (2008). The Psychology of Mass-Mediated Terrorism. *American Behavioral Scientist, 52*(1), 69–86.

140. Nathanson, Charles E. (1988). The Social Construction of the Soviet Threat. *Alternatives, 13*, 443–483.

141. Burke, Kenneth (1989). *On Symbols and Society*. Chicago: The University of Chicago Press.

142. Alexander, Jeffrey, C. (2004). From the Depths of Despair: Performance, Counterperformance, and "September 11." *Sociological Theory, 22*(1), 88–105.

143. Alexander, Jeffrey, C. (2004). From the Depths of Despair: Performance, Counterperformance, and "September 11." *Sociological Theory, 22*(1), 88–105.

144. Alexander, Jeffrey, C. (2004). From the Depths of Despair: Performance, Counterperformance, and "September 11." *Sociological Theory, 22*(1), 88–105.

145. Cowen, Tyler (2006). Terrorism as Theater: Analysis and Policy Implications. *Public Choice, 128*, 233–244.

146. Louw, P. Eric (2003). The "War against Terrorism": A Public Relations Challenge for the Pentagon. *Gazette: The International Journal for Communication Studies, 65*(3), 211–230; Weimann, Gabriel (2008). The Psychology of Mass-Mediated Terrorism. *American Behavioral Scientist, 52*(1), 69–86.

CHAPTER 5

Framing Terrorism

After reading this chapter, you will be able to

- explain framing as the process by which a media source describes and creates a political issue or public controversy;
- analyze whether media interpretations of terrorism have become one-sided; and
- discuss censorship as a framing strategy.

FRAMING: DEFINITION

This chapter explains how terrorism can be framed by the media and to what extent conventional frames about terrorism are able to influence public opinion. In media theory, **framing** is the process by which a media source, such as a news outlet, describes and creates a political issue or public controversy. Essentially, framing is a communicative strategy that steers the audience toward embracing one viewpoint over another.[1] A **frame** entails a schema of interpretation—that is, a series of anecdotes and stereotypes—that serves to organize experience and influence action and that the audience relies on to understand and respond to events. A frame determines the packaging of news so strongly that it can foster certain interpretations and discourage others. Indeed, in their representation of events or issues, the media employ essential organizing ideas that define the boundaries of those events or issues by locating them within a certain context of meaning. The media employ frames both in regard to the issues and key participants in a debate. Framing involves bias.[2] As Bernard Cohen (1963)[3] phrased it elegantly, "The media doesn't tell us what to think; it tells us what to think about" (p. 3).

News frames are representations of regulated formats for selection, highlighting, and exclusion of news. News frames offer a comprehensible interpretation and evaluation of events. They are interpretive patterns used by reporters to place a particular story within their own sphere. News frames package crucial concepts, catchphrases, and symbolic images to bolster particular ways of interpreting developments. A framing message has specific cultural resonance.[4] Decisions and common practices in news reporting promote these frames. They determine what and how events or issues are covered. Among the countless ways of reporting stories across the globe, journalists tend to use familiar news frames and interpret events (furnished by credible sources) to communicate dominant meanings, draw conclusions about the facts, emphasize headlines, and structure the storyline.[5]

Put simply, framing is a form of **news triage**, a selection process to determine what news should be reported or ignored. Framing, in essence, gives precedence to facts, images, or developments over others. In doing so, it prioritizes a particular interpretation of events. As a form of news triage, framing engages in mediatization. By definition, **mediatization** is media's performative contribution and constitutive involvement not only in describing the news but also in generating them and, eventually, interpreting them.[6] Media creations are human constructs that viewers take for granted. Fairhurst and Sarr (1996)[7] describe many possible ways for framing situations: (1) metaphors—giving an idea or constructing a new meaning by comparing it to other things; (2) stories, myths, and legends—turning a news event into an anecdote in a flamboyant and memorable fashion; (3) slogans, jargon, and catchphrases—framing a news event in an unforgettable and familiar way; (4) artifacts—enlightening corporate values through physical traces or remnants (occasionally in a way language cannot); (5) contrast—describing a subject in something that it is not; and (6) spin—describing a concept by adding positive or negative connotations.

News frames tend to perpetuate themselves; they produce their own easily recognizable histories and spheres of meanings, and are employed by the media when interpreting unfolding events. In this sense, news frames are media templates. **Media templates** refer to the myriad ways in which mass media impose a certain interpretation, organization, or story on a current news event in regard to archived images, sounds, and narratives.[8] In terms of media templates, Robert Picard (1993)[9] conceptualized four types of reporting:

- The information tradition reports news factually and reliably.

- The sensationalist tradition reports news in a style that elicits particular emotions—fear, anger, alarm, and so forth.

- The feature story tradition reports news by focusing on one person's saga, depicting him or her as hero, hood, or victim in an effort to personalize the story. At times, this focus comes to the detriment of the more essential coverage of the issues involved.

- The didactic tradition reports news to educate the audience. This potentially biased format employs documentaries and other nontraditional methods of reporting.

A media template employed extensively in the aftermath of September 11, 2001 was the Pearl Harbor attack. Public figures that were shown on television were related to traumatic histories. For example, Henry Kissinger, the U.S. Secretary of State under Richard Nixon, appeared live on CNN on the afternoon of September 11, 2001. He compared 9/11—and the response that ought to follow—with the Pearl Harbor tragedy. The presence of well-known TV personalities (usually journalists, news anchors, or retired politicians) between disasters and publics is another of mass media's framing strategies.[10] This anecdote is a reflection of Picard's "feature story" tradition of reporting.

FRAMING VS. AGENDA SETTING

Agenda-setting theory postulates that the more the media cover certain issues, the more salient (i.e., noticeable, accessible, and significant) these issues become for the audience.[11] Thus, a strong correlation exists between the focus that the media place on an issue (e.g., contingent on relative placement or magnitude of coverage) and the importance ascribed to the issue by the public. Agenda setting is grounded in memory-based structures of information processing. These structures suggest that people construct attitudes based on the most salient factors when they make decisions. In the same train of thought, agenda-setting theory explains how media gatekeepers are responsible for the everyday selection and presentation of news and how their actions influence public perceptions about the importance of events or issues. **Media gatekeepers** are editors or managers of news organizations who decide what stories will be selected for the audience and how these stories will be presented. Agenda-setting theory is a helpful theory for understanding how the underreporting or overreporting of events or issues can eventually affect public perceptions and behaviors in regard to those events or issues. It is just a matter of time: the media emphasis on particular topics leads the audience to believe those topics as more important than others.[12]

In people's minds, agenda setting makes some news more "high-ranking."[13] This is a concept called **media salience**.[14] Three dimensions of media salience need to be considered: attention, prominence, and valence. Attention depends on the volume of media coverage/exposure. Prominence is a framing tool used to emphasize or place an attribute/object in a framework that communicates its importance. The existence of news stories reported by renowned news outlets (e.g., *The Wall Street Journal*, *The New York Times*, etc.) can be a determining factor to the audience in granting news stories prominence. Valence is the affective (emotional) nature of media content. Media coverage can send signals that form the general affective salience of issues, people, and other events (e.g., how glamorous or frightening they are presented). As such, affective elements in media reporting can increase or decrease the overall salience of news.[15] A concept related to media salience is **salience transfer**, the power of media organizations to transfer issues of salience from their own media agendas to public agendas.[16]

On the other hand, framing does not refer so much to media salience; rather, it concentrates more on the methods of presentation used by the media to report events or issues in a format that matches the goal or underlying schema of the news organization, the political orientation of the media establishment, or even the culture of the audience. The consequence of framing is that the audience will interpret the world based on what they watch or hear through sound bites, news reports, newspaper stories, and so forth.[17] A **sound bite** is a very short snippet of a speech extracted from a longer speech or an interview in which an expert or media personality expresses something considered by media gatekeepers as the most important point (e.g., "We will hunt them [terrorists] down," President George W. Bush, November 21, 2001). Entman (1993)[18] contends that frames are different from agendas. In his definition, a frame is created by the structure of narratives. For him, frames

> *define problems*—determine what a causal agent is doing with what costs and benefits, usually measured in terms of common cultural values; *diagnose causes*—identify the forces creating the problem; *make moral judgments*—evaluate causal agents and their effects; and *suggest remedies*—offer and justify treatments for the problems and predict their likely effects. (p. 52)

While agenda-setting theory assumes that by making themes salient (exposing them over and over again), the media transfer their representations of salience to the public, for framing theory, media content incorporated into a specific narrative pattern will be more salient to audiences than content that is not. In later work, Entman (2003)[19] compares salience with cultural resonance as a strategy for influencing public reception of media texts.

It should be noted that framing shares a few things in common with agenda-setting. According to both theories, (1) the media control and influence discussion and perception of many day-to-day issues; (2) news events are not a reflection of reality—the media tend to filter reality; and (3) the media engage in gatekeeping. Lastly, both theories also explain how the media are managing the news. As a journalistic expression, **managing the news** refers to actions intended to affect the presentation of information within the mass media. The phrase *managing the news* is typically used in a negative sense.[20]

TYPES OF FRAMING

In spite of the globalization of communication, media coverage in general is still strikingly uneven around the world. Western Europe, North America, and developed regions of Asia, Latin America, and Oceania are more likely to have high media coverage than Africa and the poorer regions of Asia, Latin America, and Oceania. The only exception occurs if rich nations are fighting wars in those regions (especially wars of interest to rich nations).[21] In her work titled "Frames of Terrorism Provided by the News Media and Potential Communication Responses," Shannon Bowen (2008)[22] compares six types of framing prevalent in regions "more likely to have high media coverage" (as mentioned a few lines above):

• News framing is the affected reporting of news by the media. Media sources are known as *framers* because they add their own frames to mass communication. News framing explores how the media report events using dominant social frames (i.e., frames of culture resonance) as they compete for their public.

• **Attribute framing** means accentuating particular attributes of an event. The framing of attributes as positive or negative is at the preference of the reporter or media gatekeeper.

For instance, the same act can be framed as terrorism or freedom fighting, but reports either a positive or negative attribute frame.

• **Choice framing** consists of asking the audience to take a risk or make a promise about a specific decision. Framing choices has to drive people to act in a particular way. Therefore, choices are framed in a mutually exclusive manner, a method that establishes alternatives as extremely positive or extremely negative.

• **Action framing** has the goal of transforming behavioral intentions into actions. For example, Islamic media outlets such as Al Jazeera generally use action framing to report even horrifying terrorist acts in the most positive light possible.

• **Issue framing** takes up a large chunk of PR activities and attempts to define an issue. Defining an issue means deciding what facts and news are significant, or not significant, and suggesting an interpretive meaning of those facts and news. A competing issue frame surfaces and seeks to reach the status of dominant issue frame that is generally used in correspondence to the topic. For instance, the abortion debate is framed as either pro-life or pro-choice, depending on the media source. Such model of issue framing is a major cause of violence in Northern Ireland as both Catholics and Protestants fight for dominant issue frames on abortion and other moral issues.

• **Responsibility framing** ascribes causes and assigns causal accountability. It plays an important role in framing terrorist activities. Research on responsibility framing reveals that mass media focus on framing responsibility for single events (episodic framing) rather than placing events into the perspective of larger issues (thematic framing). This would lend itself to a deeper examination of the content being reported, both by the media and the audience. **Episodic frames** concentrate on the specifics of any given event, such as the Global War on Terror (GWOT). This neglects **thematic frames**, those that offer a broader and more contextualized interpretation of the root causes that lead to these issues.[23]

The media help the U.S. audience re-evaluate the notion of hero via images repeatedly shown to us on television and in print. This is an example of attribute framing. 9/11 firefighters and evacuators responded to terrorism in a noble way. They became heroes and created massive amounts of identification (e.g., the NYC police and fire department staff on 9/11). Of course, victims of the terrorist attack were usually described as heroes in unprecedented ways. As a consequence, the American audience started to define heroes and victims of terrorism in a narrower sense, one that was presented and re-presented, negotiated and renegotiated, through the visual images selected by reporters and media gatekeepers.[24]

FRAMING THROUGH THE POWER OF TELEVISION

Television is an exceptionally powerful medium in that it is visually capable of framing and reconstructing entire events. Television can achieve this by editing, beautifying, and turning past events into a format or content sufficiently appropriate for new political and cultural spheres. Television likes to project a self-image of honesty and straightforwardness. TV stations are very willing to position the stories they broadcast as accurate pieces of reality, exploiting the viewers' typical credibility that they tend to believe anything that can be seen. This is analogous to the adage that people are like sponges; they absorb anything that they see on TV. The media deform the knowledge-gaining realm because they avoid reminding the audience that whatever image or piece of information is transmitted is a function of framing. Media distortion can be done through sound bites, the angle of a particular camera, the selection of one focus over another, the structure of narratives, and so forth. The integral truthfulness that the public thinks exists in any image or piece of information that can be seen bestows television a high degree of persuasion that other media lack, particularly radio. The main corollary is that the product offered by TV stations is reality in and of itself, without considering the context and other circumstances within which these images and pieces of information are situated.[25]

As Schudson (1982)[26] points out, "[T]he way the technology is used has a relation to, but is not fully determined by, the technology itself" (p. 97). To such scholars, the technological power of television is nurtured in a market-driven for-profit and entertainment context. Accordingly, television news coverage is motivated by broadcasting organizations' prime craving for good visuals, good stories, and personalities—the main attributes for causing ratings to skyrocket. In standard news coverage, such craving is reflected through episodic coverage: real episodes or events where little contextual or thematic connection was taken into account in the reporting. When an important news event takes place, television broadcasting turns into live broadcasting. Not only does it create a colossal news hole, as exemplified by 24-hour uninterrupted news coverage (i.e., the CNN effect); it also creates the fun and buzz in both newsrooms and society at large. Live television broadcasts make celebrity news anchors and public figures star performers of a melodramatic show.[27]

Emotional Cues in Television Coverage

Researchers from various schools of thought and theoretical traditions have claimed that television is more emotionally arousing than newspapers and magazines. Influenced by the works of Marshall McLuhan (1964),[28] scholars insist that television communicates with human senses in a distinctive way: TV has a recipe of audio and visual cues, a superficial real-life tempo, a multi-dimensional juxtaposition of video images shown multiple times, and so forth. It is thus capable of producing its own forms of thinking and communicating. In addition, some contend that such technical features interrelate with market forces to fashion exceptional media logic, and a design of presentation that incorporates visual images, tempo, and rhythm in the developing of a news story and portrayals of public figures. Unsurprisingly, the role of emotions in TV coverage contributes to the dramatization of news, making television news qualitatively distinct from print-based journalism.[29]

These considerations suggest several kinds of emotional cues in television coverage, such as visual grammar (close-ups, zooms, cuts, video graphics, etc.) and emotion-evoking words.[30] **Visual grammar** is the notion that television is perceived as more emotionally arousing in comparison with print media. As a puissant broadcaster of vivid images through its usage of close-ups, zooms, slow motion, video graphics, and sound, television can overcome boundaries set by time and distance. Viewers, then, can sense some "presence."[31] This power to create real experiences is underscored by Reeves and Hass (1996),[32] who suggest that the audience responds to emotionally laden images on television just as they would in real life. Roeh (1989)[33] contends that the creative and melodramatic storytelling—including the tone, emotional signals, and verbal expressions—employed in broadcast journalism makes TV news an ideal instrument for conveying emotion over information.

Media Dependency Theory

Media Dependency Theory posits that people become increasingly reliant on media, especially in times of crises. The theory also says that dependence on a specific medium may contribute greatly to the effects that the medium has on the viewer. In the present-day media environment, it is usually the case that, for emotional reasons, people increasingly depend on television.[34] With respect to September 11, 2001, besides powerful images and emotion-loaded rhetoric, television was also instrumental for creating shared emotional moments, as premised in Media Dependency Theory. This argument was clearly substantiated by the revealing front page of the September 11, 2002 issue of *The Onion*, the satirical weekly magazine (exactly one year after 9/11 occurred). It asked the question, "Who will bring closure to a grieving nation?" The answer was plain and simple: the attention-grabbing graphic displayed the logos of the six major TV broadcasters. It points to the fact that television, as a more emotion-triggering medium than print media, causes greater emotional reactions.[35]

FRAMING TERRORISM

In the 19th century, terrorism was framed through caricatures of terrorists in newspapers (crazy-looking, bearded bombers). The media establishment started framing the idea that extreme violence was both illegitimate and crazy. Assassins were commonly depicted as lone disturbed individuals whose acts were the products of their individual pathologies, loveless lives, and unfulfilled ambitions. Suicide attacks were portrayed in a similar manner: as the irrational and abhorring actions of fanatics driven by religion or political aims.[36] Today, terrorism news frames tend to provide steady, simple, and powerful narratives rooted in the social construction of reality. Conventional frames are frames that become "majority" in the media. They furnish contextual cues and assign meaning and order to complex problems, actions, and occurrences by placing new events into familiar categories or **storyline pegs**.[37] Although the minute details of each terrorist attack tend to be unique—a suicide bomber in Tel Aviv, a detonating automobile in Sri Lanka, or abduction in Bogota—the manner in which reporters observe and narrate all these incidents is shaped by how comparable incidents have been covered in the past and by the journalist's most reliable sources of information.[38]

The media often invite controversy, especially when news coverage becomes part of the challenge to describe the social meaning of events. Covering stories about terrorism—whether 9/11, suicide bombing in the Palestinian–Israeli conflict, or bloodshed in

Chechnya—raises major questions as to how far news coverage can live up to journalistic principles of balance, truth, and objectivity. Some facts about terrorist incidents may be fairly neutral (e.g., the specific timing of the attack). However, many others remain debatable (e.g., the motives of the perpetrators or the political grievances triggering their actions). This also includes aspects of media coverage such as the language used to describe terrorist attacks, the choice, portrayal, and meaning of iconic images, and the selection of authoritative sources and experts for commentary (i.e., Should we trust Robert Gates and Janet Napolitano? Is there anyone else telling the truth here, like Ann Coulter or Al Sharpton?).

One-Sided vs. Two-Sided Coverage

News frames influence public opinion, especially if they contain one-sided messages, including what audiences learn about terrorism, how they assess the main actors and matters under contention, and how far media messages affect public concerns and perceptions of the threats and dangers of future terrorist acts. The news frame in any society is only one factor affecting public opinion, which is also influenced by real-world indicators and by personal experience and interpersonal communication.[39] In one-sided coverage, there is a general consensus about how terrorist incidents should be framed within any given community. In **one-sided coverage**, the conventional news frame is so powerful and ubiquitous that journalists, politicians, and the audience are usually unaware of this process; media coverage is seen as authoritative and relatively unquestionable. This process was illustrated by the 9/11 coverage presented to the American people by the major media outlets. By and large, the latter displayed similar formats in framing responsibility and interpreting these events.[40] For example, in the mass media, terrorism has increasingly come to refer to acts associated with agents and supporters of foreign-based terrorist movements such as Al Qaeda, rather than with the violence of homegrown activists and radicals who belong to groups such as the Animal Liberation Front, Earth First!, and the American Coalition for Life Activists (i.e., one of the founders, Paul Hill, was executed in Florida in September 2003, for murder, not terrorism).[41]

Overstating violence into the language of terrorism, the media turn it into powerful images of terror and position state-sponsored reprisals as heroic and necessary acts. One content analysis compared prominent U.S. newspapers before and after September 11, 2001. The analysis found that while the reporting on Arab-Americans after September 11 was not consistently negative, references to Arab-Americans as an in-group decreased in number. Additionally, the news created a close association between the attacks and people of Arab descent. For instance, one study examined the links among influential words in the media post–September 11, 2001. Words like *bin Laden*, *Palestinian*, *Taliban*, and *Islamic* were frequently associated to words like *terrorist* and *attack*.[42] Framing terrorism in this respect serves two main functions: cognitive and evaluative functions. **Cognitive functions** relate together disparate facts, events, and leaders. **Evaluative functions** label perpetrators, identify victims, and assign blame. Framing terrorism allows political leaders to send a coherent, simple message to the audience, while also revamping perceptions of friends and enemies. In the words of President George W. Bush, "Every nation in every region now has a decision to make. Either you are with us, or you are with the terrorists."[43]

One-sided coverage is also present in situations where state terrorists control the mass media, either by owning them directly or by imposing rules of censorship—ignoring minority views in the process. On the other hand, in **two-sided coverage**, there is usually greater awareness of the framing process, as well as of challenge and disagreement with particular portrayals by certain media outlets. In two-sided coverage, interpretations and evaluations of terrorist violence differ dramatically among sub-groups profoundly affected by the conflict. Divided communities can nevertheless share access to the mass media, as it is the case among Catholics and Protestants in Belfast, Jews and Muslims in Jerusalem, and Russians and Chechens in Grozny (the capital city of Chechnya).[44]

In two-sided conflicts that are evenly divided, intense emotional reactions to political terrorism mirror the fact that each society provides different interpretations of incidents and images—occasionally, they share virtually nothing in common. Was 9/11 committed by the very Al Qaeda or an independent group of operatives hired by Al Qaeda? Or, as some Arab pundits said, was it a Zionist conspiracy to hold Muslims responsible? The media serving each culture may reflect and, in so doing, strengthen these cultural divisions, especially if reporters and news anchors seek to bridge and conquer community differences by adopting the **fairness doctrine** (cleverly balancing contrasting viewpoints).[45] Only a few U.S. news media covered stories about German and Italian arrest warrants for CIA operatives who abducted German and Italian citizens, respectively, and transferred them to other countries so they could be tortured and questioned (they were on the terrorism watch list).[46]

"Sound-Biting" the Audience

The media and political leaders react to terrorist attacks and communicate policy imports by adopting leading cultural frames to streamline and abridge their message (e.g., "I condemn all such acts of terrorism"). Reporters "tell it like it is" within 60 seconds or within brief newspaper headlines. They select and classify main events from surrounding trivia in a quick manner; they do this by drawing on pools of stories that send familiar cues to readers. Put simply, the media are sound-biting the audience. The audience, in turn, can use frames to organize and add things up, especially when dealing with complex and unfamiliar events or people.[47]

Sound-biting the audience by using the same conventional terrorism frames is obvious when watching coverage of several terrorism-related incidents that occurred in 2002: the nightclub terrorist attack in Indonesia (i.e., the Bali bombings), the hostage taking by Chechen insurgents in the Moscow theater, the bombing of an Israeli-owned hotel in Mombassa (Kenya), the suicide bombings in Tel Aviv, or the arrest of communist rebels in the Philippines. Without being aware of much, if anything, about the particular events, people, groups, or even places involved, the sound-bited audience is being fed information by the conventional news frame of terrorism: a frame that rapidly sorts out, interprets, categorizes, and evaluates those conflicts.[48]

Never do such news frames offer an all-encompassing explanation of the main characteristics of terrorist acts. The main consequence is that important puzzles are left unresolved. The conventional news frame of terrorism mostly considers factors that best conform to the particular interpretation of events. A reverse approach is **critical media consciousness**. In this case, the audience understands the media and the manner in which stories are presented. An audience that is critically conscious does not accept, at face value, a story told or broadcast in a news frame. Such audience would attempt to learn the media's motives for presenting the story, how the story influenced social constructs and actions, and omitted facts that could make the story look different.[49]

Keeping the Audience Interested

Not all types of terrorism can be turned into equally good stories. Uninterrupted hijackings or hostage takings are more "interesting" than suicide bombings that leave journalists with mainly a messy pool of dead bodies.[50] Research has supplied evidence that, when covering incidents such as terrorist attacks, television news has a tendency to concentrate on stories about particular acts (leaving out related historical, economic, or social contexts) to keep the audience interested.[51] According to Altheide's (1987) content analysis of news coverage of terrorism,[52] there were three times as many episodic reports (e.g., repeatedly showing specific images such as planes crashing into buildings) as thematic reports (covering a terrorist incident as a whole by offering the big picture). Other content analyses have also found similar patterns in television news reports on terrorism.

Included in the television coverage of the September 11, 2001 attacks were the networks' 90-hour-plus ongoing coverage, the constant showing of horrific images and citizens' responses, and news anchors' regulated but clearly obvious displays of emotions as Americans. Television reporters hunting for information and reporting live from scenes such as Ground Zero and the Pentagon were working hard to relentlessly capture the attention of the audience as the events were unfolding. It was efficient, in part, because most of the verbal content of TV coverage was spoken "spontaneously" by emotionally struck individuals rather than written cautiously and thoroughly by print journalists. Accordingly, TV coverage turned out to be more episodic with obvious visual markers of actors and scenes. Coverage just became more interesting with respect to verbal expression.[53] Cameras also managed to expose the emotional reactions of journalists, news anchors, and show hosts who, as Americans, shared a communal sense of shock, grief, and anger. The appearance of Dan Rather in tears on *The Late Show* with David Letterman demonstrates how this can really happen, despite the fact that the national networks' coverage of 9/11 was acclaimed for being professional and emotionally restrained.[54]

Media–Military Collaboration

Now it is clear that the media do not merely report events; rather, the manner in which the media present crises becomes a crucial part of these crises. Occasionally, journalistic standard practices take the side of the military, due to an excessive dependence on the model of interpretation offered by security experts and military commentators. In the long run, such news functioning bolsters support for leaders and the security policies they put into effect. In times of conflict, the media and the military are mutually dependent to a great extent. The framing of media reporting shapes the military climate in which crises develop.[55]

Intelligence agencies that participate in Media Operations will generally pay journalists to provide a new angle to their stories or change them, for example, by including a certain fact or fabrication that the intelligence agency wants disseminated. Some intelligence agencies will actually bribe journalists to insert a particular headline and lead paragraph, and then have the journalist implant this press placement onto a totally unrelated story on which the journalists may be working. As such, there are instances of inflammatory headlines and lead paragraphs, but with the core of the story being grafted to a totally different topic, such as progress in medicine or the heritage of the pre–Columbian Olmec civilization. This sort of tactic operates on the principle that most readers only care for the headline and lead paragraph of the story, and then move on to the sports section or their horoscope. While it is a cynical approach, apparently it works.[56]

At the beginning of the War in Afghanistan, the U.S. media assisted the Pentagon in scripting the way in which the GWOT was to be waged. In fact, CNN chair Walter Isaacson was to tell his media personnel that exposing the desolation of Afghans would dangerously promote enemy propaganda.[57] Another anecdote to reflect on is the difference between surge and escalation when covering the Iraq War. In the beginning, the media employed the "surge" framing, suggesting a powerful brief, temporary increase in intensity of U.S. presence in Iraq. Again, the U.S. media simply agreed and became accommodating. However, as the Iraq War was dragging on, the growingly popular use of "escalation" in the media came with the increase in the number of U.S. troops in Iraq. This suggested that the U.S. military increased the scope of conflict in an aggressive way. It also inferred that the U.S. strategy was an enduring military presence in Iraq.[58]

Every single U.S. war since Vietnam—the Falklands (1982), Grenada (1983), Panama (1989), the Persian Gulf (1990), Somalia (1992–93), Haiti (1994), Bosnia (1992–95), Kosovo (1999), Timor (1999), Afghanistan (2001–present), and Iraq (2003–present)—has seen the military staff become gradually savvier agents of hegemonic forces. These agents became skilled not only at killing the enemy, but also at exploiting the media (especially television) as an instrumental tool of war.[59] Particularly during the 1990 Gulf War, the media became diplomatic signals and intelligence-gathering devices. Amazingly, the media humbly and submissively went along with this. The media were now a vehicle through which the military made straightforward approaches to audiences through the immediacy of television. Television became a tool of hegemony; a tool for making the use of violence against Iraq legitimate.

For the U.S. military, the 1990 Gulf War was very successful: they claimed Western hegemony over the Gulf region and created new networked (coalition) command structures. In addition, they successfully transformed the media into propaganda tools (by the deployment of PR/psy-ops) and outwardly convinced reporters to be coopted by the military.[60] Military PR staff guaranteed a stream of favorable military-created information. According to Young and Jesser (1997),[61] the purpose was "to fill the vacuum created by media restrictions. Material ranged from information provided at carefully controlled briefings which bypassed journalists on the spot, all the way to carefully sanitized television coverage of high technology weaponry in action" (p. 280).

Media–Government Collaboration

Soon after the September 11, 2001 terrorist attacks, a new interpretation of terrorism was quickly adopted in the White House as the main standard to frame friends and enemies worldwide. This interpretive frame was extended to explain and justify the George W. Bush administration's attack on the Taliban regime in Afghanistan, Saddam Hussein's Iraq, and Kim Jong-Il's North Korea. At the same time, the frame allowed the administration to warm up previously strained relations and form new international alliances, particularly with Russia, China, and Pakistan. This led U.S. journalists to develop narratives that framed a wide array of news on international security, civil wars, and global conflict.[62] Another example of such media–government collaboration is the switch from counterterrorism as law enforcement to counterterrorism as war. The preliminary response of the Bush administration to the September 11, 2001 terrorist attacks was to frame the tragedy as crime. Within hours, this framing was replaced by a war metaphor, giving rise to the GWOT. Most media organizations immediately followed suit. The difference between those two framings (i.e., law enforcement vs. war) lies in the inferred response. Crime implies bringing criminals to justice, putting them before a tribunal, and sentencing them. War, on the other hand, suggests enemy territory, military action, and more powers for the government.[63]

During the first George W. Bush administration, Baathist brutality—from the **Ba'ath Party**, a secularist political party with deep-seated socialist and Arab nationalist interests—enjoyed widespread coverage, while the killings in Fallujah received negligible coverage on U.S. news networks. Fallujah is an Iraqi city of 350,000 inhabitants that was destroyed in November 2004. Its survivors became IDPs (Internally Displaced People)—they were forced to escape as refugees in their own country. When Iraqi doctor Ali Fadhil went to the deserted town of Fallujah in December 2004, about a month after the most important U.S. military operation in occupied Iraq, to report to the British *Channel 4 News*, he discovered rotting bodies in empty homes all over town. The film *Fallujah, The Hidden Massacre* claimed that the U.S. army had committed war crimes in Fallujah, notably by using chemical weapons such as white phosphorus (which the White House had admitted to). At the same time, the media were practically silent on this.[64]

Following the September 11, 2001 terrorist attacks, members of the White House expressed worries about the media's impact on GWOT. Osama bin Laden's exploitation of the Al Jazeera network and the regular release of live and taped messages by his comrades also received attention from the Bush administration. At the invitation of Condoleeza Rice, national security advisor to President Bush, the major television stations and newspapers agreed not to air unedited reports or publish unedited texts of Osama bin Laden's speeches. By the same token, U.S. planes also bombarded the Al Jazeera TV station building in Kabul to thwart live telecast. While security concerns were used as justifications, the main reason was that unedited tapes or texts might include language inciting Muslim populations to take actions against Americans.[65] Afterward, Charlotte Beers, a Madison Avenue advertising agent, was appointed as the undersecretary of state for Public Diplomacy and Public

Affairs, with the explicit objective of fashioning a positive image of the United States and American values among young Muslims. As she said to a Congressional committee: "It's a battle for the 11-year-old mind."[66]

Frequent media reminders of the WTC terrorist attacks (e.g., monthly anniversaries, visits to the Ground Zero site by foreign leaders, and accounts of New Yorkers getting back to routine despite the terror threat) proved valuable to the Pentagon PR agenda by serving to uphold a culture of fear. These reminders were shown on most major networks. The constant replay of footage of the WTC explosions functions as useful symbols of terrorist evil. They became sufficiently justifiable for carpet-bombing Afghanistan, killing prisoners of war, and authorizing—in a November 13, 2001 military decree—the incarceration of Middle Eastern–looking males in the U.S. (and their trial by military tribunals if accused of harboring terrorism).[67]

A Clash of Civilizations in Media Framing of Terrorism

Who is to be held responsible for causing terrorist violence depends on the media located within specific cultures and how terrorism is framed. For example, while U.S. media reports often blame Palestinians (and their supporters) for the endless conflict between Arabs and Jews, non-Western media reports (e.g., Al Jazeera) often blame Israel and its supporters, especially the U.S.[68] An important consideration is the difference between Indonesian and Australian framing. In Indonesia (the world's largest Muslim country), media coverage of terrorism and Islam is significantly different from the way Australian media portray terrorists and Islamic groups—particularly Indonesian Muslims. While the frame of terrorism and Islamic groups in Australian media produces a hegemonic Orientalist image of Indonesian Muslims, Indonesian media framing of the same issues is more moderate, showing a different picture. The manner in which Australian media frame Islam cannot be equally compared with how the media in Indonesia construct Islam because of differences in cultural subjectivity in each society.[69]

Noam Chomsky (1991),[70] an American political activist and linguist, remarks that the U.S. bombings of Libya in the 1980s were calculatedly executed so they could be broadcast on network TV's evening news. This ensured that the White House's allegedly heroic response to terrorism would become appropriately timed, breaking news. While terrorists embrace mass-mediation to communicate their goals, the media are an establishment that regularly supports the prevailing perspective of terrorism. Thus, unlike reports shown on Al Jazeera, audiences in the U.S. can interpret mass-mediated images of 9/11 more as U.S. identity than human suffering. They can also view these images as threats to the nation and the heroic fight against such threats. Action flicks and other U.S. means of demonizing terrorism can be seen as clashing with the martyr videotapes (see Chapter 2) that Islamist terrorists create before committing suicide attacks.[71]

In the current context of mass-mediated images of terrorism, the global understanding of framing is increasingly important, especially since television news play a major part in constructing the conflict. The next section looks at one specific example of framing during the Palestinian–Israeli conflict: the Muhammad al-Durrah incident vs. the Vadim Norzich lynching. The objective is to analyze the power of the image.

FRAMING THE IMAGE: DURRAH VS. NORZICH

On September 30, 2000 (the second day of the Second Intifada), the Muhammad al-Durrah tragedy occurred in the Gaza Strip. While stuck in crossfire between Israelis and Palestinians, Muhammad, 12, and his father were being caught on camera by France 2 (a French television station). The boy was killed in his father's arms and became an icon of a martyr in the Muslim world. More than a decade after the tragedy, we can endorse the view that the Durrah image embodies the image of human calamity, the story that embraces the larger narrative of this blood-spattered, distant, and eternal conflict. The Netzarim junction, where he died, became a breaking point.[72] The Muhammad al-Durrah episode became another link in a chain of emblematic images that put historical events into the collective memory. Similar examples include the terrified Jewish child, his arms being raised, in a death camp; the naked nine-year-old girl running toward a photojournalist in Vietnam (her back was burning from napalm); or the Israeli soldier in the Six-Day War near the Western Wall in Jerusalem.[73]

The Palestinians drew attention to the Durrah incident and made it the most evocative icon of their suffering and the heartless cruelty of the Israeli military. As such, logos on websites displayed a collage of the last moments of Durrah with an Israeli man pointing a gun at his head. The dying episode was also repeatedly shown in lengthy excerpts on Arabic television channels featuring Durrah as the symbol of martyrdom. His photos were juxtaposed with tanks, funerals, and crying mothers. His pictures were also underscored by the sound of eulogies by popular singers, turning him into the cast for new heroes (in the form of suicide bombers). While there is no clear evidence proving that the Israeli army was responsible for killing Durrah, his image is here to stay. The Muhammad al-Durrah tragedy addresses the problem of news broadcasting on the basis of individual icons and on a method of selectivity that recycles identical stories.[74]

Two weeks after the killing of Muhammad al-Durrah, Vadim Norzich and a colleague—two reservists in IDF (Israel Defense Forces)—got lost in Ramallah and were apprehended by an angry crowd of Palestinians. Norzich and his colleague were beaten to death and hanged. This incident was granted far less media coverage by news networks across the world. The "Ramallah lynching" was hardly covered by American evening news programs on CNN, CBS, NBC, and ABC on October 12, 2000. Besides, the term *lynching* was not used in the reports of most American television news stations. Instead, the verbs *attack*, *killing*, and *murder* were used. Durrah's story, in contrast, became a journalistic exclusive worldwide. He had become Palestine's poster child for suffering.[75]

Many reasons account for the success of the Durrah image. First, his death was filmed live; it was caught by the eye of the camera. It was a coherent sequence of events, revealing, without the necessity for any words, the core of human calamity. This is a phenomenon called **photojournalism**, which refers to journalism that captures images in a timely manner to tell a news story.[76] Photojournalism has a few pluses over other types of reporting. To begin, images captured by the camera give the appearance of unmediated reality, unlike stories told by witnesses or accounts by studio anchors—these two, by definition, are mediated; they are not direct. Photojournalism, then, accords images the status of objectivity and presents a drama on the air; it creates immediate emotional involvement in the audience.

French philosopher Roland Barthes maintained that the direct connection of the camera to reality provides a greater guarantee of factualness, validity, and naturalness. However, as Barthes mentioned, this perception is also dangerous. All a photograph or camera does is frame: it selects a certain reality on which we should concentrate.[77]

Audiences worldwide watch images that have become symbols, recorded in some part of the globe. Most viewers are unaware of the framing process adopted by the media. This is the **power of the image**. Watching distant conflicts unfold in the form of personal agony speaks to the politics of empathy rather than the politics of justice. The politics of empathy, particularly when the depicted person is regarded as victim, can manage to find a middle ground with justice thanks to persuasive rhetoric. In accordance with the politics of empathy, the necessity to take urgent actions to end suffering defeats considerations of justice. Justice can enforce its rights only when suffering ceases to exist in the world.[78]

FRAMING FOR CENSORSHIP

During the George W. Bush administration, one important move was to censor information coming from satellite images. The media were particularly irritated by this move because censorship reduces the ability to report the news. **Censorship** is suppression of information believed to be offensive, sensitive, or threatening to the audience, a state, media outlets, or other controlling bodies.[79] Fifty-three percent of people surveyed in a Pew poll on November 29, 2001 (a few weeks after 9/11) agreed that the government should censor news that "it deems a threat to national security." The pollsters asked which of the two following statements mattered more: the government's power to censor or the media's power to report what was in the national interest. Four percent of respondents said that both were equally important. Sixty-one percent of respondents felt confident that the government was giving them an accurate picture about its war to terrorism, and 70% thought that national security and protection of U.S. military forces were the leading reasons for censorship.

Censorship is usually a method that governments use to address the problem of terrorism. Not only are general citizens' rights frequently a casualty of counterterrorism, but also the freedom of the press may be destroyed. Across the world, either media organizations are banned or censorship rules are imposed on media outlets the have been given permission to operate under a repressive regime. For example, in Uruguay, 41 newspapers were shut down and the media were even forbidden from using the word *Tupamaro*. The **Tupamaros** were a violent revolutionary organization in Uruguay in the 1960s and 1970s.[80] In Western Europe, various pro-PKK (Kurdish separatist group) media organizations have been closed after the Turkish state put pressure on them.[81]

Paul Wilkinson (2006)[82] believes that governments have three options when trying to maintain freedom of the press while fighting terrorism. A first option, the most welcome, is to adopt a **laissez-faire approach**, a hands-off attitude that assumes market forces will establish the norms. A second option is censorship: the government vetoes power over news reports. A third option is to let media organizations regulate themselves: journalists would behave more responsibly if they knew how to avoid serving terrorists while covering terrorist incidents.

Framing Reporters for Censorship

Griffin (2004)[83] analyzed the photo coverage of the Afghan War and the Iraq War on U.S. magazines. Overall, he found a wide array of predictable photographs that provided prompts for the dominant government version of events. These photographs rarely gave independent or new perspectives. Likewise, in a qualitative study by Kratzer and Kratzer (2003),[84] the data showed that photo editors had no authority whatsoever as to which 9/11 photographs to choose for print and which ones to choose to withhold.

During the war with Afghanistan in 2001, journalists were forced to remain in a warehouse so they could not cover one incident that involved a U.S. bombing raid hurting its own U.S. troops. The outbursts of indignation about the locking up of those journalists led the Department of Defense to issue a formal apology. New rules granted journalists greater access to the battlefronts. Nonetheless, many sites were still closed to reporters. As it had always been the case in the past, the courts took the side of the military in censorship disputes brought before them.[85] At the beginning of the Iraq War, Pentagon officials carefully chose and trained a pool of roughly 600 print and broadcast war correspondents. These journalists had to go through elementary military training to be fit to go along with their assigned units at all times. The journalists had to sign an agreement on the grounds that all stories and coverage had to be submitted to the military first, particularly stories and coverage deemed sensitive.[86]

Freedom of Information (FOI) Act

The **Freedom of Information (FOI) Act** is a law guaranteeing citizens to access governmental records. The FOI Act has not always been honored. Well-known examples of government secrecy are refusals to discuss war-related issues with journalists, concealing all information about individuals detained by the government, regulating reports about military actions in Afghanistan (e.g., only allowing reports by the secretary of defense and a few generals), and banning records of what the government knew before the September 11, 2001 terrorist attack (information that might have prevented it).[87] The Bush administration secured exclusive access to all satellite images of the U.S. bombing of Afghanistan (particularly images available from Ikonos, a civilian satellite). That acquisition prevented the media from seeing and broadcasting these high-resolution satellite images of destruction caused by U.S. attacks in Afghanistan. The decision to purchase those rights was taken immediately after reports on massive civilian casualties near Darunta (in Afghanistan) were published. Critics viewed it as heavy censorship and as a stealthy stratagem to hide terrifying scenes.[88]

Visual Determinism

The anecdote on the media coverage of the Madrid train bombings of 2004 (described in Box 5.1) symbolizes the idea of **visual determinism**, the notion that images often affect public opinion. It is a type of journalism that deletes or changes images to tell a news story.[89]

Box 5.1 Partial Photo Censorship of the Madrid Train Bombings

The **Madrid train bombings** were an organized series of 10 explosions on four passenger trains coming into Madrid (Spain) in the morning rush hour of March 11, 2004. The bombings were perpetrated by an Al-Qaeda–inspired group and killed almost 200 people and injured more than 1,800. A photo taken by Pablo Torres Guerrero of *El Pais* a few moments after the bombing made front pages around the world. *El Pais*, a Spanish daily newspaper, showed the huge photo unedited across the entire front page. However, editors elsewhere did not know what to do about a bloody severed arm that could be seen on the train tracks in the image.[90]

In London, the *Times*, the *Daily Telegraph*, the *Sun*, and the *Daily Mail* doctored the severed arm out and replaced it with stones. *The Guardian* turned the arm's color from red to grey, making it very difficult to identify. The *Independent* and the *Daily Mirror* circumvented the problem by printing the photo in black and white. As *The Guardian* noted, "for most of us the true awfulness of these scenes were edited out. Images, not words, were what the papers found so troubling." *The Digital Journalist*, the leading online magazine for photographers, was disgusted by the editing of Guerrero's photo. As an editorial said in its April edition, "[N]ewspapers are supposed to present the news in an honest context. This was a news photograph. It was not a photographic illustration. If the newspapers felt that the photograph might cause readers distress, they had the option of using another one. This is a massive breach of journalistic ethics. You may not 'clean up' a news photograph to suit your audience... If these newspapers are serious about credibility the editors who authorized this manipulation should be fired on the spot."

The *News Photographer*, published by the American National Press Photographers Association, also wrote, in an editorial about the editing of Guerrero's photo, "An image must establish the truth and context of a newsworthy moment. An altered image is a lie. We believe that the public is ill served when elements within the frame are reduced or removed in an attempt to soften the horror of the moment. If one unaltered image is too graphic for public consumption, find another. One must not alter a graphic image in an attempt to protect public sensibilities. Removing a bloody body part from a photograph sends the public an untrue and unfortunate message."

This anecdote also exemplifies the notion of visual gatekeeping. **Visual gatekeeping** is a series of decisions that are made to alter images as they move along the chain in news organizations. Shoemaker, Eichholz, Kim, and Wrigley (2001)[91] have defined the gatekeeping process as the "overall process through which the social reality transmitted by the news media is constructed" and "not just a series of in and out [italics added] decisions" (p. 233). In the context of the Madrid train bombings, censoring a victim's remains from a picture sends the message that a victim who was killed is anonymous. Removing someone's blood-soaked arm from a photo tells the audience that a victim who was killed is invisible. Casualties of terrorism must never be anonymous or invisible. Both visual determinism and visual gatekeeping are subjective.

In the same perspective, a **Nintendo war** is a media or government tactic whereby images of corpses, blood, and brutality are removed, and whereby neutral or euphemistic language is used to describe the events (e.g., *collateral damage* for *civilian deaths*). Nintendo war is the new digitized "smart weapons" war; it works efficiently thanks to various digitized communication techniques and technologies of removal. The beauty of Nintendo war is that it makes war appear spotless and bloodless. During the Vietnam War, however, and before the advent of state-of-the-art technology, carpet bombing performed by high-altitude aircrafts could not be "clean" or edited. The reality of horror was also visually clear with photos of bloody ground combat.[92]

ARGUMENTS FOR AND AGAINST CENSORING MEDIA COVERAGE OF TERRORISM

So far, we know that a major terrorist act will garner much publicity. The dilemma for the government is to figure out how to minimize publicity for terrorists without causing them to commit increasingly devastating attacks so they can get publicity. Research to explain the relationships between media and government policies, on the one hand, and the increase of terrorism, on the other, is certainly needed. Considering that terrorists become enraged when ignored, one valuable line of research would be to find out what arguments favor the censorship of media coverage of terrorism and what arguments oppose it. Schmid and de Graaf (1982)[93] developed a list of arguments for and against censoring media coverage of terrorism. The two scholars were inspired by certain events that unfolded during the Vietnam War. From the Vietnam War onward, the U.S. government has become more and more concerned about television's impact on conducting war operations. In a nutshell, war has been greatly mediatized and PR-ized.[94] Arguments for and against censoring media coverage of terrorist events, including statements released by terrorists (e.g., Osama bin Laden's tapes), are summarized below:

Arguments for Censorship

1. Terrorists exploit the media for propaganda purposes, thereby helping recruit new supporters.

2. Publicity is a key objective of terrorism.

3. Detailed reporting of terrorist incidents inspires future terrorists to commit similar actions.

4. Reporting terrorist acts can lead to imitation among ordinary citizens.

5. Describing terrorist acts might encourage sadism in some members of the audience.

6. Information broadcast during an incident can be helpful for the terrorists involved.

7. Media intrusion can put hostages in danger.

8. Media reports may unnerve or frighten kidnappers and push them to kill their victims.

9. Terrorists are people with no respect for others' lives. Therefore, they should not be allowed to draw public attention by using violence.

10. Reporting terrorist atrocities might trigger vigilantism and avenge attacks on the group to which the terrorists claim to belong.

11. News on terrorism is negative and demoralizing.

Arguments against Censorship

1. Not reporting terrorist attacks might lead people to be less critical of terrorists (i.e., showing more sympathy toward them).

2. Publicity can be a substitute for violence.

3. Censorship might cause terrorists to increase the level of violence.

4. Not reporting terrorist events would promote rumors, which might be worse.

5. Media presence can help prevent the police from taking actions. These actions would cause unnecessary deaths among both terrorists and victims.

6. Censorship allows officials to brand any dissidents as terrorists, thereby weakening legal safeguards.

7. Media credibility would decrease.

8. Lack of news might lead to a false sense of security, leaving the public unprepared to cope with terrorist attacks.

9. Lack of awareness would prevent the audience from understanding the political situation.

10. Feeling deprived of information might raise public distrust of the government.

11. Terrorists' claims that democracies do not really have freedom (i.e., of the press) would get more credibility.

Again, the main reason for developing such a list of arguments in favor or against the censorship of "inconvenient" footage and reporting came from the Vietnam War. The U.S. government believed it learned two lessons from Vietnam. First, if an antiwar consciousness rises among U.S. citizens, the war will not be won because political pressure will eventually end the war. Second, television broadcasts have the power to endorse an antiwar consciousness and upset the legitimacy of using force (even the legitimacy of the authorities).[95] The U.S. military blamed television for losing the Vietnam War because television could not deal with the complexity of war. In actual fact, the immediacy of television images left the audience with negative impressions and emotions. In his memoirs, William Westmoreland, the leading U.S. general during the Vietnam War, insisted that he wanted to block the visually dramatic, violent, and depressing news coverage of the war.[96]

FRAMING THE MEDIA AS JANUS-FACED MEANS

By definition, **Janus-faced** means two-faced. In Roman mythology, Janus was the god of gates, beginnings, endings, and time. He is described as having two faces, each looking in opposite directions. One face looks back at the past while the other looks forward to the future; in other words, both faces look simultaneously into the future and the past. For example, a Janus-faced company is a two-faced company with both formal corporate ethics guidelines and a string of giant scandals.[97] The same principle can be applied to the media. By framing the media, media organizations or the government can censor news or structure information to their advantage. The purpose is to manipulate the audience or use the media as, said Louw (2003),[98] "an avenue for diplomatic signals and intelligence gathering" (p. 219).

Janus-faced strategies of censorship were used during the 1990 Gulf War. As soon as military deployment began, media reporting was strategically controlled. Reporters were grouped into "pools" far detached from the battlefront. In these pools, the military PR was to feed reporters information. Pool reporters were only allowed to observe events that were heavily controlled. Censorship was done through denial of access to military combat. News was blacked out at the beginning of the war. All interviews had to be done in the presence of soldiers, and all recording, transcripts, and images had to be cleared by the military before transmission.[99] Journalists' general impression of the Gulf War was a bloody, unclean, and messy war. Yet, the powers that be decided that this would not be known to happen. In addition, military PR used aerial combat to create, as Franklin (1994)[100] stated, "the impression of a 'clean' techno-war, almost devoid of human suffering and death, conducted with surgical precision by wondrous mechanisms" (p. 42). This is the epitome of a Janus-faced establishment. It is two-faced.

Later, during the Afghan War, television images of aerial bombers and the distant wafting of smoke and dust caused by massive bombings became the main signature of the U.S. in the Afghan War. No civilian bodies and no blood were to be shown. In addition, no images of the destruction caused by the cluster or carpet bombings, and no unhappy locals inside Afghanistan, were to be shown on television. Certainly, the objective was to generate and transmit good televisual images to keep global audiences public "on-side."[101] This is the same old idea of framing: to focus on the public, not the state, so that the audience remembers the terrorist as bad and the U.S. as good. In democracies that have freedom of the press, elected officials will try to please audiences to maintain power. As Jean Baudrillard (1983)[102] remarked, the models of mediated reality that give rise to these feelings are "without origin or reality" (p. 2). Much media framing of terrorism embodies a false consciousness within the general public and may be conceptualized as representing self-motivated agendas formed by authorities.[103]

SUMMARY

This chapter explains how terrorism can be framed by the media and to what extent conventional frames about terrorism can influence public opinion. Framing is the process by which a media source describes and creates a political issue or public controversy. The objective is to offer a comprehensible interpretation and evaluation of events. Put simply, framing is a selection process to determine what news should be reported or ignored. Framing, in essence, gives priority to facts, images, or developments over others. Unlike framing, agenda-setting theory postulates that the more the media cover certain issues, the more salient (i.e., noticeable, accessible, and significant) these issues become for the audience. In regard to terrorism, media interpretations have become one-sided: in the mass media, terrorism has increasingly come to refer to acts associated with agents and supporters of foreign-based terrorist movements such as Al Qaeda, rather than with the violence of home-grown activists and radicals who belong to groups such as the Animal Liberation Front. Likewise, after 9/11, the U.S. media frequently associated words like *bin Laden*, *Palestinian*, *Taliban*, and *Islamic* to words like *terrorist* and *attack*. An important corollary is that the audience becomes a sound-bited audience being fed information by the conventional news frame of terrorism. On Arabic television, framing also occurs. For instance, the Muhammad al-Durrah killing in 2000 became an emblematic image that put a possibly fabricated historical event into the collective memory of the Palestinian people. As French philosopher Roland Barthes argued, all a camera does is frame: it selects a certain reality on which we should concentrate. Also part of the framing strategy is censorship: suppression of information believed to be threatening to the state or the audience. For example, in the Afghan War, there have been instances of military-imposed censorship on reporters. A practical example of censorship is visual determinism, a form of journalism that deletes or changes images to tell a news story (e.g., the editing of the main photo of the Madrid train bombings). An important conclusion of this chapter is that media organizations engaging in framing are Janus-faced (i.e., two-faced) organizations. They would rather focus on the public, not the state, so that the audience can remember the terrorist as bad and the U.S. as good.

KEY TERMS

action framing   115

agenda-setting theory   113

attribute framing   114

censorship   125

choice framing   115

cognitive functions   118

critical media consciousness   120

episodic frames   115

evaluative functions   118

fairness doctrine   119

frame   111

framing   111

Freedom of Information Act   126

issue framing   115

Janus-faced   130

laissez-faire approach   125

ENDNOTES

1. Nelson, Thomas E., Oxley, Zoe, & Clawson, Rosalee A. (1997). Toward a Psychology of Framing Effects. *Political Behavior, 19*(3), 221–246.

2. Entman, Robert M. (1993). Framing: Toward Clarification of a Fractured Paradigm. *Journal of Communication, 43*(4), 51–58; Kruse, Cowin R. (2001). The Movement and the Media: Framing the Debate over Animal Experimentation. *Political Communication, 18*(1), 67–89.

3. Cohen, Bernard (1963). *The Press and Foreign Policy*. Princeton, NJ: Princeton University Press.

4. Entman, Robert M., Matthes, Jorg, & Pellicano, Lynn (2008). Nature, Sources and Effects of News Framing. In Karin Wahl-Jorgensen & Thomas Hanitzsch (Eds.), *Handbook of Journalism Studies* (pp. 175–190). Mahwah: Erlbaum.

5. Norris, Pippa, Kern, Montague, & Just, Marion (2003). Framing Terrorism. In Pippa Norris, Montague Kern, & Marion Just (Eds.), *Framing Terrorism: The News Media, the Government, and the Public* (pp. 3–21). New York: Routledge.

6. Cottle, Simon (2006). *Mediatized Conflicts*. Boston: McGraw-Hill.

7. Fairhurst, Gail, & Star, Robert (1996). *The Art of Framing*. San Francisco: Jossey-Bass.

8. Hoskins, Andrew (2006). Temporality, Proximity and Security: Terror in a Media-Drenched Age. *International Relations, 20*(4), 453–466.

9. Picard, Robert P. (1993). *Media Portrayals of Terrorism: Functions and Meaning of News Coverage*. Iowa City: Iowa State University Press.

10. Hoskins, Andrew (2006). Temporality, Proximity and Security: Terror in a Media-Drenched Age. *International Relations, 20*(4), 453–466.

11. Edy, Jill A., & Meirick, Patrick C. (2007). Wanted, Dead or Alive: Media Frames, Frame Adoption, and Support for the War in Afghanistan. *Journal of Communication, 57*, 119–141.

12. McCombs, Maxwell, Shaw, Donald L., & Weaver, David (1997). *Communication and Democracy: Exploring the Intellectual Frontiers in Agenda-Setting Theory*. Mahwah, NJ: Lawrence Erlbaum.

13. McCombs, Maxwell, & Shaw, Donald (1972). The Agenda-Setting Function of Mass Media. *Public Opinion Quarterly, 36*, 176–187.

14. Hastie, Reid, & Park, Bernadette (1986). The Relationship between Memory and Judgment Depends on whether the Task Is Memory-Based or On-Line. *Psychological Review, 93*, 258–268.

15. Kiousis, Spiro (2004). Explicating Media Salience: A Factor Analysis of New York Times Issue Coverage during the 2000 U.S. Presidential Election. *Journal of Communication, 54*, 71–87.

16.   McCombs, Maxwell (2004). *Setting the Agenda: The Mass Media and Public Opinion.* Malden, MA: Blackwell Publishing.

17.   Snow, David A., Benford, Robert D., Worden, Steven K., & Rochford, E. Burke (1986). Frame Alignment Processes, Micromobilization, and Movement Participation. *American Sociological Review, 51,* 464–481.

18.   Entman, Robert M. (1993). Framing: Toward Clarification of a Fractured Paradigm. *Journal of Communication, 43,* 51–58.

19.   Entman, Robert M. (2003). Cascading Activation: Contesting the White House's Frame after 9/11. *Political Communication, 20,* 415–432.

20.   Zeidenstein, Harvey G. (1984). News Media Perceptions of White House News Management. *Presidential Studies Quarterly, 14*(3), 391–398.

21.   Grabosky, Peter, & Stohl, Michael (2010). *Crime and Terrorism.* Los Angeles: Sage.

22.   Bowen, Shannon A. (2008). Frames of Terrorism Provided by the News Media and Potential Communication Responses. In Dan O'Hair, Robert Heath, Kevin Ayotte, & Gerald R. Ledlow (Eds.), *Terrorism: Communication and Rhetorical Perspectives* (pp. 337–358). Cresskill, NJ: Hampton Press.

23.   Reese, Stephen D. (2003). *Framing Public Life.* Mahwah, NJ: Lawrence Erlbaum Associates; Shanto, Iyengar (1994). *Is Anyone Responsible? How Television Frames Political Issues.* Chicago: University of Chicago Press.

24.   Sparks, Lisa (2005). Social Identity and Perceptions of Terrorist Groups: How Others See Them and How They See Themselves. In H. Dan O'Hair, Robert L. Heath, & Gerald R. Ledlow (Eds.), *Community Preparedness and Response to Terrorism: Communication and the Media* (pp. 13–28). Westport, CT: Praeger.

25.   Altheide, David L., & Snow, Robert P. (1991). *Media Worlds in the Postjournalism Era.* New York: Aldine de Cruyter; Sartori, Giovanni (2007). *Homo videns: Televisione e post-pensiero.* Roma: Laterza; Soriano, Manuel T. Torres (2008). Terrorism and the Mass Media after Al Qaeda: A Change of Course? *Athena Intelligence Journal, 3*(1), 1–20.

26.   Schudson, Michael (2002). What's Unusual about Covering Politics as Usual. In Barbara Zelizer & Stuart Allan (Eds.), *Journalism after September 11* (pp. 36–47). London: Routledge.

27.   Iyengar, Shanto (1991). *Is Anyone Responsible? How Television Frames Political Issues.* Chicago: University of Chicago Press; Jacobs, Ronald N. (1996). Producing the News, Producing the Crisis: Narrativity, Television and News Work. *Media, Culture & Society, 18,* 373–397; Zelizer, Barbara (1992). CNN, the Gulf War, and Journalistic Practice. *Journal of Communication, 42*(1), 66–81.

28.   McLuhan, Marshall (1964). *Understanding Media: The Extensions of Man.* Cambridge, MA: MIT Press.

29.   Meyrowitz, Joshua (1985). *No Sense of Place.* New York: Oxford University Press.

30.   Cho, Jaeho , Boyle, Michael P. , Keum, Heejo , Shevy, Mark D. , McLeod, Douglas M. , Shah, Dhavan V. & Pan, Zhongdang (2003). Media, Terrorism, and Emotionality: Emotional Differences in Media Content and Public Reactions to the September 11th Terrorist Attacks. *Journal of Broadcasting & Electronic Media, 47*(3), 309–327.

31.   Lombard, Matthew, & Ditton, Theresa (1997). At the Heart of It All: The Concept of Presence. *Journal of Computer-Mediated Communication, 3*(2).

32.   Reeves, Byron, & Nass, Clifford (1996). *The Media Equation: How People Treat Computers, Television, and New Media Like Real People and Places.* New York: Cambridge University Press.

33.   Roeh, Itzhak (1989). Journalism as Storytelling, Coverage as Narrative. *American Behavioral Scientist, 33*(2), 162–168.

34.   Ball-Rokeach, Sandra I., & DeFleur, Melvin L. (1976). A Dependency Model of Mass-Media Effects. *Communication Research, 3,* 3–21.

35.   Cho, Jaeho , Boyle, Michael P. , Keum, Heejo , Shevy, Mark D. , McLeod, Douglas M. , Shah, Dhavan V., & Pan, Zhongdang (2003). Media, Terrorism, and Emotionality: Emotional Differences in Media Content and Public Reactions to the September 11th Terrorist Attacks. *Journal of Broadcasting & Electronic Media, 47*(3), 309–327.

36.   Turk, Austin T. (2002). Assassination. In Joshua Dressler (Ed.), *Encyclopedia of Crime and Justice* (pp. 776–781). New York: Macmillan; Turk, Austin T. (2004). Sociology of Terrorism. *Annual Review of Sociology, 30,* 271–286.

37. Norris, Pippa, Kern, Montague, & Just, Marion (2003). Framing Terrorism. In Pippa Norris, Montague Kern, & Marion Just (Eds.), *Framing Terrorism: The News Media, the Government, and the Public* (pp. 3–21). New York: Routledge.

38. Norris, Pippa, Kern, Montague, & Just, Marion (2003). Framing Terrorism. In Pippa Norris, Montague Kern, & Marion Just (Eds.), *Framing Terrorism: The News Media, the Government, and the Public* (pp. 3–21). New York: Routledge.

39. Norris, Pippa, Kern, Montague, & Just, Marion (2003). Framing Terrorism. In Pippa Norris, Montague Kern, & Marion Just (Eds.), *Framing Terrorism: The News Media, the Government, and the Public* (pp. 3–21). New York: Routledge.

40. Lakos, Amos (1986). *International Terrorism: A Bibliography*. Boulder, CO: Westview Press.

41. Turk, Austin T. (2004). Sociology of Terrorism. *Annual Review of Sociology, 30*, 271–286.

42. Persson, Anna V., & Musher-Eizenman, Dara R. (2005). College Students' Attitudes Toward Blacks and Arabs Following a Terrorist Attack as a Function of Varying Levels of Media Exposure. *Journal of Applied Social Psychology, 35*(9), 1879–1893.

43. *President George W. Bush. Address to Congress* (2001, September 20). Washington, D.C.: U.S. Congress.

44. Norris, Pippa, Kern, Montague, & Just, Marion (2003). Framing Terrorism. In Pippa Norris, Montague Kern, & Marion Just (Eds.), *Framing Terrorism: The News Media, the Government, and the Public* (pp. 3–21). New York: Routledge.

45. Norris, Pippa, Kern, Montague, & Just, Marion (2003). Framing Terrorism. In Pippa Norris, Montague Kern, & Marion Just (Eds.), *Framing Terrorism: The News Media, the Government, and the Public* (pp. 3–21). New York: Routledge.

46. Wilkinson, Tracy (2005, December 24). Court Widens Net for 22 CIA Agents to EU; Italian Prosecutors Seek to Try the Operatives in the 2003 Abduction of an Imam on a Milan Street. The Warrants Expand the Hunt to 25 Nations. *The Los Angeles Times*, p. 3; Williamson, Hugh (2006, September 22). Germany Pressed to Arrest CIA Team. *The Financial Times*, p. 11.

47. Cohen, Akiba A., & Wolfsfeld, Gafi (1993). *Framing the Intifada: People and Media*. Norwood, NJ: Ablex Publishing.

48. Norris, Pippa, Kern, Montague, & Just, Marion (2003). Framing Terrorism. In Pippa Norris, Montague Kern, & Marion Just (Eds.), *Framing Terrorism: The News Media, the Government, and the Public* (pp. 3–21). New York: Routledge.

49. White, Jonathan R. (2011). *Terrorism & Homeland Security* (7th ed.). Belmont, CA: Wadsworth.

50. Liebes, Tamar, & First, Anat (2003). Framing the Palestinian-Israeli Conflict. In Pippa Norris, Montague Kern, & Marion Just (Eds.), *Framing Terrorism: The News Media, the Government, and the Public* (pp. 59–74). New York: Routledge.

51. Ansolabehere, Stephen, Behr, Roy, & Iyengar, Shanto (1993). *The Media Game: American Politics in the Television Age*. New York: Macmillan; Carey, James W. (2002). American Journalism on, before, and after September 11. In Barbara Zelizer & Stuart Allan (Eds.), *Journalism after September 11* (pp. 71–90). London: Routledge.

52. Altheide, David L. (1987). Format and Symbol in Television Coverage of Terrorism in the United States and Great Britain. *International Studies Quarterly, 31*, 161–176.

53. Cho, Jaeho, Boyle, Michael P., Keum, Heejo, Shevy, Mark D., McLeod, Douglas M., Shah, Dhavan V., & Pan, Zhongdang (2003). Media, Terrorism, and Emotionality: Emotional Differences in Media Content and Public Reactions to the September 11th Terrorist Attacks. *Journal of Broadcasting & Electronic Media, 47*(3), 309–327.

54. Carey, James W. (2002). American Journalism on, before, and after September 11. In Barbara Zelizer & Stuart Allan (Eds.), *Journalism after September 11* (pp. 71–90). London: Routledge.

55. Brown, Robin (2003). Clausewitz in the Age of CNN: Rethinking the Military-Media Relationship. In Pippa Norris, Montague Kern, & Marion Just (Eds.), *Framing Terrorism: The News Media, the Government, and the Public* (pp. 43–58). New York: Routledge.

56. Reese, Stephen D. (2003). *Framing Public Life*. Mahwah, NJ: Lawrence Erlbaum Associates; Shanto, Iyengar (1994). *Is Anyone Responsible? How Television Frames Political Issues*. Chicago: University of Chicago Press.

57. Louw, P. Eric (2003). The "War against Terrorism": A Public Relations Challenge for the Pentagon. *Gazette: The International Journal for Communication Studies, 65*(3), 211–230.

58. Dreazen, Yochi J. (2006, December 25). Surge or Escalation in Iraq? *The Wall Street Journal.* p. A1.

59. Louw, P. Eric (2003). The "War against Terrorism": A Public Relations Challenge for the Pentagon. *Gazette: The International Journal for Communication Studies, 65*(3), 211–230.

60. MacArthur, John R. (1992). *Second Front: Censorship and Propaganda in the Gulf War.* New York: Hill and Wang.

61. Young, Peter R., & Jesser, Peter (1997). *The Media and the Military.* Melbourne: Macmillan.

62. Norris, Pippa, Kern, Montague, & Just, Marion (2003). Framing Terrorism. In Pippa Norris, Montague Kern, & Marion Just (Eds.), *Framing Terrorism: The News Media, the Government, and the Public* (pp. 3–21). New York: Routledge.

63. Lakoff, George (2004). *Don't Think of an Elephant! Know Your Values and Frame the Debate.* White River Jct., VT: Chelsea Green Publishing, p. 56; Zhang, Juyan (2007). Beyond Anti-Terrorism: Metaphors as Message Strategy of Post-September-11 U.S. Public Diplomacy. *Public Relations Review, 33*(1), 31–39.

64. Channel 4 (2005, January 11). Special Report on Fallujah. *Channel 4 News*; Monbiot, George (2005, December 22). Behind the Phosphorus Clouds Are War Crimes within War Crimes. *The Guardian*, p. A1; Thussu, Daya Kishan (2006). Televising the "War on Terrorism": The Myths of Morality. In Anandam P., Kavoori, & Todd Fraley (Eds.), *Media, Terrorism, and Theory* (pp. 3–18). New York: Rowman & Littlefield.

65. Carter, Bill, & Barringer, Felicity (2001, October 11). A Nation Challenged: The Coverage; Networks Agree to U.S. Request to Edit Future bin Laden Tapes. *The New York Times*, p. A12.

66. Reidy, Chris (2001, November 8). Hearts and Minds Madison Avenue Guru Aims to Discredit bin Laden with Ads Pitching US, Freedom to Young Muslims. *Boston Globe*, p. C1.

67. Louw, P. Eric (2003). The "War against Terrorism": A Public Relations Challenge for the Pentagon. *Gazette: The International Journal for Communication Studies, 65*(3), 211–230.

68. Turk, Austin T. (2004). Sociology of Terrorism. *Annual Review of Sociology, 30*, 271–286.

69. Mahony, Inez (2010). Diverging Frames: A Comparison of Indonesian and Australian Press Portrayals of Terrorism and Islamic Groups in Indonesia. *International Communication Gazette, 72*(8) 739–758.

70. Chomsky, Noam (1991). *Pirates and Emperors: International Terrorism in the Real World.* Montreal: Black Rose Books.

71. Meeuf, Russell (2006). Collateral Damage: Terrorism, Melodrama, and the Action Film on the Eve of 9/11. *Jump Cut, 48*, 10–21.

72. Moeller, Susan D. (2002). A Hierarchy of Innocence: The Media's Use of Children in the Telling of International News. *The International Journal of Press/Politics, 7*(1), 36–56.

73. Liebes, Tamar, & First, Anat (2003). Framing the Palestinian-Israeli Conflict. In Pippa Norris, Montague Kern, & Marion Just (Eds.), *Framing Terrorism: The News Media, the Government, and the Public* (pp. 59–74). New York: Routledge.

74. Orbach, Benjamin (2001). Usama bin Ladin and Al-Qa'ida: Origins and Doctrines. *Middle East Review of International Affairs, 5*(4), 54–68.

75. Liebes, Tamar, & First, Anat (2003). Framing the Palestinian–Israeli Conflict. In Pippa Norris, Montague Kern, & Marion Just (Eds.), *Framing Terrorism: The News Media, the Government, and the Public* (pp. 59–74). New York: Routledge.

76. Becker, Howard S. (1995). Visual Sociology, Documentary Photography, and Photojournalism: It's (Almost) All a Matter of Context. *Visual Studies, 10*(1), 5–14.

77. Barthes, Roland (1980). *La chambre claire.* Paris: Edition de l'Etoile, Gallimard.

78. Boltanski, Luc (1999). *Distant Suffering: Morality, Media and Politics.* Cambridge: Cambridge University Press; Liebes, Tamar, & First, Anat (2003). Framing the Palestinian-Israeli Conflict. In Pippa Norris, Montague Kern, & Marion Just (Eds.), *Framing Terrorism: The News Media, the Government, and the Public* (pp. 59–74). New York: Routledge.

79. Graber, Doris A. (2003). Terrorism, Censorship, and the 1st Amendment: In Search of Policy Guidelines. In Pippa Norris, Montague Kern, & Marion Just (Eds.), *Framing Terrorism: The News Media, the Government, and the Public* (pp. 27–42). New York: Routledge.

80. Hewitt, Christopher (1984). *The Effectiveness of Anti-Terrorist Polices*. Lanham, MD: University Press of America.

81. Afghanistan's Drug Trade and How it Funds Taliban Operations (2007). *Jamestown Monitor, 5*(9), p. A1.

82. Wilkinson, Paul (2006). *Terrorism versus Democracy*. New York: Routledge.

83. Griffin, Michael (2004). Picturing America's "War on Terrorism" in Afghanistan and Iraq: Photographic Motifs as News Frames. *Journalism, 5*, 381–402.

84. Kratzer, Renee Martin, & Kratzer, Brian (2003). How Newspapers Decided to Run Disturbing 9/11 Photos. *Newspaper Research Journal, 24*(1), 34–47.

85. *Flynt v. Rumsfeld*. Civ. No. 01 = 2399, DDC, Jan.8, 2002.

86. Graber, Doris A. (2003). Terrorism, Censorship, and the 1st Amendment: In Search of Policy Guidelines. In Pippa Norris, Montague Kern, & Marion Just (Eds.), *Framing Terrorism: The News Media, the Government, and the Public* (pp. 27–42). New York: Routledge.

87. Steinhauer, Jennifer (2002, July 23). Records of 9/11 Response not for Public, City Says. *The New York Times*, p. A1.

88. Graber, Doris A. (2003). Terrorism, Censorship, and the 1st Amendment: In Search of Policy Guidelines. In Pippa Norris, Montague Kern, & Marion Just (Eds.), *Framing Terrorism: The News Media, the Government, and the Public* (pp. 27–42). New York: Routledge.

89. Schwalbe, Carol B., Silcock, B. William, & Keith, Susan (2008). Visual Framing of the Early Weeks of the U.S.-Led Invasion of Iraq: Applying the Master War Narrative to Electronic and Print Images. *Journal of Broadcasting & Electronic Media, 52*(3), 448–465.

90. Moeller, Susan D. (2009). *Packaging Terrorism: Co-Opting the News for Politics and Profit*. New York: Wiley-Blackwell.

91. Shoemaker, Pamela J., Eichholz, Martin, Kim, Eunyi, & Wrigley, Brenda (2001). Individual and Routine Forces in Gatekeeping. *Journalism & Mass Communication Quarterly, 7*, 233–246.

92. Louw, P. Eric (2003). The "War against Terrorism": A Public Relations Challenge for the Pentagon. *Gazette: The International Journal for Communication Studies, 65*(3), 211–230.

93. Schmid, Alex P., & de Graaf, Janny (1982). *Violence as Communication: Insurgent Terrorism and the Western News Media*. Beverly Hills, CA: Sage.

94. Louw, P. Eric (2001). *The Media and Cultural Production*. London: Sage.

95. Young, Peter R., & Jesser, Peter (1997). *The Media and the Military*. Melbourne: Macmillan.

96. MacArthur, John R. (1992). *Second Front: Censorship and Propaganda in the Gulf War*. New York: Hill and Wang; Westmoreland, William C. (1976). *A Soldier Reports*. Garden City: Doubleday.

97. Taylor, Rabun (2000). Watching the Skies: Janus, Auspication, and the Shrine in the Roman Forum. *Memoirs of the American Academy in Rome, 45*, p. 1.

98. Louw, P. Eric (2003). The "War against Terrorism": A Public Relations Challenge for the Pentagon. *Gazette: The International Journal for Communication Studies, 65*(3), 211–230.

99. Louw, P. Eric (2003). The "War against Terrorism": A Public Relations Challenge for the Pentagon. *Gazette: The International Journal for Communication Studies, 65*(3), 211–230.

100. Franklin, H. Bruce (1994). From Realism to Virtual Reality: Images of America's Wars. In Susan Jeffords & Lauren Rabinovitz (Eds.), *Seeing through the Media* (pp. 25–43). New Brunswick, NJ: Rutgers University Press.

101. Louw, P. Eric (2003). The "War against Terrorism": A Public Relations Challenge for the Pentagon. *Gazette: The International Journal for Communication Studies, 65*(3), 211–230.

102. Baudrillard, Jean (1983). *Simulations*. New York: Semiotext(e).

103. Herman, Edward S., & Chomsky, Noam (1988). *Manufacturing Consent: The Political Economy of the Mass Media*. New York: Pantheon; Scott, John L. (2001). Media Congestion Limits Media Terrorism. *Defence and Peace Economics, 12*(3), 215–227.

Terrorism as Social Construction of Reality

After reading this chapter, you will be able to

- discuss the social construction of terrorism and the ideology of the language of terrorism;
- describe cultural programming and the formation of a cultural worldview; and
- explain how culture plays a key role in the way terrorism is perceived.

SOCIAL CONSTRUCTION OF REALITY: DEFINITION

Terrorism is a social construct; it is defined by various individuals within social and political realities. **Social construct** refers to the way people perceive reality. Societies construct a reality around a concept, determining many aspects of their lives through the meanings they give to the construct.[1] To this effect, Peter Berger and Thomas Luckmann (1966)[2] coined the term *social construction of reality*. The main idea of **social construction of reality** is that humans who interact in society create, over time, **concepts** (mental representations) of the world around them. Ultimately, these concepts become cast into reciprocal roles played by people in relation to each other. When these roles become accessible by other members of society to assume and play out, the reciprocal interactions become institutionalized. In the course of this **institutionalization**, meaning gets implanted in society. Knowledge and people's conception of reality become entrenched in the institutional fabric of society. Hence, social reality is said to be socially constructed.

The social construction of reality gives rise to the notion of consensus reality. **Consensus reality** is a method for answering the question "What is real?" It gives a "realistic" answer: reality is what we agree on through consensus. The difficult part of the question lies in the concern that people do not in fact completely understand or come to an agreement on the nature of knowledge or knowing. Consequently, it is impossible to be certain, beyond doubt, about what is real.[3] The definition of any social construct varies with the social reality of the community that created the definition—depending on the time and location of the community. The social construction of reality can be unclear, or it can be menacing when one society enforces its version of reality on another. The audience's perceptions of the September 11, 2001 terrorist attacks were, to a great extent, socially constructed. The social construction of 9/11 was based on the impact that social relations had on the existing perception of reality. Today, these perceptions might have changed for some communities—based on rumors or true facts. The main emphasis of the social construction of reality is on discourse as a vehicle for constructing the self and society, and on how discourse functions and influences social relations. Social construction, then, is conscious and occurs in the context of a discourse-based systematic relationship within society and vis-à-vis the external world.[4]

The creation of meaning for a particular concept is rooted in a social context. Groups set boundaries around their experiences and perceptions, and they define issues within these boundaries. **Meaning frameworks** are the social boundaries that surround those definitions.[5] Juergensmeyer (2003)[6] considers the conflict between modern and traditional values as a principal reason for terrorism. Religious terrorists observe the modern world and want to eliminate it. In the meaning framework of religious terrorists, it is an evil world; they reject the boundaries set by the modern world. From this vantage point, extermination will be seen as a victory by those who kill, but it will be interpreted as despicable, unjust, and incomprehensible by those who have lost a loved one.[7] The social construction of reality contributes to an ideology. As defined by Stuart Hall (1996),[8] ideology refers to "the mental frameworks—the languages, the concepts, categories, imagery of thought, and the systems of representation—which different classes and social groups deploy in order to make sense of, figure out and render intelligible the way society works" (p. 26).

TERRORISM, LANGUAGE, AND CO-CONSTRUCTION OF REALITY

Language is essential to the social construction of reality because it is the basis for the symbolic narratives that help people, groups, and systems understand and uphold the social order. It also helps restore balance and certainty when institutions falter.[9] Language connects commonsense knowledge with determinate spheres of meaning, thus allowing people, for instance, to interpret dreams through understandings related to the daytime. **Language** is conversation or communication aimed at maintaining reality in the subjective world.[10] Language represents an integral tool that results in changes to the world and social practice, and at the same time is established by social practices. Thus, language both shapes social structures and is shaped by them.[11]

Discourse

Social reality is created through news reports by linking up words with specific problems and issues. Frequent use of these words constructs public discourse.[12] **Discourse** refers to a socially constructed method for representing the world—the procedures, relations, and organizations of the material world, the social world, and the mental world of ideas, feelings, and principles. Discourses serve to identify the main themes of the world from a society's point of view. They are not loosely employed but are determined by certain conventions. Discourses are bound by the rules as to what can be written, said, or done. This is how discourses are enacted by groups of people. Yet, the degree to which they are repeated within society varies considerably, which creates a hierarchy of discourses. For example, the discourse on terrorism in the U.S. is greatly dominated by its association with Islam. In fact, it is described as one of the predominant discourses on the social scene. Discourses are ideological; they are used to maintain hegemony of the elite or the powers that be, or provinces. Ideologies represent some aspects of the world and can contribute to creating, maintaining, and altering social relations of power. Social agents who construct discourse are also bound by a consensus reality in regard to rules of grammar, acceptable style, and genre.[13]

Tracking the emergence of new discourse during a period of time is one way to assess the process of the social construction of reality.[14] As Bakhtin (1965)[15] suggested, the product of discourse is always a **co-construction of reality** of all parties involved. After 9/11, terrorism took on a whole new perspective, direction, and discourse for "our time," the "way things are today," and "how the world has changed." The ensuing campaign to incorporate fear into daily life routines had major consequences for public life, national policy, and foreign affairs.[16] Since then, terrorism has been the principal event of the 21st century. Americans have ascribed new meanings to old words: 9/11 is pronounced nine-eleven (not nine-one-one), Ground Zero means more than just the site of a catastrophic explosion, and almost everybody now believes in the significance of winning hearts and minds. In Spain, the "Madrid train station" is evocative of an epicenter of horror instead of a place to meet friends traveling across Europe. We also tend to get irritated by the names of critical individuals and groups that were unknown before the tragedy: Osama bin Laden and al-Zarqawi (militant who pledged allegiance to bin Laden), Al Qaeda, and Jemaah Islamiyah.[17] **Jemaah Islamiyah** is an Islamist terrorist group active in Southeast Asia, spanning regions such as Malaysia, Singapore, and the southern Philippine islands.[18]

Narrative

As human beings, we are **homo narrans**: when communicating, we use narratives to explain and exemplify our ideas.[19] **Narrative** is a mode of reasoning to make sense of the world. As a mode of representation, narrative is used to "tell" about the world.[20] Accordingly, narratives are discourses that provide logic and consistency to the individuals, situations, and ideas for guiding the moral conduct of a society. They also provide meaning to the lives of members of a community and are fundamental to the process of formulating policy.[21] New events are usually embedded within certain existing representations, intensifying or reviving established narratives. Representations of terrorism are always told in coherent stories. When narratives of terrorism are told in a style that the audience understands, then we have narrative fidelity. **Narrative fidelity** means that the stories, myths, or folk tales told in a community are in harmony with the culture of that community; they are part of both the sender's or receiver's heritage and allow meaning about current events and activities to emerge.[22]

As such, narratives can launch wars, lead to changes in education, or transform industrial relations. The prominent narratives on Islam and terrorism can have a profound effect on American collective identity. Studies demonstrate how the dominant narratives of the Global War on Terror (GWOT) have been adopted culturally across most aspects of U.S. society. Churches, religious broadcasting, high school and college education, popular fiction and nonfiction, children's books, television shows, newspapers, movies, documentaries, websites, think tanks, popular music, video games, cartoons, comic books, and many other narrative processes have all reproduced and intensified the core narratives by making them more popular.[23]

SOCIAL CONSTRUCTION OF TERRORISM IN THE WEST

Knowledge and skill at public discourse involve formal and informal socialization so that members jump on the bandwagon for acceptance, allegiance, and belonging. After 9/11, terrorism discourse was not confined to a specific situation but became a mainstream worldview. Domestic life became geared toward commemorating loss of life from historical terrorist incidents, preparing for and anticipating the next terrorist attack, and taking measures to prevent it. Terrorism, as a form of discourse, became an institutionalized phrase (e.g., "We all know how the world has changed since 9/11"); it documented a general (instead of specific) situation and transmitted a broadly shared meaning. Public familiarity with terrorism replaced years of news and popular culture portrayals and myths about the crime problem, terror victims, and the drug war.[24]

Symbolism

One of the most striking responses to 9/11 was the upsurge of symbolism across the country. It was a form of nationalistic pride expressed through the flood of patriotic songs, pictures, and narratives in the media. From a communicative viewpoint, patriotic symbols include the key elements and shared meanings that Americans rely on to comprehend and experience the world. From a young age, people are taught to connect such symbols with American strength, pride, survival, power, and liberty.[25] In addition, the tremendous loss of lives and property sparked patriotic slogans, countless commercial advertisements, public contributions of over $2 billion, drastic domestic and foreign policy changes, and the biggest increase in military spending in thirty-five years. Stores sold all their supplies of flags, businesses infused patriotic slogans into advertising (e.g., General Motors' "Keep America Rolling"), baseball fans sang "God Bless America" in preference to "Take Me Out to the Ball Game," and children helped raise funds for hungry Afghan children. On analyzing news reports and advertisements, it seems that popular culture and media portrayals of fear, patriotism, consumption, and victimization fueled the emergence of a collective identity and action that were shaped by elite's and authorities' propaganda.[26]

Strong action was conceived as needed, including protecting oneself and getting weapons. The Beretta gun corporation promoted its "United We Stand"—a nine-millimeter pistol with a laser-etched U.S. flag. In October 2001, the company sold 2,000 Berettas to wholesalers in just one day.[27] Anyone suggesting that the reason for the attacks was more complex and that America had enraged many political groups by its past actions was criticized (e.g., support for Israel). Bill Maher, a talk show host who said that the terrorists were not cowards, was among those denounced and got fired. Clear Channel, a radio conglomerate, circulated a blacklist of 150 songs with disturbing themes (e.g., Simon and Garfunkel's "Bridge over Troubled Water") that should not be heard on the radio.[28] Americans also showed unparalleled support for the government, expressing more eagerness to adopt increased security measures and less demand for privacy rights previously considered sacred. In fact, based on a poll in the *Washington Post* in October 2001, 94% of the respondents favored President George W. Bush's plan for striking Afghanistan.[29]

American Collective Identity

In this context, symbolism led to an **American collective identity**, a strategic theme to embrace the national, the cultural, and the social without confining any American to any one of those exclusively. American collective identity views American politics as one-sided. If one does not take the side of Americans, then one becomes unpatriotic or the "Other."[30] By the same token, if a nonresident alien wants to be accepted in U.S. society, then the nation's values infer that full assimilation is necessary; this is what Falk (2005)[31] refers to as **culture talk**, an ideology of good Muslims who adopt American values vs. bad Muslims who keep their own practices in Western society. In the aftermath of September 11, 2001, the U.S. mainstream media rushed to promote American collective identity, with major news stations displaying the flag colors and Dan Rather, the famed news anchor, declaring he was ready to take orders from the president. Architects of American culture, from the public figures who appeared at the "America: A Tribute to Heroes" telethon on September 21, 2001 to the ordinary citizens who took photos and circulated rumors in the wake of the attacks, contributed in extraordinarily purposeful ways to a new aura of patriotism, memorialization, and celebration.[32]

The country's support of an American collective identity is proportionate to moral character and a discourse of salvation to orient our way toward the new terrorism domain. The youth were beseeched to live up to the new challenge. GWOT was now their war, and the media carried youthful testimonies of refreshed loyalty and awareness that would make Sergeant Lee Ermey proud.[33] Continuously perpetuated across all facets of U.S. society, the core narratives of GWOT, particularly those concerning the grave threat posed by terrorists and their evil nature, served to produce a new social reality in which a specific group of people—terrorists, terrorist suspects, and sympathizers—were eliminated from the scope of conventional reality by the American collective.[34] American collective identity has been bestowed symbolic expression through antiterrorism steps such as the omnipresent security checks on public transport, public meetings, and access to federal buildings, as well as new banking guidelines, immigration laws, public physical barriers, public preparedness, information-gathering procedures, and terrorist threat warnings in place. Such practices serve to underscore the reality of the terrorist threat and are further strengthened by highly public government measures such as opening the Guantánamo Bay prison camp and the incarceration, without charge or trial, of innumerable suspects after September 11, 2001.[35]

United States vs. Europe

The social construction of war against Islam is the product of cultural interpretation, and this is where Europe and the United States are different. In Europe, countries may be considered to have been created based on the myth of a particular essence, what might be referred to as Frenchness or Englishness. In the United States, a nation erected on continual modern waves of immigration, the founding myth is not an essence but a melting pot. Whereas the myth of a national essence does not take non-European immigrants into consideration, that of a melting pot enables their inclusion into U.S. society.[36] Second, the concept of the American Dream, the land of opportunity, partially protects America, theoretically, from terrorism. This notion is substantiated by the Pew Research Center (2007),[37] whose poll revealed that 71 % of Muslim Americans believe in the American Dream. This European situation is the opposite, where Muslims protest discrimination in the labor market. In the United States, the all-inclusive and equal character of the American Dream are not in harmony with the belief that the country is at war with Islam, thereby making homegrown terrorism less expected than in Europe.[38]

The conception of the West as waging a war against Islam is more common among Muslim Europeans than Muslim Americans because of distinctions in their personal daily experiences. On a socioeconomic scale, European and American Muslims are clearly distinct groups. This is partially due to brain drain. **Brain drain** is human capital flight; trained and talented individuals ("human capital") migrate to better nations.[39] The United States welcomed many Muslim engineers, physicians, college professors, and businesspeople for immigration; as a result, the Muslim American community is strongly middle class, with an average income higher than that of most American families. On the other hand, Europe brought in unskilled labor to rebuild communities destroyed by World War II. The unemployment rate for the average male Muslim is significantly higher than in the rest of society; Muslim Europeans vehemently believe that they experience discrimination because of their religion.[40]

SOCIAL CONSTRUCTION OF FEAR

Fear is a basic aversive emotion that occurs in situations of perceived threat and danger to persons or their environment (the society). It allows them to respond to these situations adaptively. In many cases, responses of fear are activated automatically, enabling unconscious processing. Research documents show fear and terrorism as being highly correlated.[41] The association of terrorism with fear has fostered a **discourse of fear**, or the ubiquitous communication, symbolic familiarity, and expectation that danger and risk are a central theme of daily life. Threats to the public order—and all good citizens—are part of the emphasis of fear, but the social construction of it changes throughout time.[42] What all topics of fear have in common is denouncing the enemy, the Other, the nonmember, or the alien. **Othering** is a course of action whereby society labels an inferior group into existence. This coincides with the formation and "group sense" of symbolic boundaries of affiliation (i.e., who belongs to society and who does not). These boundaries happen through institutional processes that are grounded in daily situations and encounters, including the media, public discourse, accounts, and informal conversations.[43]

With respect to the very use of fear, an extensive use of this word in the media has been documented.[44] Indeed, journalistic accounts about terrorism mirror news organizations' dependence on official news sources to publish or broadcast entertaining reports using traditional symbols of fear, crime, and victimization about threats to citizens in the combat against terrorism.[45] A collective fear orientation is profoundly anchored into the psychic makeup of society and becomes associated with a social philosophy of conflict. Such collective fear orientation has a tendency to restrain the perspective of citizens by shaping expectations for the future solely on the basis of the past. It also creates considerable mistrust and delegitimization of the enemy.[46] In studies conducted in Israel, a negative correlation was discovered between collective fear and defense of the peace process. Lastly, the collective fear orientation is a major foundation of violence. A frightened society is more willing to fight when it has to face threatening conditions.[47]

It is unmistakable that, immediately after 9/11, a collective sense of fear, terror, and loss reigned in U.S. communities. People went to their religious establishments rather than hospitals, clinics, or mental health centers. Churches, temples, and mosques were now gathering locations to find refuge, to support the very structures that had just been assaulted (i.e., belief systems), and to regain control for the massive sense of panic and grief. The formation of physical and emotional safety is a precondition before any other intervention in the wake of a major disaster in the community.[48] Let us consider the Latin roots of the word **community**. *Communis*, "common" or "shared," highlights the social bonds between people as the core of a community. The fact that communication shares the same Latin root as community should attract our attention to the manner in which public discourse both creates and supports the myriad social relationships from which communities are built.[49]

In U.S. communities, there were now discourses about 9/11 that awakened and provoked people's reactions. Individuals started to form rhetorical strands. **Rhetorical strands** are rhetorical dimensions (about socially constructed terrorism) that are formed and interwoven in places where public discourse influences and is influenced by describing and labeling of terror, the symbolic meaning of terrorism, public discourse about terror, and the symbiotic relationship between terrorism and the media. Such rhetorical strands took the form of discussions, conversations, and the processing and internalizing of true facts or rumors. They emerged within groups and between people around the nation, if not the entire world.[50] Rhetorical strands may give a false sense of security. Security is based on the evaluation of an event(s), condition(s), or situation(s) (all are elements of a context) as a sign of threat or danger (primary evaluation) and on an appraisal of available defenses and the capacity to face the perceived threat or danger (secondary evaluation). Therefore, people develop beliefs about their own security when they do not feel any threats or dangers, or feel that the threats or dangers will eventually be overcome.[51]

SOCIAL CONSTRUCTION OF EMOTIONS

Before September 11, 2001, the U.S. had been hurt by social conflicts, by a lack of respect typical of social complexity, and even, at times, by unspeakable hostilities. After that fateful day, the national community experienced fear and considered itself united through it, through the loving kindness expressed by those who once only ran into each other in the streets, and through the civility and consideration among people who once were only friends. A deep generalization of social attention could be felt, which moved from specificity, concreteness, and idiosyncrasy to abstraction, idealization, and universality. This newfound emotional and moral situation spread from the physical to the social sphere, from the individual to the collective, from the family to the business world, from New York City to the whole United States, and from the fate of America to other civilizations across the globe.[52]

Definition of Emotions

By and large, **emotions** are response systems designed to adapt the human organism to rapid and maybe threatening changes in the environment.[53] As opposed to individual emotions, **socially constructed emotions** are emotions felt by individuals as a consequence of their membership in a particular group or society.[54] This implies that people may experience emotions, not automatically as a reaction to their own life events, but also in response to collective or societal experiences to which only specific group members are concerned. Emotional contexts influence the way society frames events. More precisely, a collective reaction to conflict—or a peace-related situation—is shaped by the temporary collective or societal emotional reaction to the experience. In any case, it is highly related to the social and emotional context.[55]

The role of emotion in the context of terrorism is evident in regard to the notion of **triggering events**, incidents that transform a person from being a passive yet enraged observer into an active and driven terrorist.[56] Looking at the incidents of Bloody Sunday on January 30, 1972 in Northern Ireland, Horgan (2005)[57] indicates how triggering events built "a sense of communal identification with the victimized, and an often unwavering, confident dedication to the preservation and importance of the memory of the particular event itself" (p. 87). The killing of thirteen unarmed demonstrators, committed by a parachute regiment of the British Army, was a catalyst for the republican community and caused them to create great intramural emotional bonds and attachment to the PIRA (Provisional Irish Republican Army). The latter became a defender of Irish welfare and rights.

Collective Emotional Orientation

Collective emotional orientation is the characterizing manner in which society expresses a certain emotion. There are some criteria to classify such characterizing tendency. For example, the emotion and the beliefs that call a specific emotion to mind are widely shared among members of a society and emerge regularly in that society's public discourse, cultural symbols, and educational materials. Collective emotional orientation may even typify entire civilizations or cultures of fear in the Western hemisphere.[58] Such orientation gives rise to three related concepts: atmosphere, emotional culture, and emotional climate. **Atmosphere** refers to emotions that surface when members of a collective focus their attention on a particular short-term event that impacts them as a group. **Emotional culture** refers to the emotional relations socialized in any culture. **Emotional climate** refers to the collective emotions felt as a consequence of a society's reaction to its sociopolitical conditions.[59]

With respect to the latter, a **negative emotional climate** is an emotional climate developed from a negative context, like a terrorist attack that has just occurred. The negative emotional climate arouses negative beliefs and emotions contributing to defensive or aggressive behavior. The resulting context may be a set of beliefs that cultivate insecurity, threat, and stress as well as emotions of fear, anger, and hate. For instance, we can look at the emotional effects of the March 11, 2004 terrorist bombings in Madrid that resulted in almost 200 deaths and over 1,800 injuries. It also resulted in the socially constructed negative climate—that is, the severe psychological aftereffects that the terrorist attack created. The way of dealing with this terrifying event shows that the bombings in Madrid influenced both collective and individual emotions in Spanish society.[60]

Emotion and Interpersonal News Diffusion

When individuals are emotionally distressed by a terrifying event, they generally feel a compulsion to engage in emotion and interpersonal news diffusion: the need to affiliate and share emotional experience with other people. This is akin to **social sharing**, whereby individuals interact with others concerning an emotion-triggering event and their own feelings.[61] In a series of experiments, Luminet, Bouts, Delie, Manstead, and Rime (2000)[62] reported that individuals who find themselves in a very negative emotional situation tend to engage in intensely more social sharing than those in non-emotional or moderately emotional situations. Other studies have also found evidence that emotion is correlated to interpersonal news diffusion. For instance, Gantz and Trenholm (1979)[63] found that expressing affect was one reason for people to pass news along to others. A relationship between negative affect and interpersonal news diffusion may reflect endeavors to deal with emotion through social contact, as mentioned before. Nevertheless, the inverse causal order can also happen. By conversing with others, people may express feelings of distress or may aggravate current negative affect. Certainly, causal order cannot be determined convincingly when examining reactions to unexpected news events.[64]

THE ROLE OF CULTURE IN TERRORISM

Culture is a socially constructed and historically transmitted system. It is a pattern of symbols, meanings, principles, rules, norms, beliefs, values, traditions, and objects that are transferred from one generation to the next, shared to a certain degree by members of a community, and become internalized when these members interact with each other.[65] What this also means is that a culture's symbols, norms, values, and so on, become more obvious when interacting with members of different cultures. These cultural differences, then, may often be a source of misunderstanding and conflict. When defining culture, one needs to consider the ideological, cognitive, motivational, and affective influences that people experience in their everyday routines. Culture defines boundaries and shows people what they are expected and allowed to do within the bounds of their status or role in society.[66]

Culture is social glue: it is a mold in which human beings are cast, and it controls their everyday lives in unpredicted ways. Culture upholds values for future generations to adopt and furnishes education, mental processes, and rules for behavior.[67] Social glue implies a similar concept called cultural determinism (or cultural blueprint). **Cultural determinism** is the belief that the culture in which humans are raised determines who they are emotionally and behaviorally. For example, some Native Americans never cry or get irritated. Culture offers a model that determines the way humans think, feel, and behave in society— a blueprint that is probably not shared by other cultures. Occasionally, cultural determinism can be so embedded within a community or society that it leads individuals to subscribe to a strong adherence to a set of beliefs even in the face of evidence that proves their beliefs wrong.[68]

Three Levels of Mental Programming

Geert Hofstede (1991)[69] refers to cultural determinism as our **software of the mind**: our way of thinking or our thinking pattern. The sources of our mental programs come from the social environment in which we grew up and gathered our life experiences. A concept for such mental software is culture. Culture involves the unwritten rules of the social game, the collective programming of the mind that differentiates a group of people from another. Culture regulates behavior in profound and persisting ways, many of which are unconscious and therefore outside of our awareness. Hofstede (2001)[70] created a model distinguishing three levels of mental programming (Figure 6.1). At the bottom is the **universal level**, the least unique but most basic level of mental programming shared by the entire humankind. This is the biological wiring of the human race that includes expressive, associative, and aggressive behaviors, as conceptualized by biologists like Konrad Lorenz (1967).[71] At the top, the **individual level** of mental programming is the most unique part. No two individuals are alike. This is the level of a person's idiosyncrasies, and it offers a wide array of alternative behaviors within a particular culture.

In the middle is the **collective level**. According to Hofstede (2001),[72] "[T]he collective level of mental programming is shared with some but not all other people; it is common to people belonging to one group or category which differ from other groups or categories" (p. 3). As Hofstede continues, "[I]t is at this middle, collective level that most of our mental programming is learned" (p. 3). The collective level of mental programming is the one we need to concentrate on. Cultural values at this level are driving principles for behavior, such as absolutism in belief. Such values are internalized by members of the culture after wide exposure to multiple sources such as national, ethnic, religious, cultural, and educational communities.[73] At any given time in history, people have lived in a society with distinctive cultural worldviews (CWVs), symbols, norms, and traditions. Synonyms for the collective level of mental programming include national character and societal influence. As social creatures, we are necessarily cultural animals. Culture is wired into us as a human species, and war and violence are especially striking cultural products.[74]

Collective Level of Mental Programming and Terrorism

This is the level at which the cultural programming of terrorism usually takes place. An analysis of a person's decision to become an Islamist fighter should consider that

Figure 6.1 Hofstede's Model of the Three Levels of Mental Programming

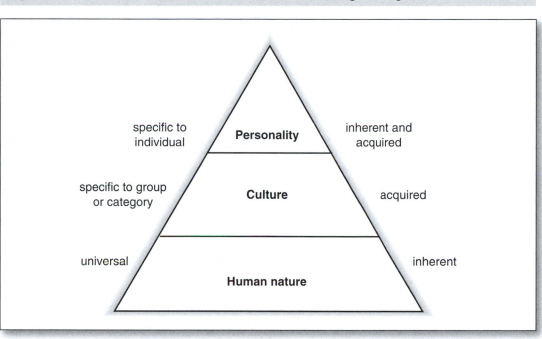

Source: Geert Hofstede, Gert Jan Hofstede, Michael Minkov, *Cultures and Organizations: Software of the Mind*, Third Revised Edition, McGrawHill 2010, ISBN 0-07-166418-1. © Geert Hofstede B.V.

person's sociocultural-political context. For example, Pakistan has numerous **madrassas** (Islamic religious schools or colleges). The curriculum of madrassas consists of learning the entire Qur'an in Arabic and exposing youth to radical rote-learning methods (from traditional Arabic sources). According to a 2008 estimate, there were more than 40,000 madrassas in Pakistan alone, serving millions of students.[75] In an analysis of Pakistani madrassas, Vicziany and the Monash Asia Institute (2007)[76] found a correlation between madrassa-based terrorism and indoctrination. In particular, madrassas in the country's border regions have been reported to turn children into future warriors for Afghanistan and Kashmir. In addition, in this part of Pakistan, most of the madrassas are **Deobandi**, a local Islamic movement that is welcoming to jihad. In a thorough study of a district in Punjab (bordering Pakistan and India), Saleem Ali (2005)[77] calculated that 80 % of Deobandi madrassas have engaged in extreme violence. Madrassas are surely a factor to consider when analyzing the relationship between the collective level of mental programming and terrorism.[78] Another example of such mental programming is the cultural worship of Osama bin Laden (Box 6.1).

Box 6.1   Cultural Worship of Osama bin Laden

One particular anecdote epitomizing the influence of the collective level of mental programming on terrorism is the cultural worship of Osama bin Laden in several places in the Middle East. Despite the fact that Osama bin Laden never officially earned, in his lifetime, the title of imam, mullah, or other religious scholar, and that he was never matriculated into an Islamic university, few Muslim detractors today question bin Laden's religious credentials. As the foundational figure for Islam is Muhammad, the Al Qaeda leader exploited this theme to the fullest; he described himself as a direct follower of Muhammad. Indeed, Osama bin Laden, too, took a heroic path, fighting great enemies, in a way that turned him into a quasi-mythic figure. Part of the reason bin Laden was mythic lies in the fact that he claimed he was part of a far-reaching struggle against Western imperialism and depravity. His actions are reminiscent of the very makeup of medieval Muslim history.[79]

Al Qaeda has tapped into a cultural worship of Osama bin Laden and has had the desired effect on its followers. Polls show that defense and sponsorship of Al Qaeda have increased in inverse relation to support for America.[80] In the aftermath of September 11, 2001, Osama bin Laden became an object of particularly intense identification. Afghan merchants sold candies in wrappers drawn with bin Laden's face. A very popular name for newborn males in the Muslim world today is Osama. For this reason, we see all the posters and stickers extolling the virtues of bin Laden in countries like Pakistan or Afghanistan.[81] He was mythologized as a hero instantly. His image was depicted on T-shirts that were displayed like iconic representations on human bodies. Recordings of his victorious words were reproduced and incessantly replayed on video and compact disc.[82] In several countries, support for bin Laden continues to remain fairly high, including 60% in Jordan and 51% in Pakistan.[83]

The example of iconic images of Osama bin Laden that have become part of those cultures are referred to as cultural materials. **Cultural materials** are concepts or symbols that are shared and understood by a given community. The more cultural materials diffuse, the more powerful they become.[84] A cultural material will have a deep impact on a community if it has cultural resonance. **Cultural resonance** is the understanding of how a movement or idea is created by and in turn creates the cultural environment. A perfectly fine cultural material can be totally worthless if it has no influence on the community. Therefore, cultural resonance is of utmost importance.[85] Cultural materials, just like madrassas, are examples of cultural capital. **Cultural capital** refers to the social assets that a culture has. Examples are cultural knowledge, local goods, material objects (e.g., books, paintings, instruments, or machines), cultural ideas, our educational system, and so forth. Parents transfer cultural capital to their children; they impart the attitudes and knowledge that make school and learning an accustomed place in which they can succeed easily.[86]

The Western media often link poverty to Islamist martyrdom. Considering that about 75% of the world's population is poor, if poverty was the root of martyrdom, then one would expect to observe similar actions happening in 75% of the world. It is not so much the sheer fact of poverty as it is cultural programming that has an overpowering effect on a person's decision to kill people.[87] Some research shows that cultural programming is particularly influential when it comes to churning out volunteers for martyrdom missions in Middle Eastern countries. Madsen (2005)[88] reported that 25% of Palestinian boys between 12 and 17 are yearning to become martyrs. In another example, Sciolino (2002)[89] reported that about 95% of young educated Saudis support Al Qaeda. Atran (2003)[90] cited studies that show approximately 70% of Palestinians and 70% of Lebanese advocating martyrdom operations and considering them necessary. Soibelman (2004)[91] reported that about 70% of Palestinians favored martyrdom missions in the summer of 2001.

Communication scholars distinguish between communication as transmission and communication as ritual. Whereas **communication as transmission** refers to disseminating information faster and to longer distances, transcending time and space, to affect the behavior or beliefs of the receivers of transmissions, **communication as ritual** refers to sacred ceremony that groups people together in fellowship and communality.[92] Communication as ritual is particularly evident in understanding the motives of martyrs to engage in suicide terrorism. Martyrs and supporting members from Islamic communities learn in fellowship that the main recompense for suicide volunteers stems from the belief that Allah will reward them. In a ritual, before the actual martyr goes on a suicidal spree, all members are also told that the persons-to-die are to be deemed martyrs and often hailed as such. As Islamist leaders told a female terrorist, "You'll gain a very special status among the women suicide bombers. You'll be a real heroine." In Palestine, Islamist martyrs always become heroes. Videos of their self-eulogy can be acquired and, many times, parents dress their babies and children in martyr costumes and have them pictured.[93] Regrettably, the destruction or death of Americans is also celebrated in those rituals. After the Columbia shuttle catastrophe in 2003, Ali Al-Timimi, an Islamic activist, said, "There is no doubt that Muslims were overjoyed because of the adversity that befell their greatest enemy. Upon hearing the news, my heart felt certain good omens that I like to spread to brothers." On the other hand, Islamic martyrs can count on their fellows to be appreciated and admired.[94]

CULTURAL WORLDVIEW (CWV)

Because we are cultural animals, we subscribe to a **cultural worldview** (CWV), a collectively embraced set of beliefs about the nature of the world and which provides persuasive answers to universal cosmological questions about life. One's CWV prescribes appropriate social roles, requirements, and principles for treasured conduct, while inculcating one's life with significance, order, and permanence. Our CWV offers some guarantee that, by living up to or surpassing the cultural standards of value, we will survive our own physical demise, either literally (e.g., by going to heaven, or paradise, or through re-embodiment) or symbolically (e.g., through recognition for good works, fame, and celebrity). In this respect, our CWV is a shield against the typical anxiety produced by the awareness that death cannot be avoided. Cultures determine the frames that individuals use to organize and interpret life, and control how individuals react when such knowledge structures are endangered. When we face the threat that terrorism poses to our CWV, we do not merely depend on our cultural sensibilities to help us understand the experience; we also vigorously hold on to our worldview, responding defensively against people who would infringe on it, or in favor of those who would buttress it.[95]

CWV plays an important role in our cultural conceptualization of terrorism, especially when it comes to forming and regulating human behavior as part of what Keen (1986)[96] calls the "phenomenology of the hostile imagination" (p. 13). Despite the fact that times and circumstances change, the "hostile imagination has a certain standard repertoire of images it uses to dehumanize the enemy" (p. 13). This process entails what Jung called the shadow archetype, which, in this case, becomes the "archetype of the enemy."[97] In a general sense, according to the **shadow archetype**, shadowy attributes and repugnant traits are projected onto others, leading to paranoia, accusations, and lack of intimacy, all of which badly affect people, groups, and even entire countries.[98]

Because humans have a CWV, they tend to support a particular cultural emphasis. A **cultural emphasis** is a notable characteristic of a culture often manifested though language and, more specifically, vocabulary; the vocabulary that individuals use indicates "what is" to that group of individuals. If there are many words to describe a particular topic in a culture, then chances are that the topic is considered important in that culture.[99] For example, according to the **Global Language Monitor (GLM)**[100]—an Austin-based company that documents, analyzes, and identifies trends in language use worldwide, especially the English language—*9/11* was the second most used word in American media during the 2000–2009 decade (#1 being *global warming*). In fact, *9/11* was the Word of the Year for 2001; *Weapons of Mass Destruction* was for 2002. In regard to the top phrases of the decade from 2000–2009, *Ground Zero*, *War on Terror*, and *Weapons of Mass Destruction* ranked #3, #4, and #5, respectively.

According to Ernest Becker (1971),[101] when there is no powerful psychological protective mechanisms, the awareness that we will die at some point creates the potential for intense fear. In the U.S., this is obvious in the cultural emphasis on using vocabulary in this manner. After 9/11, George W. Bush accentuated particular words and phrases—*us*, *them*, *they*, *evil*, *those people*, *demons*, and *Wanted: Dead or Alive*—to pigeonhole people of Arab/ Middle Eastern descent. Even the words *freedom*, *liberty*, and *justice* now possess a special type of symbolism that is distinctively applicable to U.S. values. For many Americans, those words have a quasi-sacrosanct quality—not to be tarnished or profaned.[102]

BELIEF IN A JUST WORLD

A defense mechanism for tackling terrorism is to rely on a social construct called **belief in a just world**, or the attitude that people get what they deserve. This philosophy is inculcated by parents, churches, schools, and popular culture. According to that philosophy, many people see the world as just: good people should be pleased and recompensed; bad people who have caused fear and suffering should be punished. Our **Kulturbrille** ("cultural glasses," i.e., peculiar beliefs and traditions) sways us into eliminating some facts and sensitizing us to other facts. Certain aspects of our CWV are self-deceptions that serve us well. In Africa and some parts of Asia, a certain number of cultures believe that crocodiles eat only people who have sinned. So, members of those cultures feel quite safe when they follow the reasoning that "I have not sinned, so the crocodiles will not get me." This logic decreases anxiety and makes life worth living. It is also the just-world phenomenon: "He was devoured, so he must have sinned."[103]

People who strongly subscribe to the just-world philosophy are usually more likely to derogate outsiders—for example, as a way to rationalize injustices against people who belong to the culture, religion, or ethnicity of terrorists.[104] Just-world beliefs have been reported to have a positive correlation with various ideology variables besides fear. These variables are authoritarianism, religious support, Protestant ethic, positive regard for America, and negative attitudes vis-à-vis ethnic minorities. Moreover, just-world beliefs have a positive correlation with support for government and the elite—that is, positive attitudes toward Congress, the military, corporations, and the Supreme Court.[105] Rubin and Peplau (1975)[106] suggested that the two most important social outcomes of belief in a just world are (1) "support for powerful political and social institutions" (p. 82) and (2) the "tendency to derogate victims of social injustice" (p. 82). In the post-9/11 climate, just-world beliefs may have been salient for two reasons. First, the reality that terrorists took the lives of about 3,000 civilians might have desecrated Americans' sense of a just world. Second, people with fervent just-world beliefs might believe that anti-Muslim backlash is justifiable revenge for the terrorist attacks. In sum, empirical evidence suggests that the just-world philosophy might be a central concept in understanding reactions to outsiders.[107]

A related theory is social dominance theory. **Social dominance theory** suggests that people's advocacy of group dominance can be assessed as an individual-difference variable termed *social dominance orientation*. Individuals with high social dominance orientation aspire to group inequality and support attitudes and policies that bolster social hierarchies. According to social dominance theory, cultures develop ideologies that uphold group inequality and legitimize discrimination. **Legitimizing myths** are beliefs, viewpoints, and ideologies that offer both a moral and intellectual validation for the status differences and domination of one culture over another. These legitimizing myths emerge and serve to support the preservation of group inequities.[108] In the context of terrorism, the social dominance orientation has been linked to a variety of defense mechanisms against fear. This orientation is also related to support for punitive laws and the death penalty. This implies that a program including just-world beliefs and social dominance orientation might echo a personal ideology that is projecting anti-Muslim reactions. As a matter of fact, a framework of personal ideologies that supports "you get what you deserve" and social dominance beliefs was tested by Oswald (2005)[109] and confirmed anti-Muslim prejudice and discrimination.

SYMBOLIC INTERACTIONISM

The increasing use and manipulation of up-to-date communications by terrorists have led communication and terrorism academics to reconceptualize modern terrorism within symbolic interaction theory.[110] **Symbolic interactionism** rests on the premise that people communicate through shared symbols—for example, words, definitions, roles, and gestures. Because meaning is portrayed and received within the specific culture in which one lives, meaning becomes symbolic within social interactions taking place in that culture. In addition, symbolic interactionism postulates that individuals define their own meaning of behavior and form their own social constructions of reality.[111] George Herbert Mead (1934)[112] is regarded as the forerunner to symbolic interactionism. For Mead, interaction is communication by means of significant symbols. Meltzer (1975)[113] developed Mead's ideas by claiming the following: symbolic interaction is associated with behavioral interpretation and is constructed within a particular culture.

Interpretation of events is socially created and relies on verbal and nonverbal symbols, which characterize the core elements of communication within interactions. Symbolic universes are produced to give legitimation to institutional structures. A **symbolic universe** is a group of beliefs that everybody knows. The purpose is to render the institutionalized structure credible for the individual (who might not follow or endorse the underlying logic of the institution). A symbolic universe puts things in their right place. It provides justifications for why people do things the way they do. Included in the symbolic universe are actions, behaviors, proverbs, ethical maxims, wise sayings, mythology, religions and other theological beliefs, metaphysical practices, and other value systems. They are all methods to provide legitimacy to established institutions.[114]

With respect to terrorism, symbolic interactionists have noticed that Americans are becoming "armored." Increasingly, Americans live behind walls, hire bodyguards, drive armored vehicles (e.g., hummers and SUVs), buy maces and handguns, and take martial arts classes. Taking certain actions confirms the meaning or interpretation of fear. The trouble is that these actions reaffirm and help create a sense of disorder that further actions perpetuate. Social life can become more antagonistic or unfriendly when people view their situations as fearful and commit their neighbors to that lifestyle through the discourse of fear. People come to see themselves as knowledgeable "fear realists." They get their relatives, friends, neighbors, and coworkers to socially construct their own environments with fear as well. Put simply, the symbolic interaction based on fear integrates terrorism reflexively; the actors, targets, and character of fear are established through the symbolic processes that communicate fear.[115]

As one can see, the reality of a terrorist attack is formed by a shared understanding of communication formats and symbolic meanings. The latter are conveyed more and more by media images that make the lines between fantasy, news, and reality blurry.[116] The media and popular culture are best interpreted as central elements of our symbolic milieu rather than independent causes and effects. The media do not simply set agendas. Rather, in accordance with symbolic interactionism, media that use certain symbols and encourage certain relationships between words, acts, and issues also orient the viewpoints, frameworks, language, and discourse that people use in identifying specific problems and issues. The words *crime*, *victim*, and *fear* are included in news reports about terrorism to create public discourse that suggests symbolic relationships about order, risk, and threat that may be exploited by politicians and legislators.[117]

Lastly, measures taken against terrorism are linked to the socio-historical context and fundamental structural arrangements. These measures reveal particular symbolic foundations for meaning and identity in social life. Crisis gives opportunities for presidents to portray themselves as leaders and dramatically present the situation as tragic but hopeful.

By extension, they also promise to highlight the resolve of national character. Symbolic interactionism assumes that identity and meaning are socially constructed by harnessing familiar experiences and customs to specific situations. In this sense, security and hope are related in meaningful ways.[118]

UNCERTAINTY AVOIDANCE

Hofstede (1980)[119] conducted a longitudinal study of psychological differences coming from cultural values. More precisely, in the late 1960s and 1970s, he compared those values among personnel of IBM management in sixty-four countries. Based on a statistical analysis of 200,000 responses, he created a database of social and cultural (ethno-psychological) factors. He identified and developed construct validity for four different dimensions of national values and culture across the entire world: (1) **power distance** is the degree of equality (or inequality) among subordinates and superiors in a society; (2) **individualism** is a principle by which people give preference to their own needs, rather than harmony, teamwork, and communal activities (the opposite of individualism is collectivism); (3) **masculinity** favors male "machismo" power, success, material possessions, and implementation of gender segregation while devaluing interpersonal relationships—it also makes sharp distinctions between work and roles for men and women (the opposite of masculinity is femininity); and (4) **uncertainty avoidance** represents the level of intolerance for risk or uncertain situations within a culture. Hofstede considered this fourth construct as consistent with the levels of stress and anxiety within a society.

Wiedenhaefer and colleagues (2007)[120] analyzed terrorism based on this cultural dimension of uncertainty avoidance. Based on approximately 2,200 terrorist incidents from the late 1960s to the late 1970s, their study recognized uncertainty avoidance as typical of terror-producing countries. All terrorist acts from 1968 to 1979 were found to be related to Hofstede's cultural value indices in his aforementioned 1980 study. High uncertainty avoidance, associated with terror-producing countries, confirms the powerful facilitating effect of cultural stress and anxiety for group-driven terrorist attacks. Hofstede (1991)[121] argued that different cultures experience significantly varying levels of discomfort when facing an uncertain future, and they are highly related to the level of stress in those cultures. Hofstede looked at uncertainty avoidance by examining stress and tension in IBM workplaces, the importance of rules in daily routines, and the attempt to avoid the stress of career changes. In general, cultures experiencing greater anxiety form groups that strengthen their needs for stability. Such groups are the model for terrorist groups in the situation implied here; they include like-minded individuals who share the same experiences, feelings, and values, and who are more easily "enabled" toward group behavior.

COLLECTIVISM

Collectivism is a social attitude according to which individuals consider themselves as parts of one or more groups; are principally influenced by the rules of, and obligations imposed by, those groups; are willing to privilege the goals of these groups over their own personal goals; and stress their interpersonal connectedness to and dependence on members of these groups. This philosophy, then, places a lot of emphasis on harmony, teamwork, and communal activities. Collectivism resembles a family relationship that has mutual responsibilities and obligations of protection in exchange for loyalty.[122] Schwartz (2005)[123] has characterized terrorism as a "maximally collectivist" position, where the interests of the terrorist become blended with those of the group that he or she represents. This position has also been adopted by Post (2005).[124]

According to the same study by Wiedenhaefer et al. (2007),[125] the preservation of a collective belief system was a centerpiece to many terrorist endeavors in the 1970s. As Crenshaw (1992)[126] contended, "[A] key role of leadership is to develop or maintain a collective belief system that links overall ideological orientation to the environment in which the group operates" (p. 1). To a large degree, this collective belief system is obvious in high uncertainty avoidance cultures. In addition, Schachter (1959)[127] observed the dependence of people on like-minded others (who hold similar sentiments and worldviews). Generally, they try to reach a common agreement on what they should believe. Thus, openness and sensitivity to a collective belief system (i.e., "We are good and the other group is bad") are more prominent in high uncertainty avoidance cultures.

In conditions where terrorism is constructed as a medium of collective struggle, individuals with collectivistic versus individualistic aspirations tend to be more leaning toward engaging in terrorist activities. Weinberg and Eubank (1994)[128] surveyed IBM workers in forty different nations and found that collectivists are more prone to supporting attacks against foreigners. These findings are in harmony with the results of Post, Sprinzak, and Denny (2003),[129] based on interviews conducted with imprisoned Middle Eastern terrorists. Comparing these results with reports of terrorist attacks from the "International Terrorism: Attributes of Terrorist Events 1968–1977" (ITERATE) database, Weinberg and Eubank contend that the data support their hypothesis: it is more probable that people in collectivist countries attack foreigners, while individualists are more likely to attack fellow citizens or people from other individualist cultures. They also claim that people in individualist countries feel morally inhibited from attacking innocent civilians, while collectivists have two moralities—one for their own groups, one for the outside group—and would not be morally restrained from attacking innocent civilians if they belong to the outside group.

ETHNOGRAPHY OF TERRORISM

One way to understand the social construction of reality by a terrorist group is to spend a substantial amount of time with the group itself and observe the group analytically—one such method is ethnography. **Ethnography** is the direct observation, reporting, and assessment of the behavior of a group. The ethnographer usually lives with the group, knows their language, partakes in some of their activities, and uses various observational and recording techniques. The purpose of ethnography is to understand the culture of a group and analyze the cultural patterns so as to come up with a theory of the rules for appropriate group behaviors. Ethnographers do not work in artificial settings or laboratories. They work in natural settings as participant observers. **Participant observation** is the process in which an ethnographer creates and maintains long-term rapport with multiple people in a group in its natural environment for the purpose of developing a scientific explanation of the group's culture.[130]

On analyzing the culture of a group, the ethnographer attempts to look at the group's social glue—the cultural bond that holds people together. In doing so, ethnographers develop "thick descriptions" of groups. According to Geertz (1983),[131] a **thick description** is an in-depth observation and account (from the observation) of a natural setting. The description is very much detailed and a lot of notes are taken. Thick description enables the ethnographer to comprehend systems of meaning through which individual and group actions are constructed and interpreted. The ultimate objective of the ethnographer is to portray the world as seen by the participants in the study.

Occasionally, ethnographers encounter blackmail and intimidation as they try to gain entrée to terrorist groups. Once contact and channels of communication have been opened, terrorists usually impose certain conditions under which they will be observed or answer questions of the researcher. This may lead to selective ethnography if researchers want to be promised continued access or their own safety. We know that some journalists have been abducted and killed in their efforts to talk with terrorists (e.g., Daniel Pearl; see Chapter 2).[132] Nevertheless, no ethnographer to date has been found dead while observing a terrorist group.

In her article titled "Terrorism, Myth, and the Power of Ethnographic Praxis," Cynthia Mahmood (2001)[133] wrote about the successful ethnography she conducted with **Sikh terrorists** in Punjab (northwestern India, close to Pakistan) for nine years. Sikhs' efforts toward an independent Sikh state, to be called Khalistan, have spawned a violent movement that involved thousands of adepts in the 1980s and 1990s. The Khalistani terrorists violated international laws of armed conflict and committed barbarisms against Punjabi civilians. Thousands of them were killed. On June 23, 1985, Air India Flight 182 exploded in midair (as a result of a bomb) off the coast of Ireland. Over 320 passengers were killed. The main suspects in the bombing were Sikh terrorists.[134]

For nine years, Mahmood took the risk of engaging in participant observation with Sikh terrorists, who are known to commit acts of extreme political violence and carry swords (as mandated by their religion). During her ethnography, she discovered many elements of the social glue that holds the Sikhs together. They are human beings like everybody else and communicate at different levels of language. At times, they speak formally; at other times, they do it informally, playfully, and so on. They have principles, community roles, and even factional problems. Despite their radical militancy, they do not hold animosity toward the U.S. During Sikh trials in North American courts, Mahmood provided her testimony and expertise on the Sikh issue. One of her ethnographic conclusions is that Sikhs' visualization of terror has supplanted the reality of armed conflict, among them, in Western legal and policy environments. Mahmood's ethnographic research also demonstrates how knowledge gained through face-to-face communication can add data, in great details, to judicial and legislative decisions concerning terrorism.[135]

SUMMARY

Terrorism is a social construct. The construction of terrorism is what people agree on through consensus. The audience's perceptions of 9/11 were, to a great extent, socially constructed. Language, whether through discourse or narrative, is essential to the social construction of reality. For example, the language on terrorism in the U.S. is now greatly dominated by its association with Islam. Language is ideological; it is used to maintain hegemony of the elite, or the powers that be, to represent some aspects of the world, and to fit the culture of a particular community (i.e., narrative fidelity). A striking response to 9/11 was the upsurge of symbolism across the U.S. (e.g., patriotic slogans), which led to an American collective identity: patriotism, memorialization, and celebration. Similarly, the social construction of reality implies the social construction of fear (as a way to create social bonds against a perceived enemy) and the social construction of emotions (the need to associate and share emotional experience with other people). It is clear that social construction is a consequence of people's membership of a particular group or society. In the same train of thought, the role of culture plays a pivotal role in the way terrorism is perceived. Culture is a socially constructed and historically transmitted system. It is our social glue and our software of the mind. To this effect, Geert Hofstede developed his model of three levels of mental programming: the universal, the collective, and the individual levels. The collective level is the level at which the cultural programming of terrorism usually takes place. For example, Pakistan has numerous madrassas (Islamic religious schools and colleges) that teach people how to wage jihad. And many Muslims in the Middle East continue to worship Osama bin Laden. A major effect of cultural programming is the formation of a cultural worldview (CWV). Both the West and Islamist ideology have their own belief in a just world. The reality of a terrorist attack, then, is formed by a shared understanding of communication formats and symbolic meanings (a tenet supported by symbolic interactionism). A similar approach, based on Hostede's model of cultural dimensions, led several scholars to conduct seminal studies on the influence of culture on terrorism. Overall, they found that cultures experiencing greater uncertainty have a higher tendency to create terrorist groups as it is a way to strengthen their needs for stability. Terrorist communities are also more collectivistic. Lastly, a good way to understand the social construction of reality by a terrorist group is to spend a significant amount of time with the group itself and conduct a profound analytical observation—one such method is ethnography (the direct observation, reporting, and assessment of the behavior of a group).

KEY TERMS

American collective identity   141

atmosphere   144

belief in a just world   150

brain drain   142

co-construction of reality   139

collective emotional orientation   144

communication as ritual   149

communication as transmission   149

community   143

concept   137

ENDNOTES

1. White, Jonathan R. (2011). *Terrorism and Homeland Security* (7th ed.). Belmont, CA: Wadsworth.

2. Berger, Peter, & Luckmann, Thomas (1966). *The Social Construction of Reality: A Treatise in the Sociology of Knowledge*. Garden City, NY: Doubleday.

3. Searle, John R. (1997). *The Construction of Social Reality*. New York: Free Press.

4. Gergen, Kenneth (1999). *An Invitation to Social Construction*. London: Sage.

5. White, Jonathan R. (2011). *Terrorism and Homeland Security* (7th ed.). Belmont, CA: Wadsworth.

6. Juergensmeyer, Mark (2003). *Terror in the Mind of God: The Global Rise of Religious Violence*. Berkeley: University of California Press.

7. Güss, C. Dominik, Tuason, Ma Teresa, & Teixeira, Vanessa B. (2007). A Cultural-Psychological Theory of Contemporary Islamic Martyrdom. *Journal for the Theory of Social Behaviour, 37*(4), 415–445.

8. Hall, Stuart (1996). *Modernity: An Introduction to Modern Societies*. Cambridge: Blackwell.

9. Lind, Rebecca Ann, & Salo, Colleen (2002). The Framing of Feminists and Feminism in News and Public Affairs Programs in US Electronic Media. *Journal of Communication, 52*(1), 211–228; Ryan, Michael (2004). Framing the War against Terrorism: US Newspaper Editorials and Military Action in Afghanistan. *Gazette: The International Journal for Communication Studies, 66*(5), 363–382.

10. Berger, Peter, & Luckmann, Thomas (1966). *The Social Construction of Reality: A Treatise in the Sociology of Knowledge*. Garden City, NY: Doubleday.

11. Fairclough, Norman (2003). *Analyzing Discourse: Textual Analysis for Social Research*. London: Routledge.

12. Altheide, David L., & Michalowski, R. Sam (1999). Fear in the News: A Discourse of Control. *The Sociological Quarterly, 40*, 475–503; Fowler, Roger (1991). *Language in the News: Discourse and Ideology in the British Press*. London: Routledge; Gamson, William A., Croteau, David, Hoynes, William, & Sasson, Theodore (1992). Media Images and the Social Construction of Reality. *Annual Review of Sociology, 18*, 373–393; Potter, Jonathan, & Wetherell, Margaret (1987). *Discourse and Social Psychology*. Beverly Hills, CA: Sage.

13. Fairclough, Norman (2001). *Language and Power*. Harlow: Pearson Education.

14. Altheide, David L. (2006). Terrorism and the Politics of Fear. *Cultural Studies, 6*(4), 415–439.

15. Bakhtin, Mikhail (1965). *Rabelais and His World*. Bloomington: Indiana University Press.

16. Kellner, Douglas (2003). *From 9/11 to Terror War: The Dangers of the Bush Legacy*. Lanham, MD: Rowman & Littlefield.

17. Moeller, Susan D. (2009). *Packaging Terrorism: Co-Opting the News for Politics and Profit*. New York: Wiley-Blackwell.

18. Mishal, Shaul, & Rosenthal, Maoz (2005). Al Qaeda as a Dune Organization: Toward a Typology of Islamic Terrorist Organizations. *Studies in Conflict & Terrorism, 28*(4), 275–293.

19. Wright, Kevin B., Sparks, Lisa, & O'Hair, H. Dan (2008). *Health Communication in the 21st Century*. Malden, MA: Blackwell.

20. Geist-Martin, Patricia, Ray, Eileen B., & Sharf, Barbara (2003). *Communicating Health: Personal, Cultural, and Political Complexities*. Belmont, CA: Wadsworth Press.

21. Jackson, Richard (2007). Language, Policy and the Construction of a Torture Culture in the War on Terrorism. *Review of International Studies, 33*, 353–371.

22. Gamson, William A. (1992). The Social Psychology of Collective Action. In Aldon Morris & Carol Mueller (Eds.), *Frontiers in Social Movement Theory* (pp. 53–76). New Haven, CT: Yale University Press.

23. Croft, Stuart (2006). *Culture, Crisis and America's War on Terror*. Cambridge: Cambridge University Press; Fairclough, Norman (2003). *Analyzing Discourse: Textual Analysis for Social Research*. London: Routledge; Jackson, Richard (2005). *Writing the War on Terrorism: Language, Politics and Counter-terrorism*. Manchester, England: Manchester University Press.

24. Altheide, David L. (2007). The Mass Media and Terrorism. *Discourse & Communication, 1*(3), 287–308.

25. Miller, Claude H., & Landau, Mark J. (2005). Communication and Terrorism: A Terror Management Theory Perspective. *Communication Research Reports, 22*(1), 79–88.

26. Altheide, David L. (2007). The Mass Media and Terrorism. *Discourse & Communication, 1*(3), 287–308.

27. Baker, Kevin (2001, December 9). THE YEAR IN IDEAS: A TO Z: American Imperialism, Embraced. *The New York Times*, p. 53.

28. Kellner, Douglas (2003). *From 9/11 to Terror War: The Dangers of the Bush Legacy*. Lanham, MD: Rowman & Littlefield.

29. Morin, Richard, & Deane, Claudia (2001, October 8). Public Support Is Overwhelming; Poll Finds 94% Favor Bush's Ordering Strikes on Afghanistan. *The Washington Post*, p. A5.

30. Baker, David N., & Price, Byron E. (2010). Counter-Terrorism Post 9/11: The Hidden Agenda of Exclusion. *International Journal of Criminology and Sociological Theory, 3*(2), 531–542.

31. Falk, Richard (2005). Review Essay: Imperial Vibrations, 9/11, and the Ordeal of the Middle East. *Journal of Palestine Studies, XXXIV*(3), 65–76.

32. Melnick, Jeffrey (2009). *9/11 Culture*. New York: Wiley-Blackwell; Waisbord, Silvio (2002). Journalism, Risk, and Patriotism. In Barbara Zelizer & Stuart Allan (Eds.), *Journalism after September 11* (pp. 201–219). London: Routledge.

33. Altheide, David L. (2007). The Mass Media and Terrorism. *Discourse & Communication, 1*(3), 287–308.

34. Crelinsten, Ronald (2003). The World of Torture: A Constructed Reality. *Theoretical Criminology, 7*(3), 293–318.

35. Jackson, Richard (2007). Language, Policy and the Construction of a Torture Culture in the War on Terrorism. *Review of International Studies, 33*, 353–371.

36. Sageman, Marc (2008). A Strategy for Fighting International Islamist Terrorists. *Annals of the American Academy of Political and Social Science, 618*, 223–231.

37. Pew Research Center (2007). Muslim Americans: Middle Class and Mostly Mainstream. http://pewre search.org/assets/pdf/muslim-americans.pdf.

38. Sageman, Marc (2008). A Strategy for Fighting International Islamist Terrorists. *Annals of the American Academy of Political and Social Science, 618,* 223–231.

39. Spring, Joel (2010). *The Politics of American Education.* New York: Routledge.

40. Sageman, Marc (2008). *Leaderless Jihad.* Philadelphia: University of Pennsylvania Press.

41. Gray, Jeffrey A. (1989). *The Psychology of Fear and Stress.* Cambridge: Cambridge University Press; LeDoux, Joseph E. (1996). *The Emotional Brain: The Mysterious Underpinnings of Emotional Life.* New York: Simon & Schuster; Rachman, Stanley J. (1978). *Fear and Courage.* San Francisco: W. H. Freeman.

42. Altheide, David L. (2006). Terrorism and the Politics of Fear. *Cultural Studies, 6*(4), 415–439.

43. Schwalbe, Michael, Godwin, Sandra, Holden, Daphne, Schrock, Douglas, Thompson, Shealy, & Wolkomir, Michele (2000). Generic Processes in the Reproduction of Inequality: An Interactionist Analysis. *Social Forces, 79,* 419–452.

44. Altheide, David L. (2002). *Creating Fear: News and the Construction of Crisis.* Hawthorne, NY: Aldine de Gruyter; Altheide, David L., & Michalowski, R. Sam (1999). Fear in the News: A Discourse of Control. *The Sociological Quarterly, 40,* 475–503; Glassner, Barry (1999). *The Culture of Fear: Why Americans Are Afraid of the Wrong Things.* New York: Basic Books.

45. Altheide, David L. (2006). Terrorism and the Politics of Fear. *Cultural Studies, 6*(4), 415–439.

46. Arian, Asher (1989). A People Apart: Coping with National Security Problems in Israel. *Journal of Conflict Resolution, 33,* 605–631; Gordon, Carol, & Arian, Asher (2001). Threat and Decision Making. *Journal of Conflict Resolution, 45,* 196–215; Jost, John T., Glaser, Jack, Kruglanski, Arie W., & Sulloway, Frank J. (2003). Political Conservatism and Motivated Social Cognition. *Psychological Bulletin, 129,* 339–375.

47. Bar-Tal, Daniel, Halperin, Eran, & de Rivera, Joseph (2007). Collective Emotions in Conflict Situations: Societal Implications. *Journal of Social Issues, 63*(2), 441–460.

48. Phillips, Suzanne B. (2009). The Synergy of Group and Individual Treatment Modalities in the Aftermath of Disaster and Unfolding Trauma. *International Journal of Group Psychotherapy, 59*(1), 85–107.

49. Ayotte, Kevin J., & Moore, Scott D. (2008). Terrorism, Language, and Community Dialogue. In Dan O'Hair, Robert Heath, Kevin Ayotte, & Gerald R. Ledlow (Eds.), *Terrorism: Communication and Rhetorical Perspectives* (pp. 67–92). Cresskill, NJ: Hampton Press.

50. Tuman, Joseph S. (2003). *Communicating Terror: The Rhetorical Dimensions of Terrorism.* Thousand Oaks, CA: Sage.

51. Bar-Tal, Daniel, Halperin, Eran, & de Rivera, Joseph (2007). Collective Emotions in Conflict Situations: Societal Implications. *Journal of Social Issues, 63*(2), 441–460.

52. Alexander, Jeffrey C. (2004). From the Depths of Despair: Performance, Counterperformance, and "September 11." *Sociological Theory, 22*(1), 88–105.

53. Frijda, Nico H. (1988). The Laws of Emotion. *American Psychologist, 43,* 349–358.

54. Smith, Eliot R. (1993). Social Identity and Social Emotions: Toward New Conceptualization of Prejudice. In Diane M. Mackie & David L. Hamilton (Eds.), *Affect, Cognition and Stereotyping: Interactive Processes in Group Perception* (pp. 297–315). San Diego: Academic Press.

55. Bar-Tal, Daniel, Halperin, Eran, & de Rivera, Joseph (2007). Collective Emotions in Conflict Situations: Societal Implications. *Journal of Social Issues, 63*(2), 441–460.

56. Wright-Neville, David, & Smith, Debra (2009). Political Rage: Terrorism and the Politics of Emotion. *Global Change, Peace & Security, 21*(1), 85–98.

57. Horgan, John (2005). *The Psychology of Terrorism.* New York: Routledge.

58. Bar-Tal, Daniel (2001). Why Does Fear Override Hope in Societies Engulfed by Intractable Conflict, as It Does in the Israeli Society? *Political Psychology, 22,* 601–627; Moïsi, Dominique (2007). The Clash of Emotions: Fear, Humiliation, Hope, and the New World Order. *Foreign Affairs, 86,* 8–12.

59. de Rivera, Joseph (1992). Emotional Climate: Social Structure and Emotional Dynamics. In K. T. Strongman (Ed.), *International Review of Studies on Emotion* (pp. 199–218). New York: John Wiley.

60. Bar-Tal, Daniel, Halperin, Eran, & de Rivera, Joseph (2007). Collective Emotions in Conflict Situations: Societal Implications. *Journal of Social Issues, 63*(2), 441–460.

61. Harber, Kent D., & Cohen, Dov J. (2005). The Emotional Broadcaster Theory of Social Sharing. *Journal of Language and Social Psychology, 24,* 382–400; Shaver, Phillip R., & Klinnert, Mary (1982). Schachter's Theories of Affiliation and Emotion: Implications of Developmental Research. In L. Wheeler (Ed.), *Review of Personality and Social Psychology* (pp. 37–72). Beverly Hills, CA: Sage.

62. Luminet, Oliver, Bouts, Patrick, Delie, Frederique, Manstead, Antony S. R., & Rime, Bernard (2000). Social Sharing of Emotion Following Exposure to a Negatively Valenced Situation. *Cognition and Emotion, 14,* 661–688.

63. Gantz, Walter, & Trenholm, Sarah (1979). Why People Pass on News: Motivations for Diffusion. *Journalism Quarterly, 56,* 365–370.

64. Ibrahim, Amal, Ye, Jiali, & Hoffner, Cynthia (2008). Diffusion of News of the Shuttle Columbia Disaster: The Role of Emotional Responses and Motives for Interpersonal Communication. *Communication Research Reports, 25*(2), 91–101.

65. Herskovits, Melville J. (1948). *Man and His Works: The Science of Cultural Anthropology.* New York: Knopf.

66. Güss, C. Dominik, Tuason, Ma Teresa, & Teixeira, Vanessa B. (2007). A Cultural-Psychological Theory of Contemporary Islamic Martyrdom. *Journal for the Theory of Social Behaviour, 37*(4), 415–445; Smith, Peter, & Bond, Michael (1998). *Social Psychology across Cultures.* London: Prentice Hall; Weigert, Andrew J. (2003). Terrorism, Identity, and Public Order: A Perspective from Goffman. *Identity: An International Journal of Theory and Research, 3*(2), 93–113.

67. Golden, Karen A. (1992). The Individual and Organizational Culture: Strategies for Action in Highly-Ordered Contexts. *Journal of Management Studies, 29,* 1–21; Smircich, Linda (1983). Concepts of Culture and Organizational Analysis. *Administrative Science Quarterly, 28,* 339–358.

68. Spiro, Melford, E. (2001). Cultural Determinism, Cultural Relativism, and the Comparative Study of Psychopathology. *Ethos, 29*(2), 218–234.

69. Hofstede, Geert (1991). *Cultures and Organizations: Software of the Mind.* New York: McGraw-Hill International.

70. Hofstede, Geert (2001). *Culture's Consequences: Comparing Values, Behaviors, Institutions, and Organizations across Nations.* Thousand Oaks, CA: Sage.

71. Lorenz, Konrad (1967). *On Aggression.* London: Methuen.

72. Hofstede, Geert (2001). *Culture's Consequences: Comparing Values, Behaviors, Institutions, and Organizations across Nations.* Thousand Oaks, CA: Sage.

73. Jensen, Lene A. (2003). Coming of Age in a Multicultural World: Globalization and Adolescent Cultural Identity Formation. *Applied Developmental Science, 7*(3), 189–196; Schwartz, Seth J., Montgomery, Marilyn J., & Briones, Ervin (2006). The Role of Identity in Acculturation among Immigrant People: Theoretical Propositions, Empirical Questions, and Applied Recommendations. *Human Development, 49,* 1–30; Schwartz, Seth J., Dunkel, Curtis S., & Waterman, Alan S. (2009). Terrorism: An Identity Theory Perspective. *Studies in Conflict & Terrorism, 32,* 537–559.

74. Coker, Christopher (2008). War, Memes and Memeplexes. *International Affairs, 84*(5), 903–914.

75. Hyat, Kamila (2008, September 25). No room for Doubt and Division. *The News International.*

76. Vicziany, Marika, & Monash Asia Institute (2007). Understanding the 1993 Mumbai Bombings: Madrassas and the Hierarchy of Terror. *South Asia: Journal of South Asian Studies, 30*(1), 43–73.

77. Ali, Saleem H. (2005). *Islamic Education and Conflict: Understanding the Madrassahs of Pakistan.* Washington, D.C.: U.S. Institute of Peace.

78. Bano, Masooda (2007). Beyond Politics: The Reality of a Deobandi Madrasa in Pakistan. *Journal of Islamic Studies, 18*(1), 43–68.

79. Casebeer, William D. (2008). Identity, Culture and Stories: Empathy and the War on Terrorism. *Minnesota Journal of Law, Science & Technology, 9*(2), 653–688.

80. Bergner, Daniel (2003, July 20). Where the Enemy Is Everywhere and Nowhere. *The New York Times Magazine,* 14–15; Kitfield, James (2002, November 23). Breaking Al Qaeda Means Getting Bin Laden. *National Journal,* p. 3496.

81. Abrahms, Max (2005). Al Qaeda's Miscommunication War: The Terrorism Paradox. *Terrorism and Political Violence, 17,* 529–549.

82. Alexander, Jeffrey, C. (2004). From the Depths of Despair: Performance, Counterperformance, and "September 11." *Sociological Theory, 22*(1), 88–105.

83. Bernstein, R. (2005, July 15). Muslim Approval of Terror Drops, Poll Finds. *The New York Times*, p. A8.

84. Greenblatt, Stephen (1995). Culture. In Frank Lentricchia & Thomas McLaughlin (Eds.), *Critical Terms for Literary Study* (pp. 225–232). Chicago: University of Chicago Press.

85. Ettema, James S. (2005). Crafting Cultural Resonance: Imaginative Power in Everyday Journalism. *Journalism, 6*(2), 131–152.

86. Bourdieu, Pierre (1986). The Forms of Capital. In John G. Richardson's (Ed.), *Handbook for Theory and Research for the Sociology of Education* (pp. 241–258). New York: Greenwood.

87. Güss, C. Dominik, Tuason, Ma Teresa, & Teixeira, Vanessa B. (2007). A Cultural-Psychological Theory of Contemporary Islamic Martyrdom. *Journal for the Theory of Social Behaviour, 37*(4), 415–445.

88. Madsen, Julian (2005). Murder and Martyrdom. Suicide Terror in the Third Millennium. *The Arena Journal, 23*, 97–110.

89. Sciolino, Elaine (2002, January 27). Don't Weaken Arafat, Saudi Warns Bush. *The New York Times*, p. A6.

90. Atran, Scott (2003). Genesis of Suicide Terrorism. *Science, 299*, 1534–1539.

91. Soibelman, Mali (2004). Palestinian Suicide Bombers. *Journal of Investigative Psychology and Offender Profiling, 1*, 175–190.

92. Carey, James W. (1992). *Communication as Culture: Essays on Media and Society*. New York: Routledge.

93. Levy-Barzilai, Vered (2002). *On Suicide Bombers and Humanity*. San Francisco: Independent Media Center; Oliver, Anne Marie. & Steinberg, Paul F. (2005). *The Road to Martyrs' Square: A Journey into the World of the Suicide Bomber*. Oxford: Oxford University Press.

94. Tanenbaum, Robert S. (2006). Preaching Terror: Free Speech or Wartime Incitement? *American University Law Review, 55*, 785–819.

95. Miller, Claude H., & Landau, Mark J. (2005). Communication and Terrorism: A Terror Management Theory Perspective. *Communication Research Reports, 22*(1), 79–88.

96. Keen, Sam (1986). *Faces of the Enemy: Reflections of the Hostile Imagination*. San Francisco: Harper & Row.

97. Hyde, Maggie, & McGuinness, Michael (1994). *Introducing Jung*. New York: Totem Books.

98. Hopcke, Robert H. (1989). *A Guided Tour of the Collected Works of C. G. Jung*. Boston: Shambala.

99. Hart, William B. (2005). Franz Boas and the Roots of Intercultural Communication Research. *International and Intercultural Communication Annual, 28*, 176–193; Ottenheimer, Harriet Joseph (2006). *The Anthropology of Language: An Introduction to Linguistic Anthropology*. Belmont: Thomson Higher Education.

100. Global Language Monitor (2011). *Top Words of the Decade (2000–2009)*. Austin, TX: Global Language Monitor.

101. Becker, Ernest (1971). *The Birth and Death of Meaning* (2nd ed.).

102. Miller, Claude H., & Landau, Mark J. (2005). Communication and Terrorism: A Terror Management Theory Perspective. *Communication Research Reports, 22*(1), 79–88.

103. Triandis, Harry C. (1995). *Individualism & collectivism*. Boulder, CO: Westview Press.

104. Lerner, Melvin J. (1980). *Belief in a Just World: A Fundamental Delusion*. New York: Plenum; Rubin, Zick, & Peplau, Lelita (1975). Who Believes in a Just World? *Journal of Social Issues, 31*, 65–89.

105. Lerner, Melvin J., & Miller, Dale T. (1978). Just-World Research and the Attribution Process: Looking Back and Ahead. *Psychological Bulletin, 85*, 1030–1051.

106. Rubin, Zick, & Peplau, Lelita (1975). Who Believes in a Just World? *Journal of Social Issues, 31*, 65–89.

107. Oswald, Debra L. (2005). Understanding Anti-Arab Reactions Post-9/11: The Role of Threats, Social Categories, and Personal Ideologies. *Journal of Applied Social Psychology, 35*(9), 1775–1799.

108. Sidanius, Jim, & Pratto, Felicia (1999). *Social Dominance: An Intergroup Theory of Social Hierarchy and Oppression*. New York: Cambridge University Press.

109. Oswald, Debra L. (2005). Understanding Anti-Arab Reactions Post-9/11: The Role of Threats, Social Categories, and Personal Ideologies. *Journal of Applied Social Psychology, 35*(9), 1775–1799; Pratto, Felicia, Sidanius, Jim, Stallworth, Lisa M., & Malle, Bertram F. (1994). Social dominance orientation: A personality variable predicting social and political attitudes. *Journal of Personality and Social Psychology, 67*, 741–763; Sidanius, J., & Liu, James (1991). The Gulf War and the Rodney King Beating: Implications of the General Conservatism and Social Dominance Perspectives. *Journal of Social Psychology, 135*, 685–700.

110. Weimann, Gabriel (2008). The Psychology of Mass-Mediated Terrorism. *American Behavioral Scientist, 52*(1), 69–86.

111. Goffman, Erving (1959). *The Presentation of Self in Everyday Life*. Garden City, NY: Anchor Press; Plummer, Ken (1991). *Symbolic Interactionism: Foundations and History*. Hauts, England: Edward Elgar Press.

112. Mead, George Herbert (1934). *Mind, Self and Society*. Chicago: University of Chicago Press.

113. Meltzer, Bernard N. (1975). *Symbolic Interactionism: Genesis, Varieties, and Criticism*. London: Routledge.

114. Berger, Peter, & Luckmann, Thomas (1966). *The Social Construction of Reality: A Treatise in the Sociology of Knowledge*. Garden City, NY: Doubleday.

115. Altheide, David L. (2006). Terrorism and the Politics of Fear. *Cultural Studies, 6*(4), 415–439.

116. Altheide, David, L., & Snow, Robert (1979). *Media Logic*. Beverly Hills, CA: Sage.

117. Altheide, David L. (2006). Terrorism and the Politics of Fear. *Cultural Studies, 6*(4), 415–439; Iyengar, Shanto, & Kinder, Donald M. (1987). *News That Matters*. Chicago: University of Chicago Press; Shaw, Donald L., & McCombs, Maxwell E. (1977). *The Agenda-Setting Function of the Press*. St. Paul, MN: West.

118. Perinbanayagam, Robert (1974). The Definition of the Situation: An Analysis of the Ethnomethodological and Dramaturgical View. *Sociological Quarterly, 15*, 521–541.

119. Hofstede, Geert J. (1980). *Culture's Consequences: International Differences in Work-Related Values*. Newbury Park, CA: Sage.

120. Wiedenhaefer, Robert M., Dastoor, Barbara Riederer, Balloun, Joseph, & Sosa-Fey, Josephine (2007). Ethno-Psychological Characteristics and Terror-Producing Countries: Linking Uncertainty Avoidance to Terrorist Acts in the 1970s. *Studies in Conflict & Terrorism, 30*, 801–823.

121. Hofstede, Geert (1991). *Cultures and Organizations: Software of the Mind*. New York: McGraw-Hill International.

122. Hofstede, Geert (1980). *Culture's Consequences: International Differences in Work-Related Values*. London: Sage; Hofstede, Geert (1991). *Cultures and Organizations: Software of the Mind*. New York: McGraw-Hill International.

123. Schwartz, Seth J. (2005). A New Identity for Identity Research: Recommendations for Expanding and Refocusing the Identity Literature. *Journal of Adolescent Research, 20*, 293–308.

124. Post, Jerrold M. (2005). The New Face of Terrorism: Socio-Cultural Foundations of Contemporary Terrorism. *Behavioral Sciences and the Law, 23*, 451–465.

125. Wiedenhaefer, Robert M., Dastoor, Barbara Riederer, Balloun, Joseph, & Sosa-Fey, Josephine (2007). Ethno-Psychological Characteristics and Terror-Producing Countries: Linking Uncertainty Avoidance to Terrorist Acts in the 1970s. *Studies in Conflict & Terrorism, 30*, 801–823.

126. Crenshaw, Martha (1992). Current Research on Terrorism: The Academic Perspective. *Studies in Conflict & Terrorism, 15*, 1–11.

127. Schachter, Stanley (1959). *The Psychology of Affiliation*. Stanford, CA: Stanford University Press.

128. Weinberg, Leonard, & Eubank, William Lee (1994). Cultural Differences in the Behavior of Terrorists. *Terrorism and Political Violence, 6*, 1–28.

129. Post, Jerrold M., Sprinzak, Ehud, & Denny, Laurita M. (2003). The Terrorists in Their Own Words: Interviews with 35 Incarcerated Middle Eastern Terrorists. *Terrorism and Political Violence, 15*, 171–184.

130. Geertz, Clifford (1973). *The Interpretation of Cultures: Selected Essays*. New York: Basic Books.

131. Geertz, Clifford (1983). *Local Knowledge: Further Essays in Interpretive Anthropology*. New York: Basic Books.

132. Griset, Pamala L., & Mahan, Sue (2003). *Terrorism in Perspective*. Thousand Oaks, CA: Sage; Weinberg, Leonard, & Davis, Paul B. (1989). *Introduction to Political Terrorism*. New York: McGraw-Hill.

133. Mahmood, Cynthia Keppley (2001). Terrorism, Myth, and the Power of Ethnographic Praxis. *Journal of Contemporary Ethnography, 30*(5), 520–545.

134. Kumar, Ram Narayan (1996). *The Sikh Unrest and the Indian State*. New Delhi, India: Ajanta.

135. Mahmood, Cynthia Keppley (2001). Terrorism, Myth, and the Power of Ethnographic Praxis. *Journal of Contemporary Ethnography, 30*(5), 520–545.

CHAPTER 7

Stereotyping Terrorists

> **After reading this chapter, you will be able to**
>
> - identify and evaluate the diverse ways of stereotyping the enemy, such as "guilt by association";
> - discuss the impact of the stigmatization of the enemy by stereotyping; and
> - explain Marshall McLuhan's tetradic framework of four fundamental steps of media transformation.

STEREOTYPE: DEFINITION

A **stereotype** is a simplified mental picture of a group of individuals who have certain characteristics in common. The word *stereotype* comes from the domain of printing; in the past, it was a duplicate impression of an original typographical part or text, used to print identical copies. Over the years, this became a metaphor for any collection of ideas repeated identically and with no changes. The word *stereotyping* was used for the first time by Walter Lippmann, an American journalist, in 1922. As Lippmann observed, stereotypes function as the foundations of the "fortress" of social customs.[1] People stereotype others as a way of categorizing them based on similar features. Participation in rumor mills perpetuates these prejudicial opinions and enables them to transfer to other targets too. For instance, ethnic origin is often derogated in regard to the social norms, religion, and style of dress of a certain group of people.[2] Stereotyping has also been called the *collective hunch theory* or *Gestalt*.

Gestalt is one method by which people form impressions of others. Gestalt is a broad and all-encompassing impression of an individual that is either positive or negative. We identify a few traits and, extracting information from our mental schemata, we arrive at a conclusion on the basis of these traits. The effect is an impression of the individual as a whole.[3] Gestalt gives rise to the halo effect and the horn effect. The **halo effect** is the tendency to stereotype positively, that is, to positively interpret virtually anything a person says or does because we have a positive Gestalt of the group to which that person belongs. The **horn effect** has the reverse effect: to negatively interpret anything a person says or does because we have a negative Gestalt of that person's group.[4]

Stereotyping involves three underlying ideologies. First, stereotypes display a few notable characteristics about people, and then reduce, overstate (or aggrandize), and simplify everything about the group to those characteristics in a wholesale manner. Second, stereotyping adopts a tactic of splitting. It continuously separates what is included from what is excluded or the satisfactory from the unsatisfactory. Hence, stereotyping superficially and symbolically creates boundaries and borders. Third, where flagrant inequalities of power exist, the practice of stereotyping runs rampant. Power is exploited against groups that are different and, in the process, that represent unacceptable groups. Stereotyping can preserve the social and symbolic order of a hegemonic power.[5]

Stereotyping can affect cognitive processes. In their study, Correll et al. (2002)[6] noted that subjects were more likely to misperceive an object as a weapon when held by a Black person than when held by a Caucasian. Anxiety may also contribute to the use of stereotypes. Schaller, Park, and Mueller (2003)[7] observed that anxiety caused by the dark increased participants' perception that Black males are dangerous. Maner et al. (2005)[8] showed subjects a movie clip that was made to create fear and found that the subjects were more likely to view the facial expressions of Black and Arab individuals as unfriendly than subjects who watched a neutral movie clip.

STEREOTYPING THE ENEMY

When one has no direct personal experience with a person, stereotyping that person becomes a method of filling in the blanks in regard to the expectations (or lack thereof) of those different from the person imagining them.[9] Once someone is stereotyped in a negative fashion, he or she may not even be considered as having human qualities. For example, in the Soviet Union, the stereotype of Chechens as being ruthless and bloodthirsty mountain killers was revived in the early 20th century when they resorted to terrorism to have an independent state. Presently, Chechnya's brutal efforts to separate from Russia have further stereotyped their reputation as being barbaric, violent, and inherently hostile to others. In addition, the perceived notion that Chechen separatism is driven by Islamic fundamentalism and international terrorism has shored up their image as immoral and incompatible people who choose violence over peace.[10]

Diverse Ways for Stereotyping the Enemy

Regardless of where stereotypes come from, all stereotypes are firm conceptions (*stereo* means "solid" or "firm") used over and over again; we assume that they echo the same reality—that is, they have the same meaning—whenever we use them. The literature on stereotyping has spawned various academic concepts on the subject. For example, a **normative stereotype** is an overgeneralization that draws on limited information, like the information we learn from a travel guide. The normative stereotype of Muslims, according to media news accounts, typically involves radical views, brainwashing, and terrorism. Conversely, a **non-normative stereotype** is an overgeneralization that is entirely self-projective; people project concepts from their own culture onto people of other cultures. Radical Muslims see themselves as pure and kill others who are not pure. So, according to radical Muslims, other pure cultures believe that radical Islamist terrorism is a pure action to undertake.[11]

Guilt by association, also called *bad company fallacy* or the *company-that-you-keep fallacy*, is a fallacy that something must be false because our enemies support it (e.g., "Osama bin Laden was a Muslim, so Islam is an evil religion"). Guilt by association is like collective guilt. **Collective guilt** is the notion that a group should bear guilt for all the wrongdoings of particular members. Following this logic, a person holds responsibility for what others in his or her group have done, even if that person is innocent.[12] In the U.S., the strategy of using guilt by association in immigration procedures is not new. The Immigration and Naturalization Service (INS) used guilt by association more assertively in the late 1990s, partly because in 1996 Congress gave the INS more power to do so in two statutes: the Antiterrorism and Effective Death Penalty Act and the Illegal Immigration Reform and Immigrant Responsibility Act. This type of stereotyping stems, on the one hand, from ignorance about the Arab and Muslim world and, on the other, from creating associations between terrorism and an Arab or Muslim face. Such stereotype is less costly for the government to rely on these tactics because most people are less likely to raise objections when the "victim" is one whom they have associated with terrorism.[13]

Linguistic profiling occurs when people (1) listen to someone's voice or recognize the type of first or last name that person has, (2) make deductions about that person's race or ethnicity, and (3) discriminate against him or her on the basis of the assumed race or ethnicity. A 1994 study found that subjects were biased toward Arabic-accented speech. The subjects—all freshmen at Florida State University (most of them were Anglo-American students)—showed a negative reaction to accented speech. Of the three accents—German, Spanish, and Arabic—the Arabic-accented speech had the lowest rating.[14] Likewise, in a study on discrimination in the housing market of Stockholm (Sweden), Bengtsson and Iverman (2010)[15] found that women with Swedish-sounding names were treated more positively than women with Arabic-sounding names. In another Swedish study, conducted by Rooth (2009),[16] in comparison to Swedish-sounding names, Arabic-sounding names were very much associated with words describing low productivity (e.g., ineffective) but had a low association with words reflecting high productivity (e.g., hardworking and ambitious).

Enemies can also be stereotyped by not being represented in the media. This is a phenomenon called symbolic annihilation. **Symbolic annihilation** refers to a lack of representation of which the outcome can be the reinforcement of stereotypes. In a longitudinal study (1993–1996) of TV content on ABC, CNN, and PBS, Lind and Danowski (1998)[17] found a very low amount of coverage of Arabs and even less of Arab culture. The reinforcement of stereotypes through an overpowering association with war, terrorism, and threats had led to a representation of Arabs who are violent and "identified most strongly in terms of their relations with Israel" (p. 165).

Collective Unconscious

Spillmann and Spillmann (1997)[18] explained the influence of our cultural worldview (CWV) on the collective unconscious, so much so that it comes to support the stereotyping of others as enemies. The two scholars describe the social construction of the enemy image as a syndrome of deep-seated perceptual evaluations that assume the following characteristics (pp. 50–51):

- Negative anticipation: all actions taken by the enemy (in the past, present, and future) become recognized as harmful intentions toward one's own group. Whichever act the enemy carries out is intended to destroy us.

- Putting blame on the enemy: the enemy is considered the cause of any stress on a group. The enemy is guilty of instigating the current strain and negative conditions.

- Identification with evil: the enemy's evil values have a negative correlation with our own values. The enemy wants to destroy our dominant value system as well. The enemy personifies the antithesis of what we are and strive for and wishes to extinguish our highest values. Therefore, the enemy must be stopped. Every little thing he does is tragic, like the horn effect.

- Zero-sum thinking: what is good for our enemy is bad for us; the opposite is also true.

- Stereotyping and de-individualization: "birds of a feather flock together"; any person belonging to the enemy group is automatically our enemy. This is the Gestalt or guilt by association at its core.

- Refusal to show empathy: expressing empathy toward any person of the enemy group is not advisable because of perceived threats and feelings of opposition. There is no possible alternative to that perception.

When politicians have to make decisions in an environment of deep-rooted and often unconscious stereotypes, they have a tendency to categorize and interpret facts or events based on those stereotypes rather than by making a personal and rational decision based on the specific facts of a case (i.e., judging a case on its own merit).[19] The stereotyping of all facets of a terrorist's culture as evil can stem from trumped-up prejudice or ignorance. The main corollaries are that it can perpetuate a climate of stigmatization toward people who belong to that culture and it can prevent them from entering or succeeding in various activities or fields in life.

STIGMATIZATION

Stigmatization is a problem of disempowerment and social prejudice. It refers to an invisible sign of condemnation that allows "insiders" to set boundaries around the "outsiders" to delineate the limits of inclusion in any group. Boundaries enable insiders to know which person is in and which one is out. They also permit insiders to bolster their group solidarity when outsiders violate accepted norms of conduct.[20] Sociologist Erving Goffman (1963)[21] defined **stigma** as the process by which normal identity is smeared by the response or feedback of others. The effect of stigma is a harsh social disapproval of traits or beliefs that are considered as opposing cultural norms. Etymologically, stigma is a Greek word referring to a type of tattoo mark cut or burned into the skin of criminals, slaves, or traitors. The purpose was to clearly identify them as tarnished or morally polluted. Later, a stigma came to signify a characterizing mark of social disgrace, shame, or discredit—like an eternal stain. Stigmatized persons were to be avoided or shunned, especially in public places. In ancient Greek, stigma also referred to the spots of snakes. It initially bore the meaning of "dot," "mark," "welt."[22]

Link and Phelan (2001)[23] suggest that stigmas are born when four specific elements come together: (1) people distinguish and label human variations; (2) dominant cultural beliefs link those labeled to antagonistic attributes; (3) labeled persons are categorized in distinguished groups, the goal being to create a sense of detachment between "us" and "them"; and (4) labeled persons endure status loss and discrimination leading to inequalities.

Three Forms of Stigma

There are three forms of stigma. First is the **existential stigma**: a situation in which the stigmatized individual is not responsible for his or her mistreatment or he or she has little control over the stigma. Examples are visible deformations, scars, obvious manifestations of bulimia or anorexia, leprosy, physical disabilities, and social disabilities. Second is the **achieved stigma**: a stigma that one has caused because of bad conduct or because he or she has contributed greatly to earning his or her stigma in question. Examples are deviations in terms of personality, mental illness, drug abuse, alcoholism, and criminal backgrounds. Third is the **tribal stigma**: characteristics, imagined or real, of racial groups, nationalities, or religions that are viewed as deviating from the predominant normative race, nationality, or religion.[24] An example of the tribal stigma is the image of the terrorist as the "wild man" of our modern-day imagination, entirely outside the boundaries of human civility and conscience. The wild man is usually of another race, nationality, or religion—and scary.[25]

Racial Profiling

Subsequent to the attacks on the World Trade Center and the Pentagon, and the crash of United Flight 93 in Pennsylvania, some decision makers, pundits, academics, claiming that they knew what terrorists looked like, championed the racial profiling of Arabs and Muslims as a way to achieve greater national security.[26] **Racial profiling** is a situation in which law enforcement and other officials throw a wide blanket of suspicion that entraps and harms members of racial groups—even though those members can be innocent of any wrongdoing. Generally, those who encounter such discrimination in society become most vulnerable concerning the over-inclusiveness problem. Racial profiling is a type of stigma that is over-inclusive in nature and can create false positives. After September 11, 2001, both Arabs and Muslims became subject of popular suspicion, contributing to the Arabification of Muslims and the Muslimification of Arabs.[27]

For American Muslims, the media and social construction of them as terrorists have certainly contributed to racial profiling, principally in the transportation industry. A nation-wide survey given shortly after 9/11 revealed that 35% of respondents had lower trust in American Muslims after the attacks. In the domain of legal policy, over 50% of those surveyed favored making Arabs (including Arab Americans) go through "special, more intensive security checks before boarding planes in the United States."[28] A report by CAIR (Council on American-Islamic Relations) stated that, within twelve months after 9/11, more than 60,000 American Muslims were disturbed psychologically, and sometimes physically, because of 9/11. CAIR's data include 1,200 Muslims selected and held by immigration officials and treated as if they committed a terrorist act. Other reports have kept a record of 5,000 legal visa holders being asked to undergo "voluntary interrogations."[29] Racial profiling is a tricky tool in the Global War on Terror (GWOT) because it works against, and mingles with, long-established and deep-seated stereotypes about Arabs and Muslims that not only stigmatize them even more, but that also risk distorting rational decision making.

The Case of Liban Hussein

The case of Liban Hussein in Ottawa (Canada) is a good example of racial profiling. Hussein was an immigrant from Somalia who owned a money-wiring commerce that sent funds to Somalia. On October 2, 2001, his name was put on Canada's list of terrorist entities, supposedly as a move to comply with United Nations Regulations. In the end, Hussein was found innocent for any wrongdoing and removed from the list on June 3, 2002, following an investigation from the Royal Canadian Mounted Police. Even though his name was officially taken off the list of terrorist entities, Hussein lost both his house and his business. As a result, he had no choice but move his family to his mom's house. Furthermore, owing to outdated Internet resources, he is still officially considered a member of a terrorist organization. His reputation has been irreparably smeared.[30]

In line with these contentions, on top of incurring losses because of frozen bank accounts, closed-down businesses, and damaged reputations, Arab and Muslims (and those who have their ethnic looks) have described other costs—such as encountering difficulties to fly to see a relative dying because of racial profiling by the airline industry. Racially profiled victims have missed job interviews and been turned down opportunities to attend career fairs. As a case in point, Arab employers in Windsor, Ontario have purportedly refused to hire Arab job candidates in favor of Caucasian-looking candidates because they fear that goods that are transported to the U.S. can be delayed at the borders.[31]

STEREOTYPING ARABS, ISLAM, AND TERRORISM

Even before 9/11, Arabs and Muslims were already subjected to pervasive stereotyping. In both American and Canadian mass media, Arabs and Muslims were usually depicted as zealous, violence-loving maniacs. This deeply ingrained picture of Arabs and Muslims was around well before 9/11 and has been well recorded.[32] This has had a serious impact on Westerners' perceptions of Islam as a whole. For example, in a study by Horry and Wright (2004),[33] stereotyping was shown to be related to visual attention and face recognition accuracy. After being shown terrorism-related words on a screen, anxious participants displayed an attentional bias toward Muslim faces. Non-anxious participants, in contrast, showed an attentional bias toward White faces. These results highly reflect findings from previous dot-probe studies, in which anxious participants paid more attention to threat signals—for example, angry faces and threatening words. This implies that after being prepared or nurtured to think about terrorism, participants tend to perceive the Muslim faces as threat cues based on their racial stereotypes.[34] Stereotypes become stereotypes as a result of guilt by association. Osama bin Laden was a Muslim; so was his deputy, Ayman al-Zawahiri (now Al Qaeda's #1). All nineteen hijackers on September 11, 2001 were Muslims. The late Abu Musab al-Zarqawi was a Muslim too.[35]

American Stereotypes of Arabs and Islam over the Years

Middle Easterners have lived in America since the mid-19th century. Most of the first immigrants were Chaldeans—Roman Catholics from what is today Iraq. Before September 11, 2001, the name *Arab* was used to stress the commonalty of all people of Arab descent irrespective of national origin. However, after 9/11, the use of national labels such as Palestinian, Egyptian, or Lebanese was more recurrent. This confirms the post-9/11 tensions. According to an FBI report, anti-Islamic attacks rose by 1,600% between 2000 and 2001. Many of the targets were not just Muslims, but also Sikhs, Arab Christians, South Asians, and Moroccans. A large percentage of Middle Easterners who immigrate to the U.S. are Jewish (from both Israel and Arab countries), Christian (many are Lebanese Christians), and followers of the Baha'i faith from Iran. Only 25% of Arabs who live in America today are Muslims.[36] In November 2001, Gallup polls reported that practically 25% of Americans not only thought it would be highly possible that their communities experience a terrorist attack; they also categorized Arabs as particularly devious. Forty-nine percent of Americans supported the obligation that Arabs (including Arab U.S. citizens) carry a special type of identification with them, and 58% favored the necessity that Arabs undergo a more rigorous screening process at airports.[37] This terrorism threat associated with Arabs is similar to the overstated threat of street crime associated with African Americans.[38] According to New York City police, between September 11, 2001 and March 2002, there were 117 reports of hate crimes against Muslims in that city alone.[39]

Willard Oxtoby's (1980)[40] study of U.S. perceptions of Arabs substantiates the reality that Arabs are frequently portrayed as violent, zealous, irrational, depraved, untrustworthy, and incurable barbarians determined to destroy peace. Oxtoby cites a 1976 issue of *Harper's Magazine* as an example:

> Arabs are religious fanatics devoted to a non-Western warrior religion. Their bequest to us includes the words assassin and jihad… the Arab draws his blade with gusto, and when he is finished butchering he is always that much closer to Allah. (p. 46)

In a 1991 survey conducted during the Gulf War, 59% of Americans associated *Arabic* with *terrorism*, 58% with *violence*, and two thirds said that too many Muslim immigrants were living in the U.S.[41] On April 19, 1995, the day of the Oklahoma City bombing, the media were quick to classify Middle Easterners as suspects and reported that FBI agents were on their way, looking for two males with dark hair and beards. Within hours, Arabs and Muslims became the victims of physical and verbal attacks. As the search unfolded, it turned out that an American of European ancestry, Timothy McVeigh, was responsible for the most fatal terrorist act on U.S. soil at that time.[42]

Fadel (2002)[43] did a content analysis of an Egyptian newspaper (*Al Ahram*) and an American newspaper (*USA Today*) during the three months after 9/11. According to the study, the two subjects that were the most mentioned about Arab countries in both newspapers were terrorism and Islamic fundamentalism. However, while *Al Ahram* emphasized the Arab world's strong disapproval of the attacks and of fundamentalism, *USA Today* associated Arabs with Islamic fundamentalism, terrorism, and extremism worldwide. The study also mentioned that *USA Today* "adopted a clear line of linking violence and terrorism with resisting Israeli occupation in parts of Lebanon and the Palestinian territories" (p. 451). In the fifty days following 9/11, the *Herald Tribune*, in its reports on the sources of terrorism across the world, associated terrorism with the Arab and Muslim world 96% of the time.[44]

Western Stereotypes of Arabs and Islam over the Years

One Western method for stereotyping the enemy is the use of **discursive imperialism**, a type of discourse that berates the enemy's culture. It is used by the dominant culture (usually European cultures) to attribute labels to other cultures.[45] In this context, discursive imperialism is analogous to **Orientalism**, the idea that a culture or religious movement like Islam is considered inferior, barbaric, or incompatible with democracy.[46] As Edward Said (1978)[47] put it, "Orientalism is a style of thought based upon an ontological and epistemological distinction made between 'the Orient' and most of the time 'the Occident'" (p. 2). The "Occident," or the West, is placed in contrast to and as better than the Orient. Consequently, Orientalism can be considered a Western style for dominating, reforming, and having authority over Islam.

The term *Muslim* has evolved into a frequently disparaging, general description for all Arab groups. Commonly held derogatory stereotypes about Muslims include beliefs that they are disloyal, uncivilized, radical, and either terrorists or harboring terrorism.[48] The September 11, 2001 terrorist attacks have provoked an upsurge in anti-Muslim attacks across Europe. Graffiti on a wall close to a mosque in South Shields, northeast England, authenticates the unsettling reactions to 9/11. "Avenge U.S.A." was the written message in red paint. "Kill a Muslim now" was another one. CNN reported that the anti-Islamic response post-9/11 was spreading around the world. More than a few mosques in Europe and Australia were petrol-bombed by people who thought they were "doing the U.S. a favor."[49]

While a minor issue in perspective, the veil situation in France exemplifies anti-Muslim sentiment. After long-standing disputes on the issue, the French government has prohibited "showy" religious symbols (including the veil worn by Muslim women) in public places. Though the official purpose was to maintain religious tolerance and the atmosphere of a secular state (*laïcité*), the sanction was perceived by many Muslims as stereotypical, an insult to religious freedom, and evidence of French prejudice toward Muslims. Conversely, Muslim women who opposed the ban by wearing head coverings in public were seen, at best, as rebellious and, at worst, as an insult to French cultural values.[50]

Perspectives on Racism

Racism is the view that intrinsic differences exist in people's traits and abilities that are completely due to their race, however defined, and that accordingly justify those people being mistreated. In a nutshell, racism is racial supremacy, detrimental prejudice, discrimination, or persecution on the basis of assumed racial differences.[51] Dunn and colleagues (2004)[52] succinctly categorize racism into two forms: old and new racism. **Old racism** has to do with a sociobiological conception of race—a principle of racial hierarchies and superiority. Old racism is social Darwinism. It was a part of British heritage that legitimized British colonization and annexations of territories like Australia. **New racism** has to do with **cultural differentiation**: differences of culture perceived as threats to prevailing cultural values. New racism is to be found in the context of belonging and nationalism, and relies on stereotypes of cultural characteristics that are repeated in media and political discourses. It is much more widespread in present-day society and is more embraced than old racism. New racism calls attention to nationalistic debate (e.g., about immigration, GWOT, and Islamophobia).[53]

Sheridan (2006)[54] examined degrees of self-reported racial and religious discrimination in a survey of 222 British Muslims. Participants reported that following 9/11, degrees of implicit or indirect discrimination increased by 82.6% and instances of overt discrimination by 76.3%. Thus, the study confirmed that major terrorist attacks may influence not only stereotypes of minorities but also racism toward them. In the U.S., levels of racial crimes against non-Islamic groups (e.g., Black, Hispanic, Asian) became different in the months and years following 9/11. Discha, Cavendish, and King (2011)[55] used incident-level data to examine whether the rise in crimes against Arabs/Muslims post-9/11 was comparable to trends in crimes against other racial groups. The total number of racial crimes attributed to anti-Arab/Muslim bias increased from 26 and 260, respectively, in the pre-9/11 period to 517 and 1,502 crimes in the post-9/11 period. Consistent with these rises are declines in the number of racial crimes driven by bias against Blacks, Whites, Asians, and Latinos.

MCLUHAN'S TETRADIC FRAMEWORK

In *Laws of Media: The New Science*, published posthumously by Eric McLuhan (his son), Marshall McLuhan (1988)[56] developed the **tetradic framework**, also called the tetrad of media or McLuhan's law of the media. The tetradic framework explains transformations in world life and the media through four fundamental steps. All forms of media (1) *intensify* particular aspects of media culture while, simultaneously, (2) *making* other aspects of the culture *obsolete*. At some point, people in a culture will also (3) *discover* new information about aspects in media culture that were ignored long ago (a process called retrieval)—that is, what do media retrieve that had been made obsolete earlier? Finally, (4) as this information-seeking and discovery increase, media culture is experiencing constant modification. In other words, the media *undergo a reversal* when pushed too far or extended beyond the limits of their capacity.[57] The tetradic framework can be applied to the effects of 9/11 on media reports and depictions of Muslims.

First Step

In the first step, the media amplify or intensify some aspects of world life and media culture. An example is the massive evolution from written speech (which reached a pinnacle in the early to mid-19th century) to televisual communication, which uses mostly visual images to package information.[58] In particular, stereotypical portrayals of Muslims drastically increased with the rise in mass media. In turn, negative stereotypes of Muslims in the media and by political leaders have served to justify evidence for Islamophobic prejudices.[59] Phrases such as Flying While Muslim (or Muslim While Flying) were not frequently used or heard before the advent of the Internet—especially before 9/11. **Flying While Muslim** is a phrase about racial profiling that specifically refers to the problems that Muslims on airplanes have faced since 9/11.[60] Conservative commentators such as Ann Coulter, Bill O'Reilly, and Sean Hannity argue that the airline industry has the right to consider Muslim passengers with suspicion as a result of Islamist terrorism. The Internet effect of news coverage demonized Muslims and presented them unfavorably. Many media organizations referred to the nineteen hijackers as simply "Muslims," which invigorated stereotyping of Islam and did little to help prevent the verbal and physical assaults taking place against Muslims in America at the time.[61]

As media visuals started to mature, the U.S. media establishment took the initiative of allowing sound bites to pop up like mushrooms after the rain. As such, in 2002, reverend Jerry Falwell's statement on *60 Minutes* unquestionably reached a large audience: "I think Muhammad was a terrorist. I read enough of the history of his life written by both Muslims and non-Muslims, that he was a violent man, a man of war" (CBS news, 2002).[62] Likewise, if there is one form of media that has been amplified and that has revolutionized the way Americans perceive the world, then the Internet is it. Virtually any blog on the Internet is also allowed to pop up. One of the by-products is an unprecedented stream of rumors and stereotypes about other races. As such, racial stereotypes for Middle Easterners started to emerge (e.g., "little terrorist" and "camel jockey").[63] When an innumerable number of web users engage in this form of expression, their feeling of authority and knowledge is enormous. The idea of power of the collective is enhanced. The Internet has boosted the power of traditional territorially based democracy, because the Internet is both non-territorial and geographically unlimited.

Pintak (2006)[64] asserted that the bias in American media culture after the September 11, 2001 terrorist attacks constituted **jihad journalism**. He added that such biased coverage was "the hallmark of the post-9/11 era" (p. 44). Fruit (2001)[65] called it "a result of racist jingoism." Pintak (2006)[66] also commented on Eric Rouleau of *Le Monde*, a French daily evening newspaper. Rouleau criticized the media trend to portray images of "Muslims praying, mosques or women in chadors to illustrate stories about extremism and terror" (p. 33). For Pintak, drawing on Henry Kissinger's words, it really became "a morality play between good and evil" (p. 39). At a meeting of the Global Policy Forum, Hans Giessmann of the University of Hamburg's Institute for Peace Research and Security Policy criticized the Western media for how they "fully attributed blame for the September attacks on Muslim terrorists and stopped there." He also said that "the media accepted the side effects of a stigmatization of religion, cultures, states, people and minorities and this paved the way for prejudices."[67]

Second Step

In the second step, the media make part of the media environment obsolete. After 9/11, some aspects of media culture became *passé*. One needs to ponder for a moment and read *Amusing Ourselves to Death*, by Neil Postman (1985).[68] Postman perceived television's entertainment value as a modern-day "soma," by means of which the audience's rights are traded for entertainment. The author also described how oral, literate, and televisual cultures differed dramatically in the processing and prioritization of information. Each medium, he argued, was adequate for a different type of knowledge. As readers saw in Chapters 3–5, television has become the main source of information for the audience when it comes to learning about terrorist events. What becomes obsolete, then, are the faculties required for rational inquiry (that print media used to offer). These faculties have simply been undermined by televised viewing.

For that reason, reading, a leading example used by Postman, requires profound intellectual involvement, at once interactive and dialectical. Television, on the other hand, only demands passive involvement. Additionally, as television programs are aired based on audience ratings, their content is determined by commercial feasibility, not critical judgment. Television in its current condition does not meet the circumstances or provisions for honest intellectual involvement and rational thinking. By the same token, the power of individual thinking becomes obsolete.[69] The 18th century, hailed as the Age of Reason, experienced the pinnacle for rational argument. Only in print media could complicated truths be rationally communicated.[70] Television has changed all that. The multiple media stereotypes that prevail are exclusively made of carefully chosen sound bites.

As rational judgment has been made obsolete by the rise of modern media, so has the understanding of the complexity of race and religion. In fact, the use of racism and stereotyping toward Muslims embodies the idea that many people confuse race and religion. *Sand nigger* is one of the pejorative ways Muslims are referred to.[71] *Arabic* and *Muslim* have been used interchangeably in Western media. It was certainly a prevailing misconception before 9/11, but things got worse after the terrorist attacks. In spite of the fact that many Arab nations denounced the attacks with anger, many sources in the media still failed to make a distinction between Arabs and Muslims.[72] Arabs belong to an ethnic group of people who live in North Africa and the Arabian Peninsula (i.e., the Greater Middle East). Muslims are those who have converted to Islam as their religion. The majority of Arabs (more than 90%) are Muslims. However, most Muslims are not Arabs. In fact, most

Muslims live in Indonesia, India, Malaysia, Pakistan, and Afghanistan, all of which are non-Arab nations.[73]

By extension, many voices in the media also failed to mention the differences between Arabs and Muslims, on the one hand, and terrorists, on the other. Christensen (2006a, 2006b)[74] argues that, since 9/11, the fallacy of associating *Arab* and *Muslim* with *terrorism* has run rampant. The spread of such confusion in the U.S. has been, in part, warped and imbalanced by media coverage. Christensen states that evening newscasts tend to be perceived as serious and reliable because reporting is associated in the audience's mind with objectivity and fairness. Western news stories are likely to show a mosque, a minaret, or a veiled woman notwithstanding the nature of the story, even when the story deals with terrorism. As a result of such media practices, critical thinking has been rendered even more obsolete.

Of equal relevance is the fact that 9/11 caused the transformation of most media forms, in and of themselves—hypercommunication in particular. Let us explain this further. Print media and radio became less important. For example, the events that unfolded after the first plane crash on the World Trade Center, namely, the second airliner crashing into the South Tower, were viewed on television by most Americans. Then, in an unparalleled eruption of communication, passengers on the remaining plane made mobile phone calls to their loved ones on the ground, saying goodbye and describing painful firsthand stories of the hijacking. These calls later were aired on television and published in print media for the rest of Americans to share. This event stimulated hypercommunication for weeks. A remarkable outcome of the hypercommunication around 9/11 has been the tickertapes displayed at the bottom of television screens on cable news stations. These were designed to broadcast other news stories from many countries worldwide that were pushed aside by coverage of the 9/11 attacks. Today, the American public is able to read the news while watching and listening to it.[75] As one can see, by dramatically improving television news, 9/11 literally made print media and radio less influential.

Third Step

In the third step, the media recreate or revive any older structure or environment. Despite the advent of new media forms, several old messages and media-based strategies have made a comeback. For example, after 9/11, as terrorism became a big item on the U.S. agenda, Muslims were not the only ones to be in the gaze; Latino/as started to be in the gaze too—as it was twenty years before, when it reached a pinnacle. Old frames came back; a particular one was the racial profiling of Latino/as, now portrayed as a security threat. Influenced by television and cinema, the stereotypical association of Latino/as with drugs has formed a conception of Latino/as as "narco-terrorists," like it used to be in the 1980s.[76] Already in the 1970s, the **Brown Berets**, a Latino nationalist activist group of young Mexican Americans dressed in military attire and brown berets, emulating the Black Panthers and notorious for their police brutality, helped fuel a stereotype of Latino/as as terrorists. Due to the protracted inability by the U.S. government to bring Osama bin Laden to justice, a certain number of Americans revived this image of the radical Latino/a to stereotype Mexican Americans and other Latino/as as a more accessible enemy on U.S. soil.[77]

Following the September 11, 2001 terrorist attacks, drug-producing and drug-trafficking units have come to be regarded as terrorist groups again—this time, even more. In February 2002, the Office of National Drug Control Policy revealed its initiative to inform Americans on the association between unlawful drugs and international terrorism. Within this particular context, two commercials were aired during the 2002 Super Bowl warning druggies that their addictions were contributing to the financing of terrorists. According to Congressman Mark Souder (R-IL), "Americans who buy and sell illegal narcotics are lending a helping hand to people like those who attacked America on September 11."[78] The Hispanic-led drug war added to the growth of fear with terrorism. Messages that demonized Osama bin Laden, his Taliban and Al Qaeda followers, and Islamic extremists linked them to the damaging influence of illegal drugs—particularly drug lords—in the U.S. News broadcasts and advertisements combined drug use and terrorism and helped make drugs acquire a new meaning, evolving from criminal activity to unpatriotic action. A $10 million ad campaign exposed the message from President Bush, "If you quit drugs, you join the fight against terror in America."[79]

Revitalizing the stereotypes of Latino/as as terrorists, the media got whipped up into a frenzy. The media went as far as insinuating parallels between the hunt for Osama bin Laden in the Middle East and the major U.S. mission to hunt Mexican General Francisco "Pancho" Villa in 1916 (in Mexico). An ex-ally of the U.S., as was Osama bin Laden, Villa attacked a town in New Mexico, killing seventeen Americans while stealing horses and weapons.[80] Without a doubt, since September 11, 2001, both Mexican *bandidos* and modern Latino/a gangsters have been resuscitated as terrorists. This gloomy image goes back to media and societal conceptions of Mexican American youth known as *Pachucos* in Los Angeles in the 1940s. The Pachucos were slandered in local L.A. newspapers as a foreign-born threat during World War II, leading to the alleged Zoot Suit Riots in which off-duty Anglo soldiers, and Anglo civilians, took over barrio neighborhoods to attack these Latino youth.[81] The killing of Osama bin Laden does not seem to improve the situation for Latino/a Americans.

This new trend in U.S. media culture has served to establish two sets of firm boundaries: one between Caucasians and Muslims and one between Caucasians and Latino/as. This is a process referred to as **identity politics**, the insistence on preserving strong cultural boundaries and politicizing them.[82] In this case, identity politics implies that Latino/as have been deprived of their own voice in determining the conditions of their lives. For example, many questioned their patriotism, especially illegal immigrants. In cities like San Francisco, local authorities began to tighten up on non-citizen Latino/as looking for a job. In early 2002, federal officials implemented Operation Tarmac, an immigration-enforcement policy directed at undocumented Latino/a airport employees, particularly those workers who have access to restricted zones such as airplanes, runways, and flight meal kitchens.[83] For example, the perceived importance of the English language is something to behold. Indeed, in the case of language, such harsh prerogatives to safeguard national security and to foil terrorist conspiracies were already seen as justifiable in the past on accounts of private language vigilantism. Today, bar-owners have stood up for legal challenges to English-language policies for Latino/a customers by insisting that they were maintaining peace in the bar by identifying fighting words—as one put it, "If they're speaking Spanish, how is my bartender going to know if they're cussing."[84]

Fourth Step

In the fourth step, the media, now pushed to the limit, have undergone a reversal that creates the opposite of their intended purpose. Politics is being globalized, both in the sense that political issues globally are increasingly similar, and in the sense that political matters as described in Step 3 can be perceived as obnoxious after a while—from stereotyping racial people to widespread violence in the Middle East. This media-influenced trend is being globalized thanks to the Internet, increased communications, and television entertainment, as well as modernization, traveling, education, and the popularity of English as the world's second language. The best example to illustrate Step 4 of the tetradic framework is the universal condemnation of Islamophobia. While the concept of Islamophobia was barely known before 9/11, it is now a major topic at international conferences and has even been called a threat to world peace.

Islamophobia refers to an intense fear of Islam, which has increased since September 11, 2001. The first time the word was used was in early 1991, when it appeared in a published periodical in the U.S.[85] With reference to Islam, people have either closed or open views of the religion. **Closed views** regard Islam as static and unchanging, as archaic, macho, violent, and threatening. Closed views of Islam think hostility toward Islam should be normative and are used to validate discrimination of Muslims because no common values with the religion are possible.[86] Central to closed views is Islamophobia, which was first propagated by the Western media. The assumption is that all Muslims endorse actions taken for the sake of Islam. Terrorists are referred to as Islamist fundamentalists, although a certain number of Muslims say that Islamist fundamentalists violate Islamic law and, as a result, the good ones suffer from being linked to terrorism. **Open views** regard Islam as a diverse and broad-minded religion with internal differences, disputes, and developments. Acknowledging common values with other religions and cultures, Islam is seen as equally worthy of respect. Critical views by Western thinkers and civilians are taken into account; differences and disagreements do not reduce efforts to fight discrimination while consideration is taken that criticism of Islam is not prejudicial and inaccurate.[87]

Now that billions of people worldwide can access the media in a heartbeat, certain aspects of the media, like the Internet (with its racist and hateful blogs), have been pushed to the limit, so much so that peace activists are now using the United Nations website to call for a ban on Islamophobia and criticism of Islam. Let us quickly analyze a quote from the Algiers Declaration for a Shared Vision of the Future (2006),[88] which states that "it is essential to create a Euro-Mediterranean entity founded on Universal Values." Globalized public opinion is analogous to "oneness." This is demonstrated in the idea that Islamophobia is bad. The fight against Islamophobia is proof that many people (particularly youth) have been influenced by the unprecedented evolution of media technologies and media culture. By the same token, it is also proof that Muslims understand the mechanism and advantages of the media to sensitize the world toward Islam as a religion of peace.

"Islam is a religion of peace" is an example of a **counter-stereotype** (or *reverse stereotype* or *anti-stereotype*). As Islam has been depicted as aggressive and threatening in the media for a few decades, some Islamic activists have seized opportunities to turn this stereotype into a more popular and accepted reality. We can see "Islam is a religion of peace" banners on double-decker buses in London. What it boils down to, in this fourth step, is that changes in media and world life create an opportunity for people to connect. This is the notion that humans now live in an age of **homo-contextus**, a new construction of social identity that does away with old stereotypes and signifies that people feel increasingly empowered to find like-minded others with much greater effortlessness and rapidity than was ever possible before.[89] This last step of the tetradic framework also shows that the great freedom of U.S. mass media has created a backlash against those who have abused this freedom. For instance, in contemplating a possible run for the U.S. presidency in 2012, real estate mogul, media personality, and celebrity billionaire Donald Trump faced a backlash for accusing President Obama of being a secret Muslim. Many people (most of them not Republicans) reacted to Trump's comment in the same way that people would now react to Islamophobia. In any case, the media are such that people do not have to shout loud to be heard.

STEREOTYPING TERRORISM IN HOLLYWOOD AND MOVIES

In Hollywood films, says Jackson (1996),[90] "barbarism and cruelty are the most common traits associated with Arabs" (p. 65). These stereotypes, "which tend to lump Arabs, Muslims, Middle East into one highly negative image of violence and danger" (p. 65), are perpetuated mostly through collective memory, rather than from real experience. As a result, the face of terrorism is not only that of Osama bin Laden but also all Muslims, suggesting the simulacrum of all Middle Eastern–looking males as the "Face of Terror."[91] The consequential preservation of an enemy image bolsters old ideological dichotomies of good vs. evil and us vs. them. This also solidifies a socially accepted stereotype with referential function. Over time, such an enemy image, regarded as a culturally driven, pessimistic, and stereotyped evaluation of the Other, is strengthened through mass media representations.[92]

Jack Shaheen's Studies

Many Hollywood movies have been accused of using a disproportionate number of Arabs as terrorists and of stereotyping Arabs as negatively as possible. To the eyes of the American-Arab Anti-Discrimination Committee (ADC), Hollywood depictions of Arabs can be categorized in one of the three Bs: bombers, belly dancers, or billionaires. Jack Shaheen (2009),[93] in his book *Reel Bad Arabs*, did a content analysis of over 900 Arab characters in films. Of those, only 15 or so were positive and 50 were balanced. The remaining 835 Arab characters were terrorists, machos, or aggressive individuals. Arab stereotypes in American movies have existed since the infancy of the cinema art. From 1896 until today, movie directors have stereotyped all Arabs as Public Enemy #1: cruel, coldblooded, uncivilized religious fanatics, and money-grabbing cultural aliens determined to kill Western civilians (especially Christians and Jews).

A few decades before *Reel Bad Arabs* came out, Shaheen (1980)[94] already offered examples of many television programs that portrayed Arabs as bad people. He found cases of seemingly innocent programs in the late 1970s that actually incorporated cues of prejudice in them. Examples are Hollywood-produced television series such as *Vegas*, *Fantasy Island*, and *Charlie's Angels*, and comic books such as *Brenda Starr* and *Dennis the Menace*. He also gave examples of anti-Arab and anti-Muslim broadcasts from popular news shows such as *60 Minutes* and *20/20*, along with daily news bulletins that stereotyped Arabs and Muslims as terrorists. Likewise, in *The TV Arab*, Shaheen (1984)[95] analyzed over 100 different television programs that featured Arab characters in 1975–1976 and 1983–1984. He discovered that the appearance of Arabs as terrorists was widespread. Shaheen noted that "the stereotype [of Arabs] remains omnipresent, appearing in new programs and dated reruns" (p. 113). On interviewing a CBS vice president, Shaheen said the VP confirmed the notion that he "had never seen a 'good Arab' on TV," and that Arabs are rather usually portrayed as "warmongers and/or covetous desert rulers" (p. 114).

Narrative Transportation

Narrative transportation is the degree to which someone becomes absorbed in a story while engaged with it. Narrative transportation can have an impact on how much people like movies, books, news, and other types of media. Put simply, narratives can add force to stereotypes.[96] In this respect, Frederick Forsyth (1971)[97] wrote a novel, *The Day of the Jackal*, in which an international killer known as "The Jackal" (in French, *le chacal*) is paid to assassinate French president Charles de Gaulle. This novel, erroneously believed to have been based on Ilich Ramírez Sánchez's life, is the cause of his "Jackal" nickname. Many incorrectly think that the character featured in that novel was based on Sánchez (who later established himself as a terrorist). However, the novel was published before Carlos made the news globally.

O'Brien (1986)[98] identified two types of terrorist stereotypes in narratives (both in film and in print media). First is the **hysterical stereotype**—which can be further classified into three categories. These categories are (1) terrorists who are crazy and disposed to committing mindless violence, (2) terrorists who are criminals and exploit political goals as an excuse to kill, and (3) terrorists who are actually secret agents for the other side. The general public is less likely to express sympathy toward characters that personify these traits. The second terrorist stereotype is the **sentimental stereotype**. This stereotype can be misguided and brutal as a consequence of social and political injustice or a mixture of the two. These types of terrorists can be shown sympathy by the audience, since the world seems to have left these people to their own devices; they have no choice but commit violence.

Cultivation Theory

Expanding on more than thirty years of research, George Gerbner and colleagues (2002)[99] explained how the general pattern of stereotypes of racial minorities on television has cultivated a narrow perception of social realities in the audience. One method by which media stereotypes of racial minorities can shape attitudes vis-à-vis members of those minorities is through the **accessibility principle**. Based on this principle, when someone is asked to make a social judgment, he or she will do so according to the information that comes to mind most rapidly. When media depictions of a group are primarily negative, these negative constructs are straightforwardly accessible to a person when creating a social judgment.[100]

The theory that Gerbner and colleagues' work exemplifies is cultivation theory. **Cultivation theory** posits that long-standing frequent exposure to media messages forms a person's understanding of the world in a way that corresponds to how reality is depicted in the media.[101] In the physical, three-dimensional world, terrorism is ubiquitous, used across dissimilar ideologies to establish national states, combat repression, and protect the status quo. However, in Hollywood, terrorism is reduced to the devilish work of particular groups. Images, script lines, musical scores, and sound effects are combined to affect the audience, to entrap them into a momentous Clash of Civilizations. Over time, if there is no critical thinking or thinking outside of the box, the audience might come to believe that a certain religion or racial minority is shady (with foolish, fanatical, and appalling personality types) and hostile to the Western world.[102]

SUMMARY

People use stereotypes as simplified mental pictures of other groups. They can be positive or negative. Most stereotypes, though, tend to be negative. For example, Chechens are stereotyped by Russians as ruthless and bloodthirsty. As we have seen, there are diverse ways for stereotyping the enemy: guilt by association, linguistic profiling, and so forth. Part of the reason humans engage in stereotyping stems from the fact that their cultural worldview (CWV) influences their collective unconscious. A direct consequence is stigmatization (an invisible sign of condemnation) of the Other; Arabs and Muslims have been stigmatized as a result of guilt by association. Other consequences include discursive imperialism (a type of discourse that berates the enemy's culture), racism, and stereotyping in Hollywood movies. In Hollywood, terrorism is reduced to the devilish work of particular groups. Lastly, McLuhan's tetradic framework was used to explain transformations in world life and the media through four fundamental steps. In the first step, the media amplify or intensify some aspects of world life and media culture. In the second step, the media make part of the media environment obsolete. In the third step, the media recreate or revive any older structure or environment. In the fourth step, the media, now pushed to the limit, undergo a reversal that creates the opposite of their intended purpose. The best example to illustrate this last step is globalized public opinion (thanks to worldwide access to media) and the condemnation of Islamophobia, an intense fear of Islam. An important conclusion of McLuhan's tetradic framework is that rational judgment has been made obsolete by the rise of modern media.

KEY TERMS

accessibility principle   178

achieved stigma   167

closed vs. open views of Islam   176

collective guilt   165

counter-stereotype   176

cultivation theory   179

cultural differentiation   171

discursive imperialism   170

ENDNOTES

1. Lippmann, Walter (1922). *Public Opinion*. New York: Harcourt, Brace and Company.

2. Dixon, Mark R., Rehfeldt, Ruth Anne, Zlomke, Kimberly R., & Robinson, Ashton (2006). Exploring the Development and Dismantling of Equivalence Classes Involving Terrorist Stimuli. *Psychological Record, 56*, 83–103.

3. McGarty, Craig, Yzerbyt, Vincent Y., & Spears, Russell (2002). *Stereotypes as Explanations: The Formation of Meaningful Beliefs about Social Groups*. Cambridge: Cambridge University Press.

4. Hargie, Owen, & Tourish, Dennis (2003). How Are We Doing? Measuring and Monitoring Organizational Communication. In Owen Hargie & Dennis Tourish (Eds.), *Key Issues in Organizational Communication* (pp. 234–263). New York: Routledge.

5. Jandt, Fred (2010). *An Introduction to Intercultural Communication: Identities in a Global Community* (6th ed.). Thousand Oaks, CA: Sage; Zirinski, Roni (2005). *Ad Hoc Arabism: Advertising, Culture, and Technology in Saudi Arabia*. New York: Peter Lang.

6. Correll, Joshua, Park, Bernadette, Judd, Charles M., & Wittenbrink, Bernd (2002). The Police Officer's Dilemma: Using Ethnicity to Disambiguate Potentially Threatening Individuals. *Journal of Personality and Social Psychology, 83*, 1314–1329.

7. Schaller, Mark, Park, Justin H., & Mueller, Annette (2003). Fear of the Dark: Interactive Effects of Beliefs about Danger and Ambient Darkness on Ethnic Stereotypes. *Personality and Social Psychology Bulletin, 29*, 637–649.

8. Maner, Jon K., Kenrick, Douglas T., Becker, D. Vaughn, Robertson, Theresa E., Hofer, Brian, Neuberg, Steven L., Delton, Andrew W., Butner, Jonathan, & Schaller, Mark (2005). Functional Projection: How Fundamental Social Motives Can Bias Interpersonal Perception. *Journal of Personality and Social Psychology, 88*, 63–78.

9. Green, M. (1993). Images of American Indians in Advertising: Some Moral Issues. *Journal of Business Ethics, 12*, 323–330.

10. Jersild, Austin (2004). The Chechen Wars in Historical Perspective: New Work on Contemporary Russian-Chechen Relations. *Slavic Review, 63*, 367–377; Markowitz, Fran (1999). Not Nationalists: Russian

Teenagers' Soulful A-Politics. *Europe-Asia Studies, 51*, 1183–1198; Russell, John (2005). Terrorists, Bandits, Spooks and Thieves: Russian Demonization of the Chechens before and since 9/11. *Third World Quarterly, 26*, 101–116.

11. Post, Robert (2000). Response to Commentators. *California Law Review, 88*(1), 119–126.

12. Pontikes, Elizabeth, Negro, Giacomo, & Rao, Hayagreeva (2010). Stained Red: A Study of Stigma by Association to Blacklisted Artists during the "Red Scare" in Hollywood, 1945 to 1960. *American Sociological Review, 75*(3), 456–478.

13. Cole, David (2000). Secrecy, Guilt by Association, and the Terrorist Profile. *Journal of Law and Religion, 15*(1), 267–288.

14. Johnson, Ruth & Jenks, Frederick L. (1994, March). *Native Speakers' Perceptions of Nonnative Speakers: Related to Phonetic Errors and Spoken Grammatical Errors 23–25*. Paper presented at the Annual Meeting of the Teachers of English to Speakers of Other Languages, New York.

15. Bengtsson, R., & Iverman, E. (2010). *Discrimination in the Housing Market of Stockholm: An Internet Based Field Experiment*. Stockholm: Stockholm University.

16. Rooth, Olof (2009). Automatic Associations and Discrimination in Hiring: Real World Evidence. *Labour Economics, 17*, 523–534,

17. Lind, Rebecca Ann, & Danowski, James A. (1998). The Representation of Arabs in U.S. Electronic Media. In Yahya R. Kamalipour & Theresa Carilli (Eds.), *Cultural Diversity and the U.S. Media* (pp. 156–167). Albany: State University of New York Press.

18. Spillman, Kurt R., & Spillmann, Kati (1997). Some Sociobiological and Psychological Aspects of "Images of the Enemy." In Ragnhild Fiebig-von Has & Ursula Lehmkuhl (Eds.), *Enemy Images in American History* (pp. 43–64). Providence, RI: Berghahn.

19. Bahdi, Reem (2003). No Exit: Racial Profiling and Canada's War against Terrorism. *Osgoode Hall Law Journal, 41*(2), 293–317.

20. Falk, Gerhard (2001). *Stigma: How We Treat Outsiders*. New York: Prometheus Books; Link, Bruce G., & Phelan, Jo C. (2001). Conceptualizing Stigma. *Annual Review of Sociology, 27*, 363–385.

21. Falk, Gerhard (2001). *Stigma: How We Treat Outsiders*. New York: Prometheus Books; Goffman, Erving (1963). *Stigma: Notes on the Management of Spoiled Identity*. New York: Prentice-Hall.

22. Jones, C. P. (1987). Stigma: Tattooing and Branding in Graeco-Roman Antiquity. *The Journal of Roman Studies, 77*, 139–155.

23. Link, Bruce G., & Phelan, Jo C. (2001). Conceptualizing Stigma. *Annual Review of Sociology, 27*, 363–385.

24. Goffman, Erving (1963). *Stigma: Notes on the Management of Spoiled Identity*. New York: Prentice-Hall.

25. Zulaika, Joseba, & Douglass, William (1997). *Terror and Taboo: The Follies, Fables and Faces of Terrorism*. London: Routledge.

26. Bahdi, Reem (2003). No Exit: Racial Profiling and Canada's War against Terrorism. *Osgoode Hall Law Journal, 41*(2), 293–317.

27. Bahdi, Reem (2003). No Exit: Racial Profiling and Canada's War against Terrorism. *Osgoode Hall Law Journal, 41*(2), 293–317.

28. Doyle, Pat (2001, September 30). Ethnic Profiling Revisited. *Star-Tribune*, p. A1.

29. Council on American-Islamic Relations (2002). The Status of Muslim Civil Rights in the United States: Stereotypes and Civil Liberties. http://www.cair-net.org/civilrights2002/civilrights2002.doc; Deen, T. (2002, February 5). Rights: Discrimination against Muslims increases in US. Inter Press Service. Retrieved from http://www.oneworld.net/external/?url = http%3A%2F%2Fwww.oneworld.org%2Fips2%2Fjul98%2F04_05_003.html.

30. Amendments, supra note 31. Hussein's name was removed on June 3, 2002 (SOR/2002-210); U.S. Department of State (2003). Fact Sheet: State Department Updates List of Terrorist Individuals and Groups. Washington, D.C.: U.S. Department of State.

31. Bahdi, Reem (2003). No Exit: Racial Profiling and Canada's War against Terrorism. *Osgoode Hall Law Journal, 41*(2), 293–317.

32. Ghareeb, Edmund (1983). *Split Vision: The Portrayal of Arabs in the American Media*. Washington, D.C.: American-Arab Affairs Council; Said, Edward (1981). *Covering Islam: How The Media and the Experts Determine How We See The Rest of the World*. New York: Vintage Books; Stockton, Ronald (1994). Ethnic Archetypes and the Arab Image. In Ernest McCamus (Ed.), *The Development of the Arab-American Identity* (pp. 119–153). Ann Arbor: University of Michigan Press; Weston, Mary Ann, & Dunsky, Marda (2002). One Culture, Two Frameworks: U.S. Media Coverage of Arabs at Home and Abroad. *Journal of Islamic Law and Culture, 7*(9), 132–133.

33. Horry, Ruth, & Wright, Daniel B. (2004). Anxiety and Terrorism: Automatic Stereotypes Affect Visual Attention and Recognition Memory for White and Middle Eastern Faces. *Applied Cognitive Psychology, 23*(3), 345–357.

34. MacLeod, Colin, Mathews, Andrew, & Tata, Philip (1986). Attentional Bias in Emotional Disorders. *Journal of Abnormal Psychology, 95*, 15–20; Mogg, Karin, & Bradley, Brandon P. (1999). Orienting of Attention to Threatening Facial Expressions Presented under Conditions of Restricted Awareness. *Cognition and Emotion, 13*, 713–740.

35. Ervin, Clark Kent (2006, June). Stereotyping Terrorists: The Usual Suspects. *The New York Times*.

36. Jandt, Fred (2010). *An Introduction to Intercultural Communication: Identities in a Global Community* (6th ed.). Thousand Oaks, CA: Sage.

37. Gallup (2009). *Terrorism in the United States*. Retrieved April 24, 2011 from www.gallup.com/poll/4909/Terrorism-United-States.aspx#2.

38. Eitle, David, Stewart J. D'Alessio, and Lisa Stolzenberg (2002). Racial Threat and Social Control: A Test of the Political, Economic, and Threat of Black Crime Hypotheses. *Social Forces, 81*, 557–576.

39. Evans, Martin C. (2005, July 8). London Terror: Local Muslims Decry Attacks. *Newsday*, p. W23.

40. Oxtoby, William (1980). Western Perceptions of Islam and the Arabs. In Michael C. Hudson & Ronald G. Wolfe (Eds.), *The American Media and the Arabs* (pp. 3–21). Washington, D.C.: Center for Contemporary Studies, Georgetown University.

41. Paulson, Michael (2001, September 29). U.S. Attitudes toward Arabs Souring, according to Poll. *Boston Globe*, p. A5.

42. Nacos, Brigitte L., & Torres-Reyna, Oscar (2006). *Fueling Our Fears: Stereotyping, Media Coverage, and Public Opinion of Muslim Americans*. New York: Rowman & Littlefield.

43. Fadel, S. (2002). The Image of the Arab countries in the Daily Egyptian and American Newspapers after 9/11: A Comparative Analytical Study. In *Proceedings of the Annual Scientific Convention of the Faculty of Communication* (pp. 425–457). Egypt: Cairo University.

44. Gomaa, I. (2002). The Image of Islam and Muslims in the Western Press after 9/11: An Analytical Study of American, French, and German Newspapers. In *Proceedings of the Annual Scientific Convention of the Faculty of Communication* (pp. 221–266). Egypt: Cairo University.

45. Jandt, Fred (2010). *An Introduction to Intercultural Communication: Identities in a Global Community* (6th ed.). Thousand Oaks, CA: Sage; Zirinski, Roni (2005). *Ad Hoc Arabism: Advertising, Culture, and Technology in Saudi Arabia*. New York: Peter Lang.

46. Sadowski, Yahya (1993). The New Orientalism and the Democracy Debate. *Middle East Report, 183*, 14–21.

47. Said, Edward W. (1978). *Orientalism*. New York: Vintage Books.

48. Bar-Tal, Daniel (1996). Development of Social Categories and Stereotypes in Early Childhood: The Case of "the Arab" Concept Formation Stereotypes and Attitudes by Jewish Children in Israel. *International Journal of Intercultural Relations, 20*, 341–370; Bar-Tal, Daniel, & Labin, Daniela (2001). The Effect of a Major Event on Stereotyping: Terrorist Attacks in Israel and Israeli Adolescents' Perceptions of Palestinians, Jordanians, and Arabs. *European Journal of Social Psychology, 31*, 265–280; Johnson, Stephen D. (1992). Anti-Arabic Prejudice in "Middletown." *Psychological Reports, 70*, 811–818.

49. Abdulla, Rasha A. (2007). Islam, Jihad, and Terrorism in Post-9/11 Arabic Discussion Boards. *Journal of Computer-Mediated Communication, 12*, 1063–1081.

50. Mullally, Siobhán (2011). Civic Integration, Migrant Women and the Veil: At the Limits of Rights? *The Modern Law Review, 74*(1), 27–56.

51. Miles, Robert (1989). *Racism*. New York: Routledge.

52. Dunn, Kevin M., Forrest, James, Burnley, Ian, McDonald, Amy (2004). Constructing Racism in Australia. *Australian Journal of Social Issues, 39*(4), 409–431.

53. Jayasuriya, Laksiri (2002). Understanding Australian Racism. *Australian Universities' Review, 45*(1), 40–44; Markus, Andrew (2001). *Race: John Howard and the Remaking of Australia*. Crows Nest, NSW: Allen and Unwin.

54. Sheridan, Lorraine P. (2006). Islamophobia Pre- and Post-September 11th, 2001. *Journal of Interpersonal Violence, 21*(3), 317–336.

55. Discha, Ilir, Cavendish, James C., & King, Ryan D. (2011). Historical Events and Spaces of Hate: Hate Crimes against Arabs and Muslims in Post-9/11 America. *Social Problems, 58*(1), 21–46.

56. McLuhan, Marshall, & McLuhan, Eric (1988). *Laws of Media: The New Science*. Toronto: University of Toronto Press.

57. McLuhan, Marshall, & Powers, Bruce R. (1989). *The Global Village: Transformations in World Life and Media in the 21st Century*. Oxford: Oxford University Press.

58. Headrick, Daniel R. (2002). *When Information Came of Age: Technologies of Knowledge in the Age of Reason and Revolution, 1700–1850*. Oxford: Oxford University Press.

59. Sheridan, Lorraine P. (2006). Islamophobia Pre- and Post-September 11th, 2001. *Journal of Interpersonal Violence, 21*(3), 317–336.

60. Staeheli, Lynn A., & Nagel, Caroline R. (2008). Rethinking Security: Perspectives from Arab-American and British Arab Activists. *Antipode, 40*(5), 780–801.

61. Hutcheson, John, Domke, David, Billeaudeaux, Andre, & Garland, Philip (2003). U.S. National Identity, Political Elites, and a Patriotic Press Following September 11. *Political Communication, 21*, 27–51.

62. CBS news. (2002, October 4). Falwell brands Mohammed a "Terrorist." Available at: http://www.cbsnews.com/stories/2003/06/05/60minutes/main557187.shtml.

63. Bahdi, Reem (2003). No Exit: Racial Profiling and Canada's War against Terrorism. *Osgoode Hall Law Journal, 41*(2), 293–317.

64. Pintak, Lawrence (2006). *America, Islam, and the War of Ideas: Reflections in a Bloodshot Lens*. Cairo: The American University in Cairo Press.

65. Fruit, S. (2001, September 16). Sikh Man Killed in Arizona as a Result of Racist Jingoism. *Independent Media Center*.

66. Pintak, Lawrence (2006). *America, Islam, and the War of Ideas: Reflections in a Bloodshot Lens*. Cairo: The American University in Cairo Press.

67. Abdulla, Rasha A. (2007). Islam, Jihad, and Terrorism in Post-9/11 Arabic Discussion Boards. *Journal of Computer-Mediated Communication, 12*, 1063–1081.

68. Postman, Neil (1985). *Amusing Ourselves to Death: Public Discourse in the Age of Show Business*. New York: Penguin.

69. Postman, Neil (1985). *Amusing Ourselves to Death: Public Discourse in the Age of Show Business*. New York: Penguin.

70. Nicolson, Harold (2009). *The Age of Reason: 1700–1789*. Edinburg, VA: Axios Press.

71. Bahdi, Reem (2003). No Exit: Racial Profiling and Canada's War against Terrorism. *Osgoode Hall Law Journal, 41*(2), 293–317.

72. Abdulla, Rasha A. (2007). Islam, Jihad, and Terrorism in Post-9/11 Arabic Discussion Boards. *Journal of Computer-Mediated Communication, 12*, 1063–1081.

73. Abdulla, Rasha (2007). *The Internet in the Arab World: Egypt and Beyond*. New York: Peter Lang.

74. Christensen, Christian (2006a). God Save Us from the Islam clichés. *British Journalism Review, 17*(1), 65–70; Christensen, Christian (2006b). Islam in the Media: Cartoons and Context. *Screen Education, 43*, 27–32.

75. Nacos, Brigitte (2003). The Terrorist Calculus behind 9-11: A Model for Future Terrorism? *Studies in Conflict and Terrorism, 26*, 1–16.

76. Bender, Steven W. (2005). *Greasers and Gringos: Latinos, Law, and the American Imagination*. New York: New York University Press; Gonzalez, Carmen (2002, May 3). *Political Violence, "Terrorism," and the Criminalization of the Other*. Remarks at LatCrit VII Plenary Session, Eugene, Oregon.

77. García, Ignacio M. (1997). Chicanismo: The Forging of a Militant Ethos among Mexican Americans. Tucson: University of Arizona Press.

78. Press Release (2002, February 3). *Office of National Drug Control Policy, National Youth Anti-Drug Media Campaign Links Drugs and Terror*. Available at: http://www.whitehousedrugpolicy.gov/news/press02/020302.html.

79. Altheide, David L. (2007). The Mass Media and Terrorism. *Discourse & Communication, 1*(3), 287–308.

80. Bender, Steven W. (2002). *Sight, Sound, and Stereotype: The War on Terrorism and Its Consequences for Latinas/os*. Remarks at LatCrit VII Plenary Session, Eugene, Oregon.

81. Bender, Steven W. (2002). *Sight, Sound, and Stereotype: The War on Terrorism and Its Consequences for Latinas/os*. Remarks at LatCrit VII Plenary Session, Eugene, Oregon.

82. Sampson, Edward E. (1993). Identity Politics: Challenges to Psychology's Understanding. *American Psychologist, 48*(12), 1219–1230.

83. Casey, Juliet V. (2002, February 9). Operation Tarmac Advocates: Hispanics Unfairly Targeted. *Las Vegas Review-Journal*, p. B1.

84. Monje, Kathleen (1990, October 12). Suit Accuses Tavern of Bias Against Spanish-Speakers. *Oregonian*, p. D1.

85. Runnymede Trust. (1997). *Islamophobia: A Challenge for Us All*. London: Author.

86. Sheehi, Stephen, & Churchill, Ward (2011). *Islamophobia: The Ideological Campaign against Muslims*. Atlanta: Clarity Press.

87. Esposito, John L., & Kalin, Ibrahim (2011). *Islamophobia: The Challenge of Pluralism in the 21st Century*. Oxford: Oxford University Press.

88. Algiers Declaration for a Shared Vision of the Future (2006). The European Movement International and its Mediterranean Committee, Algiers, February 26, 2006.

89. Rosen, Lawrence (1984). *Bargaining for Reality: The Construction of Social Relations in a Muslim Community*. Chicago: University of Chicago Press.

90. Jackson, Nancy Beth (1996). Arab Americans: Middle East Conflicts Hit Home. In Paul M. Lester (Ed.), *Images That Injure: Pictorial Stereotypes in the Media* (pp. 63–66). Westport, CT: Praeger.

91. Merskin, Debra (2004). The Construction of Arabs as Enemies: Post-September 11 Discourse of George W. Bush. *Mass Communication & Society, 7*(2), 157–175.

92. Fiebig-von Hase, Ragnhild (1997). Introduction. In Ragnhild Fiebig-von Has & Ursula Lehmkuhl (Eds.), *Enemy Images in American History* (pp. 1–42). Providence, RI: Berghahn.

93. Shaheen, Jack G. (2009). *Reel Bad Arabs: How Hollywood Vilifies a People*. Ithaca, NY: Olive Branch Press.

94. Shaheen, Jack G. (1980). The Arab Stereotype on Television. *The Link, 13*(2), 10–21.

95. Shaheen, Jack G. (1984). *The TV Arab*. Ohio: Bowling Green State University Popular Press.

96. Green, Melanie C., & Brock, Timothy C. (2000). The Role of Transportation in the Persuasiveness of Public Narratives. *Journal of Personality and Social Psychology, 79*, 701–721.

97. Forsyth, Frederick (1971). *The Day of the Jackal*. London: Hutchinson.

98. O'Brien, Conor Cruise (1986). Thinking about Terrorism. *The Atlantic Monthly, 257*(6), 62–68.

99. Gerbner, George, Gross, Larry, Morgan, Michael, Signorielli, Nancy, & Shanahan, James (2002). Growing Up with Television: Cultivation Processes. In J. Bryant & D. Zillmann (Eds.), *Media Effects: Advances in Theory and Research* (pp. 43–67). Mahwah, NJ: Lawrence Erlbaum.

100. Persson, Anna V., & Musher-Eizenman, Dara R. (2005). College Students' Attitudes toward Blacks and Arabs Following a Terrorist Attack as a Function of Varying Levels of Media Exposure. *Journal of Applied Social Psychology, 35*(9), 1879–1893; Shrum, Larry J. (2002). Media Consumption and Perceptions of Social Reality: Effects and Underlying Processes. In J. Bryant & D. Zillmann (Eds.), *Media Effects: Advances in Theory and Research* (pp. 69–77). Hillsdale, NJ: Lawrence Erlbaum.

101. Gerbner, George, & Gross, Larry (1976). Living with Television: The Violence Profile. *Journal of Communication, 26*(2), 172–199.

102. Boggs, Carl, & Pollard, Tom (2006). Hollywood and the Spectacle of Terrorism. *New Political Science, 28*(3), 335–351.

CHAPTER 8

Interpreting Terrorism through Rhetoric

After reading this chapter, you will be able to

- analyze interpretation of terrorism as rhetoric;
- explain the rhetorical processes for dehumanizing the enemy, such as Othering, enemification, evilification, Orientalism, Occidentalism, and the "us vs. them" dichotomy; and
- discuss various types of slogans in favor and against the Global War on Terror (GWOT).

RHETORIC: GENERAL PERSPECTIVES

Rhetoric is the art of communicating efficiently and with persuasion through language. Beyond individual expression, rhetoric influences the communication process between individuals or groups who share ideas with one another to work out a difference of opinion.[1] In his *Rhetoric*, Greek philosopher Aristotle wrote that speech can be very helpful for organizing our thinking. For Aristotle, one needs to evaluate three components of a narrative in relation to a target audience: (1) what is the ethos of the speaker, (2) what is the logos of the message being sent, and (3) does the message include the right appeals to pathos?[2]

- Ethos: this is an appeal made by the communicator to the audience to ascertain credibility. In essence, ethos is used by a speaker—indirectly or directly—to make sure that the audience can trust him or her. An example in war is a history of observance of the Law of Armed Conflict—which means to conduct a "civilized" war—and an insistence on willpower.

- Logos: this is an appeal to facts. In war, there is no better logic than use of weapons, but as revolutions confirmed throughout the 20th century, firepower (logos) alone will not lead to victory in war, and will win too few arguments.

- Pathos: this is an appeal made by the communicator to the audience's emotions. In war, pathos might be used by showing the average person on the enemy's side that the U.S. position is better.

Rhetoric is a **resource of language**, a technique used by a speaker to send people a meaning with the purpose of persuading them toward looking at an issue from a different angle or a new dimension. If rhetoric is used to misinform people, it is referred to as **sophism**, the art of using pointless or unsupported arguments for deceiving others. Rhetoric has often been associated with argumentation. **Argumentation** consists of a person's ability to defend his or her position on a controversial matter while simultaneously trying to counter another party's or person's position on the same matter. An argumentative individual rationally debates a topic and does not attack others personally. On the other hand, **verbal aggression** occurs when someone attacks the self-concept of another person; the purpose is usually to inflict psychological harm. It is a form of symbolic aggression.[3] Particularly in periods of stress and violence, speakers resort to using pluralist, evidence-based communication styles that rely on data, statistics, research, history, and context. They also guide the audience toward demonstrable and confirmable sources of information or they fall back on familiar propagandistic rhetorical strategies. To this effect, three modes of rhetoric need to be explained.

Three Modes of Rhetoric

Generally, in a debate or a speech, a person will use one of the three following modes of rhetoric: the intellectual, the rational, or the legal mode of rhetoric. Chang and Mehan (2006)[4] explain these modes well. The **intellectual mode of rhetoric** applies logical-empiricist principles that govern spot-on or appropriate inferences and logical consistency to an examination of current documents, records, policy statements, or speeches. This mode of rhetoric places events within a large historical, political, and sociological context. Journalists and scholars using the intellectual mode located the 9/11 events within the framework of the history of U.S. foreign policy, including U.S. ties with rogue states. They associated the scene and act of the September 11, 2001 attacks with the scenes and acts of events elsewhere in the world, especially events that were related to U.S. foreign policies. Historical events frequently cited have included the 1998 U.S. bombing of a pharmaceutical plant in the Sudan, the U.S. bans and bombings in Iraq, the U.S. military involvements in Libya and Nicaragua, and the U.S. interventions in the Israeli–Palestinian conflict.

The **rational mode of rhetoric** (or *technocratic mode*) employs reason, considers evidence, and evaluates costs vs. benefits so as to explain events. Critics using this mode will not likely refer to past U.S. actions—as those employing the intellectual mode of rhetoric would. The rational ones tend to evaluate the internal workings of a political or policy position. This mode invites people to make a careful, calculative assessment of the situation before them, restrain personal emotions, and adopt a cool-headed, impersonal mode of reasoning, analysis, and calculation. The **legal mode of rhetoric** is a mode that uses a logical-empiricist philosophy—but applies them to various texts. Instead of using speeches or government documents, legal arguments are rooted in instances within national and international jurisprudence. Therefore, many commentators and dissenters attempted to represent 9/11 as an act of crime or crime against humanity (instead of an act of war). In accordance with their call for a legal argumentation about these events, many advocated for having the culprits prosecuted through legal channels and legal procedures. Rather than urging for individual reasoning, it promotes legal reasoning and legal procedures to handle the situation. Any legitimate military or policy attempts would have to be approved by a legal authority, and any evidence or proof would also have to be acknowledged as legitimate by a legal authority (as stated by a legal convention).

Propaganda

As a particular form of rhetoric, **propaganda** refers to intentionally deceptive communication: public communication intended for a large group of people and designed to manipulate attitudes and behavior in times of crisis. Propaganda is also communication that employs a set of rhetorical techniques and cognitive heuristics to make specific declarations, and to generalize larger assumptions from those declarations, without providing proof or data. A rhetorical technique that corresponds to this description is the word terrorist itself.[5] Severin and Tankard (2001)[6] suggest that "two current examples of name calling [which they identify as a propaganda device] are terrorist and terrorism" (p. 112). They claim that each side in the terror–counterterror debate could provide evidence of the other's actions that would qualify for such a label. Nevertheless, labeling, especially after it has become recognized as possessing a certain meaning and connotation, means that evidence is not presented and studied on each occasion, but accepted as "read."

Propaganda stresses an essentially utilitarian perception of truth and information. Truth is subjugated to the service of expediency. In numerous visual communication narratives, truth loses value and the notions of belief and credibility become essential. The most successful propaganda campaigns use selective truth-telling extensively, but the purpose is strictly credibility.[7] Propaganda theory has made distinctions between **black propaganda** (fabrication, where distorted information is provided) and **gray propaganda**, which is not untruthful at face value but more cleverly manipulative.[8] Examples of black propaganda are cherry picking and card stacking. **Cherry picking** is the act of selecting individual cases or evidence that confirm a particular position, while turning a blind eye on a large portion of related cases or evidence that may contradict that position. **Card stacking** is a similar propaganda method that attempts to manipulate people's perception of an issue by accentuating one side and suppressing another, for example by discussing topics that highlight a specific view (e.g., a one-sided testimonial), or by ensuring that the other side is not heard. It is often used in persuasive speeches.[9]

PRO-WAR RHETORIC IN THE GEORGE W. BUSH ADMINISTRATION

Pro-war rhetoric is a type of propaganda to persuade the audience that war is necessary. Generally, pro-war rhetoric advances a national or bi-partisan agenda and is often seen as ethnocentric.[10] To convince people that war is necessary, historical figures have used strong language. For example, in his April 2, 1917 "War Message," U.S. President Woodrow Wilson advised Congress to declare war on Germany. In his speech, he maintained that the world needed to be safe for democracy and pushed for the U.S. to enter the war to "vindicate principles of peace and justice in the life of the world as against selfish and autocratic power." Likewise, on December 11, 1941, Adolf Hitler delivered a speech, in front of his Reichstag (German Parliament), declaring war on the United States of America. He made the argument that America was an evil empire to be destroyed.

Starting in September 2001, the George W. Bush administration construed 9/11 as unprovoked, original evil, because 9/11 had to become the absolute reason for all responses that would ensue. While the word *un-American* was used in the McCarthy era, the word *unpatriotic* was used in the Bush era. This labeling and framing process is exploited to emphasize the morals and motives of those who oppose U.S. military interventions.[11] Scholars and pundits who made "antimilitary" comments were targeted, even though they were not always widely broadcasted. One nonprofit organization, the American Council of Trustees and Alumni (of which Lynn Cheney, wife of Vice President Cheney, is a founding member) posted a web page denouncing multiple scholars, students, and a university president of unpatriotic attitude, condemning them as "the weak link in America's response to the attack" and accusing them of using "tolerance and diversity as antidotes to evil."[12]

The words used by the people just mentioned were basically fueling a particular **strategic political communication**, a method whereby speakers design their public language with the objective of creating, controlling, disseminating, and employing mediated messages as a political resource.[13] Such strategic political communication was enabled by **collective action frames**. These are action-oriented beliefs and meanings that motivate and legitimize social movements and campaigns. They give the media the tools to generate a desired effect from the audience. These frames enable politicians to amplify a sense of need or urgency about a specific issue presented to the audience. Accordingly, collective action frames are perfect for communicating information that contains conflict or threats that may necessitate a response on the part of the audience.[14]

According to Ronald Reid (1976),[15] professor of communication studies at the University of Massachusetts (Amherst), pro-war rhetoric uses three appeals. (1) **Territorial appeals** menace the audience's sense of territoriality. The audience is more likely to advocate waging war on the defensive rather than offensive side because of a real or threatened invasion. (2) **Ethnocentric appeals** create a division between the audience and the enemy. Ethnocentrism should be induced to a high level of emotional power to complete two goals: to despise the "inferior alien" and to show threats to cultural values. The most frequent way of evoking ethnocentric appeals is to portray the enemy's cultural values with evil traits, and the audience's as innocent. And (3) **optimistic appeals** promise the audience that victory will happen should they start war. Religion is used to establish optimism by declaring that God, or a higher power, is on the side of the audience's nation. President George W. Bush used all three appeals to start both the GWOT and the Iraq War.

The George W. Bush administration went as far as limiting dissent in multiple ways. As such, people who had T-shirts with anti-Bush slogans were taken away from events where the president spoke; those with an anti-Bush bumper sticker on their automobile that said "No More Blood for Oil" were removed from such events too; and those wearing Young Democrats shirts were forbidden from attending events. The Bush administration even published a manual that instructed how to deter potential protestors from events at which President Bush was to speak. Enclosed in the manual was a statement that local law enforcement should be asked to select a protest area "preferably not in view of the event site or the motorcade route." The rhetoric of both the Bush administration and the manual was clear: to deny dissenters an opportunity to challenge the president at meetings or even on the street. This phenomenon is referred to as **denial of the means of communication.**[16]

President Bush's Address to a Joint Session of Congress

As Black (2001)[17] suggested, because communicator intent is intrinsically difficult to identify or confirm, an emphasis on textual criteria, instead of communicator intent or audience response, is more beneficial. In his twenty-minute "Address to a Joint Session of Congress Following 9/11 Attacks" in 2001, President Bush[18] explained his views of Al Qaeda's motivations: "They hate what we see right here in this chamber—a democratically elected government. Their leaders are self-appointed. They hate our freedoms—our freedom of religion, our freedom of speech, our freedom to vote and assemble and disagree." In the Bush era, the "force of freedom" became essential to U.S. foreign policy rhetoric. The U.S. government sought to transplant freedom to "outposts of tyranny." In his address, President Bush urged "the expansion of freedom in all the world," using the word *freedom* or *free* twenty-seven times. Between 2002 and 2006, his five State of the Union addresses mentioned the word *education* 11 times, *unemployment* 3 times, and *terrorism* 122 times.[19]

In persuasion studies, **repetition** is a form of rhetorical technique using a word or phrase that is repeated time and again, thus getting stuck in the audience's head, so they can buy into the cult ideology even more. This is also referred to as **discursive control**, the process of repeating words or phrases to make messages seem unequivocal and undeniable.[20] Likewise, **argumentum ad nauseam** (or *argument from repetition* or *argumentum ad infinitum*) is a device employing assiduous repetition of an idea. An idea (i.e., a short slogan) that is repeated over and over again will eventually be seen as truth. This strategy is the most efficient when media sources are limited or controlled by the government.[21]

On hearing President Bush's "Address to a Joint Session of Congress Following 9/11 Attacks," political decision makers immediately altered propaganda passages, designed as part of the Project for the New American Century (PNAC), to stress domestic support for the new U.S. role in the world. These messages were placed into a crime-related discourse of fear, which may be described as the universal communication, symbolic awareness, and expectation that danger and risk are fundamental features of daily life.[22] PNAC was an American think tank based in Washington, D.C. that existed from early 1997 to 2006. It was created as a nonprofit educational institution by neoconservatives William Kristol and Robert Kagan. PNAC's stated goal was to stimulate American leadership in the world.[23] Soon after, an unusually large percentage of White House politicians assembled critical symbols and icons to associate terrorism with Iraq, Islam, and a large number of non-Western countries to strategically induce fear in the audience and manipulate their beliefs and assumptions about danger and risk. The purpose, of course, was to achieve key goals, including the expansion of domestic social control and the emergence of a legal mode of rhetoric as a way to legitimize the subsequent military invasions.[24]

Pro-War Rhetoric in the Media

At the beginning of the Iraq War, many reporters accepted military representatives' definitions of Iraqi fighters as criminals and thugs by propagandists working in the White House. Iraqi fighters were now gunmen or insurgents, instead of an army, soldiers, or even guerillas.[25] The 9/11 discourse was also dominated by the rhetoric of media personalities. Fairness and Accuracy in Reporting (FAIR) reported the following quotes voiced by media pundits:

- "There is only one way to begin to deal with people like this, and that is you have to kill some of them even if they are not immediately directly involved in this thing"—former U.S. Secretary of State Lawrence Eagleburger, *CNN*, September 11, 2001.

- "The response to this unimaginable 21st-century Pearl Harbor should be as simple as it is swift—kill the bastards. A gunshot between the eyes, blow them to smithereens, poison them if you have to. As for cities or countries that host these worms, bomb them into basketball courts"—Steve Dunleavy, *New York Post*, September 12, 2001.

- "It doesn't make any difference who you kill in the process of retaliation against the attacks"—Bill O'Reilly, *The O'Reilly Factor*, September 13, 2001.

- "This is no time to be precious about locating the exact individuals directly involved in this particular terrorist attack... We should invade their countries, kill their leaders and convert them to Christianity. We weren't punctilious about locating and punishing only Hitler and his top officers. We carpet-bombed German cities; we killed civilians. That's war. And this is war"—Ann Coulter, *National Review*, September 13, 2001.

Many of the phrases used by these media pundits contained **loaded language**, highly emotive language that influences audiences by appealing to emotion. Let us have a look at a few phrases here: "unimaginable 21st-century Pearl Harbor" and "this is war." These phrases exemplified the *pathos* side of rhetoric: to appeal to the audience's emotions. Such loaded language was designed to invoke a particular image of our enemies, surely for the purposes of propaganda. After 9/11, the word *madrassa* ("school" in Arabic) was loaded with negative associations by Americans and people in the West who did not know Arabic and failed to distinguish between radical Islamic schools and schools that offer primary education courses. The Yale Center for the Study of Globalization analyzed bias in U.S. newspaper coverage of Pakistan since the September 11, 2001 attacks. They discovered that the term madrassa was ascribed a loaded political meaning: "When articles mentioned 'madrassas,' readers were led to infer that all schools so-named are anti-American, anti-Western, pro-terrorist centers having less to do with teaching basic literacy and more to do with political indoctrination."[26]

The Propaganda of "World War"

As Marine Colonel Paul Melshen (2003),[27] a U.S. military official, said in a speech, "There should be no doubt, we are at war, and it is a world war." This world war was a global military operation started within a few moments after the September 11, 2001 attacks. On prime-time television, President Bush declared that America was starting a "war against terrorism." Already in the 1980s, Ronald Reagan called the Soviet Union "the focus of evil in the modern world." He requested that Americans "pray for the salvation of all those who live in totalitarian darkness" and to "pray they will discover the joys of knowing God." In 1982, owing to Reagan's Speech to the House of Commons in the British Parliament, the expression "evil empire" came to embody the Soviet Union in the Western world and "fears of terrorism" took "root in the national psyche."[28] As Lasswell (1995)[29] describes it,

> For mobilization of national hatred, the enemy must be represented as a menacing, murderous aggressor, a satanic violator of the moral and conventional standards, an obstacle to the cherished aims and ideals of the nation as a whole and of each constituent part. Through the elaboration of war aims, the obstructive role of the enemy becomes particularly evident. (p. 18)

Now, we live in a terrorism world and we claim that evil terrorists rather than dubious political tactics govern the new world. The official White House website adopted Reagan's discourses in its historical description of his occupancy of the White House: the White House stood "witness as the great moral crusader Ronald Reagan would crush the evil Soviet Empire from the Oval Office, and re-invent what it means to portray an honest, faith-loving American."[30]

The larger public discourse of this new world war comprised many core narratives, including the following: the 9/11 attacks were an act of war like the attack on Pearl Harbor, rather than a criminal act; the terrorist threat was new and unique; the threat was global in scope and theoretically disastrous to the U.S. and the civilized world; the terrorists were cruel, evil, and heartless enemies, while Americans were innocent, pacifist, heroic and united; and GWOT was a model of "good war" designed to bring the culprits to justice and make the world a safe place. These narratives were pushed on U.S. society through their constant repetition, their unmediated transmission to the audience via the mainstream media, and their intensification and hype through other social institutions.[31] This was, again, the *pathos* aspect of rhetoric.

By using the language of World War II, George W. Bush suggested that Al Qaeda was similar to the German and Japanese threats. At the core of the World War II comparison was the morality that pacification does not work; the reason is that it cannot be trusted because it covertly harbors ulterior motives that can only be foiled by the use of force. American politicians have often used the lessons of World War II to justify not appeasing their aggressors. During the Cold War, President Truman employed this analogy to rationalize opposing North Korea's invasion of South Korea. President Johnson used it to underline the costs of surrendering South Vietnam to the Vietcong.[32]

The most conspicuous observation about 9/11 is how many metaphors gained a military connotation. The general idea illustrated was that 9/11 was essentially a military strike conducted by a military group. Countless metaphors added fuel to this general theme. For instance, based on one popular interpretation, the people perpetrating the attacks were *kamikaze flyers*, *kamikaze pilots*, or *kamikaze assassins*. The airliners crashing into the towers were *kamikaze weapons* or *kamikaze flights*. The act of terrorism was also called a *kamikaze attack*, openly relating the events of 9/11 to the war with Japan and that nation's use of kamikaze tactics during World War II. This military-loaded depiction of the terrorists was also reinforced by the use of terms such as *death troop* or *suicide commandos*. Osama bin Laden was referred to as a man with a private army. In other parts of the world, the hijackers involved were called a *terrorist army*, consisting of 3,000 veterans from the war with the Soviet Union in Afghanistan. This army used camouflage and was believed to be hierarchically organized, with Osama bin Laden being the leader of the organization. And, of course, bin Laden was nicknamed a *top terrorist*, *terror chief*, *terror leader*, *terror boss*, and *senior terrorist*.[33]

PROPAGANDA CONTENT ANALYSIS CATEGORIES AND DESCRIPTORS

Table 8.1 was adapted from Lee and Lee (1939).[34] Their propaganda index sheds light on propaganda texts, whether they contain many propaganda elements. This index has become a standard table by communication scholars, because it provides great awareness of simple language analysis, and an easier direction to the more complex method of discourse analysis. With respect to the labels used in the previous section, one could easily say that the device of name-calling (NC) was mostly used when referring to the 9/11 hijackers.

Table 8.1 Propaganda Index, First Developed by Lee and Lee (1939), Later Adapted by Tilley (2005)[35]

Device	Description
Name-calling (NC)	Negative or bad labels or stereotypes (e.g., terrorists, extremists, fanatics, ferals, "rent-a-crowd") that encourage a summary negative response without examining history, complexity, or evidence related to an issue
Glittering generality (GG)	Abstract positive labeling using virtue connotators (e.g., intelligence for covert surveillance); positive-sounding euphemisms (e.g., collateral damage and friendly fire for civilian or own-troop deaths; biosolids for sewerage); broadly affirmative unverifiable adjectives (e.g., state-of-the-art, high-tech); positive abstractions (e.g., prosperity, freedom, rights, democracy, respect, common sense); vagaries (e.g., significantly increasing or highly trained, where the level of increasing or training is not defined); subjective adjectives or adverbs (beautiful, stunning) which give positive effect without evidence
Transfer positive (TF)	Process of association whereby the good of one thing rubs off onto something else (e.g., through appropriation of symbolic objects such as national flags or anthem, sponsorship, celebrity, or expert endorsement)

Device	Description
Transfer negative (TN)	Expressed or implied association with negative incidents, places, people, or symbols to rub off negative qualities to the issue being discussed or discredit by implication of an opposing viewpoint (e.g., may have links with Al Qaeda, has been seen in the company of known terrorists, etc.)
Plain folks (PF)	Implications that ideas are "of the people" (e.g., references to family values, hard working, decent folk, everyday moms and dads, average Americans, ordinary people, normal people, or middle America). PF is a values-based device that implies normalcy or rationality for an opinion and, thereby, demonizes other views as aberrant and unreasonable
Band wagon (BW)	Peer pressure or spiral of silence device (e.g., implication that everyone, most people, many people, or any large collectivized group of people, such as our school, our company, or our neighborhood thinks a particular, singular, or uniform way). Includes references to imagined communities, such as states, nations, organizations, and phrases such as *we*, *our*, *all*, *everybody*, that invite solidarity with an implied large and inclusive group, suggest mass support for an opinion, marginalize alternative views as minority, suggest collective ownership of and responsibility for the actions of a group (e.g., "our army") or obscure internal division within any group
Manifest destiny (MD)	Determinist invocation of God (or any kind of faith), destiny, fate, natural processes, or universal design, to lend support to an argument; removal of accountability for an idea or issue from individuals and attribution of responsibility to deterministic greater forces (God's will, karma, tradition, luck, history, nature)
Other (O)	A phrase that appears either neutral, with no rhetorical or persuasive effect, or persuasive but does not fit into any of the above categories

Source: "Responding to Terrorism Using Ethical Means: The Propaganda Index," by E.N. Tilley, 2005, *Communication Research Reports, 22*(1), p. 69–77.

This propaganda index may help enhance both ethics and usefulness of terror and other sensitive information outputs. The index adds to current ethics checks which either necessitate a reductionist determination of singular truthfulness, or emphasize mostly communication ends, because it allows practitioners to also evaluate the manners in which those ends are achieved and the way their specific truths or beliefs are communicated.

DEHUMANIZING THE ENEMY

Dehumanization is a process by which a group stresses the inferiority of another group through open or crafty acts or statements. Occasionally, Western governments paint enemy civilians or soldiers as inhuman so that voters will support a war even more—a war that they would otherwise see as mass murder. Dehumanization is a powerful device to dissociate a group from another by depicting the other as an animal or a beast rather than human. Worldwide, dehumanization has been exploited in the political arena for decades. For instance, during World War II, Nazis dehumanized Jews and published or broadcasted negative labels to describe them. More recently, neo-Nazis have degraded people of non-European races by calling them "mud people." On a Palestinian wall, people painted pigs and monkeys and wrote, "Sons of monkeys and pigs," making comparisons between Jews and these animals. In Islam, pigs are viewed as unclean animals.[36] Three specific techniques of dehumanization are Othering, enemification, and evilification.

Othering is labeling and degrading of cultures and groups other than one's own. Natives, women, homosexual males and females, and ethnic groups have been Othered by dominant groups in language. One customary way is to characterize the Other as the binary opposite (e.g., "colonists were hard-working; natives were lazy"). Othering is the language of oppression. The Nazis called Jews *bacilli*, *parasites*, *plague*, *disease*, and so forth. Although killing another human may be inconceivable, exterminating a disease is not. The subordination of ethnic groups became justifiable when the label *savage* was used.[37] **Enemification** is the representation of other groups as enemies—usually forever. From this perspective, it is possible to believe that referring to terrorists as evil strengthens the practice of making the enemy appear shockingly horrific. Enemification serves to identify a "legitimate" target for missiles to be launched at. It fosters a sense of unity and conviction in objectives.[38] **Evilification** is the practice of vilifying other groups and methodically classifying them as outcasts.[39] All these forms constitute **hate speech**—emotionally and psychologically hurtful words.[40] When portraying IRA bombings in 1971, money-making British newspapers qualified IRA violence with radically excessive language. For instance, headlines after IRA bombings have included "Murdering Bastards" (*Daily Star*), "Wicked Assassins" (*Sun*), and "Psychopathic Thugs" (*Daily Express*).[41]

Dehumanization during the Bush Administration

Senior spokespersons of the Bush administration regularly referred to terrorists as animals and barbarians who did not belong to any civilized community. A case in point is the U.S. ambassador to Japan declaring that the September 11, 2001 attacks were "an attack not just on the United States but on enlightened, civilized societies everywhere." Donald Rumsfeld, then U.S. secretary of defense, told journalists on a trip to Guantánamo Bay that the prisoners were "among the most dangerous, best-trained, vicious killers on the face of the earth."[42] President Bush himself repeated such statement when he said that "by their cruelty, the terrorists have chosen to live on the hunted margin of mankind. By their hatred, they have divorced themselves from the values that define civilization itself."[43] The result is that this rhetoric put terrorists outside civilized society, on the "hunted margins of mankind," and functioned to pigeonhole them as "an evil and inhuman group of men."[44]

Another relevant narrative is the conception of the terrorist enemy as a type of disease or sickness. Colin Powell frequently used the phrase *scourge of terrorism*.[45] This medical metaphor relates terrorists to filth and decay. It was reaffirmed even more overtly by Rumsfeld: "We share the belief that terrorism is a cancer on the human condition."[46] Bush, in turn, mentioned the threat to the body politic caused by "terrorist parasites who threaten their countries and our own."[47] In these rhetorical constructions, the terrorists are redesigned as threatening organisms that cause their host to be ill; they hide interiorly, sucking the lifeblood of their unsuspecting hosts and disseminating poison. It is this picture of the filthy, disease-loaded inhuman that perchance subconsciously inspired the photo of the prisoner covered with what seems to be dirt or excrement.[48]

Boomerang Effect

Demonizing terrorists through the types of rhetoric described so far can have a boomerang effect. In theory, the **boomerang effect** postulates that while people use discourses to protect their freedom, their own discourses may bite them back. According to Kapitan (2003),[49] the terrorist rhetoric may increase terrorism in four different ways:

- First, it intensifies the impact of terrorism by amplifying the fear in the target population. By demonizing terrorists, we heighten the fear and alarm caused by terrorist acts.

- Second, those who buy into the rhetoric become part of the cycle of revenge and retaliation by endorsing extreme actions taken by their own government, not only against terrorists themselves, but also against those populations from which the terrorists come. The aftereffect has been a rise in terrorist violence under the banner of retaliation or counterterrorism. For instance, since the 1950s, Israeli retaliations for violence against Jews (committed by Palestinians) have usually led to the deaths of more Arab civilians; after the hostage taking at the Munich Olympic Games in 1972, Israeli air strikes killed between 200 and 500 people, mostly civilians, in Lebanon and Syria.[50]

- Third, a violent reaction is likely to stiffen the determination of populations from which terrorists have emerged, leading them to see their enemies as people with whom one should not negotiate, and as people who, because they jump so quickly to the terrorist rhetoric, know only the language of violence. Consequently, they are more prone to matching violence with more violence.

- Fourth, people who use the rhetoric of terrorism for their own political agenda endorse actions that they know will cause or perpetuate further violence aimed at civilians (i.e., collateral damage).[51]

Based on the four tenets of the boomerang effect, it follows that the rhetoric of evil, rather than associating us with democracy, makes us participating in terrorism. Indeed, terrorism is created in and sustained by such rhetoric of evil, especially in a time of "religious violence." George W. Bush used apocalyptic connotations by referring to America as "a blessed country" called to protect and keep "God's gift to humanity" from the "designs of evil men" who are bent on eliminating freedom, liberty, and civilization with WMDs.[52]

The "Us vs. Them" Dichotomy

The **"us vs. them" dichotomy** is what some would regard as an in-group vs. out-group conflict (see Chapter 10). It is a practice that classifies people into one or the other of their multiple cultural, ethnic, or national dimensions. The outcome is a mental, emotional, and moral distinction in the audience's minds.[53] President Bush's contrasting positive and negative labels produced a separation in which the dominant positive orientator (i.e., like a "God term") was *security*, and the antagonistic "Devil term" or negative orientator was *terror*.[54] As Black (2001)[55] put it, these two "broad, all-inclusive categories of in-groups (friends) and out-groups (enemies), beliefs and disbeliefs, and situations to be accepted or rejected in toto" (p. 134) created an us vs. them binary that condemned terrorists for worsening American fear, without considering the situation's roots.[56]

The resulting us vs. them dichotomy produces a kind of close-minded mentality that advocates the separation of certain racial, religious, ethnic, or cultural groups, placing them in the hostile or alien groups. As Said (1997)[57] remarked, "sensationalism, crude xenophobia, and insensitive belligerence are the order of the day, with results on both sides of the imaginary line between 'us' and 'them' that are extremely unedifying" (p. xviii). Black's (2001)[58] assessment of propaganda theory identified such close-mindedness as a repeated practice in the media. He suggested a new definition of propaganda, based on the presence of three rhetorical traits exemplifying the us vs. them dichotomy: "simplified, pat answers (usually relayed by authoritative sources)"; "a world in which the good guys and the bad guys are readily identifiable"; and "simplistic and direct connection between causes and effects" (p. 129).

Cultural Hegemony

Cultural hegemony is a form of nationalistic rhetoric about identity enabled by the process of legitimizing feelings of dislike or superiority toward enemies. The central element in cultural hegemony is that the less powerful groups are not intimidated or forced to comply with dominant ideologies; rather, they approve them. The concept of cultural hegemony was developed by Antonio Gramsci (1971).[59] It explains relationships between groups in society and how particular ones are downgraded in discourse and stereotypical media rhetoric in a way that makes sense to the dominant group(s). Hence, the media play an important role in designing, supporting, or challenging racist or anti-Muslim perspectives in portrayals of social groups. Whether deliberate or not, media representations can justify or empower cultural racisms and contribute to Othering.[60] When politics and religion join forces, they can better propagate hegemonic beliefs. To achieve this, both political and theological communicators routinely quote images of Satan. This practice was already used by Martin Luther in the 16th century, when rebelling farmers were called "agents of the devil."[61]

Occidentalism

The term **Occidentalism** refers to negative constructions of America and dehumanizing assessments of the West. It often comes from the Islamic world and is an inversion of Orientalism, Edward Said's concept for negative Western opinions of the East. This steeped opposition to America and the West essentially echoes reactions to powers of modernization that are grounded in Western culture itself, among both idealistic radicals and nationalist conservatives who consider capitalism, liberalism, and secularism as devastating influences. Occidentalists stress the Western fervent attachment to money and purchase (as different from sharing) and the manner in which Westerners deal with each other to guarantee their individual subsistence.[62]

For years, Occidentalism has been disturbing "Oriental" countries such as Middle Eastern countries. In these places, where Islamic culture is prevailing, Occidentalism manifests itself as an aggressive force that strongly resists Western hegemony portrayed by the U.S., and at times even progresses into far-reaching armed clashes. For instance, the past and current Libyan–American hostilities, the bloodshedding battles between Iraq and the Allied Army, and the Iranian–American conflict are the most obvious cases. In these cases, Occident is also fashioned as the Other. The Occidentalism in the view of the Oriental is evidently symbolized by the Third World's anti-colonialist and anti-hegemonic movement. For Islamist extremists, Western civilization is the model of idolatrous barbarism. Idolatry is the most odious religious sin and must thus be met with all the permissible force and punishments at the true believer's disposal.[63]

Sayyid Qutb, leading activist of the Egyptian Muslim Brotherhood, employed deep-seated, hateful rhetoric against America and the West. For Qutb, Occidentals were becoming debauched and barbarous. In fact, in his writings, he made it clear that they were in a state of jahiliyyah, an Islamic notion of ignorance of divine guidance. In other words, jahiliyyah refers to any person who does not follow Islam and the Qur'an. Qutb considered the West as a huge whorehouse, embedded in immoral behavior, greed, and selfishness. His rhetoric was appealing to Muslims who had been "oppressed" and "humiliated" by Occidentals.[64] The concept of jahiliyyah is used several times in the Qur'an: for example, "Do they truly desire the law of paganism? But who is fairer than God in judgment for a people firm of faith?" (Qur'an: 5:50) and "For the unbelievers had planted in their hearts zealotry, the zealotry of lawlessness" (Qur'an: 48:26).

FREE SPEECH ABOUT TERRORISM

Public perception of terrorism has influenced the way some individuals misuse their freedom of speech. For Ward Churchill, professor of ethnic studies at the University of Colorado, America's role is to eliminate minorities. In 2003, he published a book titled *On the Justice of Roosting Chickens: Consequences of American Conquest and Carnage*,[65] in which he wrote that the 9/11 terrorist attacks were brought out by U.S. policy. He called the "technocratic corps" employed in the World Trade Center "little Eichmanns." Churchill called both America and Israel "Nazi Germany." How could anyone, in their right mind, consider Israel—the only democratic country in the Middle East that is free (from a Western perspective), where homosexuals are welcome, and where women are equal to men—Nazi Germany? In a sermon delivered just after September 11, 2001, Reverend Jeremiah Wright made comments about how America had caused the attacks to occur because of its own practice of terrorism:

> We bombed Hiroshima, we bombed Nagasaki, and we nuked far more than the thousands in New York and the Pentagon, and we never batted an eye. We have supported state terrorism against the Palestinians and black South Africans, and now we are indignant. Because the stuff we have done overseas is now brought right back into our own front yards. America's chickens are coming home to roost.[66]

Likewise, shortly after 9/11, former White House employee Van Jones, an environmental advocate, said that U.S. imperialism was the reason the terrorist attacks took place. Most types of freedom of speech are protected by the Universal Declaration of Human Rights (signed by the United Nations in 1948) and other international treaties. Put simply, they protect people's right to communicate, even though people's opinions and thoughts might contradict or offend other religions and beliefs.[67]

Anti-Semitic Rhetoric

Jews today have two safe havens: Israel and the U.S.—a country in which Jews have achieved outstanding power and wealth, and have a right, granted by the Constitution, to implement their religious traditions freely. The Jewish state secures refuge for Jews worldwide, but it is not immune of risks. Hassan Nasrallah, the leader of the Lebanese terrorist group Hezbollah, maintains that Jews need to gather in Israel to make it easier for Hezbollah, instead of having to chase them worldwide. Nasrallah's Iranian friends are on the verge of building nuclear weapons. A European poll conducted by the Anti-Defamation League revealed that 74% of Spaniards say Jews "have too much power in international financial markets," while 67% of Hungarians believe Jews "have too much power in the business world." In the U.S., at Yahoo! Finance, the forum about Goldman Sachs is replete with comments about "Jewish pigs" and the "Zionist Federal Reserve."[68] On the University of Southern California website, a Muslim call to exterminate Jews was posted by the Muslim Student Association, a branch of the Muslim Brotherhood (and supporters of jihad). Lastly, Jimmy Carter actively seeks to cut off U.S. aid to Israel, unless it surrenders to Palestinian demands.

Terrorism Slogans

An archetype of free speech is the use of slogans. A **slogan** is a memorable maxim, watchword, or phrase used as a repetitive expression of an idea or objective. Slogans are popular in political, commercial, religious, and other situations.[69] The following slogans created by terrorists are battle cries that may have been the main impetus for killing so many people in modern history:

- "One man's terrorist is another man's freedom fighter"—aphorism that became popular in the 1980s, used for the first time by Yasser Arafat in a 1974 speech before the United Nations.
- "Strike one to educate a hundred"—quoted in the memoir of the Red Brigades killer Patrizio Peci.[70]
- "Kill one, frighten a thousand"—terrorist watchword attributed to the ancient Chinese general Sun-Tzu, and later Mao Zedong.
- "We are the Soldiers of Mercy"—announced by the Armed Islamic Group, an Algerian terrorist group, during their 1994 hijacking of Air France Flight 8969.
- "Think global, act local"—Pakistan-backed Islamist terrorist slogan.
- "Bleed India with a thousand cuts"—created by an Indian militant separatist group, during India's 26/11 Operation (the 2008 Mumbai attacks).

- "Better a terrible end than an endless terror"—Nazis' terrorist slogan in the 1930s.
- "Armed people are respected people" ("Poble armat, poble respetat")—terrorist slogan calling on the Catalans to use violence against their Spanish oppressors.

These slogans are rallying mottos distinctively associated to terrorist groups' causes. Their effectiveness depends on the impact they have on both governments and audiences. The increase in mass communication, especially television and the Internet, has magnified the effectiveness of such messages. Slogans are like sound bites; they are brief, memorable statements.[71]

Counterterrorism and Antiterrorism Slogans

The selection of a slogan against terrorism depends on the personality of the president, prime minister, or other counterterrorism or antiterrorism organization. They, too, need a brief, attractive, distinctive phrase:

- "It is a global war on terror"—President George W. Bush.
- "You're either with us or you're with the terrorists"—President George W. Bush.
- "Shock and awe"—U.S. military doctrine to frighten the enemy.
- "You can run, but you can't hide"—U.S. sticker on Osama bin Laden.
- "Give peace a chance. Kill a terrorist"—Conservative slogan during President George W. Bush's presidency.
- "No Muslims—No Terrorism"—rallying cry of the Anti-Jihad League, 2003.
- "I stand against terrorism"—antiterrorism magnet by CafePress.
- "We are not afraid"—British antiterrorism slogan after the London bombings in July of 2005.

Slogans are a method of achieving group solidification and reflect a group's norms and values. Slogans emphasize a specific point, issue, or message; they arrest attention and raise consciousness about a social or global concern. For example, the taglines "You're either with us or you're with the terrorists" and "I stand against terrorism" inspire audiences to join or support a movement and to convince them to diffuse a group's message. The us vs. them metaphor serves to polarize two extreme positions. The slogan "It is a global war on terror" has made a big difference in the public opinion because it was appealing and popular right from the beginning. It resonated with the zeitgeist of the time. **Zeitgeist** refers to the general mindset, education, and morals of a given period. Put simply, it is the spirit (*Geist*) of the time (*Zeit*).[72]

Anti–Iraq War and Anti-GWOT Slogans

Slogans opposing U.S. military interventions in Iraq and Afghanistan have been plentiful. According to Bowers and colleagues (2010),[73] dissenters in the U.S. and in the U.K. have used slogans such as the following:

- "Support the troops, end the war."
- "Support our troops—Bring them home."

- "End the war now."
- "Impeach W., impeach Cheney too."
- "Wall Street gets rich, Iraqis and GIs die."
- "Drop tuition, not bombs."
- "Bush lied, they lied."
- "What do we want? Troops out. When do we want it? Now."
- "We are the veterans! The Iraq War veterans! The anti-war veterans! We are soldiers! Anti-war soldiers."
- "Quit Iraq and Afghanistan. Yes we can."

Again, most of these slogans are short. Longer statements are less memorable and less likely to be repeated sufficiently to become established as slogans. Because slogans generally attempt to elicit strong emotional responses, most of them contain words that are frequently used and familiar to most people. Human languages have a large number of familiar words. Millions of phrases are like short proverbs. They contain four to ten words.[74]

RHETORIC OF ISLAMIST TERRORIST GROUPS

In general, Islamist terrorist groups are using the media to wage a successful War of Ideas against the West because they are unable to win a conventional head-to-head war against the U.S. military. As such, Al Qaeda relies on as-Sahab (Foundation for Islamic Media Publication) and Hamas relies on al-Aqsa Television. Hezbollah uses **Al-Manar** ("the Lighthouse"), a satellite television station located in Beirut, Lebanon and affiliated with Hezbollah itself. Al-Manar television moved its operations to satellite broadcasts in 2000, propagating anti-Israel and anti-American messages to broad Muslim audiences. One Al-Manar broadcast, for example, aired a statement calling for suicide terrorism, tactfully designed as martyrdom for anti-Israel resistance: "In the culture of resistance, the culmination of humanity and human dignity is the decision to perform istishhad [martyrdom] in order to grant life to one's people and dignity to one's nation and homeland."[75] Non-terrorist Muslim governments have also their own rhetorical tactics. For instance, the Saudi media frequently air anti-American rhetoric and outwardly endorse the Palestinians' cause, combats against the Israelis in South Lebanon, and Syrian claims to the Golan Heights. Saudi rulers oppose the Western model that they see as moral decadence and an unconditional supporter of Israel.[76]

During the 1990s, one of Osama bin Laden's major rhetorical themes to his followers was that, historically, America tends to withdraw when facing asymmetrical attacks. In numerous speeches, he reminded Muslims that U.S. forces retreated from Lebanon in 1983, only four months after 260 U.S. Marines and Navy seamen were blown up in dual suicide bombings. In Al Qaeda teachings, "the most disgraceful case was in Somalia" when eighteen soldiers were killed and U.S. troops immediately evacuated the area.[77] Nevertheless, before September 11, 2001, there was virtually no congressional action or hearing on Al Qaeda, media broadcasts on Al Qaeda were rare, the American audience regularly considered terrorism a second-tier threat, and many students of international studies believed that the terrorism threat was overstated. During the 2000 U.S. presidential elections, neither George W. Bush nor Al Gore ever discussed Al Qaeda, in spite of the recorded terrorist group's criticisms of the U.S.[78] Al Qaeda's grievances against the nation have been markedly consistent. The hundreds of written and recorded statements made by Osama bin Laden and his comrades on Al Jazeera, Al Qaeda websites, and Arabic newspapers did not condemn Hollywood, U.S. crime, prostitution, or even the separation of church and government in the U.S. Instead, they concentrated on U.S. policies in the Middle East.[79]

Al Qaeda leaders describe terrorism as "a message with no words" and "the only language understood by the West."[80] Al Qaeda has been noticeably fervent about three particular policies: (1) after U.S. troops crossed the land of Saudi Arabia as part of Operation Desert Shield, Al Qaeda's founding mujahedin openly worked hard to expel the "crusader armies" from the "land of the two holy places," Mecca and Medina; (2) although never associating itself with Saddam Hussein's (secular) Baathist autocracy, Al Qaeda has incessantly opposed U.S. interference in Iraq's business, including Operation Desert Storm, later U.S.-led boycotts and weapons inspections programs, Operation Iraqi Freedom, and recent reconstruction of Iraq; and (3) Al Qaeda spokesmen have reviled the crusader–Zionist alliance, which indirectly helps Israel in its fight against the Palestinians.[81]

When releasing communiqués, Al Qaeda usually addresses a specific audience. A typical audiotape broadcast on Al Jazeera in the early 2000s would begin with such a statement: "This is a message from Osama bin Laden to the American people regarding your aggression in Iraq." By contrast, communiqués to the Muslim community are normally addressed specifically to fellow Muslims. These messages are different from those intended for Americans in a significant way: they focus on the religious element of jihad by assuring that the "victory of Islam is coming." This type of religious rhetoric is mostly instrumental. As Peter Bergen (2001)[82] observed,

> As a practical matter, the restoration of the Khalifa [Caliphate] had about as much chance as the Holy Roman Empire suddenly reappearing in Europe, but as a rhetorical device the call for its return exercised a powerful grip on bin Laden and his followers (p. 21).

Al Qaeda's religious rhetoric to fellow Muslims has three primary functions. First, it is a massive legitimizing force. Every time Al Qaeda kills innocent people, particularly if they are Muslims, the terrorist group attempts to legitimize its actions by invoking God's name. In August 1998, after the U.S. embassy bombings in Tanzania and Kenya, in which most casualties were local Muslim citizens, Osama bin Laden explained to his fellow Muslims that the attacks were conducted "with the help of God." Invoking Islam has always been pivotal to Al Qaeda because its famous leader was never a religious cleric or academic. Osama bin laden did not matriculate in any of the Islamic universities in Saudi Arabia and did not have the power to issue a fatwa on his own—he was always assisted for this.[83]

Second, Al Qaeda stresses the religious aspect of jihad to galvanize its followers. Al Qaeda is well aware that inner struggles between various Muslim factions have historically stalled efforts to fight the West. Al Qaeda often warns its followers of the "Muslim duty to ignore the minor differences among ourselves" because those engaged in an internal war will suffer "grave consequences." In messages aimed at as much to Muslims as to God, bin Laden has implored, "Oh God, unify the Muslims" and "praise be to Allah… [who] defeats factionalism." Third, Al Qaeda adroitly exploits religion to motivate its followers. Its most alarming rhetoric uses the language of religion to encourage followers to become jihadists: "destroying, fighting, and killing the enemy until, by the Grace of Allah, it is completely defeated."[84]

To stimulate his young followers, Osama bin Laden used **death cult language**, a type of rhetoric centered on the glorification of death as part of a major plan to transform the world and establish a grand Caliphate. Osama reportedly uttered statements such as "The Crusader army became dust," "Death is truth and the ultimate destiny," and "Courageous youth of Islam fear no danger." Human sacrifice had a great place in Osama's world. As opposed to the Christian martyr suffering torture and death for his or her faith, the Muslim martyr is a vigorous warrior, like a kamikaze pilot. It is the idea that Islamist terrorists will be accepted in paradise as martyrs by killing unarmed infidels. Osama bin Laden's language had historical roots. It was traced back to early terrorist cults in the Islamic world. The Assassins (see Chapter 1 for description) asserted that salvation was only for those who obeyed their leaders (i.e., imams), killed infidels, and committed ritual suicide afterward. The only acceptable weapon was the dagger. A praiseworthy Assassin was expected to die after fulfilling his duty to kill others.[85]

CASE STUDY: OSAMA BIN LADEN'S SPEECH (10/29/2004)

The following is the first half of a speech by Osama bin Laden that was broadcast by Al Jazeera on October 29, 2004.[86] This is a good case study for rhetorical appeals in terrorism:

> Praise be to Allah who created the creation for his worship and commanded them to be just and permitted the wronged one to retaliate against the oppressor in kind. To proceed:
>
> Peace be upon he who follows the guidance: People of America this talk of mine is for you and concerns the ideal way to prevent another Manhattan, and deals with the war and its causes and results.
>
> Before I begin, I say to you that security is an indispensable pillar of human life and that free men do not forfeit their security, contrary to Bush's claim that we hate freedom.
>
> If so, then let him explain to us why we don't strike for example—Sweden. And we know that freedom-haters don't possess defiant spirits like those of the nineteen—may Allah have mercy on them.
>
> No, we fight because we are free men who don't sleep under oppression. We want to restore freedom to our nation, just as you lay waste to our nation. So shall we lay waste to yours.
>
> No one except a dumb thief plays with the security of others and then makes himself believe he will be secure. Whereas thinking people, when disaster strikes, make it their priority to look for its causes, in order to prevent it happening again.

But I am amazed at you. Even though we are in the fourth year after the events of September 11th, Bush is still engaged in distortion, deception and hiding from you the real causes. And thus, the reasons are still there for a repeat of what occurred.

So I shall talk to you about the story behind those events and shall tell you truthfully about the moments in which the decision was taken, for you to consider.

I say to you, Allah knows that it had never occurred to us to strike the towers. But after it became unbearable and we witnessed the oppression and tyranny of the American/Israeli coalition against our people in Palestine and Lebanon, it came to my mind.

The events that affected my soul in a direct way started in 1982 when America permitted the Israelis to invade Lebanon and the American Sixth Fleet helped them in that. This bombardment began and many were killed and injured and others were terrorised and displaced.

I couldn't forget those moving scenes, blood and severed limbs, women and children sprawled everywhere. Houses destroyed along with their occupants and high rises demolished over their residents, rockets raining down on our home without mercy.

The situation was like a crocodile meeting a helpless child, powerless except for his screams. Does the crocodile understand a conversation that doesn't include a weapon? And the whole world saw and heard but it didn't respond.

In those difficult moments many hard-to-describe ideas bubbled in my soul, but in the end they produced an intense feeling of rejection of tyranny, and gave birth to a strong resolve to punish the oppressors.

And as I looked at those demolished towers in Lebanon, it entered my mind that we should punish the oppressor in kind and that we should destroy towers in America in order that they taste some of what we tasted and so that they be deterred from killing our women and children.

And that day, it was confirmed to me that oppression and the intentional killing of innocent women and children is a deliberate American policy. Destruction is freedom and democracy, while resistance is terrorism and intolerance.

This means the oppressing and embargoing to death of millions as Bush Sr. did in Iraq in the greatest mass slaughter of children mankind has ever known, and it means the throwing of millions of pounds of bombs and explosives at millions of children—also in Iraq—as Bush Jr. did, in order to remove an old agent and replace him with a new puppet to assist in the pilfering of Iraq's oil and other outrages.

So with these images and their like as their background, the events of September 11th came as a reply to those great wrongs, should a man be blamed for defending his sanctuary?

Is defending oneself and punishing the aggressor in kind, objectionable terrorism? If it is such, then it is unavoidable for us.

This is the message which I sought to communicate to you in word and deed, repeatedly, for years before September 11th.

And you can read this, if you wish, in my interview with Scott in Time Magazine in 1996, or with Peter Arnett on CNN in 1997, or my meeting with John Weiner in 1998.

You can observe it practically, if you wish, in Kenya and Tanzania and in Aden. And you can read it in my interview with Abdul Bari Atwan, as well as my interviews with Robert Fisk.

Unlike other speeches videotaped by Osama bin Laden, this one is unique in that, based on the rhetorical appeals used in this speech, the audience is not the worldwide Muslim community; rather, it is the U.S. audience. All one has to do is look at Paragraph 2: "People of America this talk of mine is for you and concerns the ideal way to prevent another Manhattan." And Paragraph 19 is worth mentioning too: "This is the message which I sought to communicate to you in word and deed, repeatedly, for years before September 11th." This type of rhetoric is clear and direct. Additionally, as pointed out by Tuman (2010),[87] that speech was broadcast less than a week before the 2004 U.S. presidential elections. Undoubtedly, Osama bin Laden wanted to influence the outcome of the elections by making sure that America disengages from the Middle East. This is exemplified in Paragraph 2 ("deals with the war and its causes and results"), Paragraph 9 ("the American/Israeli coalition against our people in Palestine and Lebanon"), and Paragraph 10 ("in 1982 when America permitted the Israelis to invade Lebanon").

At the beginning of his speech, it seems like bin Laden used logos on his U.S. audience, as a way to explain why he launched the attacks on September 11, 2001. This is shown in Paragraph 3 ("free men do not forfeit their security"), Paragraph 5 ("we fight because we are free men who don't sleep under oppression"), and Paragraph 18 ("Is defending oneself and punishing the aggressor in kind, objectionable terrorism?"). By the same token, bin Laden also used logos as a means to rationalize why he did not attack countries like Sweden—which has had no troops in the Middle East at all. This is obvious in Paragraph 4 ("then let him [Bush] explain to us why we don't strike for example—Sweden"). At the end of this transcript, bin Laden bragged about his terrorist accomplishments prior to 9/11. In Paragraph 21, he extolled the virtues of his feats "in Kenya and Tanzania and in Aden."

This speech also reflects bin Laden's use of ethos as he appeared supportive of martyrs (i.e., the nineteen hijackers) and hostile toward President Bush and the U.S. Indeed, on the one hand, in Paragraph 4, bin Laden told the world that he knew "that freedom-haters don't possess defiant spirits like those of the nineteen—may Allah have mercy on them," but in Paragraph 7, he made it clear that "[e]ven though we are in the fourth year after the events of September 11th, Bush is still engaged in distortion, deception and hiding from you the real causes." Another rhetorical appeal of ethos was to contrast President Bush with Osama the Savior. While Bush was evil (i.e., "the throwing of millions of pounds of bombs and explosives at millions of children," as in Paragraph 16), Osama was good. For this reason, Osama felt he had to protect the weak and wreak vengeance on the enemy, as he expressed it in Paragraph 17: "the events of September 11th came as a reply to those great wrongs."

Based on the Propaganda Index shown earlier in this chapter (Table 8.1), we can also deduce that Osama bin Laden was using glittering generalities (GG) in this speech. For example, in Paragraph 15, "destruction" is what America stands for ("freedom and democracy") and "resistance" is what the oppressed Muslims in the Middle East attempt to achieve ("terrorism and intolerance"). He was also using the technique of transfer negative (TN) as he implied a malicious association between the U.S. presidency and its overarching goal of exploiting the world. This is obvious in Paragraph 16:

[I]t means the throwing of millions of pounds of bombs and explosives at millions of children—also in Iraq—as Bush Jr. did, in order to remove an old agent and replace him with a new puppet to assist in the pilfering of Iraq's oil and other outrages.

Finally, another concept from the Propaganda Index that emerged in this speech is that of manifest destiny (MD). In this respect, Osama bin Laden invoked the name of God to lend support to his argument that, as expressed in Paragraph 9, "Allah knows that it had never occurred to us to strike the towers," but as a result of the enemy's oppression, "it came to my mind."

SELECTIVE MORAL DISENGAGEMENT

Albert Bandura's (1999)[88] theory of **selective moral disengagement** is the rhetorical effort of communicators to disengage or detach themselves from their own use of hostility or aggression. The fact that terrorists need to rationalize their deviant behavior with respect to living up to some higher societal need can be understood within the framework of social cognitive theory; how they rationalize violence can be understood in the concept of moral disengagement. According to this theory, humans do not typically resort to harmful behavior unless they have rationalized, to themselves, the morality of their actions. Bandura (2002)[89] listed six tenets that describe selective moral disengagement:

• Displacement of responsibility: pointing the finger at the victim or circumstances is an effective method that reduces responsibility. With displacement of responsibility, people see their actions as the result of social pressures and are, thus, not responsible for their actions. The action can be attributed to uncontrollable circumstances, which does not make it a personal decision.

• Diffusion of responsibility: personal responsibility can also be disguised by diffusion of responsibility. This can happen through segmentation of duties, where each segment by itself is rather innocuous, although the whole thing is harmful. Group decisions can be exploited to diffuse responsibility.

• Dehumanization of targets: people opt more for violent behavior if they do not see their targets as human beings—exposing the impersonal character of the attacks and concentrating on the targets' symbolic meaning, and by depriving the victim of human qualities. Dehumanization makes the victim subhuman—not a human with feelings and attributes.

• Euphemistic language: euphemistic language is used extensively to turn harmful behavior into a respectable action and to decrease personal responsibility for it. For instance, Al Qaeda always refers to 9/11 as an attack on symbols of American power, wealth, and consumer culture. Yet, it never mentions the killing of about 3,000 people. Euphemizing is a dangerous weapon. People act much more brutally when their violent actions are labeled with nice language than when they are labeled aggression.

- Distortion of sequence of events: moral responsibility can be reduced to a minimum by ignoring or misrepresenting the consequences of an action (i.e., claiming that the terrorist attack was merely a response to a previous action of the adversary, the government, the army, etc.). Disregarding the damaging consequences of the actions, as in selective inattention or through cognitive distortion, minimizes feelings of responsibility.

- Attribution of blame: by attributing blame to others, terrorists see themselves as victims who have been provoked. The wrongdoer's actions are now constructed as defensive or revengeful. The target of the terrorist attack, on the other hand, gets criticized and faulted for bringing the actions upon themselves.

These six tenets exemplify the idea that people often undertake disengagement practices to perform actions, which clash with their moral standards. One such practice is to reframe the moral aspect of the terrorist attack.[90] As Guttman put it (1979),[91] the terrorist "asserts that he loves only the socially redeeming qualities of his murderous act, not the act itself" (p. 525). Terrorist groups not only degrade their enemies; they also claim to be morally superior toward them. As Bandura himself suggested, Islamic extremists escalate their jihad, which is constructed as self-defense against oppressive, depraved infidels who plunder and attempt to enslave the Muslim world. Osama bin Laden portrayed his international terrorism as fulfilling a holy imperative.[92]

In his websites, Osama bin Laden argued, "We will continue this course because it is part of our religion and because Allah, praise and glory be to him, ordered us to carry out jihad so that the word of Allah may remain exalted to the heights." Thanks to the jihad, Islamists today are carrying out Allah's will as a religious duty. The main agency for the holy terror is transferred to Allah. Osama bin Laden demonized the American adversary as lowly people committing acts that "the most ravenous of animals would not descend to." The motives for terrorism are made pure, as he said, "The winds of faith have come" to eliminate the "debauched" oppressors. His support base sees itself as a group of holy warriors who will earn access to paradise through their martyrdom.[93]

The actions taken by the authorities against terrorists are greatly stressed, often with terms like *slaughter*, *murder*, *genocide*, and the like. Conversely, terrorist organizations see themselves as persecuted. This tactic depicts the organization as small, weak, and chased by a superior force or a strong state, which makes terrorists look like the underdog. A good example of this rhetoric could be seen on the Chechen terrorists' website Kavkaz-Tsentr (www.kavkazcenter.com) in late 2003. The Chechen terrorists rationalized their suicide bombings in Russian cities as the Chechens' right to self-defense. The website said that these attacks were on "the enemy's backyard," not acts of terrorism. In modern times, the Chechens have endured pain and suffering since the 1990s, and now "the time has come to die together."[94]

As one can see, moral disengagement can be effectively achieved by the institutionalization of brainwashing and similar methods. Institutionalization has been portrayed as the answer to the alleged problem of the fleeting state of mind, which is said to stimulate suicide bombers.[95] Moghaddam (2003)[96] described how volunteers hired by a Palestinian terrorist organization are usually placed into an "Institutional Phase" of training and indoctrination, where they are transformed into "living martyrs" and where they make a public commitment to the fatal course of action (i.e., suicide). This happens through a type of moral and social contract (a formal commitment), which frequently includes the video recording of a testament. Subsequent to this process, the recruits are separated from the rest of the group, or perhaps accommodated or lodged alongside other volunteers, and sent on the mission the following week. The more time passes, the more likely these martyrs-to-be will change their minds.[97]

SUMMARY

Many politicians have interpreted terrorism through rhetoric. Rhetoric is the art of communicating efficiently and with persuasion through language. In relation to a target audience, one needs to consider the ethos, pathos, and logos aspects of rhetoric. In the George W. Bush administration, pathos rhetoric was running high. For example, based on Ronald Reid's model of pro-war rhetoric, President Bush used territorial, ethnocentric, and optimistic appeals to start both the GWOT and the Iraq War. He even used the propaganda of world war to launch his long-term campaign. Part of his pro-war rhetoric was to stifle dissent from mainstream media and American citizens. Another strategy used by President Bush was repetition (e.g., between 2002 and 2006, in his five State of the Union addresses, he used the term *terrorism* 122 times). Even media pundits began using loaded language and pathos techniques to appeal to the audience's emotions. In this chapter, a propaganda index helped explain how leaders and media commentators can justify their name-calling (NC) and other sensitive information outputs. Not surprisingly, dehumanizing the enemy—whether it is Othering, enemification, evilification, Orientalism, Occidentalism, or the us vs. them dichotomy—is made easier when a whole rhetorical stratagem has been established. Osama bin Laden even used death cult language to motivate his followers. Dehumanization produces a form of close-minded mentality that advocates both the separation between the in-group and the out-group and the emergence of armed struggles. Nevertheless, much of human speech is considered free speech (for good or for ill), as it is guaranteed by both the U.S. Constitution and the Universal Declaration of Human Rights (signed by the United Nations in 1948). Lastly, an important consideration was Bandura's theory of selective moral disengagement to explain how humans rationalize their terrorist behaviors.

KEY TERMS

argumentation   186

argumentum ad nauseam   189

black propaganda   187

boomerang effect   195

card stacking   187

cherry picking   187

collective action frames   188

cultural hegemony   196

death cult language   202

dehumanization   193

denial of the means of communication   189

ENDNOTES

1. Eemeren, Frans H. van, & Grootendorst, Rob (2004). *A Systematic Theory of Argumentation: The Pragmadialectical Approach.* Cambridge: Cambridge University Press.

2. Coakley, Thomas (2003). *The Argument against Terror: The Peruvian Experience, Globalization, and US Policy.* Tel Aviv: Institute for National Security Studies.

3. Myers, Scott A., & Anderson, Carolyn M. (2008). *The Fundamentals of Small Group Communication.* Thousand Oaks, CA: Sage.

4. Chang, Gordon C., & Mehan, Hugh B. (2006). Discourse in a Religious Mode: The Bush Administration's Discourse in the War on Terrorism and Its Challenges. *Pragmatics, 16*(1), 1–23.

5. Pratkanis, Anthony R., & Aronson, Elliot (1991). *Age of Propaganda: The Everyday Use and Abuse of Persuasion.* New York: W. H. Freeman.

6. Severin, Werner J., & Tankard, James W. (2001). *Communication Theories: Origins, Methods and Uses in the Mass Media* (5th ed.). New York: Longman.

7. Altheide, David L., & Johnson, John M. (1980). *Bureaucratic Propaganda.* Boston: Allyn and Bacon; Ellul, Jacques (1965). *Propaganda: The Formation of Men's Attitudes.* New York: Knopf; Ellul, Jacques (1981). The Ethics of Propaganda: Propaganda, Innocence and Amorality. *Communication, 6,* 159–175.

8. Becker, Howard (1949). The Nature and Consequences of Black Propaganda. American Sociological Review, 14(2), 221–235.

9. Wark, Wesley, K. (2003). Introduction: "Learning to Live with Intelligence." *Intelligence and National Security, 18*(4), 1–14.

10. Ivie, R. L. (1980). Images of Savagery in American Justifications for War. *Communication Monographs, 47,* 279–294; Reid, Ronald F. (1976). New England Rhetoric and the French War, 1754–1760: A Case Study in the Rhetoric of War. *Communication Monographs, 43,* 259–286.

11. Bowen, Shannon A. (2005). Communication Ethics in the Wake of Terrorism. In H. Dan O'Hair, Robert L. Heath, & Gerald Ledlow (Eds.), *Community Preparedness and Response to Terrorism: Vol. No. III: Communication and the Media* (pp. 65–95). Westport, CT: Praeger.

12. *The Arizona Republic,* 24 November 2001, p. A11.

13. Manheim, Jarol B. (1991). *All of the People, All of the Time: Strategic Communication and American Politics.* Armonk, NY: M. E. Sharpe.

14. Wicks, Robert H. (2006). Emotional Response to Collective Action Media Frames about Islam and Terrorism. *Journal of Media and Religion, 5*(4), 245–263.

15. Reid, Ronald F. (1976). New England Rhetoric and the French War, 1754–1760: A Case Study in the Rhetoric of War. *Communication Monographs, 43*, 259–286.

16. Bowers, John W., Ochs, Donovan J., Jensen, Richard J., & Schulz, David P. (2010). *The Rhetoric of Agitation and Control*. Long Grove, IL: Waveland Press.

17. Black, Jay (2001). Semantics and Ethics of Propaganda. *Journal of Mass Media Ethics, 16*(2), 121–137.

18. Address to a Joint Session of Congress Following 9/11 Attacks, by President George W. Bush, September 20, 2001.

19. Exoo, Calvin F. (2010). *The Pen and the Sword: Press, War, and Terror in the 21st Century*. Thousand Oaks, CA: Sage.

20. Coe, Kevin, Domke, David, Bagley, Meredith M., Cunningham, Sheryl, & Van Leuven, Nancy (2007). Masculinity as Political Strategy: George W. Bush, the "War on Terrorism," and an Echoing Press. *Journal of Women, Politics & Policy, 29*(1), 31–55.

21. Rhodes, Chloe (2010). *A Certain "Je Ne Sais Quoi": The Origin of Foreign Words Used in English*. New York City: Readers Digest.

22. Altheide, David L. (2007). The Mass Media and Terrorism. *Discourse & Communication, 1*(3), 287–308.

23. Aldridge, Bob (2008). *America in Peril*. Carol Stream, IL: Hope Publishing House.

24. Altheide, David L. (2007). The Mass Media and Terrorism. *Discourse & Communication, 1*(3), 287–308.

25. Altheide, David L. (2007). The Mass Media and Terrorism. *Discourse & Communication, 1*(3), 287–308.

26. Moeller, Susan (2007, June 21). *Jumping on the U.S. Bandwagon for a "War on Terror."* New Haven, CT: Yale Center for the Study of Globalization.

27. Melshen, Paul, Marine Colonel (2003, June 27). Address to Inter-Governmental Authority on Development (IGAD) conference.

28. Kakutani, Michiko (2001, October 9). The Age of Irony Isn't Over after All. *The New York Times*, p. E1; Keen, Sam (1986). *Faces of the Enemy: Reflections of the Hostile Imagination*. San Francisco: Harper & Row.

29. Lasswell, Harold D. (1995). Propaganda. In R. Jackall (Ed.), *Propaganda* (pp. 13–25). New York: New York University Press.

30. *White House history: A Non-Partisan Evaluation of the Past*. (2004). Available at: http://whitehouse.org/history

31. Jackson, Richard (2005). *Writing the War on Terrorism: Language, Politics and Counterterrorism*. Manchester: Manchester University Press; Nacos, Brigitte (2002). *Mass-Mediated Terrorism: The Central Role of the Media in Terrorism and Counterterrorism*. Landham, MD: Rowman & Littlefield Publishers.

32. Abrahms, Max (2005). Al Qaeda's Miscommunication War: The Terrorism Paradox. *Terrorism and Political Violence, 17*, 529–549; May, Ernest (1975). *"Lessons" of the Past: The Use of Misuse of History in American Foreign Policy*. London: Oxford University Press.

33. Hülsse, Rainer, & Spencer, Alexander (2008). The Metaphor of Terror: Terrorism Studies and the Constructivist Turn. *Security Dialogue, 39*(6), 571–592.

34. Lee, Alfred McClung, & Lee, Elizabeth Briant (1939). *The Fine Art of Propaganda: A Study of Father Coughlin's Speeches*. New York: Harcourt, Brace.

35. Tilley, Elspeth N. (2005). Responding to Terrorism Using Ethical Means: The Propaganda Index. *Communication Research Reports, 22*(1), 69–77.

36. Baumeister, Roy F. (1996). *Evil: Inside Human Violence and Cruelty*. New York: Freeman; Oliver, Anne Marie. & Steinberg, Paul F. (2005). *The Road to Martyrs' Square: A Journey into the World of the Suicide Bomber*. Oxford: Oxford University Press.

37. Hillgruber, Andreas (1987). War in the East and the Extermination of the Jews. *Yad Vashem Studies, 18*, 103–132.

38. Bhatia, Aditi (2008). Discursive Illusions in the American National Strategy for Combating Terrorism. *Journal of Language and Politics 7*(2), 201–227.

39. Lazar, Anita, & Lazar, Michelle M. (2004). The Discourse of the New World Order: "Out-Casting" the Double Face of Threat. *Discourse & Society, 15*(2), 223–242.

40. Martin, Gus (2010). *Understanding Terrorism: Challenges, Perspectives, and Issues*. Thousand Oaks, CA: Sage.

41. Curtis, Liz (1998). *Ireland: The Propaganda War*. Belfast: Sasta.

42. Baker, Jr., Howard H. (2001, September 23). *Japanese Observance Ceremony for Victims of Terrorism in the US*. Retrieved February 17, 2011 from http://usinfo.state.gov/topical/pol/terror/; Rose, David (2004). *Guantánamo: America's War on Human Rights*. London: Faber and Faber.

43. Bush Jr, George W. (2001, October 20). *Remarks by the President to the CEO Summit*. Retrieved February 17, 2011 from http://usinfo.state.gov/topical/pol/terror/.

44. Baker, Jr., Howard H. (2001, September 23). *Japanese Observance Ceremony for Victims of Terrorism in the US*. Retrieved February 17, 2011 from http://usinfo.state.gov/topical/pol/terror/.

45. Powell, Colin L. (2001, October 26). *Remarks by the Secretary of State to the National Foreign Policy Conference for Leaders of Nongovernmental Organizations (NGO)*. Retrieved February 17, 2011 from http://usinfo.state.gov/topical/pol/terror/

46. Rumsfeld, Donald H. (2001, October 7). *Secretary of Defense, and Joint Chiefs of Staff, Gen. Richard Myers, "Briefing on Enduring Freedom."* Retrieved February 7, 2011 from http://usinfo.state.gov/topical/pol/terror/ .

47. George W. Bush (2002, January 29). *State of the Union Address*.

48. Jackson, Richard (2007). Language, Policy and the Construction of a Torture Culture in the War on Terrorism. *Review of International Studies, 33*, 353–371.

49. Kapitan, Tomis (2003). The Terrorism of "Terrorism." In James Sterba (Ed.), *Terrorism and International Justice* (pp. 47–66). Oxford: Oxford University Press.

50. Hirst, David (1984). *The Gun and the Olive Branch*. London: Faber and Faber.

51. Dershowitz, Alan (2002, March 18). A New Way of Responding to Palestinian Terrorism. *The Jerusalem Post*, p. A1.

52. George W. Bush (2003, January 28). *State of the Union Address*; Ivie, Robert L. (2003). Evil Enemy Versus Agonistic Other: Rhetorical Constructions of Terrorism. *The Review of Education, Pedagogy, and Cultural Studies, 25*,181–200.

53. Rogers, M. Brooke, Loewenthal, Kate M., Lewis, Christopher Alan, Amlôt, Richard, Cinnirella, Marco, & Ansari, Humayan (2007). The Role of Religious Fundamentalism in Terrorist Violence: A Social Psychological Analysis. *International Review of Psychiatry, 19*(3), 253–262.

54. Rueckert, William H. (1982). *Kenneth Burke and the Drama of Human Relations* (2nd ed.). Berkeley: University of California Press.

55. Black, Jay (2001). Semantics and Ethics of Propaganda. *Journal of Mass Media Ethics, 16*(2), 121–137.

56. Tilley, Elspeth N. (2005) Responding to Terrorism Using Ethical Means: The Propaganda Index. *Communication Research Reports, 22*(1), 69–77.

57. Said, Edward (1981). *Covering Islam: How The Media and the Experts Determine How We See The Rest of the World*. New York: Vintage Books.

58. Black, Jay (2001). Semantics and Ethics of Propaganda. *Journal of Mass Media Ethics, 16*(2), 121–137.

59. Gramsci, Antonio (1971). *Selections from the Prison Notebooks*. London: Lawrence and Wishart.

60. Mahony, Inez (2010). Diverging Frames: A Comparison of Indonesian and Australian Press Portrayals of Terrorism and Islamic Groups in Indonesia. *International Communication Gazette, 72*(8) 739–758.

61. Keen, Sam (1986). *Faces of the Enemy: Reflections of the Hostile Imagination*. San Francisco: Harper & Row; Pagels, Elaine (1996). *The Origin of Satan*. New York: Vintage.

62. Buruma, Ian, & Margalit, Avishai (2004). *Occidentalism: The West in the Eyes of Its Enemies*. New York: Penguin.

63. Ning, Wang (1997). Orientalism versus Occidentalism? *New Literary History, 28*(1), 57–67.

64. Qutb, Sayyid (1981). Milestones. Cedar Rapids, IA: The Mother Mosque Foundation.

65. Churchill, Ward (2003). *On the Justice of Roosting Chickens: Consequences of American Conquest and Carnage*. Oakland, CA: AK Press.

66. Mooney, Alex (2008, March 15). Controversial Minister off Obama's Campaign. CNNPolitics. Com. Retrieved April 29, 2011 from http://edition.cnn.com/2008/POLITICS/03/14/obama.minister/index.html.

67. Dakroury, Aliaa (2009). *Communication and Human Rights*. Dubuque, IA: Kendall Hunt.

68. Stoll, Ira (2009, April 6). Anti-Semitism and The Economic Crisis: Many People Still Blame Jews for Capitalism's Faults. *The Wall Street Journal*, p. A8.

69. Barry III, Herbert (1998). Functions of Recent U.S. Presidential Slogans. In Landtsheer Ofer & Christ'l De Feldman (Eds.), *Politically Speaking: A Worldwide Examination of Language Used in the Public Sphere* (pp. 161–169). Westport, CT: Praeger.

70. Peci, Patrizio (1983). *Io l'infame*. Milan, Italy: A. Mondadori.

71. Bellak, Leopold (1942). The Nature of Slogans. *The Journal of Abnormal and Social Psychology, 37*(4), 496–510.

72. Simonton, Dean K. (1976). Philosophical Eminence, Beliefs, and Zeitgeist: An Individual-Generational Analysis. *Journal of Personality and Social Psychology, 34*(4), 630–640.

73. Bowers, John W., Ochs, Donovan J., Jensen, Richard J., & Schulz, David P. (2010). *The Rhetoric of Agitation and Control*. Long Grove, IL: Waveland Press.

74. Barry III, Herbert (1998). Functions of Recent U.S. Presidential Slogans. In Landtsheer Ofer & Christ'l De Feldman (Eds.), *Politically Speaking: A Worldwide Examination of Language Used in the Public Sphere* (pp. 161–169). Westport, CT: Praeger.

75. Harb, Mona, & Leenders, Reinoud (2005). Know Thy Enemy: Hizbullah, "Terrorism" and the Politics of Perception. *Third World Quarterly, 26*(1), 173–197; Post, Jerrold M. (2010). "When Hatred Is Bred in the Bone": The Social Psychology of Terrorism. *Annals of the American Academy of Political and Social Science, 1208*, 15–23.

76. Hezbollah" Special Information Report (2003). Intelligence and Terrorism Information Center at the Center for Special Studies. Retrieved December 5, 2010, http://www.terrorism-info.org.il/malammultimedia/ENGLISH/IRAN/PDF/JUNE 03.

77. Abrahms, Max (2005). Al Qaeda's Miscommunication War: The Terrorism Paradox. *Terrorism and Political Violence, 17*, 529–549; *War against Americans* (1996). Fatwa by Osama bin Laden.

78. Bacevich, Andrew J. (2001). Terrorizing the Truth. *Foreign Policy, 125*, 74–75.

79. Bergen, Peter (2001). *Holy War, Inc: Inside the Secret World of Osama bin Laden*. New York: Free Press.

80. Oxford Analytica (2002). *Middle East/Afghanistan: Al Qaida Threat*. Washington, D.C.: Oxford Analytica.

81. Abrahms, Max (2005). Al Qaeda's Miscommunication War: The Terrorism Paradox. *Terrorism and Political Violence, 17*, 529–549.

82. Bergen, Peter (2001). *Holy War, Inc: Inside the Secret World of Osama bin Laden*. New York: Free Press; Text of Osama bin Laden to the United States (2003, October 18). Northeast Intelligence Network.

83. Bergen, Peter (2001). *Holy War, Inc: Inside the Secret World of Osama bin Laden*. New York: Free Press; Hoffman, Bruce (1998). Old Madness, New Methods: Revival of Religious Terrorism Begs for Broader US Policy. *RAND Review, 22*(2), 12–17.

84. *War against Americans* (1996). Fatwa by Osama bin Laden.

85. Buruma, Ian, & Margalit, Avishai (2004). *Occidentalism: The West in the Eyes of Its Enemies*. New York: Penguin.

86. Speech by Osama bin Laden (2004, October 29). Source: Al Jazeera. Retrieved on December 17, 2011 from http://www.gwu.edu/~action/2004/cands/binladen102904tr.html.

87. Tuman, Joseph S. (2010). *Communicating Terror: The Rhetorical Dimensions of Terrorism*. Thousand Oaks, CA: Sage.

88. Bandura, Albert (1999). Moral Disengagement in the Perpetration of Inhumanities. *Personality and Social Psychology Review, 3*, 193–209.

89. Bandura, Albert (2002). Selective Moral Disengagement in the Exercise of Moral Agency. *Journal of Moral Education, 31*, 101–119.

90. Smith, Allison G. (2004). From Words to Action: Exploring the Relationship between a Group's Value References and Its Likelihood of Engaging in Terrorism. *Studies in Conflict and Terrorism, 27*(5), 409–437.

91. Guttman, David (1979). Killers and Consumers: The Terrorist and His Audience. *Social Research, 46*, 517–526.

92. Weimann, Gabriel (2008). The Psychology of Mass-Mediated Terrorism. *American Behavioral Scientist, 52*(1), 69–86.

93. Ludlow, Lynn (2001, October 7). Osama Speaks: Inside the Mind of a Terrorist. *San Francisco Chronicle,* p. D-1.

94. Weimann, Gabriel (2008). The Psychology of Mass-Mediated Terrorism. *American Behavioral Scientist, 52*(1), 69–86.

95. Gambetta, Diego (2005). Can We Make Sense of Suicide Missions? In Diego Gambetta (Ed.), *Making Sense of Suicide Missions* (pp. 259–299). Oxford: Oxford University Press.

96. Moghaddam, Fathali (2003). Palestinian Suicide Terrorism in the Second Intifada: Motivations and Organizational Aspects. *Studies in Conflict and Terrorism, 26,* 65–92.

97. Soibelman, Mali (2004). Palestinian Suicide Bombers. *Journal of Investigative Psychology and Offender Profiling, 1,* 175–190.

CHAPTER 9

Euphemisms for Terrorism

> **After reading this chapter, you will be able to**
>
> - identify and analyze euphemisms of terrorism, and how both the media and politicians bury important words under jargon and ambiguous language;
> - discuss how euphemisms of terrorism have been used during both the Bush and Obama administrations; and
> - evaluate the consequences of euphemisms on society.

EUPHEMISMS: DEFINITION

Do euphemisms for terrorism help the international community? A **euphemism** is a substitution of a friendly or less offensive expression for one that implies something unpleasant or offensive to the listener. The word euphemism comes from Greek and means "good speech." A euphemistic expression can be used to obscure issues through deliberate deception or to provide tactful language.[1] The past few U.S. administrations, incapable of ignoring certain issues, have addressed these issues ambiguously, disguising their full meaning with euphemisms that deliberately divert the audience's attention from informed efficiency to perpetual hesitation.

Euphemism is **lexical ambiguity**, vagueness included in a word or phrase, which produces more than one interpretation. Lexical ambiguity is to be distinguished from the concept of polyseme. A **polyseme** is a word or concept with multiple, related meanings. For example, a mole can be a small animal, a birthmark on human skin, or a type of spy.[2] On the other hand, euphemism is **Aesopian language**, communication that carries an innocent meaning to outsiders but entails a more profound meaning to informed members with a special agenda. It is used in reference to Aesop.[3] It is mentioned by Herbert Marcuse (1964)[4] in his book *One-Dimensional Man* where it is made analogous with Orwellian language. In this perspective, Aesopian language is the idea that certain usages of language serve to "suppress certain concepts or keep them out of the general discourse within society" (p. 96).

In rhetoric, the use of euphemisms distracts attention from reality through vague and ambiguous words, such as trivialities too abstract or grandiose, which speak to sentiment and emotionality rather than facts. In 1906, Winston Churchill, then member of Parliament for Manchester North West, commented on the issues related to euphemisms and coined the phrase **terminological inexactitude**, a circumlocution of meaning (i.e., lie or untruth). Likewise, to be **economical with the truth** means to be deceiving, whether by intentionally giving false information (i.e., lying) or by deliberately omitting relevant facts. More literally, it describes a meticulous selection of facts so as not to disclose too much information.[5]

The use of language to get the audience sidetracked from reality can be explained by speech act theory. Developed by philosophers John Austin (1962)[6] and John Searle (1969),[7] **speech act theory** rests on the premise that speakers use language to accomplish intended actions and, in doing so, hearers conclude or interpret intended meaning from what speakers said. Language, then, is used not only to describe the world and phenomena, but also to serve other purposes and actions. Speech act theory emphasizes the fundamental conditions required to perform the act of speech. To know the actual meaning of words, one must understand the reasons that lie beneath discourse. There are problems related to human speech acts, such as forms of indirect speech, contextual issues, and the multifunctionality of language.[8] As explained in this chapter, the act of bombing has been romanticized with nicer language. What is the intended action here? It is to bury the profound impact of warfare under jargon.

IT'S NOT TERRORISM; IT'S THE T-WORD

Euphemisms for terrorism are linguistic changes as much as they are part of shifts in politics and power. The relationships between words and social conflict require an analytic system that can consider the reciprocal nature of meanings and power.[9] Just as we have the "F" bomb, the "N" word, and the "S" word, we also have the T-word. **T-word** is for terrorism, or dropping the "T" bomb.[10] These are examples of code words. In communication, **code words** are elements of a standardized code or convention. Each code word is designed according to the specific rules of the code and given a unique meaning. Code words are often used for factors of reliability, clarity, conciseness, or secrecy.[11] Already in the 1980s, from the controversy over word choice came the saying that one "man's terrorist is another man's freedom fighter," now a famous cliché. "That's a catchy phrase, but also misleading," President Ronald Reagan said in a radio address in 1986:

> Freedom fighters do not need to terrorize a population into submission. Freedom fighters target the military forces and the organized instruments of repression keeping dictatorial regimes in power. Freedom fighters struggle to liberate their citizens from oppression and to establish a form of government that reflects the will of the people.[12]

Increasingly, the word terrorism is not mentioned in media reports; rather, it is replaced by those euphemistic T-words. When early reports of Major Nidal Malik Hasan's killing rampage at Fort Hood, TX in November 2009, described his personal problems and did not even apply the term terrorism, activists on the right went berserk. Hasan was simply referred to as a radical or killer. Nobody dared call him a terrorist. Even worse, the Fort Hood shooting was classified as "workplace violence" by the U.S. Department of Defense. In a similar vein, in Mumbai in 2008, the horrific killing of roughly 200 innocents (and injuring another 300 people) by terrorist commandos shouting "Allah Akbar!" was mostly reduced by the international media into the cloudy maneuver of euphemisms. Al Jazeera and *The Guardian* branded the Al Qaeda–associated Islamist terrorists in Mumbai as *gunmen*; CNN labeled them *militants*. Some experts identified the primary cause as the long-running Kashmir conflict between India and Pakistan. Others, like famous psychological sage Deepak Chopra, concluded that it was the result of "collateral damage" caused by the U.S.-led Global War on Terror (GWOT) and the U.S. invasion of Iraq.[13]

The use of euphemisms often creates a situation where many ambiguous meanings are honed into one in which a single steady meaning predominates. Simple Orwellian language games may be enough to manipulate audiences.[14] In a 2005 memo, CBC News editor-in-chief Tony Burman provided much effort to argue that the terms terrorism and terrorist are not neutral and, therefore, should not be used by CBC reporters where possible. According to the memo,

> By restricting ourselves to neutral language, we aren't faced with the problem of calling one incident a "terrorist act" (e.g., the destruction of the World Trade Center) while classifying another as, say, a mere "bombing" (e.g., the destruction of a crowded shopping mall in the Middle East).[15]

The memo also said, "Rather than calling assailants 'terrorists,' we can refer to them as bombers, hijackers, gunmen (if we're sure no women were in the group), militants, extremists, attackers, or some other appropriate noun." Similarly, at first, online BBC reports of the July 7, 2005 London bombings identified the culprits as terrorists, which clashed with the BBC's internal policy. However, by the next day, Tom Gross (2005)[16] and numerous others noticed that the online articles had been edited, replacing *terrorists* with *bombers*. Two years later, in 2007, Gordon Brown became the British prime minister. After the unsuccessful terrorist attacks in Glasgow and London, Brown said that the words *Muslim* and *Islam* should not be used. Along the same lines, in 2008, as President Bush was plummeting in the polls, his administration tampered with the language commonly used by the U.S. State Department and other federal officials to refer to terrorists. In a report distributed by Homeland Security, federal officials were to avoid using the terms *jihadists* or *mujahedin*.[17] A frequent term in media coverage of Iraqi and other resistance fighters is *gunmen*. And U.S. soldiers in Iraq, who have killed families, are allowed to provide an excuse of wrath to take vengeance for a "family/teammate" member.[18]

Distancing Language

Euphemisms for terrorism work well through distancing language. **Distancing language** is phrasing employed by people to dissociate themselves from a statement, either to elude thinking about the topic or to detach themselves from its content.[19] Military staff members have used an array of distancing terms for soldiers either killing or getting killed. They have also used distancing, dehumanizing terms for fighters on the opposing side. An example is *collateral damage* for the death of innocent civilians. Rather than saying *civilian deaths*, the media may call it **collateral damage**, damage that is involuntary or incidental to the intended outcome. It can refer to both the killing of non-combatants and the destruction of their property.[20]

Many euphemisms have replaced the term *terrorism* to make the distance between reality and political agenda wider. As such, terrorist attacks have been referred to as *theater*, *Propaganda by the Deed*, *scenario reality*, and *war of nerves*.[21] One linguistic device to avoid using terrorism is by incorporating the term *war* or *warfare* inside a phrase to make the terrorist acts look more legitimate. A case in point is the term **guerrilla warfare**. Symbolically, and characteristically, guerrilla warfare is terrorism. Yet, semantically, and more technically, guerrilla warfare comes to refer to a type of irregular warfare or struggle in which a small group of rebels (including, but not limited to, armed civilians) employs military tactics to dismantle a more powerful and less mobile traditional army, or attack a vulnerable target, and retreat almost immediately. Common procedures used in guerrilla warfare are assaults, surprise attacks, entrapment, sabotage, disruptions, and extraordinary mobility.[22] While the intent and outcome described here constitute terrorism, the terrorism connection with the concept of guerrilla warfare is buried under jargon.

In British media, efforts have been made by the BBC to circumvent words such as terrorist or freedom fighter, unless they are in attributed quotes, in favor of euphemisms like militant, guerrilla, assassin, insurgent, paramilitary, or militia.[23] In regard to the relationship between terrorism and the media, it has been called an *intrinsic mutual dependency* and a *symbiotic relationship*.[24] Distancing language is the opposite of **natural language**. The latter is ordinary language, that is, any language which arises naturally, in a spontaneous and unpremeditated manner, as the result of the innate ability for language located in the human brain. Natural language is often used in interpersonal communication encounters, and may be spoken, signed, or written. Natural language also differs from constructed language.[25]

The following section looks at the different euphemisms for bombing. While a simple and straightforward word, apparently it is not to be used anymore.

No More Bombing?

Vietnam gave us new words for the old realities: bombers provided "close air support."[26] Close air support? Why not bombing? The answer is that by using nicer words, the meaning is, in part, buried under jargon. Taylor (1992)[27] calls this the creation of a **terminological fog**. Since the 1980s, such terminological fog started to be used extensively during military operations that required striking targets through massive bombings. An example of this is the euphemism of *surgical strike*. A **surgical strike** is a military attack that leads to, is intended to lead to, or is claimed to have led to only damage to the intended legitimate target, with no or minimal collateral damage to nearby people, structures, vehicles, or buildings.[28] Surgical strike was first used in medicine and surgery to refer to a cleaner and more precise operation on a person's body.[29] Put simply, it is a medical meta-phor in representations of war. As David Miller (2002)[30] contends, the term surgical strike is an oxymoron. Played up by U.S. and European forces in the Gulf War in 1991, it was supposed to portend the age of the clean war. Now, let us have a look at multiple euphe-misms for bombing below, based on various sources:[31]

- Sorties: bombing.
- Preventive reaction strike: air raid.
- Incontinent ordinance: bombs and artillery shells dropped on civilian targets (Pentagon jargon).
- Daisy cutter: a type of igniting device that detonates an aerial bomb at or above the ground.
- Neutron bomb: enhanced radiation device.
- Disruptive reentry system: nuclear-armed, intercontinental, ballistic missile.

Here, in all cases, bombing is romanticized through euphemisms that serve to distance the audience from the reality of current issues like GWOT. There are major effects caused by such euphemisms: a desensitization of the situation (because euphemisms alleviate or distort harsh realities), a lack of understanding of war among audience members (because euphemisms tone down the actual meaning of a phenomenon), and the media's vicious manipulation of reality. So, now preemptive war becomes *imminent threat*, and covert surveillance should carry the broad, vague term of *intelligence*.

No More Killing?

William Lutz (1991)[32] referred to euphemism as **gobbledygook** or **bureaucratese**, the language of bureaucracy and a tactic to overload the audience with technical, unfamiliar words. Bureaucratese has been described by various critics and scholars as a "strange and somewhat threatening foreign language,"[33] "a language which pretends to communicate but really does not,"[34] "the misuse of words by implicit redefinition,"[35] and the art of "talking out of both sides of one's mouth."[36] It may be interesting to examine how the word *kill* or *killing* has been replaced by such gobbledygook. Technical-military rhetoric is deployed which, as Brivio (1999)[37] notes, "uses acronyms and euphemisms to sterilize the horrors of war" (p. 516). As such, it makes the bad look good, the negative seem positive, and the hostile appear attractive or at least supportable.[38] During the Vietnam War, soldiers "wasted" the enemy, and some "fragged" their own officers. Even the CIA has used a verbal novelty: "termination with extreme prejudice."[39] In covert operations, to "terminate with extreme prejudice" is a command to assassinate an enemy, such as a terrorist. Its meaning was described in a *New York Times* article.[40]

The term *dead* is also critical. In the U.S., the media now call dead soldiers heroes and fallen soldiers, a popular phrase that is also applied to the death of police officers, firefight-ers, and other uniformed workers. Such discourse contributes to a surfeit of people in uniforms; all are fighting or serving on our behalf. Another tactic for limiting information, put simply, is to make it off limits. As such, journalists were barred from photographing the fallen when they were finally shown in flag-draped caskets at Dover Air Force base. The purpose was to respect the family privacy. Killing civilians presents a moral, strategic, and PR problem for any military force that rejects being labeled as terrorists, who overtly use civilian deaths as a strategy.[41] Legitimate and "civilized" states refuse to deliberately kill civilians, and any deaths happening in military operations must be called accidental. Nevertheless, a public relations problem can be noticed by the audience if too many accidental deaths occur.[42] Below is a comprehensive list of euphemisms for kill, killing, or dead, based on various sources:[43]

- Neutralize: kill (what the CIA does, according to the late stand-up comedian George Carlin).
- Depopulate: kill, according to the CIA.
- Suppress: kill.
- Waste: kill.
- Arbitrary deprivation of life: killing.
- Wetwork: murder or assassination, according to the CIA.
- Service the target: kill the enemy, according to the Pentagon.
- Eliminate with extreme prejudice: kill a suspected double agent, according to the Pentagon.
- Inanimate things: the blowing up of buildings and bridges.
- Weapons counts: dead bodies.
- KIA (killed in action): dead soldiers.
- WIA (wounded in action): wounded soldiers.
- Friendly fire: the euphemism for "troops killed by comrades." The media coverage of the friendly fire death of Pat Tillman, a professional football player, in Afghanistan confirmed the use of hero scripts to conceal a careless shooting.
- Blue on blue: NATO combatants killing each other by accident (instead of killing terrorists).
- BOBing: same as above.

These euphemisms for causing loss of life are **shifting metaphors**, uses of language that serve to connect the way people currently see a situation or issue with the way the government would like them to view the situation or issue. By imposing terms such as *neutralize*, *wetwork*, *weapons count*, and *friendly fire*, the notion of killing disappears, which, by the same token, defuses the narrative of war and conflict. Metaphor is an intrinsic element of our daily life. It not only beautifies our language; it also represents perspectives through which people relate to reality.[44] Killing reached an unusual pinnacle in Nazi Germany, and so did the language that went with it; the objective, of course, was to avoid saying so. Prisoners sent to death camps in Eastern Europe carried identity papers marked *Ruckkehr unerwunscht*, meaning "return unwanted," or death. Entire carloads of people en route to those camps were assigned to *Sonderbehandlung*, meaning "special treatment," also death. The sum of persecutions and killings was referred to as *die Endloöung*, meaning the "final solution"—again, death. Evidently, in German language, there was no use of extermination or genocide; instead, it was ethnic cleansing or purification.[45]

In his *Politics and the English Language*, George Orwell (1946)[46] wrote that the worst enemy of clear language is insincerity. Orwell advocated the use of Plain English. **Plain English** refers to both precision and elimination of ambiguity in English. It is the notion that any layperson should be able to understand the full meaning of the word or phrase uttered by the government or another person. Investigators of the aftereffects of the 2005 London bombings advised that emergency services should always use Plain English. They found that euphemisms can bring about misunderstandings that could cost lives.[47]

TERRORISM EUPHEMISMS IN THE BUSH ERA

After September 11, 2001, the Bush administration produced a plethora of persuasive metaphors to portray its relationships with its target world publics. The intent was to characterize its position toward crucial international events, and to support its important causes. Among these, it called South East Asia the "Second Front"; North Korea, Iran, and Iraq members of the "Axis of Evil"; and Germany and France "Old Europe." It wanted China to become a "Responsible Stakeholder," and the successions of pro-democracy movements in the former Communist nations in Eastern Europe were now "Color Revolutions." These euphemisms symbolically formed the U.S. strategic approaches to diverse regions across the world, developing important message strategies of the post-9/11 U.S. public diplomacy.[48]

In the summer of 2005, as the GWOT became less popular among U.S. audiences, the Bush administration streamlined its motto for the fight against Al Qaeda and other terrorist groups. It renamed GWOT the "Global Struggle against Violent Extremism," implying the idea that the long-term fight was as much an ideological struggle as a military mission.[49] Besides, many officials of the U.S. armed forces referred to GWOT as a *global counterinsurgency*. One key problem with the phrase GWOT is that its heavy legal meaning overshadows its rhetorical power. This phrase, which to many Americans in September 2001 was a great motive to get the U.S. committed to war and the confrontation with global terrorists, exceeded, by far, the rhetorical call to arms to become a prototype for U.S. military engagements (first in Afghanistan and then in Iraq). Calling something a war that is difficult to win was in fact a short-term strategy. Ultimately, one is going to get caught.[50] Think of Osama bin Laden who was finally killed in his Pakistan compound. Below is a list of several major terrorism euphemisms employed or created during the Bush era, based on various sources:[51]

- Unlawful combatant: terrorist. As opposed to the words *combatant*, *prisoner of war*, and *civilian*, the term *unlawful combatant* is not mentioned in both The Hague and the Geneva Conventions. Whereas the previous terms are well defined and clear under international law, unlawful combatant is not.

- Axis of Evil: terrorist-harboring states.

- Rogue nation: Condoleeza Rice, then national security advisor, used this label to refer to North Korea, as she applied it on October 31, 2003. In a similar fashion, President George W. Bush identified terrorists as "threats of the 21st century" and "tyrants in rogue nations intent upon developing weapons of mass destruction."

- Sectarian conflict: civil war. Sectarian conflict is a moderated, diluted, and euphemized term, which has a comparable definition to civil war. It was used by the Bush administration to elude the reality of the Iraq situation and obscure the American public's own understanding of the war.

- War of Ideas: a clashing of ideals and ideologies between the Western and Muslim worlds.

According to George Lakoff (2004),[52] professor of linguistics at Berkeley, these euphemisms would be referred to as the **politics of representation**. Such linguistic device is often associated with a coherent body of knowledge rather than isolated pieces of information. Although occasionally specific representations may not be too surprising, at other times they are very original and creative. The art of political rhetoric hinges, in part, on the use of euphemisms, metaphors, and the like to create coherence among events that would not be necessarily generated otherwise.

The Patriot Act

The **Patriot Act** is a legal sanction for the FBI, CIA, or another federal agency (1) to search citizens' phone, financial, or e-mail records without a warrant or court order, (2) to search the home or office of a suspect by law enforcement without a warrant or court order, (3) to seize and detain immigrants and suspected terrorists indefinitely, and (4) to suspend *habeas corpus* when extracting information from these people. Signed into law on October 26, 2001, policymakers understand that by calling laws "Patriot Act," Americans will probably accept them without expressing much doubt.[53] The Bush administration's positive rhetorical association of the Patriot Act has a perfect inverse relationship with negative rhetorical association, such as calling certain terrorist-harboring states the "Axis of Evil." For decades, the term *axis* has been acknowledged to have a distinctly negative connotation. During World War II, the Axis powers were the triple-threat of Mussolini's Italy, Imperial Japan, and Nazi Germany. The new "axis" label is no accident.[54] Thanks to the Patriot Act, we also have "warrantless surveillance" (and not illegal wiretapping) and "probable cause" (and not sufficient grounds) for wiretapping calls.

The Patriot Act and other domestic policies on terrorism inspired 20th Century Fox News Television to create the American television series *24*. Shown on television during eight seasons, *24* starred Kiefer Sutherland as federal agent Jack Bauer. The series helped various publics understand GWOT. An analytical reading of *24* suggests that the series imitates important elements of the Bush administration's Patriot Act and its rhetoric about GWOT, including the authentic and widespread nature of the threat posed by terrorism, and the sense of urgency that a militarized and repressive form of counterterrorism be put in place. 20th Century Fox producers and scriptwriters drew on official discourses to represent a new reality of terrorism and counterterrorism, and, thereby, make euphemisms well known to the *24* audience—euphemisms like *rendition* and *detention without charge* (i.e., Patriot Act).[55]

Unknown Unknown

U.S. Secretary of Defense Donald Rumsfeld was very involved in the evacuation of people and debris on September 11, 2001 (and the subsequent days). Rumsfeld was also shown in the media as being exceptionally cautious in giving facts and making claims. The media had to accept his messages as such.[56] Below is the transcript of a news briefing delivered by Donald Rumsfeld on February 12, 2002:[57]

There are known knowns; there are things we know that we know. There are known unknowns; that is to say, There are things that we now know we don't know. But there are also unknown unknowns; There are things we do not know we don't know.

Rumsfeld's speech mentioned the concept of unknown unknown. **Unknown unknown** refers to circumstances or outcomes that were not anticipated by an observer at any given point in time. Rumsfeld's statement on the lack of evidence linking Saddam Hussein's government with the supply of WMDs to terrorist groups was condemned as an abuse of language, but defended as mirroring a deep, almost philosophical truth. The problem is that, by avoiding proper language, the communicator is also avoiding reality; the government is not only unable to cope with unknown unknowns; it also actively ignores them.[58]

Euphemisms for Torture

Language shapes the audience's thoughts and frames the nature of public life. Language shapes the human worldview. Normal communication is always located in context; what a speaker says is assigned meaning by the context in which the speaker spoke. Context is based on the experiences of both speaker and listener. However, euphemisms impose context and a deceptive order of reality on things.[59] In the Bush administration, numerous euphemisms were created to make the meaning of torture (and related situations) evaporate. Readers should have a look at the list below, based on various sources:[60]

- Enhanced interrogation technique: torture.

- Alternative set of procedures: torture.

- Legitimate force: torture.

- Counter-resistance strategy: harsh interrogation technique, such as waterboarding and the wet-towel technique, after a "friendly" interrogation was attempted first but failed.

- Stress and duress: interrogation technique for prisoners who are decisively seen as a threat to the U.S. Such technique is alleged to produce inhuman and degrading treatment.

- Pride-and-ego down: attacking the prisoner's self-esteem to extract important information from him or her. In doing so, the prisoner vindicates him- or herself and redeems his or her pride.

- Shocking the conscience: objective of torture. It is an empty, throw-away term. This is the argument of this section: cloud the truth and prevent repercussion.

- Third degree: wreaking pain, physical or mental, to extricate confessions or statements during the interrogation of a prisoner or would-be terrorist.

- Black site: secret prison operated by the CIA.

- Extraordinary rendition: secret abduction and confinement of suspected terrorists from all over the globe. It is a U.S.-sponsored procedure of illegal kidnapping and internment of suspected terrorists. These are denied the right to trial and undergoing harsh and unusual punishments such as sleep deprivation, exposure to extreme temperatures, dog attacks, and waterboarding.

- Sleep management: torture that prevents a prisoner from getting regular sleep for about 100 hours.

Many of the euphemisms here rely on jargon. **Jargon** is what insiders use to communicate complex or difficult ideas to each other. Jargon has become a method to skim over the insupportable, inexcusable, and unspeakable. We now know of *sleep management*, which sounds like a technique to handle insomnia but is a form of torture that prevents a prisoner from getting regular sleep for about 100 hours. The use of euphemisms is a brave new world of distortion. It allows speakers to spin a word so that it means something else— something that suits the government. At times, both the speaker and listener understand the meaning, and euphemisms are an inside joke of some sort. At other times, the point of euphemism is to create confusion.[61]

TERRORISM EUPHEMISMS IN THE OBAMA ERA

In the Obama era, the national security strategy also avoids references to *Islamic extremism*, *jihad*, *Islamic radicalism*, and the like. Basically, the Obama administration has dropped references to radical Islam through euphemisms and distorting rhetoric. As terrorism analyst Daveed Gartenstein-Ross (2010)[62] said on CBN News, the Obama administration is trying to "sanitize language in a way that really presents an incoherent picture" of terrorism. The administration also avoids using the term *long war* or *GWOT*. Instead, the term *Overseas Contingency Operation* is preferred. The problem is that this terminological game suggests an attempt to minimize the terrorist threat by applying new political euphemisms. This is evident when considering the Merriam-Webster online definitions for *contingent* and *contingency* include "possible; unpredictable; an event (as an emergency) or condition that may but is not certain to occur; something liable to happen as an adjunct to or result of something else." This is in complete contrast to the more straightforward use of the word *war*. Below is a list of a few terrorism euphemisms in the Obama administration, based on various sources:[63]

- Overseas Contingency Operations: GWOT.

- Violent extremism: terrorism.

- Man-caused disaster: terrorism. In March 2009, Napolitano told *Spiegel Online*, a German newspaper's website, that although she is well aware there will always be a terrorist threat waiting for us, it is better to call terrorist attacks *man-caused disasters*.

- Outliers: rogue states. In a new episode of political correctness, language employed by the Obama administration favors *outliers* over *rogue states*. The switch was made consistent with the newly released Nuclear Posture Review—a process to identify and regulate the role of nuclear weapons in U.S. security strategy. Nations like North Korea and Iran, labeled *rogue* by the Bush administration, will no longer be subject to that adjective.

- Pirate: Islamist terrorist off the African Coast.

Do the U.S. government and the media abhor calling a spade a spade? As mentioned earlier, a new word for an Islamist terrorist off the African Coast is *pirate*. Pirate just sounds more exotic, doesn't it? It has become the euphemism of choice for cruel Islamist terrorists, particularly in countries like Somalia. These terrorists have connections to Al Qaeda, which has ruled Somali politics for many years. There is little disagreement that, immediately after 9/11, Bush's decision to use straightforward words was widely accepted by many Americans at that time. Yet, it is debatable whether the Obama administration's decision to alter the existing label for concepts such as GWOT was to fulfill political correctness motives or conceal the weak progress of U.S. military engagement in the Middle East. This situation is reminiscent of the tenets of **speech code theory**, a framework for communication in a particular speech community. A speech code is a regulation or unwritten rule that imposes, restricts, or looks down on social discourse outside the narrow cultural limitations of a community. Put simply, a speech code is, as Gerry Philipsen (1992)[64] wrote it, "a rule governing what to say and how to say it in a particular context" (p. 101). A speech code would be applied for the purpose of suppressing forms of speech believed to be disagreeable to communicators.[65]

On February 9, 2011, Janet Napolitano issued a report saying that terror threats to America may have been the most severe since 9/11. Clearly lacking in this report—though unsurprisingly so—is any reference to Islam or jihad. Not even *Islamists*, *radicalized Muslims*, or *Islamic extremists* were used. The intent here is, again, to alleviate the blow of an inconvenient reality by burying it under more syllables. Americans cannot fight an ideology that cannot be named appropriately. We all know the jihadist threat is a real threat to the U.S., irrespective of Osama bin Laden's death. Yet, in Napolitano's report, only euphemisms merit mention. What are the Obama administration's intentions: to soften the threat of terrorism and make the U.S. look weaker?[66]

BLUESPEAK

In the dictionary of the United Nations, there is a linguistic practice called **bluespeak**, the U.N. lingo for their diplomats, so they can prudently phrase evil things. For the past few decades, the U.N. has mentioned "peacekeeping" missions all over the world, "armed humanitarian interventions" in Somalia, and "safe havens" in Bosnia. The problem is that the lexicon created by the U.N. is profoundly bewildering. Differences are now being made between peacemaking (mostly diplomatic efforts), peace operations (a military all-encompassing term), peacekeeping (the conventional deployment of troops between forces that have ceased firing), peace enforcement (essentially waging war, as in the Korean War and the Gulf War) and peace building (a range of postwar operations).[67]

In bluespeak, one learns about information, and not military intelligence. Apparently, one does not spy. One refers to a battalion as a *unit* and a mechanized battalion as a *protected unit*. Bluespeak sees war as something other nations do; while nations make war, the U.N. makes peace. The euphemisms cooked up by the U.N. are reminiscent of all those jokes about John Wayne Bobbitt, whose wife (Lorena) severed his penis. In the 1990s, the Bobbitt incident inspired a whole gamut of **eponyms** (people after whom particular words are named, e.g., Obamacare, Obamanomics, etc.). The word *Bobbitt* was used as a noun for penis and as a verb, meaning "to cut off the penis by a less than surgical method."[68] And think of the June 2011 scandal of U.S. Democratic Representative Anthony Wiener's "wiener."

Bluespeak derives from an Orwellian term of deception called doublespeak. In **doublespeak**, language intentionally conceals, distorts, or reverses the meaning of words. Doublespeak may take the form of euphemisms, making the truth less disagreeable, without denying its nature. It may also be expressed as deliberate ambiguity or reversal of meaning (e.g., naming a state of war *peace*). In all cases, doublespeak clouds the nature of truth, producing a **communication bypass**. In ordinary English, bypassing means passing by a place without entering it. Accordingly, a road that is a bypass will be built around town, and traffic using that road will not enter town and, therefore, bypass it. In communication, bypassing happens when the receiver of a message infers a different meaning from the message than what was intended by the sender. Most frequently, this leads to confusion that may result from the various meanings of words—especially euphemisms.[69]

EUPHEMISMS USED BY TERRORISTS THEMSELVES

Terrorists are also skillful in their use of language. They have managed to persuade the media, many audiences worldwide, and even some governments to accept their lexicon, frames of reference, and rationalizations for their actions. For terrorists, the brutal killings of social workers, journalists, businesspeople, teachers, civil servants, and even religious leaders are "executions." From this vantage point, the interpretation is that the killings are in some way legitimate and follow due process, and comply with traditional laws of war— or at least authorized by a higher religious principle or authority. They also qualify their own captured hit men as political prisoners or prisoners-of-war, in an attempt to legitimize their crime. Killers who terrorize innocent citizens with murdering, kidnapping, or torture are not called murderers or criminals, but are glorified as freedom fighters or martyrs.[70]

A Palestinian blowing him- or herself up clearly sees him- or herself as a brave soldier and martyr, and might oppose the term *suicide bomber*, in the same way that some Americans make an objection that it should be called a *homicide bomber*. Terrorism for the IRA is called *military war of liberation*. It is a self-ascribed label to characterize their terrorist attacks against the British.[71] Terrorism, in and of itself, consists of key elements, such as the act of political violence and the meaning attached to it. Yet, long after the smoke of an explosion has disappeared, the battle over language lingers on. Contending parties want to magnify the attack or downplay it, describe it as noble, or condemn it as vile. In fact, terrorists often project the label back at their targets. In a recording played in court in March 2010, David B. Stone, Sr., leader of the Hutaree group (a Christian militia movement based in Michigan), said the government was a terrorist organization. Doku Umarov, the Chechen terrorist leader who assumed responsibility for the suicide bombings in the Moscow metro, uttered the same statement in a recorded video, saying that the real terrorist was his arch-enemy, Vladimir Putin, the Russian prime minister.[72]

Table 9.1 below has two columns. In the left column are nouns and adjectives that terrorist groups use when referring to their enemies (i.e., out-groups). Conversely, in the right column are nouns and adjectives that terrorist groups use when referring to themselves (i.e., in-groups). This model of comparison was created by Maikovich (2005):[73]

Table 9.1 Out-Group and In-Group Labeling for the Same Thing

Out-Group Labeling	In-Group Labeling
Criminal	Revolutionary
Terrorist	Guerrilla
Murderer	Freedom fighter
Gang	Army
Subversive element	Liberator
Bloodbath	Purge
Lunatic	Martyr
Mercenary	Soldier
Threat	Warning
Aggression	Preventive counter-strike
Assassin	Avenger
Propaganda	Communiqué
Extremist fanatic	Dedicated anti-imperialist
Attack	Operation
Hired killer	Example of revolutionary solidarity
Murder	Revolutionary justice

Source: "A New Understanding of Terrorism Using Cognitive Dissonance Principles," by A. K. Maikovich, 2005, *Journal for the Theory of Social Behaviour, 35*(4), p. 372–397.

Of important note in the right column are the nicer words used by terrorists to label themselves. Certainly, guerrilla sounds nicer than terrorist, warning is friendlier than threat, and communiqué is less biased than propaganda. Regardless of how terrorism is labeled, its very essence, core, and content (i.e., what terrorism is, in and of itself) remain the same. Hijacking an airliner, crashing it into a skyscraper, and causing thousands of people to die constitute terrorism, no matter what label is used to describe it. What may change, however, is the public perception of the event based on the very label ascribed to it. The use of terrorism euphemisms is a fundamentally political act with political intentions.

EFFECTS OF TERRORISM EUPHEMISMS

So, do euphemisms for terrorism help the international community? An important conclusion is that euphemisms certainly manipulate reality by burying natural language under jargon, and they are designed for audience effects. The main corollary is that the international community may view terrorism (now called militancy or rebellion) in a less negative light, a process called *desensitization*. From this perspective, euphemists may argue that they help the international community by alleviating the fear of what is going on out there (e.g., the audience may experience less psychological disturbance). Nevertheless, with euphemisms, the audience would also lack understanding of what terrorism really is, which might hurt the audience in the long term. Indeed, euphemisms could cost lives as people might lower their guard in times where they should protect themselves fully. Other consequences are the legitimization of obscurantism and the emergence of glossocracy.

Obscurantism

From the Latin *obscurans* ("darkening"), **obscurantism** is the practice of purposefully keeping the facts or full details of some issue from becoming known. Obscurantism involves two historical and intellectual denotations: (1) restricting knowledge—resisting the propagation of knowledge, a policy of concealing knowledge from the audience; and (2) deliberate obscurity—a recondite or mysterious style (as in literature and art) typified by deliberate vagueness.[74] Such obscurantism facilitates the pre-packaging of language, which has a direct effect on our thinking process. The **pre-packaging**, or the prior absorption, of words and ideas usually results in nebulousness, oversimplification, and stereotyping of language. From this perspective, one of the functions of terrorism euphemisms is to pre-pack terrorist incidents and to increase the ease with which communicators (i.e., speakers-listeners) can assimilate them.[75]

For example, with respect to the phrase *Patriot Act*, this strategic obscurantism is so vague that it encompasses hundreds of policies and details that the average Joe or Jane does not understand. This is a legislative rhetoric created as a direct result of September 11, 2001 and that fascinated the public's collective fear of terrorism. Subconsciously, it led people to positively connect the legislation with national security. Patriot Act has probably been the single most tactical discourse in the language of GWOT so far. It is also a major case of the power of subconscious rhetorical association to divert people away from the reality of what the Patriot Act really is (e.g., to arrest anybody with no warrant or court order).

Glossocracy

Creating euphemisms means distorting language, which leads to unleveled power and knowledge among individuals. A term to describe this is **glossocracy** (from Modern Greek, "government by the tongue").[76] It combines many sorts of euphemisms; it is doublespeak, semantic shift, vocabulary abuse, word tampering, and wordplay. Language can be a powerful source of manipulation—a seductive, universal language of control. When the government controls language, it controls society. Glossocracy represents the totalitarian burden of manipulative language.[77] The propensity to dismiss terrorists as thugs and murderers may be understandable, but it is dicey. It sells the terrorists short, and makes the public even less aware or knowledgeable of the fundamentally political nature of the conflict. This refusal to educate target audiences makes them defenseless against terrorist propaganda and the casuistries of terrorist supporters.

Glossocracy is risky because power through language manipulation can control the way we think and act. There is a semantic deviance in terrorism euphemisms. Perhaps the most apparent dilemmas produced by euphemisms are that the meaning and the message are separated, and communication is not well understood by the audience. This may be the actual purpose of the messenger. Should euphemisms keep growing and spilling over other areas of life, we may see the likely death of natural language at some point. Language is communication; yet, as demonstrated by both the Bush and Obama administrations, language does not communicate but often operates to inform. Communication is two-way; it is a co-construction of meaning and sharing of ideas. Information, on the other hand, is one-way and functions to shape another person's thoughts. This is particularly tricky when language advances and legitimizes the existing order and the prevailing system while the public is not cognizant of this or has little ability to take part in the exchange. Glossocracy makes the meaning and the message separate, and, in so doing, divorces language from meaning by taking the meaning away from words. Public understanding of war and terrorism depends on clear communication.[78]

Solutions

A clear understanding of language and discourse on terrorism is indispensable, and only straightforward, natural language can allow that to happen. In his *Philosophical Investigations*, Ludwig Wittgenstein (1953)[79] said that humans need to play a **language game**, meaning that speakers (or communicators) must agree on the rules of the game before communicating. There must be a common and mutually consensual understanding of the fundamentals of language. For Wittgenstein, this shared understanding comes from shared experiences and expressions of behavior that he called *forms of life*. Euphemisms do not consider these shared experiences.

Philosopher Jürgen Habermas (1979)[80] said that communication should be improved through universal pragmatics. **Universal pragmatics** is the model of mutual understanding through clear communication. The world can reach an understanding when all communicators involved agree on the same meanings about certain words or phrases. In doing so, Habermas suggested that individuals and groups achieve communicative action, which is at the core of the life world. **Communicative action** has the charge of achieving several essential social functions: reaching understanding, cultural reproduction, coordinating action plans, and socializing individuals.

The concept of Plain English was mentioned briefly earlier. The **Plain Language Movement** is a movement motivated by **semantic transparency**. The purpose is to eliminate needlessly or superfluously intricate language from government, media, academia, law, and business. The ultimate objective is that everybody should use plain, simple, and clear language.[81] To this effect, British philosopher Paul Grice (1991)[82] proposed four conversational maxims that emanate from the Plain Language Movement. The **four Gricean Maxims** are the Maxims of Quality (be truthful), Quantity (do not be too concise or too verbose), Relation (be relevant), and Manner (be clear). The objective is that everyone should understand the meaning of the claim. One of the best examples of straightforward talk about terrorists and enemies may have been delivered by one of Bush's and Obama's predecessors, Theodore Roosevelt, who once said, "Speak softly, but carry a big stick."

SUMMARY

Euphemisms for terrorism are abundant and play an active role in the lives of many Americans, but do such euphemisms help the international community? Euphemisms certainly bury natural language. A euphemism can be used to obscure issues through deliberate deception or to provide tactful language. Euphemisms for terrorism work well through distancing language. Distancing language is phrasing employed by people to dissociate themselves from a statement, either to elude thinking about the topic or to detach themselves from its content. For example, the act of bombing has been romanticized with nicer language. Likewise, while guerrilla warfare is, symbolically, terrorism, it becomes, semantically, a type of irregular warfare or struggle. The intended action is to bury the profound impact of terrorism under jargon. And it is efficient because euphemisms impose context and a deceptive order of reality on things. For this reason, even the United Nations has its own lingo: bluespeak, the practice of shrewdly phrasing evil things. When euphemisms go too far, they become doublespeak, whereby language can even reverse the meaning of words. When terrorists themselves use euphemisms, they give the impression that killings are legitimate and follow due process. Certainly, while euphemisms may help the international community by alleviating the fear of what is going on out there, they can also cause the audience to lack understanding of what terrorism really is, which might cause people to lose their life. Ultimate consequences of euphemisms are obscurantism (intentionally keeping the facts from becoming known, which has a direct effect on our thinking process) and glossocracy (government or ruling through distorted language). Although the use of terrorism euphemisms is a fundamentally political act with political intentions, terrorism, at its very essence, core, and content, remains the same.

KEY TERMS

ENDNOTES

1. Howard, Philip (1986). *Euphemisms: The State of the Language*. London: Penguin.

2. Pustejovsky, James (1995). *The Generative Lexicon*. Cambridge, MA: MIT Press.

3. Filreis, Alan (1987). Words with "All the Effects of Force": Cold-War Interpretation. *American Quarterly, 39*(2), 306–312.

4. Marcuse, Herbert (1964). *One-Dimensional Man*. Boston: Beacon Press.

5. Robinson, W. Peter (1993). Lying in the Public Domain. *American Behavioral Scientist, 36*, 359–382.

6. Austin, John L. (1962). *How to Do Things with Words*. Oxford: Oxford University Press.

7. Searle, John (1969). *Speech Acts: An Essay in the Philosophy of Language*. Cambridge: Cambridge University Press.

8. Gumperz, John (1982). *Discourse Strategies*. Cambridge: Cambridge University Press.

9. Skoll, Geoffrey R. (2007). Meanings of Terrorism. *International Journal for the Semiotics of Law, 20*, 107–127.

10. Shane, Scott (2010, April 3). Words as Weapons: Dropping the "Terrorism" Bomb. *The New York Times*, p. WK1.

11. Beckwith, Richard, & Miller, George (1990). Implementing a Lexical Network. *International Journal of Lexicography, 3*(4), 302–312.

12. Humphreys, Adrian (2006, January 17). One Official's "Refugee" Is Another's "Terrorist." *National Post*; Reynolds, Paul quoting David Hannay, Former UK ambassador (2005, September 14). UN Staggers on Road to Reform. *BBC News*.

13. Cooper, Abraham, & Brackman, Harold (2008, December 2). Mumbai: Deadly Media Euphemisms. *The New York Post*, p. A1.

14. Mehan, Hugh (1997). The Discourse of the Illegal Immigration Debate: A Case Study in the Politics of Representation. *Discourse and Society, 8*(2), 249–270; Mehan, Hugh, Nathanson, Charles E., & Skelly, James M. (1990). Nuclear Discourse in the 1980s: The Unraveling Conventions of the Cold War. *Discourse and Society, 1*(2), 133–165.

15. Gross, Tom (2005, July 5). The BBC Discovers "Terrorism," Briefly: Suicide Bombing Seems Different when Closer to Home. *The Jerusalem Post*, p. A1.

16. **Ibid.**

17. Moeller, Susan D. (2009). *Packaging Terrorism: Co-Opting the News for Politics and Profit*. New York: Wiley-Blackwell.

18. Altheide, David L. (2007). The Mass Media and Terrorism. *Discourse & Communication, 1*(3), 287–308; Mills, C. Wright (1940). Situated Actions and Vocabularies of Motive. *American Sociological Review, 5*, 904–913.

19. Anderson, Richard D., Jr. (1996). Look at All Those Nouns in a Row: Authoritarianism, Democracy, and the Iconicity of Political Russian. *Political Communication, 13*(2), 145–164.

20. Cordesman, Anthony H. (2003). *The Iraq War: Strategy, Tactics, and Military Lessons*. Westport, CT: Praeger.

21. Brunstein, Robert (1970). Revolution and Social Change: Revolution as Theatre. *Current, 118*, 3–9; Smith, D. (1974, March 30). Scenario Reality: A New Brand of Terrorism. *The Nation*, 392–394; Task Force on Disorders and Terrorism (1976). *Disorders and Terrorism*. Washington, D.C.: Government Printing Press; Weinman, Gabriel (1983). The Theater of Terror: Effects of Press Coverage. *Journal of Communication, 33*(1), 38–45.

22. Laqueur, Walter (1976). *Guerrilla Warfare: A Historical and Critical Study*. Piscataway, NJ: Transaction Publishers.

23. Humphreys, Adrian (2006, January 17). One Official's "Refugee" Is Another's "Terrorist." *National Post*; Reynolds, Paul quoting David Hannay, Former UK ambassador (2005, September 14). UN Staggers on Road to Reform. *BBC News*.

24. Damm, C. (1982). Media and Terrorism. *Journal of Security Administration, 5*(1), 7–18; Hacker, Frederick (1980). Terror and Terrorism: Modern Growth Industry and Mass Entertainment. *Terrorism, 4*(2), 143–159.

25. Dummett, Michael (1993). *Frege: Philosophy of Language*. Cambridge, MA: Harvard University Press.

26. Smith, Terence (1969, August 14). Details of Green Beret Case Are Reported in Saigon. *The New York Times*, p. A1.

27. Taylor, Philip M. (1992). *War and the Media: Propaganda and Persuasion in the Gulf War*. Manchester: Manchester University Press.

28. Hayden, Robert M. (1998). The State as Legal Fiction. *East European Constitutional Review, 7*(4), 45–50.

29. Ogilvie, David, Hamilton, Val, Egan, Matt, & Petticrew, Mark (2005). Systematic Reviews of Health Effects of Social Interventions: 1. Finding the Evidence: How Far Should You Go? *Journal of Epidemiological Community Health, 59*, 804–808.

30. Miller, David (2002). Opinion Polls and the Misrepresentation of Public Opinion on the War with Afghanistan. *Television & New Media, 3*(2), 153–161.

31. Erskine, Toni (2006). Teaching the Ethics of War: Applying Theory to "Hard Cases." *International Studies Perspectives, 7*(2), 187–203; Watson, Robert D. (1998). On the Language of Bureaucracy: Postmodernism, Plain English, and Wittgenstein. In Thomas D. Lynch & Todd J. Dicker (Eds.), *Handbook of Organization Theory and Management: The Philosophical Approach* (pp. 388–414). Boca Raton, FL: CRC Press.

32. Lutz, William (1991). The World of Doublespeak. In Christopher B. Ricks, & Leonard Michaels (Eds.), *The State of the Language* (pp. 254–264). London: Faber and Faber.

33. Roche, George (1988). Bureaucracy: Enemy of the People. In Herbert M. Levine (Ed.), *Public Administration Debated* (pp. 3–21). Englewood Cliffs, NJ: Prentice Hall, p. 14.

34. Lutz, William (1988). Fourteen Years of Doublespeak. *English Journal, 77*, 40–43, p. 40.

35. Herman, Edward S. (1992). *Beyond Hypocrisy: Decoding the News in an Age of Propaganda*. Boston: South End Press, p. 1.

36. Kehl, D. G. (1988). The 2 Most Powerful Weapons against Doublespeak. *English Journal, 77*, 57–66, p. 57.

37. Brivio, Enrico (1999). *Soundbites and Irony: NATO Information Is Made in London*. In Peter Goff & Barbara Trionfi (Eds.), *The Kosovo News and Propaganda War* (pp. 515–522). Vienna: International Press Institute.

38. Watson, Robert P. (1997). Wittgenstein on Language: Toward a Theory (and the Study) of Language in Organizations. *Journal of Management History, 3*(4), 360–374.

39. Corum, James S., & Johnson, Wray R. (2003). *Airpower in Small Wars: Fighting Insurgents and Terrorists*. Lawrence: University Press of Kansas; House, Jonathan M. (2001). *Combined Arms Warfare in the Twentieth Century*. Lawrence: University Press of Kansas; Krulak, Victor H. (1984). *First to Fight: An Inside View of the U.S. Marine Corps*. Annapolis, MD: Naval Institute Press.

40. Smith, Terence (1969, August 14). Details of Green Beret Case Are Reported in Saigon. *The New York Times*, p. A1.

41. Altheide, David L. (2007). The Mass Media and Terrorism. *Discourse & Communication, 1*(3), 287–308.

42. Louw, P. Eric (2003). The "War against Terrorism": A Public Relations Challenge for the Pentagon. *Gazette, 65*, 211–230.

43. Altheide, David L. (2006). *Terrorism and the Politics of Fear*. Lanham, MD: Alta Mira Press; Engelhardt, Tom (1994). The Gulf War as Total Television. In Susan Jeffords & Lauren Rabinovitz (Eds.), *Seeing through the Media* (pp. 81–95). New Brunswick, NJ: Rutgers University Press; Lutz, William (1991). The World of Doublespeak. In Christopher B. Ricks, & Leonard Michaels (Eds.), *The State of the Language* (pp. 254–264). London: Faber and Faber.

44. Foss, Sonja (1996). *Rhetorical Criticism: Exploration and Practice*. Prospect Heights, IL: Waveland.

45. Birn, Ruth Bettina (2001). Collaboration with Nazi Germany in Eastern Europe: The Case of the Estonian Security Police. *Contemporary European History, 10*, 181–198; Naimark, Norman M. (2001). *Fires of Hatred: Ethnic Cleansing in Twentieth-Century Europe*. Cambridge, MA: Harvard University Press.

46. Orwell, George (1946). *Politics and the English Language*. London: Horizon.

47. Gardham, Duncan (2011, March 10). 7/7 Inquests: Emergency Services Should Use Plain English. *The Telegraph*, p. A1.

48. Zhang, Juyan (2007). Beyond Anti-Terrorism: Metaphors as Message Strategy of Post-September-11 U.S. Public Diplomacy. *Public Relations Review, 33*, 31–39.

49. Schmitt, Eric, & Shanker, Thom (2005, July 27). Washington Recasts Terror War as "Struggle." *The New York Times*, p. A1.

50. Moeller, Susan D. (2009). *Packaging Terrorism: Co-Opting the News for Politics and Profit*. New York: Wiley-Blackwell.

51. Bush, George W. (2001, February 27). *Address of the President to the Joint Session of Congress*. Washington D.C.: U.S. Congress; Watkin, Kenneth (2005). *Warriors without Rights? Combatants, Unprivileged Belligerents, and the Struggle Over Legitimacy*. Cambridge, MA: Harvard School of Public Health.

52. Lakoff, George (2004). *Don't Think of an Elephant: Know Your Values and Frame the Debate*. White River Junction, VT: Chealsea Green Publishing.

53. Sinnar, Shirin (2003). Patriotic or Unconstitutional? The Mandatory Detention of Aliens under the USA Patriot Act. *Stanford Law Review, 55*(4), 1419–1457.

54. Singer, Peter (2004). *The President of Good and Evil: The Ethics of George W Bush*. New York: Dutton.

55. Van Veeren, Elspeth (2009). Interrogating 24: Making Sense of US Counter-Terrorism in the Global War on Terrorism. *New Political Science, 31*(3), 361–384.

56. Kilian, Michael (2002, January 7). The Pentagon Puzzle. *Chicago Tribune*, p. A1.

57. Rumsfeld, Donald (2002, February 12). *DoD News Briefing: Secretary Rumsfeld and General Myers.* Arlington, VA: U.S. Department of Defense.

58. Alles, Michael (2009). Governance in the Age of Unknown Unknowns. *International Journal of Disclosure and Governance, 6,* 85–88.

59. Watson, Robert D. (1998). On the Language of Bureaucracy: Postmodernism, Plain English, and Wittgenstein. In Thomas D. Lynch & Todd J. Dicker (Eds.), *Handbook of Organization Theory and Management: The Philosophical Approach* (pp. 388–414). Boca Raton, FL: CRC Press.

60. Antaki, Mark (2007). The Politics and Inhumanity of Torture. *Law, Culture and the Humanities, 3,* 3–17; Corera, Gordon (2005, April 5). Does UK Turn a Blind Eye to Torture? *BBC News*; Danner, Mark (2009, April 9). US Torture: Voices from the Black Sites. *New York Review of Books, 56*(6); Luban, David (2007). Liberalism, Torture, and the Ticking Bomb. *Intervention, Terrorism, and Torture, 5,* 249–262; Rejali, Darius M. (2007). *Torture and Democracy.* Princeton, NJ: Princeton University Press.

61. Moeller, Susan D. (2009). *Packaging Terrorism: Co-Opting the News for Politics and Profit.* New York: Wiley-Blackwell.

62. Gartenstein-Ross, Daveed (2010, July 13). Terror Euphemisms: Helping or Hurting the Enemy? Retrieved on May 3, 2011 from http://www.cbn.com/cbnnews/world/2010/July/Terror-Euphemisms-Helping-or-Hurting-the-Enemy/.

63. Charen, Mona (2010, April 10). What the Euphemisms Tell Us. *Real Clear Politics,* p. A1; Meyer, C. (2009, March 16). Away from the politics of fear. *Spiegel Online.*

64. Philipsen, Gerry (1992). *Speaking Culturally: Explorations in Social Communication.* Albany: State University of New York Press.

65. Miller, Katherine. (2005). *Communication Theories.* New York: McGraw Hill.

66. CNN Wire Staff (2011, February 9). Napolitano: Terror Threat May Be Highest since 9/11. Retrieved on April 30, 2011 at http://www.cnn.com/2011/US/02/09/terror.threat/index.html?hpt = T2.

67. Campbell, Colin (1994, August 7). On Language: Bluspeak. *The New York Times,* p. C1; Moeller, Susan D. (2009). *Packaging Terrorism: Co-Opting the News for Politics and Profit.* New York: Wiley-Blackwell.

68. Campbell, Colin (1994, August 7). On Language: Bluspeak. *The New York Times,* p. C1.

69. Baar, James. (2004). Spinspeak II: The Dictionary of Language Pollution. Bloomington, IN: AuthorHouse; Gamble, Teri Kwal, & Gamble, Michael (2009). *Communication Works* (9th ed.). Boston: McGraw-Hill; Lutz, William (1987). *Doublespeak: From "Revenue Enhancement" to "Terminal Living": How Government, Business, Advertisers, and Others Use Language to Deceive You.* New York: Harper & Row.

70. Probst, Peter S. (2007). Terrorism: Perception, Illusion and the Art of Political Warfare. In Boaz Ganor, Kathrina von Knop, & Carlos Duarte (Eds.), *Hypermedia Seduction for Terrorist Recruiting* (pp. 3–13). Amsterdam: IOS Press.

71. Tuman, Joseph S. (2003). *Communicating Terror: The Rhetorical Dimensions of Terrorism.* Thousand Oaks, CA: Sage.

72. Shane, Scott (2010, April 3). Words as Weapons: Dropping the "Terrorism" Bomb. *The New York Times,* p. WK1.

73. Maikovich, Andrea Kohn (2005). A New Understanding of Terrorism Using Cognitive Dissonance Principles. *Journal for the Theory of Social Behaviour, 35*(4), 373–397.

74. Critchley, Simon (2001). *Continental Philosophy: A Very Short Introduction.* Oxford: Oxford University Press.

75. Leech, Geoffrey (1974). *Semantics.* Harmondsworth, England: Penguin Books.

76. Mugglestone, Lynda (2005). *Lost for Words: The Hidden History of the Oxford English Dictionary.* New Haven, CT: Yale University Press.

77. Bauwens, Michel (2009). Class and Capital in Peer Production. *Capital & Class, 97,* 121–141; Bowman, John L (2005). *Socialism in America.* Bloomington, IN: iUniverse.

78. Watson, Robert D. (1998). On the Language of Bureaucracy: Postmodernism, Plain English, and Wittgenstein. In Thomas D. Lynch & Todd J. Dicker (Eds.), *Handbook of Organization Theory and Management: The Philosophical Approach* (pp. 388–414). Boca Raton, FL: CRC Press.

79. Wittgenstein, Ludwig (1953). *Philosophical Investigations.* Malden, MA: Blackwell.

80. Habermas, Jürgen (1979). What Is Universal Pragmatics? In Jürgen Habermas (Ed.), *Communication and the Evolution of Society* (pp. 1–68). London: Heinemann.

81. Cooper, Robert Leon (1989). *Language Planning and Social Change.* Cambridge: Cambridge University Press.

82. Grice, Paul (1991). *Studies in the Way of Words.* Cambridge, MA: Harvard University Press.

CHAPTER 10

Terrorism and Group Dynamics

After reading this chapter, you will be able to

- discuss terrorist groups as like-minded individuals in Communities of Practice;
- describe important group theories including Social Identity Theory, Symbolic Convergence Theory, and groupthink; and
- explain the steps of small-group radicalization and the different methods of terrorist recruitment.

GROUPS: DEFINITION

Group dynamics is a complex set of relationships between people inside a group. A **group** refers to three or more individuals working together for the purpose of completing a task. Groups are the basic building blocks of many terrorist organizations. A group exists to fulfill six important human needs, also called **interpersonal communication motives**. These needs are (1) inclusion (a need to fit in and be identified with others), (2) affection (a need for love and appreciation from others), (3) control (a need to reach and exert power over others in their environment), (4) escape (a need to communicate to avoid activities or stressful situations), (5) pleasure (a need to communicate to have fun), and (6) relaxation (a need to communicate to wind down and lower anxiety).[1]

A group is more than an aggregate. An **aggregate** is a collection of people who are together at the same time and place, but who do not constitute a unit or have a shared degree of similarity. People who stand on a street corner, an audience watching a play, and students attending a lecture are aggregates, not groups. The notion of groups necessitates **interdependence**, which exists when all group members attempt to achieve the group's purpose. This reasoning extends to group members dispersed geographically. Interdependence explains why people can accomplish something collectively as a group that individual members would have a harder time accomplishing alone. Interdependence simplifies **group cohesion**, the capacity of a group to preserve membership and accomplish its goals.[2]

Group Norms and Group Commitment

If a group wants to meet its goals successfully, there must be group norms and group commitment. In his book titled *Group Performance*, Davis (1969)[3] defines a **group norm** as a "socially accepted standard or attitude that directs the behavior or belief exhibited by the majority of the members of a group" (p. 82). A norm refers to the limits of permissible behaviors of individuals in a group. It is a guideline or rule set up to control the behaviors of group members. The more members abide by group norms, the higher the degree of cohesion. While the level of conformity to group norms by people in a group is not a sufficient criterion for cohesion by itself, if norms are lacking in the group in some form, cohesion cannot be established.

Group commitment is an allegiance or devotion of a person to the members of their primary group and the values or philosophy of that group.[4] Allen and Meyer's (1990)[5] model considers three dimensions of commitment: affective commitment, continuance commitment, and normative commitment. Affective commitment "refers to the emotional attachment, identification with, and involvement" in the group (p. 2). This element encapsulates the *want to* perspective of an individual's commitment. Affective commitment can also produce positive outcomes in the group. Continuance commitment refers to a cognizance of the consequences for leaving the group. It represents the *need to* aspect of commitment. The final dimension is normative commitment, which denotes a feeling of moral indebtedness to continue remaining a member of the group. This concept represents the *ought to* aspect of individual commitment.

Primary Groups

Research has shown that, often, successful terrorist groups are—or have begun as—primary groups.[6] A **primary group** is a small interpersonal group in which people share personal and lasting relationships. Primary groups are also referred to as expressive groups because people are emotionally connected and support each other—like a family or a small group of friends. Primary groups exist principally to meet the six interpersonal communication motives (see earlier). Primary groups play a crucial role in the development of personal identity. They are typically long term and tend to be small.[7] On examining production effectiveness in regard to group size, Olson (1965)[8] reached the conclusion that a small group was better at creating an interpersonal bond and fulfilling group interests. Studies on group dynamics by Davis (1969)[9] and Mullen and Cooper (1995)[10] agree with Olson asserting that large groups come with fundamental disadvantages such as a weak interpersonal bond between the members and the group, exploitation of group members, and lack of interests in the group tasks. An ideal situation is that of a large group with several subgroups working on their own tasks so that the entire group can achieve its goal. These subgroups would be primary groups. Some scholars have suggested that cohesion is only possible among primary groups because face-to-face interactions have an important positive effect on developing strong bonds between participants.[11]

Certainly, while face-to-face groups are favored and recommended, they are not unconditionally necessary to form cohesion within primary groups. Indeed, present-day technology has made reaching cohesion possible without face-to-face contact.[12] Since primary groups aspire to cohesion and uniformity, terrorist groups consist of like-minded people who develop bonds on prior homogeneity, at least in political attitude, and on unequivocal commitment to political goals. The terrorist group is a group in which members share a common fate, in that their outlooks and the achievement of group goals—namely, their lives—are intermingled. Members must be trustful and trustworthy of each other and not endanger the group in any way. Under such a situation of mutual interdependence, members of groups have been reported to develop the high interpersonal attraction needs that make up cohesiveness.[13] Lastly, primary groups tend to be **supergroups**, groups of peers who are task obsessed, extremely focused, greatly loyal, and producing a felt and communicable single-mindedness.[14]

GROUP SOCIALIZATION AND TERRORISM

Throughout life, humans belong to a few or manifold primary groups, and the group that is relevant to the individual is believed to vary depending on factors such as the size, context, and norms of the group. Nevertheless, one decisive factor for the survival of the group is group socialization. By and large, **group socialization** occurs when group members create agreed-on meanings as to who will do what, how the group will function, and when members learn a sufficient amount to contribute adroitly and competently to the group. Group socialization is a mutual process of group members and the group as a whole collaborating to fulfill each other's needs and accomplish goals. Put differently, individuals actively partake in the socialization process rather than passively adapt to an existing group culture. Moreover, a group's culture gets modified when a member joins because the new member might influence the others to espouse new ways of communicating or performing as a group.[15] In Islamic group dynamics, **ummah** refers to the global Muslim community. For Osama bin Laden, striking the far enemy was a method of banking on anti-American hatred and positioning himself as defender of the Muslim ummah against the evil and corruption of the Judeo-Christian West.[16]

Trust and Support

Trust is group members' willingness to have confident expectations from each other. Without trust, new members will probably not be accepted by established group members, and established members will remain suspicious of new members. The importance of trust in a terrorist group is akin to a **psychological contract** in a corporation; it contains the shared beliefs, perceptions, and informal obligations between an organization and an employee.[17] On top of trust, a terrorist group has to rely on its members' mutual support. **Support** refers to a set of positive psychosocial relationships between members and between whom mutual trust and concern exist. Positive relationships result in positive adjustment and safeguard against stressors and difficulties by offering emotional support (esteem, attachment, and comfort), instrumental support (money, material goods, and services), and information support (advice, counseling, and feedback).[18] A fourth one is peer-to-peer support, which occurs when people offer knowledge, experience, and emotional, social, or practical assistance to each other. It creates a web of trust, a feeling of potency, and a penetrating and close interpersonal atmosphere. A particular form of peer-to-peer support is **peer mentoring**: mentoring that takes place between an older or more experienced member and a novice. Peer mentoring gives people a role, which is proportionate to their prior expectations.[19]

Scholars have noted that European terrorists in the 1970s and 1980s were often students before switching to the dark side. This might allude to the importance of peer-to-peer support for moral change. Haidt (2001, 2007)[20] and Greene and Haidt (2002)[21] propose that individual moral change is hardly ever the product of private deliberation (moral reasoning), but of social interaction in primary groups. It is easy to see how small groups of students, who are constantly bathed in small, socially interactive, and emotionally charged environments, would be vulnerable to this type of moral change. The social environment can contribute to radicalization (a novel morality). It has also been postulated that indoctrination techniques—for example, bombarding people over and over again with very emotive videos along with rationalizing discourse—are the most efficient in primary groups where trust and support are high.[22] Membership of religious groups is a breeding ground for the type of trustworthy and supportive environment to which future terrorists are exposed. Hairgrove and McLeod (2008)[23] drew attention to the task of traditional Islamic study groups (usroh and halaqa) to foster "ideological conditioning" environments that turn Muslims into extremist activists. Sageman (2004)[24] found that young Muslims become jihadists and mujahedin after joining primary groups of like-minded friends and kin.

Community of Practice (CoP)

A **Community of Practice (CoP)** is an activity of group learning in which people have a mutual interest in certain subjects or problems; they also cooperate over a lengthy period to exchange ideas, find solutions, and create innovations. For Lave and Wenger (1991),[25] learning is most important to human identity. The individual is an active member in the practices of his or her group, and constructs his or her identity through that group. From this understanding emerges the concept of CoP: a group of people taking part in communal activity and constantly developing their common identity by experiencing and contributing to the practices of their group. A CoP is a learning group. Successful terrorist organizations are organizations in which people engage in mutual learning, which allows them to adapt successfully to stress. **Learning organizations** participate in their own practice for learning, for honing old skills (e.g., traditional time bombs) or developing new ones (i.e., innovative terrorist techniques), and for gaining and exchanging knowledge among each other. Improvements in the ability of weapons to kill and improvised explosive devices rarely occur by chance. Quite the contrary, they tend to be the product of trial-and-error processes, and gradual sophistication.[26]

A learning group can be explained by **Differential Association Theory**, a theory positing that individuals learn from those with whom they interact in a group. They strengthen each other's inclinations. The group grows into a "family," a term usually used pejoratively to refer to organized criminal organizations. Interpersonal bonds established in combat may also support later collaboration.[27] The battleground offers an opportunity for such terrorist socialization. Friendships formed under fire have been reported to morph into stronger, subsequent relationships in pursuance of a cause. From the end of the 1970s to the beginning of the 1980s, those fighters who resisted the Soviet occupation of Afghanistan went on to fight the U.S. twenty years later. The Afghan resistance forged the social bonds that eventually laid the foundations for Al Qaeda. This is also what happened in the 1950s when Algerian combatants in the French colonial army in Indochina went back to Algeria and became members of the National Liberation Front (FLN) that fought for Algerian independence.[28]

Group Roles

There are several important roles in primary terrorist groups. The Mastermind is a career terrorist doing his or her job. A Mastermind like Osama bin Laden remained securely in the background. This was evident when bin Laden was hiding with one of his multiple wives when the Navy Seals raided his compound. A Mastermind does mostly the planning, tends to be more oriented toward preparing terrorist operations, and has deep ideological convictions. This individual is well aware of terrorism consequences and gets the picture of the political map. The Mastermind is often a charismatic and idealist leader with an activist mentality and a strong interest in changing the world. At a smaller level, Ramzi Yousef is also believed to have been one of the Masterminds of the 1993 World Trade Center bombing. He was condemned to life imprisonment by a U.S. court.[29]

The Ring Leader is a "field captain" whose terrorism career tends to be shorter (by a few years). The Ring Leader has strong notoriety needs, adheres to deep ideological convictions, tends to be more oriented toward the social sciences, and possesses good organizational leadership. This person has a markedly high level of interpersonal charisma. He or she can stimulate the group, and could be a teacher or preacher. The Pilot/Suicide Bomber (who flies an airliner into a building) has a short terrorism career, follows very strong notoriety needs and deep ideological or religious convictions, has some scientific or technical skill-set that is advantageous to the terrorist organization, and experiences the greatest level of social isolation, which allows this individual to intentionally kill him- or herself.[30]

Finally, the Foot Soldier (who simply hijacks the airliner, or who is a suicide bomber) has also a short terrorism career, with very strong notoriety needs as well. The Foot Soldier has profound ideological or religious convictions and experiences great level of social isolation. He or she is usually the most easily recruitable, has faith in others in the organization, and is very naive (may not know he or she is dying soon). A case in point is Richard Reid, the shoe bomber who was caught in his effort to blow up American Airlines flight number 63 from Paris to Miami.[31]

TERRORISM AND SOCIAL IDENTITY THEORY (SIT)

A terrorist group orchestrates maneuvers on the basic belief that the meaning of group identity can be invigorated through in-group cohesion, through an articulated social identity in terms of "We are a group" and "They are a different group." Groups fulfill many functions, and people join for many reasons. One reason for affiliation is the establishment of a social identity and related consensual belief system that tells us who we are, how we should regard and treat others, and how others will regard and treat us. Social identity, then, provides resources for social support like those in close personal relationships.[32]

Description of SIT

Social Identity Theory (SIT) analyzes interactions between in-groups and out-groups. According to SIT, individuals develop a positive identity by defining themselves with respect to their group membership, which allows them to attribute value and emotional significance to their group membership and group objectives. Self-classification as a group member increases the tendency to see one's own group as superior to other groups, and to reassemble defensively as a group when it is felt to be under threat.[33] When people behave in a group setting, the social forces in the group have a compelling influence on their judgment and attitude (e.g., conformity). When a valued social identity is sensed to be threatened from another group (e.g., when Islam is perceived to be threatened by "the West"), then those who share strong mutual bonds will tend to disparage and hold negative views toward the threatening group. Because social identity is now part of the self-concept of the group member, a threat to the group becomes a threat to self.[34]

SIT rests on the premise that in-groups see themselves as different from out-groups, better than them, or in competition/conflict with them. **In-groups** are groups of people about whose welfare an individual is concerned, with whom that individual is ready to cooperate without asking for equitable returns, and from whom separation causes anxiety. **Out-groups**, on the other hand, are groups with which a person has something to divide, maybe unequally. They are groups that deviate on valued attributes, or groups with which a person is in conflict.[35] SIT has received empirical support from numerous studies. For example, in their study, Branscombe and Wann (1994)[36] found that subjects who had high identification as American showed a decline in collective self-esteem after watching a movie clip from Rocky IV (in which Rocky fights Ivan Drago, the Russian boxer). Additionally, subjects who had high identification as American (in comparison with low identified subjects) and who watched this movie clip had a higher tendency to derogate various out-groups, including Russians. This out-group derogation also boosted the subjects' collective self-esteem. Similar research found that in-group identification contributes to a view of the self that is in harmony with a prototypical portrayal of the group.[37]

There are four dimensions of identity: cognitive centrality, in-group affect, in-group ties, and confidence. **Cognitive centrality** is the amount of time someone thinks about being an in-group member. This variable constitutes the persistent psychological salience of group identification. **In-group affect** is the degree to which someone feels good when he or she thinks about the in-group. This variable embodies the value someone places on in-group identity. In-group ties measure how much someone feels he or she shares a group's fate. **Confidence** is the centerpiece of a group's beliefs that represent a group's identity; when the beliefs are called into question, the ensuing effects may smash group members' reality.[38]

Social Identity of Terrorists

In-group social identity enables the creation of an "interactive echo chamber." This leads to an intensification of grievances and beliefs in conspiracy to the point of hate. By moving the terms of the discourse away from long-lasting disagreements in-region vis-à-vis the "far enemy," terrorist groups such as Al Qaeda communicate significant symbolic messages about in-group identity to jihadists: they are esteemed members of a community and they should be proud of the group as a whole.[39] The perception of the enemy, then, is socially assembled.[40] In regard to Al Qaeda, this Islamist movement inculcates the importance of cohesion and in-group self-esteem. This is a process that has particular meaning in that the terrorist group trades citizen self-identity with group self-identity and, in doing so, obscures the valuableness of national designations. As Mansbach (2004)[41] explains it,

> By demarcating inclusion and exclusion on the basis of sameness and difference, moral communities draw boundaries of "inside and outside" according to which justice is distributed. Moral boundaries are also articulated authoritatively as a system of obligations and duties attached to community membership, such as jihad as defined by Islamists. In this capacity, they serve to legitimate the use of coercive power. (p. 28)

Membership in a terrorist group gives disciples a heavy and well-defined personal role, a "virtuous" purpose, the chance of avenging perceived humiliations, and the removal of limitations on the expression of otherwise proscribed behavior—protecting the member from personal blame for attacks on out-groups.[42] Shamir and Shikaki (2002)[43] found that most Palestinians identified violent acts committed by Israelis as terrorism, while only a handful of them considered acts committed by their in-group as terrorism. Conversely, Israelis mostly rated the Palestinian acts, but not the Israeli acts, as terrorism. The Groupe Salafiste pour la Prédication et le Combat (GSPC), which translates as the **Salafist Group for Preaching and Combat**, is an Algeria-based Islamist terrorist group founded in 1998 and that seeks to overthrow the Algerian government and establish an Islamic state. Islamic identity is seen by most GSPC members as a commitment to more rigid principles of faith, prescribed Islamic dress, and a more streamlined in-group identity as a faithful one.[44] A similar case would be one in which Muslims defend suicide bombers as group members who fulfilled in-group goals (e.g., making Western forces evacuate Islamic lands) to the detriment of their own lives. Although many Muslims do not advocate suicide bombing, as an in-group tradition they have defended suicide bombers as justified freedom fighters.[45]

Terrorists also engage in what Bandura (1973)[46] called slighting aggression by advantageous comparison. This concept involves highlighting the flagrant misdeeds of the government as an excuse for engaging in terrorist attacks against it. Among West German terrorist groups in the 1970s, there was a process of socialization creating a crystal-clear separation between friend and enemy: it earmarked all positive identifications for the in-group and all negative identifications for the out-groups. The enemy was seen as an abstraction, an institutional organization, rather than a group of humans. Victims had no human value to them; they were just members of institutions.[47] This philosophy resembles scapegoating, a practice whereby a group creates a crystal-clear separation by holding another group automatically responsible for all problems and by acting out widespread antipathy toward chosen out-groups. Scapegoating is an in-group's self-defense mechanism of denial. It is done through attributing responsibility and blame to out-groups. The scapegoat mechanism serves to satisfy an otherwise unquenchable animal appetite for destruction. Scapegoating is a ubiquitous group dynamic that is as old as the biblical verses describing it; possibly as old as the very first appearance of human social behavior.[48]

The social identity of terrorists implies the notion of professional socialization. **Professional socialization** is the institutionalized method whereby people are socialized into a group environment of cruelty toward out-groups. This happens through the logic of a mounting rage and a cognitive dedication to aggression. Professional socialization is important to the terrorist group because it fosters a quasi-family environment that provides the terrorist a feeling of emotional attachment to group members who are involved in the same situation. Particularly for those experiencing feelings of alienation, powerlessness, and humiliation from a real or imagined foe, joining the terrorist group supplies a palliative and creates the circumstances for a purifying or liberating sense of release.[49]

SIT and Hezbollah

In 1991, Hezbollah set up its Lebanese television station, Al-Manar ("the Lighthouse"). Al-Manar is still very popular in the Near East region. Only Al Jazeera is more popular in the West Bank and Gaza Strip. Al-Manar broadcasts many motivational videos with rousing slogans and professionally designed graphics and music. Consider, for instance, a video broadcast which showed images of Palestinian suicide bombers—that is, the Muslim in-group—blowing up an Israeli checkpoint. In another video, the footage showed a group of Israelis driving bulldozers—that is, the out-group—and destroying Palestinian habitations. A third video featured another group of Palestinian suicide bombers dying while killing members of the out-group (i.e., IDF, or Israel Defense Forces). These videos encouraged the Muslim in-group to take up the fight against the evil Jews, something that added fuel to the necessity for social identity not just for the Lebanese Hezbollah and Palestinians, but also among all Muslims in the world.[50]

Part of the reason why Hezbollah perpetrates terrorist attacks is to pave the way for being recognized as a justifiable or "right" group, not just in the Near East region but also in the larger Middle East arena, and not just for Shi'ites but also for Sunnis and all Muslims who have suffered injustice in the region. The in-group here is a gigantic one. SIT underlines the common purposes that groups share and die for. Common fate is particularly critical. If one Islamic group is hurt or even merely threatened, all Muslims should join forces. SIT teaches that the in-group will become so cohesive that it will fulfill the common objective of shielding the shared interests of the group.[51]

For French sociologist Emile Durkheim (1912),[52] groups are structured through high degrees of moral cohesion. It is a direct result of social rituals that solidify the "cult" structure of groups. For Durkheim, cults are groups of people organized around shared beliefs and consolidated by systems of traditions and customs. Durkheim developed his theory of in-group cohesion on two central concepts. First, the social structure of in-group solidarity is formed around what he called the **positive cult**, a system of group norms that prescribe the codes of expected, normative behavior. For Hezbollah, waging jihad against the infidels, combating Israel, and partaking in the Islamic resistance movement are expected norms among its members.[53] This positive cult mobilizes and assimilates Muslims into common beliefs and affinities. In brief, the positive cult is the moral influence of social norms that attracts people into group life.

Durkheim's analysis of in-group cohesion also rests on the concept of negative cult. The **negative cult** symbolizes the cultural taboos and prohibitions from which people must refrain if they are to be seen as group members. These taboos and prohibitions are the basis of group sanctions and are central to group life because they work to provide the yardstick for differentiating group membership. For example, Hezbollah members are forbidden from defecting by the Party of God (which is what "Hezbollah" means) to another country. For a certain number of Islamic groups around the world, once a Muslim leaves the religion, the person is considered an infidel and may incur severe punishment.[54]

IDF (**Israel Defense Forces**), mentioned earlier in this section, has been Hezbollah's and Hamas's greatest enemy. Yet, IDF has also managed to solidify its social identity over many decades to counter Lebanese, Palestinian, and other external threats (Box 10.1). This happened thanks to radio.

Box 10.1   Galei Tzahal

Known in Israel by its acronym Galatz, **Galei Tzahal** is a national Israeli radio network run by IDF. The station broadcasts news, music, weather forecasts, and educational programs to the general audience as well as entertainment and military news stories for soldiers. Radio played a major part in Israeli nation building. As a result of the partisan quality of the print media during the pre-state and early state era, and the nonexistence of television broadcasts (which did not appear until in 1968), radio was considered a primary method of sociopolitical socialization and cohesion.[55] Radio also contributed to the popularization of colloquial Hebrew, developing standard cultural patterns and lifestyles, and shaping the Israeli social identity and collective national memory.[56]

The supremacy of radio in establishing Israeli identity, along with the crucial role of IDF in the nascent state, led to the creation of Galei Tzahal in 1950 (thanks to David Ben-Gurion, the then Israeli Prime Minister and Defense Minister). The military role of Galei Tzahal was associated with mechanisms characteristic of a "nation-in-arms," designed to ensure a quick transition from ceasefire to a state of war. Most of the radio programs (e.g., on popular music, classical music, etc.) incorporated patriotic educational messages.[57] Galei Tzahal essentially broadcasted to the home front and was also intended from the outset at the civilian audience. The official justification for solidifying social identity in this fashion was the following: when a state is nascent, the entire nation is an army. According to this perspective, every civilian is a soldier at heart who can be asked to join forces in wartime. Galei Tzahal is now a major platform in Israeli cultural and mass media, based on the dynamics that led to its rising popularity over several decades and its struggle against assorted pressures designed to end its existence.[58]

SIT and Competition between Terrorist Groups

An often-overlooked aspect in terrorism is competition—sometimes violence—against competitors. From the point of view of SIT, threat from in-group competitors is no different than threat from an out-group enemy. The procedure is the same: to survive, the group under threat needs to form high cohesion, with subsequent high pressures for conformity and harsh punishments against deviates. Groups in competition for the same base of supporters can earn status through more severe attacks in support of the cause. Experts have suggested that the 1979 killing of Lord Mountbatten by the IRA was part of a competition with soaring attacks by the Irish National Liberation Army.[59] In regard to the IRA again, there was a fragmented faction between the Official IRA and the Provisional IRA (PIRA), which mostly committed attacks on Protestant organizations. No matter what, disputes between rival groups drastically raise the death toll.[60]

Terrorists engage in what Bandura (1990, 2004)[61] called **advantageous comparison**, which involves a group comparing its own terrorist acts with acts committed by other groups that appear worse. This comparison assuages the group's perception of the severity and moral weight of its own terrorist acts. Radicalization by competition was certainly evident in the case of the **Armenian Secret Army for the Liberation of Armenia (ASALA)**. ASALA became notorious by attacking Turks at a time when mainstream Armenian organizations were only asking for retribution for the Turkish genocide of Armenians. The Dashnaks, an older group than ASALA, reacted to the new competition by creating their own anti-Turkish terrorist organization, the Justice Commandos of the Armenian Genocide. Similarly, the 1985 hijacking of both the TWA Flight 847 airliner and the luxury cruise ship MS Achille Lauro were efforts by Islamist terrorists to show superiority over rival groups.[62] And the Palestinian Front for the Liberation of Palestine (PFLP) was forced to adopt suicide terrorism as a tactic, in spite of its materialist Marxist reasoning, when the group began to look inferior to rival groups in the Second Intifada.[63]

During the separation between the GIA (the Armed Islamic Group that wants to replace the Algerian government with an Islamic state) and the GSPC (the Group for Preaching and Combat, an Algeria-based Islamist guerrilla group), the GSPC resisted the killing of innocent people. To persuade GIA's loyalists, the GSPC increased religious proscriptions against killing civilians. As a result, some level of competition occurred between the two groups to classify followers into groups that supported the GIA and those that supported the GSPC. Different terrorist groups have different objectives. Frequently, there are many actors pursuing different tactics simultaneously. The terrorist group that can communicate its goals the most effectively will be able to inspire action and be more visible.[64]

SIT and Group "Mortality Salience"

Mortality salience refers to awareness of one's eventual death. It is a psychological process that intensifies people's connections with their in-group as a defense mechanism. This can contribute to stronger feelings of nationalism and terrorism.[65] Exposure to death-related descriptions and images, such as those contained in jihadist propaganda, leads to what psychologists call a mortality salience effect.[66] Pyszczynski, Solomon, and Greenberg

(2002)[67] have shown that mortality salience tends to increase identification with and dignity in one's country, religion, gender, race, and so forth. Remarkably, mortality salience can increase support for extremism when it is associated with group identity. For instance, one study reported that, under mortality salience circumstances, Caucasian Americans displayed more sympathy and support for other Caucasians who had racist views. Similarly, in the Middle East, Muslim university students who were reminded of death confirmed increased support for other students supporting suicide attacks. Of equal significance is the fact that the mortality salient group also expressed the idea that they wanted to participate in suicide attacks themselves.[68]

SIT and Forgiveness

The degree to which a person identifies with an in-group and embraces the group's norms has an effect on intergroup forgiveness. Members' loyalty to the group is generally stronger in conflicts where identities are under threat. This, in turn, may negatively affect in-group members' disposition to forgive an out-group because forgiveness may be perceived as disloyal to one's in-group and a repudiation of one's in-group goals. Consequently, in extended conflict such as the current terrorism phase, which can be interpreted as a Clash of Civilizations (i.e., Muslims vs. Westerners), in-group members may be more likely to bolster their social allegiance even when they do not condone some group members' actions.[69]

When forgiveness happens at the group level, victims at least discard debilitating cognitions and emotions caused by the actions of an out-group. At most, they react positively to out-groups.[70] Sherif and colleagues (1961)[71] showed that supporting rival groups for working together toward overarching, collective goals smoothed intergroup collaboration and harmony. Later, substantial research subsequently demonstrated that reclassifying out-group members as in-group members in an overarching human category enables decreased out-group prejudice and hatred.[72] Wohl and Branscombe (2005),[73] for instance, encouraged forgiveness by widening in-group inclusiveness. In their manipulation, Jewish subjects were introduced to versions of the Holocaust. Forgiveness was encouraged when the Holocaust was depicted as an example of humans acting aggressively toward humans, but not when it was depicted as Germans acting aggressively toward Jews.

SMALL-GROUP RADICALIZATION

Innes, Abbott, Lowe, and Roberts (2007)[74] define **small-group radicalization** as a process involving "significant change in an individual's or group's orienting beliefs and motivations. Through processes of radicalization some people will come to assume an extremist viewpoint, wherein they are willing to countenance or enact violence in pursuit of their goals" (p. 38). Put differently, radicalization is seen as the process by which people (or groups) modify their beliefs, embrace an extremist position, and promote (or practice) violence to reach their goals.[75] Small-group radicalization does not happen overnight. It is usually a process that follows three stages. In the first stage, **pre-radicalization**, the individual has not started the process of radicalization yet. He or she is contemplating the idea of adopting extremist views and tactics. In the second stage, the **radicalization window**, the individual is going through times during which he or she is the most vulnerable (i.e., to getting his or her views altered, etc.). In the third stage, **violent radicalization**, the new terrorist recruit has started the process of adopting extremist views and resorting to violence on the basis of a new set of beliefs.[76]

Innes and colleagues described four factors that trigger the adoption of extremist viewpoints: (1) signal events (generally negative but can be personal, group, or collective); (2) declining social control (in the form of perceived insignificance of both informal and formal ways of solving problems in their community); (3) differential association (with growing isolation from traditional contacts and increased interaction with extremists); and (4) indoctrination of the ideology and full identification with the international community as conceived by the terrorist group.

Jihadization

A notorious type of small-group radicalization is **jihadization**—behavior focused on planning an Islamist attack.[77] Sageman (2004)[78] analyzed 172 people who were or are members of extremist jihadist groups. The data came from sources in the public domain, mainly media documents and transcripts of court records. An astoundingly large percentage joined in small groups (and not as isolated people). To a large degree, joining the jihad is a group sensation. Individuals often do not join the jihad as isolated people. Rather, it is within small groups that they progressively become radicalized. In most cases, members experience a long period of deep social interaction with a small group of peers, developing strong interpersonal bonds, which alleviates their former isolation. The vast majority of jihadists follow kin and associates more than they do orders from far away. Their hard-to-penetrate social networks constitute approximately 70% friends and 20% kin.

In his study of 242 jihadists, Bakker (2006)[79] discovered that these people usually became involved in terrorism thanks to networks of friends or family and that often there were no formal ties with global Islamist networks. In brief, the people were not becoming radicalized due to attempts of an Al Qaeda recruiter. Instead, the process was happening almost separately from reputable jihadists. Small-group jihadism advocates salafiyyah (from *salaf*, the Arabic word for "ancient one" and referring to the followers of the Prophet Muhammad)—the renewal of authentic Islam—and preaches a strategy of extreme jihad, leading to an outburst of terror to eradicate what it considers local political deviation or rebellion. More recently, Arid Uka, the 21-year-old Kosovar who has acknowledged murdering two U.S. airmen in Frankfurt, was operating lonely, only adopting radical jihadist ideology a short time before killing them; he became a radical Islamist in just a few weeks.[80]

The Dutch Ministry of the Interior and Kingdom Relations (2006)[81] had concerns about European jihad and stated that this domestic threat points to a grassroots practice of radicalization, including local networks primarily active under their own control and separate from global terrorist networks. In British radical mosques, the social interactions between Muslim members taking note to the sermons create and shore up ideological commitment. The mosques present opportunities for newcomers to make new friends and further the development of an ideological devotion to the jihad, and (critically) provide associations with the jihad through members who are already connected. The Finsbury Park mosque (in London) was shut down for a lengthy period after a major police raid occurred on January 20, 2003. At that time, the police statement stated that the raid was directed specifically "at individuals who have been supporting or engaging in suspected terrorist activity from within the building. Police believe that these premises have played a role in the recruitment of suspected terrorists and in supporting their activity" (p. 102).[82]

Halaqa and Usroh

Small Islamic study groups are usually referred to as *halaqa* and *usroh*. They have been central in the radicalization and training of cadre to fulfill the agendas of mobilizers. Although the notion of small-group mobilization is not new in Islam, the calculated use of these study groups authorized by the Islamic belief system has played a crucial role in empowering high-risk activism. In Malaysia, a new usroh was launched in the 1990s, developing a link to Al Qaeda and switching their organization's name to Jemaah Islamiyah. Nevertheless, the group leaders preserved the modus operandi of the Usroh Movement cell structure and training program. Recruits came mostly from mosques and Qur'anic recitation circles at mosques where Jemaah Islamiyah recruiters selected these legitimate religious pursuits by adding the usroh training matter. After the initial indoctrination, recruits had to swear allegiance to Abu Bakar Bashir (a group leader) and be ready to go for syahid (martyrdom) for the cause of Allah to become total Jemaah Islamiyah members.[83]

There are three levels of commitment within both halaqa and usroh: (1) formal adhesion by people who agree to the outward responsibilities, but not the spirit; (2) total conversion by people who silently accept the "spirit and principles" of Islam; and (3) enforced alliance by people who are forced to stay in the Islamic alliance. The second type of conversion, total conversion of Muslims, translated into conversion into radicalism. This conversion experience is typically done through friendship, relationship, or in discipleship-based groups. Mingling with other converted Muslims in a small-group context spiritually reassures new Muslims in great depths of their encounter. These converts are psychologically conditioned and mentally controlled by their leaders; here, recruits pledge alliance to these leaders and to an imaginary world group that the leaders call the ummah, which in reality is their ummah (unlike the more standard and pluralistic meaning of ummah).[84]

GROUPTHINK

A theory developed by Irving Janis (1972),[85] **groupthink** is a situation in which (1) conflict seldom occurs as a result of high group cohesion, (2) high group cohesion is dominant when a lot of "yes men" are present in the group, (3) members are reluctant to verbalizing their unbiased opinions to avoid offending the other members of the group, and (4) members stress agreement over disagreement. Groupthink has led people to agree to group perceptions and attitudes by simply belonging to their in-group. This phenomenon is also called **individual–group discontinuity**, exemplified by the finding that people develop less distrust when in groups.[86]

As Post, Sprinzak, and Denny (2003)[87] put it, "An overarching sense of the collective consumes the individual. This fusion with the group seems to provide the necessary justification for their actions with an attendant loss of felt responsibility" (p. 176). This explanation of the submersion of individuality is highly reminiscent of Eric Hoffer's (1951)[88] statement that individuals who embark on mass campaigns "are fashioned into incomplete and dependent human beings even when they have within themselves the making of self-sufficient entities" (p. 128). Friedland (1992)[89] postulated that terrorism is not merely a group phenomenon but is undoubtedly the outcome of an interaction between social processes and individual characters. Yet, he suggests three conditions under which personal proclivity to violence is a comparatively minor factor in the terrorist turning: deprivation is strong, the in-group has ideologized its disgruntlement, and the in-group is united and clearly distinct from the out-group. He used the Palestinians as an example. Their special circumstances drive people with no special inclination toward violence to engage in terrorist acts.

A unique characteristic of terrorist groups is that they exist under conditions of intense danger and resultant stress. As Janis (1968)[90] observed, "When people are exposed to external danger, they show a remarkable increase in group solidarity. That is, they manifest increased motivation to retain affiliation with a face-to-face group and to avoid actions that deviate from its norms" (p. 80). Janis's studies of soldiers on the battlefield are relevant to this analysis of terrorist behavior. He observed, for instance, that social isolation—something that terrorists voluntarily do—also enhances dependence on the group. External danger inspires needs for reassurance, which are fulfilled through interaction with other group members. This, in turn, contributes to an intense individual motivation to remain in the group and to avoid the probability of exclusion. The risk of group expulsion reduces dispositions to diverge from group norms.

Another source of higher in-group cohesion and ideological solidarity is the person's response to the killing of comrades. Survivors frequently try to adapt to death and to offset group demoralization by unconsciously relating to dead buddies (or, as is usually the case in terrorism, those who have been captured). Through a process of introjection, or internalization of the lost object, this kind of response gives rise to a type of **postponed obedience**, or strengthened compliance with the principles represented by the fallen buddies. This heavy cost of life certainly increases group conformity.[91]

Risky Shift in Terrorist Groups

Because terrorism often occurs in a group setting, a situation known as **risky shift** (or *group extremity shift*) may emerge. Overall, risky shift is enhanced agreement on the opinion at hand, and a shift in the average opinion of members toward the opinion of the whole group. The shift is at a higher extremity on whatever side of the opinion is supported by most group members before the discussion.[92] People in groups tend to take more risks than they would if unassociated with a group. The escalation in risk-taking proclivity may encourage even more risks in the same direction. The reason is that terrorists become less constrained by the probability of negative consequences. Examinations in social psychology have found that people involved in small, face-to-face groups will accept higher risks—mostly as a result of group discussion—than they would if acting alone. Participation in a terrorist group may increase the member's inclination to consent to the great risks that participation in terrorist activity involves.[93]

As one can see, within a group setting, people progressively accept the beliefs and decisions of the group's more extreme members. With a growing emphasis on the small group, their religious faith, for example, can become more significant and more intense. The extreme divergence experienced within the group, along with a higher sense of group identity and commitment, can also help radicalize members and enable their entry into the jihad in a manner that was condoned by their new social peers. **Group polarization** is a phenomenon by which the attitudes of group members become more extreme as a consequence of joining a group. In addition to this, the open-hearted opinions of a whole group are often more extreme than those withheld by the individual members of the group.[94]

Presently, there are two theoretical models that give an explanation of risky shift. According to **relevant arguments theory**, a culturally motivated pool of arguments supports one side of the issue over the other side. An individual member samples from this pool on evaluating his or her individual opinion. Then, in group discussions, the individual listens to new arguments from others, which, coming from the same pool, are primarily in the same direction as the individual was oriented. The outcome is that individuals are rationally convinced by the imbalance of new arguments that emerged in group discussion.[95]

According to **social comparison theory**, opinions possess social values associated to them. All individuals feel pressured toward common agreement, that is, pressured to shift their opinions toward the average opinion of the group. Yet, the pressure is not equal. Individuals who are more extreme than the mean in the group-supported direction—the direction supported by most individuals before group discussion—are more appreciated. Ideological groups like terrorist organizations are ideal candidates for an event known as *social implosion* where in-group members consider former relations with out-groups less desirable and center their energy and communication almost entirely on other in-group members.[96]

Consequences of Groupthink

The effects of strong cohesiveness, pressure to obey the rules, and risky shift in terrorist groups are abundant. Strong affective relationships are developed among members, so that the degree of dependence with which members entered often grows. The returns that members were looking for almost certainly become more interpersonal than task-environmental. To be exact, the admiration of other members in the group matters more than the accomplishment of group goals. Admiration is conferred not only for decisions that help the group achieve its political goals but also for in-group compliance and acceptable ideological thinking. Under these circumstances, the purpose of the terrorist group may become self-maintenance more than the change of the political system.[97]

Additionally, terrorist leaders often regulate the flow of communication. As authorities in the collective belief system, they must regulate operational, tactical, and doctrinal communication. They generally impose a "one voice" policy where disagreement or variation is not accepted in public or even recommended in private. They manipulate motivations (and purposeful goals) for new terrorist members.[98] Another consequence of groupthink, which may give details on the escalation of terrorist violence, is the high chance of brutalization, or **graduated desensitization**. As such, the execution of terrorist attacks makes discomfort and self-censure disappear over time. Nazi violence emerged progressively from a conditioning process shared by Nazi comrades in a facilitating group context. This conditioning process, through which the individual eventually strives for destructive power, is called *brutalization*, a consequence of yielding to group pressures and abiding by a new philosophy. Even individuals who first expressed concerns and reluctance submitted to the group after a while.[99]

RECRUITMENT OF TERRORISTS

A key figure in terrorism recruitment is the activist. The activist mostly recruits within his or her social network—consisting of friends, acquaintances, or relatives. This confers recruitment and radicalization a more horizontal rather than vertical nature.[100] Each terrorist group has its favored method of recruitment and training that will best maintain its routine course of action. For example, the Malayan Communist Party made friends with Chinese locals to rapidly develop their membership. On the other hand, Al Qaeda relies strongly on relationships built over time (e.g., friendships and family bonds) to recruit truthful members and remain a secret network.[101] The way to join a terrorist group can also occur via other groups, such as in West German residential communities or prisoners' support groups. The recruitment procedure of the Basque ETA is slow but sure and effective; it is built on groups in Basque youth culture.[102]

The Importance of Identity

Terrorist recruits usually come from the segments of society that endorse or share the goals, grievances, and motivations of the terrorist group. Terrorist groups are not always made up of crazed fanatics. Groups weed out emotionally unstable people—they would pose a huge risk. Identity has been reported to play a crucial role the recruitment of terrorists. For example, in jihadist extremism, people must have a fervent sense of Muslim identity and relate strongly with the global Muslim community (i.e., the ummah).[103] Recruits constantly say that, before joining, they feel they are greatly associated with other Muslims worldwide. This global connection carries with it a certain level of responsibility for these other Muslims, even when the person has never had an encounter with them or visited their lands. Research has demonstrated that Muslims who think their identity matters more than their national or ethnic identity view topics such as jihad and martyrdom more positively.[104]

Models of Recruitment

Gewehr and Daly (2006)[105] examined four different models of **recruitments of terrorists**. In the net recruitment model, every person in a target audience (e.g., community, congregation) is considered "good enough" for terrorism recruitment. More precisely, the target audience is seen as sufficiently homogeneous and receptive to be approached without screening out anybody in the audience. An example where this approach would be efficient for Al Qaeda is a mosque led by an imam generally acknowledged as radical. Mosque-goers are likely to be asked to be recruited without additional preparation. Regionally, the net model of recruitment may work in places such as the Northwest Frontier Province of Pakistan, which is notorious for being populated by people supporting Al Qaeda.

In the funnel recruitment model, the terrorist group uses a gradual, or phased, approach of recruitment; the terrorist group deems the target audience ripe for recruitment but needs a major transformation in identity and motivation. As the term *funnel* explains, new recruits start at one end of the process and are morphed, after serious streamlining along the way, into radical group members when they emerge at the other end. Streamlining or culling often boosts the reputation of the group by giving its members elite status. In the case of Al Qaeda, recruits are required to demonstrate knowledge of radical Islam and the use of violence to accomplish the terrorist group's goals as a proof of commitment to the principles of the group.

In the infection recruitment model, an infiltrator can be placed into the target audience to gather new recruits through direct, personal appeals. This method influences the big persuasive strength of (1) source credibility, (2) social comparison and validation, and (3) particularly custom-made appeals. As recruits are gathered, the reach of the recruiting attempt improves. The purpose is to associate potential recruits with peers who are already in-group members. Infection will probably work best for a terrorist group in an organization like the police or the military, in which most members are not extremists. In this instance, the infiltrator has more chances to convert selected members who are discontented with their careers or feel resentment toward the police, the military, or even the government. For Al Qaeda, the infection recruitment model worked well in countries like Kenya and Tanzania, where most of the population was not supportive of Al Qaeda's cause, but specific people could be recruited for Al Qaeda operations.[106]

In the seed crystal recruitment model, terrorist-recruiters attempt to offer a context for self-recruitment. Metaphorically, seed crystal recruitment is akin to reducing the temperature of a glass full of water until the water cools and then ice crystals appear as the seeds of a total freeze. In this recruitment model, important variables include the kind of environmental forces used to "chill the glass" and how long the "freeze" lasts. In regard to Al Qaeda, the seed crystal model may work best in Diasporas or audiences where open recruiting is not feasible. It was efficient for recruiting the plotters of September 11, 2001 who formed the Hamburg cell.

"STAIRCASE TO TERRORISM" MODEL

The **"Staircase to Terrorism" model** is a six-step model in which a person develops, through a long-term socialization process, the aspiration to engage in terrorism. The model was developed by Fathali Moghaddam (2005).[107] The staircase has six floors, each distinguished by certain psychological processes.

Ground Floor and First Floor

On the ground floor, people acquire a degree of inclination toward terrorism through ingrained beliefs that too much deprivation and injustice exists out there, and through perceptions of infuriation and dishonor motivated by material, political, cultural, or economic circumstances. The ground floor is replete with millions of people. On the first floor, people who feel they have no options for mobility and cannot contribute to the political decision-making process may transfer the blame to an Other. Andoni (1997)[108] reports that, in Palestine, volunteers for suicide bombing feel that they are motivated by a lack of political alternatives.

Second Floor

People may proceed to the second floor, where ideological or cultural circumstances relieve them in transferring their aggression to a perceived adversary. Sprinzak (1990)[109] adds that there is a crisis of confidence in society's current rulers, followed by a conflict of legitimacy, when society itself is called into question, leading to a "break with the prevailing political order" (p. 81). With respect to young Muslims in England, they occasionally experience a sense of anomie and disconnection—a type of estrangement from mainstream British society.[110] Alienation of yuppies in Japan caused them to join Aum Shinrikyo, the doomsday cult that sought to establish a new world order by using WMDs.[111]

Innis and his colleagues (2007)[112] observed that there are four prerequisites for ideological recruitment in regard to extremist militancy: (1) inter-community separation, where a minority group is reluctant or not capable to adapt into mainstream society; (2) intra-community separation, where alienated members establish a "minority within a minority" and remove themselves from the wider minority community; (3) ideology, which fuels the individual's resentment and provides a path to restoring their grievances; and (4) group dynamics, where people buttress each other's attitudes and predispositions.

Third Floor

On the third floor, people become aware of the terrorist organization and join it. Scholars have emphasized the pivotal role that social networks play when new members join terrorist organizations. Potential recruits get into contact with the terrorist organization through relatives, friends, or acquaintances, and are caught up by the rewarding nature of interpersonal bonds.[113] For example, the Weather Underground came out as the direct offspring of a student organization. In this case, the person joins a group before it resorts to terrorism.[114] In terms of joining the terrorist organization, McCormick (2003)[115] asserts that the "individual must share something in common with a political collective to become affiliated in the first place" (p. 494). McCormick also claims that "would-be members of the underground are 'pushed' toward a particular group because of their preexisting cognitive or affective attributes and are 'pulled' into the group (and re-socialized) by forces in play within the collective itself" (p. 495). Recruits seem to choose a terrorist group based on a combination of their own frustration with society/the world and the solutions that the group can potentially offer. To some degree, the group takes advantage of an already-established disposition, a circumstantial lack of correspondence between personal and social moral valuations.

For Moghaddam (2005),[116] the group musters resources "to persuade recruits to become disengaged from morality as it is defined by government authorities (and often the majority of society) and morally engaged in the way morality is constructed by the terrorist organization" (p. 165). Moghaddam identified several tactics used by terrorist groups to motivate and preserve this moral disengagement as isolation, affiliation, secrecy, and anxiety. Kruglanski and Fishman (2006)[117] called attention to the phenomenon of **focalism**, whereby "increasing the subjective focus on a given objective leads to the suppression of alternative objectives" (p. 204). After joining the group, the new member may concentrate on the ends "assumed to be served by terrorism (e.g., a defense of one's religion)" (p. 204), and may be no longer able to see incompatible goals, such as making sure that innocent lives will not be lost.

Terrorists often believe that the actions they take are justified. They have confidence in the justice of their cause and follow their commitments accordingly. Thus, a certain number of terrorists espouse codes of self-sacrifice that are at the source of their daily lives. They deem these codes to be higher-class codes of living and that the code followers are better than those who do not follow them.[118] Benjamin and Simon (2002),[119] National Security Council staff members under President Bill Clinton, maintained that 9/11 was regarded by the nineteen hijackers as the "performance of a sacrament, one intended to restore to the universe a moral order that had been corrupted by the enemies of Islam and their Muslim collaborators" (p. 40). For terrorists driven by religion, any type of terrorist attack is justifiable if it brings them closer to their holy objective.

Fourth Floor

Further reinforcement is unmistakable on the fourth floor, where integration and absorption into the clandestine life and structure of the terrorist group, and socialization into its principles, foster an "in-group vs. out-group" and "us vs. them" dichotomy. The secretive character of the group promotes seclusion from mainstream social and political life, and new members can forget their sense of the reality of the old world outside their new world. These members can become caught up in a fantasy war and are vulnerable to groupthink. Such type of isolation brings about increased submission to the practices and radical belief system of the group.[120]

The fourth floor is the floor of peer pressure. **Peer pressure** underscores the significance of in-group dynamics in the development of violent behaviors. The value of this concept lies in its capacity to look at in-group dynamics from a new analytical perspective. More specifically, it concentrates on the power of conformity and how, within the group environment, the importance of being liked, appreciated, and respected by the other in-group members turns into a very strong emotional influence. Fear of exclusion, of scorn, or of being accused of fear or weakness can create an intense emotional impact on people. Examined from a somewhat different perspective, a fear of emotional ostracism can cause a person to control and suppress their own behavior to safeguard the uprightness, cohesiveness, and security of the group in which they are members. Forces exerted by the group, including indoctrination, repetitive training, and peer pressure, have been assumed to affect the group's violent behaviors, irrespective of whether individual members were inclined toward such behavior.[121]

On the fourth floor, peer pressure and rigid norms must be tremendously significant for individual members, very simple with no room for interpretation, and embraced continuously. This in-group normativity is developed in opposition to the norms of the out-group—the enemy, the outside world, and so forth. Taylor and Louis (2004)[122] noted the in-group's conception of the out-group's norms as absurd, determining "the form that terrorist actions take... the powerful out-group's norms signal to the terrorist group the behaviors that are most shocking" (p. 171).

Terrorist groups also subsist because of *social connectedness*, a psychological concept referring to the quality and number of connections a person has with others in his or her social circle of friends and acquaintances.[123] The IRA socialized their members through an intensifying escalation of well-though-out violent missions culminating in a "passing out ceremony." The member, in so doing, becomes attached to the cause by a terrorist act.[124] This is an illustration of habitus. **Habitus** is understood as cognitive and behavioral automation; it is a collection of acquired patterns of thought, behavior, and preferences. These patterns, or inclinations, are the product of internalization of culture or social structures through the experience of a person or group. Habitus is also acquired through gradual experience, such as training.[125]

The terrorist group regulates the environment to which the new members are exposed. Contextual stability leads to motivational stability, which the terrorist group, openly or covertly, acknowledges to be situation dependent. Palestinian terrorist organizations have been found to provide coaches, who accompany the volunteer to the heart of the location of the attack. This is the last setting the new member will encounter, and one over which the group has no control. Habitus may play a crucial part at this stage.[126] Neria et al. (2005)[127] examined the Al Qaeda written instructions given to the 9/11 terrorists. On top of passages that frame the looming massacre and death in ritualistic terms, rationalize the suicidal nature of the act, and provide moral exculpation, long segments of text are dedicated to practices that will provoke a state of altered or transcended consciousness, ignoring the necessity for deliberation, such as prayer, rituals, perpetual recitations and incantations, and total restlessness preceding the mission. Nonetheless, future suicide attackers have developed habitus by powerful environmental factors.

Fifth (and Last) Floor

The fifth (and last floor) gives the individual the cognitive resources needed to perform the terrorist act. Committing acts of terrorism against humans is not an easy moral undertaking for most people. Large military organizations have long been aware of the necessity to assimilate recruits into a brand new world to instill discipline, and to support them as they encounter, according to Procter (1920),[128] "the great strains upon human nature 'imposed by war'" (p. 36). For Procter, the combatant in World War I lost "all personal consciousness and all individual volition" (p. 43) when he went overboard; how "the habitual reactions set up in the course of his training" directed his movements" (p. 43); and how the army looked out for the dead combatants' bodies and instituted religion, because religion was "a very powerful incentive to killing Germans" (p. 44). In the army, the combatants had "no use for independent thought" (deliberation) (p. 47).

Applying Procter's argument to the terrorism situation, Moghaddam (2003)[129] described how volunteers recruited by a Palestinian terrorist organization are assimilated into an institutional phase of training and programming, where they are transformed into living martyrs and forced to publicly commit to the fatal course of action through a moral and social contract (a formal commitment). This usually includes the video recording of their testament. Subsequent to this process, the recruits are secluded from the rest of the group, or occasionally housed with other volunteers, and sent on the mission within the next few days. The more they wait, the more they may change their minds.[130] Hoffman (1993)[131] noted the value of a clerical endorsement for religious terrorists, who interpret their upcoming terrorist act as the performance of a "sacramental act or divine duty executed in direct response to some theological demand or imperative" (p. 2). The divine-driven nature of their act exempts recruits from all social and moral constraints, and justifies the extreme violence adopted by religious groups. Hoffman and McCormick (2004)[132] allude to a "deliberate recalibration of social attitudes" (p. 270) in the event of suicide terrorism, whereby "an act which under normal circumstances would be considered abnormal, if not abhorrent, has been transformed into something that is not only acceptable, but even encouraged" (p. 270).

In a study conducted by Burdman (2003),[133] in Pakistani terrorist training "summer camps," children were lionized as martyrs for Allah. The summer camp was actually a military camp for youth, with parades of both boys and girls in uniform, involved in gymnastic training exercises and even jumping through burning hoops of fire. Somewhat older boys and girls were also learning how to assemble machine guns. Drills, like constantly stabbing mannequins with bayonets, brainwashed future terrorists to react knee-jerkingly to external stimuli. Stories of barbarisms committed by the enemy were diffused through the ranks to stir up the recruits to anger and reassure them that their actions were always right.[134]

FIVE PHASES OF SOCIAL PSYCHOLOGICAL CONDITIONING

The vast literature on the social psychology of groups—including Bion's (1959)[135] basic assumption groups, Miller's (1998)[136] innovative development of those assumptions as innate biogenetic urges, and Jaques's (1996)[137] central discovery that organizations are the source of leaders' and members' disowned and projected part objects, generally echoed in disturbances of organizational functioning—provides a robust foundation for increasing our awareness of group dynamics of terrorism. In exchange for giving new members of terrorist groups meaningful existences and for living up to their affiliative emotional needs, the leader is accorded wholehearted obedience from the new recruits. Long-established members reinforce the leader's obedience requirements by exerting conformity pressure on new recruits. In this way, there is no derailment from the group's mission.[138] The recruits' initial vulnerability to this extreme obedience and conformity pressure makes them enormously susceptible to the five phases of the social psychological conditioning process used in terrorist groups, which was developed by Stahelski (2004),[139] as shown in

Table 10.1. These five phases are depluralization, self-deindividuation, other-deindividuation, dehumanization, and demonization.

Phases 1 and 2

In Phase 1, the psychological conditioning process throws out the new member's social and personal identities—a phenomenon called **depluralization**. In the case of extremist hate groups and terrorist groups, Phase 1 programs new recruits to learn how to hate and sometimes kill civilians on demand—a process called deindividuation, dehumanization, and demonization of the Other (as explained later). Many terrorist groups desire to transform this normal pluralized state by depluralizing potential recruits. Those groups generally confine themselves to isolated environments. If new members agree to live in these isolated conditions, it becomes easier for them to renounce membership in any of their former group affiliations, even including their own families (i.e., a replacement of relationships). This zealotry for creating a "milieu control" is based on the logic that old group memberships and identities would forestall the absolute commitment required by the terrorist group. The latter cannot successfully brainwash new members unless it is his or her sole group affiliation.[140]

Once the member's old group memberships and identities have been removed, he or she becomes more vulnerable to Phase 2. **Self-deindividuation** eliminates a person's individual identity, both externally and internally. For instance, many recruits in terrorist groups quit wearing civilian clothes and start wearing uniforms most of the time. Internally, all recruits are required to abandon any values, beliefs, attitudes, or behaviors that diverge from the group values and expectations.[141] It is a process called **doctrine over existence**.[142]

Phase 3

Phase 3, **other-deindividuation**, parallels joiner self-deindividuation. New members learn how to categorize their social world into those who are in the in-group (i.e., us) and those who are in the out-group (i.e., them). Many terrorist groups go a step further by identifying out-group as the enemy. The new members are then conditioned to deindividuate members of the out-group. Enemy deindividuation entails aborting all personal relationships with out-group members, knowing or calling any member of the out-group by individual name, or characterizing any individual attributes or characteristics among members of the out-group. All members of the out-group become a homogeneous, impersonal mass: they all look the same, think the same, and act the same.[143]

In this phase, the concept of deindividuation surfaces. **Deindividuation** refers to a state of lowered self-awareness, a provisional loss of individual identity as a consequence of becoming part of a group (e.g., an army or a mob); it can also occur in circumstances in which people feel anonymous. It can have extraordinary harmful effects, at times making people more willing to commit a crime, or leading police forces to use disproportionate force in an arrest. Deindividuation has been assumed to be a prime cause of rioting, such as the violent rioting that took place in South Central Los Angeles in 1992. It was a result of the acquitting of the Caucasian police officers who were caught beating Rodney King on tape. Because people in deindividuated conditions lose sense of who they are, they disregard external evaluation of themselves by others, and are unrestricted by their normal inhibitions.[144]

So, deindividuation causes someone to lose his or her social identity and behave in a way in which he or she would not normally behave. Deindividuation leads to the concept of **herd behavior**. It is a type of behavior whereby individuals abandon their sense of self, get caught up in a larger group experience, and are no longer constrained by a feeling of morality or appropriateness.[145] Terrorists have subjected their individual identity to the collective identity of the group, so that what serves the group is only what matters.[146] Since deindividuation is, in part, what forms the mental agenda for many terrorist groups, it is no surprise that massacres become normative for terrorists, who may otherwise never have considered such extreme acts as individuals. The loss of independent and critical thinking fortifies polarized, compartmental thinking, which creates psychological splitting and reversion among group members. The process of deindividuation truly relinquishes power to the terrorist group and its leadership through the initial mental programming, starting with Phase 1.[147]

Figure 10.1   The Five Phases of Social Psychological Conditioning

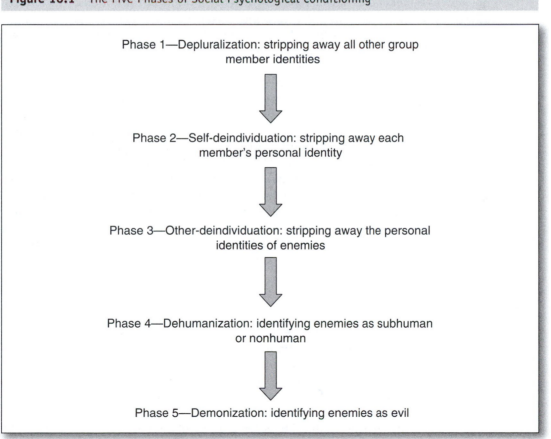

Phase 1—Depluralization: stripping away all other group member identities

Phase 2—Self-deindividuation: stripping away each member's personal identity

Phase 3—Other-deindividuation: stripping away the personal identities of enemies

Phase 4—Dehumanization: identifying enemies as subhuman or nonhuman

Phase 5—Demonization: identifying enemies as evil

Source: "Terrorists are Made, Not born: Creating Terrorists Using Social Psychological Conditioning," by A. Stahelski, 2004, *Journal of Homeland Security, 7,* p. 10–21. Copyright 2004 by Homeland Security Institute. Reprinted with permission.

Phase 4

Once terrorist members are deindividuated into "us," and enemies are deindividuated into "them," negative stereotyping of the enemy ensues. This is the evolution to Phase 4, **dehumanization**. All positive characteristics—such as moral virtue, intellect, responsibility, integrity, trustworthiness, reliability—are accredited to members of the in-group, and all negative characteristics—moral depravity, idiocy, irresponsibility, cheating, untrustworthiness, unreliability—are for members of the out-group. As explained in Chapter 8, dehumanization is a practice whereby the enemies and their characteristics are attributed nonhuman entities, such as animals, vermin, filth, and germs. In Phase 4, there is a clear blending of individual identity and group identity.[148]

This gives rise to the notion of **collective identity**. It refers to a sense of affiliation to a group (the collective) that is so powerful that someone who identifies with the group will devote his or her life to the group over individual identity; he or she will defend the group no matter what and take risks for the group, occasionally as great as loss of life. In-group cohesiveness goes beyond community, as the collective always experiences the pain of grief when a member dies. Taylor and Louis (2004)[149] introduced the notion of the terrorist **collective identity**, a normative structure within which the member "simply follows the behavioral norms specified by the collective identity" (p. 180). Large-group identity is partially created through "chosen" traumas and victories that are ritualized and even exploited politically to manipulate the members. Collective pride and collective shame can become a major part of such traumas and victories.[150]

The impact of community support has also been associated with matters of social duty and honor. The notion that people are acting altruistically in the best interest of larger groups can be a strong legitimator of violence and even martyrdom. The support and approval of the wider community, particularly if the community explicitly lionizes the terrorist as a hero in a collective fight, are likely to boost the terrorist's determination. This effect might be even more serious in cultures that stress great value on honor and dignity. For example, in the Middle East, Palestinian suicide bombers are glorified on posters and massive gatherings.[151] One particular way to fulfill the model of social duty and honor is by observing group anniversary reactions, which are popular among victimized groups and those that have suffered tragic losses, helplessness, and disgrace from another group—usually large—that cannot be properly mourned or reconciled.[152]

Phase 5

Although dehumanization justifies massive killing of unarmed civilians by terrorist group members, a last phase of conditioning helps avoid the possibility of a negative aftereffect of killing, such as remorse. **Demonization**, Phase 5 of the social psychological conditioning process, is a practice whereby terrorist group members become swayed into believing that the enemy has a pact with the devil. As most cultures define good in relativity to evil, demonization is a broadly applied conditioning strategy.[153] Referring to America as the Great Satan and Israel as the Little Satan is a case of out-group demonization by the government of Iran. Lifton's (1989, 1999)[154] description of terrorism focuses on in-group apocalyptic fantasy and pressure for a purified society, requiring destruction of the impure for a new world order. Lifton's arguments are based from studies of Aum Shinrikyo (the Japanese nerve-gas terrorist group), the Jim Jones cult (in Guyana), and the Heaven's Gate cult in San Diego.

THE PYRAMID MODEL

Group dynamics lays emphasis on the wide-ranging base of support that some terrorist activities require. McCauley (2004)[155] discussed such broad support by developing a **pyramid model**. The foundation of the pyramid is made up of sympathizers with the terrorist cause who are not necessarily ready to start engaging in terrorist activities. The base of the pyramid is the sentiment pool whose support terrorists rely on when in need. For example, in Northern Ireland, the base consists of all people who want "Brits Out." In the Islamic world, the base comprises all those who consider the U.S. harming and humiliating Muslims (i.e., the ummah) since the second half of the 20th century. The pyramid is the centerpiece for terrorist recruitment and protection. According to Silke (2003),[156]

> Even "popular" terrorist groups represent a violent and extreme minority within the immediate social group that shares the terrorists' beliefs and backgrounds. While the terrorist… may be largely tolerated within their communities, the number of individuals actively involved in the campaign of violence is always relatively low. (p. 53)

Because terrorists are few in comparison to people who are only there to accept their beliefs and feelings, terrorists may be seen as occupying the top of a pyramid. From top to bottom, higher levels of the pyramid are related to decreased numbers but greater radicalization of beliefs, feelings, and behaviors. Palestinian suicide terrorist attacks against Jews decreased considerably immediately after the Oslo Accords. Optimism of a peace agreement was accompanied by lower support for terrorism, as polls of Palestinians reported it. When the hope in the Oslo Accords was gone and the Second Intifada began, polls showed unparalleled support for terrorism and a rising number of terrorist attacks to new highs. In the vast majority of cases, terrorism increases correspondingly with popular support for terrorism. Yet, it can also decrease if popular support for terrorism does too. Nevertheless, often, more radical action leads to higher status and support to a group that competes with other groups to act for the same cause.[157]

A terrorist group is described based on a particular way of thinking. Terrorists strive not only to directly or indirectly sway opponents but also to sustain and muster support among their appropriate constituencies for reasons of recruitment, protection, and financing. For example, the reason why the IRA has not engaged in suicide attacks, unlike Hezbollah, in spite of contemplating them, considering the operational benefits of the method, can be explained through the different principles held by these terrorist organizations' respective constituencies. In Northern Ireland, the base of the pyramid in a terrorist group has comprised all members accepting the concept of "Brits Out." In Islamic terrorist groups, the base of the pyramid has comprised all people who think America has been ruining and humiliating Muslims for fifty years.[158]

Levels of Involvement of Female Terrorists

On examining the role of women in terrorism, Griset and Mahan (2003)[159] developed a classification according to four types. Any case of terrorism worldwide that includes women falls into one of four categories:

- Sympathizers: these women help the men in their terrorist operations, not by fighting alongside them but by working on the everyday chores, like cooking, sewing, and looking after the needs of the men. At this level of involvement, females also work hard to provide safe houses, move money, and traffic war equipment.

- Spies: these women are more active in their involvement in terrorism. They work as spies, gather intelligence, and act as messengers. Like sympathizers, they are discreet, but furnish the infrastructure that the terrorist organization will rely on in the future: apartments to be available as safe houses and occupations that might be beneficial to the organization, such as in banks or the government. These missions are riskier and necessitate a higher level of commitment than those carried out by sympathizers.

- Warriors: at this level, these women take part in actual combat; they fight alongside the men. They are aggressively committed to the cause and employ arms and bombs, endangering their own life, limbs, and liberty. Yet, they do not call the shots, and there is no clear plan for their status in society after the mission is accomplished.

- Leaders: these women reach governing positions in their terrorist organizations and are key figures in developing ideology, forming strategies, planning, and on occasion personally leading operations. Due to their position, stature, and skills, female terrorist leaders do not want to resume fulfilling women's traditional roles after victory is achieved. Instead, they foresee a future in which their own status and function in their societies will change drastically.

Group Failure

When popular support disappears, terrorist organizations can quickly disappear too. For instance, the Armenian Secret Army for the Liberation of Armenia (ASALA), a group operating mostly in Turkey, disappeared as soon as they lost support from its Diasporic supporters. ASALA's Diaspora strategically decided to not center their attacks exclusively on Turks any more.[160] One of the biggest dangers to a terrorist group's survival is loss of membership. Members must be enlisted and preserved. If they refuse to do it, whether in action or through desertion, the knowledge they have (and that goes with them as they leave) may put the entire organization at risk. So, at the beginning of a member's career, he or she will be subject to tactics to be "locked in." The Aum Shinrikyo group attempted to dissuade members from leaving by abducting and torturing those who tried.[161]

LaFree and Dugan (2009)[162] reported that, of 1,769 terrorist groups active between 1970 and 1997, almost 75% of them (n = 1,422) disappeared in less than a year as indicated by the time that elapsed between their first and last known terrorist attack. Only 24 terrorist organizations in the study (1.3%) existed for over twenty years (from 1970 to 1997). Jones and Libicki (2008)[163] examined 648 terrorist groups that operated between 1968 and 2006. They found that, of those terrorist groups which no longer engaged in terrorism, 43% joined political parties, 40% were stopped by police and intelligence officials (key terrorist members were caught), 10% terminated their operations because they thought their objectives had been met, and 7% were blocked by military force. Dugan, Huang, LaFree, and McCauley (2008)[164] research on ASALA and JCAG (Justice Commandos of the Armenian Genocide) points to the fact that the attrition of the support base might be a crucial reason for a terrorist group's rapid ending. Lastly, terrorist organizations might evolve into lucrative criminal groups when chances for making money occur, as has been reported in the case of Hezbollah, the Shining Path in Peru, and the FARC in Colombia.[165]

Box 10.2   Case Study—Group Failure for the Red Brigades

The **Red Brigades** (*Brigate Rosse* or *brigatisti* in Italian) were a communist terrorist organization, based in Italy. In the 1970s and 1980s, they were responsible for numerous acts of terror, such as sabotage, bank robberies, and kidnappings.[166] The Red Brigades felt that the Italian state should move away from Western ideology and NATO and, instead, espouse Soviet communism. For the terrorist group, Marxism-Leninism was the wave of the future. However, the *brigatisti* movement began to fade when the revolutionary left became increasingly split over the degree to which the state should be attacked. In addition, when the Soviet Union fell, the Red Brigades not only broke down, but they also surrendered to the Italian authorities.[167] As they wrote in one of their manifestos, the events had proven them wrong:

"The political collapse of the Warsaw Pact and of the Soviet Union itself, and the general retreat of revolutionary processes and struggles for liberation, have resulted in a change in international balances in favor of the imperialist chain and strengthen the dominance of the U.S. within it."[168]

SYMBOLIC CONVERGENCE THEORY

The situation in which terrorists strengthen in-group cohesion can be explained by **symbolic convergence theory (SCT)**, coined by Ernest Bormann (1972).[169] The theory posits that sharing group fantasies leads to symbolic convergence. Examples of fantasies are jokes, narratives, metaphors, and human interpretations of familiar events and how their feelings and moods become apparent after these events. When humans laugh together or experience anxiety together, they have a tendency to become a cohesive group. This is what is meant by symbolic convergence.[170] SCT is assigned the name *symbolic* because it has to do with fantasy, language, and symbolic facts. It is given the name *convergence* because its fundamental proposition describes the process of communication in which collectives share fantasies so they can develop their symbolic world. The basic unit of analysis of SCT is the fantasy theme. Fantasy themes are developed to accomplish rhetorical or psychological needs and can be employed to interpret a group's past, present, or future. Analogous to myth-making, a fantasy theme can be a simple word, a phrase, a sentence, or even a big paragraph.[171]

The Role of Myth in Terrorist Groups

A major principle of SCT is the role of myth. According to Malinowski (1954),[172] a *myth* "is not merely a story told but a reality lived" that satisfies "deep religious wants, moral cravings, [and] social submissions" (p. 100), "expresses, enhances, and codifies belief," and "safeguards and enforces morality" (p. 101). From this viewpoint, myth "is not an idle tale, but a hard-worked active force" that serves as a "pragmatic charter of primitive faith and moral wisdom" (p. 101). Put differently, myth both represents ideology and offers a "sacred story" that "governs our faith and controls our conduct" (p. 100). For Rowland and Theyes (2008),[173] the **symbolic DNA** of the terrorist message is a mythic symbolic scheme that functions as both a persuasive and an epistemic mechanism. Terrorists do not experience some type of satanic metamorphosis and abruptly become villains. In reality, the most threatening terrorist groups, including those performing massive attacks against innocent targets, use a mythic rhetorical design based on religion or an ideological/mythic pattern resembling religion. This pattern serves as a symbolic representation that justifies terrorism, changing it into sacramental violence.

To the outside world, the mythic system may look meaningless or irrational, but for a group of believers under the influence of their ideology, it acts as a "reality lived," creating transformation into a divinely motivated army.[174] Such a myth may produce **group delirium**—shared dreams that galvanize individuals in a political cause or religion. From such delirium, the most thorough, realistic designing and killing may be engineered.[175] Kenneth Burke (1966, 2003)[176] calls this well-designed feat a terministic compulsion leading to violence. This scheme has been noticed among terrorists whose religious views are connected to all major faiths. While a lot of attention on this subject had been paid to Al Qaeda (as the archetype of the symbolic pattern), all religious and ideological/mythic terrorist organizations tell a mythic story of how the organization, whose very identity is endangered with devastation, can recapture its strength, protect its culture, and overthrow the evil enemy it faces by going back to the heroic virtues that existed at the creation of the organization's identity.

For Rowland and Theyes (2008),[177] the symbolic DNA of terrorism can be observed in the acronym DNA itself. Religious terrorist groups, and groups that adopt an ideological/mythic pattern resembling religion, that perform massive terrorist attacks are inspired by a mythic worldview including three elements: a feeling that their identity and very existence have been denied and are endangered with destruction by some group; a total negation of the identity of people who pose the threat; and affirmation of a new identity through a foundational myth linked to the origin of the group or a millennial myth about the perfect life that the group will enjoy in the future.

To describe the mythic pattern, Lévi-Strauss (1966)[178] used the term **bricolage**. In cultural studies, bricolage is the process of developing a new social identity by appropriating symbols and artifacts from a variety of heritages and cultures. This process happens a lot within subcultures. Bricolage is apparently the terrorists' choice of the Islamic religion to use it as an instrument for supporting their actions against "the establishment." The reliance on symbols—for purposes of group identity and propaganda—to make fellow Muslims aware, endorse jihad, or recruit volunteers for a cause, is approached by bricoleurs.[179] Along with the mythic pattern, there are also three associated basic concepts. They are symbolic cue, fantasy type, and saga.

Symbolic Cue, Fantasy Type, and Saga

A **symbolic cue** is an abbreviated indication or signal like a symbol, sign, or inside joke that represents a fantasy theme.[180] Stretching the index and middle finger to form the peace sign is an example of a symbolic cue. Terrorist groups will often create flags, patches, or other identification insignias that contain symbols. While some symbolic cues have religious significance, others have a more war-like representation and some a slogan or motto. Each symbol has a specific value to the group and offers a good reason for which the group's identity can maintain group solidarity.[181]

A **fantasy type** is a standard script that employs a renowned, spectacular form to explain new events, and is an umbrella term for a collection of recurring, related fantasy themes. A fantasy type is a standard scenario repeated many times by the same or similar characters and can contain recognizable script lines, scenes, situations, and representations of individuals.[182] For the Liberation Tigers of Tamil Eelam (LTTE) in Sri Lanka, there are quite a few symbols that play an important role in the identities of the group's militants. A symbol that is particularly salient is the set of discriminatory measures taken by the Sinhalese-dominated government. A second symbol was the series of anti-Tamil massacres that occurred in 1956, 1958, 1977, 1981, and 1983.[183] The Baader-Meinhof Group in Germany in the 1970s said that Bertolt Brecht's learning-play *The Measures Taken* ("Die Massnahme") was one of their most beloved texts.[184]

A **saga** is a detailed description of the achievements in the life of an individual, group, community, organization, or country. It is a concept that seems to be unique to rhetorical groups such as those that, over time, form as a physical unit.[185] When the Prophet Muhammad was alive, militant jihad was the state's device for changing dar ul-Harb (i.e., the infidels and corrupt societies living on earth) into dar ul-Islam (the divinely perfect and righteous house of the faithful). Those who opposed the rapid propagation of Islam had to fight or die until they either submitted to Muslims or were killed by them.[186] Members of the Japanese terrorist cult Aum Shinrikyo experienced delusions that their egomaniac guru, Shoko Asahara, was both God and the Savior, that numerous rituals and machines could replicate the brainwaves of the guru, that the world was en route for Armageddon, that the cult itself would save humanity from its decadence by causing the apocalypse, and that members of Aum Shinrikyo could be born again after the global catastrophe.[187] This anecdote mirrors the notion of **violent eschatology**—when a group believes it must start a war to cleanse the earth before the second coming of a god.[188]

A famous terrorist saga is that in which they imagine themselves as soldiers. The image that terrorists radiate about themselves—namely, as soldiers acting on behalf of a duty and

higher call—can be a tactic to avoid personal responsibility for terrorist attacks. This identification is a type of self-presentation and self-perception. It is a strategy to handle the
prospect of physical danger and the emotional aftereffect of harming others. Being a soldier is better than being a terrorist. It entails being part of a cooperative enterprise that is
externally authorized. For example, in the 1970s, Italian terrorists such as the Red Brigades
imagined themselves to be at war with the government. They undertook an important
fantasy mechanism that made their resolution to violence possible.[189]

SYMBOLS IN TERRORIST GROUPS

A symbol is a mental structure, a form of knowledge representation; that is, a figure that
stands for and takes the place of something else. For example, the cross is the most important symbol of Christianity. It is through symbols that humans know and understand the
world. By conceptualizing reality through symbols, humans can interpret it too. In other
words, we come up with symbols to make sense of our world. A symbol can also be some
conventional image (i.e., an icon), a detail of an image, or even a design or color. A case in
point is the color red frequently used as a symbol for socialist parties, especially communist parties. A symbol is usually embraced only within certain cultures, religions, or areas
of life. Several hundred symbols are now recognized all over the world.[190]

Symbols and Terrorism

Symbolism is a centerpiece of terrorism. Rallying symbols are usually as vital to a terrorist group as resources. Symbols seize the imagination or feelings of neutrals and drive
commitment to altering the status quo. The purpose is to capture the hearts and minds of
the terrorist constituency by investing in social projects and overthrowing the system.
Modern terrorists and their support base have become fairly good at designing symbolic
meaning out of terrorist acts. To some degree, most terrorist targets embody the uprightness of the terrorists' cause and the evil of the enemy they are trying to kill. Symbolism can
be exploited to justify extreme terrorist acts and can be warped to fit any target into the
grouping of an enemy interest.[191]

Symbolism can craft abstract ideological connections between terrorists and their
victims. This process was observed during the upsurge of kidnappings by Latin American
left-wing terrorists in the 1970s, when terrorists abducted civilian businesspeople and
diplomats. The kidnappers said they epitomized capitalism and exploitation. Symbolic
targets can also embody enemy social or political institutions. This was the case of the 1979
IRA killing of Lord Louis Mountbatten (the uncle of Prince Philip Mountbatten, Queen
Elizabeth II's husband) and the IRA's attempted killing of Margaret Thatcher, then British
prime minister, in 1984.[192] Even whole groups of individuals can be symbolically pigeon-
holed with a label and then slaughtered. This was the case with the genocides of the
Christian Armenians by the Muslim Turks in 1915 and the Jews by the Nazis (religious and
racial), the killing fields in Cambodia (social and political), the genocide in Rwanda (ethnic
and social), and the massacres of the Darfur region of Sudan (racial).[193]

Two historical cases of lethal terrorism in the U.S. confirm the important role of symbolism from the perspective of terrorists. The first case is the Oklahoma City bombing. Timothy McVeigh intentionally chose April 19 as a symbolic date for carrying out the bombing—it was the 220th anniversary of the battles of Lexington and Concord, and the second anniversary of the Waco tragedy that killed many members of the Branch Davidians (killed by U.S. law enforcement). The second case is 9/11. It was performed by nineteen Al Qaeda hijackers on a suicidal "martyrdom mission." They perpetrated the attacks to ruin symbols of American (and Western) imperialism. This was also a reaction to what they believed to be a perpetual process of domination and exploitation of Muslim nations.[194] Perlmutter (1998)[195] found that such symbols become icons and function as paradigms of particular events or issues. In turn, audiences will always remember news through such symbols—that they see through images, texts, and so forth.

Within the Hamas terrorist group, key symbols have contributed to Palestinian identity. These symbols include Zionist presence, the rise of Islamic awakening, and the signing of the Oslo Accords. Zionist presence is the occupation of Jews in "unauthorized" lands. Islamic awakening has been fomented by the Muslim Brotherhood, the National Liberation Movement (or Fatah), the era of mosque-building and social institution formation, and the continuously active Palestinian Islamic jihad.[196] All those symbols have shaped Palestinian identity, particularly as young male Muslims were inculcated into a philosophy of service and sacrifice in support of their group. The Oslo Accords, also called *the Declaration of Principles* (DOP), endorsed mutual recognition for the rights of Palestinians and Israelis to live side-by-side peacefully. The DOP also articulated a program regarding potential negotiations on Palestinian self-governance in the occupied lands. The DOP was not accepted by Hamas because territory considered to be sacred and assigned to the Arabs and Muslims was surrendered to Israel.[197]

Symbolism in Shi'ite Terrorism

Muslims are usually either Sunnis or Shi'ites. While Sunnis compose 85% of world Muslims, Shi'ites only represent 10% to 15% of world Muslims. Almost 40% of Shi'ites live in Iran. The **Shi'ites** are often more ecstatic (i.e., euphoric, thrilled, beatific, frenzied) in religious practice and have messianic hopes that a future prophet will bring justice on earth. The main differences between the Shi'ites and the Sunnis are traced to disputes over leadership after Muhammad died. Shi'ite Muslims believe that the martyred Imam Hussein, son of Ali (Muhammad's cousin and son-in-law), should have been the official successor of Muhammad. Then, Ali's descendants should have been the subsequent leaders. The most famous Shi'ite terrorist group is Hezbollah, created in Lebanon.[198]

To harden the Shi'ite doctrine and expand its organizational structure, Shi'ite Muslims have performed all kinds of symbolic practices. These symbolic practices are often evoked in day-to-day rhetoric—for instance by Shi'ite clerics. Symbols are particularly apparent during times of struggle, in religious ceremonies, and events organized by Shi'ite leaders worldwide.[199] A good example of Shi'ite symbolism exploited by terrorism is found in the Ashura procession. The **Ashura procession** is a method to reinforce Shi'ite activism. The Ashura celebrates the day Imam Hussein, son of Ali (Muhammad's successor, as the Shi'ites see it), was killed. Each year, the Shi'ites celebrate the event with mourning rituals in which they reenact the battle. Some of the participants flog themselves in processions. They flog themselves until they bleed. The purpose is to experience the pain that Hussein endured during the battle. To the Shi'ites, the battle epitomizes the heart of the rivalry between the Sunnis and the Shi'ites.[200] In January 2009, Hezbollah used the Muslim ceremony of Ashura in Lebanon to assemble its supporters against Israel. Tens of thousands of Hezbollah supporters marched the streets of the southern suburbs of Beirut (the capital city) to honor the martyrdom of Imam Hussein.[201]

After the 1979 Islamic revolution in Iran, led by the Ayatollah Khomeini (the First Supreme Leader of Iran), various terrorist groups sprung from many Shi'ite communities. Khomeini introduced a new concept into opposition against governments and democracies: the exploitation of religious symbols as a political device. This new Shi'ite dynamic set up charity funds to help the indigent and increase the numbers of meeting places (matams).[202] As a religious symbol of the Shi'ites, the **matams** are an ancient and deep-rooted institution that was launched hundreds of years ago. In Bahrain alone, where a huge Shi'ite population lives, there are as many as 400 matams. Matams are public congregations in which Shi'ites meet for solemn reasons (e.g., to mourn the loss of a relative) and to meet before or at the end of a religious procession. They are the meeting places of Shi'ite religious tributes; they are also social and political gatherings.[203]

The problem is that matams are not just exploited to create a political bond among Shi'ite members or increase Shi'ite identity; they are also used as breeding grounds for future terrorists. Shi'ite symbolism has proved to be an intelligent choice for terrorist groups. The Shi'ites' history is laden with dichotomies between oppressors and oppressed and the grave concern for social justice.[204] As noted by Arena and Arrigo (2005),[205] concepts such as social justice are religious symbols that are socially constructed. They direct or encourage people to respond (i.e., behave) in a certain way. For Sigmund Freud, violent religious symbols arouse, and thereby release, violent impulses overall. By allowing people to give vent to their emotional states of hostility toward members of other groups, symbols of violence allow in-groups to solidify their social cohesion.[206]

Symbolism in Hezbollah

Azani (2007)[207] thoroughly studied the role of symbolism among Shi'ite terrorists. The scholar noted that Shi'ites use symbols to the fullest extent as a significant means for social mobilization. In so doing, it expands their support base, helps them recruit new activists, and inspires proactive actions to fulfill the interests of terrorist groups such as Hezbollah. The Internet is one of the most useful tools for Hezbollah to disseminate its messages and affect public opinion by using Shi'ite symbols and crafting new symbols to promote Shi'ite interests. Below is a list of other symbols used by Hezbollah to garner attention and new recruits:

- Calendar of events: Hezbollah's calendar of events contains symbolic dates (e.g., religious memorial dates) that are used to recruit potential members into the terrorist group.

- World Jerusalem Day: the ceremony was initiated by Khomeini to accomplish the Sunni and Shi'ite common goal of attacking the Jews and delivering Jerusalem.

- Month of Ramadan: Hezbollah has connections with many Shi'ite circles; the purpose is to bring people closer to Islam and broaden the support for the fight against social injustice and discrimination.

- Definition of enemies: the Great Satan is the U.S. and the Little Satan is Israel. The concept of the Great Satan (and its association with the U.S.) was invented by Khomeini and is now used by Mahmoud Ahmadinejad, the current president of Iran (also a supporter of Hezbollah).

- Individual self-sacrifice: the readiness to sacrifice one's life in jihad against the enemies of Islam. The goal is to advance the Islamic community. By establishing this principle, Khomeini laid the foundations on which the phenomenon of suicide bombing is based.

In such religious-based terrorism, symbolism aims at enlisting the society and imparting in them themes such as religious activism, determinism, and disposition to make self-sacrifices for the furtherance of jihad and other Islamic causes.[208] Hezbollah today is so successful that it is even part of the Parliament of Lebanon and received $400 million from Iran alone in 2010.[209]

SOCIAL MARGINALIZATION

Social marginalization is the process of becoming or being made marginal in society. When one is in social marginalization, one is downgraded or consigned to a lower social status or outer limit, as of social standing.[210] When socially marginalized groups experience discrimination or if they perceive that they suffer from discrimination, then within such communities, some of them will be more sympathetic to radical ideologies that support the transformation of established, mainstream society. The objective of these changes is to advance the destiny of the disadvantaged group. Socially marginalized individuals do not have much to lose if the existing social order is preserved, but possibly a lot to gain if it is radically transformed.[211] For those born or raised in a milieu where they feel discriminated against because of their connections to ethnic communities, religions, and cultures that are marginalized, terrorism may become a remedy to their frustrations. This occasionally happens, even though the host country seems to be open through its media and political discourse. The marginalized individual will nevertheless feel that the host country is roughly closed in its daily intercultural face-to-face encounters with those ethnic communities, religions, and cultures. The situation can be exacerbated if the e-mails keeping them in contact with major leaders of their culture of origin aggravate their loneliness into heroic solitude.[212]

For example, retreat into seclusion from the mainstream may escalate the strength of collective thought: on analyzing a semi-quantitative review of life histories of over 1,500 Italian and German terrorists, della Porta (1992)[213] found that increased isolation was correlated with increased separation from social reality. In a similar fashion, many factors have been recognized as key elements in inspiring the political conflict in Northern Ireland from 1969 onward and for enlarging support within Catholic communities for terrorists. In the context of the conflict in Northern Ireland, these factors included financial deprivation, unsatisfactory educational performance, and lack of political representation. Among an underprivileged Catholic population, ideologies promoting regime change always had some support and, notwithstanding continuing discrimination, ideologies sponsoring violent actions to alter the status quo attracted widespread support from some circles.[214]

Social Marginalization of Future Jihadists

Social marginalization seems to be a recurrent factor in the upbringing of most jihadist recruits. Research has demonstrated that most members of terrorist groups such as Al Qaeda joined the jihad while living in a foreign nation or when they were secluded from older friends and relatives. Frequently, these people were expatriates—students, workers, refugees—living far from home.[215] Sageman (2004)[216] found that 70% joined the jihad in a country in which they were not born and raised; 8% were second generation and might not have been totally adapted to their host culture. In total, 78% of the recruits had been isolated from their social and cultural origins, living distantly from family and relatives.

In terms of jihadist extremism, it is now clear that Muslims in the West have a tendency to experience disadvantage—regardless of whether it is just or unjust. In comparison with the U.K. population overall, there are as three times unemployed Muslims as there are unemployed British; a higher percentage of Muslims is unqualified; and a higher proportion lives in deprived districts. Muslims are considerably underperforming in secondary schools and also lack representation in higher education. A little more than a third of the British population overall is not qualified, in comparison with 43% of Muslims. Considering such levels of disadvantage, it is not shocking that many Muslims have come to see themselves as discriminatorily marginalized. Once a Muslim community and the individuals within it feel conspicuously rejected from mainstream society, they lose much willingness to preserve that society.[217]

In Europe, new terrorist networks consist mainly of European-born Muslims—sons and grandsons of Muslim immigrants who went to Europe since the second half of the 20th century—and a small but growing number of Europeans who converted to Islam. On the whole, they have only marginal connections to structured terrorist organizations such as Al Qaeda, which they only see as a source of inspiration. They also tend to have a more unstructured beginning, often arising out of small groups of childhood friends who have adopted radical Islam when joining such a group with an older and charismatic figure.[218]

"Damascus Road" Conversion

A metaphor for sudden and radical conversion, a **"Damascus road" conversion** is a situation in which a person's fundamental outlook on life is rapidly changed. According to the Bible, on the road to Damascus, the Apostle Paul converted to a Jesus follower.[219] This type of path, indicated by a long time spent in the West, seems to have been taken by Pakistani terrorist Ahmed Omar Saeed Sheikh, the lethal man whom authorities suspect engineered the scheme to abduct *Wall Street Journal* reporter Daniel Pearl. Sheikh was born and raised in London.[220]

In some instances, Muslim immigrants in the West who turn into wild boys or girls—for example, drinking, drugging, and skirt-chasing—and have an epiphany one day that their depraved lives are going too far often experience a process in which they go back to their Islamic roots and adopt a very conservative and militant version of it. In this process, they begin to "feel the pain" for the suffering of others; at the same time, they do not admit their own "bad boy" image (what they were before that conversion to radical Islam). Instead, in their reacceptance of Islam and choice for a militant fundamentalist version of it, they subsequently remove and disown the bad boy aspect of self and project it onto Western society, now the evil one.

This is currently the case with Anjem Choudary, a former British judge who, in his dissolute youth, was a drinker, spoiled himself with casual sex, and smoked cannabis and took LSD. Today, Choudary is a radical Islamist militant who defended Osama bin Laden's terrorist actions against America and the West, wants the U.S. constitution to be replaced by the sharia law, and demands the Pope's execution.[221] In the process, such types of former bad boys and now radical Muslims have determined that America and the West must be punished or demolished.[222] By associating themselves with close-knit groups of extremists, the new recruits exchange their negative image of themselves with a positive, audacious, and heroic self-image that is armored by joining the group. Allegiance, belonging, and group dynamics begin to reinforce the need for tight-knit collectivity and positive self-image, both to the detriment of losing the "good" self and in the best interests of the group.[223]

Finally, after exposure to U.S. mass communications and education, many students in the Middle East go to the U.S. or other Western nations to obtain graduate degrees. For example, it is a fact that, in 1979, when the Shah of Iran was deposed by the Iranian revolution, Iranian students composed the largest body of foreign students in America. Some of them went back to Iran when the Grand Ayatollah Khomeini became the leader. These students helped decode the fragmented CIA documents in the embassy of the United States in Tehran (then occupied by students). Likewise, most terrorists directly implicated in the hijacking of the four airliners on September 11, 2001 had stayed a long time in the U.S. or other Western nations. Not only did they learn how to fly airplanes in the U.S., but, also, most of them were students there before joining terrorist groups. It is very possible that, during this time, they became frustrated and irritated with mainstream society, to such a degree that they started to contact terrorist organizations that were associated with their religious network.[224]

SUMMARY

A terrorist group is a group in which like-minded people share a common fate. Many people become terrorists through indoctrination techniques, which are very efficient in small groups (where trust and support are high). Terrorist groups tend to be like Communities of Practice (CoPs), learning groups in which terrorists engage in mutual learning, which allows them to adapt successfully to stress. We have also seen that the role of Social Identity Theory (SIT), the idea that in-groups see themselves as different from out-groups, is important to organizations like Al Qaeda, where new members are taught to hate the out-group (i.e., America and the West) and to avenge humiliations against the ummah (the global Muslim community). If one Islamic group is hurt or even just threatened by the out-group, all Muslims should join forces. To achieve this, terrorist groups will use tactics such as "advantageous comparisons" and scapegoating. The objective is to attribute all positive identifications for the in-group and all negative identifications for the out-group. Social identity also implies group norms, duties, prohibitions, and even sanctions. Along with SIT, small-group radicalization plays a huge role in modifying new members' beliefs and turning them into killing machines. This is certainly the case with jihadization, where people become radicalized in small groups first (usually networks of friends or family). Terrorism and group dynamics imply the notion of groupthink, a situation in which conflict seldom occurs as a result of high group cohesion. In a terrorist group, leaders generally impose a "one voice" policy where disagreement or variation is not accepted. Because terrorism often occurs in a group setting, a situation known as risky shift (or group extremity shift) may emerge. Overall, risky shift is a shift in the average opinion of members toward the opinion of the whole group. With respect to the recruitment of terrorists, different models were described: Gewehr and Daly's four models of recruitment, the "Staircase to Terrorism" model (a six-step model describing a long-term socialization process), and the five phases of social psychological conditioning (depluralization, self-deindividuation, other-deindividuation, dehumanization, and demonization). Of equal relevance in this chapter is the role of the support base, the sympathizers backing the terrorist groups, based on the pyramid model. The pyramid is the centerpiece for terrorist recruitment and protection. In most cases, terrorism increases correspondingly with popular support for terrorism. Yet, it can also decrease if popular support for terrorism does too. Likewise, a huge danger to a terrorist group's survival is loss of membership. In line with these contentions, the role of symbols in terrorist groups is of utmost importance. Symbolic convergence theory (SCT) explains it well. According to SCT, sharing group fantasies (e.g., jokes, narratives, metaphors, and human interpretations) leads to symbolic convergence. The basic unit of analysis of SCT is the fantasy theme. Fantasy themes are developed to accomplish rhetorical or psychological needs and can be employed to interpret a group's past, present, or future. Overall, terrorist groups tend to rely heavily on symbols to solidify their in-group cohesion. For example, for Hamas, key symbols have contributed to Palestinian identity. These symbols include Zionist presence, the rise of Islamic awakening, and the signing of the Oslo Accords. We have also described the role of symbolism in Shi'ite terrorism (e.g., matams and the Ashura procession). Lastly, this chapter discussed the role of social marginalization for future jihadists. As a certain number of Muslims feel discrimination in the countries where their families immigrated (mostly in the West), they will undergo a "Damascus road" conversion in which their fundamental outlook on life will rapidly change and become more sympathetic to radical ideologies.

KEY TERMS

advantageous comparison   242

aggregate   233

Ashura procession   263

cognitive centrality   238

collective identity   256

Community of Practice   236

confidence   238

"Damascus road" conversion   266

Declaration of Principles   263

dehumanization   256

deindividuation   254

demonization   256

ENDNOTES

1. Myers, Scott A., & Anderson, Carolyn M. (2008). *The Fundamentals of Small Group Communication.* Thousand Oaks, CA: Sage.

2. Lott, Bernice Eisman (1960). Group Cohesiveness: A Learning Phenomenon. *Journal of Social Psychology, 55,* 275–286.

3. Davis, James H. (1969). *Group Performance.* Reading, MA: Addison-Wesley Publishing.

4. Meyer, John P., & Herscovitch, Lynne (2001). Commitment in the Workplace: Toward a General Model. *Human Resource Management Review, 11,* 299–326.

5. Allen, Natalie J., & Meyer, John P. (1990). The Measurement and Antecedents of Affective, Continuance, and Normative Commitment to the Organization. *Journal of Occupational Psychology, 63,* 1–18.

6. Reich, Walter (1990). *Origins of Terrorism: Psychologies, Ideologies, Theologies, States of Mind*. Washington, D.C.: Woodrow Wilson Center / Baltimore, MD and London: Johns Hopkins University Press; Turk, Austin T. (2004). Sociology of Terrorism. *Annual Review of Sociology, 30*, 271–286.

7. Myers, Scott A., & Anderson, Carolyn M. (2008). *The Fundamentals of Small Group Communication*. Thousand Oaks, CA: Sage.

8. Olson, Mancur (1965). *The Logic of Collective Action: Public Goods and the Theory of Groups*. Cambridge, MA: Harvard University Press.

9. Davis, James H. (1969). *Group Performance*. Reading, MA: Addison-Wesley Publishing.

10. Mullen, Brian, & Cooper, Carolyn (1994). The Relation between Group Cohesiveness and Performance: An Integration. *Psychological Bulletin, 115*(2), 210–227.

11. Cooley, Charles Horton (1930). *Sociological Theory and Social Research*. New York: Henry Holt; Lott, Bernice Eisman (1960). Group Cohesiveness: A Learning Phenomenon. *Journal of Social Psychology, 55*, 275–286.

12. Moody, James, & White, Douglas R. (2003). Social Cohesion and Embeddedness. *American Sociological Review, 68*, 103–127.

13. Cartwright, Dorwin (1968). The Nature of Group Cohesiveness. In Dorwin Cartwright & Alvin Zander (Eds.), *Group Dynamics: Research and Theory* (pp. 91–107). New York: Harper & Row; Collins, Barry E., & Guetzkow, Harold (1961). *A Social Psychology of Group Processes for Decision-Making*. New York: Wiley; Verba, Sidney (1961). *Small Groups and Political Behavior: A Study of Leadership*. Princeton, NJ: Princeton University Press.

14. Graham, William K., & Dillon, Peter C. (1974). Creative Supergroups: Group Performance as a Function of Individual Performance on Brainstorming Tasks. *The Journal of Social Psychology, 93*(1), 101–105.

15. Moreland, Richard L., & Levine, John M. (1988). Group Dynamics over Time: Development and Socialization in Small Groups. In Joseph E. McGrath (Ed), *The Social Psychology of Time: New Perspectives* (pp. 151–181). Thousand Oaks, CA: Sage.

16. Pillar, Paul R. (2010). The Diffusion of Terrorism. *Mediterranean Quarterly, 21*(1), 1–14.

17. Lester, Scott W., Kickul, Jill R., & Bergmann, Thomas J. (2007). Managing Employee Perceptions of the Psychological Contract over Time: The Role of Employer Social Accounts and Contract Fulfillment. *Journal of Organizational Behavior, 28*(2), 191–208.

18. Solomon, Phyllis (2004). Peer Support/Peer Provided Services Underlying Processes, Benefits, and Critical Ingredients. *Psychiatric Rehabilitation Journal, 27*(4), 392–401.

19. Crenshaw, Martha (1988). The Subjective Reality of the Terrorist: Ideological and Psychological Factors in Terrorism. In Robert O. Slater & Michael Stohl (Eds.), *Current Perspectives on International Terrorism* (pp. 12–46). New York: St. Martin's; Sarason, Irwin, Levine, Henry, Basham, Robert, & Sarason, Barbara (1983). Assessing Social Support: The Social Support Questionnaire. *Journal of Personality and Social Psychology, 44*, 127-139; Soibelman, Mali (2004). Palestinian Suicide Bombers. *Journal of Investigative Psychology and Offender Profiling, 1*, 175–190.

20. Haidt, Jonathan (2001). The Emotional Dog and Its Rational Tail: A Social Intuitionist Approach to Moral Judgement. *Psychological Review, 108*(4), 814–834; Haidt, Jonathan (2007). The New Synthesis in Moral Psychology. *Science, 31*, 998–1002.

21. Greene, Josh, & Haidt, Jonathan (2002). How (and Where) Does Moral Judgement Work? *Trends in Cognitive Sciences, 6*(12), 517–523.

22. Bouhana, Noémie, & Wikström, Per-Olof H. (2008). *Theorizing Terrorism: Terrorism as Moral Action*. London: University of College London Research Reports.

23. Hairgrove, Frank, & McLeod, Douglas (2008). Circles Drawing Toward High Risk Activism: The Use of Usroth and Halaqa in Islamist Radical Movements. *Studies in Conflict and Terrorism, 31*, 399–411.

24. Sageman, Marc (2004). *Understanding Terror Networks*. Philadelphia: University of Pennsylvania Press.

25. Lave, Jean, & Wenger, Etienne (1991). *Situated Learning: Legitimate Peripheral Participation*. Cambridge: Cambridge University Press.

26. Kenney, Michael (2007). *From Pablo to Osama: Trafficking and Terrorist Networks, Government Bureaucracies, and Competitive Adaptation*. University Park, PA: Pennsylvania State University Press; Grabosky, Peter, & Stohl, Michael (2010). *Crime and Terrorism*. Los Angeles: Sage.

27. Sutherland, Edwin H., & Cressey, Donald (1947). *Principles of Criminology*. Philadelphia: J. B. Lippincott.

28. Coll, Steve (2004). *Ghost Wars: The Secret History of the CIA, Afghanistan, and Bin Laden, from the Soviet Invasion to September 10, 2001*. New York: Penguin; Grabosky, Peter, & Stohl, Michael (2010). *Crime and Terrorism*. Los Angeles: Sage; Horne, Alistair (1977). *A Savage War of Peace: Algeria 1954–1962*. New York: NYRB Classics.

29. Gutman, Nathan, & Melman, Yossi (2005). Jihad Trial. *Shalom L.A., 929*, 10–14; Vaisman-Tzachor, Reuben (2007). Profiling Terrorists. *Journal of Police Crisis Negotiations, 7*(1), 27–61.

30. McDermott, Terry (2005). *Perfect Soldiers*. New York: Harper Collins.

31. Vaisman-Tzachor, Reuben (2007). Profiling Terrorists. *Journal of Police Crisis Negotiations, 7*(1), 27–61.

32. Brown, Rupert (2000). *Group Processes* (2nd ed.). Oxford: Blackwell.

33. Tajfel, Henri, & Turner, John C. (1979). An Integrative Theory of Intergroup Conflict. In William G. Austin & Stephen Worchel (Eds.), *The Social Psychology of Intergroup Relations* (pp. 33–47). Monterey, CA: Brooks/Cole.

34. Rogers, M. Brooke, Loewenthal, Kate M., Lewis, Christpher Alan, Amlôt, Richard, Cinnirella, Marco, & Ansari, Humayan (2006). The Role of Religious Fundamentalism in Terrorist Violence: A Social Psychological Analysis. *International Review of Psychiatry, 19*(3), 253–262.

35. Tajfel, Henri; Turner, John C (2004). The Social Identity Theory of Intergroup Behavior. In John T. Jost, & Jim Sidanius (Eds.), *Political Psychology: Key Readings* (pp. 276–293). New York: Psychology Press.

36. Branscombe, Nyla R., & Wann, Daniel L. (1994). Collective Self-Esteem Consequences of Out-Group Derogation when a Valued Social Identity Is on Trial. *European Journal of Social Psychology, 24*, 641–657.

37. Levy, Becca (1996). Improving Memory in Old Age through Implicit Self-Stereotyping. *Journal of Personality and Social Psychology, 71*, 1092–1107.

38. Bar-Tal, Daniel (1998). Group Beliefs as an Expression of Social Identity. In Stephen Worchel, Francisco Morales, Dario Paez, & Jean-Claude Deschamps (Eds.), *Social Identity: International Perspectives* (pp. 93–113). Thousand Oaks, CA: Sage; Cameron, James E. (2004). A Three-Factor Model of Social Identity. *Self and Identity, 3*(3), 239–262.

39. Rice, Stephen K. (2009). Emotions and Terrorism Research: A Case for a Social-Psychological Agenda. *Journal of Criminal Justice, 37*(3), 248–255; Sageman, Marc (2008). *Leaderless Jihad*. Philadelphia: University of Pennsylvania Press.

40. Aho, James (1994). *This Thing of Darkness: A Sociology of the Enemy*. Seattle: University of Washington Press, p. 6.

41. Mansbach, Richard W. (2004). The Meaning of 11 September and the Emerging Postinternational World. In Stanley D. Brunn (Ed.), *11 September and Its Aftermath: The Geopolitics of Terror*. Oxford: Routledge.

42. Stern, Jessica (1999). *The Ultimate Terrorists*. Cambridge, MA: Harvard University Press; Taylor, Maxwell &, Ryan, Helen (1988). Fanaticism, Political Suicide and Terrorism. *Terrorism, 11*, 91–111.

43. Shamir, Jacob, & Shikaki, Khalil (2002). Self-Serving Perceptions of Terrorism among Israelis and Palestinians. *Political Psychology, 23*, 537–557.

44. Eriksson, Mikael, & Wallensteen, Peter (2004). Armed Conflict, 1989-2003. *Journal of Peace Research, 41*(5), 625–636.

45. Brym, Robert J., & Araj, Bader (2006). Suicide Bombing as Strategy and Interaction: The Case of the Second Intifada. *Social Forces, 84*, 1969–1986.

46. Bandura, Albert (1973). Social Learning Theory of Aggression. In John F. Knutson (Ed.), *The Control of Aggression: Implications from Basic Research* (pp. 201–250). Hawthorne, NY: Aldine.

47. Schmidtchen, Gerhard (1981). Terroristische Karrieren: Soziologische Analyse anhand von Fahndungsunterlagen und Prozessakten [Terrorist careers: Sociological analysis based on investigation and

trial documents]. In Herbert Jager, Gerhard Schmidtchen, & Lieselotte Sullwold (Eds.), *Analysen zum Terrorismus* [*Analysis of terrorism*] (Vol. 2). Opladen: Westdeutsther Verlag.

48. Katz, Irwin, Class David A., & Cohen, Sheldon (1973). Ambivalence, Guilt, and the Scapegoating of Minority Group Victims. *Journal of Experimental Social Psychology, 9*(5), 423–436.

49. Wright-Neville, David, & Smith, Debra (2009). Political Rage: Terrorism and the Politics of Emotion. *Global Change, Peace & Security, 21*(1), 85–98.

50. Jorisch, Avi (2004). *Beacon of Hatred: Inside Hizballah's Al-Manar Television*. Washington, D.C.: Washington Institute for Near East Policy.

51. Casebeer, William D. (2008). Identity, Culture and Stories: Empathy and the War on Terrorism. *Minnesota Journal of Law, Science & Technology, 9*(2), 653–688.

52. Durkheim, Emile (1995[1912]). *The Elementary Forms of Religious Life*. New York: The Free Press.

53. Norton, Augustus Richard (2007). *Hezbollah: A Short History*. Princeton, NJ: Princeton University Press.

54. Harik, Judith Palmer (2006). *Hezbollah: The Changing Face of Terrorism*. New York: I.B. Tauris.

55. Penslar, Derek Jonathan (2003). Transmitting Jewish Culture: Radio in Israel. *Jewish Social Studies, 10*(1), 1–29.

56. Liebes, Tamar., & Kampf, Zohar (2010). "Hello! This is Jerusalem Calling": The Revival of Spoken Hebrew on Mandatory Radio. *The Journal of Israeli History, 29*(2), 137–158.

57. Ben-Eliezer, Uri (2003). Civil Society and Military Society in Israel: Neo-Militarism and Anti-Militarism in the Post-Hegemonic Era. In Majid Al-Haj & Uri Ben-Eliezer (Eds.), *In the Name of Security* (pp. 29–76). Haifa: Haifa University Press; Culbert, David (2002). Eric Barnouw's War: An Interview Concerning the Armed Forces Radio Services' Education Unit, 1944–1945. *Historical Journal of Film, Radio & Television, 22*(4), 475–490.

58. Peri, Yoram (1999). Relations between Israeli Society and Army in a State of Crisis. *Megamot, 39*(4), 375–399.

59. McCauley, Clark, & Moskalenko, Sophia (2008). Mechanisms of Political Radicalization: Pathways toward Terrorism. *Terrorism and Political Violence, 30*(3), 415–433.

60. Sirseloudi, Matenia P. (2005). How to Predict the Unpredictable: On the Early Detection of Terrorist Campaigns. *Defense & Security Analysis, 21*(4), 369–386.

61. Bandura, Albert (1990). Mechanisms of Moral Disengagement in Terrorism. In Walter Reich (Ed.), *Origins of Terrorism: Psychologies, Ideologies, States of Mind* (pp. 161–191). Cambridge: Cambridge University Press; Bandura, Albert (2004). The Role of Selective Moral Disengagement in Terrorism and Counterrorism. In Fathali M. Moghaddam & Anthony J. Marsella (Eds.), *Understanding Terrorism: Psychosocial Roots, Consequences, and Interventions* (pp. 121–150). Washington, D.C.: American Psychological Association.

62. McCauley, Clark, & Moskalenko, Sophia (2008). Mechanisms of Political Radicalization: Pathways toward Terrorism. *Terrorism and Political Violence, 30*(3), 415–433.

63. Bloom, Mia M. (2005). *Dying to Kill: The Allure of Suicide Terror*. New York: Columbia University Press.

64. Fahoum, Keely M., & Width, Jon (2006). Marketing Terror: Effects of Anti-Messaging on GSPC Recruitment. *Strategic Insights, 5*(8), 10–21.

65. Pyszczynski, Tom, Abdollahi, Abdolhossein, Solomon, Sheldon, Greenberg, Jeff, Cohen, Florette, & Weise, David (2006). Mortality Salience, Martyrdom, and Military Might: The Great Satan Versus the Axis of Evil. *Personality and Social Psychology Bulletin, 32*(4), 525–537.

66. Silke, Andrew (2008). Holy Warriors: Exploring the Psychological Processes of Jihadi Radicalization. *European Journal of Criminology, 5*(1), 99–123.

67. Pyszczynski, Tom, Solomon, Sheldon, & Greenberg, Jeff (2002). *In the Wake of 9/11: The Psychology of Terror*. Washington, D.C.: American Psychological Association.

68. Pyszczynski, Tom, Abdollahi, Abdolhossein, Solomon, Sheldon, Greenberg, Jeff, Cohen, Florette, & Weise, David (2006). Mortality Salience, Martyrdom, and Military Might: The Great Satan Versus the Axis of Evil. *Personality and Social Psychology Bulletin, 32*(4), 525–537.

69. Brewer, Marilynn B. (2007). The Importance of Being "We": Human Nature and Intergroup Relations. *American Psychologist, 62*, 728–738; Strelan, Peter, & Lawani, Angelica (2010). Muslim and Westerner

Responses to Terrorism: The Influence of Group Identity on Attitudes toward Forgiveness and Reconciliation. *Peace and Conflict, 16*, 59–79.

70. McLernon, Frances, Cairns, Ed, Hewstone, Miles, & Smith, Ron (2004). The Development of Intergroup Forgiveness in Northern Ireland. *Journal of Social Issues, 60*, 587–601; Noor, Masi, Brown, Rupert, Gonzalez, Robert, Manzi, Jorge, & Lewis, Christopher A. (2008). On Positive Psychological Outcomes: What Helps Groups with a History of Conflict to Forgive and Reconcile with Each Other? *Personality and Social Psychology Bulletin, 34*, 819–832.

71. Sherif, Muzafer, Harvey, O. J., White, B. Jack, Hood, William R., & Sherif, Carolyn W. (1961). *The Robbers Cave Experiment: Intergroup Conflict and Cooperation*. Hanover, NH: Wesleyan University Press.

72. Gaertner, Samuel L., Dovidio, John F., Banker, Brenda S., Houlette, Missy, Johnson, Kelly M., & McGlynn, Elizabeth A. (2000). Reducing Intergroup Conflict: From Superordinate Goals to Decategorization, Recategorization, and Mutual Differentiation. *Group Dynamics: Theory, Research, and Practice, 4*, 98–114.

73. Wohl, Michael J. A., & Branscombe, Nyla R. (2005). Forgiveness and Collective Guilt Assignment to Historical Perpetrator Groups Depend on Level of Social Category Inclusiveness. *Journal of Personality and Social Psychology, 88*, 288–303.

74. Innes, Martin, Abbott, Lawrence, Lowe, Trudy, & Roberts, Colin (2007). *Hearts and Minds and Eyes and Ears: Reducing Radicalisation Risks through Reassurance-Oriented Policing*. Cardiff: Universities Police Science Institute.

75. Porter, Louise E., & Kebbell, Mark R. (2010). Radicalization in Australia: Examining Australia's Convicted Terrorists. *Psychiatry, Psychology and Law, 9*(1), 1–20.

76. Innes, Martin, Abbott, Lawrence, Lowe, Trudy, & Roberts, Colin (2007). *Hearts and Minds and Eyes and Ears: Reducing Radicalisation Risks through Reassurance-Oriented Policing*. Cardiff: Universities Police Science Institute; Silber, Mitchell D., & Bhatt, Arvin (2007). *Radicalization in the West: The Home Grown Threat*. New York: New York Police Department; White, Jonathan R. (2011). *Terrorism & Homeland Security* (7th ed.). Belmont, CA: Wadsworth.

77. Silber, Mitchell D., & Bhatt, Arvin (2007). *Radicalization in the West: The Home Grown Threat*. New York: New York Police Department.

78. Sageman, Marc (2004). *Understanding Terror Networks*. Philadelphia: University of Pennsylvania Press.

79. Bakker, Edwin (2006). *Jihadi Terrorists in Europe, Their Characteristics and the Circumstances in Which They Joined the Jihad: An Exploratory Study*. The Hague: Clingendael Institute.

80. Mekhennet, Souad (2011, March 8). Frankfurt Attack Mystifies Suspect's Family. *The New York Times*, p. A5.

81. Ministry of the Interior and Kingdom Relations (2006). *Violent Jihad in the Netherlands: Current Trends in the Islamist Terrorist Threat*. The Hague, Netherlands: General Intelligence and Security Service.

82. Silke, Andrew (2008). Holy Warriors: Exploring the Psychological Processes of Jihadi Radicalization. *European Journal of Criminology, 5*(1), 99–123.

83. Hairgrove, Frank, & McLeod, Douglas M. (2008). Circles Drawing toward High Risk Activism: The Use of Usroh and Halaqa in Islamist Radical Movements. *Studies in Conflict & Terrorism, 31*, 399–411.

84. Roy, Olivier (2000). Muslims in Europe: From Ethnic Identity to Religious Recasting. *ISIM Newsletter, 5*(1), 1–9; Woodberry, J. Dudley (1992). Conversion in Islam. In H. Newton Malony & Samuel Southard (Eds.), *Handbook of Religious Conversion* (pp. 22–40). Birmingham, AL: Religious Education Press.

85. Janis, Irving L. (1972). *Victims of Groupthink*. New York: Houghton Mifflin.

86. Abrams, Dominic, & Hogg, Michael A. (1990). Social Identification, Self Categorization and Social Influence. *European Review of Social Psychology, 1*, 195–228; Insko, Chester A., & Schopler, John (1998). Differential Distrust of Groups and Individuals. In Constantine Sedikides, John Schopler, & Chester A. Insko (Eds.), *Intergroup Cognition and Intergroup Behavior* (pp. 75–107). Hillsdale, NJ: Lawrence Erlbaum.

87. Post, Jerrold M., Sprinzak, Ehud, & Denny, Laurita M. (2003). The Terrorists in Their Own Words: Interviews with 35 Incarcerated Middle Eastern Terrorists. *Terrorism and Political Violence, 15*, 171–184.

88. Hoffer, Eric (1951). *The True Believer: Thoughts on the Nature of Mass Movements*. New York: Harper Perennial.

89. Friedland, Nehemia (1992). Becoming a Terrorist: Social and Individual Antecedents. In Laurence Howard (Ed.), *Terrorism: Roots, Impact, Responses* (pp. 81–93). New York: Praeger.

90. Janis, Irving L. (1968). Group Identification under Conditions of External Danger. In Dorwin Cartwright & Alvin Zander (Eds.), *Group Dynamics: Research and Theory* (pp. 80–90) New York: Harper & Row.

91. Janis, Irving L. (1968). Group Identification under Conditions of External Danger. In Dorwin Cartwright & Alvin Zander (Eds.), *Group Dynamics: Research and Theory* (pp. 80–90) New York: Harper & Row.

92. McCauley, Clark, & Moskalenko, Sophia (2008). Mechanisms of Political Radicalization: Pathways toward Terrorism. *Terrorism and Political Violence, 30*(3), 415–433.

93. Wallach, Michael A., & Kogan, Nathan (1965). The Roles of Information, Discussion, and Consensus in Group Risk Taking. *Journal of Experimental Social Psychology, 1*, 1–19; Wallach, Michael A., Kogan, Nathan, & Bern, Daryl J. (1962). Group Influence on Individual Risk Taking. *Journal of Abnormal and Social Psychology, 65*, 75–86; Wallach, Michael A., Korgan, Nathan, & Bern, Daryl J. (1964). Diffusion and Responsibility and Level of Risk Taking in Groups. *Journal of Abnormal and Social Psychology, 68*, 263–274.

94. Pynchon, Marisa, & Borum, Randy (1999). Assessing Threats of Targeted Group Violence: Contributions from Social Science. *Behavioural Sciences and the Law, 17*(3), 339–355; Silke, Andrew (2008). Holy Warriors: Exploring the Psychological Processes of Jihadi Radicalization. *European Journal of Criminology, 5*(1), 99–123.

95. Pruitt, Dean G. (1971). Choice Shifts in Group Discussion: An Introductory Review. *Journal of Personality and Social Psychology, 20*, 339–360.

96. Levinger, George, & Schneider, David J. (1969). Test of the "Risk as a Value" Hypothesis. *Journal of Personality and Social Psychology, 11*, 165–169; Miller, Claude, Matusitz, Jonathan, O'Hair, Dan, & Eckstein, Jacqueline (2008). The Role of Communication and the Media in Terrorism. In Dan O'Hair, Robert Heath, Kevin Ayotte, & Gerald R. Ledlow (Eds.), *Terrorism: Communication and Rhetorical Perspectives* (pp. 43–66). Cresskill, NJ: Hampton Press.

97. Collins, Barry E., & Guetzkow, Harold (1961). *A Social Psychology of Group Processes for Decision-Making.* New York: Wiley; Wilson, James Q. (1973). *Political Organizations.* New York: Basic Books.

98. Crenshaw, Martha (1992). Current Research on Terrorism: The Academic Perspective. *Studies in Conflict & Terrorism, 15*, 1–11; Wiedenhaefer, Robert M., Dastoor, Barbara Riederer, Balloun, Joseph, & Sosa-Fey, Josephine (2007). Ethno-Psychological Characteristics and Terror-Producing Countries: Linking Uncertainty Avoidance to Terrorist Acts in the 1970s. *Studies in Conflict & Terrorism, 30*, 801–823.

99. Bandura, Albert (1973). Social Learning Theory of Aggression. In John F. Knutson (Ed.), *The Control of Aggression: Implications from Basic Research* (pp. 201–250). Hawthorne, NY: Aldine; Dicks, Henry Victor (1972). *Licensed Mass Murder: A Socio-Psychological Study of Some S. S. Killers.* New York: Basic Books.

100. Neumann, Peter R., & Rogers, Brooke (2007). *Recruitment and Mobilisation for the Islamist Militant Movement in Europe.* London: University of London Press.

101. Stubbs, Richard (2004). *Hearts and Minds in Guerrilla Warfare: The Malayan Emergency: 1948–1960.* Singapore: Eastern University Press.

102. Clark, Robert P. (1983). Patterns in the Lives of ETA Members. *Terrorism: An International Journal, 6*, 423–454.

103. Post, Jerrold M. (2010). "When Hatred Is Bred in the Bone": The Social Psychology of Terrorism. *Annals of the American Academy of Political and Social Science, 1208*, 15–23; Silke, Andrew (2008). Holy Warriors: Exploring the Psychological Processes of Jihadi Radicalization. *European Journal of Criminology, 5*(1), 99–123.

104. Ansari, Humayan, Cinnirella, Marco, Rogers, M. Brooke, Loewenthal, Kate M., & Lewis, Christpher Alan (2006). Perceptions of Martyrdom and Terrorism amongst British Muslims. In M. Brooke Rogers, Christopher Alan Lewis, Kate M. Loewenthal, Marco Cinnirella, Richard Amlôt, & Humayan Ansari (Eds.), *Proceedings of the British Psychological Society Seminar Series Aspects of Terrorism and Martyrdom, eCOMMUNITY: International Journal of Mental Health & Addiction.*

105. Gerwehr, Scott, & Daly, Sara (2006). *Al-Qaida: Terrorist Selection and Recruitment.* Santa Monica: RAND Corporation.

106. Rosenau, William (2005). Al Qaida Recruitment Trends in Kenya and Tanzania. *Studies in Conflict & Terrorism, 28*(1), 1–10.

107. Moghaddam, Fathali M. (2005). The Staircase to Terrorism: A Psychological Exploration. *American Psychologist, 60*(2), 161–169.

108. Andoni, Lamis (1997). Searching for Answers: Gaza's Suicide Bombers. *Journal of Palestine Studies, 26*(4), 33–45.

109. Sprinzak, Ehud (1990). The Psychopolitical Formation of Extreme Left Terrorism in a Democracy: The Case of the Weathermen. In W. Reich (Ed.), *Origins of Terrorism: Psychologies, Ideologies, Theologies, States of Mind* (pp. 65–85). Cambridge: Cambridge University Press.

110. Innes, Martin (2004), Signal Crimes and Signal Disorders: Notes on Deviance as Communicative Action. *The British Journal of Sociology, 55*(3), 335–355.

111. Lifton, Robert J. (2000). *Destroying the World to Save It: Aum Shinrikyo, Apocalyptic Violence, and the New Global Terrorism.* New York: Picador.

112. Innes, Martin, Abbott, Lawrence, Lowe, Trudy, & Roberts, Colin (2007). *Hearts and Minds and Eyes and Ears: Reducing Radicalisation Risks through Reassurance-Oriented Policing.* Cardiff: Universities Police Science Institute.

113. Bakker, Edwin (2006). *Jihadi Terrorists in Europe, Their Characteristics and the Circumstances in Which They Joined the Jihad: An Exploratory Study.* The Hague: Clingendael Institute; Clark, Robert P. (1984). *The Basque Insurgents: ETA, 1952–1980.* Madison, WI: University of Wisconsin Press; Crenshaw, Martha (1985). An Organizational Approach to the Analysis of Political Terrorism. *Orbis, 39,* 19–21; Crenshaw, Martha (1986). The Psychology of Political Terrorism. In Margaret G. Hermann (Ed.), *Political Psychology* (pp. 379–413). San Francisco: Jossey-Bass.

114. Bouhana, Noémie, & Wikström, Per-Olof H. (2008). *Theorizing Terrorism: Terrorism as Moral Action.* London: University College of London Research Reports.

115. McCormick, Gordon H. (2003). Terrorist Decision Making. *Annual Review of Political Science, 6,* 473–507.

116. Moghaddam, Fathali M. (2005). The Staircase to Terrorism: A Psychological Exploration. *American Psychologist, 60*(2), 161–169.

117. Kruglanski, Arie W., & Fishman, Shira (2006). The Psychology of Terrorism: "Syndrome" versus "Tool" Perspectives. *Terrorism and Political Violence, 18,* 193–215.

118. Martin, Gus (2010). *Understanding Terrorism: Challenges, Perspectives, and Issues.* Thousand Oaks, CA: Sage.

119. Benjamin, Daniel, & Simon, Steven (2002). *The Age of Sacred Terror.* New York: Random House.

120. Crenshaw, Martha (1985). An Organizational Approach to the Analysis of Political Terrorism. *Orbis, 39,* 19–21; Crenshaw, Martha (1988). The Subjective Reality of the Terrorist: Ideological and Psychological Factors in Terrorism. In Robert O. Slater & Michael Stohl (Eds.), *Current Perspectives on International Terrorism* (pp. 12–46). New York: St. Martin's; della Porta, Donatella (1992). On Individual Motivations in Underground Political Organizations. In Donatella della Porta (Ed.), *Social Movements and Violence: Participation in Underground Organizations.* (pp. 3–28). Greenwich, CT: JAI; Ferracuti, Franco (1982). A Sociopsychiatric Interpretation of Terrorism. *Annals of the American Academy of Political and Social Science, 463,* 129–140; Post, Jerrold M. (1984). Notes on a Psychodynamic Theory of Terrorist Behavior. *Terrorism, 8,* 241–257.

121. Clayton, Claudia, Barlow, Sally, & Ballif-Spanvill, Bonnie (1998). Principles of Group Violence with a Focus on Terrorism. In H. V. Hall & L. C. Whitaker (Eds.), *Collective Violence* (pp. 277–311). Boca Raton, FL: CRC Press; Crenshaw, Martha (1992). How Terrorists Think: What Psychology Can Contribute to Understanding Terrorism. In Laurence Howard (Ed.), *Terrorism: Roots, Impact, Responses* (pp. 405–420). New York: Praeger; Wright-Neville, David, & Smith, Debra (2009). Political Rage: Terrorism and the Politics of Emotion. *Global Change, Peace & Security, 21*(1), 85–98.

122. Taylor, Donald M., & Louis, Winnifried (2004). Terrorism and the Quest for Identity. In Fathali Moghaddam & Anthony Marsella (Eds.), *Understanding Terrorism: Psychological Roots, Consequences, and Interventions* (pp. 169–186). Washington, D.C.: American Psychological Association.

123. Myers, Scott A., & Anderson, Carolyn M. (2008). *The Fundamentals of Small Group Communication.* Thousand Oaks, CA: Sage.

124. Kenney, Michael (2007). *From Pablo to Osama: Trafficking and Terrorist Networks, Government Bureaucracies, and Competitive Adaptation*. University Park: Pennsylvania State University Press.

125. Bourdieu, Pierre (1977). *Outline of a Theory of Practice*. Cambridge: Cambridge University Press.

126. Bouhana, Noémie, & Wikström, Per-Olof H. (2008). *Theorizing Terrorism: Terrorism as Moral Action*. London: University of College London Research Reports.

127. Neria, Yuval, Roe, David, Beit-Hallahmi, Benjamin, Mneimneh, Hassan, Balaban Alana, & Marshall, Randall (2005). The Al Qaeda 9/11 Instructions: A Study in the Construction of Religious Martyrdom. *Religion, 35*, 1–11.

128. Procter, Thomas Hayes (1920). The Motives of the Soldier. *International Journal of Ethics, 31*(1), 26–50.

129. Moghaddam, Fathali (2003). Palestinian Suicide Terrorism in the Second Intifada: Motivations and Organizational Aspects. *Studies in Conflict and Terrorism, 26*, 65–92.

130. Soibelman, Mali (2004). Palestinian Suicide Bombers. *Journal of Investigative Psychology and Offender Profiling, 1*, 175–190.

131. Hoffman, Bruce (1993). Terrorist Targeting: Tactics, Trends, and Potentialities. In Paul Wilkinson (Ed.), *Technology and Terrorism* (pp. 1–11). London: Frank Cass.

132. Hoffman, Bruce, & McCormick, Gordon (2004). Terrorism, Signaling, and Suicide Attack. *Studies in Conflict and Terrorism, 27*(4), 243–281.

133. Burdman, Daphne (2003). Education, Indoctrination, and Incitement: Palestinian Children on Their Way to Martyrdom. *Terrorism and Political Violence, 15*(1), 96–123.

134. O'Leary, Michael M. (2000). A la Bayonet, or, "Hot Blood and Cold Steel." *Canadian Infantry Journal, 34*, 10–21.

135. Bion, Wilfred (1959). *Experiences in Groups*. New York: Basic Books.

136. Miller, Eric (1998). A Note on the Protomental System and "Groupishness": Bion's Basic Assumptions Revisited. *Human Relations, 51*, 1495–1508.

137. Jaques, Elliott (1996). *Requisite Organisation*. Gloucester, England: Cason Hall.

138. Stahelski, Anthony (2004). Terrorists Are Made, Not Born: Creating Terrorists Using Social Psychological Conditioning. *Journal of Homeland Security, 7*, 10–21.

139. Stahelski, Anthony (2004). Terrorists Are Made, Not Born: Creating Terrorists Using Social Psychological Conditioning. *Journal of Homeland Security, 7*, 10–21.

140. Singer, Margaret Thaler, & Lalich, Janja (1995). *Cults in Our Midst: The Hidden Menace in Our Everyday Lives*. San Francisco: Jossey-Bass.

141. Akhtar, Salman (1999). The Psychodynamic Dimension of Terrorism. *Psychiatric Annals, 29*(6), 350–355.

142. Martin, Walter, & Zacharias, Ravi (2003). *The Kingdom of the Cults*. Grand Rapids, MI: Bethany House.

143. Aronson, Elliot, Wilson, Timothy D., & Akert, Robin M. (2002). *Social Psychology: The Heart and the Mind*. New York: HarperCollins; Morgan, Stephen J. (2001). *The Mind of a Terrorist Fundamentalist: The Psychology of Terror Cults*. Cincinnati, OH: Awe-Struck E-Books.

144. Postmes, Tom, & Spears, Russell (1998). Deindividuation and Antinormative Behavior: A Meta-Analysis. *Psychological Bulletin, 123*(3), 238–259.

145. Orléan, André (1995). Bayesian Interactions and Collective Dynamics of Opinion: Herd Behavior and Mimetic Contagion. *Journal of Economic Behavior & Organization, 28*(2), 257–274.

146. Post, Jerrold M. (2010). "When Hatred Is Bred in the Bone": The Social Psychology of Terrorism. *Annals of the American Academy of Political and Social Science, 1208*, 15–23.

147. Diamond, Michael A. (2002). The Group Psychology of Terrorism. In Tushar K. Ghosh, Mark A. Prelas, Dabir Viswanath, & Sudarshan K. Loyalka (Eds.), *Science and Technology of Terrorism and Counterterrorism* (pp. 30–40). Boca Raton, FL: CRC Press. Pech, Richard J., & Slade, Bret W. (2006). Religious Fundamentalism and Terrorism: Why Do They Do It and What Do They Want? *Foresight, 8*(1), 8–20.

148. Tajfel, Henri (1982). *Social Identity and Intergroup Relations*. Cambridge: Cambridge University Press; Waller, James (2002). *Becoming Evil: How Ordinary People Commit Genocide and Mass Killing*. Oxford: Oxford University Press.

149. Taylor, Donald M., & Louis, Winnifried (2004). Terrorism and the Quest for Identity. In Fathali Moghaddam & Anthony Marsella (Eds.), *Understanding Terrorism: Psychological Roots, Consequences, and Interventions* (pp. 169–186). Washington, D.C.: American Psychological Association.

150. Volkan, Vamik (1999a). Psychoanalysis and Diplomacy: Part I—Individual and Large Group Identity. *Journal of Applied Psychoanalytic Studies, 1,* 29–55.

151. Bloom, Mia (2005). *Dying to Kill: The Allure of Suicide Terror.* New York: Columbia University Press; Pedahzur, Ami, Perliger, Arie, & Weinberg, Leonard (2003). Altruism and Fatalism: The Characteristics of Palestinian Suicide Bombers. *Deviant Behavior, 24*(4), 405–423; Post, Jerrold M. (2005). The New Face of Terrorism: Socio-Cultural Foundations of Contemporary Terrorism. *Behavioral Sciences and the Law, 23,* 451–465; Stern, Jessica (2003). *Terror in the Name of God: Why Religious Militants Kill.* New York: Harper-Collins.

152. Volkan, Vamik (1999b). Psychoanalysis and Diplomacy: Part II—Large Group Rituals. *Journal of Applied Psychoanalytic Studies, 1,* 223–247.

153. Stahelski, Anthony (2004). Terrorists Are Made, Not Born: Creating Terrorists Using Social Psychological Conditioning. *Journal of Homeland Security, 7,* 10–21.

154. Lifton, Jay (1989). *Thought Reform and the Psychology of Totalism: A Study of "Brainwashing" in China.* Chapel Hill, NC: University of North Carolina Press; Lifton, Jay (1999). *Destroying the World to Save It: Aum Shinrikyo, Apocalyptic Violence and the New Global Terrorism.* New York: Metropolitan Books.

155. McCauley, Clark (2004). Psychological Issues in Understanding Terrorism and the Response to Terrorism. In Chris Stout (Ed.), *The Psychology of Terrorism* (pp. 36–37). Westport, CT: Greenwood.

156. Silke, Andrew (2003). Becoming a Terrorist. In Andrew Silke (Ed.), *Terrorists, Victims and Society: Psychological Perspectives on Terrorism and Its Consequences* (pp. 29–53). West Sussex, England: John Wiley & Sons.

157. McCauley, Clark, & Moskalenko, Sophia (2008). Mechanisms of Political Radicalization: Pathways toward Terrorism. *Terrorism and Political Violence, 30*(3), 415–433.

158. O'Meyer, Christoph (2009). International Terrorism as a Force of Homogenization? A Constructivist Approach to Understanding Cross-National Threat Perceptions and Responses. *Cambridge Review of International Affairs, 22*(4), 647–666; Sprinzak, Ehud (2001). The Lone Gunmen: The Global War on Terrorism Faces a New Brand of Enemy. *Foreign Affairs, 10,* 72–73.

159. Griset, Pamela L., & Mahan, Sue (2003). *Terrorism in Perspective.* Thousand Oaks, CA: Sage.

160. Dugan, Laura, Huang, Julie, LaFree, Gary, & McCauley, Clark (2008). Sudden Desistance from Terrorism: The Armenian Secret Army for the Liberation of Armenia and the Justice Commandos of the Armenian Genocide. *Dynamics of Asymmetric Conflict, 1,* 231–249.

161. Grabosky, Peter, & Stohl, Michael (2010). *Crime and Terrorism.* Los Angeles: Sage.

162. LaFree, Gary, & Dugan Laura (2009). Tracking Global Terrorism Trends, 1970-2004. In David Weisburd, Thomas E. Feucht, Idit Hakimi, Lois F Mock, Simon Perry (Eds.), *To Protect and to Serve: Police and Policing in an Age of Terrorism* (pp. 43–80). New York: Springer.

163. Jones, Seth G., & Libicki, Martin C. (2008). *How Terrorist Groups End: Lessons for Countering Al Qa'ida.* Santa Monica: RAND.

164. Dugan, Laura, Huang, Julie, LaFree, Gary, & McCauley, Clark (2008). Sudden Desistance from Terrorism: The Armenian Secret Army for the Liberation of Armenia and the Justice Commandos of the Armenian Genocide. *Dynamics of Asymmetric Conflict, 1,* 231–249.

165. LaFree, Gary, & Ackerman, Gary (2009). The Empirical Study of Terrorism: Social and Legal Research. *Annual Review of Law and Social Science, 5,* 347–374.

166. Orsini, Alessandro (2011). *Anatomy of the Red Brigades: The Religious Mind-Set of Modern Terrorists.* Ithaca, NY: Cornell University Press.

167. Drake, Richard (1989). *The Revolutionary Mystique and Terrorism in Contemporary Italy.* Bloomington: Indiana University Press.

168. The Red Brigades: A Manifesto (2002, March 21). *Caserta 24: The Text of Demands of the Red Brigades.*

169. Bormann, Ernest G. (1972). Fantasy and Rhetorical Vision: The Rhetorical Criticism of Social Reality. In Bernard L. Brock (Ed.), *Methods of Rhetorical Criticism* (pp. 211–222). Detroit: Wayne State University Press.

170. Bormann, Ernest G. (1982). Fantasy and Rhetorical Vision: Ten Years Later. *Quarterly Journal of Speech, 68*, 288–305; Bormann, Ernest G. (1985). Symbolic Convergence Theory: A Communication Formulation. *Journal of Communication, 35*, 128–138.

171. Bormann, Ernest G., Cragan, John F., & Shields, Donald C. (2001). Three Decades of Developing, Grounding, and Using Symbolic Convergence Theory (SCT). In William B. Gudykunst (Ed.), *Communication Yearbook 25* (pp. 271–313). Mahwah, NJ: Lawrence Erlbaum; Bormann, Ernest G., Cragan, John F., & Shields, Donald C. (2003). Defending Symbolic Convergence Theory from an Imaginary Gunn. *Quarterly Journal of Speech, 89*, 366–372.

172. Malinowski, Bronislaw (1954). *Magic, Science and Religion and Other Essays*. Garden City, NY: Doubleday.

173. Rowland, Robert C., & Theye, Kirsten (2008). The Symbolic DNA of Terrorism. *Communication Monographs, 75*(1), 52–85.

174. Malinowski, Bronislaw (1954). *Magic, Science and Religion and Other Essays*. Garden City, NY: Doubleday; Richardson, Louise (2006). *What Terrorists Want: Understanding the Enemy, Containing the Threat*. New York: Random House.

175. Piven , Jerry S. (2007). Psychological, Theological, and Thanatological Aspects of Suicidal Terrorism. *Case Western Reserve Journal of International Law, 39*(3), 731–758.

176. Burke, Kenneth (1966). *Language as Symbolic Action: Essays on Life, Literature, and Method*. Berkeley: University of California Press; Burke, Kenneth (2003). Archetype and Entelechy, 1972. In William H. Rueckert & Angelo Bonadonna (Eds.), *On Human Nature: A Gathering While Everything Flows, 1967–1984* (pp. 121–138). Berkeley: University of California Press.

177. Rowland, Robert C., & Theye, Kirsten (2008). The Symbolic DNA of Terrorism. *Communication Monographs, 75*(1), 52–85.

178. Lévi-Strauss, Claude (1966). *The Savage Mind*. Chicago: University of Chicago Press.

179. Tattarini, Mirko (2007). Kamikaze Cyberpunk: Threats and Alternatives in the Age of Viral Power. In Boaz Ganor, Katharina Von Knop, and Carlos Duarte (Eds.), *Hypermedia Seduction for Terrorist Recruiting* (pp. 188–198). Amsterdam: NATO Science for Peace and Security Series.

180. Bormann, Ernest G., Cragan, John F., & Shields, Donald C. (2001). Three Decades of Developing, Grounding, and Using Symbolic Convergence Theory (SCT). In William B. Gudykunst (Ed.), *Communication Yearbook 25* (pp. 271–313). Mahwah, NJ: Lawrence Erlbaum.

181. Klatch, Rebecca (1998). Of Meanings and Masters: Political Symbolism and Symbolic Action. *Policy, 21*(1), 137–154.

182. St. Antoine, Thomas J., Althouse, Matthew T., & Ball, Moya A. (2005). Fantasy-Theme Analysis. In Jim A. Kuypers (Ed.), *The Art of Rhetorical Criticism* (pp. 212–240). Boston: Pearson Education.

183. Ponnambalam, Satchi (1983). *Sri Lanka: The National Question and the Tamil Liberation Struggle*. London: Zed; Tamil Information Centre (2001). *Tamils of Sri Lanka: The Quest for Human Dignity*. London: Tamil Information Centre.

184. Wessendorf, Markus (2005). Culture of Fear: Uncomfortable Transactions between Performance, Theatre and Terrorism. *International Journal of the Humanities, 3*(3), 217–228.

185. Bormann, Ernest G., Cragan, John F., & Shields, Donald C. (2001). Three Decades of Developing, Grounding, and Using Symbolic Convergence Theory (SCT). In William B. Gudykunst (Ed.), *Communication Yearbook 25* (pp. 271–313). Mahwah, NJ: Lawrence Erlbaum.

186. Gendron, Angela (2010). Confronting Terrorism in Saudi Arabia. *International Journal of Intelligence and CounterIntelligence, 23*(3), 487–508.

187. Lifton, Robert J. (2000). *Destroying the World to Save It: Aum Shinrikyo, Apocalyptic Violence, and the New Global Terrorism*. New York: Picador.

188. White, Jonathan R. (2011). *Terrorism & Homeland Security* (7th ed.). Belmont, CA: Wadsworth.

189. Ferracuti, Franco, & Bruno, Francesco (1983). Italy: A Systems Perspective. In Arnold P. Goldstein & Marshall H. Segall (Eds.), *Aggression in Global Perspective* (pp. 287–312). Elmsford, NY: Pergamon Press.

190. Deely, John (1990). *Basics of Semiotics*. Tartu, Estonia: Tartu University Press; Fiske, John (1982). *Introduction to Communication Studies*. New York: Methuen.

191. Martin, Gus (2010). *Understanding Terrorism: Challenges, Perspectives, and Issues*. Thousand Oaks, CA: Sage.

192. Martin, Gus (2010). *Understanding Terrorism: Challenges, Perspectives, and Issues*. Thousand Oaks, CA: Sage.

193. Springer, Jane (2006). *Genocide*. Toronto: Groundwood Books.

194. Lou, Michel, & Herbeck, Dan (2001). *American Terrorist: Timothy McVeigh & the Oklahoma City Bombing*. New York: HarperCollins.

195. Perlmutter, David (1998). *Photojournalism and Foreign Policy: Framing Icons of Outrage in International Crisis*. Westport, CT: Greenwood.

196. Caplan, Neil (2009). *Israel-Palestine Conflict: Contested Histories*. London: Wiley-Blackwell.

197. Arrigo, Bruce A. (2010). Identity, International Terrorism and Negotiating Peace: Hamas and Ethics-Based Considerations from Critical Restorative Justice. *British Journal of Criminology, 50*, 772–790.

198. Nasr, Vali (2006). When the Shiites Rise. *Foreign Affairs, 85*(4), 58–74; Norton, August Richard (2007). The Shiite "Threat" Revisited. *Current History, 10*, 434–439.

199. Azani, Eitan (2007). Islam & Political Symbolism: Hezbollah as a Case Study. In Boaz Ganor, Kathrina von Knop, & Carlos Duarte (Eds.), *Hypermedia Seduction for Terrorist Recruiting* (pp. 14–34). Amsterdam: IOS Press.

200. Jones, Toby Craig (2010). *Desert Kingdom: How Oil and Water Forged Modern Saudi Arabia*. Cambridge, MA: Harvard University Press.

201. Antelava, Natalia (2009, January 9). Hezbollah Woos Crowds at Ashura Rally. BBC News. Retrieved on May 1, 2011 from http://news.bbc.co.uk/2/hi/7816675.stm.

202. Bahry, Louay (2000). The Socioeconomic Foundations of the Shiite Opposition in Bahrain. *Mediterranean Quarterly, 10*, 129–143.

203. Pinault, David (1992). *The Shiites: Ritual and Popular Piety in a Muslim community*. New York: Palgrave Macmillan.

204. Bahry, Louay (2000). The Socioeconomic Foundations of the Shiite Opposition in Bahrain. *Mediterranean Quarterly, 10*, 129–143.

205. Arena, Michael P., & Arrigo, Bruce A. (2005). Social Psychology, Terrorism, and Identity: A Preliminary Re-examination of Theory, Culture, Self, and Society. *Behavioral Sciences and the Law, 23*, 485–506.

206. Juergensmeyer, Mark (2008). Martyrdom and Sacrifice in a Time of Terror. *Social Rsearch, 75*(2), 417–434.

207. Azani, Eitan (2007). Islam & Political Symbolism: Hezbollah as a Case Study. In Boaz Ganor, Kathrina von Knop, & Carlos Duarte (Eds.), *Hypermedia Seduction for Terrorist Recruiting* (pp. 14–34). Amsterdam: IOS Press.

208. Ranstorp, Magnus (1996). Terrorism in the Name of Religion. *Journal of International Affairs, 50*(1), 41–63.

209. Iran Massively Rearming Hezbollah in Violation of UN Security Council Resolution (2010, March 28). *American Chronicle*.

210. Mullaly, Bob (2007). Oppression: The Focus of Structural Social Work. In Bob Mullaly (Ed.), *The New Structural Social Work* (pp. 252–286). Don Mills, Ontario: Oxford University Press.

211. Sageman, Marc (2004). *Understanding Terror Networks*. Philadelphia: University of Pennsylvania Press.

212. Ravault, René-Jean (2002). Is there a Bin Laden in the Audience? Considering the Events of September 11 as a Possible Boomerang Effect of the Globalization of US Mass Communication. *Prometheus, 20*(3), 295–300.

213. della Porta, Donatella (1992). Political Socialization in Left-Wing Underground Organizations: Biographies of Italian and German militants. *International Social Movement Research, 4*, 259–290.

214. O'Leary, Brendan (2007). IRA: Irish Republican Army (Oglaigh na hEireann). In Marianne Heiberg, Brendan O'Leary, John Tirman (Eds.) *Terror, Insurgency and the State* (pp. 189–228). Philadelphia: University of Pennsylvania Press; Silke, Andrew (2008). Holy Warriors: Exploring the Psychological Processes of Jihadi Radicalization. *European Journal of Criminology, 5*(1), 99–123.

215. Silke, Andrew (2008). Holy Warriors: Exploring the Psychological Processes of Jihadi Radicalization. *European Journal of Criminology, 5*(1), 99–123.

216. Sageman, Marc (2004). *Understanding Terror Networks*. Philadelphia: University of Pennsylvania Press.

217. National Statistics Online (2007b). *Labour Market*. Retrieved July 10, 2008 http://www.statistics.gov.uk/cci/nugget.asp?id979; Silke, Andrew (2008). Holy Warriors: Exploring the Psychological Processes of Jihadi Radicalization. *European Journal of Criminology, 5*(1), 99–123.

218. Vidino, Lorenzo (2007). The Hofstad Group: The New Face of Terrorist Networks in Europe. *Studies in Conflict & Terrorism, 30*, 579–592.

219. Lofland, John, & Skonovd, Norman (1981). Conversion Motifs. *Journal for the Scientific Study of Religion, 20*(4), 373–385.

220. Stern, Jessica (2003). The Protean Enemy. *Foreign Affairs, 82*(4), 27–38.

221. The Unholy Past of the Muslim Cleric Demanding the Pope's Execution (2006, September 19). *London Evening Standard*, p. A1.

222. deMause, Lloyd (2002). *The Emotional Life of Nations*. New York: Karnac Books.

223. Sageman, Marc (2004). *Understanding Terror Networks*. Philadelphia: University of Pennsylvania Press.

224. Ravault, René-Jean (2002). Is there a Bin Laden in the Audience? Considering the Events of September 11 as a Possible Boomerang Effect of the Globalization of US Mass Communication. *Prometheus, 20*(3), 295–300.

Organizational Structure and Leadership in Terrorism

> **After reading this chapter, you will be able to**
>
> - describe the organizational structures of terrorist groups;
> - discuss two types of terrorist leadership: authoritarian leadership and charismatic leadership; and
> - understand social network analysis (SNA) and how social networks are used by terrorists to improve their capabilities.

TRADITIONAL ORGANIZATIONAL STRUCTURE IN TERRORISM

Terrorist organizations are able to wreak havoc thanks to the organizational structure that supports their actions. *Organizational structure* refers to the arrangement of an organization, which includes the pattern of authority and process of communication.[1] An **organization** is a collectivity consisting of and maintained by people. These people may leave, lose life, or switch allegiances, but the organization can survive. Residual members can assume the roles of those who are no longer members, new recruits can join, and the organizational structure can be expanded or revamped.[2] This section covers general perspectives on traditional organizational structure in terrorism. Specifically described here are the pyramidal (or hierarchical) structure and the horizontal structure.

Pyramidal (or Hierarchical) Structure

The way terrorists organize themselves into hierarchies is the way of the pyramid. As an analogy to compare with the ancient Egyptian edifice, the terrorist pyramidal structure displays a massive base of support culminating in a small number of terrorists (i.e., the leaders) at the top. The most common task in terrorist organizations is support, not combat. A pyramidal (or hierarchical) structure is like vertical differentiation; it has strata or gradations of hierarchy and supervision. Vertical organizations view hierarchical organizations similar to the Baader-Meinhof Group, whose operation is demarcated by an obvious set of leaders and subordinates.[3]

According to Fraser and Fulton (1984),[4] the terrorist hierarchical structure is divided into four levels. The smallest group, at the top of the pyramid, is the one that commands. Leaders establish policy and plans, and offer general guidance. The command structure in a terrorist group is usually not free to communicate straightforwardly or overtly with its members. Therefore, it finds it difficult to exercise daily operational control. The level right below the command structure is the **active cadre**, or the individuals responsible for executing the mission of the terrorist organization. Based on the organization's size, each terrorist in the cadre may be skilled in one or several areas. Other terrorists provide support to each area of expertise, but the active cadre is the unit of attack for the terrorist organization. After the command structure, the active cadre is the smallest unit in most terrorist hierarchical structures.

The third level of the pyramidal structure, a larger one (and the most important one), comprises the active supporters. These are crucial to terrorist campaigns. Any terrorist organization can perform a bombing or kidnapping, but keeping up a campaign of bombings and kidnappings requires support. Active supporters work hard to maintain the terrorists in action. They preserve communication channels, supply safe houses, collect intelligence, and make sure that all other logistical essentials are met. The fourth and largest group is the organization's passive supporters. This group can be very difficult to identify, classify, or describe because passive supporters do not always support terrorist groups openly. Nevertheless, they make up a favorable constituent of the political climate. When a terrorist organization can rally political support, it will have a considerable number of passive supporters.

Horizontal Structure

Since the 1990s, the nature of terrorist organizational structures has increasingly moved toward more horizontally complex organizations. Instead of adopting an incorporated top management, terrorist operations are grouped into divisions (based on product line or region). Thus, there is no pyramid of command. Most terrorist organizations number fewer than fifty members as active supporters, cadre, and leaders. Typically, they do not have the power to launch a long-term campaign from a few people at the top. They need to spread really thin. Under the leadership of only a handful of people, the organization is divided according to particular tasks. Intelligence sections are responsible for evaluating targets and mounting operations. Support sections supply the means needed to perform an attack. Tactical units are the ones to execute the actual terrorist action.[5] What is described here is sometimes called **strategic differentiation**, referring to organizations that have operating tasks in various areas or specialties. Terrorist groups like Hamas are horizontally structured; they assign tasks to members based on their expertise. They are also loosely organized cells in which members operate overtly through mosques and social services while others operate more secretly elsewhere—a phenomenon called **spatial differentiation**.[6] Later in this chapter, a substantial argument will be made on a few forms of horizontal structure—namely, certain types of social networks and terrorist cells.

TRADITIONAL LEADERSHIP IN TERRORISM

A distinction needs to be made, in terms of terrorist roles, between leaders and followers. While leaders tend to have more latent dispositions and features (acquired through socialization) that turn violent, stressful oppositional behavior into something attractive, followers tend to be more attracted to the organization than to its activities. Followers show significant affiliative needs.[7] For Sullwold (1981),[8] there is a remarkable difference between leaders and followers. While it is hard to conceive what a typical terrorist looks like, leaders have a higher tendency to be the ones who blend a lack of integrity with tremendous self-assurance and influence. Certainly, successful terrorist leaders are influential.

Leadership Influence

The most efficient terrorist leaders—whether through traditional or unconventional leadership—are capable of influencing terrorist activities at three levels: strategic, operational, and tactical influence.

- Strategic influence: the capacity to identify the top-level goals and missions of the terrorist organization. For instance, through his speeches and **fatwas** (i.e., legal pronouncements of death) that he frequently issued, Osama bin Laden defined the strategic missions of the new jihad.[9]

- Operational influence: the capacity to run or influence the activities and operations being performed to reach the organization's strategic goals. Examples of operational control in terrorist organizations include Osama bin Laden's plot and arrangement of the September 11, 2001 attacks and his tactful selection of targets.[10]

- Tactical influence: the capacity to run or influence the specific activities an individual member or unit of the organization fulfills on a daily basis. An example of tactical influence is the command of a cell leader; he or she directs an operation or runs the logistical or other activities that support cell members. In the September 11, 2001 scheme, Mohammed Atta had top tactical control of the operational cell, although Osama bin Laden would usually have the final say in terms of the tactical details of the operation—namely, what targets to choose and the timing of the attacks through the communication channels available at that time (particularly the few days preceding that fatal day).[11]

The following subsections look at two broad types of traditional leadership in terrorism: (1) authoritarian leadership and (2) charismatic leadership. The difference between authoritarian and charismatic leadership is fairly simple. In the first case, decision making is very centralized and the leader has more power for rewards and punishments. In the second case, the leader is not necessarily a totalitarian person but a very influential individual whose charisma (i.e., divine-like conferred power) is so strong that the followers are willing to commit any act to fulfill the mission that their leader has envisioned. An example drawing on the first type is the Provisional Irish Republican Army (PIRA). Examples used to explain the second type are Al Qaeda (mostly) and the Chechen terrorists.

Authoritarian Leadership

Leaders may exert authority by compelling or pressuring their followers. **Authoritarian leadership** is based on powerful controlling tactics and central organizational decision making. Terrorist groups that have authoritarian leaders also have closed decision-making structures and processes that are controlled by the leader and specifically designated personnel.[12] Most other members of the terrorist organization are rank-and-file members who have very few possibilities to influence decision-making processes. Authoritarian leaders make their organizations more susceptible to extreme action and aggression through polarization and groupthink.[13] The most powerful authoritarian leaders are more prone to punishing or removing group rivals. They also tend to rule group decision making ruthlessly, allowing little factionalization or dividing within the organization.[14]

The army organizational model has inspired many terrorist organizations as suggested in their organizational titles, such as the Japanese Red Army, the Red Army Faction (i.e., the Baader-Meinhof Group), and the Provisional Irish Republican Army (PIRA). In terrorist groups, as a result of the intrinsic tension between organizational control and the security conditions for secrecy and decreased communication, there is somewhat more independence at the lower level of the organization than the military model might indicate. The **Provisional Irish Republican Army (PIRA)** split from the IRA after the latter's demise in 1969. The PIRA is a typical authoritarian and hierarchical organization. It is organized like a corporation. It has positions, responsibilities, and authority distributed in a pyramidal structure. The Army Council runs and dictates the military strategy and tactics of the PIRA, such as ordering or rejecting the operations recommended by subordinate elements.[15] Military guidance is handed to either the PIRA's Northern or Southern Command—military units with spheres of responsibility, similar in organization to the U.S. Unified Command Plan. There are also the General Headquarters personnel who supervise all PIRA activities through its ten departments.[16]

The Irish Republican tradition was actually passed down from father to son (and daughter). Still today, about four decades later, familial commitment to the cause keeps filling the ranks of the PIRA. Gerry Adams (allegedly a PIRA leader since the 1970s) is not different from his predecessors. His father, grandfather, and even uncles were leading Republicans and he married a woman from a family with a similar background. This model of leadership structure is typically referred to as **follow-on terrorist leadership**—succession of terrorist leadership, often from father to son. Fathers are early leaders. They lead from the early stages of the terrorist group and inspire obedience through the strength of their command. Follow-on leaders often fall into two different categories. They either have demonstrated their ability to lead by taking part in and eventually running successful operations, or they are more prone to being selected as leaders because not only have they built a strong constituency within the group (in spite of having no operational or executive experience); they are also the children of leaders themselves.[17]

Although applying an authoritarian leadership style, the PIRA nevertheless became an umbrella. An **umbrella** is a group that protects, supports, and motivates smaller terrorist groups. The umbrella organization does not get directly implicated in terrorist activities or pretend to be a legitimate organization fighting for a political cause. The umbrella organizes regular meetings with sympathizers, suppliers, and terrorist leaders, thereby permitting terrorists to replenish, select targets, and plot. The PIRA's official end was declared in 2005. Nevertheless, the actions of Unionists and Republicans in Northern Ireland confirm the active role of the umbrella (i.e., PIRA). Both sides support legitimate political parties to push either for sustained relations with the U.K. or unity with the Republic of Ireland. The umbrella continues to deny any link to terrorist violence.[18]

Charismatic Leadership

Terrorism scholars have compared some terrorist groups to cults, and they have come to the conclusion that the cult model is relevant to terrorist groups. Most cults focus on a charismatic leader. According to Max Weber, one of the fathers of sociology, **charismatic leadership** is leadership that relies on divine-like personal traits and power. U.S. President Barack Obama is a contemporary example of a charismatic leader. Leadership is exercised in a very personal way. For Weber, the model of charismatic power was the religious cult. In a cult, the leader is usually considered an appearance of goodness, a prophet, and possibly even god-like. The cult grows through the charismatic power of that leader. The greatest obstacle to charismatic authority emerges when the leader disappears from the scene (i.e., gets old, world-weary, sick, killed, or abducted). Because the authority of the group concentrates so much on that person, his or her absence turns into a crisis.[19]

Charismatic leaders possess many of the following traits: physical presence, intellect, experience, education, skills, an aptitude to verbally and unambiguously articulate the vision and the mission, and, more importantly, powerful emotional appeal. This description is akin to the main tenet of trait theory. **Trait theory** posits that leaders are born with innate traits. As such, they are assertive, articulate, energetic, self-confident, determined, and tolerant of stress. They also adapt easily to situations, have magnetic power, are emotionally stable, and are ready to assume responsibility. Many of these traits are well suited to leadership, and those who become charismatic leaders have the right combination of traits.[20] Most new members of cults first react to the leader's message emotionally, then, later, respond to it physically and intellectually. New members say that they have finally found a leader who can answer life's mystifying questions and, hence, who is worthy of their full commitment.[21]

Some terrorist organizations revolve around the personality of a charismatic leader. For example, the Shining Path (Sendero Luminoso) in Peru centered around the magnetic power of Abimail Guzman, the Kurdish Workers' Party (PKK) around the charisma of Abdullah Öcalan, and Al Qaeda around the powerful Osama bin Laden (formerly) and now the "Egyptian doctor" (al-Zawahiri). Charismatic leadership thrives on three elements: a personality cult, a positive role model, and storytelling.

- Personality cult: a phenomenon whereby a charismatic leader gradually becomes an object of adoration as the initial principles that may have sustained the group at first lose their luster. The charismatic appeal of the leader may arouse total worship by followers. For the latter, the leader is a figurehead and often regarded as being larger than life. The leader's life (from childhood to adulthood) is deified and his or her ideas are considered unequivocal truth.[22]

- **Positive role model**: a conventional pattern of rebellion and resistance exploited for terrorist legitimacy and self-image. For instance, in late 19th century Chechnya, as a reaction to state oppression, an abrek resistance culture was born (*abrek*: a North Caucasian term for "robber"). The abreks battled the representatives of the government, sheltering their communities and clans. Today, the abrek resistance is used as a positive role model for Chechen insurgents engaging in terrorism.[23]

- Storytelling: charismatic leaders have been known to be storytellers because they can inspire followers through fascinating stories. Stories help convert new followers, foster identification, and acclimate to uncertainty and change. Stories can strengthen the terrorist organizational culture, or they can help members envision a new direction.[24]

With respect to Al Qaeda, Osama bin Laden embodied all three elements of charismatic leadership. He accomplished for jihadist terrorism what Adolf Hitler accomplished for National Socialism. Many Muslims and Arabs in the Middle East admired—and still admire—Osama bin Laden (i.e., personality cult), even if they did not always agree with his cruel tactics. For the Muslim population worldwide, bin Laden was David challenging the U.S. Goliath to unprecedented battles (i.e., positive role model). He showed Muslims that nothing is impossible, even leading a victorious battle—although temporarily—against the world's superpower. He initiated this by releasing long fatwas (in 1996 and 1998) and videotapes to help recruit followers and cultivate identification with anti-Western hatred (i.e., storytelling).[25] The point was made earlier that, because the authority of the group centers so much on a charismatic leader, his or her absence becomes a crisis. Did the death of Osama bin Laden present a crisis? Not really. The "Egyptian doctor" (al-Zawahiri) has become the new Al Qaeda leader and, according to several sources, is not only the new "most wanted terrorist" but also more operational and brutal than his predecessor.[26]

In regard to Al Qaeda again, the ideological wholesomeness of the charismatic leader must be above everything; the leader must be the paramount interpreter and communicator of the group's cause and missions. The leader, then, must make innovations or compromise with out-groups difficult or unattainable. The success of the leader also hinges on his or her interpretation of group goals and effective guidance of terrorist operations. In essence, the behavior of both the leader and followers is confined to the daily activities of the terrorist group. The leader must devote as much time to maintaining the group as to accomplishing instrumental objectives.[27]

SOCIAL NETWORKS OF TERRORISTS

Understanding terrorist networks is important for evaluating power and distribution. The distribution of roles in an organization creates specific units and differentiated tasks. Each unit develops its own interests and responsibilities. In addition, terrorist networks are made of groups that, loosely or more tightly, have common values and norms. Trust, duty, and loyalty play a major role in establishing membership in the network.[28]

Social Network: Definition

A **social network** is a pattern of connections developed by the flow of messages between communicators through space and time. **Networking** means developing an interconnected system that links groups with common goals or values. Well-placed individuals in the social network are often the central players wielding power and influence. Therefore, it can be ascertained that power depends on a person's position in the social network.[29] The basis of **social network analysis (SNA)** is that nodes (i.e., people, organizations, events, etc.) are points in the network and are linked through complex yet understandable connections that shape networks. These networks are pervasive, with a fundamental order and simple norms. The full operation of a network is a function of the extent to which members are interconnected to each other. This is the classic framework underlying SNA: strong ties guarantee high levels of trust and loyalty. To work efficiently, networks may require higher levels of trust than do other organizational structures, like hierarchies.[30]

Networks constitute the structural foundation of many events, organizations, and social processes. In counterterrorist discussions, **nodes** are points in a network where critical elements are stored or transferred. The value of a node is a function of its connection to the network.[31] The position of a node determines its centrality, which is a measure of importance or status in the network. When a node becomes highly central in the network, it becomes a **hub**. Five major parameters for nodes are:[32]

- Degree: the number of direct relationships that a node has.
- **Network density**: even if two nodes are not interconnected, they can still communicate via multiple links. Network density refers to the number of links in the network divided by the highest number of all possible links. In general, the rapidity through which information travels in a network is increasingly dependent on the density of the network. Dense networks have many links; information, then, can travel quickly from one node to any or all of the other nodes.
- **Betweenness**: the number of routes that link pairs of nodes passing through a specific node.
- **Prestige**: the important status that a node can earn when linked to other highly central nodes (hubs).
- Closeness: the number of nodes linked to one given node.

Modern war is **netwar**, an unparalleled type of war waged by terrorists and criminals thanks to a networked organizational structure. These networked structures are **virtual organizations**. These are associations that emerge through communicative, financial, and ideological links. Like a network, a virtual organization tends to have a horizontal structure and has no central leadership. It takes networks to fight networks: a similar approach is needed to fight against a network-based criminal organization.[33]

The Al Qaeda Network

In *Understanding Terror Networks*, Sageman (2004)[34] identified a massive Al Qaeda network and further subdivided it into four smaller networks. The first network is in the

Pakistan–Afghan border and comprises Al Qaeda's central staff and the global Salafist jihad. The second network is a group of active terrorists in Arab nations such as Saudi Arabia, Egypt, Yemen, and Kuwait. The third network consists of the Maghreb Arabs who, although coming from North Africa, now live in France and England. The final network is a core of people in Indonesia and Malaysia and is associated with Jemaah Islamiyah. Al Qaeda is also an example of a **covert network**. The key traits of covert networks that make them different from overt networks are (1) size (the networks may be very large, with thousands of nodes); (2) incompleteness (one characteristic of covert networks is that some links within the network will be unintentionally overlooked by intelligence-gathering teams); (3) fuzzy boundaries (the borders of any covert network will be nebulous, with people appearing to be members of different groups and different networks); and (4) dynamic (the network is always moving, changing, and non-static, with the relationships between nodes strengthening and weakening over time).[35]

During the 2004 Madrid train bombings, an Al Qaeda–affiliated terrorist group followed the network model of the **strength of weak ties**. According to this theory, weak ties—loose relationships with nodes (e.g., irregular meetings with acquaintances)—matter more than strong ones—relationships with regular people (i.e., family and friends)—when looking for information. Networks with scattered, open nodes can better access information and power than smaller, denser networks that have more interconnected nodes; weak ties allow more diverse knowledge and information.[36] The Madrid train bombings on March 11, 2004 were the result of a terrorist network based on weak ties—namely, ties with people working for the hashish trade in Spain and independent terrorists called the Abu Hafs Al Masri Brigades, consisting of Moroccan immigrants residing in Spain. Based on weak ties, the structure is horizontal and most of the connections are not based on strong or dense (e.g., familial) relationships.[37]

TYPES OF SOCIAL NETWORKS

Between nodes in a terrorist network, there is a common goal, a shared cause. The manners in which terrorist nodes communicate and collaborate are plentiful. This section lists and describes nine types of social networks, based on various sources.[38] These social networks do not comprise the entirety of such networks out there but can enlighten readers on the ingenuity of terrorist groups to organize and communicate their tactics with each other worldwide.

- All-channel network: a network where all dispersed nodes (e.g., the Al Qaeda covert network) can be interconnected for dissemination of information and instantaneous coordination concurrently. All nodes in the network are interlinked; no one is left out. The all-channel is cooperative, quick, and effective, but can be hard to maintain because of the high need of information exchange required. Nonetheless, it is the network of the digital revolution. Through technology, anyone is linked to and can communicate directly with anyone else. An all-channel network allows for round robin interaction, a method of linking new nodes to others. This type of network is similar to the loosely coupled network in that it is a horizontal, leaderless network characterized by a virtually infinite scattering of nodes. There is no control or influence at the tactical level; at most, there is little influence at the operational level—only strategic command by opinion leaders within the network.

- Chain or line network: network in which individuals are located or seated along a line, often based on their rank in the network. Communication takes place through others from a node at one end of the configuration to another node at the other end. For instance, the military arranges its leadership structure as the chain of command. Yet, there is no direct contact with others. Messages have to be relayed to others—that is, the next in line.

- Circle network: the network with the highest confidence and the highest degree of shared centrality. Equality in status and power is suggested. The disadvantage of this networked structure is that there is no perceived leader in the structure. On the whole, the circle functions to be a democratic structure for performing group operations and is perhaps the best structure for guaranteeing equal participation for all group members.

- Coupled network: network typified by the relaxing or releasing of the command and influence which leaders within the organization can apply over other components. Particularly, the looser connections between nodes and less direct channels of communication give rise to a decrease in the power of the whole organization to keep tactical unity and, occasionally even operational unity, in its components' activities.

- Dune network: type of terrorist network that uses a process of fluctuation between territorial presence and a method of disappearance. The perception of territorial presence is related to stable territorial establishments: nation-states, international markets, or ethnic societies. Conversely, disappearance tactics are closely associated to de-territorialization of a new political order. The Dune movement is quasi-random, going from one territory to another, influencing each territory, altering its features and moving on to a new destination. The Dune network is impermanent; it "attaches" and "detaches," going to new places after modifying the environment that it just occupied.

- Hub (or star, or wheel) network: the network with the lowest level of shared centrality. The hub (or star, or wheel) network has a center spoke, the leader, through whom all communication goes. Although members have the benefit of interpersonal interaction with the leader in this network, they are unable to communicate with another member directly. In this configuration, some members do not know what others are doing. Another term for this type of network is **maypole communication** (when the leader is the hub in the network and communication goes from the leader to the member and vice versa).

- Scale-free network: network that shows a power distribution (unlike a normal distribution) in which a small number of nodes may have a massive number of links, far more than the average links per node in the entire network.

- Swarming terrorist network: network with a horizontal deployment of small terrorist subgroups interacting with each other. Not a single sting would be important, but the sum total of all attacks could have lethal consequences. The metaphor is one of swarms of killer bees on the attack.

- Tightly coupled network: network in which leaders are able to exert strategic, operational, and tactical control. Thanks to effective communication means that link them to all suitable, functional parts of the group, these leaders hypothetically can conceive and implement plans for achieving complex missions, requiring the synchronization and sequencing of many different activities in different parts of the organization. The most obvious example of such tightly coupled networks is the classic pyramidal structure which, on top of specific structural characteristics, has well-defined and stable authority connections where leadership can apply various forms of control over their members.

FINANCIAL NETWORKS IN TERRORISM

We all have heard of tax havens that allow money transfer to be completely anonymous, and money laundering, the practice of concealing the sources of illegally obtained funds. Terrorist financial networks are really plentiful. The focus of this section is twofold: to make readers aware of the hawala system and to explain why it is difficult to track terrorist financial networks overall.

Hawala System

Informal financial networks pop up everywhere across the Middle East, where money is moved anonymously, without any required paperwork, and thanks to false names that can be used quite easily. A well-known informal financial network is the hawala system. **Hawala** refers to an informal Islamic banking network that connects brokers worldwide who transfer funds to depositors on a handshake and, at times, a password. It is a system of money exchange that relies on trust relationships between money dealers. A **chit**, or promissory note, is passed between two **hawaladars** (hawala dealers), and it is as worthy as cash or other swapped commodities because the trust between the two dealers ensures its value. Numerous global terrorist groups make money flow through the hawala system.[39] Hawala, Hindi for "intrust," has been active for generations in Asia and the Middle East. Islamic charities also receive billions annually, most of which is used for charitable causes, but not all. Islamist terrorists have begun taking advantage of the religious rather than the financial purposes of hawala. Al Qaeda's financial system was developed thanks to hawala. As Wolosky (2003)[40] explained, it was built "from the foundations of charities, nongovernmental organizations, mosques, websites, fundraisers, intermediaries, facilitators, banks and other financial institutions that helped finance the mujahedin throughout the 1980s. This network extended to all corners of the Muslim world" (p. 1). Based on one estimate, the amounts included in halawa transactions are probably worth billions of dollars.[41]

Difficulties in Dismantling Terrorist Financial Networks

Tracking and eliminating terrorist financial networks is a very difficult task. To begin, as terrorism expert Paul Pillar (2001)[42] explains, a terrorist attack may be supported by no financial network at all as some attacks have known to be cheap. The 1993 World Trade Center bombing cost a ridiculously low $400, and the cost of the September 11, 2001 plot has been valued at $300,000–$500,000. These amounts are relatively low, in comparison to the trillions of dollars that run through global financial networks on a daily basis.[43] Such small financial amounts are not easy to trace, and the problem is combined with the fact that much of those funds may never become part of the global financial system in the first place. Informal financial networks are only as powerful as their weakest link: those who try to hide their financial transactions will naturally hover around places that require the least paper trail.[44]

Another problem is that nations do not agree about which groups should be labeled as terrorists, which is the reason why financial procedures are applied inconsistently. The European Union (E.U.), for instance, froze assets of only two out of the twenty-eight groups that were short-listed as terrorist organizations by the U.S. The E.U. did not block any assets owned by the eleven European groups it considered friends to terrorism.[45] A third problem is the downside of unbridled capitalism. A case in point is the Benevolence International Fund (BIF), a global nonprofit charitable trust based in Saudi Arabia which supports terrorism. It moved to the U.S. in 1993 and enjoyed tax-exempt status from the IRS. It managed to raise millions of dollars within the next couple of years to endorse radical Islamist causes. The U.S. Department of the Treasury eventually banned BIF in 2002.[46]

SAFE HAVENS

A **safe haven** is a geographical location in which terrorists can successfully set up an organizational and operational base that includes one, some, or all of the following: (1) an operational base for training; access to weapons and related equipment; (2) a communications network for fast and reliable command, control, and intelligence gathering; (3) a logistics network to allow travel, the flow of money, and the access to falsified documents and weapons equipment; and (4) fundraising via different mechanisms of financing activities (e.g., trafficking and money laundering).[47]

Safe havens give terrorist networks the instruments necessary for the improvement of their organizational and operational capacities. Organizational tools support the group's existence as a cohesive unit and operational tools are for terrorists to carry out attacks. Examples of organizational tools are ideology, command structures, recruitment groups, and publicity. Natural physical barriers are the most evident geographic challenges in tracking terrorists' safe havens; leaky borders are a more unstructured challenge. Terrorists take advantage of national borders that have facilitated the mobility of humans through the progress of globalization. Greater flow of money, labor, and even ideas is now the norm, making governmental control over global commerce very difficult; and border control an even bigger problem.[48]

In 1975, police in France learned that "Carlos the Jackal" was operating a clearinghouse for terrorist mobility. His clients included the Tupamaros in Uruguay, the Quebec Liberation Front (FLQ), the IRA, the Baader-Meinhof Group in Germany, Yugoslavia's Croatian separatists, the Turkish People's Liberation Army, and the Palestinians.[49] In a similar vein, today, two examples of the advantages allowed by geographical factors are Mindanao and Yemen. Mindanao, situated at the southernmost tip of the Philippines, has a rocky mountainous landscape with small coastal plains but massive swampland. While it can be a very remote and inaccessible area for counterterrorist authorities, this did not prevent the development of training camps, such as Camp Abubakar, a 10,000-hectare compound that has allegedly trained over 2,000 Islamist terrorists in Mindanao. In Yemen, the expansive deserts and mountainous landscape facilitate terrorists' seeking of shelter among remote tribes.[50]

COLLABORATION MODELS IN TERRORISM

Many terrorist groups undertake collaborative operations at some point because they tend to be limited by the 3 Rs: resources, reciprocity, and reach. *Resources* are means, *reciprocity* refers to the open and mutual flow of ideas between people, and *reach* is an effective set of reliable, compatible contacts. As it is the case for any group competing for scarce resources, terrorists look for allies. Scarce resources can include funds, technology, manpower, knowledge, and so forth.[51] In 1986, an international terrorism congress took place in Frankfurt, Germany. It was a conference for terrorists from all over the globe to devise agendas and create collaborative projects. It was supposedly attended by at least 500 people. Meeting under the motto, "The armed struggle as a strategic and tactical necessity in the fight for revolution," the congress announced that the U.S. armed forces in Europe were the archenemy.[52] Of course, most collaborative arrangements are made secretly. This section describes various types of collaboration models in terrorism: physical exchange, information exchange, knowledge exchange, action exchange, and miscellaneous types of collaboration.

Physical Exchange

Physical exchange refers to material and physical cooperation between terrorist groups. It takes the form of shared manpower, training camps, armaments, and tactics. Terrorist groups rarely act alone because the economics of the situation may not enable solely independent actions. Al Qaeda has provided and benefited from physical exchange with various terrorist organizations since the 1990s. As such, Al Qaeda gives money to other terrorist groups to affect the strategic activities of others. It has been reported, for instance, that Osama bin Laden gave money to Algerian terrorists in the mid-1990s. Additionally, Al Qaeda provides safe haven to other Islamist groups. Lashkar-e-Tayyiba (LT), headquartered in Pakistan and created in 1990, has provided Al Qaeda trained operatives to other extreme Islamic factions fighting in Bosnia, Chechnya, and the Philippines. And South American drug gangs are investing millions of pounds of funding in Al Qaeda terrorism to guarantee the safe passage of cocaine across North Africa and en route to Europe. Islamist terrorists, aware of the barren terrain of the Sahara desert, have entered into multiple agreements. Under these agreements, they ensure armed security escorts for drug traffickers in exchange for a chunk of their profits.[53]

When the Second Intifada was launched in September 2000, Hamas smuggled arms and ammunitions through the underground tunnel network connecting Gaza with Egypt and transferred some weapons to their organization in the West Bank. This underground channel facilitated access to thousands of arms and ammunitions. Already in the 1970s, there were also large quantities of weapons in the Sinai desert left by Egyptian and Israeli forces after the Six-Day War in 1967. A certain number of Egyptians excavated weapons and sold them to Palestinian terrorist organizations (including Hamas). Those armaments and explosives were not used until the end of the First Intifada (1987–1993), when military operations conducted by Hamas, Islamic Jihad, and the PLO in Gaza intensified.[54]

Likewise, there are other examples of conspicuous collaboration between terror groups in terms of physical exchange. Libya worked out a powerful connection in Central and South America thanks to ties in Nicaragua. Until the beginning of the 1990s, the Sandinista government of Nicaragua represented the Libyan connection there. It furnished weapons, training, and logistical support to rebel groups in that region. Soon, Iran will probably be granted exclusive access to Zimbabwe's uranium in exchange for giving the country oil. A report by the United Nations' nuclear watchdog stated that Iran's Foreign and Cooperative Ministers went to Zimbabwe to make collaborative deals and sent engineers to evaluate uranium deposits. On the other side of the globe, Yemeni honey traders often abuse weak border controls and are alleged to have ties to Al Qaeda. The real value of the honey trade for Islamist extremists, along with profit, is that honey, according to Napoleoni (2003), is "considered a good product in which to conceal contraband: drugs, arms, gold, electronic equipment and cash are often smuggled in honey containers" (p. 159). The smell and reliability of honey make it great to hide weapons and drugs, and custom inspectors usually refuse to inspect honey containers that are "too messy."[55]

Information Exchange

Information exchange refers to the exchange of information between terrorist groups. Information comes from, and is rooted in, a data source. Data flows become information which, in turn, becomes knowledge. As time passes, knowledge eventually becomes wisdom. No terrorist organization can conceivably have the internal resources to create all necessary information. Just as sovereign nations depend on the intelligence of allied states, terrorist organizations use their peers for information at the local level. This can be, for example, information about the government, the physical environment, the what, why, how, and when of the military and intelligence services, financial services, and so forth. Looking back at the past, one can observe that the whole plan for the 9/11 attacks came together thanks to information exchange.[56] Intelligence-gathering about Osama bin Laden and Al Qaeda showed that their reliance on information flows developed over a long time with Afghan Arabs in Egypt and other countries. They were heavily involved in Islamic fundamentalism and terrorism against the U.S.[57]

Knowledge Exchange

As opposed to information exchange, **knowledge exchange** is executable. Anyone can surf on the Internet to learn how to build bombs. However, without the necessary knowledge to deal with such devices, their "studies" may end suddenly. The Internet offers explicit information that is easily transferrable, probably even understood. Tacit knowledge is more about experience, is not so transferrable, and is best learned through practice of observing others. Any drivers of manual transmissions know that reading about the transmission differs widely from the first time one depresses a clutch, sets the gears in motion, and tries to move forward.[58]

As this paragraph shows, two types of knowledge exist: explicit and tacit knowledge. **Explicit knowledge** is information that is codifiable and clear-cut in written form or embedded in a physical object. Because comprehending explicit knowledge is easy, it is also easily transferred between individuals. **Tacit knowledge**, on the other hand, is much less transferrable between people. Examples of tacit knowledge include the savoir-faire of terrorist bombers. Since tacit knowledge is much harder to identify, much less to codify, transfer is virtually impossible. The storage of tacit knowledge existing within a terrorist organization is essential for its operation.[59]

Unless a terrorist recruit has experienced basic training, he or she will be insufficiently prepared to live up to some conditions. At its most basic level, the purpose of training is to put the new recruit in a safe environment where he or she is exposed to what conditions would look like. The objective, of course, is to prepare the person. For instance, Zacarias Moussaoui, as his flight school records suggest, was incapable of capturing the skills required to fly a plane. This irritated Osama bin Laden, who supposedly chose all the hijackers for the September 11, 2001 attacks.[60]

Action Exchange

Action exchange refers to collaborative damage making between terrorist groups. By the mid-1990s, Osama bin Laden had created a coalition between his group (Al Qaeda) and Ayman al-Zawahiri, the leader of the al-Jihad (Holy War) group in Egypt (al-Zawahiri is now Al Qaeda's #1). The 1998 bombings of the two U.S. embassies in Tanzania and Kenya have been blamed on this collaborative alliance. Al Qaeda's active association with the Algeria's Armed Islamic Group (GIA) is another example of an action exchange. Al Qaeda was reportedly tied to the GIA and the "millennium plot"—a scheme to blow up the Los Angeles airport (LAX) in 1999. Ahmed Ressam, the originator of the plot, is an Algerian citizen who was trained at Al Qaeda camps in Afghanistan in 1998.[61]

Miscellaneous Types of Collaboration

- **Unholy triangle**: network of terrorists, drug smugglers, and government officials determined to destroy the Western world.[62]

- **Licensing agreement**: agreement to allow a terrorist organization to use a product or service for a particular purpose and duration. Jemaah Islamiyah is an extremist Islamist group active in the Southeast Asian region. It operates in places such as Malaysia, Singapore, and the southern Philippines. Jemaah Islamiyah has been reported to license training materials from Al Qaeda, both through receiving explicit knowledge (e.g., manuals and documentations) and tacit knowledge by sending members to Al Qaeda training camps in Afghanistan.[63]

- **Mergers and acquisitions**: type of collaboration whereby terrorist organizations have managed to enter into product and develop agreements and realize the effectiveness of working together. The "exclusion" of Iraq's late Al Qaeda leader, al-Zarqawi, is an example of acquisition and merger. Likewise, Hamas split from the Muslim Brotherhood in Palestine and was created in 1987 to take part in the First Intifada; that is, a giant campaign to end the Israeli military occupation of Palestine.[64]

- **Hybrid organization**: organization that has both criminal and terrorist features. As such, it can be criminal during the day, terrorist at night. Furthermore, some Islamist militants are heavily implicated in drug smuggling and rake in major financial returns from the illegal activity. The activities of a hybrid organization can concentrate on organized crime: extortion, counterfeiting, drug smuggling, and so forth.[65]

Many collaboration models between terrorist groups have taken various forms of strategic planning. The creativity to accomplish terror objectives seems endless. Another model of strategic terrorism is called the cell structure, as discussed in the next section.

MEXICAN DRUG CARTELS AND TERRORISTS: A COLLABORATION

Mexico is a principal location for the cultivation and transportation of drugs. Major Mexican drug cartels—namely, Gulf, Juarez, Sinaloa, and Tijuana—have gained political control through "cooperation" rather than appearing as competitors to the state. In this manner, drug cartels can exert greater influence within parts of the government, including the Mexican police and military.[66] Since the dawn of the 21st century, the slow decrease of state-sponsored terrorism has led many scholars to believe that terrorist groups will increasingly resort to drug trafficking and other illegal activities to acquire wealth and resources.[67] For example, Mexican drug cartels have developed connections with Mara Salvatrucha (MS-13), a radical and ultra-violent international group engaged in a broad variety of unlawful criminal activities—from human smuggling to drug trafficking. Many terrorists view drug trafficking as an abundant and risk-free source of revenue.[68] Often called **narco-guerrillas**, drug-trafficking terrorist groups often play a big role in the drug business. While some will tax drug producers, others will protect cultivators. Some might even use a direct "hands on" approach, with their own workforce, to process and smuggle narcotics.[69]

A heavy drug-trafficking Mexico has proven to lay the perfect groundwork for terrorist groups that seek to operate in North America. In fact, it is highly suspected that MS-13 and Al Qaeda have joined forces; the fear is that Al Qaeda could influence MS-13's expertise and international connections to smuggle dangerous shipment or personnel into the contiguous United States (i.e., the forty-eight interconnected U.S. states).[70] Likewise, Hezbollah, the Shi'ite Muslim terrorist organization based in Lebanon, has already penetrated the U.S. across its southwest border through drug cartel transit routes.[71] Indeed, Mexico's border with the U.S. makes it an attractive operational base for Hezbollah activities designed to infiltrate our homeland.[72] According to an FBI report in 2006,[73] Hezbollah's main strategies in Mexico are (1) to network and expand connections with the Shi'ite Muslim communities in places like Tijuana, (2) to exchange weapons and other unlawful supplies with Mexican drug cartels, and

(3) to smuggle both illegal Mexicans and Islamist terrorists across the U.S. border. The smuggling of humans (most of them terrorists or sympathizers to the Muslim cause) through the U.S.–Mexican border was showcased in the 2012 movie *Act of Valor*. The main route was an underground tunnel right underneath a milk factory. Navy Seals stopped them in the last minute.

TERRORIST CELLS: GENERAL OUTLOOK

The **cell** is the basic unit of a modern terrorist organization. Michael Collins, leader of the IRA, analyzed revolutionary tactics from the 18th and 19th centuries and created a method of insulating small units of terrorists, which he called *cells*. Each cell had a particular mission, and it was active without knowing about other cells in the area.[74] Cells have vague leadership and organizational configurations. Contemporary terrorist networks often consist of a hub that may influence the direction of a movement but that has not much direct influence and control over operational units. The latter are often autonomous or semi-autonomous cells that have their own directives, often after being inactive for a long time—as sleepers in foreign nations. The advantage of this type of organizational structure is that if one cell is identified or killed, the impact on other independent cells would be small. This structure also allows supporters overall to have "unawareness" about the tactics and targets of the cells.[75] Cells tend to be clandestine.

Clandestine Cell Structure

A **clandestine cell structure** is a method for organizing a unit in such a way that it can more efficiently resist invasions by an opposing group. Based on the unit's philosophy, its operational area, the information technologies available, and the character of the mission, a clandestine cell structure can be either a strict hierarchy or even a well-distributed organization. In a clandestine cell, terrorists work covertly to preserve the integrity of the unit and hide its plans, activities, and missions from external forces.[76] Clandestinity protects the cell and gives a group certain secretiveness. Unlike military or guerrilla forces, the terrorists' calculated surprise is designed to create an unequivocal, but seemingly omnipresent feeling of threat in the target population.[77] There are three challenges when attempting to gather information as much as possible about clandestine cells: incompleteness (with missing nodes and links that the investigators will not find), unclear boundaries (the difficulty in deciding who is in the cell and who is not), and dynamic (a clandestine cell is not static; it is always changing).[78]

Resembling overt terrorist groups, clandestine cells are to achieve a specific purpose. Acting in secrecy not only allows them to accomplish their mission, but it also fosters strong relations of trust among the group members through an "us vs. them" attitude. In a clandestine cell, the type of relationship between its members must also be private or mysterious. The best method to guarantee that bonds of loyalty and trust remain strong is to fall back on ties from previous relationships for potential recruits. While this considerably decreases the possibility for new members to join the unit, it also reduces the likelihood of a security infraction that may endanger the unit's existence.[79]

A dormant unit in a clandestine cell structure is called a sleeper cell. A **sleeper cell** is an isolated cell of sleeper agents who are members of an intelligence network or organization. The cell "sleeps" (lies dormant) within a target population until it wakes up or decides to conduct missions. A sleeper cell can be a situation in which it is clandestine until it becomes active, as with a sabotage or terror unit.[80] Some cells (or singleton agents) can be both clandestine and sleeper.

Al Qaeda Cells

Al Qaeda terrorism is widely distributed. It consists of a largely decentralized collection of individuals and cells that are not all led by a single leader or headquarters. At the operational level, the Al Qaeda network is made up of cells of a few people recruited by a cell builder. The latter tends to follow the same script: he or she recruits, activates, and then leaves. From this moment on, communication with Al Qaeda is done via the Internet. Cell builders operate to supply start-up funds. They specialize in creating new cells with no ties to any other organizational structure.[81] Al Qaeda members are only in contact with each other; they use modern technologies like the Internet, e-mail, and mobile phones. Most Al Qaeda cells are small and autonomous, with no external help needed. They only receive financial resources when sent on specific missions. For example, the cost of the bombings of the U.S. embassies in Kenya and Tanzania may have been $100,000.[82]

Al Qaeda–trained or –inspired operatives created cells in lots of countries and areas. For example, Al Qaeda cells infiltrated the following largely Islamic countries and areas: Afghanistan, Algeria, Bosnia, Chechnya, Indonesia, Iraq, Kosovo, Lebanon, Malaysia, Pakistan, the southern Philippines, Somalia, the Sudan, the West Bank, and Yemen. Other cells were secretly located in the following Western and non-Muslim nations: Britain, France, Germany, Israel, Spain, the U.S., and the Tri-Border Area (TBA) in South America (i.e., Argentina, Brazil, and Paraguay).[83]

By rearranging into a horizontal structure with shared command stretched over many actors, Al Qaeda filled its leadership void and made the most of two advantages: (1) if a particular leader in the network is arrested or killed, the full network will not be too affected by the loss, and (2) operations can be carried out rapidly without full leaders being involved.[84] Al Qaeda terrorist acts are now mainly performed by self-developing cells of acquaintances that group together for attacks, then disappear or dismantle to create new swarms. Independent studies by Nixon Center scholar Robert Leiken (2004)[85] and Sageman (2004)[86] show that over 80% of known Islamist/jihadist cells currently lie dormant in Diasporic communities worldwide. These are usually disregarded by the host society and physically detached from each other.

SELF-STARTER CELLS

Among the current extreme terrorist threats, the presence of the self-starter cell constitutes a well-defined and innovative phenomenon. A **self-starter cell** is a recent type of terrorist cell whereby a group has little or no connection with the original overarching terrorist network.[87] The term *self-starter cell* has multiple synonyms, such as *franchise*, *amateur*, *freelancer*, and *a bunch of guys*.[88] The emergence of new technologies has been influential in the growing trend of this new brand of cellular terrorism. The Internet's ease for spreading operational instructions has enlarged the current spectrum of security threats and jihadist prospects. In addition, the distinctive sociopolitical and demographic circumstances in Western Europe make this geographic area exposed to future acts of self-starter terrorism.[89]

Aidan Kirby (2007)[90] analyzed the role of self-starter cells with respect to the Al Qaeda network. Most Al Qaeda-inspired self-starter cells have little or no association with the giant Al Qaeda network. In this context, self-starter cells comprise terrorists who did not receive formal training in Al Qaeda training camps—some of the best "terrorism schools" the world has ever known. Self-starter attacks seem to occur of their own accord, without orders from an Al Qaeda leader. Since September 11, 2001, there have been many cases that symbolize this model to varying degrees. Examples are groups that committed the attacks in Casablanca in 2003, the Madrid train bombings in 2004, and the Hofstad Network of Islamist terrorists in the Netherlands. This movement is often described as the *decentralization of Al Qaeda* or the growth of horizontal Salafism as a movement. The self-starter cell is largely motivated by social dynamics but it is immersed with extreme Islamist ideology and rhetoric. The 2005 London bombers were principally an autonomous cell whose drives, cohesiveness, and ideological training were developed without any assistance from a large network or formal membership of the jihad.

As a result of the decentralization of its leadership, many parts of Al Qaeda today are run as much from the bottom-up as they are from the top-down. Cell terrorists and nonaffiliated (but sympathetic) people have more autonomous power. The Al Qaeda network seems to have diffused into independent and flexible local cells linked through loose, international connections that are hard to detect and examine by state governments. The dissemination of power into smaller cells is analogous to the manner in which the Cali and Medellin cartels dispersed during the U.S.-led War on Drugs (WOD). The WOD is still very active today because cocaine production and sales continue to be high, in spite of the disintegration of the main cartels.[91]

THE "LONE WOLF" CELL STRUCTURE

Like crime, terrorism is not always a group venture. It can be the work of one individual only. A **lone wolf** (or **lone wolf fighter**) is a person who commits terrorist acts in favor of a given group, movement, or ideology, but does it alone, independent of any command structure. Lone wolves have a broad and sometimes delusional belief that their actions will advance a superior cause against a corrupt or wicked society. Lone wolf terrorism remains a confusing and mysterious phenomenon. The boundaries of lone wolf terrorism are ill-defined and random. Lone wolf terrorists may relate with or express sympathy toward extremist movements but, by nature, are not members of these movements. The range of motivations and justifications that have been ascribed to terrorist groups equally seem to be the same for lone wolf terrorists. Many of the terrorist acts that seem to be solo endeavors conducted by rogue individuals have larger ideologies of justification behind them. These ideologies of justification clearly go beyond the spectrum of formal organization.[92]

Consequently, a terrorist cell can be as small as a lone individual. A case in point is Richard C. Reid, a British national who became a Muslim. Reid was caught by an attentive flight attendant and overcome by passengers on December 22, 2001, when he attempted to create an explosion in his shoe on a Boeing 767. Reid was seemingly associated to Al Qaeda and trained by the organization in Afghanistan.[93] Hoffman (1998)[94] made a distinction between lone wolf terrorists and **lunatic assassins**. Both may employ identical tactics and maybe even pursue the same objective (e.g., the killing of a politician), but they have different purposes. Unlike the terrorist's broader political, ideological, or religious purposes that extend beyond the direct target of his or her attacks, the lunatic assassin's purpose is more often "intrinsically idiosyncratic, completely egocentric and deeply personal" (p. 42).

Leaderless Resistance

Leaderless resistance is a lone wolf maneuver in which one person (or an extremely small, highly cohesive unit) mounts acts of anti-state terrorism outside of any movement, command structure, or support network. In leaderless resistance, no leaders—only perpetrators—are involved in terrorist attacks. Ideologues inspire or motivate the militant masses into carrying out attacks.[95] Leaderless resistance was made appealing by Louis Beam, a right-wing pastor and radical. Right-wing groups like the Phineas Priesthood and the White Aryan Resistance adopted Beam's vision by making sure that no formal organization was present in their movements. One will find no hierarchy or chain of command in leadership resistance. Activists do not depend on support from other cells. Thus, very little—if any—communication exists between operatives and their cells. Each operative is autonomous; he or she will choose the location of an attack and plot the attack on his or her own.[96]

Remarkably, left-wing groups have also embraced Beam's vision of leaderless resistance. The Earth Liberation Front (ELF), a militant environmental group, pushes its adherents to develop their own cell rather than joining an existing one. The reason is that attempts to locate an existing cell could hurt or slow down ELF's mission. ELF's cells are self-sustaining and autonomous; members are usually not aware of the identities of members of other cells; the cells are only interconnected through a shared ideology.[97]

Lone Wolf Terrorism in the U.S.

Lone wolf terrorism has been reported to be more widespread in the U.S. than most other nations. In the U.S., lone wolf terrorism has increased significantly since the 1980s; a similar rise does not seem to have taken place in other countries.[98] According to Hewitt (2003),[99] "American terrorism differs from terrorism in other countries in that a significant proportion of terrorist attacks have been carried out by unaffiliated individuals rather than by members of terrorist organizations" (p. 78). From 1955 to 1977, 7% of all victims of terrorism in the U.S. were killed by lone wolves, but between 1978 and 1999, the percentage rose to 26%.

Consider the Unabomber (Ted Kaczynski), a former math professor at Berkeley, who undoubtedly acted alone. Timothy McVeigh is also considered a textbook example of the lone wolf. Although Terry Nichols was convicted of helping him make the bomb, McVeigh was the sole planner of the Oklahoma City bombing and warned that he would hurt Nichols and his family if he refused to cooperate (i.e., helping McVeigh mix the fertilizer with other bomb ingredients).[100] More recently, the shooting spree at the military installation of Fort Hood, TX, in November 2009, was the product of lone wolf terrorism. Major **Nidal Malik Hasan**, a U.S. Army psychiatrist, shot twelve soldiers and one civilian, and wounded forty-three others. Assumptions about Hasan's motives are abounding. Hasan was vehemently opposed to the wars in Iraq and Afghanistan and believed that Muslims should not be sent on missions against other Muslims. According to media reports, Hasan used e-mail correspondence with the militant cleric Anwar al-Awlaki (based in Yemen) accused of diffusing the Al Qaeda ideology.[101]

SUMMARY

Terrorist organizations can have different organizational structures. For instance, in the pyramidal (or hierarchical) structure, leaders are at the top and passive supporters at the bottom. In the horizontal structure, where there is no pyramid of command, the organization is divided according to particular tasks and loosely organized cells. With respect to leadership, two leadership types were described: authoritarian leadership and charismatic leadership. Authoritarian leadership is based on powerful controlling tactics and central organizational decision making. Such was the case of leaders in the Provisional Irish Republican Army. In charismatic leadership, the terrorist leader has a great following thanks to his or her divine-like power and personal traits. Such was the case of Osama bin Laden. Charismatic leadership thrives on three elements: a personality cult, a positive role model, and storytelling. Additionally, this chapter provided a description of social networks of terrorists, based on social network analysis (SNA). SNA studies how an interconnected system links groups with common goals or values. Nodes are points in the network that are linked through ties. Strong ties guarantee high levels of trust and loyalty. An important premise is that it takes networks to fight networks (i.e., netwar). As we have seen, there are multiple types of social networks (e.g., all-channel, scale-free, etc.). Networks are more efficient for the simple following reason: if a particular leader in the network is arrested or killed, the full network will not be too affected by the loss. The financial networks of terrorism (e.g., the hawala system, an informal Islamic banking network that connects brokers worldwide) are difficult to track overall. Of equal relevance are the various types of collaboration models in terrorism: physical exchange, information exchange, knowledge exchange, action exchange, and miscellaneous types of collaboration. The important role of terrorist cells is something to behold. For example, the clandestine cell structure has vague leadership and organizational configurations. It protects the cell and gives a group certain secretiveness. Likewise, a sleeper cell lies dormant until it wakes up or decides to conduct missions. Cell terrorists have more autonomous power. Lastly, like crime, terrorism is not always a group venture. Lone-wolf terrorism happens when a person commits terrorist acts alone, independent of any command structure. Ted Kaczynski (the Unabomber) and Timothy McVeigh were lone-wolf terrorists.

KEY TERMS

action exchange   294

active cadre   282

authoritarian leadership   284

betweenness   287

cell   296

charismatic leadership   285

chit   290

clandestine cell structure   296

covert network   288

explicit vs. tacit knowledge   294

fatwa   283

follow-on terrorist leadership   284

hawala   290

hub   287

hybrid organization   295

information exchange   293

knowledge exchange   293

leaderless resistance   299

licensing agreement   294

lone wolf   298

lunatic assassin   299

mergers and acquisitions   295

narco-guerrillas   295

netwar   287

network density   287

networking   287

node   287

organization   281

personality cult   285

physical exchange   292

positive role model   286

pyramidal structure   281

safe haven   291

self-starter cell   297

sleeper cell   297

social network   287

social network analysis   287

spatial, strategic, or vertical differentiation   282

strength of weak ties   288

terrorist networks (types)   288–290

trait theory   285

umbrella organization   284

unholy triangle   294

virtual organizations   287

ENDNOTES

1. McKendall, Marie A., & Wagner III, John A. (1997). Motive, Opportunity, Choice, and Corporate Illegality. *Organization Science: A Journal of the Institute of Management Sciences, 8*(6), 624–648.

2. Goolsby, Rebecca (2006). Combating Terrorist Networks: An Evolutionary Approach. *Computational & Mathematical Organization Theory, 12,* 7–20.

3. Crenshaw, Martha (2001). Theories of Terrorism: Instrumental and Organizational Approaches. In David C. Rapoport (Ed.), *Inside Terrorism Organizations* (pp. 13–29). London: Frank Cass.

4. Fraser, James, & Fulton, Ian (1984). *Terrorism Counteraction.* Fort Leavenworth, KS: U.S. Army Command and General Staff College.

5. Dugan, Laura, & Gibbs, Carole (2009). *Criminology of White-Collar Crime.* New York: Springer; White, Jonathan R. (2011). *Terrorism & Homeland Security* (7th ed.). Belmont, CA: Wadsworth.

6. McKendall, Marie A., & Wagner III, John A. (1997). Motive, Opportunity, Choice, and Corporate Illegality. *Organization Science: A Journal of the Institute of Management Sciences, 8*(6), 624–648.

7. Klausner, Samuel Z. (1968). The Intermingling of Pain and Pleasure: The Stress-Seeking Personality in Its Social Context. In Samuel Z. Klausner (Ed.), *Why Man Takes Chances: Studies in Stress Seeking* (pp. 137–168). New York: Doubleday.

8. Sullwold, Lieselotte (1981). Stationen in der Entwicklung von Terroristen: Psychologische Aspekte biographischer Daten [Stages in the development of terrorists: Psychological Aspects of Biographical Data]. In Herbert Jager, Gerhard Schmidtchen, & Lieselotte Sullwold (Eds.), *Analysen zum Terrorismus [Analysis of terrorism]* (Vol. 2). Opladen: Westdeutsther Verlag.

9. Arquilla, John, & Ronfeldt, David (2001). *Networks and Netwars: The Future of Terror, Crime and Militancy*. Santa Monica: RAND.

10. Jackson, Brian A. (2006). Groups, Networks, or Movements: A Command-and-Control-Driven Approach to Classifying Terrorist Organizations and Its Application to Al Qaeda. *Studies in Conflict & Terrorism, 29*, 241–262.

11. Jackson, Brian A. (2006). Groups, Networks, or Movements: A Command-and-Control-Driven Approach to Classifying Terrorist Organizations and Its Application to Al Qaeda. *Studies in Conflict & Terrorism, 29*, 241–262.

12. Ardendt, Hannah (1968). *Totalitarianism*. New York: Harcourt Brace and World.

13. Post, Jerrold M., Ruby, Keven G., & Shaw, Eric D. (2002). The Radical Group in Context: 1. An Integrated Framework for the Analysis of Group Risk for Terrorism. *Studies in Conflict & Terrorism, 25*, 73–100.

14. Adorno, Theodore W., Frenkel-Brunswik, Else, Levinson, Daniel J., Sanford, Nevitt (1950). *The Authoritarian Personality*. New York: Harper & Bros.

15. Horgan, John, & Taylor, Max (1997). The Provisional Irish Republican Army: Command and Functional Structure. *Terrorism and Political Violence, 9*(3), 1–32.

16. Dishman, Chris (2005). The Leaderless Nexus: When Crime and Terror Converge. *Studies in Conflict & Terrorism, 28*, 237–252.

17. Garfield, Andrew (2002). PIRA Lessons Learned: A Model of Terrorist Leadership Succession. *Low Intensity Conflict & Law Enforcement, 11*(2), 271–284.

18. Dunn, Seamus, & Morgan, Valerie (1995). Protestant Alienation in Northern Ireland. *Studies in Conflict and Terrorism, 18*, 175–185; Hastings, Max (1970). *Barricades in Belfast*. New York: Taplinger.

19. Cheney, George, Christensen, Lars Thoger, Zorn, Theodore E., Jr., & Ganesh, Shiv (2010). *Organizational Communication in an Age of Globalization: Issues, Reflections, Practices* (2nd ed.). Prospect Heights, IL: Waveland Press.

20. Eisenberg, Eric M., & Goodall, H. Lloyd, Jr. (2004). *Organizational Communication: Balancing Creativity and Constraint*. Boston: Bedford/St. Martin's.

21. Morgan, Stephen J. (2001). *The Mind of a Terrorist Fundamentalist: The Psychology of Terror Cults*. Cincinnati, OH: Awe-Struck E-Books; Robbins, Thomas (1988). *Cults, Converts, and Charisma: The Sociology of New Religious Movements*. Newbury Park, CA: Sage.

22. Wilson, Loretta S., & Kwileck, Susan (2003). Are These People Crazy or What? A Rational Choice Interpretation of Cults and Charisma, *Humanomics 19*(1), 29–44, p. 30.

23. Sirseloudi, Matenia P. (2005). How to Predict the Unpredictable: On the Early Detection of Terrorist Campaigns. *Defense & Security Analysis, 21*(4), 369–386.

24. Cheney, George, Christensen, Lars Thoger, Zorn, Theodore E., Jr., & Ganesh, Shiv (2010). *Organizational Communication in an Age of Globalization: Issues, Reflections, Practices* (2nd ed.). Prospect Heights, IL: Waveland Press.

25. Scheuer, Michael (2004). *Imperial Hubris: Why The West Is Losing the War on Terror*. Washington D.C.: Potomac Books.

26. Jones, Seth G. (2011, May 3). *The Al Qa'ida Threat in Pakistan. Testimony before the Subcommittee on Counterterrorism and Intelligence, Committee on Homeland Security*. Washington, D.C.: Department of Homeland Security; Payne, Kenneth (2011). Building the Base: Al Qaeda's Focoist Strategy. *Studies in Conflict & Terrorism, 34*(2), 124–143.

27. Verba, Sidney (1961). *Small Groups and Political Behavior: A Study of Leadership*. Princeton: Princeton University Press.

28. Ackoff, Russell L., & Strümpfer, Johan P. (2003). Terrorism: A Systemic View. *Systems Research and Behavioral Science, 20*, 287–294.

29. Combs, Cindy C. (2011). *Terrorism in the Twenty-First Century*. New York: Longman; Monge, Peter, & Contractor, Noshir (2003). *Theories of Communication Networks*. Oxford: Oxford University Press; Pfeffer, Jeffrey (1992). *Managing with Power: Politics and Influence in Organizations*. Cambridge, MA: Harvard Business School Press.

30. Reed, Brian (2007). A Social Network Approach to Understanding an Insurgency. *Parameters, 7*, 19–30.

31. Arquilla, John, & Ronfeldt, David (1996). *The Advent of Netwar*. Santa Monica: RAND; Barabasi, Albert-Lazlo (2002). *Linked: The New Science of Networks*. New York: Perseus.

32. Farley, Jonathan David (2003). Breaking al Qaeda Cells: A Mathematical Analysis of Counterterrorism Operations. *Studies in Conflict and Terrorism, 26*, 399–411; Saxena, Sudhir, Santhanamb, K., & Basu, Aparna (2004). Application of Social Network Analysis (SNA) to Terrorist Networks in Jammu & Kashmir. *Strategic Analysis, 28*(1), 84–101.

33. Arquilla, John, & Ronfeldt, David (2001). *Networks and Netwars: The Future of Terror, Crime, and Militancy*. Washington, D.C.: RAND; White, Jonathan R. (2011). *Terrorism & Homeland Security* (7th ed.). Belmont, CA: Wadsworth.

34. Sageman, Marc (2004). *Understanding Terror Networks*. Philadelphia: University of Pennsylvania Press.

35. Sparrow, Malcolm (1991). The Application of Network Analysis to Criminal Intelligence: An Assessment of the Prospects. *Social Networks, 13*, 251–252.

36. Granovetter, Mark (1973). The Strength of Weak Ties. *American Journal of Sociology, 78*(6), 1360–1380.

37. Gamella, Juan F., & Rodrigo, Maria Luisa Jiménez (2004). A Brief History of Cannabis Policies in Spain (1968–2003). *Journal of Drug Issues, 34*(3), 623–659; Rodriguez, Jose (2004). *The March 11th Terrorist Network: In Its Weakness Lies Its Strength*. Barcelona Department of Sociology Analysis of Organizations, University of Barcelona.

38. Arquilla, John, Ronfeldt, David, & Zanini, Michele (1999). Networks, Netwar and Information-Age Terrorism. In Ian O. Lesser, Bruce Hoffman, John Arquilla, David F. Ronfeldt, Michele Zanini, & Brian M. Jenkins (Eds.), *Countering the New Terrorism* (pp. 39–88). Santa Monica: RAND; Arquilla, John, & Ronfeldt, David (2001). *Networks and Netwars: The Future of Terror, Crime and Militancy*. Santa Monica: RAND; Bavelas, Alex (1951). Communication Patterns in Task-Oriented Groups. In Harold Lasswell & Daniel Lerner (Eds.), *The Policy Sciences* (pp. 193–202). Stanford, CA: Stanford University Press; Leavitt, Harold J. (1964). Managerial Psychology. Chicago: University of Chicago Press; Marion, Russ, & Uhl-Bien, Mary (2003). Complexity Theory and Al-Qaeda: Examining Complex Leadership. *Emergence, 5*(1), 54–76; Matthew, Richard, & Shambaugh, George (2005). The Limits of Terrorism: A Network Perspective. *International Studies Review, 7*(4), 617–627; Mishal, Shaul (2003). The Pragmatic Dimension of the Palestinian Hamas: A Network Perspective. *Armed Forces & Society, 29*(4), 569–589.

39. White, Jonathan R. (2011). *Terrorism & Homeland Security* (7th ed.). Belmont, CA: Wadsworth.

40. Wolosky, Lee S. (2003, April 1). *National Commission on Terrorist Attacks upon the United States*. Public Hearing Delivered in New York.

41. El-Qorchi, Mohammed (2002). Hawala. *Finance and Development, 39*(4), 10–21.

42. Pillar, Paul R. (2001). *Terrorism and U.S. Foreign Policy*. Washington, D.C.: Brookings Institution Press, p. 94.

43. Francis, David R. (2004, April 8). The War on Terror Money. *Christian Science Monitor*, p. 14.

44. Bensahel, Nora (2006). A Coalition of Coalitions: International Cooperation against Terrorism. *Studies in Conflict & Terrorism, 29*, 35–49.

45. Phillips, Michael M., & Johnson, Ian (2002, April 11). U.S.-European Divisions Hinder Drive to Block Terrorists' Assets. *The Wall Street Journal*, p. A1.

46. White, Jonathan R. (2011). *Terrorism & Homeland Security* (7th ed.). Belmont, CA: Wadsworth.

47. Kittner, Cristiana C. Brafman (2007). The Role of Safe Havens in Islamist Terrorism. *Terrorism and Political Violence, 19*(3), 307–329.

48. Nassar, Jamal R. (2004). *Globalization and Terrorism: The Migration of Dreams and Nightmares*. New York: Rowman & Littlefield.

49. Raynor, Thomas P. (1982). *Terrorism*. New York: Franklin Watts.

50. Decker, Brett (2004, March 11). Out of Manila's Control. *National Review*; Stack, Megan (2004, October 18). A Bard against Bullet. *The Los Angeles Times*, p. A1.

51. Desouza, Kevin C., & Hensgen, Tobin (2007). Connectivity among Terrorist Groups: A Two Models Business Maturity Approach. *Studies in Conflict & Terrorism, 30*, 593–613.

52. Combs, Cindy C. (2011). *Terrorism in the Twenty-First Century*. New York: Longman.

53. Cronin, Audrey K., Aden, Huda, Frost, Adam, & Jones, Benjamin (2004, February 6). *Foreign Terrorist Organizations*. Washington, D.C.: Congressional Research Service; Weaver, Anne (2003). *Pakistan: In the Shadow of Jihad and Afghanistan*. New York: Farrar, Straus and Giroux; Yapp, Robin (2010, December 29). South American Drug Gangs Funding al Qaeda Terrorists. *The Telegraph*.

54. Chehab, Zaki (2007). *Inside Hamas: The Untold Story of the Militant Islamic Movement*. New York: Nation Books.

55. Davis, Brian L. (1990). *Qaddafi, Terrorism, and the Origins of the U.S. Attack on Libya*. Santa Barbara: Praeger; Laing, Aislinn (2011, March 6). Zimbabwe to Sell Uranium to Iran. *The Telegraph*, p. A1; Napoleoni, Loretta (2003). *Modern Jihad: Tracing the Dollars behind the Terror Networks*. London: Pluto Press, p. 159.

56. Desouza, Kevin C., & Hensgen, Tobin (2007). Connectivity among Terrorist Groups: A Two Models Business Maturity Approach. *Studies in Conflict & Terrorism, 30*, 593–613.

57. Ronfeldt, David, & Arquilla, John (2001). Networks, Netwars, and the Fight for the Future. *First Monday, 6*(10), 10–21.

58. Desouza, Kevin C., & Hensgen, Tobin (2007). Connectivity among Terrorist Groups: A Two Models Business Maturity Approach. *Studies in Conflict & Terrorism, 30*, 593–613.

59. Frey, Bruno S., & Osterloh, Margit (2010). *Successful Management by Motivation: Balancing Intrinsic and Extrinsic Incentives*. New York: Springer; van der Sijde, Peter, Ridder, Anne-Marie, Blaauw, Gerben, & Diesnberg, Christoph (2010). *Teaching Entrepreneurship: Cases for Education and Training*. Heidelberg, Germany: Verlag.

60. Desouza, Kevin C., & Hensgen, Tobin (2007). Connectivity among Terrorist Groups: A Two Models Business Maturity Approach. *Studies in Conflict & Terrorism, 30*, 593–613.

61. Desouza, Kevin C., & Hensgen, Tobin (2007). Connectivity among Terrorist Groups: A Two Models Business Maturity Approach. *Studies in Conflict & Terrorism, 30*, 593–613; Smith, Paul J. (2002). Transnational Terrorism and the Al Qaeda Model: Confronting New Realities. *Parameters, 32*, 33–46.

62. Combs, Cindy C. (2011). *Terrorism in the Twenty-First Century*. New York: Longman.

63. Mishal, Shaul, & Rosenthal, Maoz (2005). Al Qaeda as a Dune Organization: Toward a Typology of Islamic Terrorist Organizations. *Studies in Conflict & Terrorism, 28*(4), 275–293.

64. Desouza, Kevin C., & Hensgen, Tobin (2007). Connectivity among Terrorist Groups: A Two Models Business Maturity Approach. *Studies in Conflict & Terrorism, 30*, 593–613.

65. Dishman, Chris (2005). The Leaderless Nexus: When Crime and Terror Converge. *Studies in Conflict & Terrorism, 28*, 237–252.

66. Sullivan, John P., & Bunker, Robert J. (2002). Drug Cartels, Street Gangs, and Warlords. *Small Wars & Insurgencies, 13*(2), 40–53.

67. Dishman, Chris (2001). Terrorism, Crime, and Transformation. *Studies in Conflict & Terrorism, 24*(1), 43–58.

68. Norton, Richard (2010). Feral Cities: Problems Today, Battlefields Tomorrow? *Marine Corps University Journal, 1*(1), 50–77.

69. Clawson, Patrick, & Rensselaer, Lee (1996). *The Andean Cocaine Industry*. New York: St. Martin's Press.

70. Norton, Richard (2010). Feral Cities: Problems Today, Battlefields Tomorrow? *Marine Corps University Journal, 1*(1), 50–77.

71. Conery, Ben (2009, March 27). Hezbollah Uses Mexican Drug Routes into U.S. *The Washington Times*, p. A1.

72. Cook, Colleen W. (2007). *Congressional Research Service Report for Congress: Mexico's Drug Cartels*. Washington, D.C.: Library of Congress.

73. FBI's Mueller: Hezbollah Busted in Mexican Smuggling Operation (2006, March 30). Retrieved December 13, 2011 from http://archive.newsmax.com/archives/ic/2006/3/30/223801.shtml.

74. White, Jonathan R. (2011). *Terrorism & Homeland Security* (7th ed.). Belmont, CA: Wadsworth.

75. Martin, Gus (2010). *Understanding Terrorism: Challenges, Perspectives, and Issues*. Thousand Oaks, CA: Sage.

76. Erickson, Bonnie H. (1981). Secret Societies and Social Structure. *Social Forces, 60*(1), 188–210.

77. Sirseloudi, Matenia P. (2005). How to Predict the Unpredictable: On the Early Detection of Terrorist Campaigns. *Defense & Security Analysis, 21*(4), 369–386.

78. Sparrow, Malcolm (1991). The Application of Network Analysis to Criminal Intelligence: An Assessment of the Prospects. *Social Networks, 13*, 251–274.

79. Erickson, Bonnie H. (1981). Secret Societies and Social Structure. *Social Forces, 60*(1), 188–210.

80. de Goede, Marieke (2008). Beyond Risk: Premediation and the Post-9/11 Security Imagination. *Security Dialogue, 39*(2), 155–176.

81. Lia, Brynjar (2006). *The Al-Qaida Strategist Abu Mus'ab Al-Suri: A Profile*. Kjeller, Norway: Norwegian Defense Research Establishment; Milward, H. Brinton, & Raab, Jörg (2006). Dark Networks as Organizational Problems: Elements of a Theory. *International Public Management Journal, 9*(3), 333–360; Pillar, Paul R. (2010). The Diffusion of Terrorism. *Mediterranean Quarterly, 21*(1), 1–14.

82. McNeil, Donald G. (2001, December 2). What Will Rise if bin Laden Falls? *The New York Times*, p. A1.

83. Martin, Gus (2010). *Understanding Terrorism: Challenges, Perspectives, and Issues*. Thousand Oaks, CA: Sage.

84. Dishman, Chris (2005). The Leaderless Nexus: When Crime and Terror Converge. *Studies in Conflict & Terrorism, 28*, 237–252.

85. Leiken, Robert (2004, March 25). Bearers of Global Jihad? Immigration and National Security After 9/11. Retrieved February 2, 2011, from http://www.nixoncenter.org/publications/monographs/Leiken_Bearers_of_Global_Jihad.pdf.

86. Sageman, Marc (2004). *Understanding Terror Networks*. Philadelphia: University of Pennsylvania Press.

87. Benjamin, Daniel, & Simon, Steven (2005). *The Next Attack: The Failure of the War on Terror and Strategy for Getting It Right*. New York: Henry Holt.

88. Roy, Olivier (2004). *Globalized Islam: The Search for a New Umma*. New York: Columbia University Press; Sageman, Marc (2004). *Understanding Terror Networks*. Philadelphia: University of Pennsylvania Press; Scheuer, Michael (2005). The London Bombings: For al-Qaeda, Steady as She Goes. *Terrorism Focus, 2*(14), 10–21.

89. Kirby, Aidan (2007). The London Bombers as "Self-Starters": A Case Study in Indigenous Radicalization and the Emergence of Autonomous Cliques. *Studies in Conflict & Terrorism, 30*, 415–428, p. 416.

90. Kirby, Aidan (2007). The London Bombers as "Self-Starters": A Case Study in Indigenous Radicalization and the Emergence of Autonomous Cliques. *Studies in Conflict & Terrorism, 30*, 415–428.

91. Kenney, Michael (2007). *From Pablo to Osama: Trafficking and Terrorist Networks, Government Bureaucracies, and Competitive Adaptation*. University Park, PA: Pennsylvania State University Press; Marion, Russ, & Uhl-Bien, Mary (2003). Complexity Theory and Al-Qaeda: Examining Complex Leadership. *Emergence, 5*(1), 54–76.

92. Juergensmeyer, Mark (2000). *Terror in the Mind of God: The Global Rise of Religious Violence*. Berkeley: University of California Press; Spaaij, Ramón (2010). The Enigma of Lone Wolf Terrorism: An Assessment. *Studies in Conflict & Terrorism, 33*, 854–870.

93. Martin, Gus (2010). *Understanding Terrorism: Challenges, Perspectives, and Issues*. Thousand Oaks, CA: Sage.

94. Hoffman, Bruce (2003). *Inside Terrorism*. New York: Columbia University Press.

95. Kaplan, Jeffrey (1997). Leaderless Resistance. *Terrorism and Political Violence, 9*(3), 80–95.

96. Dishman, Chris (2005). The Leaderless Nexus: When Crime and Terror Converge. *Studies in Conflict & Terrorism, 28*, 237–252.

97. Leader, Stefan, & Probst, Peter (2003). The Earth Liberation Front and Environmental Terrorism. *Terrorism and Political Violence, 15*(4), 37–58.

98. Spaaij, Ramón (2010). The Enigma of Lone Wolf Terrorism: An Assessment. *Studies in Conflict & Terrorism, 33*, 854–870.

99. Hewitt, Christopher (2003). *Understanding Terrorism in America: From the Klan to al Qaeda*. London: Routledge.

100. Hersley, John (2004). *Simple Truths: The Real Story of the Oklahoma City Bombing Investigation*. Oklahoma City: Oklahoma Heritage Association.

101. Spaaij, Ramón (2010). The Enigma of Lone Wolf Terrorism: An Assessment. *Studies in Conflict & Terrorism, 33*, 854–870.

Diffusion of Innovations (DoI) and Terrorism

After reading this chapter, you will be able to

- discuss the application of the Diffusion of Innovations theory to the spread of terrorism;
- describe the mimetism, or imitation, of terrorism; and
- identify and evaluate the transmission of terrorist memes.

DIFFUSION OF INNOVATIONS (DOI): DEFINITION

Developed by Everett Rogers (1962),[1] **Diffusion of Innovations (DoI)** is a theory that explains how innovations (i.e., ideas, movements, or inventions) are diffused through certain channels over time across society and diverse cultures. DoI is the notion that trends, rather than emerging independently through invention, proliferate from one society to another through various types of contact and communication. A specific innovation is initiated within a given culture. Then, it is diffused by all sorts of means from this starting point. DoI involves four main elements. The first element is the innovation; it is defined by Rogers (2003)[2] as "an idea, practice, or object that is perceived as new by an individual or other unit of adoption" (p. 12). The second is the communication channel—the means by which a message moves from one person to another. The third is time—the length of time that it takes for an innovation to diffuse and be embraced, or rejected, by society. Fourth is the social system, defined by Rogers as "a set of interrelated units that are engaged in a joint problem solving to accomplish a common goal" (p. 14).

During the diffusion process, people accept innovations through five steps: knowledge, persuasion, decision, implementation, and confirmation. Knowledge is the first step and occurs when an individual is exposed to an innovation for the first time. He or she has never heard of the innovation before and has yet to decide whether he or she should look for additional information about the innovation. The second step is persuasion. This occurs when the individual is persuaded to seek additional information on the innovation and to actively obtain this information. Next, the decision step is the crucial point at which the individual assesses the benefits and drawbacks of the innovation and then decides whether or not to adopt it. In the implementation step, the individual puts the innovation into practice, gauges its actual practicality, and looks for more information about it. Finally, confirmation describes the step at which he or she finalizes his or her choice about adoption. If the person decides to fully embrace the innovation, that person will keep using it to his or her advantage.[3]

INTRODUCTION TO DOI AND TERRORISM

DoI can be easily applied to terrorism. Terrorists have exported their tactics to other places in the world and even influenced unaffiliated groups in other nations to use arms against governments.[4] An example is the diffusion of "foquismo" terrorism established by the success of the Cuban revolution (through advocates such as Che Guevara) into many Latin American countries and even to Africa and certain parts of Europe. By definition, **foquismo** refers to revolution by way of guerrilla warfare. Based on the tenets of DoI, foquismo terrorism can be applied to Laurent-Désiré Kabila's malicious tactics in the Congo, where he was the president from 1997 to 2001. Exposed to foquismo in 1960, Kabila was quickly persuaded by it. He decided to implement it in 1965, when Che Guevara arrived in the Congo with about 100 men to create a Cuban-style revolution. It was implemented and confirmed through various key battles, but it was suppressed the same year due to a lack of supplies and manpower.[5] Castro's and Guevara's writings were also helpful in inciting ethnic Tamils to resort to political violence against the Sinhalese in Sri Lanka.[6] Extremist groups in Western Europe have emulated the behaviors of Latin American terrorists, and not vice versa. From this perspective, terrorism spread from well-developed terror factions to more nascent ones.[7] As Jean Baudrillard (2002)[8] explained it,

> Terrorism, like viruses, is everywhere. There is a world diffusion of terrorism that functions as the shadow of any system of domination, everywhere ready to awaken as a double agent. It inhabits the very heart of the culture that battles it. (p. 406)

René Girard's (1996)[9] theory of **mimetic rivalry** presents terrorism as a consequence of competition between nations, when the aspiration to imitate the leading nation is stymied by the unfeasibility of doing so. Integration and economic competition are often considered the successful methods to bring about positive gains for all actors of international trade. DoI is akin to the "contagion" of terrorism. **Contagion** refers to the occurrence of terrorism in one nation that increases the probability of a neighboring nation being exposed to terrorism. This leads to a growing number of nations that transition from experiencing no terrorist incidents at all to experiencing some incidents later.[10] On explaining contagion, Midlarsky, Crenshaw, and Yoshida (1980)[11] suggested a theory of hierarchies. Prominently diplomatic countries are considered to be the first to have terrorist incidents, which then spread like a contagious disease to less prominent nations via a process of imitation. They find evidence of terrorism contagion from Latin America to Western Europe between 1973 and 1974. There are many other types of diffusion that can help spread terrorist practices, as shown below (based on various sources):[12]

- Hierarchical diffusion: research indicates that the diffusion of terrorism is mostly one of diffusing down (rather than up). In other words, influential terrorist groups diffuse innovative tactics (whether directly or indirectly) to nascent terrorist organizations.

- Knowledge diffusion: a process by which knowledge can diffuse from one place to another. The perpetual diffusion of technical knowledge translates into an ever-increasing pool of capable people from which terrorist organizations can draw. Nuclear materials are broadly spread worldwide (although they can be insufficiently secured in some facilities). Principally, the growth of religion-based terrorism and doomsday cults has been supplemented by ever-higher degrees of violence, as shown in the September 11, 2001 attacks.

- Relocation diffusion occurs when terrorist organizations move from one place to another over time.

- Relational diffusion occurs when the ideas of terrorist organizations diffuse to individuals with a shared identity. This happens fairly spontaneously through the social networks of the organization's members.

- Non-relational diffusion occurs when one terrorist organization imitates another organization's ideas without the two interacting.

- Brokerage occurs when ideas are purposely diffused from one terrorist organization to another through an intermediary. Individuals with origins in many different places and social networks are often the most effectual routes for brokerage.

- Noncontagious diffusion: collaboration between terrorist organizations in regard to intelligence, training, financial resources, and support. Noncontagious diffusion also refers to the transference and carrying of terrorist activities across nations to find weaker victims or accomplish greater impact. Both the contagion and transportation systems are key explanations of the geographic diffusion of transnational terrorism.

What these types of terrorism diffusion models exemplify is the fact that, by means of diffusionism, a major innovation in terrorist practice is anticipated to have been made in a specific time and place, and then to have been diffused to other terrorist organizations. It is obvious that the frequent occurrence of terrorist acts in one nation will increase the probability that other nations will experience terrorist incidents in the future.[13]

DOI, TERRORISM, AND SOCIAL MOVEMENT THEORY

DoI is a social process involving the communication of an idea or practice from people within the same society, and often from one society to the next, and then from one country to the next. A similar theory, **Social Movement Theory (SMT)**, attempts to explain the social production and diffusion of meaning and how people come to see themselves as a collectivity. This group shares the same values (what is right and wrong) and beliefs (interpretations of the world, characteristics of things, and means of causation).[14] The most successful movements in recruiting activists and supporters and in their ability to survive under repressive circumstances over a long period of time are those that create powerful ideas—ideas that resonate with a specific cultural and historical context. Although Islamist extremism is a supranational or transnational phenomenon, Islamist movements must cater to the local milieus in which they recruit, and then apply their ideas to form the activists' and followers' identities. More successful Islamist leaders adroitly give prominence to local issues and are inspired by local norms that match and strengthen their own ideological mission.[15]

SMT stresses the importance of **frame alignment**, the development of congruence between a person's and the movement's interests, values, and beliefs.[16] Wickham's (2002)[17] study of the Muslim Brotherhood in Egypt, for instance, highlights the importance of "ideational framing," particularly in high-risk environments. When DoI and SMT are fused together, we have **social epidemics**. These are idea-driven social movements that diffuse through a culture by exponential, rather than geometric, growth. While not everyone will be affected by the idea pushed by the movement, exponential growth echoes the notion that practically nobody is left unexposed. The central element to the shift between an idea within a culture and a full-scale epidemic is the **tipping point**, the period during which a conspicuous change takes places within the behavior or outlook of a population. These points can best be considered **snow fall**: the degree distinction between having snow and not having snow may be just one or two degrees, but the functional distinction is green grass versus white snow.[18]

Spillover Effect

A **spillover effect** is an effect observed in violent domestic conflicts that develop internationally, so that revolutions spill over national borders into the international arena.[19] An example is the uprising that started in Tunisia in January 2011 and, then, that diffused to Algeria, Egypt, Yemen, and Libya. Thousands of demonstrators staged unprecedented protests against the nations' autocratic leaders. During the revolutions, the U.S. was afraid of the rise of Islamist groups such as Al Qaeda and the Muslim Brotherhood. The uprisings in the Middle East spread the **neo-ummah**, a constructed, imaginary worldwide community of all Muslims; this can be made possible by the decline of traditional territory-bound identities and communities.[20] In some cases, all a movement or recruiter has to do is draw on a preexisting **sentiment pool**—people who already share the grumbles, objections, and attributional characteristics of the movement. Such sentiment pool involves the use of symbols, rhetoric, and various reasons for contentions.[21]

Another example of the spillover effect is what happened after the Soviet occupation of Afghanistan in 1979. A great majority of the Afghan Arabs continued their jihad in other places, becoming global mujahedin. As such, many Algerians went back home to fight alongside Muslim rebels in the brutal Algerian revolts in the 1990s. Others fought in Bosnia and earned an international reputation for their zeal, combating skills, and violence. Many Afghan Arabs reached out to Muslim communities in Asia and Africa, helping local Islamic groups in their causes. They offered technical assistance and additional resources to these groups. For instance, Filipino and Indonesian jihadists were often in contact with the Al Qaeda network and Afghan Arabs. Afghan Arabs helped Chechens against Russians, and some Chechens afterward fought alongside the Taliban in Afghanistan.[22]

Opinion Leadership

Opinion leadership is the practice whereby charismatic individuals are able to sway people's attitudes or plain behavior in a desired fashion with relative frequency. Put another way, an opinion leader has great personal influence on people; by diffusing knowledge to them, he or she can change their behaviors or attitudes.[23] With respect to terrorism, an example of an opinion leader who can successfully push people to commit acts of terror is the imam. According to Zuhdi Jasser (2008),[24] president of the American Islamic Forum for Democracy, **imams** (spiritual leaders in Muslim communities) in the Middle East have attempted to weaken the efforts of local Muslims to oppose and condemn publicly terrorist acts perpetrated for the benefit of Islam. They have also been reported to encourage the killing of "disbelievers." This was confirmed by Tahir-ul-Qadri (2010)[25] in *Introduction to the Fatwa on Suicide Bombings and Terrorism*. The author described how imams issued two fatwas (i.e., Islamic decrees) to declare the Kharijites (a tiny minority of Muslims in Iraq) disbelievers and that they should be killed. That is why imams do not condemn suicide bombings and other terrorist acts against disbelievers.

In line with these contentions, based on lengthy interviews with thirty-five imprisoned Palestinian terrorists, Post, Sprinzak, and Denny (2003)[26] found that social institutions (i.e., mosques) played a major part in the recruiting of new members in jihadist groups. Institutions like places of worship or educational services have created an atmosphere of shared experience and a degree of seclusion from infidels where "epistemic authorities," which include imams and other religious figures, can promulgate the terrorists' ideology and bring other external forces to influence potential recruits.[27]

In addition, extremist Muslim elites are also seizing opportunities and resources to be agents of cultural change—or change agents. A **change agent** is an individual who influences innovation decisions in a direction considered appropriate by a change agency. A change agent engages either intentionally in social, cultural, or behavioral change or does it through his or her natural behavior.[28] Terrorist movements rely on mechanisms and diffusers of ideas who communicate them to society through speeches, texts, leaflets, brochures, and, increasingly, Internet websites. Personal connections and small numbers enable and simplify trust and unity within the group. Diffusers successfully convey ideas through interpersonal contact that fosters personal bonds and instructs and converts recruits. In Central Asia and Azerbaijan, change agency happens through a range of informal networks—including informal Islamic circles and mahalla (neighborhood), community, tribe, region, student, and business connections.[29]

JIHAD DIFFUSING THROUGH MUSLIM COUNTRIES

Some aspects of the jihad problem today can be traced back to Iran. The revolution of 1979 generated and sponsored radical Islamist movements worldwide, particularly among the Shi'ites. The Grand Ayatollah Khomeini labeled America as the Great Satan to be blamed for the misfortunes of the Muslim countries and launched a holy war against America and Israel.[30] Exhorted by Khomeini and supported by the resources of revolutionary Iran and its zealous forces, religious leaders, mosques, schools, and media, the philosophy of Islamic revival and crusade (jihad) diffused in the Muslim world with particular importance among minority Shi'ites. Khomeini proclaimed, "Islam and the teaching of the Koran will prevail all over the world... weapons in our hands are used to realize divine and Islamic aspirations."[31]

Under the shield and with the assistance of the Association of Militant Clerics in Tehran, the Council for the Islamic Revolution, and the Revolutionary Guard Corps, the urge to change the world was proclaimed across the Muslim and Arab world for young males to migrate to Iran and become holy warriors. A plethora of men came from Libya, Palestine, Egypt, Lebanon, the Gulf States, Saudi Arabia, Egypt, and other nations. At various locations and training camps, they were exposed to religious brainwashing, weapons training, and other types of schooling. A privileged few, the "best of the best" for the jihad, became volunteers for martyrdom. They went back to their own homelands to develop local cells of revolutionary groups; others enlisted in the Iran–Iraq conflict as revolutionary combatants.[32]

The jihad diffused to the Arabian Peninsula, the civil war in Lebanon, and Egypt. When Egyptian President Anwar Sadat crushed the Muslim Brotherhood (as he anticipated a jihad annexation of power) and arrested radicals, closed publications, banned Islamic societies, and seized independent mosques, he was assassinated on October 6, 1981. The jihad had infiltrated the Egyptian army. The jihad also held Anwar Sadat responsible for having signed a truce with Israel and granted the deposed Shah of Iran a refuge the year before the assassination. In Saudi Arabia, and in neighboring states, the Saudis financed (through religious institutions) and supported fundamentalist mullahs (Islamic scholars), mosques, religious schools, social services, and charitable establishments. On top of fulfilling legitimate religious and social purposes, all such groups came to represent a religious infrastructure for jihads and religion-driven terrorists. In Pakistan, the military state also backed Islamist radicals and their religious schools as an inexpensive way to endorse terrorism in Kashmir and the Taliban in Afghanistan. The military state eventually fostered a culture of violence.[33]

The next jihad was not against America but against the Soviet Union and the communist-supported government in Afghanistan. In the 1980s, using the blueprint adopted by the Iranian Revolutionary Guards for establishing a jihad and financed by his own and Saudi funds, Osama bin Laden set up recruitment centers for mujahedin in the Middle East, North

Africa, and Asia. Volunteers clustered in Pakistani camps where they were subjected to training, indoctrination, and incentives for engaging in guerrilla battle in Afghanistan. The fight against the Soviets in Afghanistan was a victory. The U.S.-led Operation Desert Storm defeated Iraq's invasion of Kuwait and reestablished the state of Kuwait, yet it became a decisive moment in Osama bin Laden's radicalism. It was a motive for carrying out a long-term agenda to commit terrorism in the U.S.[34]

DIFFUSION OF HAMAS AND ITS IDEAS

Founded in 1987, **Hamas** (the "Islamic Resistance Movement") is a Palestinian Islamist group that rules over the Gaza Strip. In the January 25, 2006 Palestinian election, Hamas won its majority in the Palestinian parliament, while Fatah (the largest faction of the PLO) lost many seats. Many countries, including the U.S., classify Hamas as a terrorist group. One of Hamas's most important publications is *Filastin al-Muslimah*, a well-designed monthly periodical that functions as Hamas's prime voice since the group was created. The publication is run from Damascus, printed in Beirut, and continues to circulate from the U.K. to the West Bank, the Gaza Strip, Arab countries, and even Muslim areas in Europe, the U.S., Canada, and Australia. It can be accessed both in hard copies and in an Internet version.[35] Under new regulations of the Palestinian Authority, in 1995, Hamas obtained a license to publish a weekly newspaper, *Al Watan*. A little later, in 1997, another weekly, *A Risala*, started to be published in Gaza. Both these newspapers, together with the publications of the Palestinian Islamic Jihad, were the most important voices opposing the Palestinian Authority.[36]

Ever since portable radios became widely accepted in Arab countries, they have been important tools to diffuse revolutionary messages throughout national and subnational movements. As an ideological activist organization, Hamas considers the radio an important channel for disseminating its messages. Even though the group only obtained its license to direct a radio station (Sawt al Aksa) in 2003 (from the Palestinian Authority), unauthorized radio stations identified with Hamas have been active since the early days of the organization. The launch of the legal Sawt al Aksa was a defining moment in the history of the organization's media activities. Soon after the station began to transmit, it had already organized broadcasts in sequence for the major part of the day, rapidly becoming popular all over Gaza and the West Bank.[37]

A little before the 2006 general elections, Hamas received a permit to run a television channel, which became a prominent and chief tool for winning the elections. Hamas's loyal audience, which was a useful target for radio broadcasts, now also enjoyed watching the Hamas television channel, al-Aqsa TV. After winning the elections, Hamas moved to satellite broadcasts, and today al-Aqsa TV broadcasts a whole range of television shows directed to different age groups, from children's programs to shows about religion and quotidian news. For the past several years, Hamas used the Internet considerably to diffuse its messages. Hamas runs many websites including certified websites, forums, online chat rooms, online bulletin boards, a video clips site, and websites catered to children, adolescents, and women. The most famous Hamas propaganda website is the Lebanon-based "Palestine-info" network of twenty or more sites. Domains include Palestine-info-urdu.com, palestine-persian.info, and palestine-info.net.[38]

DIFFUSION OF THE MUSLIM BROTHERHOOD IN INDONESIA

There are several major forms of channels: media (one-way communication), which are usually imitative; public contact (one-way communication), which can reach out to a sizeable audience; and interpersonal contact (two-way communication), which tends to be interactive. The interactive type of channel means that both the sender and receiver have an active role, so that the diffusion of ideas occurs through interpersonal contacts. The public form has also a sender and receiver, but only the sender is active. The media form means that the source of the message is not active; rather, the receiver imitates the message through indirect contact.[39] Based on these models of diffusion of information, let us have a look at the diffusion of the Muslim Brotherhood's influence into Indonesia. The **Muslim Brotherhood** is an organization created by Hassan al Banna in 1928. The purpose was to bring back the spirit and religious purity that existed when the Prophet Muhammad and the four Rightly Guided caliphs were alive. The Muslim Brotherhood wants to establish a Caliphate (a single Muslim world) by means of education and religious reform. A militant wing of the Brotherhood was created by Sayyid Qutb, which had the same objective but through violence. The terrorist group Hamas describes itself as the Palestinian underarm of the Muslim Brotherhood.[40]

The transmission of Muslim Brotherhood's ideas to Indonesian Muslims was made through Saudi Arabia. The diffusion of the organization's ideas into Indonesia also occurred through two of the three major forms of channels: the media and interpersonal contact forms. First, the Brotherhood's influence impacted Indonesian Muslims via the print media, mostly Arabic books translated into Indonesian since the mid-1970s. Second, Indonesian students in Saudi Arabia engaged in direct contact with the sources of messages and returned to their homeland to diffuse them even more to their fellow Muslims. Those Indonesians who already knew the Muslim Brotherhood's ideas at home quickly embraced the statements and messages made by the Middle Eastern graduates. Moreover, the graduates enhanced the new ideas with the method of establishment of the movement itself, drawing on the Muslim Brotherhood's training and organizational artifacts of computer technology.[41] Today, the Muslim Brotherhood is the world's most dominant Islamist movement.

The crucial role of participants in diffusing religious ideas is characterized by their progress from their original land to foreign ones (i.e., from Indonesia to Saudi Arabia), and their return to Indonesia to diffuse the new ideas they have received from overseas. This is a process that Mandaville (2001)[42] has labeled **traveling theory**, in which not only people but also ideas travel from one country to another. Through extensive travel, however, an idea will not maintain its fundamental/extremist edge. An idea can also assume a new essential consciousness, both in itself and in shaping other ideas after enduring travel. The case of the diffusion of Muslim Brotherhood's ideas to Indonesia (and channeled through Saudi Arabia) has also produced change and revision. Fundamentalist Indonesian students have taken the Muslim Brotherhood's ideas and blended them with the revivalist dogma of Saudi Arabia. They diffused this new **syncretism** (religious or cultural synthesis) to Indonesian students in the nation's universities which had been first ruled by modernist activists.[43]

DIFFUSING SUICIDE TERRORISM

In his article titled "Nonstate Actors and the Diffusion of Innovations: The Case of Suicide Terrorism," Michael Horowitz (2010)[44] studied the diffusion of suicide terrorism thoroughly. Every now and then, desire is an insufficient criterion for adopting an innovation. Even though Al Qaeda benefited from financial resources, committed fighters, and weapons, the group transferred its members to Hezbollah (an innovating group for suicide bombings) to continue developing the experiential knowledge required to conduct its own missions. Second, organizational capacity is important too. Al Qaeda did not have a substantial operational past, leaving no records for counterterrorism organizations to study, and making Al Qaeda very flexible in designing the 1998 embassy bombings in Africa. Without an operational history that could inform counterterrorism teams on what strategies Al Qaeda would use, it was easier to venture into new territories of operations like suicide bombing. Third, one cannot understand how military power works without understanding how it diffuses. The collaboration between Al Qaeda and Hezbollah is now a critical point in the diffusion of suicide attacks worldwide. Let us look at it this way: it is a matter that linked a key innovating group in the 1980s, Hezbollah, to the prime diffuser of knowledge about suicide attacks from the mid-1990s until today, Al Qaeda.

For Horowitz, models taken from business and organizational innovation studies and traditional military books can help evaluating terrorist groups as well. For instance, while long-established or veteran terrorist groups are more able to espouse incremental or sustaining innovations, disruptive innovations that require transforming organizational rules or operational tactics can represent a serious challenge to such long-established or veteran groups. The disruptive organizational changes so necessary to adopt the suicide attack method were difficult for terrorist groups that were successful before the advent of suicide attacks, beginning in the early 1980s. Influential pre-1980s groups, such as the Palestine Liberation Organization (PLO), the Provisional Irish Republican Army (PIRA), and the Basque Fatherland and Freedom Group (ETA), were unable to adopt suicide attacks in the short-to-medium term.

Horowitz also observed that, in the terrorist world, new innovations require new levels of financial resources and organizational change for adoption. In addition, capacity is usually not exchangeable in the short and medium term. Yet, suicide bombing was a new military innovation with low financial difficulties to entry but high organizational difficulties. In essence, while capacity is not a significant matter from a financial standpoint, it has been demonstrated that not all terrorist groups have been able to successfully perform suicide attacks even if they wanted to do so. Groups that have failed suicide attacks, like the Revolutionary Armed Forces of Colombia (FARC), exemplify the notion that capacity is an important potential matter.

Theoretically, suicide attacks can diffuse through both direct and indirect mechanisms. **Direct diffusion** occurs when terrorist groups physically collaborate and train together, and when knowledge is communicated from one group to another.[45] The historical incident whereby Hezbollah operatives trained Hamas operatives in "suicide education" (after Hamas members were expelled to Lebanon in 1992) is an example of direct diffusion. **Indirect diffusion** happens when one group becomes familiar with the actions of another group and imitates those actions.[46] For example, stories about the suicide jacket created by the Tamil Tigers (LTTE) in Sri Lanka motivated Hamas to adopt similar tactics. This is indirect diffusion.[47]

The means for diffusion become the direct transmission of information from organization to organization or mimicry via vicarious learning. Although less formal than **epistemic communities** (networks of experts with recognized knowledge and skill in specific issues or areas),[48] shared beliefs about effectiveness and the manner in which to weigh costs and benefits could affect how terrorist groups make decisions as to whether to adopt an innovation. Both direct and indirect contacts between terrorist groups could drive a learning method that may resemble emulation if factors such as ethnicity, religion, and language operate as the center for diffusion.[49]

DOI AND MIMETISM: DEFINITION

A more extreme version of DoI is **mimetism**, a theory explaining the capacity of imitation (to mimic). To mimic means to copy or imitate meticulously or assume the appearance of someone or something. Within mimetism lies the word *meme*, an abbreviation of another word, *mimeme*, which comes from the Greek *mimesis* (imitation). *Meme* was introduced by Richard Dawkins (1976),[50] in his book *The Selfish Gene*. It is now part of the English language. By definition, a **meme** is a unit of cultural transmission or cultural imitation. The smiley is an example of what people might call a visual meme. Anyone who knows what a smiley is can copy, reproduce, or alter it and then show it to other people. A meme is any unit of information—such as an idea, concept, or movement—which one mind diffuses (verbally or by demonstration) to another mind. Examples of memes are thoughts, ideas, theories, attitudes, beliefs, moods, hatred, poetry, habits, dance, songs, catch-phrases, fashions, and appearances. Meme sounds like gene. Memes diffuse in the meme pool by jumping from brain to brain through a process called imitation, in the same way that genes diffuse in the gene pool by jumping from body to body through sperm or eggs.[51]

Vertical vs. Horizontal Transmission

Mimetism suggests that a process of information transmission takes place between the television screen and the brain of the individual watching the television screen. A meme can be disseminated through vertical transmission or horizontal transmission. **Vertical transmission** takes place from parents to offspring (from generation to generation). **Horizontal transmission** occurs between people of the same generation. Horizontal transmission enables cultural sharing between societies. For example, it occurs when youth are acquiring knowledge from the media. Horizontal transmission is the same as "parasite transmission."[52] The movie *Natural Born Killers* is an example of horizontal transmission because such cultural meme was not transmitted by parents but by contemporary entertainment media.

In many societies, parents can transmit—that is, vertical transmission—cooking skills to their children or even their "killing art." However, if it is the media or fellow students—as it was the case for the Muslim Brotherhood (i.e., media form and interpersonal form)—that teach others, then we are dealing with horizontal transmission. For a meme to efficiently leap from mind to mind, it must match a basic human need, want, or value to be adopted—and its indicative or characteristic behavior enacted. This can be called **resonating**. A meme must resonate with current mental concepts, or it must imply something that may be considered valuable, or desirable, before it can become popular. Resonance can be important at the individual or the group level.[53]

Meme Replication

Meme replication requires three significant elements. First, an individual must be open to the message contained in the meme. He or she must be receptive to the intent of the message or to the model in which the message is transmitted. Second, the meme must have fidelity. It must be resistant to change that may be influenced on it by the various cultures, education, and socialization that constitute the worldviews of possible hosts. If there is no such fidelity, the message contained within the meme will change or disappear as it leaps from mind to mind. Third, the meme must resonate with an inherent emotion or value already owned by, or pleasing to, the host. A meme (e.g., a terrorism meme) can only communicate its existence via the behaviors of a caring host. It must be willfully embraced and its consequential behavior displayed in acts imitating the violence embedded in the message.[54]

A **memeoid** is an individual whose behavior is deeply shaped by a meme, images they watch on television, or an icon. The hazard is that their survival is contingent on the way the meme is transmitted. A **host** is someone who has been greatly infected by a meme. A meme is successful when it travels rapidly and effectively between the sender of the meme and the host. **Infection**, then, is a person's successful encoding of a meme in his or her memory. An individual exposed to a meme, and who remembers it (consciously or unconsciously), has been infected.[55] Memes are self-replicating and ubiquitous in all cultures, present in the subconscious background, or **socio-structural white noise**, that is, the foundation of all societies. They perform the role of subconscious agents influencing an individual's decision-making process. They achieve this by creating the subliminal boundaries within which conscious decisions are made. Intrinsically, they remain "alive" within each person in a population, directing their choices and actions.[56]

Meme replication would not happen without memetic engineering. **Memetic engineering** is the process of (1) creating memes with the purpose of changing the behavior of people in society or humanity; (2) designing and developing theories or philosophies according to an analysis of societies, cultures, their modes of thinking, and the advancement of their minds; and (3) transforming beliefs and thought patterns.[57] A **memotype** is the real information content of a meme. A **meme pool** is the compilation of all memes existing in a specific population. A **memeplex** is a collection of memes often found within the same person. Memeplexes lump together easily because memes will replicate themselves much better when they are "teamed up." Examples include groups of memes such as singing and guitar playing, or the Christmas tree and Christmas dinner.[58]

DOI AND MIMETISM: TERRORISM

Memetic engineering works well for the diffusion of terrorism. With progress in information and communication technology, the diffusion of memes from brain to brain, sometimes labeled **thought contagion**, has made significant progress in the capacity to infect memeoids.[59] In the 1970s, the Grand Ayatollah Khomeini, hiding in Paris, sneaked his memes into Iran: audiotapes of his spellbinding sermons and guidelines for Muslims to establish a Caliphate. Presently, the mass media are diffusing extremist propaganda deliberately or as a supplementary outcome of news coverage. As we have seen, the Arab television network Al Jazeera operated as a powerful instrument to spread the Osama bin Laden meme by broadcasting his speeches. Contemporary communication technologies facilitate the transmission of messages for terrorists—for example, Internet websites. At the same time, they make it difficult for the state to protect its citizens from terrorism.[60] This is a standard example of horizontal transmission because this is what young people are learning from the media. Conversely, in the example of the imams (spiritual leaders) described previously, teaching Muslims to kill disbelievers is a case of vertical transmission, as an elder transmits ways and procedures to youth.

The Al Qaeda Memes

A study conducted by Smallman (1997)[61] to examine the substantial upsurge of reporting of terrorist incidents is evidence of the progress in information technology, the attention of the media, and the increase in terrorist acts themselves as the terrorist meme is imitated through these means. Before September 11, 2001, a rise in the diffusion of terrorist memes was occurring more quickly than a rise of the terrorist acts themselves. Currently, Al Qaeda is an enormous household name among Islamist terrorists. Certain groups consider it an advantage to have embraced the widely familiar Al Qaeda brand name. This resembles the way franchisees embrace commercial brand names although their origins and organizations differ from Al Qaeda and most of its objectives. Examples of the Al Qaeda household name include the Al Qaeda–branded groups in Iraq (predominantly established by the late Abu Musab al-Zarqawi) and in the western region of North Africa (mainly the Algerian group that previously called itself the Salafist Group for Preaching and Combat).

Furthermore, there are many other comparable groups that do not bear the Al Qaeda brand. Yet, like the franchisees, they have adopted the Al Qaeda's extremist Salafist ideology and proclivity for violence. They identify with some of its international objectives but also have more regionally catered objectives of their own. Al Qaeda memeoids include

Jemaah Islamiya in Southeast Asia and the Islamic Movement of Uzbekistan in Central Asia. On tops of these groups are innumerable unnamed memeoid cells and people across the globe whose love toward Al Qaeda is much more an issue of inspiration and ideology than of a command and control nature.[62] For example, the relationship between Islamist terrorists in Morocco (e.g., the May 16, 2003 attacks in Casablanca) and Al Qaeda, in spite of their ideological similarities, is not of a command and control nature. Rather, the relationship is more a matter of a franchise operation after Moroccan terrorists successfully encoded Al Qaeda memes.[63]

Al Qaeda–inspired franchises associate themselves to the group through ideological kinship, a shared brand name, and high admiration to the group's central leaders. Al Qaeda is now as much an ideology as a single organization led by a leader—since Osama bin Laden's death, it is al-Zawahiri (the "Egyptian Doctor"). Al Qaeda has gradually become a brand name, inevitably related to the various expressions of present-day Islamist militancy. This is obvious in the shifting patterns of Al Qaeda terrorism. For instance, the Al Qaeda–infected terrorists in Madrid (March 11, 2004) did not commit suicide bombings, like many previous Al Qaeda members: the audience who witnessed their deaths as a key aspect of their message ("We love death as much as you love life"). Oddly enough, the Madrid bombings were based on a short-term, influential purpose: to force the removal of Spanish troops from Iraq.[64]

Truly, during all this time that the Global War on Terror (GWOT) has been chasing and demolishing Al-Qaeda's central organization, Al Qaeda–infected groups have been active. Encoding the Al Qaeda meme, they have perpetrated a sequence of fatal attacks worldwide, from Madrid to Casablanca, from London to Istanbul, from Riyadh and Baghdad, and from Bali to Jakarta. Many of these groups already existed before Al Qaeda and have their own regional or national agendas. They do not openly communicate or coordinate their attacks with Al Qaeda. Rather, as outsiders to the Al Qaeda network, these groups only apply the Al Qaeda meme through ideology.[65] One could argue that franchising the Al Qaeda brand is precisely what the theory of memetic engineering predicts: diffusing memes to change the behavior of people and, ultimately, transforming beliefs and thought patterns.

Suicide Terrorism and Social Proof

When discussing suicide terrorism, Dennett (2006)[66] uses another mimetic term: *symbiosis*. A meme can be symbiotic because it inspires sacrifice and altruism. In the absence of these traits, we would not, as human beings, have accomplished so much. Suicide terrorism survives because the suicide memes that terrorist groups and certain doomsday cults diffuse to their followers infect the brain.[67] As Pedahzur, Perliger, and Weinberg (2003)[68] describe it, "in a society where honor is among the highest virtues, there are indeed powerful social pressures lying behind the suicide bomber's decision" (p. 420). The Prophet Muhammad said that killing an infidel symbolizes high righteousness for which the killer should be honored (Qur'an 9:111: "Allah has purchased of the believers their persons and their goods; for theirs in return is the garden of Paradise. They fight in His cause, and slay and are slain; a promise binding on Him in truth"). For the suicide terrorist, Muhammad would be social proof. In the social proof model, individuals imitate others who seem similar.

Social proof is a powerful psychological means by which we emulate others to direct our own actions. In terms of suicide, those who are willing to commit suicide have already been infected by memes (i.e., through training camps, indoctrination, religious schools, etc.). So, witnessing another person on television ready to take his or her own life—as in the case of self-made martyrdom videotapes (see Chapter 2)—gives them definitive motivation. Some violent behaviors, branded under terms such as *terrorist* or *bomber*, become memorialized in history. Therefore, a certain number of people use those immortalized people as social proof to justify their suicide attacks. What they do is project themselves into the role and conditions of such "heroes." They opt for this because particular violent acts have become memes with which they identify and through which they find validation.[69]

Mirror Neurons

The human brain has mirror neurons. As a brain cell, the **mirror neuron** is capable to seize and interpret information and imitate this as action. This constitutes the neurological foundation for an argument incorporating the copycat effect, like the one reflected in the memetic engineering design.[70] The **copycat effect** refers to the tendency of sensational publicity about extreme murders or suicides to give rise to more of the same through imitation. Mirror neurons facilitate reenactment through the copycat effect. Movies are a great source of inspiration to lethal outcomes. Each time the 1978 movie *Deerhunter* is shown on television, someone in the audience will shoot him- or herself by replicating the Russian roulette scene, where North Vietnamese soldiers forced the American captives to put one bullet in the barrel of a gun and fire at themselves; forty-three died by 1986.[71] A similar term, the **Werther effect**, is copycat suicide. It is the mirroring of another suicide that the individual attempting suicide is familiar with—either from local knowledge or thanks to accounts or portrayals of the original suicide on TV and other media. Both the copycat effect and Werther effect are examples of toxic memes. A **toxic meme** is a self-replicating pool of powerful information diffusing a message of empathy. Such message typically goes against the values and norms of society or clashes with the needs and expectations of that society. Toxic memes are self-replicating pools of nefarious information, leaping from mind to mind and searching for receptive or vulnerable hosts through which more replication can occur.[72]

SOCIAL LEARNING THEORY

Albert Bandura's (1973, 1998)[73] **social learning theory** posits that violence is a result of witnessing and imitating an aggressive model. This theory has been used to explain terrorist violence not as the result of innate aggressiveness but of cognitive "reconstrual" of moral obligations. Adolescents living in the centers of political conflict may directly observe terrorist violence and try to imitate it. They can even learn from their culture's public extolment of terrorists. An example is the common "martyr poster" alongside the streets of Shi'ite areas of Lebanon and Palestinian refugee camps. Another example is the song commending the accomplishments of the PIRA (Provisional Irish Republican Army).[74]

Social learning of the tolerability of terrorist behavior may also take an educational configuration, as exemplified in the teaching of a radical form of jihad in multiple Pakistani and Palestinian madrassas. These religious schools for young Muslim boys have been in place since the time of Muhammad. However, the recent global renaissance of Islamic fundamentalism has given rise to a high number of madrassas and probably an increase in the violence of their message. Evidence points to the fact that a minority of dominant international Islamist terrorists were schooled in madrassas.[75]

Terrorist didactic learning also happens through the diffusion of terrorist philosophy and methodology by using all forms of memetic engineering: announcements, audiovisual tapes, CDs, books, and websites. The most powerful historical example may be the 1969 *Mini-Manual* or *Handbook of Urban Guerilla Warfare* by Carlos Marighella, a Brazilian terrorist. The book has been translated in many languages and insists that readers should learn how to fly a plane.[76] The lengthy mission statement of Hamas (i.e., the "Islamic Resistance Movement") constitutes a more recent example. Article 15 of this charter stresses the importance of teaching jihad:

> We must imprint on the minds of generations of Muslims that the Palestinian problem is a religious one... I indeed wish to go to war for the sake of Allah! I will assault and kill, assault and kill, assault and kill.[77]

It seems conceivable that didactic teaching or social learning may talk some young minds into terrorism. As a symbolic gesture, terrorism is very memorable. For this reason, as well as the ease with which it can be implemented, terrorism is almost ideally imitable. The terrorist subculture creates a milieu in which violence is treasured. Social proofs such as the Tupamaros in Uruguay may be granted great prestige. The influence of such models is not weakened by their mission failures. The 1960s revolutionary crusade of the Tupamaros, for instance, climaxed in military tyranny. The mass media, especially television, are often considered key to the diffusion of information about models or social proofs. Yet, their actual influence may remain undocumented.[78]

MEME ANTIBODY

A **meme antibody** is a meme that reacts to markedly toxic ideas. It does so by neutralizing or extinguishing them, and at the same time offers immunity against them. If a child's father is extremely religious and thinks that television, video games, and rock music are evil, then the father will design a meme antibody (i.e., holding scriptures in his hand) and tell his child that only what is sacred should be followed—not television, video games, or rock music.[79]

Radical Islam

According to Gigantès (2003),[80] worldwide, many Muslims regard the U.S. as the Great Satan. As evidence, he uses several quotes of the Qur'an that make the following claims:

(1) Allah knows everything (i, 15); (2) a Muslim can do nothing about his death as the time is appointed by Allah and if he dies in a jihad—a holy war—he will go to heaven regardless of what he has done (iv, 74); and (3) in heaven, any believer who dies in jihad will be forever young and potent, and he will be given seventy virgins who will also be forever young and libidinous. There will always be wonderful fruit, rivers of milk and honey, and wine (xlvii, 15; lxxvi, 14–15; lv, 56–8). All these statements elicit powerful memetic imagery within the minds of those receptive or vulnerable to fundamentalism. In their minds, by using the Qur'an as a meme antibody against specific Western values and practices, susceptible individuals follow the will of Allah; they give good reasons for what they do. General consideration for the welfare of infidels (and non-Muslims) and clear statements for actions that should not be taken have been removed from their decision criteria. The meme antibody goes against anyone in the out-group and, therefore, the enemy of Allah.[81] Radical madrassas in southern Pakistan are an ideal environment for the creation of meme antibodies and tight-knit friendship in-groups to form. Young boys are subjected to extremist teaching and isolated from most of their kin and former friendships. The objective is to make sure that these teachings get perpetuated among people of the same age group and background.[82]

British Islamic Schools

The case of radical Islam in Pakistani madrassas is true irrespective of whether the people in question are susceptible students or hardened radicals merely associated with the radical madrassa. British Islamic schools nowadays have started to follow the same type of meme antibody indoctrination. A British network of over forty part-time Islamic schools—in which 5,000 students have been matriculated—has been applying the teachings of a Saudi Arabian government curriculum that deliberately includes anti-Semitic and homophobic lectures and activities. As stated by a BBC documentary broadcast called "Panorama," included in the curriculum of British Islamic schools is a textbook that requires children to list the "horrifying" qualities of Jews. The thirty-minute "Panorama" documentary cited the Saudi government-supplied textbook, which said that Jews "looked like monkeys and pigs," and that Zionists are determined to attain "world domination." Here, the meme antibody is Jewry overall. Children are fed memes that react to particularly toxic ideas—the idea that Jews are alive is "toxic enough."

The documentary quoted another part of the curriculum—for children as young as 6 years old—saying that any disbeliever in Islam would be condemned to death, specifically "hellfire." One of the textbooks recommended capital punishment for homosexual sex, and delineated a whole range of viewpoints as to whether execution should occur by stoning, immolation by fire, or throwing breakers of Islamic law off a cliff. Another textbook described the punishments determined by sharia law for theft, including the cutting off of both hands and feet. A BBC video, along with an article on the program's website, broadcasted a textbook drawing of a hand and a foot marked to show where exactly amputations should be performed.[83] Comparable evidence about Muslim extremism can be found in radical mosques in Britain (see Box 12.1).

Box 12.1   Radical Mosques in Britain

In 2007, Channel 4, a British television channel, reported on the alleged racist remarks made by an English lady to an Indian actress. Both were participating in *Big Brother*, a reality TV show enjoying an immense popularity around the world. The incident attracted more than 9 million viewers. During the same year, *Undercover Mosques* had a courageous journalist with a hidden camera risk his life for twelve months to make recordings of statements uttered by Muslim leaders in prominent mosques in Britain.[84] From the documentary, it followed that they preached Islamic supremacy, superiority, and hatred of kafirs (non-Muslims). Examples of statements are listed below:

"Live like a state within a state, until you take over."

"You cannot accept the rule of the kafir [non-Muslim]... we have to rule ourselves and we have to rule the others."

"If the Imam wants to crucify him, he should crucify him. The person is put up on the wood and he's left there to bleed to death for three days."

"You have to bomb the [non-Muslim] Indian businesses, and as for the Jews you kill them physically."

The viewing ratings for *Undercover Mosques* were 1–1.5 million viewers, compared to more than 9 million viewers for *Big Brother*. The Brits were interested in one thing: *Big Brother*. Does Britain not find the threat of religious persecution alarming? According to *The Sunday Times*, in an article published in the July 27, 2008 issue, close to a third of British Muslim students polled said that killing in the name of Islam can be justified. Forty percent of those Muslim students support the integration of sharia laws into British law, and a third of Muslim students favor the creation of a global Islamic state. Sharia refers to the Islamic legal code that justifies holy war, stonings, floggings, amputations, and beheadings for petty crimes, as it has been applied in countries like Saudi Arabia, Iran, Afghanistan, and the Sudan.[85]

A very high percentage of Islamist extremists in Britain have been observed through their attendance at several London mosques (shortlisted as hard-line), such as the Brixton mosque (South London) and the Finsbury Park mosque (North London). Both nationally and internationally, these mosques have gained a reputation for radical preaching that promotes the use of violence to advance the global Salafi jihad.[86] A poll by *The Daily Telegraph* found that a shocking 20% of British Muslims agree to have expressed some sympathy with the feelings and motives of the terrorists who committed the 2005 London bombings.[87]

U.S. Islamic Schools

Indoctrination of Muslim children in the U.S. is also underway. According to the *Washington Post* issue of February 25, 2002,[88] eleventh-graders at the Islamic Saudi Academy in Virginia must read a textbook that teaches them that a major sign of "the Day of Judgment will be that Muslims will fight and kill Jews, who will hide behind trees that say, 'Oh Muslim, Oh servant of God, here is a Jew hiding behind me. Come here and kill him'" (p. A1). The young students at that Islamic academy are also instructed that it is more beneficial to reject and even hate Jews, Christians, and Shi'ite Muslims than not to. Based on the same *Washington Post* article, at another Islamic school in Virginia, the Washington Islamic Academy makes children read a Pakistani textbook that describes Christianity as "nonsense" and depicts Jews as deceitful people who financially "oppress" others. In a classroom, on a map that is posted on the wall, the word *Israel* was crossed out with a marker.

Today, across the U.S., there are 300 to 600 Islamic schools, teaching no less than 30,000 full-time students and thousands more during the weekends. The Washington Islamic Academy, outside Washington, D.C., teaches approximately 1,300 youths, including children of Arab diplomats. These schools offer education from kindergarten to high school. A typical curriculum focuses on teaching Islamic values and beliefs, Islamic history, the life of Muhammad, the Arabic language, the Qur'an, and prayer. In this fashion, Islamic schools attempt to create a re-Islamization of a new generation of Muslim youths, who were or are about to be influenced by Christian and secular morals. Muslim organizations promote a philosophy of isolationism and contribute a great deal to the de-Americanization and the re-Islamization of Muslim youths. In the non-Muslim world, Saudi Arabian money has been used to build about 2,000 Islamic schools, more than 210 Islamic centers, and between 1,500 and 2,000 mosques.[89]

INDOCTRINATING PALESTINIAN CHILDREN

Based on a study conducted by Daphne Burdman (2003),[90] the official administration of the Palestinian Authority (PA) has initiated a campaign to brainwash Palestinian children into a dogma of self-sacrifice (martyrdom). Children are pressed into participating in stoning and suicide bombings against IDF (Israel Defense Forces), and taught that when they die, they become martyrs. The campaign has caused a deep impact on the psyche of Palestinian children and may linger on even when violence stops. Although PA leader Yasser Arafat signed—before his death—frequent agreements (Oslo I, Oslo II, and the Wye River Accords) to abandon violence and agitation and to assist in the peace process, he launched a comprehensive program to indoctrinate the Palestinians from the cradle into a destructive mode of behavior. To confirm Burdman's study, Pedahzur, Perliger, and Weinberg (2003)[91] reported that, among Palestinian terrorists, a large proportion of those who committed suicide attacks, unlike those who did not, were schooled in religious and fundamentalist institutions.

For Burdman, martyrdom is a centerpiece of the doctrine of Shi'ite Islam. It can be traced back to the early days of the first Caliphates and the killing of Husayn, who martyred himself. Being inactive or suspended for centuries, the idea of martyrdom was revived by the Grand Ayatollah Khomeini before the 1979 Iranian revolution. It was already growing in importance in militant Islam in the 1960s and was later embraced by the largely nationalist, Sunni Muslim Palestinian program. Palestinian children are pushed to commit violence against Jews even when they know they will be injured or die in the process. They are enthused to wish for rather than be afraid of the circumstance. After all, they will reach Paradise with Allah and will be hailed as heroes in their land since martyrdom is the highest honor in Islamic society. The various criteria used in today's PA campaign to actively promote involvement of children for military reasons include the certified textbooks used in the PA, exclusively designed teachers' training guides, summer camps for children (i.e., in reality, they are military training camps), and the culminating factor of a superb television campaign highlighting a message of violence. All these tactics serve to indoctrinate children so they engage in self-sacrifice for Palestine and especially for Allah.

In September 2000, the PA Ministry of Education Curriculum Committee introduced the first of a series of textbooks designed by the PA itself.[92] The PA published supplementary guidebooks that overtly lead teachers toward particular didactic methods. About thirty guidebooks of the pre-2000 books were reviewed.[93] Thorough investigations by Palestine Media Watch (PMW), an Israeli NGO, of newspapers and television programs prior to and during the Second Intifada suggest that PA television greatly escalated its presentations of many clips that encouraged children to sacrifice their lives for jihad in the fight against the Jews.[94] In 1998, a "Jihad for Kids" video showed kids recite and sing refrains: "Ask from us blood, we will drench you," "When I wander into Jerusalem I'll turn into a *feda'ye* [warrior who sacrifices himself], in battledress, in battledress, in battledress," which elicits exclamations of approval "Bravo, Bravo, Bravo" from the teacher.[95] Around the year 2000, television clips of child violent participation in jihad recurrently aired on official PA media—sometimes, up to about 90% of broadcasting time. These clips carried the Palestinian television station logos. A television clip by the PA recorded in May 2001 showed an adult tell 7- and 8-year-old children the following: "The time for toys and games is over, throw away your toys, pick up rocks!" and then showed this happening.[96]

Textbooks are of two separate historical periods: those written prior to September 2000 (by Egypt and Jordan in 1948) and those published under the sponsorship of the PA Ministry of Education Curriculum Committee; they were introduced in an astounding fashion over a five-year period that started in September 2000. Examples of quotations from the pre-2000 books include poems to be learned from memory, for first-graders: "The youth will not tire, They desire to be free or perish, We draw our water from death, And will not be as slaves to the enemy" (Ref: Palestinian National Education for First Grade, "My Homeland," pp. 67–68).

Box 12.2   The Case of Omar Rezaq

Oma Rezaq, member of the Abu Nidal Organization (ANO), a Palestinian terrorist group in the 1970s and 1980s, played a key role in seizing the EgyptAir airliner (it was forced down in Malta in 1985).

(Continued)

(Continued)

Rezaq killed five hostages (two Israeli women and three Americans) before the failed SWAT team attack by Egyptians caused over fifty deaths. Guilty for murder by Malta, Rezaq was given amnesty and released after seven years. Yet, soon after, he was arrested by the FBI for "skyjacking." Rezaq was schooled in a refugee camp funded by UNESCO. His teacher was affiliated with the Palestinian Liberation Organization (PLO) and a member of Fatah, a secular Palestinian group. His teacher told Rezaq and his classmates (then young) that the only way to be a man was to become a jihadist and defend the lands stolen from their parents and grandparents. Each morning, Rezaq learned reading, writing, and arithmetic; each afternoon he was trained to be a jihadist, learning how to handle small weapons, booby traps, explosives, and exercising in obstacle courses.[97]

Rezaq had been saturated with the indoctrination of victimization ever since he was a little boy. He had been taught that it was the enemy, Israel the Occupier, that was the reason for all of Palestinian families' difficulties. The statement, "It's not us; it's them; they are responsible for our problems" offers a psychologically satisfying justification for what goes wrong in the lives of those who become jihadists. After graduating from intermediate school, Rezaq enrolled in technical school under U.N. sponsorship. Branches of the revolution existed in this school; each group wanted to recruit new students. Rezaq became more profoundly immersed in politics. He was taught that the only way to regain his country was to engage the PLO into fighting Israel. Without a doubt, history recorded that he was increasingly resolute to join that fight.[98]

As another example: "Know my son, that Palestine is your country… that its pure soil is drenched with the blood of martyrs" (Ref: Our Arabic Language for Fifth Grade, pp. 64–66). In terms of denigration of Jews: "Racism: Mankind has suffered from this evil both in ancient as well as modern times, for indeed Satan has, in the eyes of many people, made their evil actions appear beautiful… Such a people are the Jews…" (Ref: In Islamic Education for Eighth Grade, p. 95).

These mental constructs are used not only in civics textbooks and textbooks on Islam but also in all subjects taught. These include Arabic language and grammar exercises, such as, "Determine what is the subject, and what is the predicate, in the following sentences: The jihad is a religious duty of every Moslem man and woman" (Ref: Our Arabic Language for Fifth Grade, p. 167). The post-2000 textbooks continue to stress the religious duty to fight to recapture Palestine while avoiding, mostly, the use of actual words citing Israel and Jews directly. While no direct support of terror can be observed, there is constant admiration for fedayeen and shahedeen (martyrs), undoubtedly suggesting the necessity for and advocacy of terrorism. Delegitimization of Israel remains the same. Tolerance of other religions is only for Christianity, but not modern Judaism.[99] A particular case of indoctrination of Palestinian children is the case of Omar Rezaq (see Box 12.2).

In general, the indoctrination of Palestinian children in schools and the case of Omar Rezaq confirm the reality that systems and interrelationships that surround children have a deep impact on all aspects of their development. Immediate environments such as schools are external forces that influence children's early development and conception of the Other.[100]

DOI AND RESPONSE TO TERRORISM

Rogers and Seidel (2002)[101] studied the diffusion of the 9/11 news in detail. The September 11, 2001 news event was the first to be analyzed in which mobile phones and the Internet were largely accessible to the public. A few moments after the terrorist attacks on September 11, 2001, there was a system overload of telephone calls and the Internet. Mobile phones were used to call relatives and friends in their cars with news of the terrorist incident. Rogers and Seidel's survey data showed that telephone calls were not a particularly crucial channel of communication to diffuse the news event. The study was based on Everett Rogers's theory of Diffusion of Innovations (DOI).

The rate of diffusion consists of the cumulative percentage of people to whom the news event had diffused over time. Rogers and Seidel surveyed 127 respondents. By 12 p.m. on Tuesday, September 11, 2001, over 99% of the survey's participants were aware of the news. Most of them were aware of the news by 9:30 a.m. (Albuquerque, NM time), less than three hours after the first airliner flew into the North Tower of the World Trade Center. Tuesday is a weekday, which means that many people go to work or school. Mayer and colleagues (1990)[102] stated that "people tend to hear of the occurrence of a major news event from another person when the event takes place during a weekday, but from the media when the event takes place on a weekend" (p. 114).

Rogers and Seidel found that television (32%) and radio (27%) played an important part in how people were first aware of the 9/11 news event. Broadcasting channels can respond rapidly to a fast-breaking news story. Person-to-person communication (26%) and telephone (14%) were also crucial in diffusing knowledge of the terrorist incident. None of the 127 respondents reported that newspapers were a source/channel for first hearing about the news. Many Americans watch television on waking up, for the purpose of obtaining the latest news. Basil and Brown (1990)[103] stated that "when a story is personally relevant to people, a person is more likely to pass the news on to others" (p. 316). Mayer and colleagues pointed out that "news of an important event quickly diffuses throughout the populace by word-of-mouth, while people discover the occurrence of a less important event through the media" (p. 114).

Bonitz (1991)[104] found two main features of the scientific communication system: (1) it is holographic and (2) it adheres to the principle of utmost speed. These features actually describe the information and give details about researchers' behavior within the system. Being **holographic** signifies that, from the time the information penetrates the communication system (i.e., published in some form), it is virtually everywhere—in books, articles, conference proceedings, reports, advances, e-mail, and so forth. All channels of communication provide access to this information. **Utmost speed** means that the information reaches its destination in the quickest way and shortest time possible. Modern technological development allows the attainment of these principles.

Consequently, the degree of their application is contingent on the degree of technological development of the time.

What this study has demonstrated is that, as a result of the general dependence on both vertical and horizontal diffusion in Western cultures and societies (now facing the threat of Islamist ideology), the power to incorporate a message into the social network of a particular group could be done non-technologically—especially for diffusing anti-jihadist memes. Using person-to-person communication (i.e., gossip and informal talk) instead of technology or literacy-dependent alternatives will guarantee increased awareness.[105]

SUMMARY

Diffusion of Innovations (DoI) explains how innovations (i.e., ideas, movements, or inventions) are diffused through certain channels over time across society and diverse cultures. In the domain of terrorism, DoI is akin to "contagion," which refers to the occurrence of terrorism in one nation increasing the probability of a neighboring nation being exposed to terrorism. There is evidence of terrorism contagion from Latin America to Western Europe in 1973–1974. Many other types of diffusion can help spread terrorism. For example, in knowledge diffusion, nuclear materials are now broadly spread worldwide. A theory related to DoI is Social Movement Theory (SMT), which explains the social production and diffusion of meaning and how people come to see themselves as a collectivity. The most successful terrorist movements in recruiting activists and supporters are those that create powerful ideas resonating with a specific cultural and historical context. In a similar vein, opinion leaders and change agents are diffusers of ideas: they sway people's attitudes or behavior in a desired fashion and, in the process, infuse innovative extremist ideologies into entire populations. Put simply, most of the jihad problem today can be traced back to Iran, which started in 1979. The urge to change the world was proclaimed across all Muslim and Arab nations. Hamas diffused its ideology through traditional media (newspapers), mass media (radio and television), and the Internet. The Muslim Brotherhood diffused its ideas in Indonesia through two of the three major forms of channels: the media (mostly Arabic books translated into Indonesian) and interpersonal contact (Indonesian students in Saudi Arabia who returned home to diffuse ideas to fellow Muslims). Likewise, Hezbollah diffused its ideas of suicide terrorism to Al Qaeda through transfer of membership. A more extreme version of DoI is mimetism, the theory explaining the capacity of imitation (to mimic), which one mind diffuses to another mind. A meme can be disseminated through vertical transmission or horizontal transmission. Of course, meme replication would not happen without memetic engineering, the various tactics used to create and spread memes. Al Qaeda memes are plentiful: Al Qaeda–branded groups in Iraq, high admiration to the group's central leaders, and so forth. As social learning theory predicts, adolescents living in the centers of political conflict may directly observe terrorist violence and try to imitate it (e.g., the common "martyr poster" alongside the streets of Shi'ite areas of Lebanon and Palestinian refugee camps). Along with the meme, there is a meme antibody, a meme that reacts to very toxic ideas. For example, by using the Qur'an as a meme antibody against specific Western values and practices, susceptible individuals follow the will of Allah; they give good reasons for engaging in holy war (jihad). According to various sources, meme antibody indoctrination is happening in both British and U.S. Islamic schools. A whole section was devoted to the indoctrination of Palestinian children, who are being fed memes of anti-Semitism and jihad through textbooks and videos.

KEY TERMS

brokerage   309

change agent   311

contagion   308

copycat effect   320

Diffusion of Innovations   307

direct vs. indirect diffusion   316

epistemic community   316

foquismo   308

frame alignment   310

Hamas   313

horizontal vs. vertical transmission   316

host   317

infection   317

meme   316

meme antibody   321

memeoid   317

memeplex   318

meme pool   318

meme replication   317

memetic engineering   317

memotype   317

mimetism   316

mimetic rivalry   308

mirror neuron   320

Muslim Brotherhood   314

neo-ummah   310

opinion leadership   311

resonating   317

sentiment pool   310

social epidemics   310

social learning theory   320

Social Movement Theory   310

social proof   320

socio-structural white noise   317

spillover effect   310

syncretism   315

thought contagion   318

tipping point   310

toxic meme   320

traveling theory   314

Werther effect   320

ENDNOTES

1. Rogers, Everett (1962). *Diffusion of Innovations* (1st ed.). New York: Free Press.

2. Rogers, Everett (2003). *Diffusion of Innovations* (5th ed.). New York: Free Press.

3. Bhattacherjee, Anol (2001). Understanding Information Systems Continuance: An Expectation-Confirmation Model. *MIS Quarterly, 25*(3), 351–370.

4. Wilkinson, Paul (1986). *Terrorism and the Liberal State*. New York: New York University Press.

5. Schatzberg, Michael G. (1997). Beyond Mobutu: Kabila and the Congo. *Journal of Democracy, 8*(4), 70–84.

6. Laqueur, Walter (1999). *The New Terrorism*. Oxford: Oxford University Press; Raby, Diana L. (2006). *Democracy and Revolution: Latin America and Socialism Today*. London: Pluto Press.

7. Braithwaite, Alex, & Li, Quan (2007). Transnational Terrorism Hot Spots: Identification and Impact Evaluation. *Conflict Management and Peace Science, 24*(4), 281–296; Heyman, Edward, & Mickolus, Edward (1980). Observations on "Why Violence Spreads." *International Studies Quarterly, 24*(2), 299–305.

8. Baudrillard, Jean (2002). L'Esprit du Terrorisme. *South Atlantic Quarterly, 101*(2), 403–415.

9. Girard, René (1996). Eating Disorders and Mimetic Desire. *Contagion: Journal of Violence, Mimesis, and Culture, 3*, 1–20.

10. Braithwaite, Alex, & Li, Quan (2007). Transnational Terrorism Hot Spots: Identification and Impact Evaluation. *Conflict Management and Peace Science, 24*(4), 281–296.

11. Midlarsky, Manus I., Crenshaw, Martha, & Yoshida, Fumihiko (1980). Why Violence Spreads: The Contagion of International Terrorism. *International Studies Quarterly, 24*, 262–298.

12. Baylouny, Anne Marie (2006, March 14). NS4300: Social Mobilization and Conflict in the Middle East. Monterey, CA: Naval Postgraduate School; Falkenrath, Richard A., Newman, Robert, & Thayer, Bradley A. (1998). *America's Achilles' Heel: Nuclear, Biological, and Chemical Terrorism and Covert Attack*. Cambridge, MA: MIT Press; Heyman, E. S. (1980). *Monitoring the Diffusion of Transnational Terrorism*. Gaithersburg, MD: IACP; Tarrow, Sidney, & McAdam, Doug (2005). Scale Shift in Transnational Contention. In D. Della Porta and S. Tarrow (Eds.), *Transnational Protest and Global Activism* (pp. 121–150). New York: Rowman and Littlefield.

13. Braithwaite, Alex, & Li, Quan (2007). Transnational Terrorism Hot Spots: Identification and Impact Evaluation. *Conflict Management and Peace Science, 24*(4), 281–296.

14. Snow, David, Rochford, E. Burke, Worden, Steven, & Benford, Robert (1986). Frame Alignment Processes, Micromobilization, and Movement Participation. *American Sociological Review, 51*, 464–481.

15. Collins, Kathleen (2007). Ideas, Networks, and Islamist Movements Evidence from Central Asia and the Caucasus. *World Politics, 60*, 64–96.

16. Snow, David, Rochford, E. Burke, Worden, Steven, & Benford, Robert (1986). Frame Alignment Processes, Micromobilization, and Movement Participation. *American Sociological Review, 51*, 464–481.

17. Wickham, Carrie Rosefsky (2002). *Mobilizing Islam: Religion, Activism, and Political Change in Egypt*. New York: Columbia University Press.

18. Sullivan, Andrew Brian S. (2009). Innovations in Strategic Communications: A New Approach. *Canadian Army Journal, 12*(1), 75–88.

19. Martin, Gus (2010). *Understanding Terrorism: Challenges, Perspectives, and Issues*. Thousand Oaks, CA: Sage.

20. Roy, Olivier (2004). *Den globaliserede islam*. København: Vandkunsten.

21. Collins, Kathleen (2007). Ideas, Networks, and Islamist Movements Evidence from Central Asia and the Caucasus. *World Politics, 60*, 64–96; della Porta, Donatella (1992). On Individual Motivations in Underground Political Organizations. In Donatella della Porta (Ed.), *Social Movements and Violence: Participation in Underground Organizations* (pp. 3–28). Greenwich, CT: JAI.

22. Martin, Gus (2010). *Understanding Terrorism: Challenges, Perspectives, and Issues*. Thousand Oaks, CA: Sage.

23. Myers, James H., & Robertson, Thomas H. (1972). Dimensions of Opinion Leadership. *Journal of Marketing Research, 9*(1), 41–46.

24. Jasser, M. Zuhdi (2008). Exposing the "Flying Imams." *Middle East Quarterly, 15*(1), 3–11.

25. Tahir-ul-Qadri, Muhammad (2010). *Introduction to the Fatwa on Suicide Bombings and Terrorism*. Lahore, Pakistan: Minhaj-ul-Quran International (MQI).

26. Post, Jerrold M., Sprinzak, Ehud, & Denny, Laurita M. (2003). The Terrorists in Their Own Words: Interviews with 35 Incarcerated Middle Eastern Terrorists. *Terrorism & Political Violence, 15*(1), 171–184.

27. Kruglanski, Arie W., & Fishman, Shira (2009). Psychological Factors in Terrorism and Counterterrorism: Individual, Group and Organizational Levels of Analysis. *Social Issues and Policy Review, 3*(1), 1–44.

28. Ottaway, Richard N. (1983). The Change Agent: A Taxonomy in Relation to the Change Process. *Human Relations, 36*(4), 361–392.

29. Keck, Margaret, & Sikkink, Kathryn (1998). *Transnational Advocacy Networks*. Ithaca, NY: Cornell University Press; Olson, Mancur (1971). *The Logic of Collective Action*. Cambridge, MA: Harvard University Press; Radnitz, Scott (2005). Networks, Localism, and Mobilization in Aksy, Kyrgyzstan. *Central Asia Survey, 24*(4), 405–424.

30. Oberschall, Anthony (2004). Explaining Terrorism: The Contribution of Collective Action Theory. *Sociological Theory, 22*(1), 26–37.

31. Wright, Robin (2001). *Sacred Rage: The Wrath of Militant Islam*. New York: Simon & Schuster, p. 27.

32. Oberschall, Anthony (2004). Explaining Terrorism: The Contribution of Collective Action Theory. *Sociological Theory, 22*(1), 26–37.

33. Luttwak, Edward (2001, October 2). Foreign Policy Remade, but for How Long? *The New York Times*, p. A27; Stern, Jessica (2000). Pakistan's Jihad Culture. *Foreign Affairs, 79*, 115-126; Weaver, Mary Anne (2000). *A Portrait of Egypt: A Journey through the World of Militant Islam*. New York: Farrar, Straus and Giroux; Wright, Robin (2001). *Sacred Rage: The Wrath of Militant Islam*. New York: Simon & Schuster, p. 27.

34. Oberschall, Anthony (2004). Explaining Terrorism: The Contribution of Collective Action Theory. *Sociological Theory, 22*(1), 26–37; Rashid, Ahmed (2001). *Taliban*. New Haven, CT: Yale University Press.

35. Mozes, Tomer, & Weimann, Gabriel (2010). The E-Marketing Strategy of Hamas. *Studies in Conflict & Terrorism, 33*(3), 211–225.

36. Nossek, Hillel, & Rinnawi, Khalil (2003). Censorship and Freedom of the Press under Changing Political Regimes. *Gazette: The International Journal for Communication Studies, 65*(2), 183–202.

37. Salama, Vivian (2006). Hamas TV: Palestinian media in transition. Retrieved May 8, 2011 at http://www.tbsjournal.com/salamapf.html.

38. Mozes, Tomer, & Weimann, Gabriel (2010). The E-Marketing Strategy of Hamas. *Studies in Conflict & Terrorism, 33*(3), 211–225.

39. Hirsch, Paul M. (1972). Processing Fads and Fashions: An Organization-Set Analysis of Cultural Industry Systems. *The American Journal of Sociology, 77*(4), 639–659.

40. White, Jonathan R. (2011). *Terrorism & Homeland Security* (7th ed.). Belmont, CA: Wadsworth.

41. Hasan, Noorhaidi (2002). Faith and Politics: The Rise of the Laskar Jihad in the Era of Transition in Indonesia. *Indonesia, 73*, 145–170.

42. Mandaville, Peter (2001). *Transnational Muslim Politics: Reimagining the Umma*. New York: Routledge.

43. van Bruinessen, Martin (2002). Genealogies of Islamic Radicalism in Post-Suharto Indonesia. *South East Asia Research, 10*(2), 117–154.

44. Horowitz, Michael C. (2010). Nonstate Actors and the Diffusion of Innovations: The Case of Suicide Terrorism. *International Organization, 64*, 33–64.

45. Giugni, Marco G. (2002). Explaining Cross-National Similarities among Social Movements. In Jackie G. Smith, Hank Johnston (Eds.), *Globalization and Resistance: Transnational Dimensions of Social Movements* (pp. 13–29). Lanham, MD: Rowman & Littlefield Publishers.

46. Soule, Sarah A. (2004). Diffusion Processes within and across Movements. In David A. Snow, Sarah Anne Soule, Hanspeter Kriesi (Eds.), *The Blackwell Companion to Social Movements* (pp. 294–310). New York: Wiley-Blackwell.

47. Horowitz, Michael C. (2010). Nonstate Actors and the Diffusion of Innovations: The Case of Suicide Terrorism. *International Organization, 64*, 33–64.

48. Haas, Peter M. (1992). Introduction: Epistemic Communities and International Policy Coordination. *International Organization, 46*(1), 1–35.

49. Gray, Virginia (1973). Innovation in the States: A Diffusion Study. *American Political Science Review, 67*(4), 1174–1185.

50. Dawkins, Richard (1976). *The Selfish Gene*. Oxford: Oxford University Press; Dawkins, Richard (1998). *Unweaving the Rainbow*. New York: Penguin Press.

51. Coker, Christopher (2008). War, Memes and Memeplexes. *International Affairs, 84*(5), 903–914.

52. Brown, William Michael (2001). Genomic Imprinting and the Cognitive Architecture Mediating Human Culture. *Journal of Cognition and Culture, 1*(3), 251–258.

53. Pech, Richard J., & Slade, Bret W. (2005). Imitative Terrorism: A Diagnostic Framework for Identifying Catalysts and Designing Interventions. *Foresight, 7*(1), 47–60.

54. Dawkins, Richard (1976). *The Selfish Gene*. Oxford: Oxford University Press; Dawkins, Richard (1998). *Unweaving the Rainbow*. New York: Penguin Press.

55. Henson, H. Keith (2002). Sex, Drugs, and Cults: An Evolutionary Psychology Perspective on Why and How Cult Memes Get a Drug-Like Hold on People, and What Might Be Done to Mitigate the Effects. *The Human Nature Review, 2*, 343–355.

56. Sullivan, Andrew Brian S. (2009). Innovations in Strategic Communications: A New Approach. *Canadian Army Journal, 12*(1), 75–88.

57. Marsden, Paul S. (1998). Memetics: A New Paradigm for Understanding Customer Behaviour and Influence. *Marketing Intelligence & Planning, 16*(6), 363–368.

58. Blackmore, Susan (2001). Evolution and Memes: The Human Brain as a Selective Imitation Device. *Cybernetics and Systems, 32*(1), 225–255; Dawkins, Richard (1998). *Unweaving the Rainbow*. New York: Penguin Press.

59. Lynch, Aaron (1998). *Thought Contagion*. New York: Basic Books.

60. Lin, Chin-Huang, Liou, Dian-Yiang, & Wu, Kang-Wei (2007). Opportunities and Challenges Created by Terrorism. *Technological Forecasting and Social Change, 74*(2), 148–164.

61. Smallman, Clive (1997). Read All about It—Risk Trends in the Media: A Research Note. *Disaster Prevention and Management, 6*(3), 160–164.

62. Fishman, Brian (2008). Using the Mistakes of Al Qaeda's Franchises to Undermine Its Strategies. *The Annals of the American Academy of Political and Social Science, 618*, 46-54; Pillar, Paul R. (2010). The Diffusion of Terrorism. *Mediterranean Quarterly, 21*(1), 1–14.

63. Kalpakian, Jack (2005). Building the Human Bomb: The Case of the 16 May 2003 Attacks in Casablanca. *Studies in Conflict & Terrorism, 28*, 113–127.

64. Haynes, Jeffrey (2005). Al Qaeda: Ideology and Action. *Critical Review of International Social and Political Philosophy, 8*(2), 177-191.

65. Karon, Tony (2004, March 17). Why the Al Qaeda Threat Is Growing. *Time Magazine*, p. 2.

66. Dennett, Daniel C. (2006). *Breaking the Spell: Religion as a Natural Phenomenon*. New York: Viking Adult.

67. Liddle, James R., Bush, Lance S., & Shackelford, Todd K. (2010). An Introduction to Evolutionary Psychology and Its Application to Suicide Terrorism. *Behavioral Sciences of Terrorism and Political Aggression, 10*, 1–22.

68. Pedahzur, Ami, Perliger, Arie, & Weinberg, Leonard (2003). Altruism and Fatalism: The Characteristics of Palestinian Suicide Bombers. *Deviant Behavior, 24*(4), 405–423.

69. Pech, Richard J., & Slade, Bret W. (2005). Imitative Terrorism: A Diagnostic Framework for Identifying Catalysts and Designing Interventions. *Foresight, 7*(1), 47–60.

70. Kohler, Evelyne, Keysers, Christian, & Umilta, M. Alessandra (2002). Hearing Sounds, Understanding Actions: Action Representation in Mirror Neurons. *Science, 297*(2), 846–848.

71. Coleman, Loren (2004). *The Copycat Effect: How the Media and Popular Culture Trigger the Mayhem in Tomorrow's Headlines*. New York: Pocket Books.

72. Pech, Richard J., & Slade, Bret W. (2005). Imitative Terrorism: A Diagnostic Framework for Identifying Catalysts and Designing Interventions. *Foresight, 7*(1), 47–60.

73. Bandura, Albert (1973). *Aggression: A Social Learning Analysis*. New York: Prentice Hall; Bandura, Albert (1998). Mechanisms of Moral Disengagement. In Walter Reich (Ed.), *Origins of Terrorism: Psychologies, Ideologies, Theologies, States of Mind* (pp. 161–192). Washington, D.C.: Woodrow Wilson Center Press.

74. Crenshaw, Martha (1992). How Terrorists Think: What Psychology Can Contribute to Understanding Terrorism. In Laurence Howard (Ed.), *Terrorism: Roots, Impact, Responses* (pp. 405-420). New York: Praeger; Kelly, Robert, & Rieber, Robert (1995). Psychosocial Impacts of Terrorism and Organized Crime: The Counterfinality of the Practico-Inert. *Journal of Social Distress and the Homeless, 4*, 265–286; Taylor, Maxwell, & Quayle, Ethel (1994). *Terrorist Lives*. London: Brassey's.

75. Armstrong, Karen (2000). *Islam*. New York: The Modern Library; Atran, Scott (2003). Genesis of Suicide Terrorism. *Science, 299*, 1534–1539; Kepel, Gilles (2002). *Jihad: The Trail of Political Islam*. Cambridge, MA: Belknap; Marshall, Tyler, & Danizewski, John (2001, September 9). Pakistan's Muslim Schools Offer a Dark View of U.S. *Los Angeles Times*, p. A1; Sageman, Marc (2004). *Understanding Terror Networks*. Philadelphia: University of Pennsylvania Press.

76. Saper, Bernard (1988). On Learning Terrorism. *Terrorism, 11*, 13–27.

77. Alexander, Yonah (2002). *Palestinian Religious Terrorism: Hamas and Islamic Jihad*. Ardsley, NY: Transnational Publishers.

78. Bandura, Albert (1973). Social Learning Theory of Aggression. In John F. Knutson (Ed.), *The Control of Aggression: Implications from Basic Research* (pp. 201–250). Hawthorne, NY: Aldine; Midlarsky, Manus I., Crenshaw, Martha, & Yoshida, Fumihiko (1980). Why Violence Spreads: The Contagion of International Terrorism. *International Studies Quarterly, 4*, 262–298.

79. Christiansen, Morten H., & Chater, Nick (2008). Language as Shaped by the Brain. *Behavioral and Brain Sciences, 31*, 489–558.

80. Gigantès, Philippe (2003). *Power & Greed: A Short History of the World*. London: Robinson.

81. Pech, Richard J., & Slade, Bret W. (2006). Religious Fundamentalism and Terrorism: Why Do They Do It and What Do They Want? *Foresight, 8*(1), 8–20.

82. Magouirk, Justin (2008). Connecting a Thousand Points of Hatred. *Studies in Conflict & Terrorism, 31*, 327–349.

83. Burns, John F. (2010, November 22). Lessons of Hate at Islamic Schools in Britain. *The New York Times*, p. A8.

84. Conlan, Tara, & Tryhorn, Chris (2007, August 24). Channel 4 Rests Celebrity Big Brother. *The Guardian*; Doward, Jamie (2007, January 7). Revealed: Preachers' Messages of Hate. *The Observer*.

85. Otto, Jan Michiel (2008). *Sharia and National Law in Muslim Countries: Tensions and Opportunities for Dutch and EU Foreign Policy*. Amsterdam: Amsterdam University Press, p. 7; Taher, Abul (2008, July 27). A Third of Muslim Students Back Killings. *The Sunday Times*, p. A1.

86. Silke, Andrew (2008). Holy Warriors: Exploring the Psychological Processes of Jihadi Radicalization. *European Journal of Criminology, 5*(1), 99–123.

87. Saggar, Shamit (2009). Boomerangs and Slingshots: Radical Islamism and Counter-Terrorism Strategy. *Journal of Ethnic and Migration Studies, 35*(3), 381–402.

88. Strauss, Valerie, & Wax, Emily (2002, February 25). Where Two Worlds Collide: Muslim Schools Face Tension of Islamic, U.S. Views. *The Washington Post*, p. A1.

89. Frum, David, & Perle, Richard (2003). *An End to Evil: How to Win the War on Terror*. New York: Random House.

90. Burdman, Daphne (2003). Education, Indoctrination, and Incitement: Palestinian Children on Their Way to Martyrdom. *Terrorism and Political Violence, 15*(1), 96–123.

91. Pedahzur, Ami, Perliger, Arie, & Weinberg, Leonard (2003). Altruism and Fatalism: The Characteristics of Palestinian Suicide Bombers. *Deviant Behavior, 24*(4), 405–423.

92. Press Release from Francois Zimeray, Member of European Parliament for France (2001). Controversy about new books culminated in Amendment 177 to prevent funding of antipeace projects.

93. Itamar, Marcus (2000). *Report: Palestinian Authority Teachers' Guides* (CMIP).

94. Burdman, Daphne (2003). Education, Indoctrination, and Incitement: Palestinian Children on Their Way to Martyrdom. *Terrorism and Political Violence, 15*(1), 96–123.

95. "Jihad for Kids!" videocassette produced by and available from Peace for Generations (P.O. Box 55, Union, N.J. 07083-0055, USA, peace4gen@aol.com).

96. Burdman, Daphne (2003). Education, Indoctrination, and Incitement: Palestinian Children on Their Way to Martyrdom. *Terrorism and Political Violence, 15*(1), 96–123.

97. Post, Jerrold M. (2000). Murder in a Political Context: Profile of an Abu Nidal Terrorist. *Bulletin of the Academy of Psychiatry and the Law, 28*, 171–178.

98. Post, Jerrold M. (2010). "When Hatred Is Bred in the Bone": The Social Psychology of Terrorism. *Annals of the American Academy of Political and Social Science, 1208*, 15–23.

99. Groiss, Arnon, & Manor, Yohanan (2001). *Jews, Israel and Peace in Palestinian School Textbooks 2000-2001 and 2001-2002*. Jerusalem: Center for Monitoring the Impact of Peace (CMIP).

100. Bronfenbrenner, Urie (1979). *The Ecology of Human Development: Experiments by Nature and Design*. Cambridge, MA: Harvard University Press.

101. Rogers, Everett M., & Seidel, Nancy (2002). Diffusion of News of the Terrorist Attacks of September 11, 2001. *Prometheus, 20*(3), 209–219.

102. Mayer, Michael E., Gudykunst, William B., Perrill, Norman K., & Merrill, Bruce (1990). A Comparison of Competing Models of the News Diffusion Process. *Western Journal of Speech Communication, 54*, 113–123.

103. Basil, Michael D., & Brown, William J. (1990). Interpersonal Communication in News Diffusion: A Study of "Magic" Johnson's Announcement. *Journalism Quarterly, 71*(2), 305–320.

104. Bonitz, Manfred (1991). The Existence of Simple Principles Governing Human and Scientific Behavior in a System of Scientific Communication. *Library and Information Science Research, 13,* 61–66.

105. Sullivan, Andrew Brian S. (2009). Innovations in Strategic Communications: A New Approach. *Canadian Army Journal, 12*(1), 75–88.

The Globalization of Terrorism

After reading this chapter, you will be able to

- discuss global transnational terrorism and the progress of terrorism via globalization;
- explain the impact of cyberterrorism; and
- describe how terrorist groups use social media and covert communication, or steganography, to spread their ideas and recruit supporters.

GLOBALIZATION: DEFINITION

Since the 1990s, the study of globalization has attracted the attention of many scholars. By and large, **globalization** brings into international networks parts of the globe that were isolated or disconnected. Thanks to globalization, human beings are unified in unprecedented ways. This global interconnection has been growing rapidly since the beginning of the 20th century. Accordingly, today, people find themselves living in a world of seamless and inseparable webs of interconnected parts, regardless of the borders that divide the world's many nations.[1] Globalization can be looked at from three dimensions: (1) material—the movement of humans, goods, information, and wealth along the channels of a global transportation and communication network; (2) spatio-temporal—the revolution of time and space by networks that traverse political borders and considerably decrease transaction time; and (3) cognitive—the change in public awareness of how remote events affect local events and, therefore, in the view of what represents a meaningful world.[2]

Globalization implies **liberalization**—that is, the removal of national restrictions on trade and foreign exchange as well as the lessening of controls on flows of capital, labor, knowledge, and technology.[3] From this vantage point, globalization implies the spread of the logic of capital, the proliferation of democracy in information and financing, and the diffusion of technology. Globalization not only creates a world horizon but also revamps the very fabrics of national states that used to characterize the political, economic, and social world. Again, globalization links humans together and brings fresh commonalties into experience.[4] Lastly, the concept of globalization involves a dialectical process. On the one hand, globalization entails a process of **cultural Westernization**—standardization of Western mass culture that travels around the world and produces sameness and homogeneity in all places. The growth of global markets for goods, services, and capital forces local cultures to transform their cultural practices. On the other hand, globalized culture facilitates the ubiquitous expansion of unique appropriations and developments, thus diffusing hybridity, difference, and heterogeneity. Each local culture has its own appropriation and transformation of global products, thus propagating difference and diversity.[5]

GLOBAL TRANSNATIONAL TERRORISM (GTT)

On a global level, terrorism now consists of people or territory of more than one state. **Global transnational terrorism** (GTT) refers to terrorism whereby violent non-state actors (VNSAs) are active in multiple territories. The global aspect involves groups that focus on the far enemy. They operate beyond their local and regional constituencies and concerns, and target the main enemy that hurts the near enemies. GTT organizations such as Al Qaeda and Jemaah Islamiyah generally enjoy more extensive network capabilities and are then harder to eliminate.[6]

Violent Non-State Actors (VNSAs)

In GTT, a **violent non-state actor** (VNSA) refers to any actor or group on the global level which is not a state. It uses extreme violence to accomplish its objectives; in so doing, it challenges the domination on violence of the state. Examples of VNSAs are armed groups, like groups such as Al Qaeda, and criminal organizations, like international drug cartels.[7] The growth of VNSAs is a powerful argument to demonstrate the reduced role of the state in the age of globalization. The importance of the VNSA has enabled terrorist organizations to circumvent direct associations with the state and, in particular, with states that support terrorism. Terrorist groups have increasingly begun to use non-state actors and non-state financial sources. This advantage of globalization makes GTT harder to monitor and to predict. It also restricts the effectiveness of traditional political and diplomatic means, which cannot be applied efficiently against amorphous VNSAs.[8] This is exemplified by the Tri-Border Area (TBA) in Box 13.1.

The progress of globalization and the proportion of VNSAs are so significant that they cause changes in the organizational structures of terrorist groups. The global operations of multinational corporations (MNCs) have provided a model that terrorist organizations can emulate, particularly in regard to how they can plan, organize, and accomplish their goals at the international level. Much like these MNCs, terrorist groups have metamorphosed organizationally. As it was explained in Chapter 11, terrorist groups are now moving from hierarchical, or pyramidal, structures to more horizontal and flexible organizational arrangements. The ability to adapt to changes, as modeled from the best blueprints of MNCs, has permitted numerous terrorist groups to recruit supporters, to protect finances and resources, and to obscure operations in the face of global attempts to kill terrorist activities.[9]

Box 13.1   Tri-Border Area (TBA)

The **Tri-Border Area (TBA)** is the area where Argentina, Brazil, and Paraguay join (where the Iguazú and the Paraná rivers converge). It is also referred to as the Triborder Region and the Triple Frontier (Spanish: *La Triple Frontera*; Portuguese: *Tríplice Fronteira*). A lot of GTT activity has taken place in the TBA. It has been reported that the Paraguayan side is being used as a sanctuary for terrorist operations. The sad reality is that Paraguay has no antiterrorism laws. Thus, helping terrorist organizations—whether directly or indirectly—is not punishable by law; rather, suspected terrorists are arrested for tax evasion and other similar charges. The Paraguayan city of Ciudad del Este is especially notorious for its lawlessness. The TBA is also inhabited by over 20,000 Middle Eastern immigrants. Hamas, Hezbollah, and other terrorist organizations have frequented the area.[10]

The TBA is a haven for global terrorist support, and possibly even operations. The bombings in Buenos Aires were traced back to terrorists passing through or operating in the region. In 1996, Marwan Al Safadi, presumed to belong to the group that bombed the World Trade Center in 1993, was apprehended in Paraguay. In 1999, El Said Ali Mohamed Mokles, an alleged Egyptian terrorist, was captured in Chuy, Uruguay, after having spent some time in the TBA.[11] In 2002, and again in 2006, the U.S. Treasury Department wrote in a memo that there are "clear examples" of Islamist organizations in the area that put money into terrorist activities. Besides Al Qaeda and Hezbollah, other VNSAs such as the Islamic Jihad Movement (from Palestine), and al-Gama'a al-Islamiyya (from Egypt) are thought to get some of their funding from activities in the TBA.[12]

Hezbollah and GTT

Hezbollah, the "Party of God," a Shi'ite terrorist group created in Lebanon in 1982, has had much contact with terrorist groups and networks globally. An example of the Hezbollah global connection is the group's establishment of camps that have trained operatives from terrorist organizations like the IRA, the Kurdish Workers Party (PKK), the Basque Fatherland and Freedom (ETA), and Italy's Red Brigades. In addition to Iran, Africa, and North America, one of the fastest-growing and key areas of the world to the global efforts of Hezbollah is the TBA itself. According to Paraguayan officials, between 1998 and 2001, Arab communities in the TBA have contributed financial sums of $50–$500 million (U.S.) to Islamist terrorist organizations in the Middle East—Hezbollah has been a major recipient.[13]

Hezbollah takes advantage of modern communications to engage in terrorist activities and even has its own television network: Al-Manar or "The Beacon" (as it was discussed in Chapter 8). In tandem with the American telethon style, Hezbollah has drawn considerable cash donations with its twenty-four-hour televisions station. Many of the profits are siphoned to Palestinian terrorist activities in Israel. These funds are then funneled to a few Lebanese-based banks whose assets, by law, cannot be frozen or confiscated by the government. These banks, in turn, collaborate with many large U.S. banks; this proves beneficial in the siphoning of funds abroad for terrorist activities. Among these banks are such prestigious banks as Bank of New York, Wachovia, and JP Morgan Chase.[14]

By striking their enemies throughout the globe, Hezbollah has compelled the world community to take notice. This growing global attention breeds sympathetic groups emerging in other places and completes the boomerang strategy used by Hezbollah in its attempt to achieve its objective. Although Hezbollah's direct and concrete mission involves the regional politics in Israel and Lebanon, the group has mounted attacks on a Kuwaiti aircraft in Thailand and a U.S. aircraft in Denmark. It has also hijacked a TWA flight from Athens to Rome. These actions did not have an instrumental impact of changing policies in Israel or Lebanon. Instead, relying on the boomerang effect and leverage politics, these actions were taken to achieve goals by exerting international pressure on Hezbollah's side.[15]

New Weapons and Better Technologies

Before the era of globalization, terrorism was rare because geographical barriers did not allow it to grow. For instance, people subjugated by a European colonial power in the 19th century could not strike Europe and slay massive numbers of innocents.[16] Modern technologies have changed the horizon by reducing distance and providing weapons. Globalization, thanks to international trade and transportation, has given new opportunities for terrorist groups to obtain and use better and deadlier weapons, and to carry out more enormous and more destructive acts. It has also made things easier for terrorist organizations in terms of targeting. Faster travel and communication technologies smooth the progress of terrorist operations and facilitate the diffusion of radical ideas that may arouse large constituencies. This, in turn, helps terrorists get funds, recruit followers, and muster support for their cause.[17]

There has been much debate of the transformations that globalization has engendered or enabled among radical groups—what Stanislawski (2004)[18] calls **Transnational Bads**. This term means that terrorists have exploited the shift to unprecedented global relations and the logistical advantages that come with it. More advanced technologies and communications have given rise to new ways for transporting weapons, laundering money, establishing secret logistical networks, and sharing information.[19] These opportunities for transformation allow new models for terrorist organizations to emerge. Although GTT has existed for a few decades, it has become increasingly common and often more difficult to combat.

The reliance on exceptional technologies as means of destruction also exposes new configurations of power and nascent forms of terrorism. Modern-day technologies diffuse power, emboldening irate disempowered individuals, leveling the playing field, and spreading the use and application of information technology and technologies of mass destruction. Many technologies used in the military can now be acquired by terrorists to use against power blocs. This frightening access to technology creates a situation of asymmetrical warfare in which the weaker one can target superpowers. Truly, globalization allows innovative forms of warfare. Terrorist threats from CBRN (chemical, biological, radiological, and nuclear weapons) make the national defense of overdeveloped countries more vulnerable and provide a boon for weaker states or groups to go after stronger ones.[20]

PARALLEL GLOBALIZATION OF TERROR AND ONTOLOGICAL INSECURITY

The terrorist attacks of September 11, 2001 were interpreted, by German Chancellor Gerhard Schröder (2001), as "a declaration of war against all of civilization" (§20). As the dark side of globalization, terrorism has power that is equal to the bright side of globalization. Put another way, terrorism is parallel to the benefits of globalization.

Parallel Globalization of Terror

The idea that terrorism plays such a huge role in globalization is referred to as **parallel globalization of terror**. Intrinsically, globalization is both a benevolent process and a process of terror. This is an unfortunate state of affairs, because globalization is such that it determines the fate of the world's free economies and, by the same token, the world's free societies. It is by looking at the dark side of globalization that the terrorist element emerges. As globalization plays a major part in defining our future, the dark side of it heralds a dark scenario for the coming years. Diffusions of terrorism and terrorist networks operate on the same principle by which economic and cultural globalization is thought to work. They all diffuse via the infrastructure of globalization.[22]

Globalization has upsides and downsides, advantages and disadvantages. They are generally interconnected and are, therefore, essentially ambiguous. New technologies can be used for good or for ill. In fact, they are simultaneously empowering (and productive) and disempowering (and destructive), and are, thereby, replete with paradoxes. Globalization allows the emergence of international terrorist networks and networks of commerce and communication. The movement of commodities, technologies, ideas, funds, and humans enable networks of terror, along with trade and travel. Before September 11, 2001, Bill Clinton repeatedly said that terrorism was the dark side of globalization. After that fateful day, Colin Powell viewed the terrorist tragedy in like manner. GTT is threatening, partly because globalization continuously splits the world into haves and have-nots, creates conflicts and competition, and encourages long-festering animosities and grievances. At the same time, globalization brings people together, fashioning new relations and interactions, and novel hybridities.[23]

Ontological Insecurity

Ontological insecurity refers to the fear of the incapacity to maintain global order because terrorism is a perpetual threat.[24] By identifying modern terrorism with the rise of globalization, which the West believes creates this global order (as well as national orders), following the Cold War, terrorism has been construed as an existential danger. Terrorism-induced global insecurity causes reflection on the very **ontology** (i.e., the study of being, existence, nature, and the world) of the situation in which humans are.[25] In the perspective of U.S. politics, 9/11 was so in-depth and dramatic that it turned the political world upside down, set new issues in motion (e.g., GWOT), and altered the political, cultural, and economic atmosphere virtually from top to bottom. The September 11, 2001 terrorist attacks and consequent Bush administration military reaction in Afghanistan and Iraq have, once again, placed the centrality of globalization in the spotlight. These reflect the present experience and the necessity for proper conceptualizations and responses to it.[26]

The September 11, 2001 terrorist attacks also exposed the vulnerable aspect of a globally interconnected society and the contradictions, surprises, and inadvertent consequences that arise from the multifaceted processes of globalization. Al Qaeda exemplified a hidden and mysterious decentered network devoted to destroying America. Their Afghanistan base was what theorists referred to as *wild zones* or *zones of turmoil* that sprung out of the boundaries of safe zones" of globalized mega-places such as Wall Street and Northern Virginia.[27]

Twenty-first-century terrorism is mostly founded on a fight to transform the entire world, with accountability only to a deity or a transcendental conception and a desire for martyrdom. Data on terrorism identify the Muslim world as particularly predisposed toward extreme conflict with other civilizations. In the definition of globalization, the term was analogous to cultural Westernization, which can deeply alter traditional (and local) ways of life. In response, this has triggered opposition of large segments in the affected societies, giving them a reason to engage in terrorism. Globalization has weakened national boundaries by rendering them less relevant. Global economies that are mutually dependent have shifted national identities to ones that only include ethnicity and religion, providing justification for extreme xenophobic and fundamentalist antagonism toward Western political and cultural hegemony.[28]

TERRORISM IN CYBERSPACE

Terrorists are well aware that our notion of time has changed thanks to globalization. While methods like face-to-face and phone conversations require the simultaneous presence of both parties of the communication process (i.e., sender and receiver), technologies like the Internet (e.g., e-mail) and interactive multimedia free us from such constraints. Hence, an important distinction exists between synchronous and asynchronous communication. **Synchronous communication** restricts communication to episodes where both parties are present or available. **Asynchronous communication**, on the other hand, gives the sender (i.e., Internet user) the opportunity of leaving a message without needing the receiver to be present at the time the message is transmitted. Asynchronous communication is communication outside real time.[29]

Cyberspace: Definition

Cyberspace refers to the "virtual world" or the World Wide Web. The term *cyberspace* was made popular for the first time in William Gibson's (1984)[30] classic work titled *Neuromancer*. Cyberspace mixes textual interactions and virtual worlds for supreme global communication among people. It offers a wide array of communication channels; e-mails, chat rooms, and VR (virtual reality) simulations are well-known examples. The development of cyberspace is mainly interpreted to be organic rather than centrally directed. No single central player can run it, though some players have more power than others.[31] Cyberspace has been compared to the second media age. While the **first media age** includes broadcast forms of media like newspapers, radio, and television, where a handful speak to many (i.e., one-way communication), the **second media age** marks a departure from the supremacy of broadcast forms of media like newspapers, radio, and television. Pointedly, the announcing of a second media age is nearly exclusively grounded in the expansion of cyberspace and interactive media (i.e., two-way communication).[32]

Marshall McLuhan (1962)[33] referred to this phenomenon of an interconnected world as the **Global Village**—today, it has become a metaphor to describe the Internet and the World Wide Web. The Internet globalizes communication by enabling users worldwide to connect with each other. By extension, web-connected computers can make people link their websites together. The Global Village is more a chronological period than a place. It was immediately heralded by what McLuhan referred to as the **Gutenberg Galaxy** (a label for the historical period of the mass media, particularly the printing press). While its roots can go back to the invention of the "phonetic alphabet" (McLuhan's designation for phonemic orthography), the Gutenberg Galaxy, like the subsequent Global Village, was marked by a technological innovation: Gutenberg's movable press, which revolutionized the mass production of books and other types of publications.

Terrorists Exploiting Cyberspace

Cyberspace expands and de-territorializes, at the same time, the social interactions between local and international terrorists. The advantage of the Internet in smoothing the development of self-starters cannot be overemphasized. Cyberspace has intensely transformed the way in which current terrorist networks run their activities. Of equal relevance is the manner in which it has improved the range of possibilities for potential or future terrorists. On top of the large amounts of radicalizing content, cyberspace has successfully eliminated many of the functional barriers that once restricted entry into the diffusion of terrorist propaganda.[34] In a malignant fashion, the Internet allows terrorists to blossom in the autonomy that democracies provide. The exhaustive coverage in the media about a terrorist act produces anticipated psychological effects. Terrorist attacks are mounted in a manner that creates a strategically high communicative effect, while demanding minimal resources. Now that we have cyberspace, the symbiotic relationship between terrorism and the (new) media works even better in the terrorists' favor. The perpetrators have an even higher impact through Internet publicity. Terrorists *are* exploiting cyberspace.[35]

Under these circumstances, terrorist weapons today are not just the traditional machine guns and bombs. Now, they also include mobile phones, laptop and desktop computers, and the Internet and the World Wide Web. Without a doubt, mostly thanks to cyberspace—and the quasi-unlimited range of communications opportunities that it offers—the ability of terrorist communication has now reached a point at which terrorists can painlessly and successfully be in charge of the communication of their ideology of hatred, intolerance, and violence. As such, they can control the content, context, and channel over which their message is launched—and toward exactly the multiple audiences they try to reach.[36]

For terrorists, cyberspace has become a virtual haven to make up for the loss of their physical sanctuaries and continues to give details on training and instruction (e.g., the means and methods of planning and carrying out terrorist attacks). As Gabriel Weimann (2006),[37] professor at Haifa University, noted in his influential study *Terror on the Internet*, when he began examining this phenomenon at the end of the 1990s, there were just about twelve terrorist group websites. When he completed his research in 2005, the number had jumped to more than 4,300. This translated into a rate of proliferation of approximately 4,500% every year.[38] By the time the book was published in 2006, the number had grown to over 5,000 terrorist websites. By December 2007, the number of terrorist websites was reported to have increased to about 7,000.[39]

Communicating Jihadist Terrorism through Cyberspace

The implications of the expansion of cyberspace are beyond compare. Once considered a tool for education and enlightenment, cyberspace has now become an enormously useful vehicle for terrorists with which to market their decentered propaganda and multifarious conspiracy theories and rally their followers to committing violence.[40] Between 2001 and 2006, websites propagating Islamist messages have spread from fewer than 20 to over 3,000 (with about 70 admittedly militant sites collectively constituting a virtual jihadist university).[41] A quote lifted from what could easily be portrayed as a "jihad-friendly" website is symptomatic of a type of discourse that seeks to induce specific emotional responses among a target audience; responses which are, in turn, used to garner a new community of resistance: "Know, my beloved brother, that the path of jihad is not paved with roses, rather it is a path that is paved with severed limbs and blood, and it is full of fear and danger."[42]

Distressingly, such websites offer an increasingly persuasive and accepted alternative viewpoint to the terrorists' multi-colored audiences. This was certainly what Al Qaeda's purpose was when the group launched its first website, www.alneda.com, and maintained various successor sites ever since: to offer a "better" source for news and information over which the group itself could exert total control.[43] Likewise, an October 2005 posting by Ahmad Al-Wathiq bi-Llah, "deputy general emir" of the Al-Zarqawi-affiliated Global Islamic Media Front, re-released a 2003 announcement for the "Al Qaeda University of Jihad Studies... a tangible reality for the enemies of the Nation and the Faith; a decentralized university without geographical borders, present in every place."[44] Graduates, he explains, go through "faculties" that further the cause of a global Caliphate through great encouragement (and bombings!). Graduates also specialize in "electronic jihad, media jihad, spiritual and financial jihad." Now, let us have a look at a message about their Internet strategy, appearing on an Al Qaeda website, aimed at Muslim Internet professionals:

> Due to the advances of modern technology, it is easy to spread news, information, articles, and other information over the Internet. We strongly urge Muslim Internet professionals to spread and disseminate news and information about the Jihad through email lists, discussion groups, and their own websites. If you fail to do this, and our site closes down before you have done this, be held you to account before Allah on the Day of Judgment.[45]

As equally open and deliberate, the following message was posted on an Al Qaeda website four months prior to the Madrid train bombings on March 11, 2004:

> In order to force the Spanish government to withdraw from Iraq, the resistance should deal painful blows to its forces… It is necessary to make the utmost use of the upcoming general election in March next year. We think that the Spanish government could not tolerate more than two, maximum three blows, after which it will have to withdraw as a result of popular pressure.[46]

A Hezbollah website specifically addressed reporters and called them to interact with the group's press office via e-mail communication. Most of the terrorist organization's websites provide content in several languages to expand its international audience. The sites especially use English and major languages (in addition to the local version of Arabic for the organization's supporters). On looking at the content of many of the sites, it can easily be deduced that reporters represent another bystander target audience. Press releases by Hezbollah and similar organizations are often posted on the sites.[47]

Online Do-It-Yourself Jihad

Do-it-yourself jihad refers to the sharing of instructions on jihad published in monthly magazines, online forums, chat rooms, and state-of-the-art virtual camps. All of these have facilitated a do-it-yourself era of jihadist terror in the same way that the Internet has allowed the development of online education, business, and manifold hobbies and pursuits.[48] To use Fareed Zakaria's (2004)[49] term, it has given rise to the *democratization of violence*. It has initiated a de-formalized experience in which a low-profile Al Qaeda sympathizer is now blessed with a drastically better opportunity to become a full-fledged jihadist. The military wing of Hamas has created an online military academy offering courses that teach how to make bombs, including a fourteen-lesson course. In 1996, the Hamas website published "The Mujahideen Poisons Handbook," a twenty-three-page handbook on how to prepare poisons and toxins.[50]

The Madrid train bombings of March 11, 2004 were committed by the Abu Hafs Al Masri Brigades and were attributed to Moroccan immigrants residing in Spain. They were linked to each other through loose and informal ties. The terrorists who mounted the attacks managed to download strategies and tactics from the Internet and make use of the attacks for direct political objectives, while formulating their rhetoric in jihadist philosophy. Judiciously, the attacks were executed on behalf of Al Qaeda and not at Al Qaeda's request.[51]

Websites also contain precious technical information like maps, plans, how to make suicide belts or extract toxins, conspiracy theories, radical texts, Qur'anic interpretations, and detailed antiterrorist agendas.[52] The kind of urban warfare training necessary to accomplish the 2005 London attacks (i.e., 7/7) could be easily downloaded from the Internet. In Al Qaeda's Internet journal *Mu'asker al-Battar*, various contributors provided instructions as to how to prepare and successfully conduct an urban attack. Such detailed explanation shed light on the planning of the 7/7 attack. Video footage of the terrorists' obvious "dry-run" nine days prior to the actual attack reinforces this possibility even more.

The painstaking preparation and well-choreographed reconnaissance demonstrated in the case of 7/7 hint at the tradecraft that is usually featured in quasi-oriented instruction material like *Mu'asker al-Battar*.[53]

TERRORISTS AND ONLINE SOCIAL MEDIA

For terrorists, online social media have been useful for organizing operations, while websites have been valuable for circumventing media editorial controls and communicating directly with supporters and new recruits. Online social media allow communication from one person to another in a virtual world. This is the marvel of globalization: all one needs is an Internet connection. Social media give humans immediate connections with others.[54] About 100 million Internet users are believed to have joined online discussion forums to share information, advice, and social support via the user-created content of messages (available in the public domain). The fast development of online discussion group membership implies that participation in these groups is a great benefit to members, including both informational and social support to those who participate.[55] Today, millions of web users interact in chat rooms, **blogs** (interactive web pages or online forums allowing visitors to post comments), and message boards. Online forums are mostly arenas for individual users where they can express their viewpoints publicly and discuss almost any topic. Users can post short messages or longer articles, and write comments on other postings. They can also form relationships via social networking sites.[56]

Virtual Community

The concept of **virtual community** refers to a social network of people who communicate through specific online media, potentially moving beyond geographical and political boundaries to pursue mutual interests or objectives. One of the most universal forms of virtual community includes social networking services, which are composed of various online communities.[57] A virtual community is an example of **interactive communication**, a sharing of ideas where all participants are active and can have an influence on one another. It is a dynamic, two-way exchange of information. Unlike face-to-face communication, a virtual community gives opportunities for greater thought and deeper reflection on the matters discussed. Part of the reason is that it can be asynchronous communication and, thereby, give users more time to think on a subject.[58] The present-day successful terrorist is a hypercommunicator. A **hypercommunicator** is an engaged communicator who abundantly relies on both conventional and electronic media platforms to socially absorb or link individuals and virtual communities. Hypercommunicators are cutting-edge users of new communication tools to communicate and achieve their goals.[59]

A virtual community allows individuals to communicate immediately through only a few mouse clicks away. It is a decentralized meeting place that cannot be put under control or restriction. It gets no censorship and provides access to anyone who wants it. A virtual community, then, is like a global network. A **global network** is a type of communication network that covers the entire planet. Global networks have transfigured human communication on several occasions. The first to achieve this was the electrical telegraph. Its impact was so significant that it has been nicknamed the Victorian Internet. Its coverage was expanded many times thanks to the introduction of radiotelegraphy, and with text messaging using telex machines. The World Wide Web has allowed totally new forms of social interaction, endeavors, and organizing, on account of its basic features like widespread usability and access, and immediate communication from any connected point to another.[60]

Terrorists as Online Social Communicators

Cyberspace is offering a social networking platform for terrorists, enabling them to regularize their behavior and build up a sense of persecution. Blogs or online forums are also exploited to give terrorists and their supporters a feeling of belonging. Websites bolster members in their belief that they are not nonconformists or loners. Websites have their own icons or symbols—horses, flags, and sunrises have the same value as scarves in a tri-dimensional world. Hezbollah and Hamas offer souvenirs featuring logos. Local terrorist incentives (e.g., in Chechnya, Afghanistan, and Saudi Arabia) may be different, but their websites grant them a global jihad angle. The youngest, least educated, and not-so-literate (religious converts in particular) are intensely influenced by propaganda in online social media.[61]

The Internet constitutes a supreme propaganda tool, and, consequently, most extremist groups have an online presence. Websites and blogs are inexpensive to run and can still look professional, which makes a cause look even more valid and legitimate. It is fairly easy for extremists to use online social media that, again, attract less-literate youths. In the past, to obtain press coverage, terrorist organizations had to grab the attention of the mass media and, even so, could still be eclipsed by a competing story or ignored by an editor. Today, however, groups are able to sidestep these gatekeepers and interact straightforwardly with supporters and potential recruits.[62]

Additionally, terrorists use online social media to bond, interact socially, and plan and mount attacks. Blogs, chat rooms, and message boards are able to impact a wider audience, especially supporters and would-be militants.[63] Potential new recruits are referred to as **armchair jihadists**, and online forums are run by terrorist groups to facilitate such potential new recruitment. They are e-mailed or otherwise contacted directly by an ideologue who will indoctrinate and train the recruit. After being fully prepared, they are transferred to an operational leader, who will be in charge of tactical training in distinctive skills such as counter-surveillance, target selection, and bomb-making. The armchair jihadists are then ready to set up a cell offline, and additional support will be available on the ground.[64]

A classic example illustrates how people, who have never been in contact before with the jihadist community, use online resources to get in touch with established organizations and high-profile jihadists. Zachary Chesser, a 20-year-old from Virginia, was caught on July 21, 2010 on attempting to board an airliner bound to Africa. He was arrested on charges of backing Al-Shabaab, a Somalia-based terrorist organization. He owned and ran AlQuranWaAlaHadeeth, a YouTube website, and themujhidblog.com (a blog), which he used to upload videos and mediate discussions pertaining radical Islam. Chesser became an active member of the al-qimmah online forum, which he claims was Al-Shabaab's official forum. It was certainly his online participation that allowed him to be connected with Al-Shabaab, whose members told him that "he would have no problem in getting into Al-Shabaab when he reached Somalia."[65]

This recent anecdote demonstrates that online forums are breeding even more jihadists than before. While many forums are protected by passwords, the procedure to become a member seems simple; one has to sign up or contact the mediator of the site to become a member. The password protection is not set up to screen members but to make sure the forums will not be overloaded. Nevertheless, the forums do apply internal censorship. Apparently, it is the mediator's task to control the postings posted on the site and take down those that the mediator does not like or that do not live up to the terms of the site. Generally, the mediator will publish messages on the forum to declare that nonconformist postings or those against jihadist ideology are considered controversial and will be removed. For instance, this was the case in the aftermath of the London bombings in July 2005.[66]

MOTIVES FOR ONLINE TERRORIST RECRUITMENT

The blending of globalization and terrorism in the 21st century has spawned a new, flexible, and complex form of networked asymmetric enemy. For many terrorist organizations, cyberspace has become not only a virtual sanctuary, where new dimensions of warfare are unfolding online; it has also given rise to a virtual university that teaches potential new recruits how to make bombs, gather more followers, raise money, and even indoctrinate little children. Cyberspace offers an all-inclusive capability to a level that is quasi-limitless.[67] Weimann and von Knop (2008)[68] describe, in detail, seven motives for which terrorists exploit cyberspace for recruitment:

• Psychological warfare: the Internet enables to deliver threats and diffuse multimedia content to create fear and panic, as witnessed in Iraq. Virtually all insurgent factions in Iraq have media teams that publish statements and upload videos and web broadcasts.

• Online indoctrination: the Internet is now a tool used for radicalization and brainwashing by modern terrorists. Many of the contemporary terrorist attacks in Europe, North Africa, and the Middle East were perpetrated by individuals indoctrinated on the Internet.

• Recruitment and mobilization: the Internet and advanced technology are powerful instruments for recruiting and mobilizing group members, through networked communications.

• Planning and coordination: terrorist organizations make the most of new technologies such as encryption, voice-over-IP, and secure messaging systems to enhance the ease, rapidity, and cost of their communications. This facilitates the exchange of information such as training videos and manuals, improving their planning efforts and dexterity in an ever-evolving environment.

• Fundraising: terrorist organizations influence a massive number of Internet users and online front groups to promote aggressive funding drives, gathering vast amounts of money through online payment systems that are hard to track.

- Data mining: data mining consists of collecting information to smooth the progress of terrorists' strategic knowledge of an enemy and to facilitate terrorist attacks. A bleeding-edge repertoire of open-source technologies is used, such as search engines and website analytics, to gather intelligence on adversaries, potential recruits, and funding targets.

- Disinformation: an intentional dissemination of conspiracy theories that destabilize public confidence and trust both in the state and traditional media.

These seven motives demonstrate that cyberspace offers terrorists expanded possibilities of influencing and manipulating potential new recruits. Whether it is through blogs or other Internet tools, cyberspace allows terrorist organizations to send messages more easily and with few constraints than through other channels of communication.

THE TERRORISTS' ONLINE AUDIENCE

As a rule, a terrorist organization's website will outline the history of the organization; details about its political and ideological objectives (i.e., what it stands for); a thorough examination of its social and political background; accounts of its "accomplishments"; profiles of its leaders, founding members, and heroes; harsh condemnation of its enemies; and current news. Nationalist and separatist terror groups even display maps of the territories in dispute. For instance, the Hamas website displays a map of Palestine, the FARC website presents a map of Colombia, and the LTTE (Liberation Tigers of Tamil Eelam) site shows a map of Sri Lanka.[69] Now, what types of audience do terrorists target through their websites? According to Tokar (2007),[70] the content of the websites suggests four types of online audience:

Four Types of Online Audience

- Current and potential supporters: terrorist websites rely heavily on slogans. They also exhibit items for sale, such as T-shirts, badges, flags, videos, and audiocassettes, all obviously directed to sympathizers. Typically, an organization will aim at its local sympathizers with a website using the local language, and will give detailed content on the activities and internal politics of the organization, its partners, and its opponents.

- International public opinion: the international public—not directly involved in the struggle—who may be interested in the issues in question. Such public is cozied up to with websites written in languages other than the local language. Most websites are in several languages. For example, ETA's website writes its content in Castillian Spanish, German, French, and Italian, while the MRTA (the Túpac Amaru Revolutionary Movement, a Peruvian Marxist terrorist group) website offers Japanese and Italian besides its English and Spanish versions. The IMU (Islamic Movement of Uzbekistan) website provides content in Arabic, English, and Russian. To appeal to global audiences, the websites publish fundamental information about their organizations and their historical backgrounds.

- Specific audiences: on reading the content of many terrorist websites, it looks like foreign media are also targeted. Press releases tend to be posted on the websites to insert the terrorist organization's viewpoint into the traditional media. The detailed background information of the organization can also help international reporters and politicians themselves. One of Hezbollah's sites explicitly addresses reporters, inviting them to communicate with the organization's press office through e-mail.

- The enemy public: attempts at reaching the enemy public (i.e., citizens of those states that the terrorists consider opponents) are not as obvious from the content of many websites. Yet, some sites try to undermine their enemies, by threatening to attack them and producing feelings of guilt about the opponent's behavior and motives.

The Internet is ideal for terrorists as hypercommunicators. Through networks of mediated exchange, terrorists can speak to multiple audiences.

Hamas Audiences

According to Mozes and Weimann (2010),[71] Hamas websites regularly modify their formats and design by including new features, adding new links, using new online technologies, and embracing recent innovations in cyberspace (such as Facebook and YouTube). For the two scholars, four types of audience log on to Hamas websites:

- Audiences that are Hamas-oriented: these are people who overtly endorse Hamas and who search for information about the terrorist group as a social organization, a Palestinian political movement, or an operating militant corps.

- Audiences generally interested in the Palestinian issue: this audience expresses interest in Palestinian history or politics and looks for information about Palestinians, their struggle against Israel, and their background.

- Audiences that are anti-Western: these are people opposed to the West; they are anti-American and very frequently anti-Semitic.

- Audiences interested in human rights: this audience expresses an interest in learning about human rights violations.

Chaffey and colleagues (2000)[72] introduced three levels of positioning information that were promoted on terrorist groups' websites: "Brochureware," "Interaction," and "Representation" (web self-service). Most groups' websites emphasize information presentation according to the **Brochureware** style. The information displayed on some websites tends to be of a reporting style and distances itself from propaganda content. In addition, all terrorists' websites adopt the Interactive mode: on all websites, there are opportunities to register and obtain information from the site through e-mail or by using the RSS service (which stands for "Really Simple Syndication"). RSS allows the distribution and gathering of content from sources across the Internet, like newspapers, magazines, and blogs. The last positioning measure is Representation. In the case of Hamas, Representation is made up of links to Hamas forums and chat rooms, which includes an additional dimension of interactivity. Hamas supporters use many online forums. Some of them are run or controlled by Hamas operatives.[73]

ONLINE RADICALIZATION

Internet-savvy terrorists have launched a process of online radicalization, especially of youth, through virtual communities and online social bonding. Online radicalization is an ideal instrument of ideological recruitment. In fact, over the past few years, face-to-face radicalization has been replaced by online radicalization. This type of interactivity, as typically found in Islamist or extremist forums, can change people's beliefs. The same support, endorsement, and justification that youth used to get from face-to-face groups are now found in online forums all over the world. They glorify the image of terrorist heroes, market extremist ideas, connect users to virtual radical movements, offer them guidance, and coach them on various tactics. The real leader of this virtual radical movement is the collective discourse on innumerable online forums. They are revolutionizing terrorist movements, recruiting ever younger individuals and—more importantly—females to take part in the discussions.[74]

The Public Sphere (Habermas)

Jürgen Habermas (1974),[75] a German sociologist and philosopher, defines the **public sphere** as an entity that comes into existence "when private individuals assemble to form a public body. They then behave neither like business or professional people transacting private affairs, nor like members of a constitutional order subject to the legal constraints of a state bureaucracy" (p. 49). Online radicalization can be set in motion through the public sphere. Individuals are now radicalized in the new-fangled terrorist public sphere by way of multiple means. These include competing independent online news pathways and official media, Islamist social networking sites, and prominent high-profile figures and intellectuals who post messages. Through these channels, a gigantic terrorist Diaspora can increasingly keep in contact with the politics of the terrorist arena and actively engage with them thanks to information and communication technology—whether by viewing Al Jazeera podcasts in Seattle or by e-mailing friends from Sweden.[76] Immediately after September 11, 2001, Islam Online—a very prominent and wide-ranging Islamic propagandist site—enjoyed a spectacular increase in visitor numbers. Its page views rose from an average of 24 million to 150 million every year.[77]

The age of the public sphere as face-to-face interaction has passed its prime. Today, the public sphere is based on the idea that it is a mediated and mediating place. Terrorist groups can narrow their radicalization and recruitment to the online public sphere. Contrary to powerful group dynamics of traditional three-dimensional radicalization and recruitment, networked groups can now be in contact electronically and experience a fundamentally different group psychology, **virtual group dynamics**, which greatly impacts their decision making and risk taking, and has critical security effects.[78] Online radicalization is also a form of techno-terrorism. **Techno-terrorism** is a terrorist means of satellite communications, e-mail, and the World Wide Web. The jihadist networks have exploited the Internet and a variety of other information technologies to diffuse their message, indoctrinate people, find new recruits, muster support, plan and prepare activities, impart operational information, and raise funds.[79]

Stages of Online Radicalization

According to various scholars,[80] online radicalization does not happen overnight—as it was already the case with face-to-face or in-group radicalization. Rather, it is a five-phase process. In the first phase, the Searching Phase, the users have to restrain an individual interest or desire that leads them to look for radical websites. The users seek particular answers that may offer full or partial fulfillment of their needs. In the second phase, the Seduction Phase, the users now visit specific sites and are, therefore, being exposed to the radical ideology. In the third phase, the Captivation Phase, the users join blogs, forums, and chat rooms, and become lured by their charming messages. That is why this phase is seen as the most important one. In the fourth phase, the Persuasion Phase, the users decide to become participants in the online exchange and are full-fledged members of the online community. For most users, the road stops here. In the fifth phase, the Operative Phase, the user is exposed to an assortment of operative activities of the online community and/or a particular terrorist group. It should be remarked that, all the way through the stages of the online radicalization process, the user does not stop interacting with the three-dimensional environment (i.e., usually relatives, friends, and the mass media).

STEGANOGRAPHY: COVERT COMMUNICATION

Terrorists also communicate via predetermined codes that are generally sent through ancient personal messenger systems. This is particularly true for complex operation moves during the few steps that precede the actual execution.[81] One of these ancient personal messenger systems is steganography.

Steganography: Definition

Steganography (also abbreviated as **stego**) derives from Greek and literally means "covered writing" (*steganos* for "covered" and *graphy* for "writing"). It is an ancient practice of concealing messages within texts, pictures, and objects. In ancient Greece, steganography consisted of judiciously sending warnings of an impending attack by writing them on the wood underneath a wax tablet. To the naked eye, the tablet itself simply looked blank, but to the intended receiver of the message, the seemingly blank tablet contained a message underneath the wax. Another way of applying steganography in ancient Greece was to tattoo a secret message onto a messenger's head that was shaved. The messenger was dispatched to a specific location, while his hair was growing back during his travel to the destination, and on arrival, his head was shaved again to reveal the message. As a reported method of terrorist communication, steganography represents complex symbolism.[82]

Steganography is an example of **covert communication**—the art of communicating without making the communication noticeable, thereby making communication totally anonymous. This stratagem can facilitate absolute anonymity and asynchronous communication between two parties that may not even know each other. This is the principle on which steganography operates: it conceals the fact that communication is taking place on top of actually concealing a message. It is encoded as minute variations to the color of the pixels in a JPEG image. The message is so tiny that it goes undetected by the casual observer. To the latter, it is merely a picture, but to the terrorist group that sent the message and to the intended recipient, there is a message hidden there. They are the only ones to be aware of it and understand it. A terrorist organization can select a "spy" who will sign up for a free, anonymous e-mail account, and with whom other terrorist members can easily communicate. In other cases, the terrorist organization can produce a web-based file that has other types of files covertly implanted inside. They can also embed a message in a text file or within an image. Such text file or image can be posted secretly on many websites. Again, not only is the message astutely hidden; the reality that a message is lurking in there is also hidden and unknown.

Cryptography

Today, terrorist organizations can communicate without making it known through avant-garde technology. They use computers, the Internet, steganography, and encryption to get down to business. If their cryptography is of high quality, it can take years and years to crack. Cryptography enables terrorists to encrypt their communications. **Cryptography** (also known as **crypto**) encodes messages in such a way that not one person can read it, except the one to whom the message was sent. Cryptography relies on **ciphertext**, information written in a covertly encoded form, what some people designate *garbled information*. The meaning of the messages in ciphertext is masked. The opposite, of course, is plaintext. **Encryption** involves muddling information in such a manner that only the intended recipient, who possesses the key to decode the encrypted messages, can detect the data. Any other person intercepting the message could not read it.[83]

It has even been reported that terrorists have embedded encrypted data inside pornographic files, which are then unearthed and decoded by other terrorists. To be more precise, the senders encode maps and photos of likely targets on pornographic bulletin boards. Covert messages can even be transmitted through spam e-mails. Cryptography involves the garbling of messages, so that they can be slipped into seemingly innocent pictures or files. It is a rapid, low-cost, and secure way of assigning lethal instructions. This is the core of globalization: the messages, concealed in websites, could be accessed by any person, from any place in the world, and at virtually no cost to the user. It is also believed that cybercafés in developing countries and anonymous computer stations (in general) have played a major role in allowing terrorists to access their encrypted messages.[84] When encryption is solid, no one can break it. U.S. federal agencies incapable of reading covert messages have developed **inference tracking**, a method that does not enable counterterrorism agencies to decode messages. Instead, it gives some cues as to whether messages exist and as to what is afoot. Otherwise stated, it is evident from the message that something big is about to happen.[85]

Examples of Steganography in Terrorism

In one particular example, reported by *ABC News* in October 2001, French detectives believed that suspects caught in an alleged conspiracy to bomb the U.S. embassy in Paris intended to send, covertly, the go-ahead for the attack within a picture posted on the web. The detectives found a notebook replete with secret codes on one of the suspects, who was identified as a computer nerd savvy in steganography.[86] Many terrorist groups have web-sites or will upload videos on video-sharing sites such as YouTube. These can be embedded with hidden codes; straightforward graphics such as a terrorist holding his or her machine gun in the left hand will be shown. However, displaying a similar picture with the gun in the right hand can be a special signal for a terrorist group and be virtually indiscernible to the intelligence agencies monitoring it.[87]

Steganography has been used in the form of an **electronic dead drop**. An electronic dead drop refers to an invisible "go-between" on the web—that is, a signal implanted within an Internet photo or text that is posted in an online forum, and then downloaded by the intended recipient. For a terrorist organization, the aim of having an electronic dead drop is to allocate crime activities or random tasks to unknown parties—to warn others that they have to follow guidelines, such as picking up a piece of luggage (that contains a time bomb) placed underneath the counter of a cafeteria. An electronic dead drop is a superior method toward face-to-face communication. Two terrorist groups that have never seen each other (or that may not even know each other) but that belong to the same network can use an electronic dead drop as a go-between: without even coordinating a face-to-face appoint-ment. No trace can be detected: no e-mail exchanged between them, no communication through Internet Relay Chat or a chat room, no remote login, or no instant messaging.[88]

Khalid Sheikh Mohammed (KSM), a suspected mastermind behind 9/11 who was famously waterboarded in Guantánamo Bay, and who faces the death penalty if convicted, is believed to have sent directives through an electronic dead drop; messages were written but never sent. Rather, KSM saved them as drafts. Then, the intended recipient read them from the draft message folder of a shared e-mail account. Other terrorists have also used this method, including one of the sentenced killers behind the 2004 Madrid train bombings.[89]

CYBERTERRORISM

Globalization facilitates the wicked exploitation of cyberspace, which can be an important terrorist weapon against computer-based networks. One such method is called cyberter-rorism. **Cyberterrorism** refers to the use of information technology to launch attacks and capture attention from the state. Cyberterrorists will usually use information technology such as telecommunications, the Internet, or computer systems as a method to choreo-graph attacks.[90] By and large, cyberterrorist attacks on diverse targets can theoretically disrupt networked services. For instance, cyberterrorists could prevent networked emer-gency systems from working or delve into networks that house indispensable information to interrupt those very networks. There is some dissent over the degree of the existing danger posed by cyberterrorism.[91] In theory, it has the power to cause a **cascading failure**—a series of failures (i.e., cascade) engendered by the removal of a vital node (i.e., a key point or location in an infrastructure) from a network.[92]

Cyberterrorism Different from Hacking and Cyberwar

A computer-whiz kid looking for glory and who disrupts the whole computer system of a university would not be labeled a cyberterrorist if (1) the act of hacking is unpremeditated and (2) the act of hacking is not intended to cripple a large network. Therefore, the term **hacker** does not automatically suggest that he or she is a cyberterrorist. Hackers infiltrate systems or networks but do not seek to damage them. It is important to realize that, under a U.S. Congress law called "Act 2001,"[93] if the destruction caused by the computer-whiz kid is substantial, then he or she will still be punished. In any case, a cyberterrorist is an intentional, malicious hacker. Hackers turned malicious users are also considered cyberterrorists.[94]

In line with these contentions, **cyberwar** has been described by security expert Richard A. Clarke (2010),[95] in his book *Cyber War*, as "actions by a nation-state to penetrate another nation's computers or networks for the purposes of causing damage or disruption" (p. 6). In contrast to cyberterrorism, cyberwar involves the state and/or the military. On the other hand, cyberterrorism usually involves non-state actors. The following is a real example of cyberterrorism that occurred in 2000: an Australian cyberterrorist was charged with delving into the Maroochy Shire Council's computer network and operating it to release raw sewage into the Sunshine Coast (in Australia), causing overflowed contamination. The Australian cyberterrorist was a discontented consultant who was denied a position at a water treatment facility. In retaliation, he infiltrated a sewage treatment network from a remote position and discharged 264,000 gallons of raw sewage into rivers and parks.[96]

The Postmodern Condition

Cyberterrorism is an indicator of the postmodern condition. The term *postmodern* was already used in Chapter 1, but no thorough definition was provided. **Postmodernism** is a cultural movement of the late 20th century that embraces the philosophy that humans live in an age of personal freedom from imposed rules and social limitations. Postmodernism is a shift away from spatialization and a victory over linearity. While modernism is analogous to the early 20th century machine age, postmodernism is analogous to the age of simulation, of online selves, and of computer and electronic means.[97] The cyberterrorist can incorporate a virus that causes damage for one week, then stops, and then re-emerges a year later to destroy computers and networks again. Fundamentally, a digital tool like a virus can be encoded to operate or "explode" at a specific time or only if a specific condition is met. By contrast, no non-digital (i.e., analog) weapon—not even a time bomb—could achieve such feat. Once it goes off, it goes off. Think of the landmine; it will explode only one time. It will not reappear or go off a second time ever. From this vantage point, while traditional weapons are **analog**—that is, they are used in a linear sequential manner—postmodern cyberterrorist weapons are **digital**—that is, they do not depend on a linear sequential order.[98]

Cyberterrorism is postmodern because it is more hyperreal than real. Coined by Jean Baudrillard (1983),[99] **hyperreal** represents the blurring of differences between the real and the unreal. The postmodern perspective of cyberspace is that it makes the fine line between the real and the unreal collapse into itself. What cyberterrorists benefit from is hyperreality. The hyperreal means that the sense of placeness as humans know it in the three-dimensional world has no value in cyberspace. That is why cyberspace is considered the postmodern condition. What humans witness are new worlds that appear; although real, they are not physical. What humans witness are new spaces that appear; although extensive, they are instant and the sense of remoteness no longer makes sense. Cyberterrorists' spatial-temporal methods of conducting attacks are not inflexible and uniformed. This brings an end to geography. They are just a few mouse clicks away from causing serious damage. This even signifies the death of time. As Mitchell (1995)[100] suggests,

> The Net negates geometry; it is fundamentally and profoundly antispatial. It is nothing like the Piazza Navona or Copley Square. You cannot say where it is or describe its memorable shape and proportions or tell a stranger how to get there. But you can find things in it without knowing where they are. The Net is ambient—nowhere in particular and everywhere at once. (p. 8)

The more Internet- and technology-reliant a culture is, the more defenseless it becomes toward cyberterrorism. Not surprisingly, there are grave concerns about this terrorist method that can potentially disrupt networked societies. Paul Virilio (1998),[101] a French cultural theorist, suggested the scary possibility of the breakdown of cyberspace after a disastrous technological event brings about its shutdown. The scholar was thinking of disruptions caused by cyberterrorist attacks, worms, Trojan horses, and viruses. For Virilio, the catastrophe that the Internet faces is "the accident of accidents," as he refers to it. It is the total collapse of global Internet- and technology-dependent systems of communication and information, and consequently the global economy.

SUMMARY

Global transnational terrorism (GTT) refers to terrorism whereby violent non-state actors (VNSAs) are active in multiple territories. The progress of globalization and the proportion of VNSAs make GTT harder to monitor and to predict. For example, The Tri-Border Area (TBA), where Argentina, Brazil, and Paraguay join, is being used as a sanctuary for terrorist operations. Paraguay has no antiterrorism laws. Arab communities in the TBA have contributed financial sums of $50–$500 million (U.S.) to terrorist organizations like Hezbollah (a major recipient). Globalization, thanks to international trade and transportation, has given new opportunities for terrorist groups to obtain and use better and deadlier weapons. Modern-day technologies diffuse power and level the playing field for terrorists. As the dark side of globalization, terrorism has power that is equal to the bright side of globalization (a phenomenon called *parallel globalization of terror*). Ontological insecurity refers to the fear of the incapacity to maintain global order because terrorism is a perpetual threat. In line with these contentions, terrorism plays a huge role in cyberspace. Terrorism exploits the Global Village. Cyberspace, like the Global Village, expands and de-territorializes. It has intensely transformed the way in which current terrorist networks run their activities. Jihadist terrorism can be easily communicated through cyberspace. By December 2007, the number of terrorist websites was reported to have increased to about 7,000. There is even an online do-it-yourself jihad; it posts handbooks that explain how to make bombs. A great advantage of the Internet is the emergence of online social media and virtual communities. The youngest, least educated, and not-so-literate are intensely influenced by propaganda in online social media. As a result, online media are breeding even more jihadists than before. Many of the contemporary terrorist attacks in Europe, North Africa, and the Middle East were perpetrated by individuals indoctrinated on the Internet. An important conclusion here is that online radicalization is made easy. As we have seen, Weimann and von Knop (2008) found seven motives for which terrorists exploit cyberspace for recruitment. With respect to the terrorists' online audience, four types were identified: current and potential supporters, international public opinion, specific audiences, and the enemy public. Hamas, too, has its four types of online audience. Terrorists also communicate via predetermined codes that are generally transmitted through old personal messenger systems. Such a method is steganography (an ancient practice of concealing messages within texts, pictures, and objects). By and large, it is covert communication that makes it totally anonymous. Lastly, terrorists can turn into cyberterrorists. Cyberterrorism is the use of information technology such as telecommunications, the Internet, or computer systems as a method to mount attacks. Cyberterrorism can theoretically disrupt networked services, even provoking cascading failures. Part of the reason is that cyberterrorist weapons are digital and postmodern.

KEY TERMS

analog   353

armchair jihadists   345

(a)synchronous communication   340

blog   344

Brochureware   348

cascading failure   352

ciphertext   351

covert communication   350

cryptography   351

cultural Westernization   336

cyberspace   340

cyberterrorism   352

cyberwar   353

digital   353

do-it-yourself jihad   343

electronic dead drop   352

encryption   351

first and second media age   341

globalization   335

global network   344

global transnational terrorism   336

Global Village   341

Gutenberg Galaxy   341

hacker   353

Hezbollah   337

hypercommunicator   344

hyperreal   353

inference tracking   351

interactive communication   344

liberalization   335

ontological insecurity   339

parallel globalization of terror   339

postmodernism   353

public sphere   349

steganography   350

techno-terrorism   349

Transnational Bads   338

Tri-Border Area   337

violent non-state actor   336

virtual community   344

virtual group dynamics   349

ENDNOTES

1. Nassar, Jamar R. (2004). *Globalization and Terrorism: The Migration of Dreams and Nightmares*. Lanham, MD: Rowman & Littlefield.

2. Rojecki, Andrew (2005). Media Discourse on Globalization and Terror. *Political Communication, 22*, 63–81.

3. Sullivan, Arthur, & Sheffrin, Steven M. (2002). *Economics: Principles in Action*. Upper Saddle River, NJ: Pearson Prentice Hall.

4. Beck, Ulrich (2000). *What Is Globalization?* Cambridge: Polity Press; Friedman, Thomas (1999). *The Lexus and the Olive Tree*. New York: Farrar, Straus, Giroux; Friedman, Thomas (2005). *The World Is Flat*. New York: Farrar, Straus, Giroux.

5. Ritzer, George (1993). *The McDonaldization of Society*. Thousand Oaks, CA: Pine Forge Press.

6. Magouirk, Justin, Atran, Scott, & Sageman, Marc (2008). Connecting Terrorist Networks. *Studies in Conflict & Terrorism, 31*(1), 1–16.

7. Rochester, Martin J. (2002). *Between Two Epochs: What's Ahead for America, the World, and Global Politics in the Twenty-First Century*. Upper Saddle River, NJ: Prentice Hall.

8. Gotchev, Atanas (2006). Terrorism and Globalization. In Louise Richardson (Ed.), *The Roots of Terrorism* (pp.103–120). New York: Routledge.

9. Gotchev, Atanas (2006). Terrorism and Globalization. In Louise Richardson (Ed.), *The Roots of Terrorism* (pp.103–120). New York: Routledge.

10. White, Jonathan R. (2011). *Terrorism & Homeland Security* (7th ed.). Belmont, CA: Wadsworth.

11. Costa, Thomaz G., & Schulmeister, Gastón H. (2007). The Puzzle of the Iguazu Tri-Border Area: Many Questions and Few Answers Regarding Organised Crime and Terrorism Links. *Global Crime, 8*(1), 26–39.

12. Goldberg, Jeffrey (2002, October 28). In the Party of God: Part 2 of 2. *The New Yorker*, p. A1.

13. Asal, Victor, Nussbaum, Brian, & Harrington, D. William (2007). Terrorism as Transnational Advocacy: An Organizational and Tactical Examination. *Studies in Conflict & Terrorism, 30*, 15–39.

14. Mannes, Aaron (2004). *Profiles in Terror: A Guide to Middle East Terrorist Organizations*. Lanham, MD: Rowman & Littlefield Publishers.

15. Asal, Victor, Nussbaum, Brian, & Harrington, D. William (2007). Terrorism as Transnational Advocacy: An Organizational and Tactical Examination. *Studies in Conflict & Terrorism, 30*, 15–39.

16. White, Jonathan R. (2011). *Terrorism & Homeland Security* (7th ed.). Belmont, CA: Wadsworth.

17. Matusitz, Jonathan, & O'Hair, Dan (2008). The Role of the Internet in Terrorism. In Dan O'Hair, Robert Heath, Kevin Ayotte, & Gerald R. Ledlow (Eds.), *Terrorism: Communication and Rhetorical Perspectives* (pp. 383–407). Cresskill, NJ: Hampton Press.

18. Stanislawski, Bartosz H. (2004). Transnational "Bads" in the Globalized World. *Public Integrity, 6*(2), 155–170.

19. Arquilla, John, & Ronfeldt, David (1996). *The Advent of Netwar*. Santa Monica: RAND Corporation; Basile, Mark (2004). Going to the Source: Why Al Qaeda's Financial Network Is Likely to Withstand the Current War on Terrorist Financing. *Studies in Conflict and Terrorism, 27*(3), 169–186; Cronin, Audrey Kurth (2003). Behind the Curve: Globalization and International Terrorism. *International Security, 27*(3), 30–58; Laurance, Edward J. (2002). Shaping Global Public Policy on Small Arms: After the UN Conference. *The Brown Journal of World Affairs, 9*(1), 193–201.

20. Greider, William (1998). *Fortress America: The American Military and the Consequences of Peace*. New York: Public Affairs.

21. Schröder, Gerhard (2001, September 19). *The Terrorist Attacks in the United States and the Decisions Taken by the United Nations Security Council and NATO*. Berlin: Bulletin der Bundesregierung, No. 61-1.

22. Rasmussen, Mikkel Vedby (2002). "A Parallel Globalization of Terror": 9-11, Security and Globalization. *Cooperation and Conflict, 37*(3), 323–349.

23. Kellner Douglas (2007). Globalization, Terrorism, and Democracy: 9/11 and Its Aftermath. *Frontiers of Globalization Research, 11*, 243–268.

24. Rasmussen, Mikkel Vedby (2002). "A Parallel Globalization of Terror": 9-11, Security and Globalization. *Cooperation and Conflict, 37*(3), 323–349.

25. Willis, Jerry W. (2007). *Foundations of Qualitative Research: Interpretive and Critical Approaches.* Thousand Oaks, CA: Sage.

26. Kellner Douglas (2007). Globalization, Terrorism, and Democracy: 9/11 and Its Aftermath. *Frontiers of Globalization Research, 11*, 243–268.

27. Mann, Michael (2001). Globalization and September 11. *New Left Review, 12*, 51–72.

28. Barber, Benjamin R. (1995). *Jihad vs. McWorld.* New York: Crown; Friedman, Thomas (2002). *Longitudes and Attitudes: The World in the Age of Terrorism.* New York: Anchor; Stevens, Michael J. (2002). The Unanticipated Consequences of Globalization: Contextualizing Terrorism. In Chris Tout (Ed.), *The Psychology of Terrorism: Theoretical Understandings and Perspectives* (pp. 31–54). Westport, CT: Praeger.

29. Cheney, George, Christensen, Lars Thoger, Zorn, Theodore E., Jr., & Ganesh, Shiv (2010). *Organizational Communication in an Age of Globalization: Issues, Reflections, Practices* (2nd ed.). Prospect Heights, IL: Waveland Press.

30. Gibson, William (1984). *Neuromancer.* New York: Ace.

31. Matusitz, Jonathan (2007). The Implications of the Internet for Human Communication. *The Journal of Information Technology Impact, 7*(1), 21–34.

32. Holmes, David (2005). *Communication Theory: Media, Technology and Society.* Thousand Oaks, CA: Sage; Poster, Mark (1995). *The Second Media Age.* New York: Polity.

33. McLuhan, Marshall (1962). *The Gutenberg Galaxy: The Making of Typographic Man.* Toronto: University of Toronto Press.

34. Kirby, Aidan (2007). The London Bombers as "Self-Starters": A Case Study in Indigenous Radicalization and the Emergence of Autonomous Cliques. *Studies in Conflict & Terrorism, 30*, 415–428; Ranstorp, Magnus (2007). The Virtual Sanctuary of Al Qaeda and Terrorism in an Age of Globalization. In Johan Eriksson and Giampiero Giacomello (Eds.), *International Relations and Security in the Digital Age* (pp. 31–54). New York: Routledge.

35. Katz, Elihu, & Liebes, Tamar (2007). "No More Peace!" How Disaster, Terror and War have Upstaged Media Events. *International Journal of Communication, 1*, 157–166.

36. Hoffman, Bruce (2007). Countering Terrorist Use of the Web as a Weapon. *CTC Sentinel, 1*(1), 4–6.

37. Weimann, Gabriel (2006). *Terror on the Internet: The New Arena, the New Challenges.* Washington, D.C.: U.S. Institute of Peace Press, p. 105.

38. Remarks by Professor Gabriel Weimann, book launch event held at the U.S. Institute of Peace, Washington, D.C. on April 17, 2006.

39. Hoffman, Bruce (2007). Countering Terrorist Use of the Web as a Weapon. *CTC Sentinel, 1*(1), 4–6.

40. Brown, Tina (2005, May 19). Death by Error. *Washington Post*, p. A1.

41. Ariza, Luis Miguel (2005, December 26). Virtual Jihad: The Internet as the Ideal Terrorism Recruiting Tool. *Scientific American, 294*(1), p. 18.

42. Abu Usamah Al-Hazin (2008). To the One Who Falls Imprisoned: Messages of Advice. Retrieved May 17, 2011 http://tibyan.wordpress.com/2008/06/06/to-the-one-who-falls-into-imprisonment-messages-of-advice/.

43. Brown, Tina (2005, May 19). Death by Error. *Washington Post*, p A1.

44. Al-Farouq Jihadi Forum (2005, October 7). Retrieved February 2, 2011 from http://www.al-farouq.com/vb/.

45. From the Al Qaeda Website called "Azzam," cited in *Jihad Online: Islamic Terrorists and the Internet*, published by the Anti-Defamation league (ADL) in 2002, at http://www.adl.org/internet/jihad_online.pdf

46. Al Qaeda (2003). *Jihadi Iraq: Hopes and Dangers.* Al Qaeda Manual published in September 2003 and dedicated to Yusef Al-Ayeri. Retrieved December 5, 2010, http://www.mil.no/felles/ffi/start/article.jhtml?articleID = 71589.

47. Weimann, Gabriel (2008). The Psychology of Mass-Mediated Terrorism. *American Behavioral Scientist, 52*(1), 69–86, p. 78.

48. Kirby, Aidan (2007). The London Bombers as "Self-Starters": A Case Study in Indigenous Radicalization and the Emergence of Autonomous Cliques. *Studies in Conflict & Terrorism, 30*, 415–428.

49. Zakaria, Fareed (2004). *The Future of Freedom*. New York: W.W. Norton and Company.

50. Weimann, Gabriel (2006). Virtual Training Camps: Terrorists' Use of the Internet. In James Forest (Ed.), *Teaching Terror: Strategic and Tactical Learning in the Terrorist World* (pp. 110–132). Lanham, MD: Rowman & Littlefield.

51. Ward, Blake (2005). *Osama's Wake: The Second Generation of Al Qaeda*. Washington, D.C.: USAF Counterproliferation Center; Wright, Lawrence (2004, August 2). The Terror Web, a Reporter at Large. *The New Yorker, 80*(21), p. A1.

52. Brown, Ian, & Korff, Douwe (2009). Terrorism and the Proportionality of Internet Surveillance. *European Journal of Criminology, 6*(2), 119–134.

53. *BBC News* (2005, September 20). London Bombers Staged "Dummy Run." *BBC News*; Scheuer, Michael (2005). The London Bombings: For al-Qaeda, Steady as She Goes. *Terrorism Focus, 2*(14), 10–21.

54. Turkle, Sherry (1997). *Life on the Screen: Identity in the Age of the Internet*. New York: Simon & Schuster.

55. Rainie, Lee (2005). *Internet: The Mainstreaming of Online Life*. Pew Internet & American Life Project; Ridings, Catherine, & Wasko, Molly (2010). Online Discussion Group Sustainability: Investigating the Interplay between Structural Dynamics and Social Dynamics over Time. *Journal of the Association for Information Systems, 11*(2), 95–121.

56. Warschauer, Mark, & Grimes, Douglas (2007). Audience, Authorship, and Artifact: The Emergent Semiotics of Web. *Annual Review of Applied Linguistics, 27*, 1–23.

57. Rheingold, Howard (1998). *The Virtual Community*. New York: Simon & Schuster.

58. Van Raaij, W. Fred (1998). Interactive Communication: Consumer Power and Initiative. *Journal of Marketing Communications, 4*(1), 1–8.

59. Vevere, Velga (2005). Existence and Communication: Challenge of the Times. *Analecta Husserliana, 84*, 165–175.

60. Castells, Manuel (2001). *The Internet Galaxy, Reflections on the Internet, Business and Society*. Oxford: Oxford University Press.

61. Bird, Juliette (2006). *Terrorist Use of the Internet*. The Second International Scientific Conference on Security and Countering Terrorism Issues, Moscow State University Institute for Information Security Issues, 25–28 October; Labi, Nadya (2006). Jihad 2.0. *Atlantic Monthly, 7*, 102–107.

62. Brown, Ian, & Korff, Douwe (2009). Terrorism and the Proportionality of Internet Surveillance. *European Journal of Criminology, 6*(2), 119–134.

63. Ryan, Johnny (2007). *Countering Militant Islamist Radicalisation on the Internet: A User Driven Strategy to Recover the Web*. Dublin: Institute of European Affairs.

64. Shahar, Yael (2007). *The Internet as a Tool for Counter-terrorism: Patrolling and Controlling Cyberspace*. Garmisch-Partenkirchen, Germany: NATO Advanced Research Workshop.

65. Kennedy, Jonathan, & Weimann, Gabriel (2011). The Strength of Weak Terrorist Ties. *Terrorism and Political Violence, 23*(2), 201–212.

66. Rogan, Hanna (2006). *Jihadism Online: A Study of How al-Qaida and Radical Islamist Groups Use the Internet for Terrorist Purposes*. Oslo: FFI Rapport.

67. Ranstorp, Magnus (2007). The Virtual Sanctuary of Al Qaeda and Terrorism in an Age of Globalization. In Johan Eriksson and Giampiero Giacomello (Eds.), *International relations and Security in the Digital Age* (pp. 31–54). New York: Routledge.

68. Weimann, Gabriel, & von Knop, Katharina (2008). Applying the Notion of Noise to Countering Online Terrorism. *Studies in Conflict & Terrorism, 31*, 883–902.

69. Tokar, Luibomyr (2007). Hypermedia Communication as a Modern Means for the Creation of Terrorist and Counterterrorist Consciousness. In Boaz Ganor, Katharina Von Knop, and Carlos Duarte (Eds.), *Hypermedia Seduction for Terrorist Recruiting* (pp. 105–115). Amsterdam: NATO Science for Peace and Security Series; Weimann, Gabriel (2006). *Terror on the Internet: The New Arena, the New Challenges*. Washington, D.C.: U.S. Institute of Peace Press.

70. Tokar, Luibomyr (2007). Hypermedia Communication as a Modern Means for the Creation of Terrorist and Counterterrorist Consciousness. In Boaz Ganor, Katharina Von Knop, and Carlos Duarte (Eds.), *Hypermedia Seduction for Terrorist Recruiting* (pp. 105–115). Amsterdam: NATO Science for Peace and Security Series.

71. Mozes, Tomer, & Weimann, Gabriel (2010). The E-Marketing Strategy of Hamas. *Studies in Conflict & Terrorism, 33*(3), 211–225.

72. Chaffey, Dave, Mayer, Richard, Johnston, Kevin, & Ellis-Chadwick, Fiona (2000). *Internet Marketing.* Harlow, England: Pearson Education.

73. Weimann, Gabriel (2007). Using the Internet for Terrorist Recruitment and Mobilization. In Boaz Ganor, Katharina Von Knop, and Carlos Duarte (Eds.), *Hypermedia Seduction for Terrorist Recruiting* (pp. 47–58). Amsterdam: NATO Science for Peace and Security Series.

74. Kohlmann, Evan F. (2008). "Homegrown" Terrorists: Theory and Cases in the War on Terror's Newest Front. *Annals of the American Academy of Political and Social Science, 618,* 95–109; Sageman, Marc (2008). A Strategy for Fighting International Islamist Terrorists. *Annals of the American Academy of Political and Social Science, 618,* 223–231.

75. Habermas, Jürgen (1974). The Public Sphere: An Encyclopedia Article. *New German Critique, 1*(3), 49–55.

76. Walker, Karen M. (2007). Proposing a Joint Enterprise for Communication and Terrorism Studies: An Essay on Identity Formation and Expression within the Arab Public Sphere. *Review of Communication, 7*(1), 21–36.

77. El-Kashef, Injy (2005, October 13). Islam dot com. *Al Ahram Weekly,* 764.

78. Post, Jerrold M., Ruby, Keven G., & Shaw, Eric D. (2000). From Car Bombs to Logic Bombs: The Growing Threat from Information Terrorism. *Terrorism and Political Violence, 12*(2), 97–122.

79. Jackson, Richard (2007). Constructing Enemies: "Islamic Terrorism" in Political and Academic Discourse. *Government and Opposition, 42*(3), 394–426.

80. Benjamin, Daniel, & Simon, Steven (2005). *The Next Attack: The Failure of the War on Terror and a Strategy for Getting It Right.* New York: Henry Holt and Company; Fair, Christine (2007). Militant Recruitment in Pakistan: Implications for Al Qaeda and Other Organizations. *Studies in Conflict & Terrorism, 27*(6), 489-504; Hoffman, Bruse, Rosenau, William, Curiel, Andrew, & Zimmermann, Doron (2007). *The Radicalization of Diasporas and Terrorism.* Santa Monica: RAND; Sageman, Marc (2004). *Understanding Terror Networks.* Philadelphia: University of Pennsylvania Press.

81. Ranstorp, Magnus (2007). The Virtual Sanctuary of Al Qaeda and Terrorism in an Age of Globalization. In Johan Eriksson and Giampiero Giacomello (Eds.), *International relations and Security in the Digital Age* (pp. 31–54). New York: Routledge.

82. Cole, Eric (2003). *Hiding in Plain Sight: Steganography and the Art of Covert Communication.* New York: Wiley.

83. Cimato, Stelvio, & Yang, Ching-Nung (2011). *Visual Cryptography and Secret Image Sharing.* Boca Raton, FL: CRC Press.

84. Fridrich, Jessica (2009). *Steganography in Digital Media: Principles, Algorithms, and Applications.* Cambridge: Cambridge University Press.

85. Cole, Eric (2003). *Hiding in Plain Sight: Steganography and the Art of Covert Communication.* New York: Wiley.

86. Ross, Brian (2001, October 4). A Secret Language. *ABCNEWS.com.*

87. Charvat, G. (2007). *Cyber Terrorism: A New Dimension in Battlespace.* Ankara, Turkey: Centre of Excellence Defense against Terrorism.

88. Hedges, Joshua W. (2008). Eliminating the Learning Curve: A Pragmatic Look at Jihadist Use of the Internet. *Journal of Applied Security Research, 3*(1), 71–91.

89. Cyber-Jihadists Weave a Dangerous Web (2005, October 27). *Agence France-Presse*; Johnson, Keith (2005, February 14). Terrorist Threat Shifts as Groups Mutate and Merge. *The Wall Street Journal,* p. A1.

90. Matusitz, Jonathan (2009). A Postmodern Theory of Cyberterrorism: Game Theory. *Information Security Journal: A Global Perspective, 18*(6), 273–281.

91. Matusitz, Jonathan (2008). Postmodernism and Networks of Cyberterrorists. *Journal of Digital Forensic Practice, 2*(1), 17–26.

92. Matusitz, Jonathan (2008). Cyberterrorism: Postmodern State of Chaos. *Information Security Journal: A Global Perspective, 17*(4), 179–187.

93. Archick, Kristin (2003). Cybercrime: The Council of Europe Convention. In John V. Blane (Ed.), *Cybercrime and Cyberterrorism* (pp. 1–6). Hauppauge, NY: Novinka Books.

94. Vegh, Sandor (2002). Hacktivists or Cyberterrorists? The Changing Media Discourse on Hacking. *First Monday, 7*(10), 12–25.

95. Clarke, Richard A. (2010). *Cyber War*. New York: HarperCollins.

96. Clem, A., Galwankar, Sagar, & Buck, George (2003). Health Implications of Cyber-Terrorism. *Prehospital and Disaster Medicine, 18*(3), 272-275; Lenzner, Robert, & Vardi, Nathan (2007). The Next Threat. *Forbes, 174*(5), 15–21.

97. Docherty, Thomas (1993). *Postmodernism: A Reader*. London: Harvester Wheatsheaf; Jameson, Fredric (1991). *Postmodernism, or the Cultural Logic of Late Capitalism*. Durham, NC: Duke University Press.

98. Matusitz, Jonathan (2008). Cyberterrorism: Postmodern State of Chaos. *Information Security Journal: A Global Perspective, 17*(4), 179–187.

99. Baudrillard, Jean (2003). *Simulacra and Simulation*. Ann Arbor: The University of Michigan Press.

100. Mitchell, William J. (1995). *City of Bits*. Cambridge, MA: MIT Press.

101. Virilio, Paul (1998). *The Virilio Reader*. Oxford: Blackwell.

One-on-One with the Terrorist: Interpersonal Perspectives

After reading this chapter, you will be able to

- describe hostage negotiation through both the dyadic and triadic models of hostage negotiation;
- evaluate why hostage negotiation failed or succeeded in specific case studies; and
- explain the use of interpersonal communication in interrogating suspected terrorists.

INTERPERSONAL COMMUNICATION: DEFINITION

Interpersonal communication denotes the exchange of symbols to achieve, in part, interpersonal goals. It consists of message sending and message reception between two or more people. This can include all characteristics of communication such as listening, influencing, declaring, engaging in nonverbal communication, and so forth. A chief concept of interpersonal communication deals with communicative acts when a few people are involved. In this sense, interpersonal communication can be about one-on-one conversations or people interacting with others within a group.[1]

Six Assumptions

Canary, Cody, and Manusov (2003)[2] describe how interpersonal communication rests on six assumptions:

(1) Interpersonal communication is based on an exchange between individuals: at a minimum, one individual sends a message to another. In very fundamental terms, this is an act, or one behavior.

(2) Interpersonal communication takes place between individuals who are themselves developing; they look for meaning and create strategies to adapt to their social world.

(3) Interpersonal communication entails the use of symbols, which includes verbal and nonverbal depictions of ideas.

(4) Interpersonal communication is strategic (i.e., it is objective-relevant communication behavior).

(5) Interactants (communicators) must be skilled at using interpersonal communication to accomplish their objectives. This is what is designated as **communication competence**, including factors like empathy, interaction management, and involvement.

(6) Interactants should reflect on how their communication impacts others.

Successful interpersonal communication assumes that both message senders and message receivers will interpret and understand the messages based on these six assumptions.

Negotiation

Individuals who share interpersonal goals are interdependent. One way to reach such interdependence is through negotiation. Negotiation is a social activity that involves parties (i.e., human groups). As defined by Deutsch and Coleman (2000),[3] **negotiation** is a process by which strategies are used to "determine the circumstances that allow the conflicting parties to arrive at a mutually satisfactory agreement that maximizes their joint outcomes" (p. 17). In this context, negotiation is analogous to discourse. **Discourse** means back-and-forth communication. Discourse is actually derived from a Latin phrase that means "running to and fro."[4] Good negotiators are capable of achieving good results based on their superior communication skills. If truth be told, everybody uses negotiation strategies to reach a preferred outcome or solution to a conflict. In many cases, negotiation happens when the parties in dispute, either directly or by way of third-party intervention, make offers (or counter solutions) to each other until some agreement is reached. If successful, both parties will see their issues as resolved. If unsuccessful, then the conflict will constantly be on the table.[5]

Just as negotiators and conflict management practitioners are essential to organizational success, hostage negotiators are increasingly used by counterterrorist agents for managing hostage crises (which have arisen since the second half of the 20th century). One type of interpersonal skill in negotiation is the use of language. **Language** is the means by which negotiators develop relationships and make decisions that will impact the very situation. Negotiation relies on skillful language to reach solutions. Thanks to linguistic strategies that initiate de-escalation, de-mystification, and diffusion of conflict, the supreme goal is the same: collaboration between parties.[6]

HOSTAGE NEGOTIATION

Hostage taking is not a new phenomenon. It has been prevalent in South America and in East Asia for decades. Since 1967 and the upsurge of urban guerilla movements, political kidnapping has gained momentum in regard to perceived threat and media publicity over criminal kidnapping.[7] With respect to global terrorist events, hostage-taking incidents constitute 14.2% of all such incidents: 9.44%, kidnappings; 2.88%, skyjackings; 1.42%, barricade missions; and 0.46%, non-aerial hijackings. The larger proportion of skyjackings relative to barricade events is due to the greater challenge that authorities face in their attempt to end a skyjacking, in comparison to the capture or seizure of a building.[8] For this reason, meticulous hostage negotiation is required.

Interpersonal communication fits well within the perspective of hostage negotiation. A hostage is an individual held by a captor (here, a terrorist). A **hostage crisis** occurs when terrorists hold individuals against their will and try to resist the established order by force, threatening to execute the hostages if irritated or attacked. **Hostage negotiation** involves negotiation with a terrorist, or groups of terrorists, for the liberation of one or more hostages.[9] Hostage takers can be classified into absolute and contingent terrorists. **Absolute terrorists** view the terrorist acts themselves as objectives. They generally resist any negotiation and no one can communicate with them. **Contingent terrorists** employ hostages as leverage. Terror is used to accomplish other instrumental aims such as media attention, ransom, or liberation of prisoners in exchange for hostages taken.[10]

Terrorist-Negotiators

Terrorist-negotiators feel a sense of victory when authorities negotiate with them to respect political demands. The hostage-taking incidents in Lebanon (in the 1980s) were, in part, driven by the ambition to obtain the release of prisoners held in Kuwait. In many cases, Israel has negotiated the exchange of prisoners to obtain the freedom of its citizens. Even when political demands are not fulfilled, negotiating with terrorists gives them a certain level of legitimacy, whether merited or not.[11] Sometimes, terrorists benefit from the **one-down effect**, a situation in which terrorist-negotiators, who have fewer alternatives than their counterpart, lean toward using extreme measures to attain power dominance. Terrorists like to believe they have fewer alternatives and apply extreme measures to keep their momentum. Hostage taking is an appealing bargaining chip established to knock down the existing power structure.[12]

Governments frequently adopt the public position never to negotiate with terrorists. However, governments often do not keep this commitment. This is because the loss with which the terrorists are able to burden a state (e.g., executing hostages) may be so significant that the state would be wiser to abandon its initial decision never to negotiate. A case in point is the TWA Flight 847 hijacking on June 14, 1985 in Beirut; one U.S. hostage was killed. By their readiness to slay a hostage, the hostage takers demonstrated that high costs certainly exist when one party does not negotiate. The hostage crisis was over after Israel liberated over 700 Lebanese and Palestinian prisoners in exchange for the captives.[13]

Dyadic and Triadic Hostage Negotiation

According to the **dyadic hostage negotiation** model (see Figure 14.1), the hostage taker makes straightforward requests to the hostage negotiator, the powers that be (i.e., the government), or even sharpshooters. The hostage situation is uncomplicated and takes the form of a dynamic duo.[14]

Figure 14.1   Dyadic Hostage Negotiation

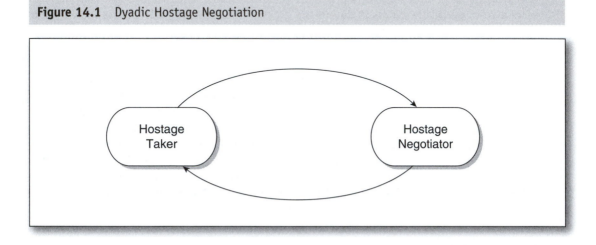

The figure above represents a script for a dual role play. At the same time, it may be the case that the hostages themselves engage in communication with the hostage negotiator or other parties trying to save them. According to the **triadic hostage negotiation** model (see Figure 14.2), what makes hostage negotiation different from most other cases of interpersonal violence is that hostage negotiation can often be triadic as well. The hostage taker may try to employ the hostage as a "go-between," who unavoidably becomes a participant of the hostage situation, even at a distance.

Figure 14.2   Triadic Hostage Negotiation

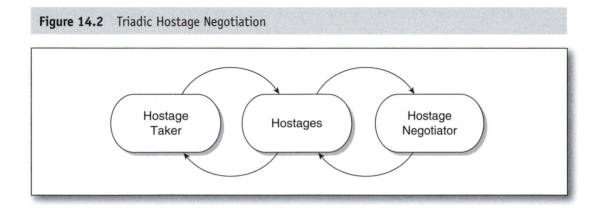

The figure above is a script for a trio—a triadic structure role play. The hostage taker sends a warning to the hostages; the hostages make requests to the hostage negotiator (or the general audience). Naturally, as they are the go-betweens, the hostages will report back to the hostage taker. The terrorist hopes that the message communicated by the hostage to the hostage negotiator (or the audience) will be received and responded to in a positive manner (to the terrorists themselves).[15]

Levels of Negotiation Behavior

Most early conceptions of negotiation have highlighted the importance of distinguishing acts of bargaining along the lines of Avoidant (withdrawn), Distributive (antagonistic), and Integrative (cooperative) behavior. Early stages of interpersonal interaction will probably involve the least amount of contact. The reason is that the overwhelming situation can escalate an extreme crisis or elude response that causes hostage takers to withdraw from active participation in the situation (Avoidant). On becoming aware of the unavoidability of negotiation, hostage takers may display some level of collaboration by following an active role in interactions, though they remain impacted by the stress of crisis and turn to self-served aggressive and coercive tactics (Distributive). As the hostage negotiation unfolds, hostage takers may be convinced that the collaboration of both sides will eventually lead to a reasonable solution. Accordingly, they put significant emphasis on normative and collaborative communication as a method of integrating the parties' divergent interests (Integrative).[16]

RELATIONAL DEVELOPMENT

For the terrorists, like the few other types of hostage takers, the taking of hostages is usually well planned or rehearsed in advance. They are also equipped with sophisticated weapons. Hence, tactful communication with terrorists is of utmost importance.[17] For the past few decades, the increasing pressure to manage or put an end to hostage crises through negotiation has pushed the authorities to underscore the importance of applying informed knowledge of both the psychological and communicative methods involved in interpersonal communication.[18] Based on this reality, Mark Knapp (1984)[19] took the initiative to develop a theory called **relational development**. This theory posits that relationships evolve into stages as a result of interpersonal dialogue. Such dialogue sheds light on the interactants' positive or negative experiences and modifications of their intimacy or communication styles. One method for solving a relationship crisis is to either enhance positive feelings or reduce certain negative feelings to make the other party content during the dialogue.[20]

Relational Development in Hostage Negotiations

Relational development with hostage takers is undoubtedly critical to obtain the release of the hostages. Like a mediator in organizational conflict management, the hostage negotiator evaluates the goals, desires, and behavior of the hostage takers. The mission of the negotiation team is to give advice or suggestions to the on-scene commander in terms of what strategy should be best used.[21] Donohue and Roberto (1993)[22] applied organizational philosophy and regarded relational development between terrorists and hostage negotiators as a "negotiation within a negotiation." This is particularly evident in their statement that, as negotiating parties communicate, "they implicitly make, accept, and reject proposals that define the relational limits of the interaction. These implicitly created limits become the relational structures that function as a subtext to the explicit negotiations centering around the release of hostages" (p. 176).

Donahue and Roberto conducted a meticulous analysis of dialogues between hostage negotiators and hostage takers across ten authentic hostage negotiations. Spatial and indirect (or informal) verbal immediacy language indicators were employed to operationalize affiliation and interdependence in each statement made across all ten negotiations. The results showed that when parties produced a "moving against" and "moving away" relational pattern, they had a harder time developing a relational agreement during the negotiations. Conversely, when parties vacillated between "moving toward" and "moving with" relational phases, they were more able to develop relational consensus. The results also disclosed that both parties in hostage negotiations elaborate relational rhythms by operating within rather stable collaborative or competitive relational patterns.

As stated by the principles of relational development, hostage crises may be centered on interpersonal attachment issues, generally beginning as a strong-willed argument that moves to a hostage-barricade situation. After many hours have passed, negotiators may feel completely exhausted in their interactions with the hostage taker. The latter, nonetheless, seems to possess unlimited energy and switches from thought to thought, issue to issue, forestalling any type of consistent communication or interpersonal relationship from developing. In such events, negotiators may want to bring in new partners in the game so they can keep the conversation going or divert the terrorists away from contemplating the idea of harming their captives.[23]

The Role of Language

Proper language use can be as efficient in hostage negotiations as it is in relational development. Language is the channel through which negotiators establish rapport; they depend heavily on conversation to develop relationships with their counterparts. Because one of the main goals of hostage takers is to gain publicity and attention, an initial bond with hostage takers should be easy to elaborate. Words are the main tools of the initial bond and constitute the main components of ensuing contact and communication. Voice inflection, tone, and rate of delivery will have an influence on the communication and negotiation processes.[24] Another strategy of proper language use is counter-maneuvering.

Counter-maneuvering is an effective application of language in which subtle words are chosen to attenuate anger and to affect and change the behavior of the interactant. In hostage negotiations, subtle utterances can infiltrate the unconscious mind of the hostage takers and, thereby, allow the negotiator to glide into their world. After rapport has been established, the negotiator can then set the agenda for the remainder of the negotiation process.[25] Through strategies like counter-maneuvering, negotiators let terrorists become interactants on an equal level. They are locked in a transaction of moves and countermoves that ends only when the communication cycle becomes disrupted.[26]

Hostage negotiations that include relational development between people who speak different languages are increasingly common.[27] After all, to fight GWOT, it is necessary to tackle terrorism where it starts. The U.S. must send missions to help foreign governments in their fight against terrorism through support and training. This requires U.S. personnel to recruit people who speak foreign languages both here and abroad.[28] A great advantage of using interpreters in hostage negotiations has to do with the timing and synchronicity of the situation. Interpreting the interaction between both parties can suspend the evil intentions of the hostage takers and buy time for the negotiators to investigate alternative options. In the same train of thought, this postponement can cause hostage takers to think more about future alternatives. Finally, being knowledgeable in the language and culture of the terrorist allows a skilled interpreter to give the negotiators practical information.[29]

Besides, linguistic differences in a hostage situation represent a primary impediment to identification. Both parties would more likely remain estranged from each other. They would keep on being an unknown entity and humanizing the circumstances would less likely happen. In the case of skyjacking, linguistic impediments may create an odd division in which the Hostage Identification Syndrome (HIS)—explained later in this chapter— crosses the minds of some passengers, who speak the terrorists' language, but not of others, as it was demonstrated by the 1977 Japanese Red Army skyjacking.[30]

Moluccans' Hijacking in the Netherlands

The Moluccans' hijacking of a train occurred in the Netherlands in 1975. Moluccans come from southeastern Pacific islands and were colonized by Dutch settlers when the king of the Netherlands invaded the Dutch East Indies. After WWII, the Dutch government allowed the Moluccans to move to the Netherlands.[31] On December 2, 1975, seven Moluccan youths (aged 19–25) took over a train in the northeastern part of the country and held fifty passengers captive for twelve days. They murdered the engineer as well as two passengers, in cold blood, before television cameras.[32] The hostage takers issued a statement to the Dutch government, stipulating that they meet the Moluccans' demands that peace and faith be maintained and that the subjugated Moluccans be seriously considered.[33]

At first, negotiations were not effective. However, after several days, the negotiators realized that it was necessary for a successful solution that they engage in relational development. The first step adopted by the negotiators was to communicate with the terrorists in regard to the current state of affairs. They informed the hijackers that the counterterrorist teams had total control over the scene. There was already a huge constraint imposed on the Moluccans as they could not escape. The only action possible was to commit suicide after killing the remaining hostages. The second step was to avoid confrontations. What is remarkable about this hijacking incident is that the negotiators were determined to smooth things down, rather than aggravating them. Their patience was something to behold: while the hostage-taking incident lasted for twelve days, no other hostage was killed. This was due to the negotiators' immaculate and tactful communication.[34]

The last step was persuasion, perhaps the most contributive element to the victory of the negotiation process. In practical terms, the Dutch negotiators used a form of persuasive discourse that secured them a reciprocally favorable deal whereby the hostage takers would not be sentenced to capital punishment if all hostages would be freed. After many hours of negotiation, the seven Moluccan youths finally gave up, liberated the hostages, and surrendered to the Dutch established order.[35] The triumph over Moluccan terrorists reached a pinnacle in the art of relational development and demonstrated that hostage negotiation skills can bring positive outcomes. Negotiation is discourse; it is a social undertaking that adopts a bargaining approach. The next section illustrates two historical tragedies caused by the lack of relational development with hostage takers. In both cases, the result was a fiasco.

Hostage Negotiation Fiascos

The conclusion was easy to reach: the philosophy of relational development in both hostage situations was completely ignored and the negotiation (and rescue mission) failed. In the first case, the well-intended objective was to rescue high-profile Colombian politicians from the Colombian Revolutionary Armed Forces (FARC) in 2003. **FARC** is an antigovernment terrorist group that vows to kidnap important personalities of the political arena. In exchange for freeing them, FARC requests the liberation of their imprisoned fellows. Here is how the fiasco happened: before the Colombian government considered opening channels of communication with FARC and developing gradual relationships to meet their demands, a Colombian Special Forces team stormed the hostage site and caused the hostage takers to draw their firearms on the hostages, slaying ten of them, including two key Colombian officials, Guillermo Gaviria and Gilberto Echeverri. Had negotiations grounded on relational development been followed (instead of operating an abrupt raid that caused hostages to die), there likely would have been a much higher chance of survival for more, if not all, the captives.[36]

In like fashion, the Munich massacre taught us a lesson: continuing relationship development is vital during all stages of the hostage negotiation process. The failed rescue mission at the 1972 Olympic Games in Munich is no different from the scenario described above. A counterterrorist team made an attempt at using divisive tactics as well as manipulative and hostile efforts to rescue the Israeli hostages (who were athletes) from Black September, the Palestinian terrorist group. Those tactics lethally backfired. Sixteen hours after Black September held the athletes hostage, the German forces botched it by ending negotiations prematurely. German snipers were precipitately ordered to kill the terrorists while the captives were still at gunpoint, a violation of the agreement that was made between the hostage takers and the German government. Without a hesitation, the terrorists shot eleven of the hostages. Without a doubt, this failed tactic wrecked all chances of reaching a mutually beneficial resolve. If German negotiators had applied the principles of relational development, they would have never witnessed antagonisms, detrimental confrontation, and, above all, the death of many hostages.[37]

HOSTAGES INTERACTING WITH TERRORISTS

Generally, the more face-to-face interaction, the higher the likelihood of the identification process with captors. In those situations in which terrorist "guards" form regular interaction with captives, a bond seems to occur. During a long-lasting hostage taking—several days or weeks—after the initial crisis has passed, a smart move involves preserving healthy interpersonal relations with captors and other hostages. On a plane, it would also involve remaining alert and staying away from emotional deterioration when the confined cabin is increasingly nasty, exceeding 100 degrees in temperature, without food supplies, and in a stressful period (with many hostages beyond their emotional capacity).

Uncertainty Reduction Theory (URT)

Developed by Berger and Calabrese (1975),[38] **Uncertainty Reduction Theory (URT)** posits that on meeting for the first time, strangers will go through certain steps and checkpoints to decrease uncertainty about each other and develop an impression of whether one likes or dislikes the other. As humans communicate, they cook up plans to accomplish their goals. During highly uncertain times, we become more cautious and count more on facts available in the situation. URT also postulates that greater levels of uncertainty create detachment between individuals and that nonverbal expressiveness is more likely to help decrease uncertainty. According to the theory, there are three strategies to decrease uncertainty: passive strategies (i.e., observing the other); active strategies (i.e., asking others about the individual or searching for information); and interactive strategies (i.e., asking questions, self-disclosure).[39]

URT is applicable to hostage-taking situations. Some counterterrorism experts argue that it would be helpful for hostages to have some "humanizing" interaction with their captors, showing them pictures of their children and asking about their family. The purpose is that the hostage should make him- or herself a known person whom terrorists will not kill in case of a crisis.[40] In any event, in interactions with hostage takers, one should (1) be courteous, calm and collected, and not servile or pleading; (2) volunteer little information (certainly not overloading terrorists with information); (3) offer no political or controversial opinions, even if requested for one; and (4) listen respectfully to any political agenda the hostage takers want to advance. Furthermore, hostages need to try to maintain as neutral a presence (from the standpoint of their captors) as possible. Holding one's routine will make the hostage appear regular and planned (not impromptu). With respect to interactions between hostages and their captors, a frequent consequence of URT is **script breakdown**, a by-product of intrapersonal processes, whereby many hostages may perceive their captors as victims of the situation. It ultimately leads to more normalized interpersonal relationships between hostages and hostage takers. This also implies that some positive feelings are virtually inevitable.[41]

European singer Demis Roussos was one of the hostages on TWA Flight 847 that was seized by Islamist terrorists on June 14, 1985. Famously, the hostage takers celebrated the singer's birthday as they were astounded to have taken, as a hostage, a prominent celebrity in Europe. Nevertheless, this successful anecdote is an exception. In hostage-taking incidents, normal patterns of interpersonal relationships are often disrupted. Interaction under severe pressure (both among fellow travelers and with the terrorists) will certainly be affected and not look natural. Befriending terrorists even for tactical purposes remains a risky business.[42] It can also be impossible to do. Indeed, to thwart relational development, hostages have been hooded or muzzled to minimize the humanizing process. In addition, the hostage guards can be replaced frequently or prohibited from speaking with the hostages. Sir Geoffrey Jackson was a British ambassador in Uruguay in 1969. He was abducted by Tupamaro guerrillas in 1971, undergoing captivity for eight months. After his liberation, he went back as an official for the Foreign Office. During his eight-month experience, he was never able to develop interpersonal relationships with his captors.[43]

Stockholm Syndrome

The **Stockholm syndrome** is a psychological phenomenon in which hostages show admiration and have positive feelings for their captors that appear irrational considering the danger or risk incurred by the victims, essentially confusing a lack of abuse from their captors with an act of compassion. Victims who develop the Stockholm syndrome often see the hostage taker as giving life by simply not killing it. From this perspective, the captor becomes the one in control of the hostage's basic needs for survival and his or her life itself.[44] In 1974, Patty Hearst was held hostage by the Symbionese Liberation Army (SLA). After two months, she sided with her captors and participated in a bank robbery that was planned by the SLA. Her failed legal defense was that she suffered from the Stockholm syndrome and was pressured to help the SLA. She was convicted and incarcerated for her participation in the robbery, though her punishment was over in February 1979 thanks to President Jimmy Carter. She obtained a Presidential pardon from President Bill Clinton on January 20, 2001 (one of his last presidential acts before leaving office).[45]

The Stockholm syndrome has been scientifically examined from the viewpoint of interpersonal communication, using simulated captivity. Two central interpersonal dimensions—control (dominance-submission) and affiliation (friendliness-hostility)—were involved. The less the "hostages" viewed the simulated hostage takers as dominant and the more they saw them as pleasant, the higher was the hostage adjustment. Likewise, the more the captors considered their hostages kind, the nicer the experience was for the hostages.[46] Strentz (1979)[47] indicated that development of the syndrome is contingent on the interaction of three factors: how much time passes, whether victims are isolated, and whether contact between the captor and the captive is positive or negative. In general, if captors maintain daily contact with the hostages (e.g., by being in the same room), and if it is a positive contact (or simply not negative; e.g., no beatings, rape, or verbal aggressiveness), then the more time passes, the higher the development of the syndrome. Conversely, if the captor abuses the victims or isolates them—for example, by moving them to a separate room or making them wear hoods—time will not be a major factor in development of the syndrome.

There is an alternate form of the Stockholm syndrome called the **Hostage Identification Syndrome (HIS)**, a situation in which positive interactions lead the hostage taker to identify with the victim. Here, it is in the hostage's favor. In many cases, the relationship between captor and captive becomes a two-way interchange.[48] HIS has also been called the **Lima syndrome**, a phenomenon by which abductors develop sympathy for their captives. The name comes from a Lima (Peru) kidnapping at the Japanese embassy in 1996. Members of MRTA (a Peruvian terrorist group) took hundreds of party attendees as hostages at the official residence of the Japanese ambassador. Due to sympathy expressed toward the hostages, within a few hours, the terrorists liberated most people, including the most important ones.[49]

INTERROGATION AS AN INTERPERSONAL FORM

Human intelligence is the first step to end terrorism. Therefore, it is important to interrogate suspected terrorists and to be aware of false information during an interrogation. After the 9/11 terrorist attacks, increased support for interrogation of suspected terrorists emerged in the mass media. Yet, the May 2004 disclosure of U.S. Army "enhanced interrogation techniques" (i.e., torture) of Iraqi prisoners at the Abu Ghraib prison (Baghdad) started to stifle overall enthusiasm for harsh interrogations.[50] On the program *60 Minutes* (September 22, 2002), Harvard professor Alan Dershowitz asserted that torture of a suspected terrorist is not against the Fifth Amendment. For him, every democratic nation should use torture if it is the best way to save 500 or 1,000 lives by obtaining information about a bomb ready to explode.[51] In this section, however, the issue at hand is not about torture, but about interrogation. Interrogation is legal.

Interrogation: Definition

Interrogation refers to a method of obtaining a maximum amount of true information from a prisoner or suspect in a minimum amount of time, using legal measures. Interrogation involves interaction and conversation with a person who appears initially reluctant to giving information. If the person is present by choice and is disposed to talk, then the situation is a **debriefing**, not an interrogation. The difference is in the rapport between the interrogator and source (i.e., the interrogatee), and the physical setting.[52] Each interpersonal interaction between the interrogator and the interrogatee varies to some level because of their idiosyncrasies (individual characteristics) and because the circumstances of each interaction and the physical environment change too. The interrogation of suspected terrorists constitutes a rare occasion for direct face-to-face contact with the enemy.

Essentially, an interrogation is a greatly interpersonal dynamic. This unique aspect of interrogation sets it apart from other means of intelligence gathering: interrogation is much more reactive in both time and character than all other types of intelligence collection. For example, it does not entail the passive collection of signals or the distant sensing of images.[53] The art of interrogation is still a misunderstood nature of warfare (even by military forces).[54] Alfred McCoy, professor of history at the University of Wisconsin, Madison, has published books on the CIA experiments in coercing suspects. For McCoy, suspects become so hungry for human interaction that "they bond with the interrogator like a father, or like a drowning man having a lifesaver thrown at him. If you deprive people of all their senses, they'll turn to you like their daddy."[55]

Walton (2002)[56] considered interrogation as a category of information-seeking dialogue, where the aims, conversational rules, participants, and strategies of interrogation are identified. A good (correct, accurate) argument is one that advances the objective of the dialogue. A bad (incorrect, false) argument is one that obstructs the objective of the dialogue. At its core, the interrogation is an unbalanced type of dialogue, meaning that the objectives and techniques of argumentation adopted by the one side widely differ from those on the other side. The interrogator wants to extract any sort of information out of the interrogatee that is key—for example, knowing what action to take to prevent harm or complementing an investigation. The interrogatee wants to pursue his or her own interests (or the ones of his or her group).[57]

Interrogation of Suspected Terrorists

Since the first bombing of the World Trade Center in 1993, U.S. interrogation of Al Qaeda–affiliated subjects has had successful results. Interrogation techniques were refined over the following years, integrating lessons learned along the way. They seemed to be effective in the interrogation of Al Qaeda suspects associated with the Tanzania and Kenya embassy bombings in 1998, the attack on the USS Cole in 2000, and the September 11, 2001 tragedy. In all cases where interrogation has the objective of extracting reliable information, a rapport-based approach is first recommended.[58] Just as it is for hostage negotiations, the model of relational development is crucial in interrogations.

Establishing interpersonal contact with the interrogatee may gain his or her respect. This does not imply trying to persuade the person to like the interrogator, trust the latter, or become his or her friend. Such actions would be considered superficial by the interrogatee and be immediately exposed as a red flag. It does not mean being excessively gracious or well-mannered. Perceived weakness leads to attack and motivates the suspect to try to take control over the interrogation process. Rapport building aims at developing shared understanding and respect between both parties. The interrogator seeks to develop a bond based on common ground and shared experiences in the interrogation room.[59]

Through an approach of personal appearance, good conduct, and communication, the interrogator should exude self-confidence, self-respect, and respect for the suspect. Above all, the interrogator should avoid any maneuver that demeans his or her self-respect. Suspects intuitively believe that if an interrogator cannot respect him- or herself, then the interrogator should not merit the suspect's respect, rapport, and, ultimately, a confession that goes against the suspect's interests. At the same time, the interrogator should uphold high standards and self-discipline in the interrogation room, without judging the suspect's misconduct. After a few encounters, that respect will likely become mutual, and rapport born out of reciprocal respect becomes a useful lubricant when attempting to obtain critical information.[60]

The interrogator needs to involve the suspect in a prolonged conversation and build a relationship that helps shed light on the suspect's motivations. In addition, other specific considerations can have an influence on the "fit" between interrogator and suspects such as Middle Eastern Arab Al Qaeda–related subjects. For example, age should be taken seriously when matching or assigning an interrogator to a subject; this is due to high respect for elders and seniority in the Arab and Muslim world. Interrogations are also beneficial when both parties can be paired regularly. Middle Eastern Arabs tend to give the best responses when interrogated by the same person rather than by multiple parties or through a "whoever is available" assignment procedure.[61]

DECEIVERS AMONG SUSPECTED TERRORISTS

In matters of deception, there is no **Pinocchio response**, that is, a behavior or pattern of behaviors present in all humans, and across all situations, when lying.[62] Suspected terrorists will likely respond differently, based on their training and/or religious background.

The Most Likely to Deceive among Suspected Terrorists

Among suspected terrorists, there are two categories to take into consideration for interrogation purposes: fundamentalist zealots (the zealots do not show hesitations; they follow Al Qaeda principles to the letter and lead others to strict observance of these principles) and **religious idealists**. These idealists get their strength from mimicking the **fundamentalist zealots**. They have faith in the destructive interpretation of Islam—as instructed by the zealots—as a moral and social ideology. However, in some cases, religious idealists will later move away from strict obedience and will be coerced by their handlers, on being threatened of torture or death to relatives, to execute terrorist acts.[63]

Verbal, vocal, and nonverbal behaviors can be reliable indicators of truth or deception from the suspected terrorist. The cultural or economic background of each of them gives clues into the interpretation of their behavioral responses as well as their classification—that is, as to which of the two categories they belong to (as discussed above).[64] Fundamentalist zealots, in particular, raise three obstacles to the interrogator's strategy. First, they are trained to countermeasure or defeat interrogation procedures. Second, they are indoctrinated into the moral justification for the killing, torture, or massive destruction which they cause on behalf of jihad. For this reason, they feel no regret for their deeds. Third, those who possess the most vital information are the ones who are the most capable of resisting harsh interrogation. That is, those who possess vital information have actually been hand-picked and trained to hold back true information when tortured and to make false confessions to their captors when interrogated.[65]

Inbau, Reid, and Buckley (1986)[66] compared two types of suspected terrorists: emotional offenders and non-emotional offenders. **Emotional offenders** usually commit their crimes in reaction to unrestrained but basic human drives, experience some level of remorse, try to understand their criminal behavior, and are susceptible (during interrogations) to concepts such as minimization of the consequences of their conduct or the placing of blame for the criminal behavior on others, including the victim. In contrast, **non-emotional offenders** are often calculating in their behavior, experience little to no remorse, are undecided about empathy from others, and are prone to confessing only if they think the act of confessing can directly benefit them. These two distinctions apply to foreign terrorist suspects too.

Matheny (1995)[67] recommends that the interrogator be disciplined in the way he or she listens (i.e., aggressive listening) and observes the suspect at all points in the interrogation. **Aggressive listening** includes perfecting recall, so that minutiae of a suspect's statements can be extracted from memory (the same day or even days later). The objective here is to refute an alibi/explanation and, thus, wear down the suspect's confidence in his or her skill to deceive the interrogator. Aggressive listening for details and intricacies in the suspect's statements can prod follow-up questions which unavoidably are much more productive than the initial scripted questions. Repetition operates against the deceiver, so the interrogator should not be reluctant to asking the same questions hours, days, or weeks after these questions were asked. So, the interrogator should aggressively listen for, and call attention to, inconsistencies. At the same time, he or she should observe the suspect in every side of his or her demeanor for deception.

Intercultural Complications

In the context of the current Global War on Terror (GWOT), interrogations of suspected terrorists are often muddled by intercultural differences. More often than not, when U.S. intelligence agents interrogate Middle Eastern suspects, questions and answers are first translated by a qualified interpreter. Language interpretation is the facilitation of discourse or interchange between people speaking different languages. If an interpreter is necessary, his or her role must be plainly explained and constantly underlined so that he or she does not play the role of a surrogate interrogator. A **surrogate interrogator** is a person who stands next to the actual interrogator and who routinely edits, adds, or subtracts information uttered by one or more parties. The interrogator must be the one to regulate the interrogation, not the interpreter. The latter must be, and assume the appearance of being, subordinate to the interrogator—someone assisting and working for the interrogator. As a pragmatic solution, it has been considered beneficial to have the interpreter sit behind the suspect.[68]

Individuals from different cultures differ greatly in the way they display emotional and nonverbal expressions and in their inclination to give false confessions under pressure.[69] If there is no familiarity with the culture of the suspect, interrogators will be more likely to misinterpret behavior. Research has demonstrated that the capacity to determine whether a person is being deceptive is worse when the evaluator comes from a different culture than the interrogatee.[70] Thus, intercultural differences are expected to increase the risk of error of the current error-prone judgments as to whether a suspect is being deceptive or withholding information. Such judgments can even be the effect of conscious or nonconscious stereotyping and prejudice. Prejudice may cause interrogators to go after suspects for torture just by looking at their physical appearance. They can also use torture based on erroneous stereotypes about behavioral signals.[71]

ANALYZING DECEPTION IN INTERROGATIONS

Deception is the cover-up of true information. It can be of three types: **manipulating information** (distancing oneself from the message, so if the message turns out to be false, the deceiver can extricate him- or herself; thus, the deceiver can use vague generalities and discuss other people or things); **strategically controlled behavior** (the suppression of signals that might show that one is lying; e.g., a deceiver's face may be more emotionless and body more rigid); and **image management** (e.g., smiling or nodding more). The last two are forms of nonverbal communication. While verbal communication is expressed by the words that we choose and constitutes about 7% of communication, **nonverbal communication** is the process of sending and receiving wordless messages and comprises 93% of communication.[72] The average person can make differences between lies and truths at a rate only marginally better than chance—approximately 54% where chance accuracy is 50%.[73] Experts with adequate professional training (e.g., interrogators, polygraphers, customs officers) do somewhat better; they can detect deception at a rate that is slightly above chance.[74] For example, being fully aware of the different categories of suspected terrorists (as explained previously) is a plus.

The capacity to conceal one's actions to commit an unexpected attack relies, in part, on deception and the skill at masking nonverbal cues. In terms of terrorism, knowing how to interpret nonverbal behavior is key to survival. During interrogations, several studies[75] have reported that suspected terrorists have shown symptoms of deceptive facial behavior such as masking and simulation. **Masking** consists of communicating an emotion that is totally different from the one that a person is experiencing. **Simulation** involves acting like one feels an emotion when there is no such emotion.[76] Accurately detecting nonverbal behavior, such as facial expression and body language, is a difficult task, particularly when a suspect is intentionally covering up his or her intent. The human face is the main channel of expression that interrogators rely on and, consequently, in deceitful behavior such as that of suspected terrorists, the latter are likely to manage their facial expressions adroitly.[77]

Microexpressions and Leakage

Dr. Paul Ekman was a professor of psychology at the University of California, San Francisco. He is still recognized as the world's most prominent face reader. He coined the term **microexpressions** to refer to minuscule facial expressions that are performed for less than a quarter of a second. They often occur accidentally or unpredictably and can reveal emotions that deceivers are trying to hold back. Deceivers may not even be aware of those tiny facial expressions. Microexpressions are brief and incomplete and occur on people's faces very rapidly after being exposed to a specific interrogation. Such a channel is likely an impediment to the covering up of deception. Negative microexpressions can be fleetingly leaked through several forms: unpredictable voice shifts, rapid head shaking, and more importantly negative facial expressions.[78]

A microexpression is an example of **leakage**, the unconscious nonverbal signals about an internal state. Leakage includes nonverbal disclosure of a message about one's internal state, which may be counter-productive to the deceptive message the person is attempting to express. Ekman and Friesen (1969)[79] also coined the term **leakage hierarchy** to refer to some behavioral channels that are harder to control than others, in spite of efforts to hide them. Ekman (2001, 2003)[80] also argued that the face has more leakage than the body or voice because of the involuntary nature of human emotion.

A fundamental principle is that suspects under interrogation reveal such leakage. Verbal, vocal, and nonverbal behaviors are external, visible symptoms of anxiety, and they occur involuntarily as the body's defense mechanism to decrease internal anxiety. Symptoms of stress can be read correctly under the condition that they are observed for timing (i.e., in reaction to particular inquiries or stimulus during the interrogation), clusters (i.e., no isolated behavior symptom can be considered important), and changes from the suspect's personal or cultural norm. Within the context of interrogation, the suspected terrorist who exudes well-timed clusters of behavior symptoms, which are uncharacteristic for the issue at hand or his or her culture, is probably deceptive.[81]

Facial Action Coding System

U.S. federal agencies frequently hire Dr. Paul Ekman to teach the distinctions of facial expressions for use during interrogations of accused Al Qaeda terrorists.[82] To this effect, U.S. counter-intelligence agencies are attempting to use the **Facial Action Coding System (FACS)**, which was developed by Paul Ekman and Wallace Friesen (1978).[83] FACS has already been applied by the Transportation Security Administration (TSA) as part of its behavioral profiling plan. Using a repertoire to create more than ten thousand facial muscle combinations, Ekman and Friesen created FACS as an all-embracing, anatomy-based program for evaluating all visually decipherable facial movements.[84] FACS thus claims to standardize a system of detecting facial behavior for signs of deception. According to the FACS model, even when attempting to purposefully or unconsciously deceive, human emotions still appear as microexpressions, which last for less than a quarter of a second.[85] Identifying terrorism on the basis of body language is called **behavioral detection**. It is our hope that, in the future, all interrogators and members of security staff will be thoroughly trained to detect deceitful body language and facial expressions.[86]

SUMMARY

According to the dyadic hostage negotiation model, the hostage taker makes straightforward requests to the hostage negotiator, the powers that be (i.e., the government), or even sharpshooters. According to the triadic hostage negotiation, the hostage taker sends a warning to the hostages; the hostages make requests to the hostage negotiator (or the general audience). Naturally, as they are the go-betweens, the hostages will report back to the hostage taker. In hostage crises, when confronting terrorists at the interpersonal level, superior communication and negotiation skills are required. One psychological and communicative method for solving a hostage crisis is relational development, the idea that relationships evolve into stages as a result of interpersonal dialogue. Words are the main tools of the initial bond between hostage negotiators and hostage takers. For example, counter-maneuvering is an effective application of language in which subtle words are chosen to attenuate anger and to affect and change the behavior of the captor. In addition, being well versed in the language and culture of the terrorist allows a skilled interpreter to give the negotiators practical information. Because relational development was used during the Moluccans' hijacking in the Netherlands in 1975, the remaining hostages were safely released. Negotiation is discourse. Yet, it was not used when facing the Colombian Revolutionary Armed Forces (FARC) in 2003, which resulted in a fiasco (so was the 1972 Munich massacre). Along the same lines, the role of Uncertainty Reduction Theory (URT) is important too. URT posits that on meeting for the first time, strangers will go through certain steps to decrease uncertainty about each other. Based on the tenets of the theory, it would be helpful for hostages to have some humanizing interaction with their captors. The objective is to normalize interpersonal communication with hostage takers. Lastly, the role of interpersonal communication in interrogation of suspected terrorists is of utmost importance too. In all cases where interrogation has the objective of extracting reliable information, a rapport-based method is first recommended, using an approach of personal appearance (including appropriate age), good conduct, and tactful communication. The technique of aggressive listening (for details and intricacies in the suspect's statements) is recommended. Among suspected terrorists, one category (i.e., fundamentalist zealots) is most likely to deceive than another (i.e., religious idealists). The use of a surrogate interrogator (i.e., interpreter) has proved useful too. During interrogations, being aware of microexpressions (tiny facial emotions that last for less than a quarter of a second) and leakage (the unconscious nonverbal signals about an internal state) helps determine the true character of the suspected terrorist.

KEY TERMS

absolute terrorists   363

aggressive listening   374

behavioral detection   376

communication competence   362

contingent terrorists   363

counter-maneuvering   366

debriefing   371

deception   374

discourse   362

dyadic hostage negotiation   364

emotional offender   373

Facial Action Coding System   376

fundamentalist zealot   373

hostage crisis   363

Hostage Identification Syndrome   370

hostage negotiation   363

image management   375

interpersonal communication   361

interrogation   371

language   362

leakage   375

leakage hierarchy   375

Lima syndrome   371

manipulating information   374

masking   375

microexpressions   375

negotiation   362

non-emotional offender   373

one-down effect   363

Pinocchio response   373

relational development   365

religious idealist   373

script breakdown   369

simulation   375

Stockholm syndrome   370

strategically controlled behavior   375

surrogate interrogator   374

triadic hostage negotiation   364

Uncertainty Reduction Theory   369

ENDNOTES

1. Kelley, Harold H. (1979). *Personal Relationships: A Theory of Interdependence*. New York: Wiley.
2. Canary, Daniel J., Cody, Michael J., & Manusov, Valerie L. (2003). *Interpersonal Communication: A Goals-Based Approach* (3rd ed.). New York: Bedford/St. Martin's.
3. Deutsch, Morton, & Coleman, Peter (2000). *The Handbook of Conflict Resolution: Theory and Practice*. San Francisco: Jossey-Bass.
4. Puhn, Laurie (2006). *Instant Persuasion: How to Change Your Words to Change Your Life*. New York: Penguin.
5. Fisher, Roger, & Ury, William (1981). *Getting to Yes: Negotiating Agreement without Giving in*. Boston: Houghton Mifflin; Pruitt, Dean G., & Carnevale, Peter J. (1993). *Negotiation in Social Conflict*. Buckingham: Open University Press; Rubin, Jeffrey (1994). Models of Conflict Management. *Journal of Social Issues, 50*, 33–45.
6. Boltz, Jr., Frank, Dudonis, Kenneth J., & Schulz, David P. (2001). *The Counterterrorism Handbook: Tactics, Procedures, and Techniques*. Boca Raton, FL: CRC Press; Breslin, J. William, & Rubin, Jeffrey Z. (1991). *Negotiation Theory and Practice*. Cambridge, MA: Program on Negotiation Books.
7. Clutterbuck, Richard (1975). *Living with Terrorism*. London: Faber.
8. Gaibulloev, Khusrav, & Sandler, Todd (2009). Hostage Taking: Determinants of Terrorist Logistical and Negotiation Success. *Journal of Peace Research, 46*(6), 739–756.
9. Greenstone, James L. (2005). *The Elements of Police Hostage and Crisis Negotiations: Critical Incidents and How to Respond to Them*. New York: Taylor and Francis; Strentz, Thomas (2006). *Psychological Aspects of Crisis Negotiation*. Boca Raton, FL: CRC Press.
10. Zartman, William (2003). Negotiating with Terrorists. *International Negotiation, 8*, 443–450.
11. Islam, Muhammad Q., & Shahin, Wassim N. (2001). Applying Economic Methodology to the War on Terrorism. *Forum for Social Economics, 31*(1), 7–26.
12. Donohue, William A., & Taylor, Paul J. (2003). Testing the Role Effect in Terrorist Negotiations. *International Negotiation, 8*, 527–547.
13. Islam, Muhammad Q., & Shahin, Wassim N. (2001). Applying Economic Methodology to the War on Terrorism. *Forum for Social Economics, 31*(1), 7–26.
14. Slatkin, Arthur A. (2009). *Training Strategies for Crisis and Hostage Negotiations: Scenario Writing and Creative Variations for Role Play*. Springfield, IL: Charles C. Thomas.
15. Soskis, David A., & Van Zandt, Clinton R. (1986). Hostage Negotiation: Law Enforcement's Most Effective Nonlethal Weapon. *Behavioral Sciences & the Law, 4*(4), 423–435.
16. Sillars, Alan L. (1980). Attributions and Communication in Roommate Conflicts. *Communication Monographs, 47*, 180–200; Taylor, Paul J. (2002). A Cylindrical Model of Communication Behavior in Crisis Negotiations. *Human Communication Research, 28*(1), 7–48.
17. Soskis, David A., & Van Zandt, Clinton R. (1986). Hostage Negotiation: Law Enforcement's Most Effective Nonlethal Weapon. *Behavioral Sciences & the Law, 4*(4), 423–435.
18. Giebels, Ellen (1999). A Comparison of Crisis Negotiation across Europe. In Otoo Adang & Eellen Giebels (Eds.), *To Save Lives: Proceedings of the First European Conference on Hostage Negotiations* (pp. 13–20). Amsterdam: Elsevier.
19. Knapp, Mark L. (1984). *Interpersonal Communication and Human Relationships*. Boston: Allyn & Bacon.
20. Knapp, Mark L., & Daly, John (2002). *Handbook of Interpersonal Communication* (3rd ed.). Beverly Hills, CA: Sage.
21. Fuselier, G. Dwayne (1981). A Practical Overview of Hostage Negotiations: Conclusion. *FBI Law Enforcement Bulletin, 50*(7), 10-15; Strenz, Thomas (1986). Negotiating with the Hostage Taker Exhibiting Paranoid Schizophrenic Symptoms. *Journal of Police Science and Administration, 14*, 12–16.
22. Donohue, William A. & Roberto, Anthony J. (1993). Relational Development as Negotiated in Hostage Negotiation. *Human Communication Research, 20*, 175–198.

23. Miller, Laurence (2007). Negotiating with Mentally Disordered Hostage Takers. *Journal of Police Crisis Negotiations, 7*(1), 63–83.

24. Rogan, Randall G., & Hammer, Mitchell R. (1995). Assessing Message Affect in Crisis Negotiations: An Exploratory Study. *Human Communication Research, 21*(4), 553–574; Wargo, M. G. (1990). Communication Skills for Hostage Negotiators. *Police Marksman, 2*, p. 52.

25. Cutshall, Charles R. (1982). Culprits, Culpability, and Crime: Stocktheft and Other Cattle Maneuvers among the Ila of Zambia. *African Studies Review, 25*(1), 1–26.

26. O'Hair, Dan, & Heath, Robert (2005). Conceptualizing Communication and Terrorism. In Dan O'Hair, Robert Heath, & Gerald Ledlow (Eds.), *Community Preparedness, Deterrence, and Response to Terrorism: Communication and Terrorism* (pp. 1–12). Westport, CT: Praeger.

27. Matusitz, Jonathan, & Breen, Gerald-Mark (2006). Negotiation Tactics in Organizations Applied to Hostage Negotiation. *Journal of Security Education, 2*(1), 55–73.

28. Roth, Mitchel, P., & Sever, Murat (2007). Barriers to International Police Cooperation in the Age of Terrorism. In Huseyin Durmaz, Bilal Sevinc, Ahmet Sait Yayla, & Siffidk Ekici (Eds.), *Understanding and Responding to Terrorism* (pp. 42–55). Amsterdam: IOS Press.

29. Matusitz, Jonathan, & Breen, Gerald-Mark (2006). Negotiation Tactics in Organizations Applied to Hostage Negotiation. *Journal of Security Education, 2*(1), 55–73.

30. Turner, James L. (1985). Factors Influencing the Development of the Hostage Identification Syndrome. *Political Psychology, 6*(4), 705–711.

31. Stevens, Mark (1975). Strangers on a Train: Hostages Held by South Moluccan Guerrillas. *Newsweek, 86*, 59–60.

32. Herman, Valentine, & Laan Bouma, Rob van der (1981). Nationalists without a Nation: South Moluccan Terrorism in the Netherlands. In Juliet Lodge (Ed.), *Terrorism: A Challenge to the State* (pp. 119–146). Oxford: Martin Robertson.

33. Van Drevan, W. P. (1977). Came the Dawn: South Moluccan Terror in the Netherlands. *Counterforce, 1*, 15–21.

34. Hughes, Edward (1976). Terror on Train 734: Hostages Taken by South Moluccan Guerrillas. *Reader's Digest, 109*, 64–69.

35. Van Drevan, W. P. (1977). Came the Dawn: South Moluccan Terror in the Netherlands. *Counterforce, 1*, 15–21.

36. Felbab-Brown, Venda (2009). *Shooting Up: Counterinsurgency and the War on Drugs*. Washington, D.C.: Brookings Institution Press; Forero, Juan (2003, May 6). Rebels Execute 10 Hostages in Colombia. *The New York Times*, p. A14.

37. Soskis, David A., & Van Zandt, Clinton R. (1986). Hostage Negotiation: Law Enforcement's Most Effective Nonlethal Weapon. *Behavioral Sciences & the Law, 4*(4), 423–435.

38. Berger, Charles R., & Calabrese, Richard J. (1975). Some Exploration in Initial Interaction and Beyond: Toward a Developmental Theory of Communication. *Human Communication Research, 1*, 99–112.

39. Berger, Charles R. (1986). Uncertain Outcome Values in Predicted Relationships: Uncertainty Reduction Theory Then and Now. *Human Communication Research, 13*(1), 34–38.

40. Savage, Peter (1999). *The Safe Travel Book*. Lanham, MD: Lexington Books; Snyder, Rodney A. (1994). *Negotiating with Terrorists: TWA Flight 847*. Washington, D.C.: Institute for the Study of Diplomacy, School of Foreign Service, Georgetown University.

41. Wilson, Margaret, & Smith, Alaster (1999). Rules and Roles in Terrorist Hostage Taking. In David Canter, & Laurence Alison (Eds.), *The Social Psychology of Crime: Groups, Teams and Networks* (pp. 127–151). Ashgate, England: Aldershot.

42. Turner, James L. (1985). Factors Influencing the Development of the Hostage Identification Syndrome. *Political Psychology, 6*(4), 705–711.

43. Turner, James L. (1985). Factors Influencing the Development of the Hostage Identification Syndrome. *Political Psychology, 6*(4), 705–711.

44. de Fabrique, Nathalie, Romano, Stephen J., Vecchi, Gregory M., & van Hasselt, Vincent B. (2007). Understanding Stockholm Syndrome. *FBI Law Enforcement Bulletin, 76*(7), 10–15.

45. Scodel, Ruth (1998). The Captive's Dilemma: Sexual Acquiescence in Euripides Hecuba and Troades. *Harvard Studies in Classical Philology, 98,* 137–154.

46. Auerbach, S. M., Kiesler, D. J., Strentz, T., Schmidt, J. A., & Serio, C. D. (1994). Interpersonal Impacts and Adjustment to the Stress of Simulated Captivity: An Empirical Test of the Stockholm Syndrome. *Journal of Social and Clinical Psychology, 13,* 207–221.

47. Strentz, Thomas (1979). Law Enforcement Policies and Ego Defenses of the Hostage. *FBI Law Enforcement Bulletin, 48*(4), 1–12.

48. Turner, James L. (1985). Factors Influencing the Development of the Hostage Identification Syndrome. *Political Psychology, 6*(4), 705–711.

49. Fowler, Michael Ross (2007). Relevance of Principled Negotiation to Hostage Crises. *Harvard Negotiation Law Review, 12,* 251–318.

50. Hersh, Seymour M. (2004, May 10). Annals of National Security: Torture at Abu Ghraib. *The New Yorker,* p. A1.

51. CBS News Transcripts (2002, September 22). *60 Minutes.* Burrelle's Information Services (available on Lexis-Nexis, Academic Universe).

52. Arrigo, Jean Maria, & Wagner, Richard V. (2007). Psychologists and Military Interrogators Rethink the Psychology of Torture. *Peace and Conflict: Journal of Peace Psychology, 13*(4), 393–398; Fein, Robert A., Lehner, Paul, & Vossekuil, Bryan (2006). Intelligence Science Board Study on Reducing Information. Washington, D.C.: National Defense Intelligence College.

53. Kleinman, Steven M. (2009). The Promise of Interrogation v. the Problem of Torture. *Valparaiso University Law Review, 43*(4), 1577–1589.

54. Mackey, Chris, & Miller, Greg (2005). *The Interrogators: Task Force 500 and America's Secret War against Al Qaeda.* New York: Back Bay Books.

55. Mayer, Jane (2007, August 13). The Black Sites: A Rare Look inside the C.I.A.'s Secret Interrogation Program. *The New Yorker,* p. A1.

56. Walton, Douglas (2002). The Interrogation as a Type of Dialogue. *Journal of Pragmatics, 35,* 1771–1802.

57. Levy, Earl J. (1999). *Examination of Witnesses in Criminal Cases* (4th ed.). Scarborough, ON: Carswell.

58. Borum, Randy (2004). Counterterrorism Training Post-9/11. In Rohan Gunaratna (Ed.), *The Changing Face of Terrorism* (pp. 60–81). Singapore: Eastern Universities Press.

59. Mullenix, Philip A. (2007). Interrogation Strategies for an Unconventional Extremist Enemy. *Polygraph, 36*(3), 121–132.

60. Mullenix, Philip A. (2007). Interrogation Strategies for an Unconventional Extremist Enemy. *Polygraph, 36*(3), 121–132.

61. Nydell, Margaret K. (2002). *Understanding Arabs: A Guide for Westerners* (3rd ed.). Yarmouth, MA: Intercultural Press; Walters, Stan (2002). *Principles of Kinesic Interview and Interrogation* (2nd ed.). Boca Raton, FL: CRC Press.

62. Krapohl, Donald, & Sturm, Shirley (2002). Terminology Reference for the Science of Psychophysiological Detection of Deception. *Polygraph, 31*(3), 154–239.

63. Mullenix, Philip A. (2007). Interrogation Strategies for an Unconventional Extremist Enemy. *Polygraph, 36*(3), 121–132.

64. Mullenix, Philip A. (2007). Interrogation Strategies for an Unconventional Extremist Enemy. *Polygraph, 36*(3), 121–132.

65. *Al Qaeda Jihad Training Manual.* (2001). Retrieved May 18, 2011 at http://cryptome.org/alq -terr-man.htm; Costanzo, Mark A., & Gerrity, Ellen (2009). The Effects and Effectiveness of Using Torture as an Interrogation Device: Using Research to Inform the Policy Debate. *Social Issues and Policy Review, 3*(1), 179–210.

66. Inbau, Fred E., Reid, John E., & Buckley, Joseph P. (1986). *Criminal Interrogation and Confessions* (3rd ed.). Baltimore: Williams & Wilkins.

67. Matheny, Richard E. (1995). Communication in Cultivation and Solicitation of Major Gift Donors. *New Directions for Philanthropic Fundraising, 1995*(10), 33–44.

68. Puar, Jasbir K., & Rai, Amit S. (2002). Monster, Terrorist, Fag: The War on Terrorism and the Production of Docile Patriots. *Social Text, 20*(3), 117–148; Ramsay, Maureen (2006). Can the Torture of Terrorist Suspects Be Justified? *The International Journal of Human Rights, 10*(2), 103–119.

69. Leo, Richard A., Costanzo, Mark, & Shaked-Schroer, Netta (2009). Psychological and Cultural Aspects of Interrogations and False Confessions: Using Research to Inform Legal Decision-Making. In Daniel Krauss & Joes Lieberman (Eds.), *Psychological Expertise in Court* (pp. 25–55). Surrey, England: Ashgate Publishing; Matsumoto, David (2004). *Culture and Modern Life*. Pacific Grove: Brooks-Cole.

70. Bond, Charles F., Omar, Adnan, Mahmoud, Adnan, & Bonser, Richard Neal (1999). Lie Detection across Cultures. *Journal of Nonverbal Behavior, 14*, 189–204.

71. Costanzo, Mark A., & Gerrity, Ellen (2009). The Effects and Effectiveness of Using Torture as an Interrogation Device: Using Research to Inform the Policy Debate. *Social Issues and Policy Review, 3*(1), 179–210.

72. Moore, Nina-Jo, Hickson, III, Mark, & Stacks, Don W. (2010). *Nonverbal Communication: Studies and Applications* (5th ed.). Los Angeles: Roxbury Publishing Company.

73. DePaulo, Bella M., Lindsay, James J., Malone, Brian E., Muhlenbruck, Laura, Charlton, Kelly, & Cooper, Harris (2003). Cues to Deception. *Psychological Bulletin, 129*, 74–118.

74. Vrij, Aldert (2004). Why Professionals Fail to Catch Liars and How They Can Improve. *Legal and Criminal Psychology, 9*, 159–181; Vrij, Aldert, & Mann, Samantha (2001). Who Killed My Relative? Police Officers' Ability to Detect Real-Life High-Stake Lies. *Psychology, Crime, and Law, 7*, 119–132.

75. Costello, Brian, & Axton, JoAnn (2006). A New Forensic Picture Polygraph Technique for Terrorist and Crime Deception System. *Journal of Instructional Psychology, 33*(4), 1–23; Vrij, Aldert (2008). Detecting Deception. In Mark R. Kebbell & Graham M. Davies (Eds.), *Practical Psychology for Forensic Investigations and Prosecutions* (pp. 89–102). New York: Wiley.

76. Moore, Nina-Jo, Hickson, III, Mark, & Stacks, Don W. (2010). *Nonverbal Communication: Studies and Applications* (5th ed.). Los Angeles: Roxbury Publishing Company.

77. McKenzie, Frederic, Scerbo, Mark, & Catanzaro, Jean (2003). Generating Nonverbal Indicators of Deception in Virtual Reality Training. *Journal of WSCG, 11*(1), 10–21.

78. Ekman, Paul (1985). *Telling Lies: Clues to Deceit in the Marketplace, Politics, and Marriage*. New York: Norton.

79. Ekman, Paul, & Friesen, Wallace V. (1969). Nonverbal Leakage and Cues to Deception. *Psychiatry, 32*, 88–106.

80. Ekman, Paul (2001). *Telling Lies: Clues to Deceit in the Marketplace, Politics, and Marriage*. New York: W. W. Norton & Co; Ekman, Paul (2003). *Emotions Revealed: Recognizing Faces and Feelings to Improve Communication and Emotional Life*. New York: Henry Holt & Co.

81. *United States Army Interrogation Training Manual* (1996). Washington, D.C.: Department of Defense.

82. Coniff, Richard (2004, January 15). Reading Faces. *Smithsonian Magazine*, p. A5.

83. Ekman, Paul, & Friesen, Wallace V. (1978). *Facial Action Coding System: A Technique for the Measurement of Facial Movement*. Palo Alto, CA: Consulting Psychologists Press.

84. Rosenberg, Erika L. (1997). The Study of Spontaneous Facial Expressions in Psychology. In Paul Ekman & Erika L. Rosenberg (Eds.), *What the Face Reveals: Basic and Applied Studies of Spontaneous Expression Using the Facial Action Coding System (FACS)* (pp. 3–17). New York: Oxford University Press.

85. Herbert, Lenese C. (2007). Othello Error: Facial Profiling, Privacy and the Suppression of Dissent. *Ohio State Journal of Criminal Law, 5*, 79–129.

86. Milmo, Dan (2010, November 28). Airport Security Rules Give Terrorists an Advantage. *The Guardian*, p A1.

CHAPTER 15

One-on-One with the Terrorist: International Perspectives

> **After reading this chapter, you will be able to**
>
> - explain the role of negotiation in international communication;
> - discuss the roles of third-party intervention, intercultural competence, and diplomacy between two parties in conflict; and
> - explain the Dialogue among Civilizations as an alternative to global cultural conflict.

INTERNATIONAL COMMUNICATION AND INTERNATIONAL DIALOGUE

The importance of negotiation was already emphasized in the previous chapter. In this one, the role of negotiation will be taken from a different angle—that is, as a direct resolution between parties that are in conflict. During the course of history, military commanders have acknowledged that there is usually no military solution to struggles waged by individuals who employ methods of terror.[1] To this end, it might prove interesting to look at international communication and international dialogue more closely.

Definitions

International communication refers to communication that occurs beyond national borders. It has traditionally dealt with government-to-government information flows in which key powerful nations determine the communication agenda.[2] International communication involves a sociopolitical and economic examination of communication across international borders. Most international communication takes place among First World countries.[3] This international focus or medium through which relations are observed or analyzed has been modified substantially, in part, since the end of WWII and the far-reaching changes it has caused; this includes political shifts and readjustments across Europe.[4]

International dialogue involves an array of methods designed to decrease the possibility of lapsing or relapsing into conflict by bolstering dialogue between warring parties (scattered geographically) for conflict management and to lay the groundwork for peace and development. Political processes and state-to-state interactions are the centerpiece of international dialogue. The rationale behind international dialogue is simple: as parties in conflict explain their criticisms or concerns and present them for international discussion, the uncertainty of intentions that raises insecurity may be reduced. Other parties will then articulate policies with greater knowledge and less insecurity. This will help funnel attention on zones of joint gain and thus eschew disruptive conflicts that jeopardize international security.[5] Both international communication and international dialogue include the notion of voice. **Voice** refers to the opportunities and motivations for global players to present their sides in the public domain and be heard.

At the Negotiation Table with Terrorists?

Bringing opposing parties at the negotiation table so that they can commence serious dialogue is generally difficult. Most states are disinclined to negotiate with terrorists. Often, the reason is that negotiation shows weakness and may lead to additional acts of terrorism. Nevertheless, parties that cannot bring terrorist attacks to an end may determine that the political costs of maintaining the status quo prevail over the risks of initiating dialogue or barring voices from emerging. Concessions from both parties may be essential to arrive at this point. Negotiating with terrorists is a good occasion for appeasing those who would kill innocent targets. It offers an opportunity to negotiate cease-fires and advance toward the peaceful resolve of armed struggles. Grievances from both parties must be heard and legitimate concerns attended to. By all means, this is not equivalent to giving in to terrorism. Rather, continuous dialogue is a preemptive approach of reducing the possibility of future terrorist acts. Dialogue may be entered into by diplomatic, political, military, and religious persons.[6] According to Habermas (1979),[7] in his philosophy of communicative action, dialogues are symmetrical interactions typified by "reciprocal expectations regarding the truth, appropriateness, and sincerity of statements" (p. 104).

For example, à propos the Arab–Israeli peace negotiations, the suspicion and conception that each side feels about the other are grounded, in part, in the dissimilarities between the negotiating cultures within which each party is located. For instance, some cultures can be categorized as goal-oriented or process-oriented cultures (e.g., the Israelis), while others are more relationship-oriented cultures (e.g., the Arabs). Additionally, the Israeli and Arab stances vis-à-vis the negotiating process are rooted in the divergences in their social make-ups and negotiating cultures. The Arabs tend to underscore elements of trust in the relationship, whereas the Israelis are keen on contractual, binding agreements. Because of the differences between the parties' cultural standpoints, success in any potential negotiations may entail adopting what is referred to as a **perceptual pluralism** approach, in which fundamental issues (e.g., security, financial matters, and diplomatic relations) should be tackled simultaneously at a negotiation table, thus allowing to find points of agreement.[8]

NEGOTIATION THEORY

Negotiation is a procedure of common decision making between parties that share joint interests but also diverge as to what should be accomplished in a conflict. As shared decision making, negotiation requires that the warring parties reach some decision together about what the future holds. **Negotiation theory** centers on how parties come to a solution rather than what solution they select.[9] Negotiation can be cooperative or competitive. When it is cooperative, it merges formal bargaining techniques with many skills imparted in basic interpersonal communication courses. These skills include careful listening, assertiveness, supportiveness, and collaborative communication. However, when negotiation is competitive, one party (or both parties) tends to exaggerate the importance of its (or their) concessions, be dishonest, hide information, argue forcefully, or prevail over the other.[10] Budjac Corvette (2006)[11] argues that, in negotiation theory, there are four key **negotiating temperaments**:

- Harmonizer (pacifier): the harmonizer is aware of the big picture and undertakes problems with a broad perspective. He or she tends to address multiple issues together or switch freely from one to another. It is hard to make the harmonizer focus on details. He or she shares viewpoints without making or looking for judgment. The harmonizer, when going overboard, becomes the pacifier. Once the pacifier is at the negotiating table, a true resolution will not be likely.

- Controller (bull): the controller has a well laid-out plan and cannot wait for a decision or resolution. The controller is resolute, decisive, and methodical. He or she succeeds through structure and order and wants things his or her way. Although controlling, the controller does not want conflict, but wants harmony or, at least, peace. Yet, the problem is that, since he or she has strong opinions, he or she can become confrontational, with a propensity to see things as unchanging, right/wrong, and black/white. One can tell there is a controller at the negotiating table by looking at his or her sense of the big picture combined with a strong determination. The controller, when going overboard, may become the bull. Once the bull shows up, a true resolution will not be likely.

- Pragmatist (street fighter): the pragmatist likes details, looks at specifics, and approaches things sequentially. Pragmatists see facts and figures as well as definite and tangible results. They are real-world, hands-on, and bottom-line oriented. They are organized and anxious for reaching a solution. Pragmatists are so resolute to be right that they will usually not accept alternatives or make concessions. As a result of loss of control, the pragmatist-turned-street fighter regards the negotiation as a win/lose situation. The street fighter wants to win; being #2 would be losing. The best manner to confront a street fighter is to give him or her some time to cool off.

- Action seeker (high roller): action seekers also approach situations sequentially, but they can wait for resolution. They are practical and realistic. Action seekers are spur-of-the-moment and action-oriented people. They like thrills and gratification. Since action seekers do not necessarily rely on structure or completion, they can be distracted in a blink of an eye. Action seekers disregard rules, and they are not predictable.

Historically, President John F. Kennedy's involvement in the 1962 Cuban missile crisis is an example of the controller negotiation strategy. To begin, the Soviet Union had started to ship missiles and nuclear warheads to Cuba. In reaction, JFK launched a naval blockade of all Soviet cargoes to Cuba. He said plainly that this blockade would go on unless and until the Soviets ended all additional shipments and destroyed all the missiles and nuclear warheads that had been sent. Put plainly, JFK was following the reasoning that "I have started doing something that punishes you and will continue doing it until you conform to my wishes."[12] This anecdote mirrors the concept of thromise. A **thromise** (a combination of "threat" and "promise") is a form of communication that sounds like a promise (i.e., if you do x, you will receive y) but operates like a threat. Indeed, the compliance may hurt the message receiver, not just failing to receive a benefit. An example of making a thromise is to say that he or she offers to continue giving something to the other if the latter does something in return.[13]

On the other hand, President Barack Obama has been considered a harmonizer when attempting to negotiate peace in the Middle East. On June 4, 2009, Obama gave a speech in Cairo asking for peace between Muslims and the West, emphasizing that "Islam is not part of the problem in combating violent extremism—it is an important part of promoting peace" and that "Islam has a proud tradition of tolerance." Unfortunately, Obama's pacifying stance has been ineffective as it defies the reality of Islam in the very country in which he delivered his speech (i.e., Egypt). Indeed, a sample group of 1,000 Egyptians was surveyed in face-to-face interviews in April and May of 2010 for the U.S.-based Pew Research Center. According to this massive survey, 84% believe apostates from Islam should face the death penalty, 82% believe adulterers should be stoned to death, and 77% believe thieves should be flogged or have their hands cut off. In addition, for the speech, Obama had openly invited the Muslim Brotherhood, the threats of which were explained in Chapter 12.

TACTICS AND STRATEGIES IN NEGOTIATION

Strategies are different from tactics. A *strategy* is a general plan of action to accomplish a particular goal—usually for just one situation. A *tactic* is a particular observable behavior that takes a conflict in a certain direction (consistent with the strategy). In *Managing Conflict through Communication*, Cahn and Abigail (2010)[14] list and describe various tactics and strategies to negotiate with enemies:

- **Concession**: a situation in which a party gives something of high value to the other party, or when the party ceases making demands on the other. For example, Israel has made concessions on the West Bank and Gaza, involving retreat from and reduction of the physical territory of the land of Israel.[15] Likewise, Palestinians have also made concessions on three settlement blocs in the West Bank, agreeing that the Israeli neighborhoods of East Jerusalem would stay as such, and agreeing to Israeli early-warning positions in the West Bank.[16]

- **Fair division** (or *cake-cutting problem*): the process of dividing a resource in such a manner that each party believes it has received its fair share. For instance, to conclude the Iran hostage crisis, President Reagan freed close to $8 billion in Iranian assets in exchange for the fifty-two hostages at the embassy in Tehran.[17] It is a difficult problem because each recipient may have a different perception of how much the resource is worth. In the cake-cutting option, one recipient may like marzipan, another like apples, and so on.

- **Logrolling**: a procedure by which each party grants those issues to which the other party gives top priority. Both sides make concessions, but not on issues to which they attribute top priority. Logrolling is the exchange of favors or quid pro quo ("something for something"). Opposing sides have to desire several items (not just one), but only press for the top priority because of its importance and not the others because they are not as important. This is precisely a lingering problem between Israel and Palestine. Both parties, it seems, are willing to make concessions that are not important to the other party.

- **Compensation**: a method whereby one party grants something of value (usually financial) to the other to compensate for losses caused by the other party's behavior or that result from its own demands. For example, the U.S. government has agreed to rebuild parts of Afghanistan (e.g., by building schools) after destroying many settlements there.

- **Bridging**: a strategy whereby a new option is offered that meets both parties' most significant needs. No compensation and no more than one piece for each side are involved. For instance, at the conclusion of the 1978 Camp David Accords, the U.S. committed itself to grant financial aid to both Egypt and Israel. On the one hand, Israel had to withdraw from the Sinai Peninsula (which it seized after the Six-Day War in 1967). On the other hand, Egypt had to grant Israel the free movement of Israeli ships through the Suez Canal and the recognition of the Strait of Tiran (and other straits) as international passages.[18]

Certain tactics can be unfair or contentious, in which one party benefits tremendously from the other or exploits the other exceedingly, as the examples below describe:

- **Threat**: statement that associates the other party's refusal to comply with negative consequences. A party that constantly follows through on threats may gain better cooperation than a party that does not carry them through. Consistency leads to greater credibility. Al Qaeda threatened to commit terrorist attacks if the West sent troops to places like Iraq. With the Madrid train bombings that occurred on March 11, 2004, Spain was forced to withdraw its 1,300 troops from Iraq.[19] A big advantage of threats is that they tend to be persuasive.

- **Hard bargaining**: confrontational, competitive bargaining that considers the opponent as an enemy to overcome, rather than a partner with whom to collaborate. This is certainly the case between Israel and Palestine, both of which tend to view each other as enemies. Hard bargaining is contrasted with **soft bargaining**, which is highly pacifying to the point of conceding important positions.

- **Pie metaphor**: a distributive strategy in which the negotiator's goal is to obtain all that he or she can, irrespective of equity or how the other party feels. Using the common pie metaphor, the objective is to secure the whole pie or at least a large chunk of it. For instance, Islamist terrorists want the entire world to become a grand Caliphate—the entire world, not just some parts of it.

- Persuasive argumentation: winning arguments through reasoning and logical appeals. Both Israel and Arab countries have employed arguments such as, "We need your money because our lives depend on it." Israel is asking the U.S. for money to help them resist attacks from neighboring countries. Arab countries may be doing it for similar (and additional) reasons.

- **Ingratiation**: a strategy in which a party tries to make itself more appealing to the other to set up the other for subsequent exploitation. The usefulness of ingratiation comes from the other's very unawareness of the party's ultimate intentions. Through ingratiation, one party attempts to do the other party favors, and so lower their guard. Specific ingratiation tactics include flattery, concurring with the other party's views, and doing them unimportant favors. Ingratiation involves praising and using flattery to make the target feel more confident. The purpose, of course, is to influence the party. Ingratiation tactics are designed to persuade the recipient that they are held in high regard. Doing whatever others want is a good way to show that a party thinks favorably of their ideas. Ingratiation is the art of opening channels of communication, building relationships, putting others in a good mood (i.e., especially before making a request), getting into "opinion conformity," and acting friendly.

- **Tit-for-tat**: the biblical "eye for an eye" and "tooth for a tooth." Tit-for-tat is rewarding the other party when it is cooperative and punishing them when uncooperative. For instance, Terry Jones, the controversial Floridian pastor who was ready to burn multiple Qur'ans in September 2010, eventually agreed to abstain from doing it. Nevertheless, his intentions alone were profound infractions to the eyes of radical Muslims worldwide. To this effect, the tit-for-tat response was the killing of U.N. staffers by Muslims in Afghanistan a few months later.[20]

THIRD-PARTY INTERVENTION

The term **third-party intervention** refers to a type of intermediacy by an individual or team of people who get involved in a conflict to help the conflicting parties manage or resolve it. Fisher and Keashly (1991)[21] provide a constructive basis for understanding the various possible roles of the third party. Using their framework, one could say that some third parties participate in conciliation. **Conciliation** involves a third party—a trusted one—that offers an informal communication link between the parties with the goal of identifying the issues, decreasing tensions, and motivating the parties to change their negotiating positions.

The third party can also engage in **problem solving** (adopting an alternative that meets the aspirations of both sides).[22] Problem solving should happen during negotiation or with the help of an outside intervener. It is usually a form of consultation whereby a third party helps analyzing the conflict and develops alternatives through communication and fact-finding based on a thorough understanding of conflict processes. For instance, President Jimmy Carter at Camp David provided such type of mediation assistance (along with his aides). Egypt and Israel undertook such a process when they entered into an agreement to disengage in the Sinai Peninsula. Israel withdrew from the Sinai Peninsula. Despite all the obstacles, Jimmy Carter reached a joint solution, otherwise conflict would have endured and collective distress would have ensued.[23]

The advantage of third-party mediation is that both parties can see the outside inter-vener as an arbitrator. An **arbitrator** attends to presentations made by both sides, assesses written materials and other evidence concerning the case, and then draws a conclusion as to who is right and who is wrong, or how conflict should be managed.[24] In the case of the Israel–Egypt conflict, both President Sadat of Egypt and Prime Minister Begin of Israel were engaging in inaction, which governed much of the proceedings. This was not because the main actors were unintelligent, fumbling decision makers. It was the design: each party waited continually for the other's next move. To resolve the stalemate created by this mutual inaction, President Carter ultimately imposed a deadline, beyond which he made it clear that he would withdraw from the negotiations. This motivated the parties to take action.[25]

Another form of third-party intervention is **peacekeeping**, which involves providing military personnel by a third party (or parties) to supervise and control a cease-fire, to take part in humanitarian activities, or work to avert hostilities between the parties. The final form of third-party intervention, **mediation**, consists of the intervention of a third party to facilitate a negotiated settlement of the main issues in the conflict. The emphasis is on the role and importance of mediation in internationalized conflicts, like the conflict in Northern Ireland. Here, third parties might act as facilitators; they can organize meetings, set agendas, and conduct productive discussions. Mediation allows the third party to assume a more active or formal role in the process. Unlike arbitration, it is voluntary and ad hoc in nature. It is designed for a specific problem or task. For example, in the mid-1990s, George Mitchell—a U.S. envoy working for the Clinton administration—became the co-chairman of the All-Party Talks in Northern Ireland. His task was to manage the conflict between the Catholics and the Protestants in that nation. Mitchell's personal intervention with the par-ties was crucial to the success of the talks.[26]

In international disputes, mediation over border issues, cease-fires, and civil conflicts can use high-ranking international mediators like former U.S. President Jimmy Carter. As such, the **Carter Center** is a nongovernmental, nonprofit organization founded in 1982 by Jimmy Carter. Carter has been involved in various national and international public policy, conflict management, human rights, and charitable causes. For instance, the Carter Center has been involved in several African countries' peace and democracy efforts since 1991. In particular, it was actively engaged in the 2005 electoral process in Liberia, where it orga-nized an international observer delegation. The Center negotiated the Nairobi Agreement in 1999 between the Sudan and Uganda. Furthermore, the Center led a team of eighty observers in monitoring legislative elections in the Palestinian territories and Jimmy Carter's mission to North Korea in 1994 initiated the debate of a U.S.–North Korea pact on nuclear issues.[27]

It is important to note, however, that third-party intervention does not always work. For instance, the Norwegian attempts to secure a cease-fire between the Colombo government in Sri Lanka and the Liberation Tigers of Tamil Eelam (LTTE) in 2002 demonstrate the difficulty in convincing terrorists to drop their weapons. Norway mediated a cease-fire agreement (CFA) and supervised interim peace talks until 2005. Under that agreement, substantial autonomy was granted to the LTTE, but both sides resorted to full-scale war in 2006 as a result of violations of the cease-fire. In addition, a more hard-line Sinhalese government, led by President Rajapakse, emerged and insisted on military victory.[28] The Sinhalese represent the largest national group (74%), while the Tamils are the largest minority (a Hindu minority), constituting 18% of the population.[29] In a similar vein, the failure of the Oslo Accords in 2000 and the resulting erosion of Israeli–Palestinian relations have predictably contributed to profound debates over the role of third parties.

STRATEGIC AMBIGUITY AS A COMMUNICATION STRATEGY

Strategic ambiguity attaches importance to the symbolic and dialogic aspect of language and the multicultural sources for interpretations of meanings. It also emphasizes unified diversity so essential to the formation of resilient organizations that operate in environments with high uncertainty.[30] According to Goodall, Trethewey, and McDonald (2006),[31] the goal of strategic ambiguity as a form of communication should be the new policy. Five principles to guide strategic ambiguity are as follows:

(1) Practice strategic engagement, not global salesmanship: strategic engagement involves applying strategic ambiguity to public diplomacy objectives. This means demonstrating a willingness to consider the messages of other leaders and representatives without engaging in immediate closure or pressing for the integral "rightness" of our messages. It also means viewing communication as a two-way interchange and meanings as emergent over time. For example, in the 1960s, President Lyndon B. Johnson botched a chief political opportunity in U.S.–Egyptian relations when he took offense at what he believed were aggressive comments by President Nasser. Nasser later explained his comments were only directed to Arab audiences while he sought to collaborate in a diplomatic backchannel with the U.S. Being aware of deeply embedded cultural norms and values, and their effect on communication patterns, requires an engaged attitude, not an "our way or no way" attitude.[32]

(2) Do not repeat the same message, using the same means, with the same spokespersons and expect new or different results (i.e., repetition breeds contempt): using the same model to participate in public diplomacy is inefficient because it makes spokespersons repeat the same fundamental ideas and messages without taking the meaning-making practices of target audiences into account. Therefore, it is important to replace repetition with strategic communication as a guiding standard of interaction with diverse audiences.

(3) Do not attempt to influence a message's meaning in cultures that are not fully understood: monopolizing favored communications is a misleading objective in a diverse mediated communication world. There is an inverse relationship between domination of

a message's meanings and our understanding of the distant culture in which it will be interpreted. The less awareness of distant cultures (as well as languages and religions), the less control over the probable meanings ascribed to diplomacy messages. For example, in January 1991, at a meeting in which Tariq Aziz (the foreign minister of Iraq) met with James Baker (the U.S. secretary of state), there was miscommunication. On analyzing Baker's words, the latter was very clear that the U.S. would attack if Iraq did not pull out of Kuwait. However, he expressed it in a calm voice. The miscommunication occurred because Saddam Hussein's brother was sitting next to Aziz. Hussein paid attention only to Baker's nonverbal communication (i.e., how he talked, rather than what he said). As he reported back to Baghdad, "The Americans will not attack. They are weak. They are calm. They are not angry. They are only talking." Western individualist cultures look mostly at the content of communication, whereas Eastern collectivist cultures look mostly at the context of communication. From this vantage point, Western individualist cultures tend to be more **low-context**, whereas Eastern collectivist cultures tend to be more **high-context**. Low-context cultures focus more on clear and objective messages, codes, data, facts, and theories than high-context cultures.[33]

(4) Be aware that message clarity and perception of meaning are a function of relationships, not just a function of word usage: diplomatic efforts should concentrate on building trust and credibility based on a longer term and more profound understanding of cultures, languages, and religions. It is in the framework of building long-lasting relationships and being alert to the interpretations of others that we can better design productive messages that have authentic value and that resonate among a wide array of audiences.

(5) Search for "unified diversity" based on global collaboration instead of "focused wrongness" based on pure dominance and power: it is necessary to acknowledge that shared meaning is not the only objective, but common principles and goals are meaningful in and of themselves. So, we need to learn to expect and develop multiple meanings in local cultures and communities that endorse larger agreements of U.S. principles or goals. We also need to expect that those audiences will adjust and co-opt those messages based on their own needs and resources. Forming coalitions of engaged communication should vigorously and overtly improve coalitions of military force and be organized with them.

THE ROLE OF DIPLOMACY

Nations have many tools to communicate with each other, such as state-to-state written exchanges, executive treaties, security commitments, and agreements. A tool that needs to be explored is diplomacy.

Definition

From the Greek word *diploun* (in reference to an official, folded document), **diplomacy** refers to the official method by which sovereign states manage affairs with one another and enter into agreements on their respective postures. Diplomacy is the art and practice of leading negotiations between representatives of institutions or nations. It is conducted through the use of tact to obtain strategic advantage, one set of instruments being the articulation of statements in a non-argumentative or social manner. Diplomacy is useful in counteracting the signaling problems characteristic to an uncivilized world. For this reason, diplomacy has been called the "the best line of defense."[34] Diplomatic rights were initiated in the mid-17th century in Europe and have expanded across the world. These rights were ratified by the 1961 Vienna Convention on Diplomatic Relations, which shields diplomats from persecution or prosecution while on a diplomatic assignment. If a diplomat commits a serious offense while in a host country, he or she may be considered **persona non grata** (unwanted person). Such diplomats are often put on trial for the offense in their homeland.[35]

Traditionally, diplomats have been allowed to take documents with them without being searched. The procedure for this is the purported **diplomatic bag** (or, in some nations, the *diplomatic pouch*). Because of international terrorism, however, signals intelligence has caused this use of diplomatic bags to be widely discarded.[36] Nevertheless, the sanctity of diplomats has been a long practice, which is referred to as **diplomatic immunity**. In some instances, diplomats have been killed, which is generally regarded as a great breach of honor. Genghis Khan and the Mongols were famous for fiercely insisting on the rights of diplomats, and they would often wreak dreadful revenge against any group that violated these rights.[37] Diplomacy is akin to **representative negotiation**—negotiation done through representatives. For example, U.S. citizens hastily hire a lawyer when things go wrong. Not surprisingly, representative negotiation is a crucial element of the practice of law. In fact, most U.S. lawsuits are settled through negotiation without ever moving to court. The same is true in international law.

The Middle East and other parts of the world have a very different conception of diplomacy. Already in the past, in the Ottoman Empire, Persian diplomats (and those from other states) were viewed as a guarantee of acceptable behavior. If a state broke a treaty or if their nationals committed a crime, the diplomats would be punished. Diplomats were exploited as an enforcement apparatus on treaties and international law. To confirm that punishing a diplomat carried important weight, rulers were looking for high-ranking figures. This tradition is generally considered as the basis of the 1979 Iranian hostage crisis. Student-supporters of the Iranian Revolution sought to punish the U.S. for its alleged transgressions by holding their diplomats captive.[38]

Intercultural Competence

Negotiating the peace process in the face of the Global War on Terror (GWOT) involves navigating "thick" cultures. Because the thick cultures that distant states represent are complex (linguistically, symbolically, materially, and culturally), they tend to behave in manners that are unstable, are subject to change or inconsistency, are fleeting and diverse, are unanticipated and, in the extreme, seem nonsensical. Navigating through this mediation course—one that is immersed in history, conflict, and difference—is a challenge.[39] Put simply, part of the success of diplomacy hinges on intercultural competence. **Intercultural competence** is the ability to embark on successful communication with individuals of other cultures. An interculturally competent diplomat grasps and understands, when communicating with diplomats from foreign cultures, their unique concepts in perception, thinking, feeling, and acting.[40]

Negotiation between opposing parties should not hinge on cultural ignorance or misunderstanding. In January 1991, a striking intercultural mishap occurred between the delegates of the U.S. and Iraq in Geneva. The U.S. sent a female envoy, April Glaspie, as its ambassador to Iraq. The ambassador's gender and her position as a "Westerner" made her a very unpersuasive delegate to the eyes of the Iraqis. The Iraqis concluded that the Americans were not serious about making negotiations. At other times, there can also be troubles of translation. For instance, at the peak of the Cold War, a nonchalant statement made by Soviet Premier Nikita Khrushchev to a British diplomat was translated as "We will bury you." The accurate translation of his comment was, "We will be present at your burial." In conflict, misconstruals are not uncommon because people interpret statements in diverse ways.[41]

A universal principle of intercultural competence requires one side to pay attention while the other speaks (and vice versa). This is an example of **cultural diplomacy**, a type of diplomacy that carries a series of prescriptions which are material to its successful practice; these prescriptions involve the clear recognition and awareness of foreign cultural dynamics and observance of the principles that dominate basic dialogue. Cultural diplomacy prescribes the adherence to such principles and for parties to be inspired by their enlarged cultural understanding when negotiating. This paradigm enables a dialogue that lends to straightforward collaboration. Parties may opt to conduct dialogues through an interpreter or by using a **lingua franca** (i.e., a common international language, such as English or French). Nonverbal communication also plays a major role in this process. Foreign conceptions of body language and other forms of nonverbal communication must be taken into account to avoid uncertainty or obscurity during a dialogue. There is a darker side which may lead to hostile or unfamiliar forms of dialogue: disproportionate intonation or the decision to be speechless for long periods in a meeting. Being familiar with the tenets of cultural diplomacy facilitates the creation of a collaborative platform on which there is a cultural understanding that moves negotiations toward solutions that are mutually satisfying to both parties.[42]

MULTI-TRACK DIPLOMACY

Multi-track diplomacy can be defined as diplomatic measures taken by official state or non-state actors to turn a dispute into a positive outcome. This can be done by finding innovative ways to impart information, proposing novel solutions, and directly guiding the crisis by using newfangled carrots and sticks that can help move things toward beneficial bargaining positions. Multi-track diplomacy is the combination of five track diplomacies: Track I, Track II, Track III, Track IV, and Track V. In essence, it is an interaction of peacemaking endeavors thanks to multi-leveled categories of diplomats, each using their own track.[43]

Track I Diplomacy

Track I diplomacy involves the input and interaction of state or official diplomats in their attempts to resolve conflict. These actors are sent on behalf of their state or institutions. The previous section on diplomacy is mostly representative of this type of diplomacy. It is a process which employs the skills, resources, and plans of those state or official actors. Track I diplomacy is not always efficient (that is why other tracks were implemented). For example, both the Israelis and Palestinians have gradually become skeptical about the use of Track I diplomacy in the U.S.-driven "Road Map for Peace." Israelis contend that they will give too much land by accepting the Road Map, while Palestinians argue that the proposal only benefits the interests of the U.S. as a friend of Israel.[44]

Track II Diplomacy

Track II diplomacy is more semi-formal, off the record, and personal. It involves actors representing NGOs (nongovernmental organizations) involved in activity at the grassroots level and backchannel initiatives. Track II diplomacy is crucial in preserving support at the local level for negotiated bargains and provisions to a peace settlement. Track II diplomacy is conducted through informal channels using facilitators such as high-profile figures and social activists (like Bono, U2's frontrunner). In this case, it is called **celebrity diplomacy**.[45] Celebrities have long been associated with the contemporary world of diplomacy. Benjamin Franklin—often hailed as the first American celebrity—diligently curried favors (on behalf of America) with the French Court of Louis XVI. And the great reputation of Lawrence of Arabia remains permanently linked to the Paris Peace Conference of 1919. More recently, Youssou N'Dour, the Senegalese singer, gave a speech during a media conference at the G8 Summit in Scotland in 2005. N'Dour is probably Africa's most acclaimed celebrity advocate for interreligious and inter-civilizational diplomacy.[46]

Hollywood stars George Clooney, Don Cheadle, and Angelina Jolie have benefited from their star power to capture international attention to the unending humanitarian crisis in Darfur. Together, they have produced documentaries and a book, made manifold media appearances, and exerted pressure on world leaders.[47] Track II diplomats want dialogue, with the purpose of conflict management or confidence building. Track II leaders are differentiated from both top-tier leaders (government spokespersons and Track I diplomats) and grassroots leaders (local leaders and community organizers). Track II diplomats are midlevel leaders. They tend to enjoy both top-down effects with their support base as well as bottom-up effects in the sense that they usually get the attention of official leaders. Midlevel leaders can have a direct influence on the media as well.[48]

Track II diplomats can also be academics or representatives of think-tanks. During the initial Palestinian–Israeli negotiations, only backchannel congregations were taking place. Thanks to the neat planning of a Norwegian sociologist, Terje Rod Larsen, talks began between Yair Hirschfeld, an Israeli Jewish academic, and Abu Alaa, a PLO official (and ex-director of finances for Yasser Arafat). They began to convene in secret, and, owing to sustained commitment by both parties, the Norwegian government began to endorse additional meetings between the two men, and ultimately their respective parties. Thanks to these meetings, the Declaration of Principles was drafted between the officials of the two parties. The initial base created by Track II diplomats on both sides was used until the parties were sufficiently comfortable to back and publicly champion the negotiations and their content.[49]

A similar example of Track II diplomacy is the Dartmouth Conference, which was introduced in 1959 when U.S. President Dwight D. Eisenhower requested that Norman Cousins make arrangements to get private U.S. and Soviet citizens to meet to discuss U.S.–Soviet relations. These meetings, initially organized at Dartmouth College in October 1960, were prolonged on a regular basis for over twenty-nine years. They led to better U.S.–Soviet communications and relations as well as understanding on a whole range of issues.[50]

Track III Diplomacy

Track III diplomacy refers to diplomacy between businesspeople (businessperson to businessperson). It deals with interactions in the private sector, free enterprise, and multinational corporations (MNCs). The most recurrent example of Track III diplomacy is that of American business tycoon Armand Hammer. Hammer played a crucial role in improving U.S.–Soviet relations by promoting trade between the U.S. and the ex-Soviet Union during the Cold War. Armand Hammer was president and CEO of Occidental Petroleum, a U.S.-headquartered oil and gas exploration and production company established in 1920. Through his business interests worldwide and his business-driven diplomacy, Hammer developed a massive network of friends and acquaintances on both sides of the Pacific Ocean.[51]

Track IV Diplomacy

Track IV diplomacy refers to citizen-to-citizen exchange programs of all sorts, such as university, high school, educational, academic, scientific, linguistic, cultural, film, music, art, and sports exchanges. For example, the Fulbright Program, created by an act of Congress in 1946, has allowed thousands of U.S. scholars to live and do research abroad, and for thousands of foreign scholars to live and do research in the U.S. After the Madrid and London bombings, Western states have customized their response to particularly improve their "citizenship awareness" programs. They have tackled the kind of sociopolitical alienation that Muslim immigrants feel. For instance, in the Netherlands, the effort is to avert radicalization by stimulating and reinforcing sociopolitical integration.[52] In doing so, the development of new methods of communication between citizens (i.e., Muslims and non-Muslims) was put in place. The intent was to re-integrate at-risk communities and show the world that Muslims are welcome in Western Europe. The Dutch approaches have involved mandatory integration courses, language tests that are to be given before immigration, the official observance of national oaths, the obligatory watching of cultural films about Western values, the opportunities of having "homework support cafés" for marginalized youths, and increasing government recruitment movements in minority circles.[53]

Track V Diplomacy

Track V diplomacy refers to media-to-media endeavors to expose and educate large sections of the population who have expressed hatred toward the philosophy, beliefs, culture, and needs of the other national, religious, or ethnic group with whom they are in conflict. One example of Track V diplomacy is a series of thirty episodes of five-minute public service announcements (PSAs) that looked like television documentaries. These were produced by CNN in 1989 and explored the concept of Track V diplomacy by concentrating on an assortment of national and international armed struggles and presenting diverse possible approaches to resolve or assuage these struggles.[54] Likewise, in a study of a few Ramadan TV series shown on Arab TV channels and dealing with topics on terrorism, Mernissi (2004)[55] observed that those shows were products of a deep-rooted tradition in which Arab states used the vehicle of the Ramadan soap opera to educate the audience about issues considered important. For instance, in 2005, the popular topic on terrorism of the TV series echoed a willingness on the part of states confronting problems with Islamists to diffuse antiterrorism messages. *Hollywood 9/11*, an entertainment industry group formed to improve America's image abroad, requested help from Muhammad Ali, the famed Muslim boxer, to appear in TV advertisements. These commercials were broadcasted in the Arab language on the A1 Jazeera network.[56] A1 Jazeera is what Secretary of State Colin Powell referred to as the "voice of terrorism" and "the most vitriolic, irresponsible" television channel.[57]

VOICE OF AMERICA (VOA)

Track V diplomacy is something to behold, especially in its promotion of **Voice of America** (**VOA**). VOA is the official international radio and TV broadcasting service of the U.S. federal government. It was established in 1942. Its oversight body is the Broadcasting Board of Governors. VOA offers a wide variety of programs for broadcast on radio, TV, and the Internet worldwide and in about fifty languages. The objective is to promote a positive image of America. It broadcasts some 900 hours of original programming each week.[58] Before the September 11, 2001 attacks, VOA's top five nations (in terms of audience ratings) were China, Bangladesh, Ethiopia, Nigeria, and Afghanistan. VOA found that, in 2000, 80% of men in Afghanistan listened to VOA news at least once a week (in the Pashto or Dari language, the principal ones in that country). The Taliban would not allow a poll of women. After 9/11, President George W. Bush selected a new VOA director—a person with strong conservative records. Congress seemed to support the White House decision by voting, on November 7, 2001, to create Radio Free Afghanistan to emit American news and entertainment to Afghans in their local languages. The vote was 405 to 2 and was barely a vote of confidence in the VOA. The broadcasts were to emulate Radio Free Europe.[59] In fact, Radio Free Europe/Radio Liberty, its Iraqi arm (Radio Free Iraq), and Al-Hurra TV are now actively taking part in U.S. strategic communication attempts, though with questionable results. All this has happened, in part, by getting resources from VOA.[60]

VOA exemplifies the philosophical concept of the agora. In ancient Greek city-states, the **agora** was an open "place of assembly." Greece was among the earliest civilizations to use space as an expression of both concrete and intangible meanings. For instance, Athenian citizens would regularly congregate in the agora, in which they would share ideas, debate politics, and conduct business.[61] A present-day agora where humans can meet is satellite broadcasting or the Internet. The latter could be an agora for public exposure and encounter of opposing views on a planetary scale. A case in point is a program that used live satellite connections to enable intercultural exchanges across geopolitical, cultural, and religious borders. Soon after 9/11 and before the war in Afghanistan, it brought together studio audiences based in New York and Islamabad.[62]

DIALOGUE AMONG CIVILIZATIONS

In November 2008, at the request of multiple Islamic organizations, including the Organization of Islamic Cooperation (OIC), a global organization comprising fifty-seven Muslim nations, the United Nations General Assembly condemned the defamation of religions, stating that "Islam is frequently and wrongly associated with human rights violations and terrorism." All countries in the world were charged with the goal of taking "all possible measures to promote tolerance and respect for all religions and beliefs."[63] Such notion of a **Dialogue among Civilizations** was introduced by Mohammed Khatami, the former Iranian president. It is a type of interfaith dialogue or global peace dialogue. It is also an alternative to the unavoidability of global cultural conflict as suggested by Samuel Huntington's theory of Clash of Civilizations—see Chapter 1—between the West and the Islamic countries in the Middle East.[64]

Global Opinion Theory

A Dialogue among Civilizations is an example of **global opinion theory**. This theory argues that countries develop interpretations of world opinion whose frame and content are in line with their interests and values. Then, a procedure of negotiation follows among the countries in question to resolve these interpretations. Countries that do not abide by any resulting consensus incur the risk of being isolated from the international community. World opinion is described as the moral judgments of critics or commentators that states must respect in the global arena, or, again, they could incur the risk of being isolated. Global opinion theory implies the phrase of the *world as a unit* deriving concepts such as world community, world public, or civilized nations as synonyms in its examinations.[65] According to Rusciano (2003),[66] for world opinion to efficiently sway audiences, it has to follow six major components:

- Moral component: values shared by all countries in their assessments of world opinion.

- Pragmatic component: interests shared by all countries in their assessments of world opinion.

- Power of world opinion: its obvious influence on world events and countries' behaviors.

- Nation's image: reputation, in world opinion, as it is interpreted by itself and other countries.

- World considered as a unit: a global community that may judge and react to other countries' behaviors.

- Threat of international isolation: threat which functions as a possible punishment for countries that do not respect the guidelines of world opinion.

As Rusciano (2001)[67] sees it, global opinion theory posits that states acquire a certain status as key global players by "agreeing" with world opinion that, in turn, will boost their global influence even more. A procedure of negotiation then arises among the involved states to create interpretations of how the new world order should be. The objective, of course, is to arrive at an international consensus.

Kissing the Enemy?

Kissing the enemy is a phrase used by right-wing conservatives to refer to global peace activists who adhere to fantasies of peace as their best answer to solve global conflicts. For example, according to detractors, in his après-presidency, Jimmy Carter's foreign policy has consisted, on some occasions, of kissing world-class tyrants and murderers. As such, he kissed Cuban dictator Fidel Castro in the same way that he kissed Soviet dictator Leonid Brezhnev during the Vienna Summit meeting in 1979. Other dictators on whose cheeks Carter put his lips were President Ceaușescu of Romania (of whom Carter said, "Our goals are the same"), Syrian mass executer Hafez al-Assad, Ethiopian mass executer Mengistu, and North Korean dictator Kim Jong Il—said Carter of the latter, "I don't see that they are an outlaw nation." Metaphorically, the kiss-your-enemy practice is also reflected through Carter's aggressive efforts to save terrorists from trouble. In June 2009, Carter asked President Obama to remove Hamas from the Terrorist List. Hamas, the Palestinian terrorist organization, admits to killing Jews, Christians, gays, and infidels. Carter has supported Hamas for a long time.[68]

Indulging in sentiment with terrorist groups such as Hamas and Hezbollah—and praising them for being "anti-imperialist" powers—is a sign of kissing the enemy. Hezbollah is regarded as a terrorist organization by the U.S., Israel, Egypt, several European countries, Canada, and Australia. In June 2009, Javier Solana, the European Union's (E.U.) Foreign Affairs Chief, held a peaceful meeting with Hussein Hajj Hassan, a Hezbollah lawmaker. The meeting was a widespread effort by the E.U. to reach out to Hezbollah. England has also created connections with Hezbollah's political wing. Hezbollah legislator Hussein Hajj Hassan called his meeting with Javier Solana a "goodwill gesture from the European Union toward Hezbollah." In a similar fashion, Spain's former Prime Minister Zapatero liked to brand himself as a politician of dialogue, harmony, and plurality. He started peace talks with ETA, the armed Basque nationalist and separatist organization considered a terrorist group by both the U.S. and the E.U.[69]

This type of behavior is happening worldwide. In April 2004, Romano Prodi, then president of the European Commission, broke with E.U. protocol and welcomed Libyan leader Muammar Gaddafi as a friend of Europe. Prodi's step toward global unity was not only dangerous; it also caused dismay as Gaddafi was supporting terrorism in the 1980s.[70] French philosopher René Girard (2008)[71] views human beings as the most mimetic or imitative of all living creatures. They are so imitative that the inclination to mimic the observable actions (and even the apparent attention) of others represents an existential roadblock to logic and rationality.

Kissing the enemy can be symbolized through the publishing of literature or promotion of books that support the destruction of people and ideals in the West. In England, extremist literature exists at six public libraries (three in London, two in the Midlands, and one in the North of England). In an investigation called "Hate on the State," Gardham (2007)[72] warned that some British public libraries have become flooded with Islamist books calling for the killing of non-Muslims. Hundreds of Islamist books on those library shelves exalt terror and advocate holy war and acts of terrorism. Council taxpayers' money in England has been used to buy these Islamist books and place them in those public libraries.

Schmoozing with Terrorists

Many celebrities of the Western world have been called *schmoozers*. The root of **schmoozing** is *schmooze*, a Yiddish word for casual conversation or gossip. In *Schmoozing with Terrorists: From Hollywood to the Holy Land, Jihadists Reveal Their Global Plans—to a Jew!*, Aaron Klein (2007)[73] pleads Muslim jihadists to respond to the habitual sweet talk of American global peace activists such as Jimmy Carter, House Speaker Nancy Pelosi, and entertainment personalities like Rosie O'Donnell, Sean Penn, and Jane Fonda. These peace activists continue to call terrorists freedom fighters, side with terror-supporting nations, or even consider the 9/11 attacks as an inside job by the U.S. government.

Klein explains that, in a 2005 sweet-talk presentation, Sean Penn, who visited his pal Ahmadinejad in Tehran, referred to Iran as a "great country," called Bush and Cheney "villainous and criminally obscene people," and even said that Iran has the right to have a nuclear weapon because, after all, the U.S. has a nuclear arsenal. For American stand-up comedian Rosie O'Donnell, terrorists are people too. As O'Donnell said, "Don't fear the terrorists. They're mothers and fathers." O'Donnell even doubted whether Al Qaeda should be held responsible for the 9/11 attacks. In fact, she questioned whether Khalid Sheikh Mohammed—the confessed 9/11 mastermind—was the one planning the attacks. She also suggested that the Iranian seizure of fifteen British Royal Navy personnel in March 2007 was a swindle to give Bush an excuse to attack Iran.

SUMMARY

When facing terrorists one-on-one, both international communication and international dialogue are important. Negotiating with terrorists is difficult as parties may have different objectives and cultural backgrounds. As shared decision making, negotiation requires that the warring parties reach some decision together about what the future holds. Various tactics and strategies in negotiation were listed and described. An example is concession, a situation in which a party gives something of high value to the other party. Certain tactics can be unfair or contentious (e.g., threat, tit-for-tat, etc.). In addition, the concept of third-party intervention can be useful in that an individual (or team of people) can help the conflicting parties manage or resolve it. The third party can engage in problem solving, arbitration, peacekeeping, and mediation. Third-party intervention was efficient in the conflict between the Catholics and the Protestants in Northern Ireland in the mid-1990s. According to Goodall, Trethewey, and McDonald (2006), there are five principles to guide strategic ambiguity as a form of communication. For example, the U.S. government should practice strategic engagement, not global salesmanship. This entails viewing communication as a two-way interchange and meanings as emergent over time. Another point to consider is that

Western individualist cultures tend to be more low-context, while Eastern collectivist cultures tend to be more high-context. The next important method is diplomacy, the art and practice of leading negotiations between representatives of institutions or nations. Negotiating the peace process with terrorists involves navigating "thick" cultures. Therefore, intercultural competence and cultural diplomacy are of paramount importance. A case in point is the decision to be speechless for long periods in a meeting, which can be a bad move when negotiating with enemies. A specific type of diplomacy is multi-track diplomacy, the combination of five track diplomacies: Track I, Track II, Track III, Track IV, and Track V. For instance, Track II diplomacy is celebrity diplomacy, in which a rock star like Bono will step in to improve inter-civilizational diplomacy. A specific model of Track V diplomacy is Voice of America (VOA), the official international radio and TV broadcasting service of the U.S. federal government to promote a positive image of America. Lastly, global opinion theory, of which the concept of Dialogue among Civilizations is an example, posits that nations acquire a certain status as key global players by agreeing with world opinion that, in turn, will boost their global influence even more. A direct consequence is that key countries will eventually form a world as a unit. The problem is that, when confronting enemies, currying favors with them may be seen as kissing the enemy or, as Aaron Klein (2007) wrote it, "schmoozing with terrorists."

KEY TERMS

Agora   396

arbitrator   389

bridging   387

Carter Center   389

celebrity diplomacy   394

compensation   387

concession   386

conciliation   388

cultural diplomacy   393

Dialogue among Civilizations   397

diplomatic bag   392

diplomatic immunity   392

diplomacy   391

fair division   387

global opinion theory   397

hard vs. soft bargaining   387

high- vs. low-context culture   391

ingratiation   388

intercultural competence   392

international communication   383

international dialogue   384

kissing the enemy   398

lingua franca   393

logrolling   387

mediation   389

multi-track diplomacy   393

negotiating temperament   385

negotiation theory   385

peacekeeping   389

perceptual pluralism   384

persona non grata   392

pie metaphor   388

problem solving   388

representative negotiation   392

schmoozing   399

strategic ambiguity   390

third-party intervention   388

threat   387

thromise   386

tit-for-tat   388

Voice of America   396

ENDNOTES

1. Imre, Robert, Mooney, T. Brian, & Clarke, Benjamin (2008). *Responding to Terrorism*. Farnham, England: Ashgate.
2. Thussu, Daya (2006). *International Communication: Continuity and Change*. London: Bloomsbury.
3. Park, Hong-Won (1998). A Gramscian Approach to Interpreting International Communication. *Journal of Communication, 48*(4), 79–99.
4. McPhail, Thomas L. (2005). *Global Communication: Theories, Stakeholders, and Trends*. New York: Wiley-Blackwell.
5. Nye, Joseph, S. (1974). Collective Economic Security. *International Affairs, 50*(4), 584–598.
6. Imre, Robert, Mooney, T. Brian, & Clarke, Benjamin (2008). *Responding to Terrorism*. Farnham, England: Ashgate.
7. Habermas, Jürgen (1979). *Communication and the Evolution of Society*. Boston: Beacon.
8. Mishal, Shaul, & Morag, Nadav (2002). Political Expectations and Cultural Perceptions in the Arab–Israeli Peace Negotiations. *Political Psychology, 23*(2), 325–353.
9. Cahn, Dudley D., & Abigail, Ruth Anna (2010). *Managing Conflict through Communication* (4th ed.). Boston: Pearson/Allyn & Bacon.
10. Pruitt, Dean G., & Kim, Sung Hee (2004). *Social Conflict: Escalation, Stalemate, and Settlement*. Boston: McGraw-Hill.
11. Budjac Corvette, Barbara A. (2006). *Conflict Management: A Practical Guide to Developing Negotiation Strategies*. New York: Prentice Hall.
12. Stern, Sheldon (2005). *The Week the World Stood Still: Inside the Secret Cuban Missile Crisis*. Palo Alto, CA: Stanford University Press.
13. Chase, Lawrence J., & Kneupper, Charles W. (1974). A Literary Analog to Conflict Theories: The Potential for Theory Construction. *Communication Monographs, 41*(1), 57–63.
14. Cahn, Dudley D., & Abigail, Ruth Anna (2010). *Managing Conflict through Communication* (4th ed.). Boston: Pearson/Allyn & Bacon.
15. Amara, Muhammad (2003). The Collective Identity of the Arabs in Israel in an Era of Peace. *Israel Affairs, 9*(1), 249–262.
16. Ross, Dennis (2004). *The Missing Peace: The Inside Story of the Fight for Middle East Peace*. New York: Farrar, Straus and Giroux.
17. Abrahms, Max (2005). Al Qaeda's Miscommunication War: The Terrorism Paradox. *Terrorism and Political Violence, 17*, 529–549.
18. Eisenberg, Laura Zittrain, & Caplan, Neil (2010). *Negotiating Arab-Israeli Peace: Patterns, Problems, Possibilities*. Bloomington: Indiana University Press
19. Spain PM Orders Iraq Troops Home (2004, April 18). BBC News. Retrieved June 3, 2011 from http://news.bbc.co.uk/2/hi/3637523.stm.
20. Schifrin, Nick, Afgha, Aleem, Ferran, Lee, & Gutman, Matt (2011, April 1). U.N. Staffers Killed in Afghanistan Over Terry Jones Koran Burning, Police Say. ABC News. Retreived June 3 from http://abcnews.go.com/Blotter/staffers-killed-terry-jones-stunt/story?id = 13275234.
21. Fisher, Ronald, & Keashly, Loraleigh (1991). The Potential Complementarity of Mediation and Consultation within a Contingency Model of Third Party Intervention. *Journal of Peace Research, 28*(1), 29–42.
22. Johnson, Ralph A. (1992). *Negotiation Basics: Concepts, Skills, and Exercises*. Thousand Oaks, CA: Sage.
23. Stein, Kenneth W. (1999). *Heroic Diplomacy: Sadat, Kissinger, Carter, Begin and the Quest for Arab-Israeli Peace*. New York: Routledge.
24. Noussia, Kyriaki (2010). *Confidentiality in International Commercial Arbitration: A Comparative Analysis of the Position under English, US, German and French Law*. New York: Springer.
25. Pruitt, Dean G., & Kim, Sung Hee (2004). *Social Conflict: Escalation, Stalemate, and Settlement*. Boston: McGraw-Hill.

26. Curran, Daniel F., & Sebenius, James K. (2003). The Mediator as Coalition-Builder: George Mitchell in Northern Ireland. *International Negotiation: A Journal of Theory and Practice, 8*(1), 111–147.

27. Bekoe, Dorina A. (2008). *Implementing Peace Agreements: Lessons from Mozambique, Angola, and Liberia.* New York: Palgrave-Macmillan.

28. Beardsley, Kyle (2009). Intervention without Leverage: Explaining the Prevalence of Weak Mediators. *International Interactions, 35*(3), 272–297.

29. Thompson, James (2007). Performance, Globalization and Conflict Promotion/Resolution: Experiences from Sri Lanka. In Helmut Anheier and Yudhishthir Raj Isar (Eds.), *Conflict and Tensions* (pp. 296–305). Thousand Oaks, CA: Sage.

30. Weick, Karl, & Sutcliffe, Kathleen (2001). *Managing the Unexpected: Assuring the High Performance in an Age of Complexity.* San Francisco: Jossey-Bass.

31. Goodall, Bud, Trethewey, Angela, & McDonald, Kelly (2006). *Strategic Ambiguity, Communication, and Public Diplomacy in an Uncertain World: Principles and Practices.* Tempe, AZ: Consortium for Strategic Communication.

32. Banks, Stephen P., Ge, Gao, & Baker, Joyce (1991). Intercultural Encounters and Miscommunication, In Nikolas Coupland, Howard Giles, & John M. Wiemann, (Eds.). *Miscommunication and Problem Talk* (pp. 103–120). London: Sage.

33. Triandis, Harry C. (2000). Culture and Conflict. *International Journal of Psychology, 35*(2), 145–162.

34. Barston, Ronald Peter (2006). *Modern Diplomacy.* Upper Saddle River, NJ: Pearson Education; Plischke, Elmer (1979). Diplomacy. In Elmer Plischke (Ed.), *Modern Diplomacy: The Art and the Artisans* (pp. 30–40). Washington, D.C.: American Enterprise Institute for Public Policy Research.

35. Kleiner, Juergen (2009). *Diplomatic Practice: Between Tradition and Innovation.* Hackensack, NJ: World Scientific Publishing Company.

36. Ure, John (1996). *Diplomatic Bag: An Anthology of Diplomatic Incidents and Anecdotes from the Renaissance to the Gulf War.* London: John Murray Publishers Ltd.

37. Weatherford, Jack (2005). *Genghis Khan and the Making of the Modern World.* New York: Broadway.

38. Zulaika, Joseba (2009). *Terrorism: The Self-Fulfilling Prophecy.* Chicago: University of Chicago Press.

39. Arrigo, Bruce A., & Williams, Christopher R. (2003). Victim Vices, Victim Voices, and Impact Statements: On the Place of Emotion and the Role of Restorative Justice in Capital Sentencing. *Crime and Delinquency, 49,* 603–626.

40. English, Fenwick, & Larson, Robert (1996). *Curriculum Management for Educational and Social Service Organizations.* Springfield, IL: Charles C. Thomas Publishers.

41. Eckhardt, William, & White, Ralph L. (1967). A Test of the Mirror-Image Hypothesis: Kennedy and Khrushchev. *The Journal of Conflict Resolution, 11*(3), 325–332; Kimmel, Paul R. (1994). Cultural Perspectives on International Negotiations. *Journal of Social Issues, 50*(1), 179–196.

42. Finn, Helena K. (2003). The Case for Cultural Diplomacy. *Foreign Affairs, 82*(6), 15–20.

43. Bercovitch, Jacob, & Jackson, Richard (1997). *International Conflict: A Chronological Encyclopedia of Conflicts and Their Management, 1945–1995.* Washington, D.C.: Congressional Quarterly; Crumm, Eileen M. (1995). The Value of Economic Incentives in International Politics. *Journal of Peace Research, 32*(3), 313–330; Dixon, William J. (1996). Third-Party Techniques for Preventing Conflict Escalation and Promoting Peaceful Settlement. *International Organization, 50*(4), 653–681; Frazier, Derrick, & Dixon, William (2006). Third-Party Intermediaries and Negotiated Settlements, 1946–2000. *International Interactions, 32*(4), 385–408; Jackson, Richard (2000). Successful Negotiation in International Violent Conflict. *Journal of Peace Research, 37*(3), 323–343; Regan, Patrick M., & Aydin, Aysegul (2006). Diplomacy and Other Forms of Intervention in Civil Wars. *Journal of Conflict Resolution, 50*(5), 736–756.

44. Böhmelt, Tobias (2010). The Effectiveness of Tracks of Diplomacy Strategies in Third-Party Interventions. *Journal of Peace Research, 47*(2), 167–178.

45. Dieter, Heribert, & Kumar, Rajiv (2008). The Downside of Celebrity Diplomacy: The Neglected Complexity of Development. *Global Governance, 14,* 259–264.

46. Cooper, Andrew F. (2008). *Celebrity Diplomacy.* London: Paradigm Publishers.

47. Eke, Chinedu (2008). Darfur: Coverage of a Genocide by Three Major US TV Networks on Their Evening News. *International Journal of Media & Cultural Politics, 4*(3), 277–292.

48. Chataway, Cynthia J. (1998). Track II Diplomacy: From a Track I Perspective. *Negotiation Journal, 14*(3), 269–287.

49. Diamond, Loise, & McDonald, John W. (1996) *Multitrack Diplomacy: A Systems Approach*. Sterling, VA: Kumarian.

50. Vorhees, James (2002). *Dialogue Sustained: The Multilevel Peace Process and the Dartmouth Conference*. Washington, D.C.: United States Institute of Peace.

51. Gillette, Philip S. (1981). Armand Hammer, Lenin, and the First American Concession in Soviet Russia. *Slavic Review, 40*(3), 355–365.

52. Wilner, Alex S., & Dubouloz, Claire-Jehanne (2010). Homegrown Terrorism and Transformative Learning: An Interdisciplinary Approach to Understanding Radicalization. *Global Change, Peace & Security, 22*(1), 33–51.

53. Jongman, Berto (2007). Terrorism and Diasporas in the Netherlands. In Bruce Hoffman (Ed.), *The Radicalization of Diasporas and Terrorism* (pp. 13–19). Santa Monica: RAND.

54. McDonald, John W. (1991). Further Exploration of Track Two Diplomacy. In Louis Kriesberg & Stuart J. Thorson (Eds.), *Timing the De-Escalation of International Conflicts* (pp. 201-220). Syracuse, NY: Syracuse University Press.

55. Mernissi, Fatema (2004). The Satellite, the Prince, and Scheherazade: The Rise of Women as Communicators in Digital Islam. *Transnational Broadcasting Studies, 12*, 10–21.

56. Rutenberg, Jim (2001, December 23). Ali Joins Hollywood's Corner to Explain War to Muslims. *The New York Times*, p. A1.

57. Sardar, Ziauddin (2001, October 22). Sultan of Spin—or of Truth. *New Statesman*.

58. Krugler, David F. (2000). *The Voice of America and the Domestic Propaganda Battles, 1945–1953*. Columbia: University of Missouri Press.

59. Hachten, William A., & Scotton, James F. (2002). *The World News Prism: Global Media in an Era of Terrorism* (6th ed.). Iowa City: Iowa State Press.

60. Curtis, Lisa (2007, April 26). *Efforts to Deal with America's Image Abroad: Are They Working?* Testimony before the House Committee on Foreign Affairs Subcommittee on International Organizations, Human Rights, and Oversight, Washington, D.C.

61. Mitchell, Don (1995). The End of Public Space? People's Park, Definitions of the Public, and Democracy. *Annals of the Association of American Geographers, 85*(1), 108–133.

62. Cottle, Simon (2006). Mediatizing the Global War on Terror: Television's Public Eye. Kavoori, Anandam P., & Todd Fraley (Eds.), *Media, Terrorism, and Theory* (pp. 19–48). New York: Rowman & Littlefield.

63. Bandow, Doug (2009, June 1). Obama's Interfaith Dialogue: Let's Talk Persecution. *Lebanon Daily Star*.

64. United Nations Year of Dialogue among Civilizations (2001). Retrieved June 4, 2011 from http://www.un.org/Dialogue/background.html.

65. Rusciano, Frank Louis (1998). *World Opinion and the Emerging International Order*. Westport, CT: Praeger.

66. Rusciano, Frank Louis (2003). Framing World Opinion in the Elite Press. In Pippa Norris, Montague Kern, & Marion Just (Eds.), *Framing Terrorism: The News Media, the Government, and the Public* (pp. 159–179). New York: Routledge.

67. Rusciano, Frank Louis (2001). World beyond Civilizations: New Directions for Research on World Opinion. *International Journal of Public Opinion Research, 13*(1), 10–24.

68. Bennett, William J. (2007). *America: The Last Best Hope (Volume I): From the Age of Discovery to a World at War*. Nashville: Thomas Nelson; Engel, Joel (2003, May 27). Too smart to be so dumb: The moral tyranny of IQ. *The Weekly Standard*; Nordlinger, Jay (2004, July 26). There he goes again. *National Review*; Zuckerman, Mortimer (2008, April 18). The Damage of Jimmy Carter: Carter's Hamas Meeting Legitimizes Terrorism. *U.S. News & World Report*.

69. Burnett, Victoria (2008, March 10). Zapatero: Spain's Bold Liberal. *The New York Times*, p. A2; Senior EU Official Holds Talks with Hezbollah (2009, June 15). *The Wall Street Journal*, p. A1.

70. Gaddafi welcomed by EU chief (2004, April 28). Daily Mail, p. A1.

71. Girard, René (2008). *Anorexie et Désir Mimétique*. Paris: L'Herne.

72. Gardham, Duncan (2007, September 6). Report: Libraries Stock Islamic Terror Books. *The Daily Telegraph*, p. A1.

73. Klein, Aaron (2007). *Schmoozing with Terrorists: From Hollywood to the Holy Land, Jihadists Reveal Their Global Plans—to a Jew!* Santa Monica: WND Books.

CHAPTER 16

Crisis Communication and Intelligence

After reading this chapter, you will be able to

- discuss how effective crisis communication can respond to terrorism;
- explain interorganizational communication (interorganizational networking communication linkages among actors in the system) through the use of technologies such as mobile phones; and
- describe intelligence and deceitful tactics such as misinformation, disinformation, and rumors.

CRISIS COMMUNICATION: GENERAL PERSPECTIVES

The anthrax attack in the weeks after 9/11 was possibly one of the most public and troublesome public health emergencies in modern U.S. history. Although there are much bigger and widespread health risks, such as the avian flu, SARS (sudden acute respiratory syndrome), the upsurge in skin cancer, and the West Nile virus occurrences, anthrax was new in regard to the perceived danger and the premeditated nature of the attack.[1] The anthrax attack, in and of itself, represented a crisis. A **crisis** is a major incidence with a potentially negative consequence impacting a country or organization. A crisis disrupts normal everyday transactions and can even jeopardize the existence of individuals.[2]

Crisis Management

Crisis management is a procedure of strategic planning for a crisis or serious predicament. It is a process that eliminates part of the risk and uncertainty from the negative event and thereby enables the country or organization to better control its own destiny.[3] According to Timothy Coombs (1999),[4] crisis management is a four-step process: prevention, preparation, response, and learning. *Prevention* includes approaches that are adopted to decrease risks and vulnerabilities to a crisis. *Preparation* involves forming a crisis management plan, establishing and training a crisis management team, and practicing the principles of that plan. For instance, after the 9/11 attacks, many local and state governments created crisis management plans to handle bioterrorist attacks. Rehearsing for those types of terrorist attacks can help alleviate the impact of an attack when it happens. *Response* implies the actual measures adopted when a crisis occurs. *Learning* involves reviewing the strengths and weaknesses of the crisis management plan to see how future plans can be enriched. For example, in the aftermath of 9/11, police and fire departments investigated the breakdown of two-way radio systems during the tragedy and have since made sure to improve these communication systems in the event of a similar crisis.

Crisis Communication: Definition

Crisis communication refers to the analysis and use of cleverly designed messages sent through selected sources (mediated and interpersonal) to transmit relevant information to intended audiences in crisis situations that have the following characteristics: (1) uncertainty, (2) strong emotion, (3) disparate audience, (4) time being "of the essence," and (5) rapid communication of tailored and effective strategic messages.[5] Crisis communication entails the dialogue between the state and its various audiences before, during, and after the crisis.[6]

Crisis communication also involves the sending and receiving of messages "to prevent or lessen the negative outcomes of a crisis and thereby protect the organization, stakeholders, and/or industry from damage" (Coombs, 1999, p. 4).[7] As such, it finds itself within the broader crisis management function. Crisis communication tries to describe the particular event, identify potential consequences and outcomes, and transmit specific harm-reducing messages to affected groups in a truthful, fair, quick, accurate, and complete manner.[8] Fearn-Banks (2002)[9] suggests that "crisis communication is verbal, visual, and/or written interaction between the organization and its stakeholders (often through the media) prior to, during and after a negative occurrence" (p. 480). These communication processes are meant to decrease and assuage harm, give precise information to stakeholders, initiate and improve recovery, control image and opinions of blame and responsibility, restore legitimacy, produce support and assistance, defend and validate actions, apologize, and encourage healing, learning, and change.[10]

Crisis Communication: Indicators

States and people employ three forms of indicators to evaluate the potential threat of terrorism. These can be described as general threat indicators, local threat indicators, and specific threat indicators. **General threat indicators** are used to conclude whether, within the country, there are conditions that might motivate or provoke terrorism. For example, politically, the existence of a disliked, authoritarian, or corrupt government is seen as a positive indicator of the likelihood of terrorism. **Local threat indicators** are used to measure more specific and localized risks of terrorism. The creation of radical groups;

accounts of stolen weapons, ammunition, and explosives; and hostility toward local property are reasonable local threat indicators. **Specific threat indicators** are used to assess the susceptibility or weakness of a particular target to terrorism.[11]

DIFFERENCES WITH RISK COMMUNICATION

Risk is described as the socially constructed perception of the likelihood that a negative event will occur. The interpretation of risk stems from the interface of many factors but can be more simply understood as the combination of control and dread. Control is the felt level of choice or predictability related to a risk.[12] With respect to terrorist attacks, risk consists of the projected number of lives lost, people injured, property damaged, and economic activity interrupted as a result of a terrorist attack. **Risk management** is the assessment of the importance of a particular risk and an evaluation of how significant the risk is. There are two factors to this: **risk assessment**, the measure of the risk from data to produce a risk probability, and **risk evaluation**, the perception that a society attributes to the risks that face them in agreeing on what steps to take about the risks.[13]

One of the main differences between crisis communication and risk communication has to do with their origins. Crisis communication is generally linked to public relations and is rooted in attempts to strategically control and frame public perceptions of a crisis so that harm is lessened for both the state and the people who are affected. **Risk communication**, in contrast, is usually associated with the detection of risks to public health and attempts to persuade the audience to assume healthier, less risky behaviors.[14] Accordingly, public campaigns on the dangers of cigarette smoking are the epitome of risk communication. This may also involve diffusing information about harm alleviation resources and procedures (e.g., trying an e-cigarette), and about the potential of additional harm (e.g., smoking and quitting exercising at the same time).[15]

In addition, risk communication includes the diffusion of information on environmental hazards such as chemical and toxic contaminates, carcinogens, pathogens, and similar hazards. This is a type of constant communication that stimulates lasting behavioral and environmental changes.[16] As Heath (1994)[17] suggests, "risk communication deals with risk elements, whether they are appropriately tolerable, and risk consequences" (p. 257). Covello (1992)[18] defines risk communication as "the exchange of information among interested parties about the nature, magnitude, significance, or control of a risk" (p. 359). The National Research Council (1989)[19] describes risk communication as "an interactive process of exchange of information and opinion among individuals, groups, and institutions" (p. 2). From this perspective, risk communication is highly correlated with the sensing and assessment of threats. Reynolds and Seeger (2005)[20] developed a model (Table 16.1) that compares features of crisis communication with those of risk communication:

In a similar fashion, fundamental tenets of effective communication have also added to the practice of risk communication. The public tends to simplify messages. Credibility matters significantly to the effectiveness of messages. Risk messages tend to include a certain level of self-efficacy action designed to decrease the risk. Messages are more

Table 16.1 Distinguishing Features of Risk and Crisis Communication

Risk communication	Crisis communication
Messages regarding known probabilities of negative consequences and how they may be reduced; addressing technical understandings (hazards) and cultural beliefs (outrage)	Messages regarding current state or conditions regarding a specific event; magnitude, immediacy duration and control/remediation; cause, blame, consequences
Principally persuasive, i.e., advertising and public education campaigns	Principally informative, i.e., news disseminated through media or broadcast through warning system
Frequent/routine	Infrequent/non-routine
Sender/message centered	Receiver/situation centered
Based on what is currently known, i.e., scientific projections	Based on what is known and what is not known
Long-term (pre-crisis) message preparation, i.e., campaign	Short-term (crisis) less preparation, i.e., responsive
Technical expert, scientist manager, technical experts	Authority figures/emergency
Personal scope	Personal, community, or regional scope
Mediated; commercials, ads brochures, pamphlets	Mediated; press conferences, press releases, speeches, websites
Controlled and structured	Spontaneous and reactive

Source: "Crisis and Emergency Risk Communication as an Integrative Model," by B. Reynolds & M. W. Seeger, 2005, *Journal of Health Communication*, *10*, p. 43–55. Copyright 2005 by Taylor & Francis.

persuasive when they are well tailored to audience needs, morals and principles, background, culture, and experience. Effective risk messages are clear and simple, speak to reason and emotion, and provide solutions to problems.[21]

TEN PRACTICES IN CRISIS COMMUNICATION

In a sense, crisis communication is a type of **social amplification**. Its objective is to observe signals that a terrorist attack is underway and to educate audiences about the potential risks by developing communication between society and the risks themselves.[22] A warning sign that a terrorist attack may happen is labeled a **prodrome**. Local media in the affected communities are often the first to inform government officials of the crisis (i.e., public-to-agency communication). They can also provide coverage of the event from the community ground level from its infant stages. First responders frequently fall back on media reports as these are perceived as the most reliable and direct information as to how a disaster is unfolding.[23] Looking at these facts, Seeger (2006)[24] described ten practices that function as basic standards for crisis communication. These standards offer guidelines that generate an efficient plan and response:

- Process methods and policy development: communication is an essential element of crisis communication and should be integrated into all points of the process. Crisis and risk communication need to develop a constant and cohesive process in place.

- Pre-event planning: having a plan ready is indispensable. A plan functions as a signal of potential problems and can be a guideline for people to follow in preventing and facing a crisis.

- Partnerships with the public: the public is a valid and equal associate that should be notified and educated during the course of the crisis. The public can also be a resource rather than an encumbrance if they are considered a partner.

- Attend to the public's concern and understand the audience: a state or organization must attend to the concerns of the public and take them into consideration.

- Honesty, truthfulness, and openness: these concepts are elements of a whole range of elements; honesty is the best policy and must be the yardstick of measure across all situations; truthfulness has to do with imparting the whole truth even when it may reflect negatively on the state or organization; and openness, by definition, is accessibility and closeness that transcends a simple response.

- Cooperate and make arrangements with credible sources: planners and communicators should constantly look for validation that permits their sources to communicate and cooperate successfully with all stakeholders. Making appropriate arrangements is crucial and should not fail during a crisis.

- Match the needs of the media and stay accessible: involve the media with open and truthful communication. Efficient use of the media is vital in reaching the general public.

- Communicate with compassion, concern, and responsiveness: compassion, concern, and responsiveness will improve message credibility and apparent legitimacy of the messenger prior to and after the crisis.

- Accept uncertainty and ambiguity: in all cases, there is some degree of uncertainty; hence, it is imperative to recalibrate messages as additional information is learned.

- Messages of self-efficacy: inform audiences what steps they can take to reduce harm. These messages will help alleviate part of the uncertainty in a crisis.

People who are directly involved (e.g., first-responders, etc.), who have an interest in crisis communication, or who can be affected by a crisis should take these ten principles seriously. A key objective of this list is to reach **containment**, the effort to restrict the duration of a crisis or to prevent it from proliferating to other regions affecting the nation.[25]

An institution that tends to promote these ten practices is the **Consortium for Strategic Communication (CSC)**, a think-tank at Arizona State University. Its objective is to put communication research into practice in the fight against terrorism, to support national security, and to promote public diplomacy worldwide.

IMPROVING TERRORISM PREPAREDNESS: INTERORGANIZATIONAL COMMUNICATION

In his article titled "Improving Terrorism Preparedness for Hospitals: Towards Better Interorganizational Communication," Jonathan Matusitz (2007)[26] offers insights on the principal remedy for improving terrorism preparedness for hospitals: enhanced interorganizational communication between hospitals and other agencies. **Interorganizational communication** refers to interorganizational networking and communication linkages within a system. Such linkages among actors in the system are essential to accomplish legitimate, productive, and powerful emergency response planning objectives, to identify shrewd terrorist activities (e.g., an often-ignored anthrax case), to smooth the progress of the treatment of mass casualties, and so forth. In this manner, cooperative decision making and joint program implementation will yield better results, unlike solutions coming from individual or independent actions.[27] To date, such form of strategic communication planning has been a neglected area in counterterrorism, especially in matters such as interruption of terrorist communication.[28] For instance, many hospitals in the U.S. are still inadequately prepared should a major terrorist attack occur.

Five Reasons Why Hospitals Are Not Prepared

Encounters with devastating terrorist attacks have generated five reasons that shed light on this lack of preparedness. First, hospitals have taken a long time to participate in joint planning efforts. This lack of endeavor is attributable to hospitals operating individually and not trying to interorganizationally communicate their planning intents.[29] Second, trained staff is lacking too. Hospitals have fewer members in their workforce and, with a decrease in the ratio of qualified healthcare employees to patients, personal workload is rising. This is especially true in the greater patient–nurse ratios that have burgeoned since the early 2000s. Consequently, it is common to see many hospitals that cannot keep their doors open. The day-to-day workload stress leads to an upsurge in personnel turnover that, in turn, leads to a reduction in level of experience of hospital staff. Now, envision a state of affairs in which terrorists strike a region with many medical facilities shut down: the gargantuan burden would fall on those healthcare centers that remain—those that are meant to serve a larger community.[30]

Third, disaster planning does not work as it was initially planned. The explanation is that hospital staffs (i.e., nurses) are often unaware of their clinics' emergency preparedness processes. Whereas emergency medical response personnel often engage in training drills with firefighters and police (i.e., to prepare for terrorist attacks), hospitals rarely ask their staff to take part in such exercises.[31] Fourth, the healthcare system on the whole is in financial shambles. This unavoidably impacts preparedness for mass casualty incidents. For example, many hospitals have only a low amount of on-site storage of sterile resources, vital equipment, and pharmaceuticals to meet instant requirements. Some inadequately funded hospitals may even be unwilling to offer costly disaster preparedness training if it unsettles their financial needs.[32] Fifth, the perception of urgency of preparedness seems to have declined in some hospitals. This is largely caused by the assumption that a terrorist attack is not likely to occur. Furthermore, regional hospitals might have different views on terrorism and disaster than urban hospitals do. As such, they have fewer rigorous training requirements and fewer incentives in that domain.[33]

Interorganizational Communication as the Main Remedy

The main remedy for enhancing preparedness in hospitals is to concentrate on one particular aspect of interorganizational collaboration: interorganizational communication, such as communication between hospitals and other organizations. Which organizations should be involved? Major hospitals, local health centers, smaller public health agencies, pharmacies, clinicians, off-site healthcare shelters, secondary assessment centers, local private physicians, mental health professionals, emergency response units, poison control centers, decontamination facilities, hazardous materials teams, fire departments, police departments, federal law enforcement agencies (e.g., FBI and CIA), counterterrorism agents, schools, nonprofit organizations (e.g., International Red Cross, Habitat for Humanity, Boy Scouts and Girl Scouts of America), industries, professional societies, 911 centers, public officials, media, and general public.[34]

Interorganizational communication is tantamount to interorganizational networking, communication linkages in interorganizational systems, operational interorganizational teamwork, manifold communication channels, and the bridging of the interorganizational communication disparities between hospitals and other agencies. All things considered, interorganizational communication is synergy. **Synergy** (from the Greek *syn-ergos*, meaning "working together") is the phenomenon in which two or more individual agents join forces to produce an effect bigger than they would if they acted separately. It is a mutually beneficial unification in which the whole is greater than the sum of the parts.[35] The idea that the whole is greater than the sum of the parts is the key principle of **systems theory**. Interorganizational communication can be the by-product of a giant system. All units or parts within the system are correlated and influence each other to make the whole system function properly. A system is the sum of all its parts coupled with the effects of interdependency among those parts. Thus, a system is greater than just the sum of its parts. The whole affects the nature of the parts; the parts cannot be separated from the whole.[36]

From this vantage point, synergy is interdependence. **Interdependence** is the notion that actors in the system organize their efforts to achieve their task together. When an incident happens to, or affects, one agent in the system, it will have an effect on the rest of the members in the system. Synergy leads to improved decision making and collaboration that, in turn, yields better results, which is set against solutions stemming from an individual agent or independent actions. The synergy-based outcomes, then, can contribute to enhanced community development and fortify the public health system overall.[37]

It is plain to see that interorganizational communication can improve both collaboration and communication between various organizations. Such crisis communication also integrates the interoperability of electronic devices, such as hand-held data devices, mobile phones, and satellite telephone networks. When it comes down to it, communication certainly increases the capacity to construct shared meanings among people, organizations, and groups.[38] As will be explained in the next section, one method to safeguard quick and effective communication among key organizations is the use of electronic communications devices, like cell phones, wireless networks, and the Internet. They bypass methods that are more vulnerable to terrorist attacks and natural disasters. The Internet is a helpful tool for interactive communication when there is a crisis created by, say, a bioterrorist attack. Because hospitals increasingly rely on the Internet and computer-based technologies to function, emergency communication system providers have set up massive hospital-to-hospital communication channels via the Internet. Telephone and radio systems are gradually becoming outdated.[39]

CRISIS RESPONSE THROUGH THE WEB

Use of online communications throughout a crisis carries considerable importance to the examination of crisis communication. The Internet has become a pivotal communication device during a crisis. By offering an immediate channel of response, the web facilitates communication to the public and the media. In organizations, disaster plans must deliver information and assistance to employees, particularly those who are unable to receive messages via traditional communication channels. Indeed, since the September 11, 2001 attacks, both states and organizations have relied on diverse types of online communications to diffuse information to their diverse audiences.[40]

The websites of United Airlines and American Airlines, which usually displayed information such as flights, ticket purchases, and corporate data, were turned (after the attacks) into a resource center for various publics. These ranged from the press to family members of victims. Possibly the biggest task was to satisfy the information needs of all those publics simultaneously. In the wake of the crisis, the web allowed both United Airlines and American Airlines to provide an instant response to terrorist attacks, to give regular updates about the flights, and to share their crisis process to an assortment of publics at the same time.[41]

The conventional media sources (e.g., television, radio, and print media) have been replaced by the web. It is the web which must now be exploited to produce mass awareness of crisis response. On examining emergency communication during the World Trade Center catastrophe, Libenau (2003)[42] came across the fact that firefighters' radios were not coordinated with police, other clusters of firefighters, or other emergency services. Therefore, the failing radios were limiting the amount of synchronization across agencies. Since the September 11, 2001 attacks, the topic of interoperability has been the emphasis of governmental organization endeavors and research. Technologies such as mobile phones, computer database systems, and geographic information systems (GIS) are used more and more. They can help transmit information between organizations during a crisis; yet, they will only work well if the equipment and operating procedures match. Such information sharing is called **interoperability**.

The often-ignored communication dynamic between first responders (at all organizational levels) and first communicators of the media and audiences (often represented by citizen journalists) is important for understanding and handling response effectiveness. **Citizen journalists** are mainstream citizens who use innovative mobile digital technology to give journalistic accounts of events—usually to the mass media but sometimes directly to online social networks such as Facebook, Flickr, and Twitter. This practice occurs increasingly; citizens are now active participants in the crisis communication process. On the other hand, **participatory journalists** are independent journalists who report both in mainstream media and in Internet-based outlets (public-to-public communication).[43]

CRISIS RESPONSE AS RESTORATIVE RHETORIC

In their article titled "The Rhetoric of Atonement," Koesten and Rowland (2004)[44] argued that crisis response can be examined based on the framework of restorative rhetoric. **Restorative rhetoric** is rhetoric focused on helping those affected by a crisis handle loss. In this case, the rhetor is not directly defending him- or herself. Rather, the rhetor functions as a facilitator and sense-maker. His or her task is not just to manage the crisis; it is also to handle the recovery process from disaster to restoration. According to Rowland (1991),[45] three significant factors to the development of a genre exist. First, there must be a perceived need. For example, in the days following September 11, 2001, local communities that were affected, and even the country overall, needed to listen to leaders to make sense of the crisis. Second, there must be a purpose. The chief purposes of restorative rhetoric are to restore faith in a fundamental group of values and beliefs; facilitate healing for people directly hurt by the crisis and broader audiences that witnessed the destruction; generate a feeling of security throughout the resolution of the crisis; and to prepare a vision for the future. Third, a genre has societal limitations in terms of what is an adequate response. With respect to 9/11, it was crucial for Mayor Rudy Giuliani to be truthful with the people and not to be condescending to them. He felt obligated to create a balance between controlling high levels of anxiety caused by the terrorist attack and fashioning a perception of hope that the tragedy would ultimately be closured.[46]

Restorative rhetoric moves post-crisis communication from decreasing the offensiveness of the event, and upholding a positive image, to enabling dialogue between audiences and crisis leaders, and assisting victims and the general public in making sense of the crisis. Restorative rhetoric includes a more generative and natural dialogue that is formed not only as a reaction to the crisis itself, but also by the contextual and social components that structure the crisis and affect response to it.[47] Two important characteristics inspire restorative rhetoric: (1) although there are usually recognizable victims of terrorist attacks, there is a broader audience that is also devastated and, consequently, must be considered in the response dialogue; and (2) crisis sense-making is an active, transactive course of events; it is neither linear nor unidirectional.[48]

Restorative rhetoric adheres to five stages: (1) initial reaction, (2) assessment of the crisis, (3) issues of blame, (4) healing and forgiveness, and (5) corrective action and rebuilding through rhetorical vision.[49] These five stages can be applied to Mayor Rudy Giuliani's handling of 9/11. For the most part, Mayor Giuliani's initial reaction was calm and collected. He voiced grief-stricken emotions about the loss of human life, but his composure, equanimity, and demeanor did not waver or falter—at any time before the cameras. Later on that tragic day, in his early assessment of the crisis, Mayor Giuliani organized a press conference in which he did not speculate about the number of dead people. Rather, he remarked that the number was "more than any of us can bear."[50] In the handful of public comments that Mayor Giuliani uttered in that afternoon, he plainly rose as a leader—even a rhetorical hero—by showing an understanding of his audience's desolation and fear.[51]

On issuing blame, Mayor Giuliani called the terrorists cowards. Nevertheless, Giuliani refused to make far-reaching indictments. His main focus of blame was on the very hijackers who flew the planes and were directly involved in the terrorist attacks.[52] Giuliani often used *we* to confirm his unity and solidarity with the residents of New York City, thereby developing a shared sense of identity and acting as an inspirational person in the handling of the crisis. Mayor Giuliani had evolved from his initial reactions—where he merely provided facts and figures on what had just happened and what actions to take—to assuming his new role. It was now the role of encouraging and accepting his responsibility as the restorer. Put another way, the mayor dedicated the majority of his time—days, weeks, and even months after the tragedy—using the last two stages of restorative rhetoric: healing and forgiveness, and corrective action and rebuilding through rhetorical vision. On top of attending or holding events that gathered a national audience, Giuliani also delivered speeches at innumerable funerals of firefighters and police officers. Evidently, one of Giuliani's principal strategies in his attempt to foster healing was the use of spiritual language. He regularly made references to God, faith, and prayer.[53]

COUNTERTERRORISM VS. ANTITERRORISM

International terrorism became a federal crime in America in 1984 after a huge bomb destroyed U.S. Marine barracks in Lebanon, killing 220 Marines and 21 Navy medical personnel. The law became the Act to Combat International Terrorism. Laws against domestic terrorism were implemented in 1996, after the Oklahoma City bombing. It led to the Antiterrorism and Effective Death Penalty Act of 1996. The attacks against the World Trade Center and Pentagon on September 11, 2001 gave rise to the enactment of the USA Patriot Act on October 26, 2001. These three laws—(1) the 1984 Act to Combat International Terrorism, (2) the Antiterrorism and Effective Death Penalty Act of 1996, and (3) the USA Patriot Act—are the principal laws criminalizing terrorism.[54] On September 20, 2001, nine days after the 9/11 terrorist attacks, President George W. Bush announced in his State of the Union Address that he intended to start the Global War on Terror (GWOT). He stated, "Our War on Terror begins with Al Qaeda, but it does not end there. It will not end until every terrorist group of global reach has been found, stopped, and defeated."

Based on these measures, it would be interesting to compare counterterrorism with antiterrorism. **Counterterrorism** refers to offensive strategies designed to stop an enemy, in a broader conflict, from successfully employing the method of terrorism. According to the U.S. Department of Defense (2007),[55] of which the definition matches the definitions used by NATO and other military agencies, counterterrorism refers to "operations that include the offensive measures taken to prevent, deter, preempt, and respond to terrorism" (p. 1). Put simply, counterterrorism uses a series of techniques to deny an enemy the use of terrorism-based strategies, just as counter-air relies on a series of techniques to prevent the enemy from using attack aircraft.[56]

Six major components of a "group dynamics" perspective intended to counter terrorism are to (1) prevent would-be terrorists from joining terrorist groups, (2) create disagreement within the groups, (3) enable exit from the groups, (4) decrease support for the groups, (5) make their leaders less legitimate, and (6) protect the target audience from the objectives of the terrorist group.[57] Conversely, antiterrorism has a different meaning. According to the same U.S. Department of Defense, **antiterrorism** is defensive. It seeks to decrease the probability of an attack that employs terrorist methods at specific points, and to diminish the vulnerability of potential targets to such methods. Specifically, antiterrorism refers to "defensive measures used to reduce the vulnerability of individuals and property to terrorist acts, to include limited response and containment by local military and civilian forces" (p. 2).

INTELLIGENCE: KNOW THY ENEMY

Sun Tzu, an Ancient Chinese philosopher and military strategist, said "Know thy enemy." No one can defeat an enemy without knowing how enemies operate and why they do so (i.e., "If you only know yourself, but not your opponent, you may win or may lose"). Today, the tactics and information gathered to know our enemies are called *intelligence*.

Definition

Intelligence is the collection of data to create an information database about terrorist actions and to make predictions about their behavior. In the U.S., the Federal Bureau of Investigation (FBI) enacts domestic intelligence collection, and the Central Intelligence Agency (CIA) operates outside of the country. The National Security Agency (NSA) is the technological body of U.S. intelligence. In Great Britain, MI5 handles domestic intelligence while MI6 takes care of international collection.[58] In the U.S., law enforcement agencies tend to follow a four-step process: basic information (analysts begin work after receiving an in-depth, multi-disciplinary training); applied information (analysts collect information about a particular problem); real-time information (analysts obtain actual information as it is forwarded from various sources); and analyzed information (analysts create intelligence on the basis of analyzed information).[59]

An example of U.S. intelligence is the **Communication Management Unit**. It is a recent label for an independent group within a unit in the U.S. Federal Bureau of Prisons that harshly limits, manages, and observes all outside communication (telephone, mail, or visitation) of inmates in the unit. Included in the Bush administration's GWOT, the April 3, 2006 Federal Register recommended rules by the Federal Bureau of Prisons (FBOP) that "limited communication for terrorist inmates."[60] **Human intelligence** (known as **HUMINT**) is a collaborative undertaking with open intelligence agencies and law enforcement officials. Situations may also necessitate the covert manipulation of people associated with terrorist organizations or their support base. The objective is to persuade them to become intelligent agents. The manipulation process can involve invoking prospective spies' sense of justice or patriotism, giving them money and other "treasures," and providing them with something that they could not obtain in any other way (e.g., asylum for their relatives in a Western nation).[61]

Signal Intelligence

Signal intelligence (known as **SIGINT**) refers to the use of state-of-the-art resources to intercept financial data, monitor communications (e.g., conversations via cell phones), and read e-mail content. Satellite imagery is also frequently used by intelligence agencies, and leading-edge computers specialize in code breaking.[62] Below is a list of examples of SIGINT, based on various sources:[63]

- Carnivore: a surveillance system that can watch and examine Internet communications. By early 2001, Carnivore was re-dubbed DCS-1000. The system is capable of reading Internet traffic that moves through collaborating Internet service providers.

- Echelon: a satellite surveillance network and a universal "wiretap" that filters through communications. Echelon uses antennae, satellites, and similar technologies. Internet transfers, phone conversations, and data transmissions are examples of communications that can allegedly be intercepted.

- Dark Web Project: a group of computational experts using advanced technology and groundbreaking approaches to track terrorism on the web. The Dark Web Project systematically collects and examines all terrorist-generated content on the Internet. This is a colossal task as there are over 5,000 websites launched and maintained by terrorist groups. The vast majority of these sites are in foreign languages.

- Web spidering: a method to search discussion threads and other content to identify the "dark corners" of the web where terrorist attacks are being planned.

- Writeprint: a method to automatically extract thousands of multilingual, structural, and semantic characteristics to identify who is generating anonymous content online (relating to terrorism). Using Writeprint, online bulletin board postings can be analyzed and compared with writings found in other places on the Internet.

Computers and the Internet, it seems, can be useful tools for investigating terrorism. The Internet, in particular, and the skills of intelligence officials to "bug" or "snoop on" e-mail and phone calls, became leading tools in the attempt to locate the architects behind the September 11, 2001 attacks.

INFORMATION ENVIRONMENT: MISINFORMATION, DISINFORMATION, AND RUMORS

To be successful, U.S. forces need to obtain and maintain information superiority. **Information** is a strategic resource that is essential to national security. Military maneuvers are determined by information and information systems for multiple concurrent and integrated activities. The **information environment** is the collection of people, organizations, and systems that gather, process, diffuse, or take actions based on information.[64] Of course, not all content in the information environment is accurate. Two major problems are misinformation and disinformation.

Misinformation is inaccurate information that is disseminated unintentionally. It is differentiated from disinformation by motive; misinformation is purely erroneous. Among the obstacles encountered in educating audiences, the main obstacle is dissipating facts and things that everyone thought was correct. Also designated as *urban legends*, misinformation embodies a fundamental problem that must be tackled before our communities can be effectively educated and prepared.[65] Once it is encoded, misinformation may keep influencing the reasoning process, even if people later find out that the information is incorrect. The constant dependence on such misinformation, even when individuals can remember a correction or retraction, has been referred to as the **continued influence effect**.[66]

Disinformation

Conversely, **disinformation** is deliberately inaccurate information, including the spread of fabricated intelligence. Disinformation is the intentional dissemination of false information to mislead a group as to one's position or maneuver. For instance, information can be issued to create discord and distrust or to otherwise influence the group's behavior. It can also be used to diffuse harmful propaganda about terrorist groups and their leaders—under these circumstances, it would be called *black propaganda* (see Chapter 8).[67] Jihadist media strategy is highly advanced in that it seemingly uses disinformation too. This mainly consists of spreading rumors that portray the apostates, Jews, and infidels in a negative light. Even though jihadist messages fall somewhere on a continuum between fantastic and irrational to the Western public, the disinformation is tailored to appeal to the prejudices of the jihadists' followers, making them more open to arguments on legitimation and propagation.[68]

As Winston Churchill once said, "In wartime, truth is so precious that she should always be attended by a bodyguard of lies." The jihadists and other terrorists have used the tactic of disinformation for a long time. In the early 1980s, a rumor diffused from Morocco to Indonesia that Neil Armstrong heard the Islamic call to prayer when he was on the moon and converted to Islam. Yet, he told nobody out of fear that he would lose his job. In regard to terrorism and U.S. actions, examples of disinformation, from various sources,[69] include the following:

- The U.S. Marine Corps grilled or roasted Somali babies.
- The South Asian tsunami in Indonesia was caused by a nuclear bomb detonated by the U.S. Navy.

- On September 11, 2001, both the CIA and the **Mossad** (the Israeli secret service) warned 4,000 Jews that they should not show up at work in the Twin Towers of the World Trade Center.

- Wealthy Jews (e.g., Jewish bankers) caused 9/11 to happen because they intend to dominate the world by dividing existing political parties and nations, triggering unnecessary global conflicts (remember what Mel Gibson said!) and, thereby, giving Jews greater power and control in the world.

- A jihadist warned his non-Muslim girlfriend to be at another location than the World Trade Center on September 11, 2001.

- Arabic cab drivers vanished from the streets of lower Manhattan on September 11, 2001.

- President George W. Bush, at the very least, had some knowledge about the plan to attack the U.S.

- President George W. Bush did not take all necessary actions against Osama bin Laden because the Al Qaeda leader came from a wealthy Saudi family with ties to the Bushes.

- Osama bin Laden was not involved in 9/11 or was on the payroll throughout the whole story.

- The Twin Towers collapsed not because of the aircrafts that hit them but because of bombs placed at their base.

- United 93 did not hit the ground in Pennsylvania but was shot down.

- The Pentagon was not hit by an airliner but by missiles.

- Not a single steel-framed building before or after 9/11 has ever fallen down as a result of fire.

- No official agency has ever issued a list of the 9/11 passengers. However, a few hours after the tragedy, the FBI published a list of the nineteen hijackers.

- Arab-American teenagers celebrated the collapse of the World Trade Center in front of a library in South Paterson, New Jersey (a town that is largely Arab).

- Coca-Cola, perfume, sponges, and diapers were contaminated by anthrax.

This type of disinformation fulfills the legitimation dream of disinformers by positioning the West (and the U.S. in particular) as double-dealing and evil, as a power that Muslims must resist. Every occasion to disrepute U.S. accounts of events is taken to cast doubts about America's motives, just as every physical attack on a Muslim in the U.S. or Europe is perceived as further proof that the U.S. despises Islam. The truth, for instance, is that many Jews were killed in the World Trade Center on 9/11. Then, why would Jews seek to dominate the world by killing others of their kind? Yet, disinformation has the bonus of being very difficult to disprove. It has the power of making sense of an enormous crisis like 9/11. People felt that they were faced with strong and mysterious thoughts: hateful Arabs, evil elites, conniving Jews, Israeli agents, the U.S. military with ulterior motives, and double-dealing U.S. politicians. Those who believe in LIHOP (Let It Happen on Purpose) or MIHOP (Made It Happen on Purpose) have an advantage: if all this disinformation successfully infects minds and diffuses widely enough, it will push officials to take defensive responses (as it was the case with the WTC/Jews rumor). In turn, these responses can be hijacked by the jihadists as even further proof of Western treachery.[70]

It is important to note that disinformation can also be committed by the U.S. military. For example, in military jargon, **Information Operations** (IO) centers on human-related properties of information use. IO collects information functions that include the military spokespersons corps, called *public affairs*, *electronic warfare*, *computer network operations*, *military deception*, and *psychological operations*. What this means is that individuals whose traditional task has been to inform the media and disclose truthfully what they can tell now work very closely with those whose task it is to reinforce battlefield missions with information (some of which may be inaccurate). Taken as a whole, the objective of IO is to affect, interrupt, corrupt, or appropriate human and automated decision-making from the enemy while safeguarding the U.S. military's own.[71]

Rumors

Rumors are often discussed with respect to both misinformation and disinformation. By and large, a **rumor** is an unconfirmed account or explanation of events that diffuses from individual to individual. It usually pertains to an object, event, or issue of public interest.[72] In his article titled "A Psychology of Rumor," Robert Knapp (1944)[73] stated that negative rumors are more likely to be spread than positive ones. It is particularly in times of crisis that rumors tend to proliferate. Understanding the power of the informal rumor channel as a goldmine of information dissemination, and recognizing that more conventional channels may be discredited in crisis, humans will naturally spread false rumors to the loss of true information.

Within a few hours after the Oklahoma City bombing in 1995, a rumor was spread uncontrollably: the bombers were Arabs or Muslims. No facts existed, but the claim made powerful sense. The terrorist act fit a **template**, a category of belief explanations. The analysis of rumors increased our understanding that thinking is permanently socially influenced, a crucial claim of what is called **cognitive sociology**. What humans think is neither universal nor particular. Rather, it is linked to what other humans in their community think. They think in harmony with what they have been taught by those around them. By the same token, thought works through **social mnemonics**, methods by which people recall what their group considers to be important.[74]

As such, when we take rumors into account, we unconsciously rely on our sense of how the world functions and use the templates with which we feel comfortable. The objective, of course, is to decide that one rumor is plausible while another is not likely, even if factual sources of both are equally questionable. Rumors in the aftereffects of disasters usually follow a pattern: crisis management, blame, and conspiracy. The reason is that people are confused, even scared; they ask others what new things they have learned, compare notes, and feel ready to do something. This is the process of **improvised news**.[75] Individuals have to get through the day, demanding to know what threats are hovering around and how they should respond to the crisis. So, as soon as the World Trade Center collapsed, rumors spread about arsons in the Washington Mall, attacks on the White House, and plots in other U.S. metropolitan areas.[76]

The main by-product of rumors is conspiracy theory. A **conspiracy theory** is a story that explains a historical or current event by combining plausible elements. It relies on **cultural grammar**, a nexus of beliefs, not all of which are backed by any conclusive evidence. Put simply, a conspiracy theory is a quasi-theory or fringe theory. Its power is to associate rumors with documented, official evidence. The evidence provides a foundation for belief in other claims that have not been verified. The objective is to create **motive talk**—to give people the motivation to make their own assessment of a situation. Now, people have a valid reason to believe in all those conspiracies.[77] Nevertheless, since the 1950s, the U.S. has established **rumor control centers** to help diffuse accurate information (hoping, of course, that there is true information out there) during crises, terrorist attacks, or natural disasters. For instance, the Department of Homeland Security in Iowa has public emergency information dissemination programs that use rumor control centers.[78]

FUSION CENTERS

A **fusion center** is a terrorism prevention and response center. Between 2003 and 2007, many fusion centers were the products of collaboration between the Department of Homeland Security and the U.S. Department of Justice's Office of Justice Programs. Fusion centers collect information from both government sources and their associates in the private sector. They are designed to store all intelligence in a single center, fusing various agencies in a single unit to investigate all sorts of threats. Thus, a fusion center combines information—earning the label *fusion*—into a single method of data analysis. A standard fusion center may employ experts and agents from multiple law enforcement and intelligence agencies, military personnel, and local police officers and criminal specialists.[79] In the summer of 2009, the Department of Homeland Security (DHS) reported that there were already over seventy-two fusion centers in the U.S. For example, the Florida Fusion Center is located in Tallahassee, the state capital. It is Florida's chief fusion center that collects, processes, examines, and spreads information on terrorism, law enforcement, and homeland security.[80]

Every person working in a fusion center gathers and forwards information, and transforms it into actionable intelligence. **Actionable intelligence** is information that law enforcement agencies, military corps, or other security units can use to stop an attack or operation. This information is redirected to the NCTC (National Counterterrorism Center) where it is compared with information from other sources in the counterterrorism network. Then, this freshly created actionable intelligence is sent back to the fusion centers as an intelligence product. An **intelligence product** is any result or output of examined information that can be used by law enforcement agencies, military corps, or other security units to take actions immediately.[81]

Actionable intelligence is also created to detect pre-incident indicators and predictive profiling. Pre-incident indicators are the criminal and social actions of people and groups prior to a terrorist attack. **Predictive profiling** is a procedure of threat assessment that predicts and classifies the ability of criminal and/or terrorist modus operandi (i.e., methods of operation). Predictive profiling is done on the basis of observed behavior, information, situations, and/or objects. It is to be distinguished from racial profiling in that the latter uses race and ethnicity as the only criteria against which to assess potential threats.[82]

COLOR-CODED TERRORISM

Color-coded terrorism refers to the degree of severity of terrorism as indicated by an alert warning system. The term comes from color-coding, a practice of presenting information by using different colors. In the U.S., the **Homeland Security Advisory System** is a threat advisory scale using color-coded terrorism. The different colors prompt specific actions by federal, state, and local agencies, and they influence the degree of security at specific airports and other public facilities. The media often call it the terror alert level.[83] The system was established by Homeland Security Presidential Directive 3 on March 11, 2002. It was divulged to the public the next day, on March 12, 2002, by Tom Ridge, then the Assistant to the President for Homeland Security. It was designed to offer a comprehensive and effective method for spreading information about the risk of terrorist attacks to federal, state, and local authorities and to people living in America.[84]

The system ended in April 2011 and was supplanted with a new system called the **National Terrorism Advisory System**, a two-level terrorism threat advisory scale of the U.S. Department of Homeland Security (DHS). Based on this new system, alerts are sent under the category of "elevated" or "imminent" and tell what actions Americans should take. The Homeland Security Advisory System was considered a failure as it established no real efficient value in its nine years of existence and unnecessarily loaded Americans with fear.[85] It was even the object of jokes in late-night shows in the U.S. According to the **Homeland Security Advisory System Scale**, this is what color-coded terrorism used to be:

- Severe was red and meant severe risk.
- High was orange and meant high risk.
- Elevated was yellow and meant significant risk.
- Guarded was blue and meant general risk.
- Low was green and meant low risk.

In February 2003, before Operation Iraqi Freedom began, DHS increased the official national terrorism alert to the orange (high-risk) level, citing "recent intelligence reports." DHS made it clear that Americans should be ready for another terrorist attack. To prepare for this, Americans had to make a household disaster supply kit that contained duct tape and plastic sheeting. These were to seal a room against radiological, chemical, or biological chemicals.[86] DHS underscored that its new security preparedness tactics would heighten Americans' sense of security by teaching them how to keep themselves safer. It was akin to the 1960s elementary schoolchildren being asked to cover from an atomic blast by hiding underneath the fragile protection of their desks. The media expressed the concern that, even if Americans survived an initial attack, no practical local or national policy existed for faring well during the following days and weeks.[87]

The alert level was increased again in 2004, the presidential election year, leading some critics to wonder if the Bush administration had not used them for political purposes—rather than security reasons.[88] In his book titled *The Test of Our Times: America*

Under Siege... and How We Can Be Safe Again, Tom Ridge (2009),[89] with Larry Bloom, claimed that high-profile aides to President George W. Bush, including Donald Rumsfeld (the U.S. secretary of defense) and John Ashcroft (the U.S. attorney general), put pressure on Ridge to increase the alert level right before the November 2004 presidential election. Ridge rejected the recommendation.

SUMMARY

Crisis communication is the analysis and use of well-designed messages sent through various channels to transmit relevant information to intended audiences in crisis situations. Crisis communication is to be differentiated from risk communication. The latter refers to the detection of risks to the public health and attempts to persuade the audience to assume healthier, less risky behaviors. Table 16.1 was able to distinguish features of risk and crisis communication. Matthew Seeger (2006) provided ten practices that function as basic standards for crisis communication (e.g., partnerships with the public, acceptance of uncertainty and ambiguity, etc.). In a similar vein, the importance of improving terrorism preparedness for hospitals cannot be underestimated, especially if the method is interorganizational communication (interorganizational networking communication linkages among actors in the system). The actors are hospitals, private institutions, federal agencies, and so forth. Interorganizational communication works because it is, in essence, synergy and interdependence between key agencies. Crisis response through the web has also been shown to be effective, as the web facilitates communication to the public and the media. Technologies such as mobile phones can also help a great deal. At the semantic or philosophical level, an approach to crisis response is restorative rhetoric, which is rhetoric focused on helping those affected by a crisis cope with loss. Restorative rhetoric, exemplified by Mayor Rudy Giuliani's handling of 9/11, moves post-crisis communication from decreasing the offensiveness of the event, and upholding a positive image, to enabling dialogue between audiences and crisis leaders. The second section of the chapter dealt with intelligence, the collection of data to create an information database about terrorist actions. When it is a collaborative undertaking with open intelligence agencies and law enforcement officials, it is called human intelligence (HUMINT). When it is the use of state-of-the-art resources to intercept financial data or monitor communications, it is called signal intelligence (SIGINT). Intelligence may be thwarted by both misinformation (inaccurate information that is disseminated unintentionally) and disinformation (deliberately inaccurate information, including the spread of fabricated intelligence). In relation to both misinformation and disinformation, rumors play a big role in misleading the public. Humans naturally spread false rumors to the loss of true information. As we have seen, countless rumors emerged when the World Trade Center was hit by airplanes. A valuable tool of intelligence gathering is the fusion center, a terrorism prevention and response center that stores all intelligence in a single center, fusing various agencies in a single unit to investigate all sorts of threats. Lastly, color-coded terrorism, as epitomized by the Homeland Security Advisory System, is an alert warning system that has several degrees of terrorist threats. It has been replaced by a two-level terrorism threat advisory scale.

KEY TERMS

actionable intelligence   420

antiterrorism   415

citizen vs. participatory journalists   413

cognitive sociology   419

color-coded terrorism   421

Communication Management Unit   415

Consortium for Strategic Communication   410

conspiracy theory   420

containment   409

continued influence effect   417

counterterrorism   410

crisis   405

crisis communication   406

crisis management   405

cultural grammar   420

disinformation   417

fusion center   420

Homeland Security Advisory System   421

human intelligence   416

improvised news   419

information   417

information environment   417

Information Operations   419

intelligence   415

intelligence product   420

interdependence   411

interorganizational communication   410

interoperability   413

misinformation   417

National Terrorism Advisory System   421

predictive profiling   420

restorative rhetoric   413

risk communication   407

rumor   419

rumor control center   420

signal intelligence   416

social amplification   408

social mnemonics   419

synergy   411

systems theory   411

template   419

threat indicators   406

ENDNOTES

1. Reynolds, Barbara, & Seeger, Matthew W. (2005). Crisis and Emergency Risk Communication as an Integrative Model. *Journal of Health Communication, 10*, 43–55.

2. Fearn-Banks, Kathleen (2011). *Crisis Communications: A Casebook Approach*. New York: Routledge.

3. Dezenhall, Eric, & Weber, John (2011). *Damage Control: The Essential Lessons of Crisis Management*. Key West, FL: Prospecta Press.

4. Coombs, W. Timothy (1999). *Ongoing Crisis Communication: Planning, Managing, and Responding*. Thousand Oaks, CA: Sage.

5. Sparks, Lisa, Kreps, Gary L., Botan, Carl, & Rowan, Katherine E. (2005). Responding to Terrorism: Translating Communication Research into Practice. *Communication Research Reports, 22*(1), 1–5.

6. Fearn-Banks, Kathleen (2011). *Crisis Communications: A Casebook Approach*. New York: Routledge.

7. Coombs, W. Timothy (1999). *Ongoing Crisis Communication: Planning, Managing, and Responding*. Thousand Oaks, CA: Sage.

8. Seeger, Matthew W., Sellnow, Timothy L., & Ulmer, Robert R. (1998). Communication, Organization and Crisis. In Michael E. Roloff (Ed.), *Communication Yearbook 21* (pp. 231–275). Thousand Oaks, CA: Sage.

9. Fearn-Banks, Kathleen (2002). *Crisis Communications*. Mahwah, NJ: Lawrence Erlbaum.

10. Seeger, Matthew W., Sellnow, Timothy L., & Ulmer, Robert R. (2003). *Communication, Organization and Crisis*. Westport, CT: Quorum.

11. Combs, Cindy C. (2011). *Terrorism in the Twenty-First Century*. New York: Longman.

12. Venette, Steven J. (2003). *Risk Communication in a High Reliability Organization: APHIS PPQ's Inclusion of Risk in Decision Making*. Ann Arbor, MI: UMI Proquest Information and Learning; Venette, Steven J. (2008). Risk as an Inherent Element in the Study of Crisis Communication. *Southern Communication Journal, 73*(3), 197–210.

13. Combs, Cindy C. (2011). *Terrorism in the Twenty-First Century*. New York: Longman.

14. Freimuth. Vicki, Linnan, Huan W., & Potter, Polyxeni (2000). Communicating the Threat of Emerging Infections to the Public. *Emerging Infectious Diseases, 6*, p. 4; Reynolds, B., & Seeger, M. W. (2005). Crisis and Emergency Risk Communication as an Integrative Model. *Journal of Health Communication, 10*, 43–55.

15. Mileti, Dennis S., & Sorensen, John H. (1990). *Communication of Emergency Public Warnings*. Washington, D.C.: Federal Emergency Management Administration; Sorensen, John H. (2000). Hazard Warning Systems: Review of 20 years of Progress. *Natural Hazards Review, 1*(2), 119–125.

16. Powell, Douglas A., & Leiss, William (1997). *Mad Cows and Mother's Milk: The Perils of Poor Risk Communication*. Buffalo, NY: McGill-Queen's University Press.

17. Heath, Robert L. (1994). Environmental Risk Communication: Cases and Practices along the Texas Gulf Coast. In Brant R. Burleson (Ed.), *Communication Yearbook 18* (pp. 225–277). Newbury Park, CA: Sage.

18. Covello, Vincent T. (1992). Risk Communication: An Emerging Area of Health Communication Research. In Stanley A. Deetz (Ed.), *Communication yearbook 15* (pp. 359–373). Newbury Park, CA: Sage.

19. National Research Council. (1989). *Improving Risk Communication*. Washington, D.C.: National Academy Press.

20. Reynolds, Barbara, & Seeger, Matthew W. (2005). Crisis and Emergency Risk Communication as an Integrative Model. *Journal of Health Communication, 10*, 43–55.

21. Egbert, Nichole, & Parrott, Roxanne (2001). Self-Efficacy and Rural Women's Performance of Breast and Cervical Cancer Detection Practices. *Journal of Health Communication, 6*, 219–233; Freimuth. Vicki, Linnan, Huan W., & Potter, Polyxeni (2000). Communicating the Threat of Emerging Infections to the Public. *Emerging Infectious Diseases, 6*, p. 4; Murray-Johnson, Lisa, Witte, Kim, Liu, Wen-Ying, & Hubbel, Anne P. (2001). Addressing Cultural Orientations in Fear Appeals: Promoting AIDS-Protective Behaviors among Mexican Immigrant and African American Adolescents and American and Taiwanese College Students. *Journal of Health Communication, 6*, 335–358.

22. Sirseloudi, Matenia P. (2005). How to Predict the Unpredictable: On the Early Detection of Terrorist Campaigns. *Defense & Security Analysis, 21*(4), 369–386; Vardalos, Marianne, Letts, Guy Kirby, Teixeira, Hermínio Meireles, Karzai, Anas, & Haig, Jane (2009). *Engaging Terror: A Critical and Interdisciplinary Approach*. Boca Raton, FL: BrownWalker Press.

23. Auf der Heide, Erik (1989). *Disaster Response: Principles of Preparation and Coordination*. St. Louis, MO: The CV Mosby Company.

24. Seeger, Matthew W. (2006). Best Practices in Crisis Communication: An Expert Panel Process. *Journal of Applied Communication Research, 34*, 232–244.

25. Ulmer, Robert R., Sellnow, Timothy L., & Seeger, Matthew W. (2010). *Effective Crisis Communication: Moving from Crisis to Opportunity*. Thousand Oaks, CA: Sage.

26. Matusitz, Jonathan (2007). Improving Terrorism Preparedness for Hospitals: Towards Better Interorganizational Communication. *International Journal of Strategic Communication, 1*(3), 169–189.

27. Danowski, James A., Barnett, George A., & Friedland, Matthew H. (1986). Interorganizational Networks via Shared Public Relations Firms: Centrality, Diversification, Media Coverage, and Public's Image. In M. L. McLaughlin (Ed.) *Communication Yearbook 10* (pp. 808–830). Beverly Hills, CA: Sage; Evan, William (1976). *Interorganizational Relations: Selected Readings*. London: Penguin; Roger, David L., & Whetten, David A. (1982). *Interorganizational Coordination: Theory, Research, and Implementation*. Ames: Iowa State University Press.

28. Bolz, Frank, Dudonis, Kenneth, Schulz, David (2002). *The Counterterrorism Handbook: Tactics, Procedures, and Techniques*. Boca Raton: CRC Press.

29. Barbera, J., & Macintyre, A. (2002). The Reality of Modern Bioterrorism Response. *The Lancet, 360*(9350), 33–34.

30. Sorelle, Ruth (2001a). Crisis Pushes California EDs to the Breaking Point. *Emergency Medicine News, 23*(30), 58–60; Sorelle, Ruth (2001b). Ratios Pit Nurses against Hospitals, Doctors. *Emergency Medicine News, 23*(3), 1–29.

31. Glass, Thomas A. (2001). Understanding Public Response to Disasters. *Public Health Reports, 116*(2), 69–73.

32. Buerhaus, Peter I., & Staiger, Douglas O. (1999). Trouble in the Nurse Labor Market? Recent Trends and Future Outlook. *Health Affairs, 18*(1), 214–222; Cohn, Jonathan (2007). *Sick: The Untold Story of America's Health Care Crisis and the People Who Pay the Price*. New York: HarperCollins.

33. Jarrett, Mark P. (2007). Defining "Community" in Emergency Preparedness. *Annals of Internal Medicine, 146*(1), p. 72.

34. Matusitz, Jonathan (2007). Improving Terrorism Preparedness for Hospitals: Towards Better Interorganizational Communication. *International Journal of Strategic Communication, 1*(3), 169–189.

35. Lasker, Roz D., Weiss, Elisa S., & Miller, Rebecca (2001). Partnership Synergy: A Practical Framework for Studying and Strengthening the Collaborative Advantage. *The Milbank Quarterly, 79*(2), 179–205.

36. Luhmann, Niklas (1995). *Social Systems*. Stanford, CA: Stanford University Press.

37. Myers, Scott A., & Anderson, Carolyn M. (2008). *The Fundamentals of Small Group Communication*. Thousand Oaks, CA: Sage.

38. Comfort, Louise K. (2007). Crisis Management in Hindsight: Cognition, Communication, Coordination, and Control. *Public Administration Review, 67*(1), 189–197.

39. Matusitz, Jonathan (2007). Improving Terrorism Preparedness for Hospitals: Towards Better Interorganizational Communication. *International Journal of Strategic Communication, 1*(3), 169–189.

40. Coombs, Timothy (2007). *Ongoing Crisis Communication: Planning, Managing, and Responding*. Thousand Oaks, CA: Sage; Kiger, Patrick (2001). Lessons from a crisis: how communication kept a company together. *Workforce, 80*, 28–36.

41. Greer, Clark F., & Moreland, Kurt D. (2003). United Airlines' and American Airlines' Online Crisis Communication Following the September 11 Terrorist Attacks. *Public Relations Review, 29*(4), 427–441.

42. Libenau, Jonathan (2003). Communication during the World Trade Center Disaster: Causes of Failure, Lessons, Recommendations. In A. Michael Noll (Ed.), *Crisis Communication: Lessons from September 11* (pp. 45–54). Lanham, MD: Rowman & Littlefield.

43. Pechta, Laura E., Brandenburg, Dale C., & Seeger, Matthew W. (2010). Understanding the Dynamics of Emergency Communication: Propositions for a Four-Channel Model. *Journal of Homeland Security and Emergency Management, 7*(1), Article 55.

44. Koesten, Joy, & Rowland, Robert C. (2004). The Rhetoric of Atonement. *Communication Studies, 55*(1), 68–87.

45. Rowland, Robert C. (1991). On Generic Categorization. *Communication Theory, 1*, 128–144.

46. Griffin-Padgett, Donyale R., & Allison, Donnetrice (2010). Making a Case for Restorative Rhetoric: Mayor Rudolph Giuliani & Mayor Ray Nagin's Response to Disaster. *Communication Monographs, 77*(3), 376–392.

47. Griffin-Padgett, Donyale R., & Allison, Donnetrice (2010). Making a Case for Restorative Rhetoric: Mayor Rudolph Giuliani & Mayor Ray Nagin's Response to Disaster. *Communication Monographs, 77*(3), 376–392.

48. Seeger, Matthew W., & Griffin-Padgett, Donyale R. (2010). From Image Restoration to Renewal: Approaches to Understanding Post-Crisis Communication. *Review of Communication, 10*(2), 127–141.

49. Griffin, Donyale R., & Allison, Donnetrice (2007, April). *Making a Case for Restorative Rhetoric: A Comparative Analysis of Mayor Ray Nagin and Rudolph Giuliani's Response to Disaster*. Paper presented at the annual conference of the Eastern Communication Association, Providence, RI.

50. *Attack on America: September 11, 2001* [Videorecording]. (2001). New York: NBC Nightly News.

51. Hyde, Michael J. (2005). The Rhetor as Hero and the Pursuit of Truth: The Case of 9/11. *Rhetoric & Public Affairs, 8*(1), 1–30.

52. Giuliani, Rudy (2001). Remarks at the Fire Department Promotions Ceremony. Archives of Rudolph W. Giuliani, 107th Mayor. Retrieved February 19, 2011 from http://www.nyc.gov/html/records/rwg/home.html.

53. Griffin-Padgett, Donyale R., & Allison, Donnetrice (2010). Making a Case for Restorative Rhetoric: Mayor Rudolph Giuliani & Mayor Ray Nagin's Response to Disaster. *Communication Monographs, 77*(3), 376–392.

54. Skoll, Geoffrey R. (2007). Meanings of Terrorism. *International Journal for the Semiotics of Law, 20*, 107–127.

55. U.S. Department of Defense (2007, July 12). *Joint Publication 1-02 Department of Defense Dictionary of Military and Associated Terms*. Arlington, VA: U.S. Department of Defense.

56. Kemsley, Harry (2007). Air Power in Counter-Insurgency: A Sophisticated Language or Blunt Expression? *Contemporary Security Policy, 28*(1), 112–126.

57. Post, Jerrold M. (2010). "When Hatred Is Bred in the Bone": The Social Psychology of Terrorism. *Annals of the American Academy of Political and Social Science, 1208*, 15–23.

58. Graham, Bob, & Nussbaum, Jeff (2008). *Intelligence Matters: The CIA, the FBI, Saudi Arabia, and the Failure of America's War on Terror*. Lawrence: University Press of Kansas.

59. White, Jonathan R. (2011). *Terrorism & Homeland Security* (7th ed.). Belmont, CA: Wadsworth.

60. Eggen, Dan (2007, February 25). Facility Holding Terrorism Inmates Limits Communication. *Washington Post*, p. A1.

61. Clark, Robert (2009). *Intelligence Analysis: A Target-Centric Approach*. Washington, D.C.: CQ Press.

62. Martin, Gus (2010). *Understanding Terrorism: Challenges, Perspectives, and Issues*. Thousand Oaks, CA: Sage.

63. Chen, Hsinchun (2007). Exploring Extremism and Terrorism on the Web: The Dark Web Project. *Intelligence and Security Informatics, 4430*, 1–20; Combs, Cindy C. (2011). *Terrorism in the Twenty-First Century*. New York: Longman; Martin, Gus (2010). *Understanding Terrorism: Challenges, Perspectives, and Issues*. Thousand Oaks, CA: Sage.

64. Information Operations (2006, February 13). Washington, D.C.: U.S. Department of the Army.

65. Black, Alistair (1999). Information Management in Business, Libraries and British Military Intelligence: Towards a History of Information Management. *Journal of Documentation, 55*(4), 361–374; Gill, Peter (2004). Securing the Globe: Intelligence and the Post-9/11 Shift from "Liddism" to "Drainism." *Intelligence and National Security, 19*(3), 467–489.

66. Johnson, Hollyn M., & Seifert, Colleen M. (1994). Sources of the Continued Influence Effect: When Misinformation in Memory Affects Later Inferences. *Journal of Experimental Psychology: Learning, Memory, and Cognition, 20*, 1420–1436.

67. Hiebert, Ray Heldon (2003). Public Relations and Propaganda in Framing the Iraq War: A Preliminary Review. *Public Relations Review, 29*(3), 243–255.

68. Paz, Reuven (2005). Global Jihad and WMD: Between Martyrdom and Mass Destruction. *Current Trends in Islamist Ideology, 2*, 74–86; Paz, Reuven (2007). *Reading Their Lips: The Credibility of Jihadi Web Sites in Arabic as a Source for Information*. Jerusalem: Project for the Research of Islamist Movements (PRISM).

69. Fine, Gary Alan, & Ellis, Bill (2010). *The Global Grapevine: Why Rumors of Terrorism, Immigration, and Trade Matter*. Oxford: Oxford University Press; Herman, Carl (2011, March 17). Did US Secret Weapons Cause Japan's Earthquake and Tsunami? *Examiner*; Melnick, Jeffrey (2009). *9/11 Culture*. New York: Wiley-Blackwell; Taylor, Phillip M. (2002). Perception Management and the "War" against Terrorism. *Journal of Information Warfare, 1*(3), 16–29.

70. Taylor, Phillip M. (2002). Perception Management and the "War" against Terrorism. *Journal of Information Warfare, 1*(3), 16–29.

71. Information Operations (2006, February 13). Washington, D.C.: U.S. Department of the Army.

72. Peterson, Warren, & Gist, Noel (1951). Rumor and Public Opinion. *The American Journal of Sociology, 57*(2), 159–167.

73. Knapp, Robert H. (1944). A Psychology of Rumor. *Public Opinion Quarterly, 8*, 22–37.

74. Olick, Jeffrey, & Robbins, Joyce (1998). Social Memory Studies: From Collective Memory to the Historical Sociology of Mnemonic Practices. *Annual Review of Sociology, 24*, 105–140.

75. Shibutani, Tamotsu (1966). *Improvised News: A Sociological Study of Rumor*. New York: Irvington publishing.

76. Fine, Gary Alan, & Ellis, Bill (2010). *The Global Grapevine: Why Rumors of Terrorism, Immigration, and Trade Matter*. Oxford: Oxford University Press.

77. Frankfurter, David (2006). *Evil Incarnate: Rumors of Demonic Conspiracy and Ritual Abuse in History*. Princeton, NJ: Princeton University Press; Hewitt, John, & Hall, Peter (1973). Social Problems, Problematic Situations, and Quasi-Theories. *American Sociological Review, 38*, 367–374.

78. Weinberg, Sanford B., & Eich, Ritch K. (1978). Fighting Fire with Fire: Establishment of a Rumor Control Center. *Communication Quarterly, 26*(3), 26–31.

79. Monahan, Torin (2009). The Murky World of "Fusion Centers." *Criminal Justice Matters, 75*(1), 20–21; Monahan, Torin, & Palmer, Neal A. (2009). The Emerging Politics of DHS Fusion Centers. *Security Dialogue, 40*(6), 617–636.

80. Florida Department of Law Enforcement (2011). What Is a Fusion Center? Retrieved March 3, 2011 from http://www.fdle.state.fl.us/Content/getdoc/9ebab176-ddff-4e62-80cd-869934ab7090/FUSION-Home .aspx.

81. White, Jonathan R. (2011). *Terrorism & Homeland Security* (7th ed.). Belmont, CA: Wadsworth.

82. Daniels, Ronald J., & Roach, Ken (2001). *Securer Freedom for Whom: Risk Profiling and the New Anti-Terrorism Act: The Security of Freedom: Essays on Canada's Anti-Terrorism Bill*. Toronto: University of Toronto Press.

83. Schneier, Bruce (2004). The Nonsecurity of Secrecy. *Communications of the ACM, 47*(10), p. 120.

84. Wise, Charles R., & Nader, Rania (2002). Organizing the Federal System for Homeland Security: Problems, Issues, and Dilemmas. *Public Administration Review, 62*, 44–57.

85. National Terrorism Advisory System (2011). Washington, D.C.: U.S. Department of Homeland Security.

86. Brown, Michael (2003, February 14). Letters to the Editor. *The New York Times*.

87. Moeller, Susan D. (2009). *Packaging Terrorism: Co-Opting the News for Politics and Profit*. New York: Wiley-Blackwell.

88. Kamen, Al (2004, October 13). Will Terror Alert Level Show Its True Colors? *Washington Post*, p. A19.

89. Ridge, Tom, & Bloom, Lary (2009). *The Test of Our Times: America Under Siege... And How We Can Be Safe Again*. New York: Thomas Dunne Books.

Glossary

Absolute terrorists: terrorists who view the terrorist acts themselves as objectives. They generally resist any negotiation and no one can communicate with them (Ch. 14).

Académie Française: an elite French learned body on matters dealing with the French language (Ch. 1).

Accessibility principle: according to this principle, when someone is asked to make a social judgment, he or she will do so according to the information that comes to mind most rapidly (Ch. 7).

Achieved stigma: a stigma that one has caused because of bad conduct or because one has contributed greatly to earning his or her stigma in question (Ch. 7).

Actionable intelligence: information that law enforcement agencies, military corps, or other security units can use to stop an attack or operation (Ch. 16).

Action exchange: collaborative damage-making between terrorist groups (Ch. 11).

Action framing: transforming behavioral intentions into actions (Ch. 5).

Active cadre: the individuals responsible for executing the mission of the terrorist organization (Ch. 11).

Advantageous comparison: practice involving a group comparing its own terrorist acts with acts committed by other groups that appear worse (Ch. 10).

Aesopian language: communication that carries an innocent meaning to outsiders but entails a more profound meaning to informed members with a special agenda (Ch. 9).

Agenda-setting theory: theory postulating that the more the media cover certain issues, the more salient (i.e., noticeable, accessible, and "significant") these issues become for the audience (Ch. 5).

Aggregate: a collection of people who are together at the same time and place, but who do not constitute a unit or have a shared degree of similarity (Ch. 10).

Aggressive listening: recalling minutiae of a suspect's statements by extracting them from memory (Ch. 14).

Agora: in ancient Greek city-states, it was an open "place of assembly." Today, it is the "public domain" (Ch. 15).

Al Jazeera television: a small and fast-growing Arabic news channel based in Qatar (Ch. 2).

Al-Manar: a satellite television station located in Beirut (Lebanon) and affiliated with Hezbollah (Ch. 8).

Alternative set of procedures: torture (Ch. 9).

American collective identity: a strategic theme to embrace the national, the cultural, and the social without confining any American to any one of those exclusively (Ch. 6).

Amplification effect: when terrorist attacks are shown in the media to an audience much larger than what the audience would be at the place where the attacks occur (Ch. 3).

Analog: in a linear sequential manner (Ch. 13).

Animal Liberation Front (ALF): a European-based terrorist group that commits unlawful actions in quest of animal liberation (Ch. 2).

Anomie: a reaction against or withdrawal from the mainstream controls of society (Ch. 1).

Antiterrorism: strategies seeking to decrease the probability of an attack that employs terrorist methods at specific points, and to diminish the vulnerability of potential targets to such methods (Ch. 16).

Arbitrary deprivation of life: killing (Ch. 9).

Arbitrator: mediator who attends to presentations made by warring parties and draws a conclusion as to who is right and who is wrong, or how conflict should be managed (Ch. 15).

Argumentation: a person's ability to defend his or her position on a controversial matter while simultaneously trying to counter another party's or person's position on the same matter (Ch. 8).

Argumentum ad nauseam: a device employing assiduous repetition of an idea (Ch. 8).

Armchair jihadists: potential new recruits using online media to become jihadists (Ch. 13).

Armed propaganda: the idea that terrorism and the media feed on each other (Ch. 3).

Armenian Secret Army for the Liberation of Armenia: Armenian terrorist group notorious for attacking Turks in retribution for the Turkish genocide of Armenians (in 1915) (Ch. 10).

Arousal hypothesis: theory positing that unusual or exceptional media content can intensify a viewer's desire to act aggressively (Ch. 4).

Aryan Brotherhood: a group of devious bikers formed in U.S. prisons (Ch. 1).

Ashura procession: a method to reinforce Shi'ite activism and that celebrates Imam Hussein, son of Ali (Muhammad's successor, as the Shi'ites see it) (Ch. 10).

Assassination: tactic of surprise killing invented by the Assassins cult in the Middle Ages (Ch. 1).

Assassins: in 11th century Persia, it was a religious sect striking terror against the empire of Saladin and resisted the armies of the Ottoman Empire (Ch. 1).

Asymmetric warfare: the use of random/unpredictable violence by a weak group against a stronger power (Ch. 1).

Asynchronous communication: communication outside real time (Ch. 13).

Atmosphere: emotions that surface when members of a collective focus their attention on a particular short-term event that impacts them as a group (Ch. 6).

Attribute framing: accentuating particular attributes of an event (Ch. 5).

Audience: a group of people who participate in an event, either passively or actively (Ch. 4).

Audience identification: strategic communication adopted by terrorists, in their justification for violence, to attract and engage particular audiences (Ch. 4).

Aum Shinrikyo: a deadly Japanese cult that committed a sarin gas attack in the Tokyo subway in 1995 (Ch. 1).

Authoritarian leadership: leadership based on powerful controlling tactics and central organizational decision making (Ch. 11).

Axis of Evil: terrorist-harboring states (Ch. 9).

Baader-Meinhof Group: a German terrorist group active from the 1970s to the 1990s (Ch. 1).

Ba'ath Party: a secularist political party with deep-seated socialist and Arab nationalist interests (Ch. 5).

Back-stage: the physical or social space in which people are more genuine and less "performing" (Ch. 4).

Baghdad Sniper: an alleged Islamist sniper who has killed over 600 U.S. soldiers (Ch. 2, Box 2.1).

Barrack buster: the nickname given to a homemade mortar developed since the 1970s (Ch. 2).

Behavioral detection: identifying terrorism on the basis of body language (Ch. 14).

Beheading video: video released by Islamist terrorist groups showing interviews by hostages. At the end of the video, one of the captors is shown to pull his knife out and behead (slowly) the hostage (Ch. 2).

Belief in a just world: the attitude that people get what they deserve (Ch. 6).

Bellum omnium contra omnes: the war of all against all (Ch. 1).

Berlo's Model of Communication: model describing a two-way interactive communication process (Ch. 2).

Betweenness: the number of routes that link pairs of nodes passing through a specific node (Ch. 11).

bin Laden, Osama: late founder of Al Qaeda (Ch. 6, Box 6.1).

Black propaganda: fabrication, where distorted information is provided (Ch. 8).

Black September: a Palestinian terrorist group that committed the Munich massacre (Ch. 3, Box 3.3).

Black site: secret prison operated by the CIA (Ch. 9).

Black Widows: female Chechen suicide bombers who are widows of men killed by the government (Ch. 1).

Blog: interactive web page or online forum allowing visitors to post comments (Ch. 13).

Blue on blue: NATO combatants killing each other by accident (instead of killing terrorists) (Ch. 9).

Bluespeak: the U.N. lingo for their diplomats so they can prudently phrase evil things (Ch. 9).

BOBing: NATO combatants killing each other by accident (instead of killing terrorists) (Ch. 9).

Bolo: an emblematic bush knife unique to the Philippines to kill opponents in broad daylight (Ch. 2).

Boomerang effect: model postulating that while people use discourses to protect their freedom, their own discourses may bite them back (Ch. 8).

Brain drain: human capital flight; trained and talented individuals who migrate to better nations (Ch. 6).

Bricolage: the process of developing a new social identity by appropriating symbols and artifacts from a variety of heritages and cultures (Ch. 10).

Bridging: a strategy whereby a new option is offered that meets both parties' significant needs (Ch. 15).

Brochureware: information displayed on websites that tends to be of a reporting style (Ch. 13).

Brokerage: when ideas are diffused from one terrorist organization to another through an intermediary (Ch. 12).

Brown Berets: a Latino nationalist activist group of young Mexican Americans dressed in military attire and brown berets, emulating the Black Panthers, and notorious for their police brutality (Ch. 7).

Bureaucratese: the language of bureaucracy and a tactic to overload the audience with unfamiliar words (Ch. 9).

Caliphate: a grand Arab-Muslim state (Ch. 1).

Card stacking: a similar propaganda method that attempts to manipulate people's perception of an issue by accentuating one side and suppressing another (Ch. 8).

Carnivore: a surveillance system that can watch and examine Internet communications (Ch. 16).

Carter Center: a nongovernmental, nonprofit organization involved in various national and international public policy, conflict management, human rights, and charitable causes (Ch. 15).

Cascading failure: a series of failures engendered by the removal of a vital node from a network (Ch. 13).

CBRN: chemical, biological, radiological, and nuclear weapons (pronounced C-BURN) (Ch. 1).

Celebrity diplomacy: diplomacy conducted through informal channels using facilitators such as high-profile figures and social activists (Ch. 15).

Cell: the basic unit of a modern terrorist organization, with vague leadership and organizational structure (Ch. 11).

Censorship: suppression of information believed to be offensive, sensitive, or threatening to the audience, a state, media outlets, or other controlling bodies (Ch. 5).

Chain or line network: network in which individuals are located or seated along a line, often based on their rank in the network (Ch. 11).

Change agent: an individual who influences innovation decisions (Ch. 12).

Charisma: divine-like conferred power (Ch. 11).

Charismatic leadership: leadership that relies on divine-like personal traits and power (Ch. 11).

Cherry picking: the act of selecting individual cases or evidence that confirm a particular position, while turning a blind eye on a large portion of related cases or evidence that may contradict that position (Ch. 8).

Chit: promissory note (Ch. 11).

Choice framing: asking the audience to take a risk or make a promise about a specific decision (Ch. 5).

Ciphertext: information written in an encoded form, what some people designate "garbled information" (Ch. 13).

Circle network: network with the highest confidence and the highest degree of shared centrality (Ch. 11).

Citizen journalists: mainstream citizens who use innovative mobile digital technology to give journalistic accounts of events (Ch. 16).

Clandestine cell structure: a method for organizing a unit in such a way that it can more efficiently resist invasion by an opposing group (Ch. 11).

Clash of Civilizations: theory positing that cultural and religious differences between civilizations worldwide have become the primary source of terrorism today (Ch. 1).

Classical terrorism: terrorism whereby group warfare is direct and with few casualties (Ch. 1).

Closed view of Islam: view that Islam is static, unchanging, archaic, macho, violent, and threatening (Ch. 7).

Co-construction of reality: social construction of reality through discourse (Ch. 6).

Code: sign system (Ch. 3).

Code words: elements of a standardized code or convention (Ch. 9).

Cognitive centrality: the amount of time someone thinks about being an in-group member (Ch. 10).

Cognitive functions: in framing theory, cognitive functions co-relate disparate facts, events, and leaders (Ch. 5).

Cognitive sociology: the notion that thinking is permanently socially influenced (Ch. 16).

Collateral damage: damage that is involuntary or incidental to the intended outcome. It can refer to both the killing of non-combatants and the destruction of their property (Ch. 9).

Collective action frames: action-oriented beliefs and meanings that motivate and legitimize social movements and campaigns (Ch. 8).

Collective Communication Model of Terrorism: model positing that the psychological impacts of terrorist threats can be seen as a collective communication process that occurs between terrorists and their potential targets (Ch. 2).

Collective emotional orientation: the characterizing manner in which society expresses a certain emotion (Ch. 6).

Collective identity: a sense of affiliation to a group (the collective) that is so powerful that someone who identifies with the group will devote his or her life to the group over individual identity (Ch. 10).

Collective guilt: the notion that a group should bear guilt for all the wrongdoings of particular members (Ch. 7).

Collective level of mental programming: level of mental programming shared with some but not all other people; it is common to people belonging to one group or category which differ from other groups or categories (Ch. 6).

Collectivism: a social attitude according to which individuals consider themselves as parts of one or more groups, and are principally influenced by the rules of, and obligations imposed by, those groups (Ch. 6).

Color-coded terrorism: the degree of severity of terrorism as indicated by an alert warning system. The term comes from "color coding," a practice of presenting information by using different colors (Ch. 16).

Communication: the act of conveying a message from a sender to a receiver (Ch. 2).

Communication as ritual: sacred ceremony that groups people together in fellowship and communality (Ch. 6).

Communication as transmission: disseminating information faster and to longer distances, transcending time and space, to affect the behavior or beliefs of the receivers of transmissions (Ch. 6).

Communication bypass: linguistic strategy whereby the receiver of a message infers a different meaning from the message than what was intended by the sender (Ch. 9).

Communication competence: empathy, interaction management, and involvement (Ch. 14).

Communication Management Unit: an independent group within a unit in the U.S. Federal Bureau of Prisons that harshly limits, manages, and observes all outside communication (telephone, mail, or visitation) of inmates in the unit (Ch. 16).

Communicative action: Habermas's model of communication to achieve essential social functions: reaching understanding, cultural reproduction, coordinating action-plans, and socializing individuals (Ch. 9).

Community: the social bonds between people (Ch. 6).

Community of Practice (CoP): an activity of group learning in which people have a mutual interest in certain subjects or problems (Ch. 10).

Compassion fatigue: a gradual avoidance of sensitivity toward dramatic events; it is desensitization (Ch. 4).

Compensation: a method whereby one party grants something of value (usually financial) to the other to compensate for losses caused by the other party (Ch. 15).

Comprador ruling elites: Third World ruling elites perceived to be in power (despite being shady, incompetent, and sanguinary) because the West put them or has kept them in power (Ch. 1).

Concept: mental representation (Ch. 6).

Concession: a situation in which a party gives something of high value to the other party (Ch. 15).

Conciliation: an informal communication link by a third party between warring parties with the goal of identifying the issues (Ch. 15).

Conduit metaphor: the notion that, when communicating, humans use the media for encoding purposes (Ch. 2).

Confidence: the centerpiece of a group's beliefs that represent a group's identity; when the beliefs are called into question, the ensuing effects may smash group members' reality (Ch. 10).

Consensus reality: the idea that reality is what we agree on through consensus (Ch. 6).

Consortium for Strategic Communication: a think tank at Arizona State University. Its objective is to put communication research into practice in the fight against terrorism, to support national security, and to promote public diplomacy worldwide (Ch. 16).

Conspiracy theory: a quasi-theory that explains an event by combining plausible elements (Ch. 16).

Contagion: the occurrence of terrorism in one nation which increases the probability of a neighboring nation being exposed to terrorism (Ch. 12).

Contagion effect of media reporting: the idea that the rapid dissemination of ideas, doctrines, or emotional conditions through the media impacts the potential behavior of like-minded extremists (Ch. 3).

Containment: the effort to restrict the duration of a crisis or to prevent it from proliferating to other regions affecting the nation (Ch. 16).

Content analysis: a careful, thorough, systematic analysis and interpretation of the content of texts (or images) to identify patterns, themes, and meanings (Ch. 1).

Contingent terrorists: terrorists who employ hostages as leverage. Terror is used to accomplish other instrumental aims such as media attention, ransom, or liberation of prisoners in exchange for hostages taken (Ch. 14).

Continued influence effect: constant dependence on misinformation, even when individuals can remember a correction or retraction (Ch. 16).

Copycat effect: the tendency of sensational publicity about extreme murders or suicides to give rise to more of the same through imitation (Ch. 12).

Counter-maneuvering: an effective application of language in which subtle words are chosen to attenuate anger and to affect and change the behavior of the interactant (Ch. 14).

Counter-resistance strategy: harsh interrogation technique like waterboarding and the wet-towel technique (Ch. 9).

Counter-stereotype: stereotype that has been turned into a more popular and accepted reality (Ch. 7).

Counterterrorism: offensive strategies designed to stop an enemy, in a broader conflict, from successfully employing the method of terrorism (Ch. 16).

Coupled network: network typified by the relaxing or releasing of the command and influence which leaders within the organization can apply over other components (Ch. 11).

Covert communication: the art of communicating without making the communication noticeable (Ch. 13).

Covert network: dynamic network with fuzzy boundaries (Ch. 11).

Critical media consciousness: when the audience understands the media and the manner in which stories are presented (Ch. 5).

Crisis: a major incidence with a potentially negative consequence impacting a country or organization (Ch. 16).

Crisis communication: the analysis and use of cleverly designed messages sent through selected sources (mediated and interpersonal) to transmit relevant information to intended audiences in crisis situations (Ch. 16).

Crisis management: a process that eliminates part of the risk and uncertainty from the negative event and thereby enables the country or organization to better control its own destiny (Ch. 16).

Cryptography: technique that encodes messages in such a way that not one person can read it, except the one to whom the message was sent (Ch. 13).

Culpable-media model: model that identifies a causal relationship between media and terrorism, which calls for media regulation (Ch. 3).

Cultivation theory: theory positing that long-standing frequent exposure to media messages forms a person's understanding of the world in a way that corresponds to how reality is depicted in the media (Ch. 7).

Cultural capital: the social assets that a culture has (e.g., cultural knowledge, local goods, material objects) (Ch. 6).

Cultural determinism: the belief that the culture in which humans are raised determines who they are emotionally and behaviorally (Ch. 6).

Cultural differentiation: differences of culture perceived as threats to prevailing cultural values (Ch. 7).

Cultural diplomacy: a type of diplomacy involving a clear recognition and awareness of foreign cultural dynamics and observance of the principles that dominate basic dialogue (Ch. 15).

Cultural emphasis: a notable characteristic of a culture often manifested though language and, more specifically, vocabulary (Ch. 6).

Cultural grammar: a nexus of beliefs (Ch. 16).

Cultural hegemony: a form of nationalistic rhetoric about identity enabled by the process of legitimizing feelings of dislike or superiority toward enemies (Ch. 8).

Cultural materials: concepts or symbols that are shared and understood by a given community (Ch. 6).

Cultural resonance: the understanding of how a movement or idea is created by and in turn creates the cultural environment (Ch. 6).

Cultural Westernization: a standardization of Western mass culture that travels around the world and produces sameness and homogeneity in all places (Ch. 13).

Cultural worldview: a collectively embraced set of beliefs about the nature of the world and which provides persuasive answers to universal cosmological questions about life (Ch. 6).

Culture: a socially constructed and historically transmitted system. It is a pattern of symbols, meanings, principles, rules, norms, beliefs, values, traditions, and objects that are transferred from one generation to the next, and shared to a certain degree by members of a community (Ch. 6).

Culture of Terror: a collapse (both physically and figuratively) of America and the West through massive killings and the constant availability and uses of WMDs or CBRN weapons (Ch. 1). It is also referred to as the spectacle of killing, torture, and evil bewitchment (Ch. 4).

Culture talk: an ideology of good Muslims who adopt American values vs. bad Muslims who keep their own practices in Western society (Ch. 6).

Cyberspace: virtual world or the World Wide Web (Ch. 13).

Cyberterrorism: the use of information technology such as telecommunications, the Internet, or computer systems as a method to mount attacks (Ch. 13).

Cyberwar: actions by a nation-state to penetrate another nation's computers or networks for the purposes of causing damage or disruption (Ch. 13).

Daisy cutter: a type of igniting device that detonates an aerial bomb at or above the ground (Ch. 9).

"Damascus road" conversion: a situation in which a person's central outlook on life is rapidly changed (Ch. 10).

Dark Web Project: a group of computational experts using advanced technology and groundbreaking approaches to track terrorism on the web (Ch. 16).

Dar ul-Harb: the infidels and corrupt societies living on earth (Ch. 10).

Dar ul-Islam: the divinely perfect and righteous house of the faithful (Ch. 10).

Death cult language: a type of rhetoric centered on the glorification of death as part of a major plan to transform the world and establish a grand Caliphate (Ch. 8).

Death of Statecraft: situation in which diplomats fail to negotiate with their counterparts or nation-states make no attempt at engaging in communicative action (Ch. 1).

Debriefing: situation in which someone willingly informs others (Ch. 14).

Deception: the cover-up of true information (Ch. 14).

Declaration of Principles: see Oslo Accords (Ch. 10).

Dehumanization: a process by which a group stresses the "inferiority" of another group through open or crafty acts or statements (Ch. 8).

Deindividuation: a state of lowered self-awareness, a provisional loss of individual identity as a consequence of becoming part of a group (Ch. 10).

Demonization: a practice whereby terrorist group members become swayed into believing that the enemy has a pact with the devil (Ch. 10).

Demonstrative terrorism: a type of terrorism enacted mainly for publicity reasons (Ch. 2).

Denial of the means of communication: an act in which the authorities deny dissenters an opportunity to challenge a speaker at meetings or even on the street (Ch. 8).

Deobandi: an Islamic movement at the border of Pakistan and India that is welcoming to jihad (Ch. 6).

Depluralization: a conditioning process that throws out the new member's social and personal identities (Ch. 10).

Depopulate: kill, according to the CIA (Ch. 9).

Destabilizing the enemy: creating a sense of unrest and heightening a sense of fear that the state is incapable to provide security and stability to its people (Ch. 4).

Dialogue among Civilizations: a type of interfaith dialogue or global peace dialogue (Ch. 15).

Diaspora: the dispersal of an ethnic or religious group worldwide (Ch. 1).

Differential Association Theory: theory positing that individuals learn from those with whom they interact in a group (Ch. 10).

Diffusion of Innovations: a theory that explains how innovations (i.e., ideas, movements, or inventions) are diffused through certain channels over time across society and diverse cultures (Ch. 12).

Digital: that which does not depend on a linear sequential order (Ch. 13).

Diplomacy: the art and practice of leading negotiations between representatives of institutions or nations (Ch. 15).

Diplomatic bag: diplomats taking documents with them without being searched (Ch. 15).

Diplomatic immunity: sanctity of diplomats (Ch. 15).

Direct diffusion: when terrorist groups physically collaborate and train together, and when knowledge is communicated from one group to another (Ch. 12).

Disaster created for PR: a strategic and managed intervention, well calculated for an increasingly dominant extremist agenda (Ch. 3).

Disaster for PR: expressive communication, symbolic hatred, a desire for martyrdom, and a crazy, almighty aspiration to dominate the world (Ch. 3).

Discourse: a socially constructed method for representing the world (Ch. 6). It also means back and forth communication (Ch. 14).

Discourse of fear: the ubiquitous communication, symbolic familiarity, and expectation that danger and risk are a central theme of daily life (Ch. 6).

Discursive control: the process of repeating phrases to make messages seem unequivocal and undeniable (Ch. 8).

Discursive imperialism: a type of discourse that berates the enemy's culture (Ch. 7).

Disinformation: deliberately inaccurate information, including the spread of fabricated intelligence (Ch. 16).

Disinhibition hypothesis: theory based on the premise that news stories detailing terrorism decrease the inhibition of the viewer to engage in extreme violence, which in turn increases the viewer's readiness to engage in aggressive behavior (Ch. 4).

Disruptive reentry system: nuclear-armed, intercontinental, ballistic missile (Ch. 9).

Distancing language: phrasing employed by people to dissociate themselves from a statement (Ch. 9).

Doctrine over existence: when new recruits are required to abandon any values, beliefs, attitudes, or behaviors that diverge from the group values and expectations (Ch. 10).

Do-it-yourself jihad: the sharing of instruction on jihad published in monthly magazines, online forums, chat rooms, and state-of-the-art virtual camps (Ch. 13).

Doublespeak: language that intentionally conceals, distorts, or reverses the meaning of words (Ch. 9).

Downward terror spiral: situation in which "rebels" and repressive states escalate their violence (Ch. 4).

Dramaturgical Analysis: theory that individuals engage in public performance—activities in the front of observers (i.e., an audience) (Ch. 4).

Dune network: type of terrorist network that uses a process of fluctuation between territorial presence and a method of disappearance (Ch. 11).

Dyadic hostage negotiation: negotiation in which the hostage taker makes straightforward requests to the hostage negotiator (Ch. 14).

Earth Liberation Front (ELF): a European eco-terrorist organization (Ch. 2).

Echelon: a satellite surveillance network and a universal "wiretap" that filters through communications (Ch. 16).

Economical with the truth: deceiving, whether by intentionally giving false information (i.e., lying) or by deliberately omitting relevant facts (Ch. 9).

Electronic dead drop: an invisible "go-between" on the web; that is, a signal implanted within an Internet photo or text that is posted in an online forum, and then downloaded by the intended recipient (Ch. 13).

Electronic media: radio, television, facsimile (fax), cell phones, and text messaging (Ch. 3).

Eliminate with extreme prejudice: kill a suspected double agent, according to the Pentagon (Ch. 9).

Emotional climate: the collective emotions felt as a consequence of a society's reaction to its sociopolitical conditions (Ch. 6).

Emotional culture: the emotional relations socialized in any culture (Ch. 6).

Emotional offender: offender committing a crime in reaction to unrestrained but basic human drives (Ch. 14).

Emotion and interpersonal news diffusion: the need to join and share emotional experience with others (Ch. 6).

Emotions: response systems designed to adapt the human organism to rapid and maybe threatening changes in the environment (Ch. 6).

Emotive narratives: stories loaded with emotional appeals and often combined with pictures (Ch. 2, Box 2.1).

Encryption: method to muddle information in such a manner that only the intended recipient, who possesses the key to decode the encrypted messages, can detect the data (Ch. 13).

Enemification: the representation of other groups as enemies (Ch. 8).

Enhanced interrogation technique: torture (Ch. 9).

Episodic frames: frames that concentrate on the specifics of any given event (Ch. 5).

Epistemic community: network of experts with recognized knowledge and skill in specific issues or areas (Ch. 12).

Eponyms: people after whom particular words are named (Ch. 9).

Ethnocentric appeal: an appeal that creates a division between the audience and the enemy (Ch. 8).

Ethnography: the direct observation, reporting, and assessment of the behavior of a group (Ch. 6).

Etymology: the study of the origin and evolution of words (Ch. 1).

Euphemism: a substitution of a friendly or less offensive expression for one that implies something unpleasant or offensive to the listener (Ch. 9).

Evaluative functions: in framing theory, functions that label culprits, identify victims, and assign blame (Ch. 5).

Evilification: the practice of vilifying other groups and methodically classifying them as outcasts (Ch. 8).

Existential stigma: a situation in which the stigmatized individual is not responsible for his or her mistreatment or he or she has little control over the stigma (Ch. 7).

Explicit knowledge: information that is codifiable and clear-cut in written form (Ch. 11).

Extraordinary rendition: secret abduction and confinement of suspected terrorists from all over the globe (Ch. 9).

Facial Action Coding System: an all-embracing, anatomy-based program for evaluating all visually decipherable facial movements (Ch. 14).

Fair division: the process of dividing a resource in such a manner that each party believes it has received its fair share (Ch. 15).

Fairness doctrine: cleverly "balancing" contrasting viewpoints (Ch. 5).

Fantasy type: in symbolic convergence theory, it is a standard script that employs a renowned, spectacular form to explain new events, and is an umbrella term for a collection of recurring, related fantasy themes (Ch. 10).

FARC: a Colombian terrorist group that vows to kidnap important personalities of the political arena (Ch. 14).

Far enemy: non-Islamic powers or countries outside the jurisdiction of Islam (i.e., the West, the U.S., and Israel) that do not embrace the jihadist view (Ch. 1, Box 1.1).

Fatwa: legal pronouncement of death (Ch. 11).

Fear: a basic aversive emotion that occurs in situations of perceived threat and danger to persons or their environment (the society) (Ch. 6).

Fear narrative: the widespread communication, symbolic awareness, and expectation that danger is constantly present or imminent (Ch. 4).

Fedayeen: suicide squads who are not bombers (Ch. 1).

Fickle friend: the notion that the media always search for novelty and that, from the terrorists' perspective, novelty can be created by the terrorists themselves (Ch. 3).

First media age: form of media such as newspapers, radio, and television (Ch. 13).

First Wave of terrorism: terrorism that occurred in the late 19th and early 20th centuries (Ch. 1).

Fixity: trauma that media exposure to terrorism causes (Ch. 4).

Flickr.com: a website that allows users to post photographs for free (Ch. 3).

Flying While Muslim: a phrase about racial profiling that specifically refers to the problems that Muslims on airplanes have faced since 9/11 (Ch. 7).

Focalism: technique whereby increasing the subjective focus on a given objective leads to the suppression of alternative objectives (Ch. 10).

Focality: a focal place, individual, or event that must be well visible, have some unforgettable features, and be associated with a successful story line (Ch. 4).

Follow-on terrorist leadership: succession of terrorist leadership, often from father to son (Ch. 11).

Foot Soldier: the most easily recruitable in a terrorist group (Ch. 10).

Foquismo: revolution by way of guerrilla warfare (Ch. 12).

Force multiplier: a technique to increase the impact power of a method without increasing the number of people involved in an attack (Ch. 2).

Fourth Wave of terrorism: terrorism symbolized by religious justification for killing and international scope, introduced by the September 11, 2001 terrorist attacks (Ch. 1).

Frame: a schema of interpretation—that is, a series of anecdotes and stereotypes—that serves to organize experience and influence action and that the audience relies on to understand and respond to events (Ch. 5).

Frame alignment: the development of congruence between a person's and the movement's interests, values, and beliefs (Ch. 12).

Framing: a communicative strategy that steers the audience toward embracing one viewpoint over another (Ch. 5).

Franc-tireurs: "free shooters"; French and Russian peasants committing acts of terror against German occupiers in the 19th century (Ch. 1).

Freedom of Information (FOI) Act: a law guaranteeing citizens to access governmental records (Ch. 5).

Friendly fire: the euphemism for "troops killed by comrades" (Ch. 9).

Front-stage: the physical or social space in which performances are enacted (Ch. 4).

Fundamentalist zealot: terrorist who follows Al Qaeda principles to the letter and leads others to strict observance of these principles (Ch. 14).

Funnel recruitment: recruitment model according to which the terrorist group uses a gradual, or phased, approach of recruitment (Ch. 10).

Fusion center: a terrorism prevention and response center that stores all intelligence in a single center, fusing various agencies in a single unit to investigate all sorts of threats (Ch. 16).

Galei Tzahal: a national Israeli radio network run by IDF (Israel Defense Forces) (Ch. 10, Box 10.1).

General threat indicators: indicators used to conclude whether, within the country, there are conditions that might motivate or provoke terrorism (Ch. 16).

Gestalt: a method by which people form impressions of others (Ch. 7).

Globalization: the unification of parts of the globe that were isolated or disconnected (Ch. 13).

Global Language Monitor: an Austin-based company that documents, analyzes, and identifies trends in language use worldwide, especially the English language (Ch. 6).

Global network: a type of communication network that covers the entire planet (Ch. 13).

Global opinion theory: theory positing that states acquire a certain status as key global players by "agreeing" with world opinion that, in turn, will boost their global influence even more (Ch. 15).

Global transnational terrorism: terrorism with violent non-state actors active in multiple territories (Ch. 13).

Global Village: a metaphor to describe the Internet and the World Wide Web (Ch. 13).

Glossocracy: government by the tongue; it is the totalitarian burden of manipulative language (Ch. 9).

Gobbledygook: the language of bureaucracy and a tactic to overload the audience with unfamiliar words (Ch. 9).

Graduated desensitization: when the execution of terrorist attacks makes discomfort and self-censure disappear over time (Ch. 10).

Gray propaganda: propaganda that is not untruthful at face value but more cleverly manipulative (Ch. 8).

Greater jihad: the struggle a person has within him- or herself to fulfill what is right (Ch. 1, Box 1.1).

Gricean Maxims: Maxims of Quality, Quantity, Relation, and Manner (Ch. 9).

Group: three or more individuals working together for the purpose of completing a task (Ch. 10).

Group cohesion: the capacity of a group to preserve membership and accomplish its goals (Ch. 10).

Group commitment: an allegiance or devotion of a person to the members of their primary group and the values or philosophy of that group (Ch. 10).

Group delirium: shared dreams that galvanize individuals in a political cause or religion (Ch. 10).

Group dynamics: a complex set of relationships between people inside a group (Ch. 10).

Group norms: the limits of permissible behaviors of individuals in a group (Ch. 10).

Group polarization: a phenomenon by which the attitudes of group members become more extreme as a consequence of joining a group (Ch. 10).

Group socialization: when group members create agreed-on meanings as to who will do what, how the group will function, and when members learn a good amount to contribute adroitly and competently to the group (Ch. 10).

Groupthink: a situation in which conflict or disagreement seldom occurs due to high group cohesion (Ch. 10).

Guerrilla warfare: a type of irregular warfare or struggle in which a small group of rebels (including, but not limited to, armed civilians) employs military tactics (Ch. 9).

Guillotine: a device for decapitation (Ch. 2).

Guilt by association: a fallacy that something must be false because our enemies support it (Ch. 7).

Gutenberg Galaxy: a label for the historical period of the mass media, particularly the printing press (Ch. 13).

Habitus: cognitive and behavioral automation; it is a collection of acquired patterns of thought, behavior, and preferences (Ch. 10).

Hacker: computer experts who infiltrate systems or networks but do not seek to damage them (Ch. 13).

Hakimiyya: true sovereignty of Allah over nation-states or civil laws (Ch. 1, Box 1.1).

Halo effect: the tendency to positively interpret virtually anything a person says or does (Ch. 7).

Hamas: a Palestinian Islamist group that rules over the Gaza Strip (Ch. 12).

Hard bargaining: competitive bargaining that considers the opponent as an enemy to overcome (Ch. 15).

Hasan, Nidal Malik: the Fort Hood, TX killer in November 2009 (Ch. 11).

Hashashins: "hashish eaters" in the Middle Ages, giving rise to the term *assassins* (Ch. 1).

Hate speech: emotionally and psychologically hurtful words (Ch. 8).

Hawala: an informal Islamic banking network that connects brokers worldwide (Ch. 11).

Hawaladars: hawala dealers (Ch. 11).

Herd behavior: a type of behavior whereby individuals abandon their sense of self, get caught up in a larger group experience, and are no longer constrained by a feeling of morality or appropriateness (Ch. 10).

Hezbollah: a Shi'ite terrorist group created in Lebanon in 1982 (Ch. 13).

Hierarchical diffusion: the diffusion of terrorism that is mostly one of diffusing down (rather than up) (Ch. 12).

High-context culture: culture focusing on the context of communication, not on clear messages (Ch. 15).

Holographic: from the time information penetrates the communication system (i.e., published in some form), it is virtually everywhere (Ch. 12).

Homeland Security Advisory System Scale: a threat advisory scale using color-coded terrorism until 2011 (Ch. 16).

Homo-contextus: a new construction of social identity that does away with old stereotypes and signifies that people feel increasingly empowered to find like-minded others (Ch. 7).

Homo narrans: when communicating, humans use narratives to explain and exemplify their ideas (Ch. 6).

Horizontal transmission: diffusion between people of the same generation, like cultural sharing (Ch. 12).

Horn effect: the tendency to stereotype negatively; to negatively interpret anything a person says or does (Ch. 7).

Host: someone who has been greatly infected by a meme (Ch. 12).

Hostage crisis: when terrorists hold individuals against their will and try to resist the established order (Ch. 14).

Hostage Identification Syndrome: a situation in which positive interactions lead the hostage taker to identify with the victim (Ch. 14).

Hostage negotiation: negotiation with terrorists for the liberation of one or more hostages (Ch. 14).

Hub: a highly central node in the network (Ch. 11).

Hub and spoke design: structure in which nodes in the network communicate with the center (Ch. 1).

Hub network: network with the lowest level of shared centrality (Ch. 11).

Human intelligence: a collaborative undertaking with intelligence agencies and law enforcement officials (Ch. 16).

Hybrid organization: organization that has both criminal and terrorist features (Ch. 11).

Hypercommunicator: an engaged communicator who abundantly relies on both conventional and electronic media platforms to socially absorb or link individuals and virtual communities (Ch. 13).

Hyperreal: the blurring of differences between the real and the unreal (Ch. 13).

Hypodermic model: model in which the sender of the message selects an appropriate communication channel (e.g., face-to-face, phone, radio, e-mail, etc.) and sends a message to the receiver (Ch. 2).

Hysterical stereotype: stereotype that terrorists are crazy and disposed to committing mindless violence, are criminals and exploit political goals as an excuse to kill, and so on (Ch. 7).

Identity: the distinct personality of a person (Ch. 1).

Identity cues: a set of characteristics of a person's identity (Ch. 1).

Identity politics: the insistence on preserving strong cultural boundaries and politicizing them (Ch. 7).

Ideologies: systems of belief derived from worldviews that frame human social and political conditions (Ch. 1).

Image management: smiling or nodding more (Ch. 14).

Imam: spiritual leader in Muslim communities (Ch. 12).

Improvised news: process by which people in a crisis ask others what new things they have learned, compare notes, and feel ready to do something (Ch. 16).

Inanimate things: the blowing up of buildings and bridges (Ch. 9).

Incontinent ordinance: bombs and artillery shells dropped on civilian targets (Pentagon jargon) (Ch. 9).

Independent variable: a thing that causes another thing to change (Ch. 4).

Index: in semiotics, it is what the sender intends to accomplish (Ch. 3).

Indirect diffusion: when a group becomes familiar with the actions of another group and imitates them (Ch. 12).

Individual–group discontinuity: by simply belonging to their in-group, people agree to group perceptions and attitudes (Ch. 10).

Individualism: a principle by which people give preference to their own needs, rather than harmony, teamwork, and communal activities (the opposite of individualism is collectivism) (Ch. 6).

Individual level of mental programming: the most unique level of mental programming. No two individuals are alike. This is the level of a person's idiosyncrasies (Ch. 6).

Individual terror: a form of revolutionary terror involving the murder of isolated individuals with the purpose of promoting a political movement or causing political changes (Ch. 2).

Infection: a person's successful encoding of a meme in his or her memory (Ch. 12).

Infection recruitment: recruitment model according to which an infiltrator can be placed into the target audience to gather new recruits through direct, personal appeals (Ch. 10).

Inference tracking: a method that does not enable counterterrorism agencies to decode messages. Instead, it gives some cues as to whether messages exist and as to what is afoot (Ch. 13).

Information: a strategic resource that is essential to national security (Ch. 16).

Information environment: the collection of people, organizations, and systems that gather, process, diffuse, or take actions based on information (Ch. 16).

Information exchange: exchange of information between terrorist groups (Ch. 11).

Information Operations: practice that centers on human-related properties of information use (Ch. 16).

Information overload: too much information (Ch. 4).

Infotainment: news stories that are entertaining for the public (Ch. 3).

Ingratiation: a strategy in which a party tries to make itself more appealing to the other to set up the other for subsequent exploitation (Ch. 15).

In-group: group of people about whose welfare an individual is concerned, with whom that individual is ready to cooperate without asking for equitable returns, and from whom separation causes anxiety (Ch. 10).

In-group affect: the degree to which someone feels good when he or she thinks about the in-group (Ch. 10).

In-group ties: measure of how much someone feels he or she shares a group's fate (Ch. 10).

Institutionalization: practice whereby meaning gets implanted in society (Ch. 6).

Intellectual mode of rhetoric: type of rhetoric that applies logical-empiricist principles that govern spot-on or appropriate inferences and logical consistency to an examination of current documents, records, policy statements, or speeches (Ch. 8).

Intelligence: the collection of data to create an information database about terrorist actions and to make predictions about their behavior (Ch. 16).

Intelligence product: any result or output of examined information that can be used by law enforcement agencies, military corps, or other security units to take actions immediately (Ch. 16).

Interactive communication: a sharing of ideas where all participants are active and can have an influence on one another (Ch. 13).

Intercultural competence: the ability to embark on successful communication with other cultures (Ch. 15).

Interdependence: situation in which group members attempt to achieve the group's purpose (Ch. 10). It is the notion that actors in the system organize their efforts to achieve their task together (Ch. 16).

International communication: communication that occurs beyond national borders (Ch. 15).

International dialogue: dialogue between warring parties scattered geographically (Ch. 15).

International rule of law: the standard by which all nations are subject to and bound by supranational legal covenants (Ch. 1).

Interorganizational communication: interorganizational networking and linkages within a system (Ch. 16).

Interoperability: information sharing among agencies through technologies such as mobile phones, computer database systems, and geographic information systems (GIS) (Ch. 16).

Interpersonal communication: the exchange of symbols to achieve, in part, interpersonal goals (Ch. 14).

Interpersonal communication motives: important human needs that a group can fulfill (Ch. 10).

Interpretant: the viewer's interpretation or the resulting effect in the mind of the interpreter (Ch. 3).

Interpretive community: the idea that the audience reacts or responds to a message (Ch. 4).

Interrogation: a method of obtaining a maximum amount of true information from a prisoner or suspect (Ch. 14).

Irgun: a Jewish terrorist group that operated in the British mandate of Palestine between 1931 and 1948 (Ch. 1).

Irish Republican Army (IRA): an anti-British terrorist organization founded in Ireland in 1919 (Ch. 11).

Islamic: Muslim related (Ch. 1).

Islamist: an extreme version of "Islamic" that has connotations of militancy and terrorism (Ch. 1).

Islamophobia: an intense fear of Islam, which has increased since September 11, 2001 (Ch. 7).

Israel Defense Forces: the military forces of Israel, and Hezbollah's and Hamas's greatest enemy (Ch. 10).

Issue framing: framing that takes up a large chunk of PR activities and attempts to define an issue (Ch. 5).

Jahiliyyah: an Islamic notion of ignorance of divine guidance (Ch. 8).

Janus-faced: two-faced; said of a media organization that pretends to be fair but that "looks the other way" (Ch. 5).

Jargon: what insiders use to communicate complex or difficult ideas to each other (Ch. 9).

Jellabiya: long robe worn by Muslim males (Ch. 1).

Jemaah Islamiyah: an Islamist terrorist group active in Southeast Asia, spanning regions such as Malaysia, Singapore, and the southern Philippine islands (Ch. 6).

Jihad: "struggle" or "holy war" (Ch. 1, Box 1.1).

Jihadization: behavior focused on planning an Islamist attack (Ch. 10).

Jihad journalism: after the 9/11 attacks, it was a bias in U.S. media culture against Arabs and Muslims (Ch. 7).

Jihad vs. McWorld: model describing the struggle between jihad and "McWorld" (globalization and the political process controlled by corporations) (Ch. 1).

Kafir: those who disbelieve in Allah (Ch. 1, Box 1.1).

KIA (killed in action): dead soldiers (Ch. 9).

Kissing the enemy: a phrase used by right-wing conservatives to refer to global peace activists who adhere to fantasies of peace as their best answer to solve global conflicts (Ch. 15).

Kneecapping: firing a shot in the back of a victim's knee joint, thus shooting off the kneecap (Ch. 2).

Knowledge diffusion: a process by which knowledge can diffuse from one place to another (Ch. 12).

Knowledge exchange: exchange of information that is executable or based on experience (Ch. 11).

Kulturbrille: "cultural glasses" in German; peculiar beliefs and traditions (Ch. 6).

Laissez-faire approach: a hands-off attitude that assumes market forces will establish the norms (Ch. 5).

Language: conversation or communication aimed at maintaining reality in the subjective world (Ch. 6). It is also the means by which negotiators develop relationships and make decisions that will impact the very situation (Ch. 14).

Language game: the idea that speakers must agree on the rules of the game before communicating (Ch. 9).

Leaderless resistance: a lone-wolf maneuver in which one person mounts acts of anti-state terrorism outside of any movement, command structure, or support network (Ch. 11).

Leakage: unconscious nonverbal signals about an internal state (Ch. 14).

Leakage hierarchy: behavioral channels that are harder to control than others (Ch. 14).

Learning organizations: organizations that participate in their own practice for learning, for honing old skills or developing new ones (Ch. 10).

Legal mode of rhetoric: type of rhetoric that uses a logical-empiricist philosophy—but applies them to various texts (Ch. 8).

Legitimate force: torture (Ch. 9).

Legitimizing myths: beliefs, viewpoints, and ideologies that offer both a moral and intellectual validation for the status differences and domination of one culture over another (Ch. 6).

Lesser jihad: the external, physical effort to defend Islam (including terrorism) (Ch. 1, Box 1.1).

Lexical ambiguity: vagueness included in a word or phrase, which produces more than one interpretation (Ch. 9).

Liberalization: the removal of national restrictions on trade and foreign exchange as well as the lessening of controls on flows of capital, labor, knowledge, and technology (Ch. 13).

Licensing agreement: agreement to allow a terrorist organization to use a product or service for a particular purpose and duration (Ch. 11).

Lima syndrome: a phenomenon by which abductors develop sympathy for their captives (Ch. 14).

Lingua franca: a common international language, such as English or French (Ch. 15).

Linguistic profiling: type of discrimination whereby people (1) listen to someone's voice or recognize the type of first or last name that person has, (2) make deductions about that person's race or ethnicity, and (3) discriminate against him or her on the basis of the assumed race or ethnicity (Ch. 7).

Loaded language: highly emotive language that influences audiences by appealing to emotion (Ch. 8).

Local threat indicators: indicators used to measure more specific and localized risks of terrorism (Ch. 16).

Logrolling: a procedure by which each party grants those issues to which the other party gives top priority (Ch. 15).

Lone wolf: a person who commits terrorist acts alone, independent of any command structure (Ch. 11).

Low-context culture: culture focusing on clear and objective messages, codes, data, facts, and theories (Ch. 15).

Lunatic assassin: assassin whose purpose is intrinsically idiosyncratic and deeply personal (Ch. 11).

Madrassa: Islamic religious school or college (Ch. 6).

Madrid train bombings: bombings perpetrated by an Al Qaeda–inspired group at the Madrid train station on March 11, 2004 and that killed almost 200 people (Ch. 5).

Mala in se acts: crimes that are immoral or wrong in themselves (Ch. 1).

Mala prohibita acts: crimes that are made illegal by legislation (Ch. 1).

Managing the news: actions intended to affect the presentation of information within the mass media (Ch. 5).

Man-caused disaster: terrorism (Ch. 9).

Manipulating information: distancing oneself from the message, so if the message turns out to be false, the deceiver can extricate him- or herself (Ch. 14).

Martyr: in counterterrorism jargon, it is a person considered a terrorist for the West but a hero for terrorist groups (and their sympathizers) (Ch. 2).

Martyrdom: dying or suffering as a hero; martyrdom is associated with jihad and praised through videos, poetry, songs, and web postings (Ch. 1, Box 1.1).

Martyrdom video: a video recording, usually from Islamist activists, advocating the participation in a suicide attack and the death as a "hero" during the intended actions (Ch. 2, Box 2.1).

Masculinity: principle that favors male "machismo" power, success, material possessions, and implementation of gender segregation while devaluing interpersonal relationships (Ch. 6).

Masking: communicating an emotion that is totally different from the one that a person is experiencing (Ch. 14).

Mass communications: the institutions and methods by which news organizations use technical mechanisms (e.g., press, radio, films) to distribute content to sizable, heterogeneous, and widely diffused audiences (Ch. 3).

Mastermind: a charismatic and idealist leader with a strong interest in changing the world (Ch. 10).

Matams: public congregations in which Shi'ites meet for solemn reasons (Ch. 10).

Maypole communication: when the leader is the hub in the network and communication goes from the leader to the member and vice versa (Ch. 11).

Meaning framework: the social boundaries that surround definitions (Ch. 6).

Mean World Syndrome: the idea that interpretations of the world, through media coverage with violent content, are modified by means of cultivation; audience members are more prone to believing that the world is more dangerous than it truly is (Ch. 4).

Media: transmission channels that are used to store and deliver information (Ch. 3).

Media congestion effect: a phenomenon whereby media coverage of one group singles out coverage of other groups (Ch. 4).

Media Dependency Theory: theory positing that people become increasingly reliant on media, especially in times of crises (Ch. 5).

Media logic: the process through which media display or communicate information (Ch. 4).

Media-oriented terrorism: terrorism deliberately carried out to attract attention from the media and, accordingly, the general public (Ch. 3, Box 3.2).

Media salience: the notion that the agenda setting of the media makes some news more "high ranking" (Ch. 5).

Media templates: the myriad ways in which mass media impose a certain interpretation, organization, or story on a current news event in regard to archived images, sounds, and narratives (Ch. 5).

Media terrorism: media's use of fear to frighten and pressure the masses to act (Ch. 3).

Mediation: intervention of a third party to facilitate a negotiated settlement in the conflict (Ch. 15).

Mediatization: media's performative contribution and constitutive involvement not only in describing the news but also in generating them and, eventually, interpreting them (Ch. 5).

Meme: any unit of information which one mind diffuses (verbally or by demonstration) to another mind (Ch. 12).

Meme antibody: a meme that reacts to markedly toxic ideas (Ch. 12).

Memeoid: an individual whose behavior is deeply shaped by a meme (Ch. 12).

Memeplex: a collection of memes often found within the same person (Ch. 12).

Meme pool: the compilation of all memes existing in a specific population (Ch. 12).

Meme replication: when an individual receives a meme and enacts in real life (Ch. 12).

Memetic engineering: the process of creating memes with the purpose of changing the behavior of people (Ch. 12).

Memotype: the real information content of a meme (Ch. 12).

Mergers and acquisitions: type of collaboration whereby terrorist organizations have managed to enter into product and develop agreements and realize the effectiveness of working together (Ch. 11).

Message Influence Model: model in which the message is a conduit for conveying information to a receiver. The purpose is to make sure that he or she understands the information in the same way as the source (Ch. 2).

Metteur en scène: director of choreographer of something (Ch. 4).

Microexpressions: minuscule facial expressions that are performed for less than a quarter of a second (Ch. 14).

Mimetism: a theory explaining the capacity of imitation (to mimic) (Ch. 12).

Mimetic rivalry: concept describing terrorism as a consequence of competition between nations (Ch. 12).

Mirror neuron: a brain cell that is capable to seize and interpret information and imitate this as action (Ch. 12).

Misbaha: a necklace; prayer beads (Ch. 1).

Mise en scène: the idea of directing and choreographing something (Ch. 4).

Misinformation: inaccurate information that is disseminated unintentionally (Ch. 16).

Model of terrorism and its target audiences: a model showing there are multiple audiences for the terrorist messages (Ch. 4).

Model of terrorism as a communication process: model in which the terrorist conveys a message to a target audience (i.e., the general public, the government, an organization, etc.) by committing an act of violence. The message, in and of itself, is not the violence. Instead, it is encoded within such an activity (Ch. 2).

Modern terrorism: terrorism whereby attacks are more indiscriminate and destruction is much higher (Ch. 1).

Mortality salience: awareness of one's eventual death (Ch. 10).

Mossad: the Israeli secret service (Ch. 16).

Motive talk: anything that motivates people to make their own assessment of a situation (Ch. 16).

Mourning sickness: a collective emotional grieving by individuals at the death of media personalities or victims of violence (Ch. 4).

Mujahedin: Muslims doing the jihad (Ch. 1).

Mullah: Islamic scholar (Ch. 12).

Multi-track diplomacy: the combination of five track diplomacies: Track I, Track II, Track III, Track IV, and Track V (Ch. 15).

Muslim Brotherhood: an organization created in 1928 to bring back the spirit and religious purity that existed when the Prophet Muhammad and the four Rightly Guided caliphs were alive (Ch. 12).

Mutaween: religious police in Saudi Arabia (Ch. 1).

Narco-guerrillas: drug-trafficking terrorist groups that play a big role in the drug business (Ch. 11).

Narodnaya Volya: a Russian terrorist organization notorious for the killing of Czar Alexander II of Russia (Ch. 2).

Narrative: a mode of reasoning to make sense of the world (Ch. 6).

Narrative fidelity: when stories, myths, or folk tales told in a community are in harmony with the culture of that community (Ch. 6).

Narrative transportation: the degree to which someone becomes absorbed in a story while engaged with it (Ch. 7).

National Terrorism Advisory System: a two-level terrorism threat advisory scale of the U.S. Department of Homeland Security (DHS). It has been used since 2011 (Ch. 16).

Natural language: ordinary language; any language that arises naturally, in a spontaneous and unpremeditated manner (Ch. 9).

Near enemy: Muslim government and form of Islamic law that do not embrace the jihadist view (Ch. 1, Box 1.1).

Negative cult: a system of group norms that symbolizes the cultural taboos and prohibitions from which people must refrain if they are to be seen as group members (Ch. 10).

Negative emotional climate: an emotional climate developed from a negative context, like a terrorist attack that has just occurred (Ch. 6).

Negotiating temperament: type of negotiating style (Ch. 15).

Negotiation: a process by which strategies are used to determine the circumstances that allow the conflicting parties to arrive at a mutually satisfactory agreement (Ch. 14).

Negotiation theory: how parties come to a solution rather than what solution they select (Ch. 15).

Neo-ummah: a constructed, imaginary worldwide community of all Muslims (Ch. 12).

Net recruitment: recruitment model according to which every person in a target audience is considered "good enough" for terrorism recruitment (Ch. 10).

Netwar: a war waged by terrorists and criminals thanks to a networked organizational structure (Ch. 11).

Network density: the number of links in the network divided by the highest number of all possible links (Ch. 11).

Networking: developing an interconnected system that links groups with common goals or values (Ch. 11).

Neutralize: kill (which is what the CIA does, according to late stand-up comedian George Carlin) (Ch. 9).

Neutron bomb: enhanced radiation device (Ch. 9).

New Islamic world order: an expressed will to power and a tremendous ambition to rebuild a Caliphate (Ch. 1).

New racism: type of racism that is to be found in the context of belonging and nationalism, and relies on stereotypes of cultural characteristics that are repeated in media and political discourses (Ch. 7).

New terrorism: terrorism that is indiscriminate, causes as many casualties as possible, and uses extreme violence. It is also driven by religious fanaticism (Ch. 1).

News event: a newsworthy topic that captures broad public attention (Ch. 3).

News frame: representation of regulated formats for selection, highlighting, and exclusion of news (Ch. 5).

News media: news sources like television, radio, print journalism, and the Internet (Ch. 3).

News triage: a selection process to determine what news should be reported or ignored (Ch. 5).

New world order: a wide-ranging global agenda intended to change the world, establish new ideologies, and eventually replace sovereign nation-states (Ch. 1).

Nintendo war: a media or government tactic whereby images of corpses, blood, and brutality are removed, and whereby neutral or euphemistic language is used to describe the events (Ch. 5).

Node: point in a network where critical elements are stored or transferred (Ch. 11).

Noncontagious diffusion: collaboration between terrorist organizations (Ch. 12).

Non-emotional offender: offender who is calculating and experiences little to no remorse (Ch. 14).

Non-normative stereotype: an overgeneralization that is entirely self-projective; people project concepts from their own culture onto people of other cultures (Ch. 7).

Non-relational diffusion: diffusion that occurs when one terrorist organization imitates another organization's ideas without the two interacting (Ch. 12).

Nonverbal communication: the process of sending and receiving wordless messages (Ch. 14).

Normative stereotype: an overgeneralization that draws on limited information, like the information we learn from a travel guide (Ch. 7).

Object: the "referent"; what the sign refers to or symbolizes (Ch. 3).

Obscurantism: the practice of purposefully keeping the full details of some issue from becoming known (Ch. 9).

Occidentalism: negative constructions of America and dehumanizing assessments of the West (Ch. 8).

Oklahoma City bombing: terrorist incident in which Timothy McVeigh blew up a governmental building in April 1995 (Ch. 3, Box 3.2).

Old racism: type of racism that has to do with a sociobiological conception of race—a principle of racial hierarchies and superiority (Ch. 7).

Old terrorism: terrorism that strikes only selected targets (Ch. 1).

One-down effect: a situation in which terrorist-negotiators, who have fewer alternatives than their counterpart, lean toward using extreme measures to attain power dominance (Ch. 14).

One-sided coverage: biased coverage whereby the conventional news frame is so powerful and ubiquitous that journalists, politicians, and the audience are usually unaware of this process (Ch. 5).

Ontological insecurity: the fear of the incapacity to maintain global order because terrorism is a threat (Ch. 13).

Ontology: the study of being, existence, nature, and the world (Ch. 13).

Open view of Islam: view of Islam as a diverse and broad-minded religion with internal differences, disputes, and developments (Ch. 7).

Opinion leadership: the practice whereby charismatic individuals are able to sway people's attitudes or plain behavior in a desired fashion with relative frequency (Ch. 12).

Optimistic appeal: in persuasion, it is an appeal that promises the audience that victory will happen should they start war (Ch. 8).

Organization: a collectivity consisting of and maintained by people (Ch. 11).

Orientalism: the idea that a culture or religious movement like Islam is considered inferior, barbaric, or incompatible with democracy (Ch. 7).

Oslo Accords: also called the *Declaration of Principles* (DOP), they were accords that endorsed mutual recognition for the rights of Palestinians and Israelis to live side-by-side peacefully (Ch. 10).

Other-deindividuation: when new members learn how to categorize their social world into those who are in the in-group (i.e., "us") and those who are in the out-group (i.e., "them") (Ch. 10).

Othering: a course of action whereby society labels an inferior group into existence (Ch. 6). It also means labeling and degrading cultures and groups other than one's own (Ch. 8).

Out-group: group with which a person has something to divide, maybe unequally (Ch. 10).

Outliers: rogue states (Ch. 9).

Overseas Contingency Operations: Global War on Terror (GWOT) (Ch. 9).

Oxygen of publicity: a phrase used in the 1980s by Margaret Thatcher, then PM of Britain, to refer to the daily IRA bombings and killings reported on the newspapers' front pages and the 6 p.m. TV news (Ch. 2).

Paradigm: a way of interpreting the world that has been accepted by a group of people (Ch. 1).

Paradigm shift: when a paradigm changes and people interpret the world differently (Ch. 1).

Parallel globalization of terror: the idea that terrorism has power equal to the bright side of globalization (Ch. 13).

Parasocial interaction: the degree to which the audience has a personal relationship with a celebrity (Ch. 4).

Participant observation: the process in which an ethnographer creates and maintains long-term rapport with multiple people in a group in its natural environment (Ch. 6).

Participatory journalists: independent journalists who report both in mainstream media and in Internet-based outlets (Ch. 16).

Patriot Act: a legal sanction for the FBI, CIA, or another federal agency to search citizens' phone, financial, or e-mail records without a warrant or court order (Ch. 9).

Peacekeeping: providing military personnel by a third party to supervise and control a cease-fire (Ch. 15).

Peer mentoring: mentoring that takes place between an older or more experienced member and a novice (Ch. 10).

Pejorative term: a term that is fraught with negative and derogatory meanings (Ch. 1).

People Against Gangsterism and Drugs: established in 1996, PAGAD launched a crusade of violence to object to the values of an "immoral" South African society (Ch. 4).

People of the Book: the term for non-Muslim monotheistic peoples (mostly Jews and Christians) (Ch. 1, Box 1.1).

Perceptual pluralism: differences between the parties' cultural standpoints (Ch. 15).

Performance as Political Action: theory that rests on the premise that humans participate in a performance-centered method of communicating with the purpose of changing the audience's behavior (Ch. 4).

Personality cult: a phenomenon whereby a charismatic leader gradually becomes an object of adoration (Ch. 11).

Personalization of an attack: the effect that a terrorist attack has on the audience that is not directly struck by the attack (Ch. 4).

Persona non grata: unwanted person (Ch. 15).

Persuasion: a form of influence whereby the sender attempts to make the receiver adopt or change an idea, attitude, or action (Ch. 4).

Philosophy of the bomb: the idea that bombing enemies was the only viable social noise and means of social change (Ch. 2).

Photojournalism: journalism that captures images in a timely manner to tell a news story (Ch. 5).

Physical exchange: material and physical cooperation between terrorist groups (Ch. 11).

Physical spectacle: when a terrorist act creates a spectacle by overpowering the audience's senses (Ch. 4).

Pie metaphor: a distributive strategy in which the negotiator's goal is to obtain all that he or she can (Ch. 15).

Pinocchio response: a behavior or pattern of behaviors present in all humans when lying (Ch. 14).

Pirate: Islamist terrorist off the African Coast (Ch. 9).

Plain English: precision and elimination of ambiguity in English (Ch. 9).

Plain Language Movement: a movement motivated by semantic transparency (Ch. 9).

Politics of representation: linguistic device often associated with a coherent body of knowledge rather than isolated pieces of information (Ch. 9).

Polyseme: a word or concept with multiple, related meanings (Ch. 9).

Popular Front for the Liberation of Palestine: a Palestinian Marxist movement considered a terrorist organization by over 30 countries (Ch. 2).

Positive cult: a system of group norms that prescribe the codes of expected, normative behavior (Ch. 10).

Positive role model: a conventional pattern of rebellion and resistance exploited for terrorist legitimacy and self-image (Ch. 11).

Postmodernism: a cultural movement of the late 20th century that embraces the philosophy that humans live in an age of personal freedom from imposed rules and social limitations (Ch. 13).

Postmodern terrorism: terrorism that uses CBRN or launches attacks against "symbols" of the enemy (Ch. 1).

Postponed obedience: strengthened compliance with the principles represented by the fallen buddies (Ch. 10).

Power distance: the degree of equality (or inequality) among subordinates and superiors in a society (Ch. 6).

Predictive profiling: a procedure of threat assessment that predicts and classifies the ability of criminal or terrorist modus operandi (i.e., methods of operation) (Ch. 16).

Pre-incident indicators: the criminal and social actions of people and groups prior to a terrorist attack (Ch. 16).

Pre-packaging: the prior absorption of words and ideas that usually results in nebulousness, oversimplification, and stereotyping of language (Ch. 9).

Pre-radicalization: stage during which the individual has not started the process of radicalization yet (Ch. 10).

Preventive reaction strike: air raid (Ch. 9).

Pride-and-ego down: attacking the prisoner's self-esteem to extract important information from him or her (Ch. 9).

Primary group: a small interpersonal group in which people share personal and lasting relationships (Ch. 10).

Print media: newspapers, journals, magazines, and books (Ch. 3).

Problem solving: adopting an alternative that meets the aspirations of both sides (Ch. 15).

Prodrome: a warning sign that a terrorist attack may happen (Ch. 16).

Professional socialization: the institutionalized method whereby people are socialized into a group environment of cruelty toward out-groups (Ch. 10).

Propaganda: intentionally deceptive communication (Ch. 8).

Propaganda by the Deed: terrorism used as a tool of communication to galvanize the masses and trigger a revolution (Ch. 2).

Provisional Irish Republican Army: terrorist group that split from the IRA in 1969 (Ch. 11).

Pro-war rhetoric: a type of propaganda to persuade the audience that war is necessary (Ch. 8).

Proxemics: the study of space and distance (Ch. 4).

Psychological contract: the shared beliefs, perceptions, and informal obligations between an organization and an employee (Ch. 10).

Public character of terrorism: by witnessing a terrorist act, the audience publicly interacts with terrorists (Ch. 4).

Public sphere: when private individuals assemble to form a public body (Ch. 13).

Pyramid model: vertical model of which the foundation is made up of sympathizers with the terrorist cause who are not necessarily ready to start engaging in terrorist activities. Terrorists may be seen as occupying the top of the pyramid (Ch. 10).

Pyramidal structure: structure that displays a massive base of support culminating in a small number of terrorists (i.e., the leaders) at the top (Ch. 11).

Qutb, Sayyid: leading activist of the Egyptian Muslim Brotherhood who employed deep-seated, hateful rhetoric against America and the West (Ch. 8).

Racial profiling: a situation in which law enforcement officials throw a wide blanket of suspicion that entraps and harms members of racial groups—even though those members can be innocent of any wrongdoing (Ch. 7).

Racism: the view that intrinsic differences exist in people's traits and abilities that are completely due to their race, however defined, and that accordingly justify those people being mistreated (Ch. 7).

Radicalization window: in the radicalization stages, the individual is going through times during which he or she is the most vulnerable (i.e., to getting their views altered, etc.) (Ch. 10).

RAND: a California-based nonprofit global policy institution that is a major frontrunner in terrorism and counterterrorism studies (Ch. 1).

Rational mode of rhetoric: type of rhetoric that employs reason, considers evidence, and evaluates costs vs. benefits so as to explain events (Ch. 8).

Red Brigades: a communist terrorist group from Italy in the 1970s and 1980s (Ch. 10).

Redemptive terrorism: a form of terrorism that attempts to coerce a higher force into ceding specific human (e.g., prisoners) or material (e.g., money) resources (Ch. 2).

Regicide: the killing of kings (Ch. 1).

Reign of Terror: a campaign of large-scale violence by the French state during the French Revolution (Ch. 1).

Relational development: theory that relationships evolve into stages as a result of interpersonal dialogue (Ch. 14).

Relational diffusion: diffusion that occurs when the ideas of terrorist organizations diffuse to individuals with a shared identity (Ch. 12).

Relevant arguments theory: theory positing that a culturally motivated pool of arguments supports one side of the issue over the other side (Ch. 10).

Religious idealist: terrorist who has faith in the destructive interpretation of Islam as a moral ideology (Ch. 14).

Relocation diffusion: diffusion that occurs when terrorist organizations move from one place to another (Ch. 12).

Repetition: a form of rhetorical technique using a word or phrase that is repeated time and again, thus getting stuck in the audience's head (Ch. 8).

Representamen: the actual sign itself; what something is (Ch. 3).

Representative negotiation: negotiation done through representatives (Ch. 15).

Resonating: the idea that a meme must match a basic human need, want, or value to be adopted (Ch. 12).

Resource of language: a technique used by a speaker to send people a meaning with the purpose of persuading them toward looking at an issue from a different angle (Ch. 8).

Responsibility framing: framing that ascribes causes and assigns causal accountability (Ch. 5).

Restorative rhetoric: rhetoric focused on helping those affected by a crisis handle loss (Ch. 16).

Rhetoric: the art of communicating efficiently and with persuasion through language (Ch. 8).

Rhetorical strands: rhetorical dimensions that are formed and interwoven in public places (Ch. 6).

Ring Leader: a "field captain" (Ch. 10).

Risk: the socially constructed perception of the likelihood that a negative event will occur (Ch. 16).

Risk assessment: the measure of the risk from data to produce a risk probability (Ch. 16).

Risk communication: the detection of risks to the public health and attempts to persuade the audience to assume healthier, less risky behaviors (Ch. 16).

Risk evaluation: the perception that a society attributes to the risks that face them in agreeing on what steps to take about the risks (Ch. 16).

Risk management: the assessment of the importance of a particular risk and an evaluation of how significant the risk is (Ch. 16).

Risky shift: enhanced agreement on the opinion at hand, and a shift in the average opinion of members toward the opinion of the whole group (Ch. 10).

Rogue nation: nation intent on developing weapons of mass destruction (Ch. 9).

Rumor: an unconfirmed account or explanation of events that diffuses from individual to individual (Ch. 16).

Rumor control center: center that helps diffuse accurate information (hoping, of course, that there is true information out there) during crises, terrorist attacks, or natural disasters (Ch. 16).

Safe haven: a geographical location in which terrorists can successfully set up an organizational and operational base (Ch. 11).

Saga: in symbolic convergence theory, it is a detailed description of the achievements in the life of an individual, group, community, organization, or country (Ch. 10).

Salafist Group for Preaching and Combat: an Algeria-based Islamist terrorist group founded in 1998 and that seeks to overthrow the Algerian government and establish an Islamic state (Ch. 10).

Salafiyyah: the renewal of authentic Islam (Ch. 10).

Salience transfer: the power of media organizations to transfer issues of salience from their own media agendas to public agendas (Ch. 5).

Scale-free network: network that shows a power distribution in which a small number of nodes may have a massive number of links (Ch. 11).

Scapegoating: a practice whereby a group creates a crystal-clear separation by holding another group automatically responsible for all problems (Ch. 10).

Schmoozing: casual conversation or gossip (in this context, with terrorists) (Ch. 15).

Script breakdown: normalized interpersonal relationships between hostages and hostage takers (Ch. 14).

Second-hand terrorism: a practice whereby media outlets excessively stress the possibility for anyone of being a direct victim of terrorism (Ch. 3).

Second media age: age of cyberspace and interactive media (Ch. 13).

Second party: the idea that the audience is the immediate target of the message (Ch. 4).

Second Wave of terrorism: colonial wave of terrorism, confined within national geographical boundaries from 1921 until today (Ch. 1).

Sectarian conflict: civil war (Ch. 9).

Seed crystal recruitment: recruitment model according to which terrorist-recruiters attempt to offer a context for self-recruitment (Ch. 10).

Selective moral disengagement: the rhetorical effort of communicators to disengage or detach themselves from their own use of hostility or aggression (Ch. 8).

Selective terrorism: selectively targeting people in a terrorist attack (Ch. 2).

Self-deindividuation: elimination of a person's individual identity, both externally and internally (Ch. 10).

Self-esteem and self-actualization values: values referring to having feelings of accomplishment, inner harmony, self-respect, and wisdom (Ch. 4).

Self-starter cell: a recent type of terrorist cell whereby a group has little or no connection with the original overarching terrorist network (Ch. 11).

Semantic transparency: method to eliminate needlessly or superfluously intricate language from government, media, academia, law, and business (Ch. 9).

Semiotics: the study of signs and symbols, especially their processes and systems (Ch. 3).

Sensation-seeking: looking for personal reward, including the thrill of the combative lifestyle and a feeling of empowerment, through violence (Ch. 1).

Sentimental stereotype: stereotype of terrorists who can be shown sympathy by the audience (Ch. 7).

Sentiment pool: people who already share the grumbles, objections, and attributional characteristics of the movement (Ch. 12).

Service the target: kill the enemy, according to the Pentagon (Ch. 9).

Shadow archetype: shadowy attributes and repugnant traits are projected onto others, leading to paranoia, accusations, and lack of intimacy (Ch. 6).

Shahid: suicide bomber (Ch. 2).

Sharia: "Islamic law"; the required implementation of virtuous vs. materialistic, status-driven behavior based on group interpretation (Ch. 1, Box 1.1).

Shifting metaphors: uses of language that serve to connect the way people currently see a situation or issue with the way the government would like them to view the situation or issue (Ch. 9).

Shi'ites: composing 10% to 15% of world Muslims, Shi'ites are often more ecstatic in religious practice and have messianic hopes that a future prophet will bring justice on earth (Ch. 10).

Shock advertising: a form of advertising that is controversial, distressing, and graphic (Ch. 2).

Shock and awe tactics: tactics that form a traumatic spectacle and that can be justified as a humane method of restraint (Ch. 4).

Shocking the conscience: objective of torture (Ch. 9).

Sica: short sword used by the Sicarii ("sica" is the first four letters of the group's name) (Ch. 1).

Sicarii: a Zealot-affiliated religious sect fighting against Roman occupiers in 66–73 CE (Ch. 1).

Sikh terrorists: terrorists in Punjab (northwestern India, close to Pakistan) who fight to have an independent Sikh state to be called Khalistan (Ch. 6).

Sign: something that stands for something else (Ch. 3).

Signal: in semiotics, it is a statement conveyed from a sender to a receiver (Ch. 3).

Signal intelligence: the use of state-of-the-art resources to intercept financial data, monitor communications (e.g., conversations via cell phones), and read e-mail content (Ch. 16).

Signature method: a method that is strongly associated with the operational activities of a terrorist group (Ch. 2).

Signified: the absent part of a sign; it is symbolic (Ch. 3).

Signifier: the visible, or material, part of a sign (Ch. 3).

Simulation: the act of feeling an emotion when there is no such emotion (Ch. 14).

Sleeper cell: an isolated cell of sleeper agents who are members of an intelligence network or organization (Ch. 11).

Sleep management: torture that prevents a prisoner from getting regular sleep for about 100 hours (Ch. 9).

Slighting aggression by advantageous comparison: highlighting the flagrant misdeeds of the government as an excuse for engaging in terrorist attacks against it (Ch. 10).

Slogan: a memorable maxim, watchword, or phrase used as a repetitive expression of an idea or objective (Ch. 8).

Small-group radicalization: a process involving significant change in an individual's or group's orienting beliefs and motivations (Ch. 10).

Snow fall: the degree distinction between having snow and not having snow may be just one or two degrees, but the functional distinction is green grass versus white snow (Ch. 12).

Social amplification: observing signals that a terrorist attack is underway and educating audiences about the potential risks by developing communication between society and the risks themselves (Ch. 16).

Social communication: communication that can be noticed, transmitted, and understood by all (Ch. 2).

Social comparison theory: theory positing that opinions possess social values associated to them (Ch. 10).

Social construct: the way people perceive reality (Ch. 6).

Social construction of reality: the model according to which humans who interact in society create, over time, concepts of the world around them (Ch. 6).

Social dominance theory: theory suggesting that people with high social dominance orientation aspire to group inequality and support attitudes and policies that bolster social hierarchies (Ch. 6).

Social epidemics: idea-driven social movements that diffuse through a culture by exponential, rather than geometric, growth (Ch. 12).

Social Identity Theory: theory analyzing interactions between in-groups and out-groups (Ch. 10).

Social learning theory: theory that violence is a result of witnessing and imitating an aggressive model (Ch. 12).

Socially constructed emotions: emotions felt by individuals as a consequence of their membership in a particular group or society (Ch. 6).

Social marginalization: the process of becoming or being made marginal in society (Ch. 10).

Social mnemonics: methods by which people recall what their groups consider to be important (Ch. 16).

Social Movement Theory: theory that explains the social production and diffusion of meaning and how people come to see themselves as a collectivity (Ch. 12).

Social network: a pattern of connections developed by the flow of messages between communicators through space and time (Ch. 11).

Social network analysis: theory positing that nodes (i.e., people, organizations, events, etc.) are points in the network and are linked through complex yet understandable connections that shape networks (Ch. 11).

Social noise: a practice of being conspicuously noticeable by means of noisy or controversial actions (Ch. 2).

Social proof: a powerful psychological means by which we emulate others to direct our own actions (Ch. 12).

Social sharing: situation in which individuals interact with others concerning an emotion-triggering event and their own feelings (Ch. 6).

Socio-structural white noise: when memes are self-replicating and ubiquitous in all cultures, present in the subconscious background (Ch. 12).

Soft bargaining: bargaining which is highly pacifying to the point of conceding important positions (Ch. 15).

Software of the mind: our way of thinking, our thinking pattern, and the sources of our mental programs (Ch. 6).

Sophism: the art of using pointless or unsupported arguments for deceiving others (Ch. 8).

Sorties: bombing (Ch. 9).

Sound bite: a very short snippet of a speech extracted from a longer speech or an interview (Ch. 5).

Spatial differentiation: when organizations are loosely organized cells in which members operate in different places (Ch. 11).

Specific threat indicators: indicators used to assess the susceptibility or weakness of a particular target (Ch. 16).

Spectacle: a major human event portrayed as a form of drama or "theater" (Ch. 4).

Spectaculturization: spectacle of violence used to confirm the fears of the audience and their feelings of unrest during times of emergency and political uncertainty (Ch. 3).

Speech act theory: theory positing that speakers use language to accomplish intended actions and, in doing so, hearers conclude or interpret intended meaning from what speakers said (Ch. 9).

Speech code theory: a framework for communication in a particular speech community (Ch. 9).

Spillover effect: an effect observed in violent domestic conflicts that develop internationally, so that revolutions "spill over" national borders into the international arena (Ch. 12).

"Staircase to Terrorism" model: a six-step model in which a person develops, through a long-term socialization process, the aspiration to engage in terrorism (Ch. 10).

Status conferral: the amount of attention given to particular people (Ch. 3).

Steganography: an ancient practice of concealing messages within texts, pictures, and objects (Ch. 13).

Stereotype: a simplified mental picture of a group of people who have certain characteristics in common (Ch. 7).

Stern Gang: a militant Zionist group that sought to expel the British from Palestine in the 1940s (Ch. 1).

Stigma: the process by which normal identity is smeared by the response or feedback of others (Ch. 7).

Stigmatization: an invisible sign of condemnation which allows "insiders" to set boundaries around the "outsiders" to delineate the limits of inclusion in any group (Ch. 7).

Stockholm syndrome: a psychological phenomenon in which hostages show admiration and have positive feelings for their captors (Ch. 14).

Storyline pegs: new events placed into familiar categories (Ch. 5).

Storytelling: charismatic leaders have been known to be storytellers because they can inspire followers through fascinating stories (Ch. 11).

Strategically controlled behavior: the suppression of signals that might show that one is lying (Ch. 14).

Strategic ambiguity: attaching importance to the symbolic and dialogic aspect of language and the multicultural sources for interpretations of meanings (Ch. 15).

Strategic differentiation: when organizations have operating tasks in various areas or specialties (Ch. 11).

Strategic political communication: a method whereby speakers design their public language with the objective of creating, controlling, disseminating, and employing mediated messages as a political resource (Ch. 8).

Strength of weak ties: theory positing that, when looking for information, "weak ties" matter more than "strong ties" (Ch. 11).

Stress and duress: interrogation technique for prisoners who are seen as a threat to the United States (Ch. 9).

Suicide bombing: the act of blowing oneself up and other people in the process (Ch. 2).

Supergroup: group of peers who are task obsessed, extremely focused, greatly loyal, and producing a felt and communicable single-mindedness (Ch. 10).

Supersize terrorism: overstate the threat of terrorism (Ch. 3).

Support: a set of positive psychosocial relationships between members characterized by mutual trust and concern (Ch. 10).

Suppress: kill (Ch. 9).

Surgical strike: a military attack that leads to, is intended to lead to, or is claimed to have led to only damage to the intended legitimate target (Ch. 9).

Surrogate interrogator: a person who stands next to the actual interrogator and who routinely edits, adds, or subtracts information uttered by one or more parties (Ch. 14).

Survival, safety, and security values: values referring to comfortable living, being in a world at peace, and enjoying equality, freedom, national security, and deliverance (or redemption) (Ch. 4).

Swarming terrorist network: network with a horizontal deployment of small terrorist subgroups interacting with each other (Ch. 11).

Symbiotic relationship: terrorism–media relationship in which terrorism attracts cameras, and cameras attract terrorism (Ch. 3).

Symbol: a mental structure, a form of knowledge representation—that is, a figure that stands for and takes the place of something else (Ch. 10).

Symbolic annihilation: a lack of representation of which the outcome is the reinforcement of stereotypes (Ch. 7).

Symbolic convergence theory: theory positing that sharing group fantasies leads to symbolic convergence. Examples of fantasies are jokes, narratives, and metaphors (Ch. 10).

Symbolic cue: in symbolic convergence theory, it is an abbreviated indication or signal like a symbol, sign, or inside joke that represents a fantasy theme (Ch. 10).

Symbolic DNA (of terrorism): a mythic symbolic scheme that functions as both a persuasive and an epistemic mechanism (Ch. 10).

Symbolic interactionism: theory positing that people communicate through shared symbols—for example, words, definitions, roles, and gestures (Ch. 6).

Symbolic universe: group of beliefs that "everybody knows" (Ch. 6).

Synchronous communication: communication restricted to episodes where both parties are present (Ch. 13).

Syncretism: religious or cultural synthesis (Ch. 12).

Synergy: the act of working together; interdependence (Ch. 16).

Systems theory: theory positing that the whole is greater than the sum of the parts and the parts depend on each other (Ch. 16).

Tacit knowledge: knowledge that is much less transferrable between people (Ch. 11).

Takfir: disbelief in Allah (Ch. 1, Box 1.1).

Technorati.com: website that collects blogs from all over the world (Ch. 3).

Techno-terrorism: a terrorist means of satellite communications, e-mail, and the World Wide Web (Ch. 13).

Template: a category of belief explanations (Ch. 16).

Terminological fog: a circumlocution of meaning (i.e., lie or untruth) (Ch. 9).

Terminological inexactitude: a circumlocution of meaning (i.e., lie or untruth) (Ch. 9).

Territorial appeal: in persuasion, it is an appeal that threatens the audience's "sense of territoriality" (Ch. 8).

Terror: from the Latin *terrere*, it means "frighten" or "tremble" (Ch. 1).

Terror cimbricus: in ancient Rome, it was a state of panic and emergency in response to the coming of the Cimbri tribe killers in 105 BCE (Ch. 1).

Terrorism: the use of violence to create fear (i.e., terror, psychic fear) for (1) political, (2) religious, or (3) ideological reasons (Ch. 1).

Terrorist organization: an illicit clandestine organization that generally consists of planners, trainers, and actual bombers/killers (Ch. 1).

Terrorist spectaculars: when large terrorist attacks are carried out to attract rising attention through the intensification of horror (Ch. 4).

Tertiary identities: identities are exclusive to those who have indirectly witnessed a terrorist attack (Ch. 4).

Tetradic framework: McLuhan's law of the media that explains transformations in world life and the media through four fundamental steps (Ch. 7).

Theater: the idea that a terrorist spectacle has a "looking" or visual character, a visual dimension (Ch. 4).

Thematic frames: frames that offer a broader and more contextualized interpretation of the root causes that lead to issues (Ch. 5).

Thick description: an in-depth observation and account (from the observation) of a natural setting (Ch. 6).

Third degree: wreaking pain, physical or mental, to extricate confessions or statements during the interrogation of a prisoner or would-be terrorist (Ch. 9).

Third party: the idea that the audience is the target beyond the immediate target of the message (Ch. 4).

Third-party intervention: a type of intermediacy by an individual or team of people who get involved in a conflict to help the conflicting parties manage or resolve it (Ch. 15).

Third Wave of terrorism: contemporary wave of terrorism; it introduced international terrorism, crossing national boundaries, which began in the 1960s (Ch. 1).

Thought contagion: the diffusion of memes from brain to brain (Ch. 12).

Threat fatigue: a gradual avoidance of sensitivity toward threat warnings after being overexposed to them (Ch. 4).

Thromise: a combination of "threat" and "promise" (Ch. 15).

Thugs of India: Hindu worshippers who strangled sacrificial victims from the 13th to the 19th century (Ch. 1).

Tightly coupled network: network in which leaders are able to exert strategic and tactical control (Ch. 11).

Tipping point: the period during which a conspicuous change takes places within the behavior or outlook of a population (Ch. 12).

Tit-for-tat: the biblical "eye for an eye" and "tooth for a tooth" (Ch. 15).

Toxic meme: self-replicating meme of nefarious information (Ch. 12).

Trait theory: theory positing that leaders are born to lead (i.e., with innate traits) (Ch. 11).

Transgressive spectacle: a situation in which the terrorist act creates a spectacle by commanding the audience's gaze for the simple reason that the terrorist act is an infringement on widely established rules (Ch. 4).

Translating well: the idea that terrorist violence is a dramatic form of spectacle—something that is so engaging that the audience stops and takes notice (Ch. 4).

Transnational Bads: terrorists who have exploited the shift to unprecedented global relations (Ch. 13).

Traveling theory: theory positing that both people and ideas travel from one country to another (Ch. 12).

Triadic hostage negotiation: negotiation in which the hostage taker sends a warning to the hostages; the hostages make requests to the hostage negotiator (or the general audience). Naturally, as they are the "go-betweens," the hostages will report back to the hostage taker (Ch. 14).

Tribal stigma: characteristics, imagined or real, of racial groups, nationalities, or religions that are viewed as deviating from the predominant normative race, nationality, or religion (Ch. 7).

Tri-Border Area: the area where Argentina, Brazil, and Paraguay join (Ch. 13, Box 13.1).

Triggering events: incidents that transform a person from being a passive yet enraged observer into an active and driven terrorist (Ch. 6).

Trust: group members' willingness to have confident expectations from each other (Ch. 10).

Tupamaros: a violent revolutionary organization in Uruguay in the 1960s and 1970s (Ch. 5).

T-word: terrorism, or dropping the "T" bomb (Ch. 9).

TWA flight 847: famous incident in which an airliner was hijacked by Hezbollah on June 14, 1985 (Ch. 2).

Two-sided coverage: coverage in which there is usually greater awareness of the framing process, as well as of challenge and disagreement with particular portrayals by certain media outlets (Ch. 5).

Tyrannicide: the killing of tyrants (Ch. 1).

Umbrella: a group that protects, supports, and motivates smaller terrorist groups (Ch. 11).

Ummah: the global Muslim community (Ch. 10).

Unabomber: Ted Kaczynski, an anarchist against technological progress who committed a mail bombing spree (Ch. 3, Box 3.1).

Unabomber Manifesto: the Unabomber's 35,000-word essay ("Industrial Society and Its Future") (Ch. 3, Box 3.1).

Uncertainty avoidance: principle that represents the level of intolerance for risk or uncertain situations within a culture (Ch. 6).

Uncertainty Reduction Theory: theory positing that, on meeting for the first time, strangers will go through certain steps to decrease uncertainty about each other (Ch. 14).

Unholy triangle: network of terrorists, drug smugglers, and government officials determined to destroy the Western world (Ch. 11).

Universal level of mental programming: the least unique but most basic level of mental programming shared by the entire humankind (Ch. 6).

Universal pragmatics: the model of mutual understanding through clear communication (Ch. 9).

Unknown unknown: circumstances that were not anticipated by an observer at any given point in time (Ch. 9).

Unlawful combatant: terrorist (Ch. 9).

Uses and Gratifications Theory: theory assuming that audiences are in control of choosing media that meet their needs (Ch. 4).

"Us vs. them" dichotomy: a practice that classifies people into one or the other of their multiple cultural, ethnic, or national dimensions (Ch. 8).

Utmost speed: when information reaches its destination in the quickest way and shortest time possible (Ch. 12).

Verbal aggression: when someone attacks the self-concept of another person (Ch. 8).

Vertical differentiation: structure that has strata or gradations of hierarchy and supervision (Ch. 11).

Vertical transmission: diffusion from parents to offspring (from generation to generation) (Ch. 12).

Violent eschatology: when a group believes it must start a war to cleanse the earth before the second coming of a god (Ch. 10).

Violent extremism: terrorism (Ch. 9).

Violent non-state actor: any actor or group on the global level that is not a state (Ch. 13).

Virtual community: a social network of people who communicate through specific online media (Ch. 13).

Virtual group dynamics: networked groups that are in contact electronically (Ch. 13).

Virtual organization: association that emerges through communicative, financial, and ideological links (Ch. 11).

Visual culture: the importance attached to the visual, as opposed to the oral or written (Ch. 3, Box 3.2).

Visual determinism: the notion that images often affect public opinion (Ch. 5).

Visual gatekeeping: a series of decisions that are made to alter images as they move along the chain in news organizations (Ch. 5).

Visual grammar: the notion that television is perceived as more emotionally arousing in comparison with print media (Ch. 5).

Visual rhetoric: the art of visual persuasion, visual communication, and visual images (Ch. 2, Box 2.1).

Voice: the opportunities and motivations for global players to present their sides in the public domain (Ch. 15).

Voice of America: the official international radio and TV broadcasting service of the U.S. federal government. Its objective is to promote a positive image of America (Ch. 15).

Vulnerable-media model: model that considers the media as only victims of terrorism, not causes of it (Ch. 3).

War of Ideas: ideals and ideologies that clash between the West and the Muslim world (Ch. 1).

War without front lines: a war waged in the shadows against an indescribable enemy (Ch. 1).

Waste: kill (Ch. 9).

Weapons counts: dead bodies (Ch. 9).

Weather Underground: a U.S. radical left organization that committed terrorist acts against the U.S. government (Ch. 1).

Web spidering: a method to search discussion threads and other content to identify the "dark corners" of the web where terrorist attacks are being planned (Ch. 16).

Weekend terrorists: phrase referred to the Red Brigades, whose terrorist acts were frequently committed on Saturday because they knew that, in Italy, newspaper circulation on Sunday was the highest (Ch. 2).

Werther effect: the mirroring of another suicide that the individual attempting suicide is familiar with (Ch. 12).

Wetwork: murder or assassination, according to the CIA (Ch. 9).

Wheel design: structure in which nodes communicate with each other without going through the center (Ch. 1).

WIA (wounded in action): wounded soldiers (Ch. 9).

WMDs: weapons of mass destruction (Ch. 1).

World Jerusalem Day: ceremony initiated by the Ayatollah Khomeini to accomplish the Sunni and Shi'ite common goal of attacking the Jews and delivering Jerusalem (Ch. 10).

Writeprint: a method to automatically extract thousands of multilingual, structural, and semantic characteristics to identify who is generating "anonymous" content online (relating to terrorism) (Ch. 16).

Yale Model of Persuasion: model explaining that a variety of message, source, and audience factors can influence the degree to which audiences can be persuaded; these factors bring about opinion, attitude, affect, and action change (Ch. 4).

Zawahiri, Ayman (al-): Al Qaeda's new "number one" (Ch. 1).

Zeitgeist: the general mindset, education, and morals of a given period (Ch. 8).

Index

Surnames starting with al- are alphabetized by the subsequent part of the name.

About the Author

Dr. Jonathan Matusitz (Ph.D., University of Oklahoma, 2006) is currently an Associate Professor in the Nicholson School of Communication at the University of Central Florida (UCF). He studies globalization, culture, and terrorism. On top of having 85 academic publications and over 100 conference presentations, he taught at a N.A.T.O.-affiliated military base in Belgium in 2010. Originally from Belgium himself, he migrated to the United States in 2000. In 2012, he was honored with a prestigious teaching award by the College of Sciences at UCF.

◎SAGE research**methods**

The essential online tool for researchers from the world's leading methods publisher

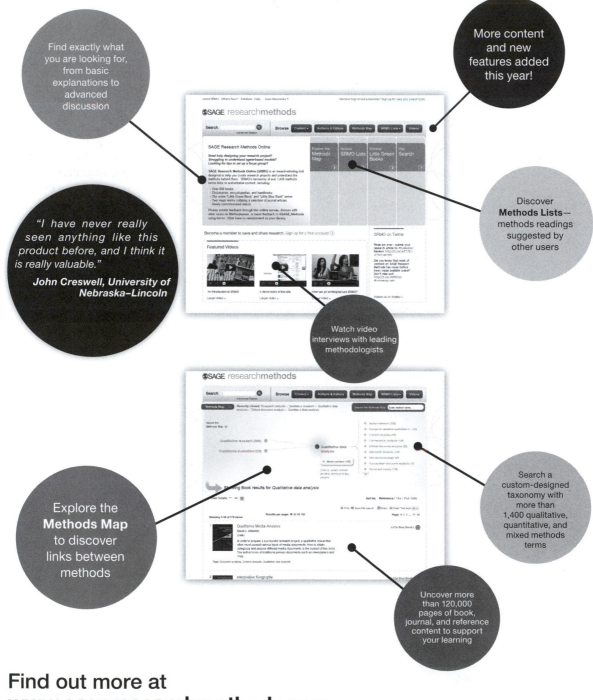

Find exactly what you are looking for, from basic explanations to advanced discussion

More content and new features added this year!

"I have never really seen anything like this product before, and I think it is really valuable."

John Creswell, University of Nebraska–Lincoln

Discover **Methods Lists**— methods readings suggested by other users

Watch video interviews with leading methodologists

Explore the **Methods Map** to discover links between methods

Search a custom-designed taxonomy with more than 1,400 qualitative, quantitative, and mixed methods terms

Uncover more than 120,000 pages of book, journal, and reference content to support your learning

Find out more at
www.sageresearchmethods.com